WHITE MAN'S LAW

NATIVE PEOPLE IN
NINETEENTH-CENTURY CANADIAN JURISPRUDENCE

White Man's Law

NATIVE PEOPLE IN NINETEENTH-CENTURY CANADIAN JURISPRUDENCE

SIDNEY L. HARRING

Published for The Osgoode Society for Canadian Legal History by
University of Toronto Press
Toronto   Buffalo   London

ISBN 0-8020-0503-9 (cloth)

Printed on acid-free paper

Canadian Cataloguing in Publication Data

Harring, Sidney L., 1947–
White man's law : native people in nineteenth-century Canadian jurisprudence

Includes bibliographical references and index.
ISBN 0-8020-0503-9

1. Law – Canada – History – 19th century.   2. Indians of North America–
Legal status, laws, etc. – Canada – History – 19th century.   3. Indians of
North America – Canada – Government relations.   I. Osgoode Society for
Canadian Legal History.   II. Title.

KE7709.H376 1998   349.71'089'97   C98-931768-4
KF8205.H376 1998

University of Toronto Press acknowledges the financial assistance to its
publishing program of the Canada Council for the Arts and the
Ontario Arts Council.

To my grandmother, Ina Oelke Olds,
who was born in 1906 in Princeton, Wisconsin,
and who died there eighty-nine years later
as I was working on this book

Contents

Foreword

THE OSGOODE SOCIETY
FOR CANADIAN LEGAL HISTORY

The purpose of The Osgoode Society for Canadian Legal History is to encourage research and writing in the history of Canadian law. The Society, which was incorporated in 1979 and is registered as a charity, was founded at the initiative of the Honourable R. Roy McMurtry, a former attorney general for Ontario, now chief justice of Ontario, and officials of The Law Society of Upper Canada. Its efforts to stimulate the study of legal history in Canada include a research-support program, a graduate student research-assistance program, and work in the fields of oral history and legal archives. The Society publishes volumes of interest to the Society's members that contribute to legal-historical scholarship in Canada, including studies of the courts, the judiciary, and the legal profession, biographies, collections of documents, studies in criminology and penology, accounts of significant trials, and work in the social and economic history of the law.

Current directors of The Osgoode Society for Canadian Legal History are Jane Banfield, Tom Bastedo, Brian Bucknall, Archie Campbell, J. Douglas Ewart, Martin Friedland, Charles Harnick, John Honsberger, Kenneth Jarvis, Allen Linden, Virginia MacLean, Wendy Matheson, Colin McKinnon, Roy McMurtry, Brendan O'Brien, Peter Oliver, Paul Reinhardt, Joel Richler, James Spence, Harvey Strosberg, and Richard Tinsley.

The annual report and information about membership may be obtained by writing: The Osgoode Society for Canadian Legal History, Osgoode Hall, 130 Queen Street West, Toronto, Ontario. M5H 2N6.

In recent years numerous important books have appeared which deal with the history of aboriginal populations in early Canada. Although these studies add enormously to our understanding of the role played by native peoples in the British North American and Canadian communities, there has been to date no significant study of the dynamic and at times tragic relationship between Euro-Canadian law and the legal traditions of aboriginal populations.

Professor Sidney L. Harring now addresses that lacuna in this sweeping reinvestigation of Canadian legal history. In the nineteenth century, many Canadians commented proudly on what they regarded as this country's liberal treatment of Indians. In challenging that conception, Professor Harring draws on scores of nineteenth-century legal cases. His study demonstrates that colonial and early Canadian judges were sublimely ignorant of British policy concerning Indians and their lands and arrogantly indifferent to native rights and traditions. A great strength of the study is its account of the remarkable tenacity of First Nations in continuing their own legal traditions despite obstruction by the settler society that came to dominate them.

Today, legal decisions respecting native rights and land claims reverberate throughout our society, affecting the rights and obligations of all Canadians. This study helps us to understand and come to terms with how we arrived at our present condition. It leaves no doubt that Canadian native legal culture requires further study by scholars and that aboriginal history demands more serious attention by courts in rendering decisions.

R. Roy McMurtry
President

Peter N. Oliver
Editor-in-Chief

Acknowledgments

Anyone who writes legal history knows that we owe all of this work to those who hold the legal stories that, in the end, add up to a book. I am indebted to all of the people and institutions who shared such stories with me, as well as to the historians who have covered much of the same ground for different reasons. My principal debt is to native people, who hold that their own histories simply cannot be put into words. We can only hope that the ultimate promise of *Delgamuukw* will be broadly met, with the oral histories of the First Nations finally given full weight in the rewriting of the legal history of Canada.

This particular work has its roots in another book, *Crow Dog's Case: American Indian Sovereignty, Tribal Law, and United States Law in the Nineteenth Century*. I first intended to ignore the border between the United States and Canada as I wrote the various chapters of that book, seeing the border as an artifact of the colonial carving up of North America, having nothing to do with the native nations. Indeed, many of the chapters of that book crossed and recrossed the border: Sitting Bull and many Dakota fled to Canada after their victory over American troops at Little Big Horn, and the Tlingit not only lived in both the United States and Canada but also occupied an important place in international trade. The Six Nations' long history in the northeast had been divided between two countries. Even the Copper Inuit, living deep within the Canadian Arctic, had seen their lands occupied by Canadian authorities as an assertion of Canadian sovereignty against the incursions of American and Scandinavian whalers.

This very good idea, however, could not survive the complexity of the project. Just as United States historians sometimes describe John Brown's raid on Harper's Ferry as 'the best plan that ever failed,' I soon realized that the distinct political and legal cultures of the United States and Canada made the idea unworkable. The Copper Inuit chapter was then published separately and, with a Canadian Studies Grant from the Canadian Embassy, in Washington, I pursued the Canadian portion of the Six Nations' story. That opened up for me the native legal history of Upper Canada and set the context for this book.

I am grateful for the support that I have received from a number of sources and acknowledge that, without this support, this work could not have been written. The D'Arcy McNickle Center for the History of the American Indian at the Newberry Library in Chicago provided a Rockefeller Fellowship to write *Crow Dog's Case* and, eight years later, provided a National Endowment for the Humanities/Lloyd Lewis Fellowship to spend a year there working on this project. Fred Hoxie, formerly director of the McNickle Center and currently vice-president of the Newberry Library, has now provided support for two of my books. The Newberry prides itself in building a unique community of fellows who, although typically working on diverse projects, support and learn from each other. Nancy Shoemaker, Tim Gilfoyle, Elliot Gorn, and Elisa Weaver provided insights into my thinking about this work at every stage and I appreciate their help very much. The Newberry Library holds an amazing collection of materials on native history and it is always a pleasure to work there. The Canadian Embassy in Washington provided two Canadian Studies Research Grants, which I used to do research in Ontario and the west.

Subsequently, the University of Saskatchewan College of Law provided me with a year of support as the Law Foundation of Saskatchewan Chair in Law and Public Policy. Not only did the opportunity provide a year of access to a first-rate Canadian library, a necessity for an American scholar of Canada, but it also provided access to the Native Law Centre and native students, several of whom gave me important leads involving their communities. Sakej Henderson, research director of the Native Law Centre, shares his wisdom freely with anyone who seeks him out, and I learned a good deal from him. Tim Quigley, Dan Ish, Marie Ann Bowden, and Shelley Wright, all faculty members at the College of Law, helped me understand Canadian law and the Canadian legal tradition, and Norman Zlotkin helped me figure out some of the intricacies of native law in Canada. Dean Peter MacKinnon was consistently supportive of this work and, under his leadership, the College of Law financed a number of research trips to archives across Canada. At the final stages, the University of Victoria Faculty of Law invited me to give the McLean Lecture, an opportunity that financed two days of searching through thousands of photographs for illustrations. The Humanities Research Centre of Australian National University provided a visiting fellowship during the summer of 1997 so that I could do the final writing, revising, and editing.

The staffs of a dozen archives are the unsung authors of much of this history. Without exception, they were helpful, bringing me piles of documents as I worked my way across Canada, archives by archives. Research for this work was carried out in the Provincial Archives of British Columbia, the Archives of Ontario, the National Archives of Canada, the Saskatchewan Archives Board, the Glenbow Museum and Library, the Osgoode Hall Law Library, the Yukon Territory Archives, the Prince of Wales Northern History Centre, the Wisconsin State Historical Society, the Newberry Library, the Alaska State Archives, the University of Saskatchewan Library, the University of Saskatchewan College of Law Library, the Six Nations Library at Brantford, and the Walpole Island Heritage Centre. Written queries went out to other libraries that were always answered by mail or phone; the institutions that assisted me in this way include the Provincial Archives of Nova Scotia, the Provincial Archives of Manitoba, and the Hudson's Bay Company Archives. I would like to thank every archivist who assisted me and apologize for not listing all of their names.

A number of scholars also gave me advice, even encouragement, and helped me to understand many things that were not always evident to me. This was particularly important given that I am an outsider to Canadian history. I did the best I could and thank many Canadians who had the patience to help me understand Canadian history and Canadian law. In no particular order I want to thank Jim Miller, Lou Knafla, Jon Swainger, Hamar Foster, John McLaren, John Borrows, David McNab, Constance Backhouse, Donald Smith, Frank Tough, Russell Smandych, Barry Cottam, Tony Gulig, Peter Oliver, Wes Pue, and Tony Hall. Any author producing a book like this one necessarily uses a number of secondary sources. In doing so I acknowledge the large number of scholars who have so changed the field of native history over the past two decades. In each generation, history is written from the work of those who have gone before, and this book would not have been possible without the careful research of others. Two judges, Michelle Bourassa, of the Territorial Court of the Northwest Territories, and Jeremy Nightingale, of the Provincial Court of Saskatchewan, invited me to accompany their court parties to native communities in the north.

The Osgoode Society for Canadian Legal History and the University of Toronto Press have both been supportive as publishers, creating an environment that makes researching and writing a pleasure. Laura Macleod, Gerald Hallowell, Emily Andrew, Marilyn MacFarlane, and Peter Oliver worked very hard to make this book happen. Curtis Fahey is a superb editor and his careful work greatly improved the manuscript.

A lot of this book was written 'on the road' and most of that travelling was done in a truck with a canoe on top. Law is about people and their relationship to each other and their land and I learned very much simply being out there. While doing this book, for example, I camped in British Columbia, Alaska, and Yukon three months in a row – in the rain. My wife, Michelle, and I – and our dog, Betyar – ran two hundred miles of the Yukon River, fighting hypothermia in late July, and a hundred miles of the Churchill River in warm August sun with the fish biting on anything we threw in the water. A Cree fisherman turned his boat and came to the far corner of a large lake to ask us if we were lost and laughed when I told him that we were trying to get lost. There is no question that human events of great power have repeatedly occurred on this harsh and expansive Canadian landscape. Mackenzie King, of course, ignored native history when he noted that 'Canada has so much more geography than history,' but that geography has clearly been a potent force in Canadian legal history. In this respect, it might be simply pointed out that, while the North-West Mounted Police was created to take the Queen's law to the farthest corners of Canada, native people have long developed many ways to keep their laws and traditions to themselves when they wished – often beyond the reach of Canadian law. Thus, in a real sense, Canada's vast geography has helped shape Canadian legal history.

Still, law, as a system of rules and a set of social institutions, has great power. The meeting of a conservative European law and an expansive native land is an inherently poor fit. We are still living that poor fit today, all over the world. I am, for example, one of the thousands of Western scholars who have worked in Africa, trying to contribute what I could. A European legal order is superimposed over a broad range of human and environmental problems. I cannot pretend to have the creativity and imagination to sort all of this out well.

Putting this material all together in one legal history has been a great challenge. More than once I was daunted by trying to write the book, thinking I should leave it for someone with a better understanding than

I, and I know of a number of people who could tell this story better. But the fact remains that the more often different versions of these stories are told, the more we will understand. This, I trust, is a help, but I, like others, hope that more of the First Nations will share more of their histories with us.

WHITE MAN'S LAW

NATIVE PEOPLE IN
NINETEENTH-CENTURY CANADIAN JURISPRUDENCE

Introduction

But savage as those distant tribes are, they have their treaties, their peace and war agreements, constantly in their minds; they would insist upon their presents established by long custom, and if not complied with on representation, they would do themselves justice to their own satisfaction, and we should soon find them most formidable enemies.[1]

Writing in 1827, Sir George Ramsay, Earl of Dalhousie, governor-in-chief of Canada, was impressed by the strength of the legal traditions of the Indians, and, as a matter of sound policy, he urged that their law be respected. Now, almost two centuries later, while Canada's tortured relationship with its First Nations can be studied on many levels,[2] the legal nature of these issues still occupies a unique place in Canadian history. In the past twenty years an impressive body of literature has set out to reinterpret Indian/white relations in a number of disciplinary contexts, producing hundreds of scholarly works that cast Canada's relationship to indigenous people in new ways.[3] Lawyers have drawn on this research in dozens of cases, representing some of the most complex litigation in the world, that have turned on historical, anthropological, or sociological evidence. Simultaneously, new and original research on diverse areas of Indian rights has become common as the First Nations bring renewed legal claims against the Canadian government.[4]

Although Canadian law has by no means come to terms with First Nations sovereignty and land rights, some of the common law world's most ambitious indigenous rights litigation has occurred in Canada. Cases like *Calder, Guerin, Bear Island, Sioui, Sparrow, Badger, Van der Peet,* and *Delgamuukw* share in common the depth to which they are rooted in history – sometimes bad judicial history.[5] The First Nations themselves, without needing (but sometimes with) the help of scholars, have set about recasting their relationship to Canada.[6] This resurgence of Indian sovereignty has led to armed stand-offs, a handful of gunfights, the creation of Nunavut, an Inuit territory within Canada, the demise of the Meech Lake Accord at the hands of the Cree legislator Elijah Harper, symbolically holding an eagle feather, countless lawsuits, any number of arrests, and perhaps thousands of local assertions of indigenous rights on the widest possible range of issues.[7] But, as Lord Dalhousie observed, these difficulties follow from an historical denial of Indian law and legal rights and need to be understood in the context of a wide-ranging legal history.

CANADIAN LAW AND INDIGENOUS PEOPLE

Indians, as individuals, and the First Nations, as sovereignties, have, since the late eighteenth century, repeatedly taken their claims to court, forcing the courts to redefine their relationship with first the British crown and, later, the Canadian state. Canadian courts, through the 1960s, were generally (but not always) unreceptive to First Nations legal claims.[8]

There are reasons why Indians repeatedly returned to court. The first is that they had few alternatives, given their poverty and lack of representation in the political process. Another reason is that legal concepts such as property ownership, sovereignty, and land, water, and hunting and fishing rights are deeply rooted in the common law, and consequently, once natives experienced reverses on all these fronts, they naturally turned to the law to reinforce the various political strategies they employed to recover lost ground. Finally, there can be no question that the Canadian courts in recent years have been increasingly receptive to the First Nations' legal rights. The result has been a great amount of native-rights litigation, over a full range of issues.

The most important native-title case of the 1990s, *Delgamuukw* v. *the Queen*, a complex legal argument that Gitksan and Wet'suwet'en chiefs brought forth from their unique traditional history and took to the Supreme Court of British Columbia, was bluntly rejected out of hand by the trial judge, who treated chiefs, elders, and an ancient culture with great disrespect.[9] *Delgamuukw* required 318 days to introduce the evidence and 56 days to argue. The record includes 23,503 pages of evidence at trial, 5,898 pages of argument, 9,200 exhibits, totalling over 50,000 transcript pages, draft outlines of argument running to 3,250 pages for the plaintiffs and 1,975 pages for the province – all told making the case one of the most extensive ever tried anywhere in the world.[10]

The Supreme Court of Canada set aside the *Delgamuukw* holding seven years later, in December 1997, on the grounds that the lower court had erred in ruling that the oral histories of the Gitksan and Wet'suwet'en witnesses were not entitled to be accorded independent weight as evidence and that the natives' land title had been extinguished. The case was sent back for retrial.[11] While this decision removes part of the stain of the trial court's insensitivity towards the chiefs and their culture, and sends a clear directive to Canadian judges that they must give independent weight to aboriginal oral history in all present and future cases, the legal rights of the Gitksan and Wet'suwet'en remain unresolved after more than a decade of litigation.[12]

Section 35 of the Constitution Act of 1982 recognizes 'existing Aboriginal and treaty rights' without a definition of what those rights are.[13] Obviously, if those rights amount to nothing, there was no point including them in the document. *Sparrow* suggests that the potential limits of those rights are broad. In this case, Ronald Sparrow, a member of the Musqueam nation, had been charged with fishing illegally, and in the ensuing trial his defence – that he was merely excercising his traditional right to fish – was rejected.[14] The conviction was overturned, with the Supreme Court of Canada not only making new law but potentially charting out a new Canadian jurisprudence of indigenous rights by carefully analysing their history. *Sparrow* required a complex analysis of aboriginal history to determine the precise nature of the aboriginal right in dispute, and then another analysis of both Canadian and aboriginal history to determine if that right had been extinguished.[15] The same court, however, retreated from this prospect of a broad jurisprudence of 'existing aboriginal rights' in *R. v. Badger* and in *Van der Peet* v. *The Queen*, leaving the broad legal question of the scope of 'existing aboriginal rights' still poorly defined.[16] The aboriginal right of self-government, in particular, has been consistently evaded by the Supreme Court of Canada.[17]

A number of scholars have challenged the whole constitutional paradigm upon which these cases are based. Mary Ellen Turpel focuses on the cultural bias of the entire constitutional scheme, beginning with the statement in the Constitution Act's preamble that 'Canada is founded upon principles that recognize the supremacy of God and the rule of law.' Such a statement is a 'story of multicultural dominance,' in Turpel's analysis. She goes on to describe the discourse over 'rights' (including 'Indian rights') as one that disguises the existing economic and political interests which dominate Canada, imposes a European conception of individual rights into traditional societies based on collective rights, and removes a whole range of differences from the purview of the constitution and from law. At the same time, native law and the cultural forces that define native society have been left out of the whole constitutional process. Her analysis ends by arguing that the 'rights paradigm and interpretative context of Canadian constitutional law is so unreceptive to cultural differences that ... it is oppressively hegemonic in its perception of its own cultural authority.'[18]

John Borrows argues both that the First Nations have always retained their sovereignty, therefore making sovereignty an 'existing aboriginal right' entrenched in the constitution, and that the First Nations themselves hold the key to freeing Canadian law from its Eurocentric roots by insisting on the recognition of Indian law by Canadian courts. He then shows in a legal history of his own Ojibwa family how this traditional law has survived.[19] Russel Barsh and James [Sakej] Youngblood Henderson have attacked the *Van der Peet* trilogy (*Van der Peet* was handed down the same day as *Gladstone et al.* v. *The Queen* and *N.T.C. Smokehouse* v. *the Queen*) for freezing aboriginal rights in historical time and thus limiting them.[20] The 'frozen rights' theory is that aboriginal rights must be 'truly' aboriginal, in the sense of being rooted in traditional aboriginal society, and then recognized only in this historically defined form.[21] *Sparrow* held out the prospect of aboriginal rights interpreted 'in a contemporary form rather than in their primeval simplicity and vigor.'[22] *Van der Peet* took a more limited view, holding that the Sto:lo had no aboriginal right to 'commercial fishing' in a case involving the illegal sale of ten salmon.[23] A dissent criticized the opinion as mischaracterizing the nature of the right, referring instead to a long Sto:lo history of fishing in order to earn a livelihood.[24] Thus, even voluminous historical research and aboriginal oral history in a case involving ten salmon did not resolve the issue. Rather, it provided the raw material for two inconsistent interpretations of the meaning of 'existing aboriginal rights' under the constitution.[25]

Noel Lyon has argued for a broad interpretation of section 35 as a fresh constitutional mandate for reconsidering claims of aboriginal and treaty rights in light of modern standards of constitutional and international law.[26] Such a view may result in a fundamental reinterpretation of 'existing aboriginal rights' and thus lead to broader recognition of sovereignty and land rights, but that is not yet clear. A basic reconceptualization of the framework of aboriginal rights is not only difficult from the standpoint of Canadian constitutional law, but must also recognize that unique historical and legal issues are specific to particular aboriginal rights and Indian nations. *Van der Peet* illustrates how complex the process of fact-finding and interpretation in each of these cases can be.[27]

Youngblood Henderson sets out a new regime of treaty federalism which includes a framework for this fresh constitutional mandate. He argues that section 35 'conceived a new Canadian society,' consolidating a new treaty federalism and the former provincial federalism into a 'shared rule in Canada.'[28] In this new federalism the sovereignty of the First Nations would be recognized and they would assume a role in a new federal system of government.

The crisis in the Canadian law of indigenous rights is doubly ironic in that it is fundamental to Canadian legal history that the Canadian frontier was a legally structured frontier, one that used the law to govern Indian and Euro-Canadian relations and to avoid the violent 'collision' of the two cultures. This model is often juxtaposed against the violence of the American frontier.[29] The result, however, was very much the same, with Indians killed by disease, impoverished, and deprived of their lands in both countries. While there were very real historical differences between United States and Canadian Indian policy, it is impossible to describe the results of these policies in terms of differences in the lives of indigenous people today.[30]

The uniquely historical nature of Indian law, an area of law that requires historical analysis and argument in every case, brings the study of Canadian legal history out of its normal relegation to the borders of legal scholarship. Indeed, even the 'weight of history' itself is a legal argument, providing a legal basis for government actions done in violation of law – so long as they were done long enough ago.[31] Canadian legal history, like American and commonwealth legal history, is in a state of important change. Traditional legal history, the history of judges, courts, and cases, has given way to a 'new' legal history focusing on the social impact of law on the various peoples and processes that make up Canada.[32] Particularly important have been a number of legal histories of women and family life and of the application of the criminal law to the lives of ordinary people.[33] There is a small but growing literature on the legal history of native peoples in Canada, best seen in the important work of Hamar Foster.[34] The legal history of the native peoples of Canada, however, is still underdeveloped, in contrast to a large literature on the history of Canadian Indian policy.[35]

George Stanley has reminded all of those 'embarking' on any historical study of Indian-white relations that we are all prisoners of our culture. Every interpretation that we make is subject to layers of misunderstanding, of value judgments, of diverse underlying philosophies. Overlaying these difficulties are problems of evidence: European law and culture have been recorded in written form for thousands of years, while indigenous law and culture have survived in oral tradition.[36] Issues of racism and ethnocentrism also structure this historical discourse. The European powers that took possession of the New World may have been awed by much of what they saw, but they did not defer to or generally respect the social, cultural, or political values of the indigenous peoples of the Americas: traditional indigenous law was not only not honoured, it was ignored, devalued, and, often, forcibly swept away.[37]

This kind of legal history develops in the context of the 'new' Indian history as well. Traditional history relegated Indians to the margins of Canadian history, if not 'doomed to extinction' then, beyond their role in the fur trade, irrelevant to the development of Canada.[38] Similarly, native institutions were dismissed with the analysis that, after European contact, there was 'a complete breaking down of the old social order, of the systems of law, government, and religion on which their societies rested.'[39] Beginning in the 1970s a rich historiography developed, emphasizing the continuing strength of Indian cultures in Canada as well as the complex and central place of Indians in Canada's history. In this view Indians were conscious historical actors with their own cultures as well as their own vision, if not of Canada at least of their own nations.[40]

Aboriginal people had their own laws and legal institutions, but these traditions were bound up with all other aspects of their societies. Law, leadership, religion, family, band and national structures, and economic activity were not differentiated the way they were in British and European societies. At the time of colonization there were dozens of Indian nations in Canada, organized at different levels into hundreds of bands, speaking fifty languages, each with its own culture and history and its own network of relations with other native peoples.[41] By the nineteenth century, these traditions included various levels of interaction with whites and with European, Canadian, and American institutions, sometimes dating back over three hundred years. Indigenous laws and legal traditions varied widely from nation to nation but were often characterized by an integrative and mediative quality designed to resolve disputes efficiently and restore traditional relationships. There is a substantial literature on these legal traditions that has been largely left out of Canadian law.[42] Assuming that many native people still follow their own law and have a traditional right to do so, then the constitutional recognition of 'existing' aboriginal rights must recognize all of this law that 'exists.' Each First Nation has its own legal history, currently substantially unwritten.[43]

Indigenous legal history involves three distinct sets of inquiry. First, the focus must be on the scope, content, and meaning of the various laws of the individual Indian nations. These laws are part of the Canadian legal tradition and must be considered by Canadian courts whenever it is appropriate. Fully known only to the elders, although pieces of this history have been studied and written about by scholars,[44] native legal traditions were not fixed but evolved with changing conditions. The fur trade, for example, altered traditional law well ahead of colonial settlement as Indians changed their traditional laws of property and international relations to deal with their new roles as commercial trappers and traders.[45] Other changes in social and economic activity within indigenous societies similarly effected their law.[46]

A second distinct inquiry into First Nations legal history concerns not Indian law but the interaction of two legal orders, Indian and European. There was both an Indian reception of Canadian law and also, but less known, a Canadian reception of Indian law. Indians were not ignorant of the structure and claims of Canadian and English law. As colonial and Canadian officials increasingly used their law in ways that affected the lives of Indians, the latter developed strategies for responding. Most of these strategies must be inferred from indigenous actions because the contents of the meetings when colonial law was discussed were unrecorded and are known only to aboriginal people through oral tradition. The Indian reception of Canadian law was recorded by Canadian and colonial officials, although they often did not understand or give legitimacy to Indian legal activity. Frequently, this reception took the form of an explicit meeting of two laws. Indigenous leaders negotiated, or attempted to negotiate, appropriate compromises between their laws and Canadian ones.[47] Some of these negotiations are well documented. Perhaps the best known is Joseph Brant's negotiation of the legal status of the Six Nations' lands. Many of the treaty negotiations are also recorded, clearly showing a negotiation of two sets of laws with Indians attempting to reach an accommodation that would protect their traditional laws and cultures and permit two societies to live alongside each other.

John Phillip Reid has demonstrated the Canadian use of Indian law in the fur trading culture of the northwest. Under frontier conditions, Indian legal traditions emphasizing blood revenge for killings and exchanges of property to mediate other kinds of disputes and restore normal trading relations were incorporated into the Canadian and American fur trade. Such law was not only more efficient than English or American law, it was also more just and more immediately satisfying to the parties involved. There were unknown hundreds of these cases, involving dozens of killings and untold numbers of less serious crimes.[48]

The third model, and the most well-known model of colonial law, is that of imposed law.[49] In this model the dominant colonial power imposes its law over acquired lands and peoples through its superior military and police power. Most legal history of indigenous/colonial contact describes this model: at its simplest level, indigenous people have their lands taken away by colonial law and are forced to live isolated lives on the margins of the colonial society. This is a miserable legal history of oppression, violence, and domination. Indigenous people were victims of every kind of legal violence, fraud, and theft. They lacked the education and means to use the civil courts to protect their interests. This legal chicanery was the subject of a number of official reports in nineteenth-century Upper Canada (Ontario) and the Maritimes.[50]

Two major areas of modern concern are particularly open to historical analysis in ways that clearly have constitutional implications: the legal history of Indian sovereignty and land rights. Canada's Indian nations remained sovereign political communities long after colonial contact, either because early authorities de facto recognized that sovereignty, or because they lacked the power to interfere with it. Exactly how that sovereignty survived British and Canadian authority opens up an important range of legal and political questions.[51] Similarly, Indians, under their own laws, did not need a common law title to the lands they occupied: they had property rights, defined in their own laws, but obviously they could not define their title in terms of the English common law.[52] To the extent that the cession of Indian lands was coerced, various legal remedies may be available today. While it is clear that Indians have an aboriginal title to their lands, the precise nature and content of that title is still unresolved and, again, turns on a variety of historical and cultural factors.[53]

THE LIBERAL TREATMENT OF INDIANS

Canada's Indian policy, rooted in Great Britain and Upper Canada's earlier policies, was both politically and legally a policy of 'liberal treatment.' Its elements included a legal procedure for the orderly purchase of lands, the reservation for the Indian nations of sufficient land, the provision of 'presents' as a sign of comradeship and good faith, and the full application of legal rights under English and Canadian law. Later, after the passage of the early Indian Acts beginning in Upper Canada in 1837, a policy of paternalism and protection was imposed over this 'liberal treatment' framework and was in contradiction with it. For example, a policy protecting indigenous people from exploitation also kept Indian farmers from selling their produce and stopped Indians who had been voting from exercising that right of citizenship.[54]

The policy of 'liberal treatment of Indians' is restated repeatedly in government reports of the day, and it occupies a key position in Chancellor John Alexander Boyd's opinion in *St. Catherine's Milling and Lumber Company*: 'The liberal treatment of the Indians, and the solicitude for their well-being everywhere manifested throughout this treaty [Treaty 3], are the outgrowth of that benevolent policy which before Confederation attained its highest excellence in Upper Canada.'[55]

The use of the term 'liberal' in this context means more than benevolent. It has a political meaning derived from the colonial relationship. Indians were involved in a two-level colonial relationship, the first level being with the colony of Upper Canada, and the second with Great Britain. The actual use of the term 'liberal treatment' to describe the relationship between Indians and the crown may derive, in an analogy understood at the time, from the nature of the tie between Upper Canadian settlers and the crown. Richard Cartwright, Jr, a prosperous Kingston merchant rhetorically asked when describing the prosperity of the new colony: 'To what is to be ascribed the present state of improvement and population in this country? Certainly not to its natural advantages, but to the liberality which Government has shown towards the loyalists who first settled it.'[56]

To Cartwright, 'Government' meant the king and parliament and 'liberality' meant the material benefits bestowed on the colonists as well as the secure political structure afforded them by 'English laws and form of government.'[57] 'Liberality', then, refers to the economic and political benefits of the colonial relationship, a relationship founded on paternalism and benevolence. The use of the term to refer to Britain's relationship with the

Indian nations carries the same general meaning but the context of that paternalism and benevolence was very different. Euro-Canadians were being prepared for a fully functioning role within the empire, including local self-government, economic prosperity, and rich social and cultural lives. Indians were being prepared for a position on the margins of Canadian society, working as farmers and labourers, living on small reserves under the despotic control of petty local officials, deprived of their own cultures and traditions, and subject to the regular incursions of settlers. While 'liberality' in the context of loyalists meant the provision of free lands, the 'liberal' material benefits bestowed on Indians were minimal educational and social support, designed to speed up their assimilation.

As used in 'liberal democracy,' the word 'liberal' connotes 'equal,' the fundamental equality of all human beings. A corollary of this ideology is the idea that each individual is free to achieve her or his own free and independent development in a free market.[58] Liberal treatment also implicitly meant 'non-violent,' once again in reference (and in deliberate contrast) to the United States and its violent Indian policy. Chancellor Boyd, also in his *St. Catherine's Milling* opinion, referred to a legal policy that promoted the immigration of Europeans in such a way so that 'their contact in the interior might not become collision.'[59] Non-violence was implicit in the ideology of liberalism: people treated equally, according to the law, did not need to resort to violence. A just society was also a nonviolent society. Canadians were committed to a frontier without the kind of warfare that they saw just below their border. This commitment had underlying reasons of economy as well as morality, for, as some nineteenth-century observers noted, the cost of Indian wars to the United States in the decade of the 1870s exceeded the entire Canadian budget.[60] But it was also a moral policy.

Accordingly, the policy of 'liberal treatment' can be read in any number of ways. Clearly, it can be understood within the paradigm of nineteenth-century liberalism, a dominant political ideology celebrating individual integrity and autonomy. In this sense it was a legal policy, committed to the idea of the rule of law and of the according of the full range of English and Canadian legal rights to Indians (as long as they assimilated, became enfranchised, and, in essence, ceased being Indians). But it can also be understood in ironic, even cynical ways. 'Liberal' means benevolent, generous, and sometimes paternalistic, a well-meaning slogan of colonial authorities determined to take Indian land and then, with Christian humanitarianism, provide for the needs of impoverished Indians. Thus, the policy of 'liberal treatment' was filled with contradictions. In the context of Canada, 'liberal' was also a relative term, meaning simply better treatment than that accorded American Indians, a broad political claim that went to the heart of how Canadians saw their political practice and ideology.

CONCLUSION: THE PLAN OF THE STUDY

What follows, considering issues of both indigenous and Canadian law, will analyse the nineteenth- and early-twentieth century context of Canadian law as it was applied to Indians and Indian rights. This legal history is put in a particular geographical context: the first half of the study concerns the development of Canadian Indian law in Upper Canada/ Ontario. First, it will look at the creation of the Indian law and policy of Upper Canada within its British colonial setting. The actual creation of an English and Canadian law of Indian rights in Upper Canada will be explored in two distinct contexts, one indigenous, the struggle over the definition of Indian law on the Six Nations' Grand River lands, the other judicial, the record of Upper Canada's most important judge, John Beverley Robinson, in the area of Indian law. The reported cases that judicially defined indigenous rights in nineteenth-century Ontario are studied, together with a few early-twentieth-century cases that cast light on the earlier cases. The legal doctrine of *St. Catherine's Milling*, Canada's leading nineteenth-century 'Indian title' case, will be analysed in its historical context. Finally, the study will examine the application of Canadian law to Indian people. An effort will be made to understand how Indians saw Canadian law and attempted to deal with the law's intrusion into their world. This attempt at an ethno-legal history of Indians is necessarily speculative but is an important part of Canadian legal history. Finally, the meaning of Indian law against the background of nineteenth-century Ontario legal culture will be considered.

The book's Ontarian core is then expanded outward to the rest of Canada. Some parts of this history precede the foundation of Ontario, some are contemporary with it, and some follow it. Much colonial Indian law and policy developed in isolation, the product of local colonial elites, either operating independently of the Colonial Office or deliberately ignoring its directives in order to advance local interests, and often doing a certain amount of lying to cover up their actions. The Indian law of the French regime in Quebec and the Maritimes, for example, was all but ignored by British colonists. Colonial law in Nova Scotia incorporated some of the New England colonial legal tradition, directly linking U.S.

Indian law with Canadian Indian law. British Columbia Indian policy was a hybrid, with elements borrowed from New Zealand but then loaned to Hudson's Bay Company (HBC) men who applied a rough frontier tradition. Finally, a dominion government dominated by Ontario approaches sought to extend Ontario Indian policy to the prairies, a policy that met with failure and Canada's major native rebellion.

The book ends there. It does not extend its analysis much beyond the turn of the twentieth century, and it does not consider important twentieth-century legal and historical developments. As well, the legal history of the north is beyond its scope. Nor is the legal history of the Metis, who are recognized in Canada as having aboriginal rights, considered here. Finally, in spite of limited references to events in the United States, I have avoided presenting a comparative analysis of Indian law and policy in the two countries. There is no question that Canadian Indian law and policy developed in an awareness of American events and that more comparative analysis is needed. Indeed, when one looks at the vast number of scholarly books and articles written about United States and Canadian Indian policy, given the parallel development of the two countries, it is surprising that there is so little comparative work. That, quite simply, is another book.

Besides making a contribution to the modern understanding of the context of Canadian Indian law, the present book seeks to make a contribution to an understanding of Canadian legal history. This history has not been much informed by the First Nations, and the same can be said of the role of law in structuring the relationship of Indians with modern Canada. To the extent that law is seen as a force in structuring indigenous/white relations in Canada, it is depicted in one-dimensional terms: much is said about the law acting against indigenous people, but lacking is an understanding of how Indians acted to structure the impact of Canadian law on their lives.

Louis Knafla, a Canadian legal historian, has noted that Canadian legal history has largely been written and understood regionally, with few works devoted to broad, Canada-wide themes.[61] Certainly, there are large risks in writing about the legal histories of Indian people in Canada. On the one hand, each of these histories is not only regional but specific to each First Nation, often to each native community. On the other hand, however, there is a legal history here that is national and even international. Themes do reappear Canada-wide; legal ideas, both of Indians and of the colonial and Canadian governments, did spread, not only from province to province but around the world. The present account is organized not chronologically but regionally, recognizing the regional, particularly Ontarian, core of legal history in Canada. Any study of such a broad topic is exposed on a broad range of fronts. Much has been left out; many of the legal histories have not been included. Those are inherent risks in writing a Canadian rather than a regional legal history. Similarly, there is an oral history that the First Nations have not yet revealed, for reasons that are entirely their own.

The past fifteen years have produced a large number of works analysing the legal doctrine of Indian rights in Canada. Since 1973, when the Supreme Court of Canada in *Calder* first recognized aboriginal title as a legal right derived from the Indians' historic occupation of their tribal lands, and, nine years later, the patriation of the Canadian constitution with its recognition of 'existing aboriginal rights,' there have been signficant changes in the basic doctrine of the Canadian law of aboriginal rights along with a renewed interest by legal scholars in these matters. This study does not focus on the legal doctrine of aboriginal rights, itself very complex and rooted in both its own history and the living history of Indians in Canada. Rather, the focus is on the social history of Indians and Canadian law in the nineteenth century, the social history of a complex and changing legal relationship. As a social history, it is concerned about people as much as it is about law, and about people as legal actors. Using or not using law is a matter of human choice. The British might have occupied (or tried to occupy) Canada through sheer military force, without any recourse to the language of law. The political choice to use one form of occupation and domination rather than another structures the shape of the colonial relationship. What follows, then, is the history of a theme at the heart of the Canadian experience, the country's legal relationship with the First Nations.

1

'The Privilege of British Justice':
Colonialism and Native Rights

Canadian Indian policy until 1860 was directed from the Colonial Office in London, which was responsible to parliament.[1] The problems of the Indian nations in Canada, while not unnoticed, were secondary on the colonial agenda, far less important than the central task of orderly settlement. In the 1830s and 1840s, reforms in colonial policy included the recognition of some legal rights for indigenous people. The Colonial Office itself was reorganized during this period, made more efficient and bureaucratic in response to the growth of empire. The business of the Colonial Office in the early nineteenth century was focused on Canada, Australia, New Zealand, the West Indies, and southern Africa, with numerous other colonies constituting less significant administrative problems.[2] While native issues were a concern of the Colonial Office before the 1820s, and a concern of British military authorities before there was a Colonial Office, by the 1830s and 1840s, formative years in Canadian Indian policy, British officials were deeply involved in the administration of native policy because they were convinced that local settlers could not be trusted in this area.[3] In turn, native policy was influenced by a growing anti-slavery movement, with an ideology denying that the indigenous peoples of the world were inferior to Europeans.

The core of colonial policy in Canada was the idea of an orderly frontier, regulated by the rule of law and extending 'the privilege of British justice' to all of Canada's inhabitants.[4] Sir Peregrine Maitland, as lieutenant governor of Upper Canada, put this policy simply: 'The speedy settlement of the Colony, however desirable, is a secondary object compared to its settlement in such a manner as shall best secure its attachment to British Laws and Government.'[5]

Through the Constitutional Act of 1791 and early related efforts, most of the features of English law and courts were brought to Upper Canada. The Court of King's Bench was established by the Judicature Act of 1794. Lieutenant Governor Simcoe believed that 'every regulation in England should be proper' in Upper Canada, upsetting local interests who thought that the great distances involved and distinct local differences required some modification of English law.[6] The centrality of the rule of law in Canadian history is repeated in study after study, distinguishing Canadian colonial history from that of other colonial societies.[7] This distinction had a number of different meanings.

Symbolically, it was important for Canadians to distinguish the nature of their political order from that of the United States, and the ideas of legality and an orderly frontier contrasted sharply with popular Canadian views of the comparable situation in the United States. Colonialism itself was not a pejorative term at that time but rather stood for the extension of the highest ideals of British justice and humanitarianism around the world.[8] The rich substance of the common law, interpreted in a formalistic manner by a conservative judiciary and a government under the powerful unifying symbol of the crown, was fundamental to this colonial ideology. The rulers and ruling class of Canada were Tories, living embodiments of conservatism in all its forms.[9] The rule of law was one of the bulwarks of Tory ideology. Finally, as a practical matter the British intended to govern Canada more effectively than they had governed the American colonies. The rule of law was the technical framework for that good government; administrators proclaimed good laws (or imported them from England), and then saw to their efficient administration. This legal policy was paternalistic, relying on both the common law and legislation, 'Indian Acts,' designed to protect and support the Upper Canadian Indians until they could be assimilated: a policy of 'liberal treatment.'[10] From 1791 British legal authorities apparently assumed that all provisions of English and Canadian law equally applied to all persons, including Indians, but it was easier to state this as a policy than to apply it, especially in frontier conditions.[11] And there clearly was an ambivalent commitment to this policy, even in settled areas of Canada. In Rupert's Land, the area west of Upper Canada, there was a policy of leaving native legal matters unmolested as long as they did not interfere with the fur-trading activities of the HBC.[12] Ultimately, the difficulties of bringing

Indians under English and Canadian law resulted in the creation of a legal duality, later incorporated into the Indian Acts, which legally established different rights for Indians and non-Indians.[13]

The British colonies became models of colonial administration with a class of professional administrators promoted from colony to colony. Issues of local politics and culture mattered little to the Colonial Office: John Beverley Robinson, by far the most important legal official in Upper Canada, was routinely offered a promotion to the position of chief justice of Mauritius.[14] As early as the 1790s judges, accompanied by retinues of legal officials, were riding to remote parts of Upper Canada to administer British justice.[15] Judge William Dummer Powell, a Montreal lawyer and, like Robinson, admitted in the London Inns of Court, in 1789 carried English law to a community of 4000 French and Indian settlers at Detroit, a thirty-nine day journey from Montreal.[16]

This law-centred policy as it pertained to native people had two purposes: first, to avoid unnecessary colonial wars by protecting indigenous people from the uncontrolled usurpation of their lands by local colonists; and second, to re-socialize indigenous people so as to accommodate them to the new colonial order. Law, an instrument of social control, took an equal place with education and religion in the acculturation of indigenous people.[17] But the imposition of the common law on indigenous people was never a goal of British colonization. In fact, English law was applied to indigenous people for two contradictory reasons. On the one hand, it was an efficient tool of domination. The imposition of prison sentences accompanied the loss of aboriginal land and the impoverishment of aboriginal people. But law was also applied with a paternalistic and colonial view which recognized the basic humanity of indigenous people by according them the full legal rights of Englishmen.[18] Ironically, Indians in Upper Canada who met the legal property qualifications could vote on the same terms as Euro-Canadians until the later Indian Acts took away the franchise.

EARLY-NINETEENTH-CENTURY BRITISH POLICY
TOWARDS INDIGENOUS PEOPLE

The essence of colonial native policy was an ethnocentric paternalism, designed both to protect indigenous people from the depredations of settlers and to re-socialize them with Christian religion and education in preparation for marginal roles in the colonial economy.[19] Liberal reformers in parliament linked the plight of indigenous people in the colonies with slavery. Once the slave trade was finally abolished in 1833, their attention turned to indigenous peoples in the colonial settler societies.[20] The extension of the full legal rights of British citizens to indigenous people was a central feature of this policy: an 1839 report of a parliamentary subcommittee emphasized the need to establish religious and educational institutions accessible to indigenous people, as well as to grant them the legal privileges of all Englishmen.[21]

It was common knowledge in governmental circles in early-nineteenth-century England that indigenous peoples in Canada faced serious problems. Events of the previous generation surrounding the American Revolutionary War, the flight of large numbers of American Loyalists to Canada and, finally, the War of 1812 had the effect of undermining Indian sovereignty, ruining tribal economies, and creating large numbers of refugees. Indian policy had been a matter of military expediency in the eighteenth and early nineteenth centuries, but the military alliance with the Indian nations against the United States became all but irrelevant after the War of 1812.[22] From this point until Confederation, there was no centralized Indian policy: the Maritime colonies, Lower Canada,[23] Upper Canada, and, much later, British Columbia were administered separately and developed different approaches. These governments were often ignorant of Indian policy in other colonies, pursuing local programs advancing the interests of settlers.[24] And, because until the American revolution British Indian policy had included all of the North American colonies, some of the policies followed in the thirteen colonies that became the United States also influenced Indian policy in Canada.

Settler violence against indigenous people in Australia, New Zealand, and the Cape Colony resulted from unrestrained occupation of aboriginal lands and was basic to the new colonial aboriginal policy.[25] Canada, although it presented a more controlled settlement practice, did not escape the critical notice of the Colonial Office. The problems in Canada were not entirely unlike those in other parts of the empire as local elites displaced indigenous people from their lands. Chief Joseph Brant and the Six Nations were effective in carrying their dispute with Upper Canadian authorities over their land title to London. The apparent extermination of the Beothuk population in Newfoundland by the late 1820s also attracted attention in the England of the 1830s, coinciding with the recognition that settlers in Australia and New Zealand might engage in a similar form of genocide unless they were controlled by British authorities. In fact, Newfoundland and Tasmania had virtually nothing in common, except that both were island colonies in which the indigenous inhabitants were purported to have been exterminated within a few years of each other, a fact that linked them in the minds of reformers.[26] The rapid displacement and impoverishment of the Indian population of New Brunswick and Nova Scotia also greatly concerned the Colonial Office in the 1820s and 1830s.[27]

The language of liberal benevolence towards Indians was self-congratulatory and political, reflecting two strains of colonial policy. At a minimum, even proponents of a bold imperial policy wanted to avoid uncontrolled frontier violence against aboriginal peoples. Not only was there a political reason for this, a deliberate contrasting of the benevolence of British policy with the violence of the Americans, but colonial wars were expensive and nasty. Other colonial policy makers genuinely sought to protect indigenous people for moral reasons.[28] By the 1830s and 1840s the Colonial Office was increasingly concerned that colonial governments were potentially the instruments of local forces that had an interest opposed to indigenous rights: colonies were driven by ever-increasing expansion into cheap and plentiful aboriginal lands.[29]

The differences between the two policies could be cast in humanitarian as well as legal terms. Legal matters in the Colonial Office were under the control of Sir James Stephen. In 1813 Stephen, a lawyer in private practice, had been hired as a legal adviser to the Colonial Office. In 1825 his part-time post was made full-time and, in 1836, he became permanent under-secretary in the Colonial Office, serving until 1846. The Colonial Office had primary responsibility for reviewing and approving colonial legislation, and this broad power gave Stephen substantial influence over local matters in all British colonies.[30]

Stephen's attention to legal detail was amazing. With dozens of colonies under his jurisdiction, he routinely examined thousands of laws. He had been trained for this tedious duty through his earlier work when he had commented on colonial laws for a fee of three guineas each. Rarely did this involve fewer than 150 laws per year, reaching as high as 277 for 1817 and 272 for 1821.[31] Stephen had a special interest in aboriginal matters and viewed rapacious colonial policies as immoral. Commenting on the destruction of Australian aborigines, he lamented that 'we take possession of their Country, introduce amongst them the most profligate habits and the severest Law of Europe – and having tainted them with our vices, and oppressed them with our injustice, we execute against them all the severity of our own Law merely for having too well learnt the lessons we have taught them.'[32] Later, referring to the failure of planters to protect former slaves in the colonial laws of the various West Indian colonies, Stephen noted that colonial law was subject to the political influence of local interests: 'The English Statute Book from one end to the other shows the influence of self-love and self-interest on the law-giver.'[33] Yet, although Stephen was blunt about indigenous policy in Australia, New Zealand, and the Cape Colony, Canadian matters never aroused the same strong language. Stephen's view was that a sound British native policy was already in place in North America, dating from the eighteenth century.

His legal research on New Zealand native title made wide use of the American Chief Justice John Marshall's first major opinion on aboriginal title, *Johnson* v. *McIntosh*.[34] In this opinion Marshall had analysed the history of Indian property rights in British North America. Stephen studied the case carefully and then wrote a lengthy memorandum on its impact on Maori title in New Zealand. This memorandum is important because, at a time when Canadian judges seldom referred to American cases, it is the first reference to United States law in relation to the British colonial law of native rights. Stephen, misunderstanding the facts of the case because the Indian lands involved had previously been surrendered by treaty to the United States, noted:

The case of John and Mackintosh [*sic*] proves that a grant from an Indian Tribe of Lands in the State of Ohio would confer on the grantee no valid Title in defiance of a Title derived under a grant from the United States. It shows that the whole Territory over which those Tribes wandered was to be regarded as the property of the British Crown in right of discovery and conquest – and that the Indians were mere possessors of the soil on sufferance.

Such is American Law. The British Law in Canada is far more humane, for there the Crown purchases of the Indians before it grants to its own subjects.

Whatever may be the ground occupied by international jurists they never forget the policy and interests of their own Country. Their business is to give to rapacity and injustice, the most decorous veil which legal ingenuity can weave. Selden, in the interest of England maintained the doctrine of what was called Mare Clausum, Vattel in the interest of Holland laid down the principles of open Fisheries. Mr. Marshall, great as he was, was still an American and adjudicated against the rights of the Indians. All such law is good, just as long as there is power to enforce it, no longer.

Besides what is this to the case of New Zealand? The Dutch, not we, discovered it. Nearly a hundred years ago [*sic*] Captain Cook landed there, and claimed the Sovereignty for King George the III. Nothing has ever been done to maintain and keep alive that claim. The most solemn Acts have been done in repudiation and disavowal of it. Besides the New Zealanders are not wandering Tribes, but bodies of men, till lately, very populous, who have a settled form of Government, and who have divided and appropriated the whole Territory amongst them. They are not huntsmen, but after their rude fashion, Agriculturists.

The two cases seem to me altogether dissimilar, and the decision of the Supreme Courts of the United States, though it may be very good American Law, is not the Law we recognize and act upon on the American Continent [Canada].[35]

The result of this memorandum was the application of a form of Britain's treaty-based Upper Canadian Indian policy, designed to stem the uncontrolled movement of settlers to indigenous lands, to New Zealand and, through New Zealand and in a distorted form, to British Columbia.[36] William Hobson, British consul to New Zealand, was directed to treat the Maoris 'mildly and justly.' He was told that only the crown could acquire land from the Maoris, and then only through purchase, with the contracts carefully explained to the Maori and the Maori left with sufficient lands for their own use. Hobson, acting on these instructions, a clear reflection of the Royal Proclamation of 1763, then proceeded to negotiate the famous Treaty of Waitangi by which the Maori ceded their lands to England.[37]

James Bushby, appointed British resident in the Bay of Islands, New Zealand, in 1832, was one of the drafters of the Treaty of Waitangi. An employee of the Colonial Office, he was cognizant of *Johnson* v. *McIntosh* but read it to embody the same policy set out in the Royal Proclamation. He intended, through the treaty, to acquire Maori land rights in exactly the same way that Marshall had held that the United States acquired Indian land rights: 'The word in the English version of the Treaty, is used in the technical sense, in which it has always been used in dealing with the American Indians ... that is, as an exclusive right to deal with them for their lands.'[38] Governor George Gipps of New South Wales also referred to the Marshall opinions in a reading of the New South Wales bill which prohibited New Zealand settlers making direct land purchases from Maori chiefs.[39] *Regina* v. *Symonds*, the first case (1847) involving the nature of Maori land title in New Zealand, is also the first non-American case to cite John Marshall's Indian title jurisprudence.[40]

Symonds, in turn, became the first British colonial case in which the colonial judiciary addressed directly the matter of native title, although it was never cited in nineteenth-century Canada. The background of *Symonds* was not unlike that of any number of potential Canadian cases: the Treaty of Waitangi of 1840 had guaranteed the Maori 'full, exclusive, and undisturbed possession of their lands and ... fisheries ... so long as it is their wish and desire to retain the same in their possession.'[41] Not surprisingly, the Maori took this language to mean that they had retained ownership of their lands, a position resisted by colonial authorities and settlers and setting the stage for the Maori wars. Parliament appointed a select committee to investigate and report on the New Zealand lands question and the committee adopted the settler position that the Maori retained possession of only the lands that they actually occupied. This was much less land than the Maori believed was protected by the treaty.[42]

The crown, however, did not adopt this interpretation but retained the policy that it had used in Upper Canada. This required the purchase of every piece of land used for settlement, regardless of whether the Maori used it or not, a practice that recognized that the Maori claimed every part of New Zealand just as Indians in North America claimed every part of the continent. This practice was confirmed by the New Zealand Supreme Court in *Symonds:* 'Whatever may be the opinion of jurists as to the strength or weakness of the Native title, whatsoever may have been the past vague notions of the Natives of this country, whatever may be their present clearer and still growing conception of their own dominion over land, it cannot be too solemnly asserted that it is entitled to be respected, that it cannot be extinguished (at least in times of peace) otherwise than by the free consent of the Native occupiers.'[43]

Stephen, of course, was every bit as selective and political as John Marshall in his colonial use of law.[44] Not only did he, as a colonial administrator, selectively use *Johnson* v. *McIntosh*, but even the legal history of New Zealand's unique relationship with the Maori disappeared from British colonial law by the time of the Maori wars of the early 1860s – two decades after Stephen left office. His reference to *Johnson* v. *McIntosh* ignored Marshall's later cases where he recognized the inherent sovereignty of the Indian nations and accorded them a status as 'domestic dependent nations,' using the European analogy that when nations put themselves under the authority of a more powerful king they still keep their national sovereignty under the crown.[45] Stephen knew of those cases and the implications of Marshall's 'domestic, dependent nations' analysis on British colonial law.[46] Obviously, Stephen could not incorporate into English law any notion of national sovereignty to any of the peoples within the British empire, not the Scottish or the Irish and certainly not the Six Nations, Ojibwa, Cree, Zulu, Basotho, Maori, or Australian aborigine.

Stephen's belief that Canadian authorities were engaged in the process of purchasing Indian lands by treaty, according Indians the full measure of English and Canadian law, and following a humane policy of education and christianization was myopic, for he also knew of the various Upper Canadian reports on Indian affairs, of the land thefts at Grand River and elsewhere in Upper Canada, and of the wholesale dispossession and impoverishment of Indians in the Maritimes.[47] Yet Canada, partly because of its closeness to the United States, was far ahead of other colonies on the road to self-government. Therefore, the Colonial Office, with limited resources and a limited capacity to intervene in societies thousands of miles from London, often deferred to Canadian authorities in Indian matters.

THE PARLIAMENTARY SELECT COMMITTEE ON ABORIGINES REPORT: CANADA

The combined forces of the Anti-Slavery Society, the Aborigines' Protection Society, the Church Mission Society, and a wide range of Christian and liberal forces in Britain forced a parliamentary inquiry into native policy in 1836.[48] Friends of these groups in parliament constituted a select committee expressly to promote their political agenda. While conditions varied among the colonies, one central issue forced the investigation: widespread reports that the various colonial governments either engaged in or permitted wholesale theft of native lands, a process that was often accompanied by the violent removal of indigenous people. The thrust of the report was directed at Australia and Cape Colony, but Canada also figured prominently in the investigation. The committee's conclusion was clear: indigenous people had a legal right to their lands that both needed to be respected by settlers and enforced by colonial authorities. Politics could not protect indigenous people in colonial societies; there were intense pressures on local governments, far removed from the direct supervision of the Colonial Office in London, to open cheap land to settlers. Recourse to the law, interpreted by a professional colonial judiciary loyal to the principles of the common law, however, could – at least in the view of these parliamentarians – check local political forces and protect indigenous rights.[49]

While some parts of the eighty-seven-page report were polemical, it consistently urged that indigenous people be accorded the full legal rights of British subjects, including a legal right to their lands, and called on colonial authorities to extend 'British justice' to indigenous people. Such, officially, was already the legal situation in Upper Canada, but there were many accounts from Canada that revealed the duplicity of this policy.[50] Some of the report's recommendations were generic to colonial situations, while others focused on particular colonies. The report refused to make specific recommendations for colonies in North America solely because they [members of the select committee] understand that Her Majesty's Government have for some time past been engaged in correspondence respecting it [North America] with the Lieutenant-governor of Upper Canada, and that the case ... will probably engage the attention of Parliament whenever the estimates for the expenses of what is called the Indian department shall be brought under the consideration of the House of Commons.'[51]

Appended to the report, however, were hundreds of pages of evidence and a collection of government papers organized around a theme common to all of the colonies: indigenous people were being unjustly – and illegally – deprived of their lands at great human cost. Settlers were not only engaging in outright frauds against indigenous people, they were also killing them. Dispossessed indigenous communities, in turn, became impoverished and socially disorganized, with high levels of crime, violence, and alcoholism.[52] The colonial governments of New Brunswick and Nova Scotia, conscious of potential trouble from the Colonial Office over their Indian policies, refused to respond to inquiries from the select committee.[53] This tactic was not successful: the committee used the extermination of the Beothuk as an example of the violence of the Indian policy of the Atlantic colonies.

The select committee took a careful stance on British North America. While it deferred making policy recommendations on Canada, it included a description of the Indian situation in the British North American colonies that was devastating. The Indians of New Brunswick were described as 'dwindling in numbers' and 'in a wretched condition.' Government intervention was urgently called for in Upper Canada 'on behalf of hapless individuals whose landed possessions, where they have any assigned to them, are daily plundered by their designing and more enlightened white brethren.' The Six Nations were described as 'degenerate' as a result of government policy.[54] A report of General H.C. Darling, chief superintendent of the Indian Department from 1828 to 1830, urged that Indians in Upper Canada remain under the protection of the crown because abandonment 'would be the general signal for plunder and persecution.' He went on to point out that 'an Indian cannot legally defend himself' and that, if such acts of plundering that had already occurred had taken place under the protection of the crown, it was impossible to imagine what would happen if that protection were withdrawn.[55] As if to illustrate this point, over sixty pages of official papers on two Lower Canada land disputes, between the Jesuits and the Mohawks of Caughnawaga and the Hurons of Lorette, were included.[56] Underlying these disputes (discussed in chapter 8) were Six Nations assertions of title to the land in question.[57] The purpose of chronicling this dispute in the report of the select committee was to illustrate that Indians could not defend their lands in Canadian courts.[58]

The committee's recommendations were minimal compared to the scope of its investigation, a recognition of the reality of colonial politics. It recommended that native policy be kept under British control rather than transferred to colonial officials, since local forces tended to align against indigenous people. The acquisition and sale of land was to be regulated: only transactions through the crown were legal, the same policy originally set out in the Royal Proclamation. This position, however, failed to protect Indian land rights in Canada because most fertile lands in Upper and Lower Canada by the 1830s had already been acquired by the crown and largely alienated to individuals. Irrelevant in Canada, but appropriate to plantation societies, labour contracts requiring periods of forced service from natives were to be illegal. Missionaries were to be encouraged, religious instruction and education promoted, and the sale of liquor banned, all predictable recommendations consistent with Christian colonialism. The criminal law was to be extended to Indians, as well as to settlers beyond the frontier, in order to create a legally structured society and minimize extra-legal violence.[59] This put a great faith in the neutrality of colonial law in criminal matters, a faith that the committee did not extend to matters of land tenure. In any case, over the subsequent hundred years of expanding British colonialism, the committee's recommendations regarding the recognition of the legal rights of indigenous peoples were largely ignored.

TREATIES IN COLONIAL LAW

A final recommendation of the select committee defied one of the foundations of British Indian policy in North America, the centrality of treaty making in formal relations between the crown and Indians going back to the beginning of colonial America. The committee recommended that 'as a general rule it is inexpedient that treaties should be frequently entered into between the local Governments and the tribes in their vicinity.'[60] The committee's objection, however, had nothing to do with the role of the treaty in negotiations between the crown and sovereign indigenous nations. Instead, it turned on a legal argument: the treaties were most often negotiated 'on terms of such entire disparity' that they created rather than resolved disputes between aboriginal people and the crown. Moreover, since the British colonists were more educated and had drafted the treaties, they were more expert in evading and interpreting them, again cheating aboriginal peoples because of an inherent disparity in the process.[61] These legal objections were drawn, not from international law, but from the law of contract: unfair and unequal contracts were unconscionable. Of course, the committee's recommendation on this point was inconsistent with the legal foundation of the treaty-based policy of land acquisition set out in the Royal Proclamation of 1763.

British colonialism was too deeply bound up in the treaty system to abandon it. Indeed, there was no other method consistent with 'liberal treatment' for acquiring Indian lands; the system remained the best political alternative to the problem of local settlers negotiating their own land deals. However, Britain did shift the treaty-making function to colonial governments, most often politically dominated by those same settler interests. The Treaty of Waitangi followed the select committee's recommendation by scarcely three years.[62] Ten years later, in the Robinson Treaties of 1850, Canada began its final round of treaty making, a process that by 1880 had acquired for the crown most aboriginal lands from the northern shore of Lake Huron to the Rocky Mountains, well north into the boreal forest.[63]

Treaties, in the sense of contracts or agreements between nations, went back to before the fifteenth century. European expansion led to a number of such agreements with peoples around the world, beginning as trade agreements in Africa, the Middle East, India, Southeast Asia, and the Pacific but soon including the recognition of legal control and sovereignty over trading areas.[64] It was North America, however, that witnessed the most frequent use of treaties. There, a growing colonial-settler society inhabited the edge of a continent owned and occupied by powerful Indian nations. From the first years of settlement, each of the colonies had recognized that settlers could not be randomly let loose in Indian lands. Dozens of wars followed, some with heavy settler casualties, threatening entire colonies.[65] Local colonial laws, therefore, forbade molesting Indians on their lands and required that all lands first be acquired by colonial authorities. Hundreds of these negotiations occurred, the origin of the nineteenth-century treaty-making process. After this practice was legally institutionalized in most colonies, Britain enshrined it in the Royal Proclamation, which applied to much of Canada as well as to the Thirteen Colonies.[66]

The early operation of treaty policy in the United States has been well documented. Colonial officials in Nova Scotia operated with the same legal framework as those in New England, a policy that recognized Indians' right to their lands. In fact, the first British Indian treaties applying to Canada were negotiated in Boston in 1725 with Mi'kmaq (Micmac) from what is now New Brunswick and Nova Scotia, thereby incorporating the legal history of New England treaty policy into Canada.[67] Following the American revolution, however, Indian lands in Nova Scotia and New Brunswick were overrun by Loyalists, who often ignored the legal requirement that such lands be purchased from the Indian nations by the crown.[68]

In the old province of Quebec after the American revolution, the treaty-making process moved swiftly as British authorities sought to establish a new colonial empire in North America while avoiding the problems that had destroyed the old. Governor Haldimand in 1784 granted Britain's Six Nations allies a huge tract of land along the Grand River that he had purchased a few months before through a treaty with the Mississauga. In the space of a decade, the Mississauga, an Ojibwa people, yielded up most of their lands north of Lake Ontario, the modern settled core of Ontario, leaving them impoverished.[69] Over the next twenty years most of what is now southern Ontario was surrendered. This area was occupied by a large number of Indian nations, with rich and diverse traditions, many of them resettled from the United States.[70] While some treaties of surrender followed the appropriate legal procedures set out in the Royal Proclamation, others did not. Many different kinds of dishonesty were practised. Some treaties were coerced, some were secured on false representations, some poorly described the lands transferred, some were not reduced to writing and recorded, and some of the promised payments were not made.[71] And, as the select committee anticipated, even those treaties that followed legal procedures did not adequately protect Indian lands: First Nations oral history today is replete with accounts of fraud and misrepresentation in the treaty process and the outright disregard of treaty agreements.[72]

The Nova Scotia situation was as dismal but lacked the procedural formality of Upper Canadian land surrender. Initially, British authorities claimed that when they took the land there was no Indian title: the French, who had previously held the colony, had extinguished it.[73] A series of early peace treaties between the Mi'kmaq and the Massachusetts colony had ended a devastating series of colonial wars, recognizing some kind of Indian title. These peace treaties were not land surrenders but political agreements and, as noted, put Nova Scotia more within the model of New England colonies than within the model established in the rest of Canada.[74] In practice, however, Nova Scotia authorities permitted settlers to push the Mi'kmaq off their lands, forcing them deeper and deeper into interior forests, without even the pretense of negotiated land surrenders.[75] The large numbers of Six Nations Indians in Upper Canada, their substantial political power, and their high visibility made the deprivation of their lands more difficult and set the stage for the complex legal dispute over the Six Nations land title.

This long history of treaties negotiated in what is now eastern Canada led to the alienation of almost all Indian lands, leaving Indians impoverished and dependant – exactly the evil that the select committee feared and, through its recommendations, sought to avoid. Treaty negotiations, like contract negotiations, require an equality between the parties that did not exist under these political and economic conditions.

THE COMMISSIONS TO INVESTIGATE INDIAN AFFAIRS
IN UPPER CANADA

Problems in Indian policy in the nineteenth century produced a thoroughly documented historical record through formal commissions of inquiry. There were six in Upper Canada alone during the mid-nineteenth century, as well as others in the Maritimes and in Lower Canada. While most of the issues concerned in these investigations were not legal in nature, some were.

Following the War of 1812, the Colonial Office had transferred administration of Indians from civil to military authorities, a move designed to protect Indians from the avariciousness of local legislatures as well as to reduce the cost of Indian administration. The role of the Indian Department in Upper Canada – issuing presents, paying annuities, and treating for Indian lands – remained the same, even as it was moved among various colonial administrative structures.[76] Later, in the 1820s and 1830s, the underlying goal of Indian policy gradually changed from one of co-existence between two distinct cultures, envisioned at the time of the Haldimand grant to the Six Nations, to one of christianizing the Indians, converting them to small farmers, and gradually assimilating them into Canadian society: the policy, in other words, of 'liberal treatment.' The process of assimilation went badly: although some Indians converted to Christianity and became small farmers, costs were high in the face of Indian resistance.[77] Broad policies, directed by the Colonial Office and implemented through officials sent from Great Britain, were subject to a variety of local constraints in their actual adminstration.

The picture that emerges from the successive investigations into native affairs in Upper Canada is chaotic. The first inquiry, ordered by Viscount Goderich, the colonial secretary in 1827, was aimed most directly at the Indian Department's finances. Major-General H.C. Darling conducted a full investigation of the Department. His report, completed in July 1828, held that the return of the Indian Department from military to civilian administration would be 'a general signal for Plunder [sic] and persecution, since Indian people were not in a position to defend their property against the advancing tide of settlement.'[78] This acknowledgment of the severity of the problems of regulating settlement did not achieve the narrow result the cost-conscious Colonial Office wanted: it did not recommend any reduction in the expenses of the Indian Department.

The next inquiry stemmed from the policy of assimilation put into place in the 1820s and 1830s. It was obvious at the time that the policy was not succeeding, because the Indians did not choose to assimilate or to become self-sufficient small farmers. In 1836 Sir Francis Bond Head, the new lieutenant governor of Upper Canada, abandoned the 'civilization' program; he intended, instead, to remove the Indians from settled Upper Canada to Manitoulin Island, segregate them from settlers, and let them continue to exist by hunting, tending gardens, and fishing.[79] Bond Head's removal policy had never been approved by the Colonial Office and soon drew resistance from many quarters, including reformers, government officers, and missionaries. Judge James B. Macaulay, a former member of Upper Canada's Executive Council, was chosen to make another inquiry. Macaulay had sat at the Niagara assizes and had first-hand familiarity of Indian/white relations on the Grand River. He worked on his report for only about two months, limiting his research to a study of state papers, visiting no reserves, and interviewing no government officials. The final report ran to almost four hundred pages and reflected his experience as a judge. Central to Indian administration, in his view, was the need to recognize individual Indian property and civil rights in order to ensure that Indians, like new immigrants, would prosper in a growing colony.[80] This idealistic report satisfied no one.

Another inquiry reported in 1840. This body was composed entirely of legal officials – Judge Macaulay, Robert Jameson, another judge and former attorney general then serving as vice-chancellor, and William Hepburn, registrar of the Court of Chancery – and was conceived more broadly than Macaulay's investigation, as part of an effort to study all departments of government in Upper Canada following the 1837 rebellion.[81] By now, it was clear that Indian policy was in shambles: all of the Indian reserves were overrun with squatters, thousands of dollars of Indian trust funds were missing and unaccounted for (a fact suggesting massive corruption and incompetence in the Indian Department), and the government was besieged with Indian complaints. The first of the Upper Canadian Indian Acts, passed in 1839, provided criminal penalties to protect Indian lands from trespass and the looting of natural resources but it had not adequately been enforced.[82] These conditions, as outlined in the 1840 report, describe nothing less than the complete political and legal abandonment of Indians in Upper Canada. For all of the legal talent on the commission, however, its recommendations avoided the major legal issues. The problem of the corruption of Indian agents, for example, was met with a recommendation that better records be kept in the future, as though keeping records prevented further corruption. Similarly, the problem of squatters reflected a general weakness of rural law enforcement generally, as well as the reluctance of local officials to arrest settlers for trespassing on Indian lands.[83]

Sir Charles Bagot, the new governor-in-chief, appointed another commission in 1844. While Hepburn was a member of this body, too, its chairman was Rawson W. Rawson, a career civil servant who had recently arrived in the colony to take up the post of civil secretary. Unlike the perfunctory investigations of the earlier commissions, the 1844 inquiry produced a report with a hundred appendices containing reserve-by-reserve information about Indians in Upper Canada.[84]

Like its 1840 predecessor, the commission recommended that reserve lands be granted to individual Indians in fee simple. The 'peculiar' nature of Indian title, in the view of the commissioners, excluded Indians from the political franchise (voting was based on property qualifications), taxation, and liability for debt. All of the Indian nations protested this recommendation. Not only was individual ownership of property inconsistent with the traditional law of the various Indian nations, it was also a thinly veiled land grab.[85] After individual allotments were granted, the rest of reserve lands would be immediately alienated to squatters. The result of the Bagot commission was an increase in Indian legislation in Upper Canada. The particular statutory enactments increased penalties for squatter trespasses, protected Indians from private debts, exempted Indians from property taxes while on their reserves, and prevented them from pawning their property for liquor.[86]

The last of the commissions, the Pennefather commission of 1856, recommended transferring control of Indian affairs in Canada from Britain to the colonial government, a step taken in 1860.[87] By this time it was apparent that the civilization of Indians was not to be accomplished in a few years and that expense of Indian affairs would be a continuing one; indeed, reports on the success or failure of Indian education, agriculture, or missionary work were to be ongoing through the twentieth century.[88] The Pennefather commission's conclusions were predictable. Its report claimed that the communal ownership of Indian lands retarded development, noted that the depredations of local settlers were continuing, and lamented the anomalous nature of the legal position of Indians.[89]

Britain's subsequent decision to surrender control over Indian affairs was a result of the increasing movement towards self-government in Canada.[90] The influence of British colonial reformers such as the Aborigines' Protection Society, along with the experience of Australia, New Zealand, and South Africa, had prolonged direct colonial administration of native affairs primarily because of the well-grounded fear that local settlers would steal Indian lands. The crown also recognized a special relationship with indigenous people that transcended local politics, stemming from the treaty process and from military alliances. But the crown now abandoned this relationship for financial reasons and deferred to Canadian self-government.[91]

THE COLONIAL INDIAN ACTS

The several commissions into native affairs had presented abundant information revealing not only that Indian affairs in Canada were corruptly administered but that tribal lands and resources were being stolen by squatters. Canadian authorities took cognizance of these crimes symbolically by enacting limited protections of Indian lands in statutes that were the forerunners of the federal Indian Act of 1876. But enforcement was lax, perhaps merely symbolic. The Gradual Civilization Act of 1857 stemmed directly from the various commissions of inquiry and was the final imperial Indian policy initiative prior to the transfer of responsibility for Indian matters to the colonial government.[92] This act, passed by the legislature of the united Canadas, bridges the earliest protective legislation, an act of 1839 designed to protect Indian lands from squatter encroachment, and the broad-based policy of legal dualism that is now equated with the Indian policy of the national government.[93] Indeed, the Gradual Civilization Act of 1857 was the most lasting colonial legacy in dominion Indian law: it was the basis of the dominion Indian Act of 1876, both in law and in policy. In this sense the colonial Indian policy survived, evolving directly into twentieth-century national policy. At the time the Gradual Civilization Act was passed, Upper Canadian Indians objected to it strenuously. One tribal leader claimed that its goal was to 'break them to pieces.'[94]

Prior to 1857 there had been a number of acts designed to offer limited protection to Indians, primarily to Indian lands and other property.[95] These derived from the same political forces that promoted the protection of indigenous rights in the empire, centring on the demands of the Aborigines' Protection Society. The Gradual Civilization Act, however, charted a whole new course. It did not narrowly protect Indian rights from settler intrusion; instead, it defined an inferior legal status for Indians, creating a system of legal dualism, denying them the franchise, and placing them in a distinct legal category, under the paternalistic protection of the government. Legally holding Indians in this condition, the government could subject them to unique forms of social control, educate and Christianize them, and 'gradually' train them for the full responsibilities of citizenship. Then, when each Indian arrived at that level, a special board of examiners would examine his moral character, education, and personal habits, and, if all was satisfactory, would award him forty acres of land and the full privileges of citizenship that went along with it, including the right to vote.[96]

This policy of 'gradual civilization,' conceived in colonial Canada and elaborated in subsequent Indian Acts, failed. Indians refused to cooperate and almost no Indians were enfranchised. Yet the Indian Act, repeatedly amended, is still fundamental law governing Indian rights in Canada, often characterized as a 'cradle to grave set of rules, regulations, and directives.'[97] It is a legal regime imposed on Indians without their consent, denying their rights and controlling their lives, even purporting to define who is an Indian.[98]

CONCLUSION

Canadian Indian policy was a British colonial policy until Canada attained self-government. The empire offered some legal protection of indigenous rights, but legal measures along these lines put Colonial Office objectives in direct conflict with local landowning interests, as well as with colonial governors who were responsive to political pressures. Indigenous rights did not fare well within this system.

Although the Colonial Office had legal functions, and colonial policy was centred on a liberal conception of legality governing relations with indigenous people, these matters could not practically be administered from London. Judges were dispatched from London to the colonies (and later recruited from the colonial elite) to provide local justice, a practice that was consistent with broad Colonial Office policy but that was difficult to administer at such great distances. Furthermore, the underlying legality of British conceptions of colonialism was undermined by contradictory legal goals. Matters of law and order, imposing English criminal law first on communities that were initially composed of settlers and the indigenous people who worked with them and then gradually extending into hinterlands, were the first objects of colonial law. Laws regarding land and commerce followed, punishing violators and providing a framework for organizing land and resources so that development could go forward. Inherent in this same legal order, however, were quite different legal values: liberal British conceptions of humanity, equality, and justice that required that indigenous people be given the full benefit of English law. By the end of the nineteenth century, when Britain dominated a quarter of the globe, it had become increasingly difficult to imagine that such values were anything but cynical. Yet these values had been the foundation of British colonial policy in the 1830s and 1840s. The legacy of this policy in the legal history of the First Nations in Canada reflects the aspirations of the policy of 'liberal treatment' as well as its failures.

2

'A Condescension Lost on Those People': The Six Nations' Grand River Lands, 1784–1860

Contemporary disputes over indigenous rights most often involve either land or sovereignty, and the lengthy (and still continuing) litigation over the Six Nations' Grand River lands brings these legal issues together.[1] The Six Nations Confederacy believes that it retains the sovereign right of self-government and the ownership of its lands. Their private sale of lands, beginning in the late eighteenth century and continuing into the nineteenth, initiated years of litigation between those holding title from the Six Nations and others holding title from the crown. To compound this, squatters occupied land without legal title. Two distinct stories intersected here and set the stage for the legal confusion that followed: first, the Six Nations' persistence in maintaining their sovereignty and land rights led to what is among the most documented native-rights disputes in Canadian history; second, the settlers' persistence in taking lands by a wide variety of illegal means itself became law as their political and economic power influenced the government to refuse to enforce its own land laws protecting the Six Nations against settler interests.

The law of property is at the core of English common law but little in the history of English land law helped structure the distribution of land on the frontier; indeed, an analysis of the land problem reveals the disorder of early Canadian law. The issue was centred on the Six Nations' Grand River lands.[2] This was due both to the tenacity of the Six Nations themselves, who from the 1780s claimed a special status as 'allies' of the crown, entitled to the rights associated with that status, as well as to the choice location of their extensive lands in a settled part of southern Ontario.[3] There was a historical basis for their claim to a special status. Upper Canada was settled by Loyalists who had lost their lands in the United States for defending the crown in the American revolution.[4] The Six Nations fell precisely in that category – except they were Indian.[5]

Within Upper Canada a disproportionate number of reported legal cases arose involving the Six Nations or their Grand River lands: twenty-nine nineteenth-century cases, nearly half of the sixty-four reported. These Grand River cases are foundational in Canadian Indian law for a number of reasons, although none of them is of continuing doctrinal importance. First, these cases produced the first substantial body of law on Indians. Second, the position of Chief Justice John Beverley Robinson, the leading legal figure and an important political leader in Upper Canada, adds to their significance: Robinson authored thirteen published opinions on Indian legal issues during his thirty years on the bench, including six from Grand River.[6] Third, the legal chaos surrounding the Grand River lands challenged the capacity of English common law to resolve frontier legal matters. Ultimately, the law failed in creating an 'orderly' Canadian frontier.

THE LEGAL STATUS OF THE SIX NATIONS CONFEDERACY

In 1784 Lieutenant Governor Frederick Haldimand, in recognition of the Six Nations' loyalty during the American revolution, issued them a grant to a large tract of land along the Grand River. This grant authorized the Six Nations Confederacy to 'take Possession of, & settle upon the Banks of the River called Ours or Grand River, running into Lake Erie, allotting to them for that Purpose Six Miles deep from each side ... which them & their posterity are to enjoy forever.'[7]

The grant extended for six miles on either side of the Grand River, most of the way across Upper Canada,[8] and consisted of land that the Mississauga had surrendered to the British by treaty.[9] Thus, while the lands of the other Indians in Upper Canada were subject to the common law of aboriginal title and to the Royal Proclamation of 1763, the lands of the Six Nations had been purchased by the British from the Mississauga and, argued the Six Nations, granted them in fee simple for services rendered as allies in the Revolutionary War.[10] The Six Nations' title was not an 'Indian' title but involved lands on which the Mississauga Indian title had been extinguished under existing colonial law.[11] The racism underlying colonial land policy in the early to mid-nineteenth century either did not exist or was not apparent to the Six Nations in the late eighteenth century: they believed that they held their lands in fee simple on the same basis as European settlers and American Loyalists.[12]

After obtaining the grant, the Six Nations chiefs, including the war chief Joseph Brant (Thayendanegea), and about 2000 Six Nations Indians – Seneca, Mohawk, Cayuga, Oneida, Tuscarora, and Onondaga, together with a few hundred members of allied Indian nations – moved onto a twelve-mile-wide strip of land south of present-day Hamilton along the Grand River, some of the most valuable land in Upper Canada.[13] Soon, the Six Nations began to grant, lease, and sell parts of their lands to settlers. The reasons are complex and included Brant's personal egotism as well as his desire to live among European settlers, a belief that money from these land sales could be used to improve the Six Nations' living conditions, and even corruption. At the same time, other settlers took advantage of the confusion and moved onto Six Nations' lands. The result was fifty years of instability in land tenure, a problem detailed in several governmental investigations[14]:

... the extent and isolation of the Indian Lands in Upper Canada, the impossibility of exercising a surveillance over those vast tracts, and still more, the uncontrollable force of those natural laws of society to which even Governments must bend, have prevented the efficient protection of the Indian Reserves, any more than the Crown and Clergy Lands under similar circumstances.

These Reserves contain some of the finest and most valuable land in the Province. Hence they have attracted the attention of the indigent emigrant, and the fraudulent speculator, who, either in ignorance or with a view to future gains, have settled upon portions of them, sometimes without leave or observation, but more frequently under color of titles obtained from individual Indians.[15]

The Six Nations were divided on the issue. Over time, from the 1790s through the 1830s, an accommodationist faction led first by Brant and then by a larger group that included his son, John, became dominant. For them, the right to alienate these lands was a measure of their sovereignty, a recognition of their status as 'allies' of the crown and of the equality of the rights of Indians with those of settlers.[16] Initially, their goal was to hold a tract of land large enough to sustain a traditional way of life. Recognizing that they were to live in a country with a large settler population, they believed that a sizable tract of land would allow the Six Nations to structure their frontier on favourable terms. Individual Indians who wanted to acculturate to settler ways could live on the edges of the Six

Nations' lands, as Brant himself did. A traditionalist faction resisted all such assimilationist ideas, seeking to preserve their way of life within the boundaries of their own lands.

As early as 1787, the huge size of the tract, the perception of some of the chiefs that the confederacy needed money, and perhaps a desire to put settlers on the borderlands of Indian settlements to facilitate assimilation had led Brant and certain other chiefs to agree to sell some of the land to individual settlers.[17] By 1798 large-scale sales of lands labelled blocks 1 through 6, intended to provide a substantial income to the Six Nations, were the source of a number of legal disputes because these sales were both illegal under English law and poorly documented.[18] In later sales it seems that some Indians realized that the continuation of a traditional economy was impossible and therefore that a large proportion of their lands could be alienated as surplus: the Six Nations had far more land than they could use.[19] It has also been argued that, for Brant, selling some of their lands would allow the Six Nations to obtain both the money and the non-Indian neighbours they needed to become acculturated and to acquire agricultural skills. To the extent this was true, just as Britain had an 'Indian policy,' Brant had his own policy for transforming and assimilating the Six Nations.[20] It was a policy, however, that was rejected by the traditionalists within the Six Nations, who adamantly opposed all land sales.[21]

Peter Russell, senior member of Upper Canada's Executive Council and administrator of the province, was unprepared for this struggle with Brant over the legal status of the Six Nations' lands. After repeatedly burying the chief in procedural formalities and delays, Russell exhausted Brant's patience. Brant made a formal statement accusing the Russell administration of 'trifling so often with the Indians that they lost all confidence in it.'[22] This disagreement was about many things connected to the complexity of the meeting of two cultures, but it was also about law. Russell was using the language of law to delay and frustrate Brant's goals.

Brant insisted that Lieutenant Governor John Graves Simcoe had promised the Indians deeds to their lands. Simcoe had issued a patent on the Grand River lands to the Six Nations in 1793, but it did not help resolve the title dispute. Like the Haldimand grant, the Simcoe patent used the language of a deed:

To them the Chiefs Warriors Women and people of the Six Nations and to and for the sole use and behoove of them and their heirs for ever freely and clearly of and from all and all manner of Rents, fines, and services whatever to be rendered by them or any of them to Us or Our Successors ... Giving and Granting and by these presents confirming to the said Chiefs Warriors Women and people of the Six Nations and their heirs the full and entire possession use benefit and advantage of the said District ... securing to them the free and undisturbed possession and enjoyment of the same.[23]

The patent went on to restrict the rights of the Indians to alienate those lands to anyone except the crown.

Officially, the purpose of the Simcoe patent was to 'confirm' the Haldimand grant, but it restricted the terms of the original grant in limiting the right of the Six Nations to sell the land. While this made the grant consistent with the terms of the Royal Proclamation restricting the alienation of Indian lands, the Six Nations took the position that they held these lands as allies of the crown and not as Indians. Indeed, these former 'Indian lands' had been alienated from the Mississauga according to the terms of the Royal Proclamation.[24] Both documents have the appearance of deeds and were clearly understood as deeds by the Six Nations. It is unclear precisely what Haldimand and Simcoe meant, but they may have had a duplicitous intent: on the one hand, they wanted to satisfy their Indian allies with a substantial land grant, at a time when huge land grants in fee simple were being made to Loyalists[25]; and, at the same time, both deliberately hedged by using legally ambiguous language that sounded like the language of a deed but that did not include the key language appropriate to a fee simple deed. All the same, the language, on balance, is the language of a deed, a large land grant understood to be 'forever' that could be passed on to heirs and sold, albeit only to the crown.[26]

By this time the real issue underlying the dispute was the sovereignty of the Six Nations and not the law of property. Brant insisted on his right to sell the land because ownership of lands was central to the Six Nations' independence and their political status as 'allies of the Crown.' Moreover, Brant argued that Six Nations law governed the disposition of such lands, a forceful assertion of the political sovereignty of the confederacy. As one element of this assertion of the supremacy of tribal law, Brant maintained that under Six Nations law women had to agree to land cessions.[27] He also secured a personal 'power of attorney' from Six Nations chiefs empowering him to sell tribal lands.[28]

Russell was afraid of trouble with Brant and ultimately, in a series of negotiations, the government confirmed antecedent Brant land sales in spite of the explicit prohibition of those sales in the Simcoe patent.[29] This action reinforced Brant's view that the lands belonged to the Six Nations and could be disposed of at their will. The result seems simple: the chiefs could not understand why the title they held to their lands was any different than the titles of the Loyalists to adjacent lands.[30] They had been given their Grand River lands to replace lands that they had owned in the Mohawk valley, just as Loyalists had been granted lands to replace those abandoned and lost to the Americans.[31] This was a tenable legal position, one that followed the simple logic of English law. Any different position depended on a Six Nations' understanding of a unique (and inferior) legal status for Indians which was unknown in late-eighteenth-century Canada. Even British authorities had not settled their own views of the legal status of Indian lands.[32] Indeed, Brant hired the services of Alexander Stewart, a prominent lawyer, to arrange the confederacy's land sales as well as to assist non-Indian purchasers in the proper procedural requirements of their land transactions.[33]

The fact that the British authorities confirmed the Six Nations' land sales convinced the Indians that they did, indeed, own those lands in fee simple. William Dummer Powell, a leading Upper Canada jurist, noted the legal impact of their understanding:

The pretension of a part of the Six Nations, under the direction of Joseph Brant, to a right of alienation, without Control, of the tract purchased for their use by General Haldimand, underwent much discussion last year, and from various circumstances, sufficiently untoward, the President and Council were induced to accede to those pretensions in part, a condescension lost on those people, who consider it as the result of fear, and who consequently will not only persist themselves in the exercise of their presumed right, but instill the same notions into the other neighboring Indians.[34]

The legal structuring of land title on the Six Nations' Grand River lands involves two considerations. First, there was a formal system of land acquisition for settlers that was either poorly enforced or unenforced. This was coupled with a system for the legal control of Indian lands that was still in the making, its parameters not yet understood by any of the colonial authorities. The result was chaos in frontier land title. At a minimum, there was great miscommunication between two cultures about the legal status of the Grand River lands. But that dismisses too easily British responsibility for the ambiguous legal positions that the colonial government was relaying to the Six Nations. Both the Six Nations and Canada devoted a great deal of effort to the legal structuring of their relationship.

The Six Nations sought legal recognition of their sovereignty and their land title; colonial authorities, mindful of the potential political cost of this legal recognition, and perhaps unwilling to see Indians as their juridical equals, deliberately hedged in every way they could. The result still shapes Indian law in Canada.

SQUATTERS ON THE SIX NATIONS' GRAND RIVER LANDS: A LEGAL HISTORY

The squatter issue brought the legal dispute to a head and received extensive attention in the 1840 and 1844 reports on Indians in Upper Canada.[35] The term 'squatters' loosely applied to anyone who moved onto any lands without a legal title: thus, it was understood by all at the time as a legal category. While now the term has a pejorative meaning, this was not as true in the nineteenth century.[36] Government reports put squatters into two categories, deserving and undeserving, and, in the context of the land shortage of the time, a large proportion of early-nineteenth-century Upper Canadian farmers started off as squatters. Upper Canada gained nearly one million people in the fifty years between 1800 and 1851.[37] The legal regulation of this huge influx of settlers, often in frontier areas far from government offices and courts, was a difficult matter even with the best of intentions to protect Indian land rights. The more extensive of the two reports, done in 1844, deferred to the facts of the 1840 report on the squatter question and reached the same conclusion: that the crown could not protect Indian lands from squatters: 'That complete protection of such [Indian] property can only be looked for as the result of that change which shall assimilate the Indians with people accustomed from infancy to the idea of separate and individually appropriated property, where each is, under the Law, the protector of his own possessions; but they are also of the same conviction.'[38]

This conclusion served the purpose of forcing Indian land surrenders. According to its reasoning, the land of individual Indians could be protected only on their reserves[39] after it had been broken up and allocated in small parcels. This made land policy a part of the general policy of 'civilization' and assimilation. The government's professed inability to protect Indian lands belies both logic and reality, a fact the Six Nations pointed out at the time. No crime is more easy to detect than squatting, which, by definition, is open and prolonged. (Before the passing of special acts in 1837 punishing squatters on Indian land, squatting was merely a civil offence, that of common law trespass.) The Six Nations' Grand River lands alone in 1840 had, by one count, 400 settler families, including about 2000 individuals, occupying 45,000 acres out of a total of 160,000 acres.[40] Surely these squatters, roughly equal in number to the Indian population (about 2200) and occupying 20 per cent of the land, could not have been difficult to find and punish. The political repercussions of such a massive forcible expulsion of squatters in the Upper Canada of the 1840s would have been a quite different matter.

Political reality, however, should not be confused with the law. The government had formed an unambiguous legal policy regarding squatters as early as 1794. The Executive Council found that squatters lived in every township in Upper Canada: the problem was not limited to Indian lands and could occur on any unoccupied land. When squatters became troublesome to land surveyors, the council set out legal measures to deal with them. Deputy surveyors were to report suspected trespassers to the surveyor general who, 'if the trespassing was proved, was to issue a notice requiring them to vacate immediately.' If this warning was not obeyed he was to report the measure to the council so that the attorney general could take legal action. All squatters who refused to vacate would never be allowed any grant of crown lands.[41]

Nor can it be said that the Six Nations did not protest. A lengthy resolution of the Six Nations' council on 1 March 1809 detailed a number of specific encroachments by name and requested Canadian authorities to take action:

There is a part of our lands that Mr. Mallory pretends to claim a little distance above the place our mill stood; this we disallow of, as we knew nothing about it ...

The next place we come to, is that of John Nelles, we were not generally acquainted with the quantity of the manner in which it was granted by our late Chief; but we imagine that he has caused the survey to pass the limits and he has behaved very improper to some of our people ... Mr. Anderson agreed to keep a mill in order when 200 acres of land was granted him, but he has extended his limits, left the Mill ... and rents it to people that in general are not agreeable to us – we also lay this before him ... A piece of land that was given to a John Huff for the good of his family who are of a Delaware mother – we find he is selling off – therefore as we have forbid these sales it is our request that all those who have attempted to purchase be expelled and his family left in peaceable possession ... We had forgot to mention 4800 acres marked out for Mr. Augustus Jones near the Delaware village – as we have never agreed to this we forbid his getting it – there are others below there who we wish to get off.[42]

The same council meeting listed other tracts that the Indians recognized as being in the hands of settlers under a valid Indian title. For example, a grant to John Dochester had been divided, with Dochester selling a piece that exceeded his grant to a Mr Canby. Since the Six Nations expected Canby to make payments to Dochester's family, they did not oppose the transaction, but when Canby did not make payments, the council asked that 'justice be done them.'[43] Apparently, a continuing sense of obligation ran with land occupancy under Six Nations law.

Sir Isaac Brock, administrator of Upper Canada in 1812, issued a proclamation on the Indian lands that acknowledged the law. The proclamation admitted that 'many white persons are settled on the Indian land in the County of Haldimand (including Grand River) without due authority or License.' It went on to state that 'by law all white persons are forbidden to establish themselves or reside in any Indian Village or Country without such license, under a penalty for the first offense of ten pounds, and for the second and every other subsequent offense of twenty pounds.' Finally, Brock announced that by issuing the proclamation he was making it clear that settlers could not 'pretend ignorance of the law.' All those claiming to reside on Indian lands under some valid licence were required to report themselves to William Claus, deputy superintendent general of Indian affairs.[44]

Although a number of squatters did report under the proclamation, given the confused state of the land titles and the absence of written records, this could not have resolved most title problems. Ezra Hawley, for example, reported purchasing a hundred and seventy-five acres of land granted to William Crum, a volunteer under Joseph Brant in the Revolutionary War, together with fifty acres granted to Benjamin Fairchild, another associate of Brant; he also paid Stephen Carpenter $900 for a farm that was under a 999-year lease. Thus, Hawley's farm, of average size, involved two separate grants and one long-term lease, all unrecorded.[45] No major removals of squatters followed from the Brock proclamation. Rather, in retrospect, Brock's proclamation highlights the ineffectiveness of government land policy: the government was ignoring its own laws regulating squatters from the beginning of the nineteenth century.

Government reports equivocated on the squatter problem. On the one hand, they described the extent of the depredations of squatters who often, for example, clear-cut thousands of acres of valuable oak forest and moved on; many, men of the 'lowest sort,' were engaged in liquor traffic or illicit and corrupt trade with the Indians. On the other hand, such reports did not recommend either punishing squatters or protecting Indian land. This inconsistency cannot be understood from the standpoint of legal doctrine: it was a political compromise.[46]

Objections more rooted in policy than morality were raised by A.J. Russell, assistant commissioner of crown lands, in his report of 1854–5: 'Squatting is injurious to the future character of the settlement. The land is taken up by a poorer and inferior class of settlers. The best lands are picked out by them before the survey takes place, to the exclusion of settlers with more means who cannot be expected to join in the squatting or settle on the inferior lots afterwards.'[47] Yet, in direct contradiction to such a claim, government officials also asserted that many of the squatters were honest and hard-working farmers who had secured their lands either by mistake or by an honest reliance on a sale or lease from an Indian[48]: 'The interests of the Indians, and a humane consideration for the numerous families of white settlers ... alike require that measures should be speedily taken for the adjustment of difficulties.'[49]

The reports are so contradictory that they often make inconsistent policy recommendations within a single page. One report asserted that 'an indiscriminate removal of the white settlers would be most prejudicial to, and was not at all desired by the Indians; while by a judicious arrangement, that estate might be managed to their great and manifest advantage.' Then, a page later, it went on to state the opposite: 'Repeated remonstrances had been made by the Indians against the encroachments of the whites, and the injury their property was daily sustaining from the plunder carried on by the intruders; and the faith of the Government was as often pledged, that steps should be taken to redress the grievance.'[50]

The view that squatters were innocent settlers, deserving the consideration of the crown rather than removal and punishment, is repeatedly expressed and reflects local political sentiment. But it is impossible to believe that, in the Upper Canada of the 1840s, any settler did not know that land could be lawfully obtained only by a written patent from the crown.[51] Brock's 1812 proclamation was specifically intended to remove any defence of ignorance of land laws from the squatters' claims. Such persons were to be dispossessed and evicted.[52] Indeed, one of the salient central themes of Ontario history is the centrality of an orderly land policy in provincial development.[53] Conversely, every squatter must also have known that it was illegal under English and Canadian law to secure land in a private transaction with an Indian.[54] The crown commissioners failed to give effect to the government's elaborate legal policies governing the settlement of either crown or Indian lands, making these policies very close to a dead letter on the Indian reserves. The squatters, in fact, were relying on the unwillingness of the Canadian government to remove them and believed ultimately that they would get legal title to their lands. The result was a de facto land law at odds with the statutory land law: frontier settlers relied on the unwritten law.

Several of the squatter cases that reached the courts or legislative assembly bear out this claim. The longest case in duration involved a dispute between Thomas Clark and Nelson Cozens that also illustrates the unsettled state of Upper Canadian land law. In 1806 Clark attempted to purchase lands in block 4, originally sold by Joseph Brant.[55] Cozens objected to the purchase, claiming that his father, Joshua Cozens, had purchased the lands – an entire township of 92,160 acres – in 1796 from Brant personally, although the deed was never recorded and had, through a series of accidents, been lost.[56] Cozens claimed that the transaction was so well known that it should be given legal effect.[57] In the meantime, the legal history of the deed came to include 'a lost deed, the theft of legal papers, fraudulent practices upon the person of an old man, an old trunk containing valuable papers left in a garret, and other details.'[58] While at one point the House of Assembly passed a resolution supporting Cozens's claim, he lost in the Executive Council and finally, in 1836, in an appeal to the colonial secretary.[59] He had kept his claim alive for thirty years, through all of the legal processes of Canada, and at substantial legal expense, with no documentary proof whatever.[60]

Mary Martin, an Onondaga woman, lived alone on a cultivated lot on the Six Nations' Grand River lands.[61] She was very poor, living on the proceeds of a few vegetables and a government payment of £6 a year from Indian funds. Desiring to make her lot more profitable, she thought it would be better to have it worked by whites rather than by Indians and asked James Hagar to work it on shares. They made an oral agreement that he would farm the land for five years, giving her one-third of the proceeds.

Upon hearing of the agreement, Onondaga chiefs persuaded Martin to break it off. The Indians had been involved in an ongoing land dispute with Hagar, a squatter, dating back to 1832 when he settled on land which he had illegally 'bought' from an individual Onondaga but which the Onondaga had opposed because it contained a sacred site used in the white dog ceremony. Unable to remove Hagar legally because they lacked recourse to Canadian authorities, the Onondaga took the law into their own hands and attacked Hagar, striking him in the head with an axe and leaving him for dead. He lived, however, and went to court against

both his assailants and the Onondaga, later getting his illegal title confirmed.[62] Mary Martin, deferring to the will of her nation, agreed to ter-
minate the lease and informed Hagar of her decision. He defied the Six
Nations and insisted that she honour the agreement, while also planting
wheat on the disputed land. The Indian superintendent charged Hagar
with making a lease for Indian lands without the consent of the crown.
Upon conviction Hagar appealed, arguing that the statute referred only
to 'legal leases' not informal ones. The Court of Common Pleas broadly
construed the statute, citing its language prohibiting such leases 'in any
manner or form, or upon any terms whatsoever.'[63]

In fact, the court addressed the policy behind these statutes in response
to Hagar's argument that his agreement was a benefit to Martin. To give
effect to such an agreement, stated the court, would be to legislate instead
of administer the law. Characterizing the statute as 'designed to protect
the Indians from all contracts made by them in respect to lands set aside
for their use, in consequence of their own improvidence,' the court
denied any interest in the substance of the bargain, limiting its inquiry to
the question of whether the crown had given consent.[64] Indians were, as a
matter of law, improvident even when they made a good bargain for land
they did not want. The same logic did not follow when Indians sold their
lands to the crown: while 'improvident' Indians needed protection from
legal dealings with settlers, they did not need such protection from the
crown, their protector.

Hagar defied the Six Nations and Canadian land law for twenty years.
He appears to have been very aggressive in his pursuit of Onondaga land,
dealing with individual Indians under circumstances that we cannot
know. While the Six Nations prevailed in this case, they could not evict
him from tribal lands that he held under other pretexts. Hagar became an
established and prosperous farmer, living in the middle of Indian lands
and evidently using whatever ingenious chicanery he could to gain access
to additional land. Like other local settlers, he may have been quite hostile
to Indians, a hostility fuelled by repeated land disputes.[65]

This same kind of aggressiveness on the part of a squatter emerges in
another case, The Queen v. Strong.[66] The Indians involved in this case had
requested the assistance of the crown in removing trespassers from their
lands, with Peter Smith, an Indian leader and interpreter, providing the
evidence.[67] James Strong was among many squatters at Grand River
whose ejectment was sought by the Indians. He mounted a substantial
defence against an action against him for trespass, grounded in procedural issues and formalities of land title. Losing before the two crown

lands commissioners, he appealed. Among his arguments was the claim that there was insufficient evidence to prove that the lands in question were Indian lands, a claim based on the fact that there was no adequate system of land registration on the frontier. Yet Strong had been charged with trespass on Indian lands because, like most squatters, he made no effort to purchase the land, and so the court could not evade deciding that the lands in question were Indian lands within the meaning of the statute. The Court of Chancery, in 1850, rejected Strong's argument, holding that the parole testimony of one Indian witness was sufficient to establish that the lands in question were occupied by Indians although ceded to the province.[68] The fact that Strong, in 1850, went to Chancery Court on such a basic question as how the crown could prove that Indian lands were in fact Indian lands is one illustration of the tenacity of squatters.

At the bottom of the whole case was the legal issue of whether Indian land title, not formally recorded as most settler titles were, could be established by Indian testimony that lands were 'Indian lands.' The courts ruling in the affirmative was a necessary step to protecting Indian lands beyond the reach of written land records.[69]

The case of James Wilkes, another squatter on the Six Nations' Grand River lands, also wound up in the Executive Council.[70] Wilkes's case is nothing short of amazing: having already made a fortune, and secured the patents to valuable land that he had squatted on, he petitioned the Executive Council for a grant of even more land to repay him for all of his work and investment in opening up the Grand River lands to settlement. All this when, had a simple law been enforced, he would have gone to jail as a thief and a trespasser.[71]

Five or six years earlier (about 1833), Sheldon, Dutcher and Company had won a judgment against Augustus Jones, a government surveyor, for a large sum of money and taken out an execution against his goods in the Gore District. Jones held a Brant lease to 1260 acres of Six Nations lands but had 'disposed' of most of it, retaining 208 acres. The sheriff seized the land and sold it to William Andruss at a sheriff's sale. Wilkes purchased the land from Andruss. The Six Nations intervened, arguing that the sheriff had no right to sell Indian land, and blocked Wilkes's attempt to register his title. When he could not get legal title through the courts, Wilkes petitioned the Executive Council for redress.

Wilkes, incredibly for the late 1830s, argued that the Indians had a legal right to dispose of their lands and that the lease should be confirmed. Moreover, he made an equity argument that, relying on his title, he had made extensive improvements, including the surveying of the front of the tract into town lots, greatly increasing the value of adjacent Indian lands and providing for the creation and expansion of the town of Brantford.[72]

The Executive Council denied the legal basis of Wilkes's claim. The law was well settled: the right of Indians to alienate their lands 'has been repeatedly denied, and this denial has been confirmed by Her Majesty's Government, specially in the case of Nelson Cozens.'[73] Citing a long history of permitting the purchase of such lands, for reasons of equity the council stated that Wilkes would probably have been allowed to purchase his lands at the ordinary price of farm lands. The problem, stated the council, was that Wilkes had the 'sagacity' to recognize that a new town would develop on the site of these lands. The government could not, as trustee for the Indians, let one Indian family make an alienation of land so detrimental to the interests of the nation as a whole: placing a village of settlers on Six Nations lands. The land was ordered surveyed, with the proviso that 'the utmost favor be shewn to Mr. Wilkes consistent with the interests of the Indians.'[74]

The survey revealed that, although an extensive village had sprung up, Wilkes had exaggerated both the extent and the value of his improvements. In fact, his lots were unimproved but included a mill race worth £1300. Wilkes was a land speculator. Still, the council insisted on seeing his actions as a benefit to the Indians:

In all their deliberations upon those claims, the Council have carried to their consideration a just sense of the benefits which are likely to result to the Indians from Mr. Wilkes' sagacity in discovering the great natural advantages which Brantford possesses; and from his activity and energy in ascertaining the development of those advantages, by his spirited and judicious exertions from Bringing them into early operation ... They have been disposed ... to grant him every indulgence which a reasonable regard to the interests of the Indians would permit.[75]

Wilkes was granted several lots outright and allowed to purchase others at their pre-development price.

Superintendent of Indian Affairs Samuel P. Jarvis opposed this action. In a memorandum to the council, he set out the history of Wilkes's 'sagacity' at Brantford. Wilkes, together with his father, John, and brother, also named John, had settled on the lands where Brantford now stands in 1823 and, by 1840, they had already survived seventeen years as squatters. The father had operated a store 'frequently filled with Indians in their original garb.'[76] He had leased 200 acres of Indian land from

Ester Hill, a widow, and John Hill, her son, for a term of twenty-one years at a rent of £3 15s per year. This was wild land with no 'Indian improvements' which might be legally sold or leased. After three years Wilkes renegotiated the lease, this time for a 999-year term at a small increase in the rent of £2 10s per year. In 1829 Brantford was laid out, with Wilkes's lot in the centre of it, holding the valuable mill privilege.[77] As soon as the town was laid out and the legal dispute began, Wilkes stopped paying his annual rent, thereby impoverishing the Hill family. The family, consisting of four children, were deprived of all their lands by this lease. For Jarvis, the lease was in violation of the common rules of law and equity. Wilkes, having knowledge of the likelihood of a town site developing, acquired a huge amount of land on unfair terms. His mill site alone was worth £1300 at the same time as he was failing to pay an annual rent of £3 15s. The crown's policy behind the growth of Brantford was to increase the value of Indian lands, but the greatest part of that value was being distributed to speculators.[78]

Jarvis's memorandum – and the several others he wrote afterwards – fell on deaf ears. Although the 1840 report had recommended a strengthened law against squatters, the government, intent on occupying Upper Canada with settler/farmers, was unwilling even to pretend to enforce it.[79] The existing Act for the Protection of Indian Reserves permitted the appointment of special commissioners to investigate and try cases. The 1844 report went much farther, urging the appointment of Indian 'rangers' to enforce the laws against squatters and extending the act to Indians who sold or leased their lands to settlers as well as to settlers who took advantage of those illegal land transactions.[80] The final appendix of the 1844 report extensively cited the case of the Cherokee Rangers, who had been created to enforce similar laws.[81] But the idea of empowering armed Indians to patrol their lands with the legal authority to arrest trespassers was politically unacceptable and never seriously discussed.

The Wilkes case follows a distinction in the 1840 report: there were two classes of squatters: one set was 'deserving' and should be protected by law, the other was venal:

As to the course to be adopted with respect to Squatters upon Indian lands. These may be divided into two classes – First, of those who have taken illegal possession of the Land, either under some pretended license from individual Indians, or without even such a color of title, for the purpose of farming alone, and have cleared and cultivated, and built upon the land.

Secondly. Such whose illegal possession is accompanied by circumstances of a

still more objectionable nature – such as cutting and plundering the valuable Timber – keeping houses for the sale of spirituous liquors, and otherwise disseminat-
ing the vices into which the Indians, so easily fall ...

The first class by the valuable improvements upon and attached to the lands,
have given a sort of security for their ultimately making to the Indians full compensation for their temporary usurpation and their cases may for the present be
postponed ...

The second class of squatters, your Committee conceive to be entitled to no
consideration ... but that the Commissioners appointed under the Act for the protection of Indian Reserves, ought to be instructed promptly to enforce the law
against them.[82]

This analysis is revealing for it shows that legality had nothing at all to
do with the difference between 'deserving' settlers, like Wilkes, who
deserved every consideration from the government, and those 'undeserving.' Those who took their lands through some direct agreement with
Indians were grouped with those who took their land from the Indians by
pure theft and trespass. The critical issue was not title but whether a
squatter was productively farming the land. Many, like Wilkes, placed
themselves in the deserving category by falsely claiming improvements
or by putting up 'instant' improvements, shabby buildings and cheap
fences, to mask their depredations on the land.

This level of uncertainty of Grand River land tenure at the highest legal
and political levels set a stage for the squatter controversies which followed: the Cozens and other cases tied up over 187,000 acres of prime
lands – almost 300 square miles – for up to forty years during a period of
rapid settlement. Some measure of the extent of the aggressiveness of
squatters and their success in using these methods to gain control of land
can be seen in the 1840 report's reference to the squatter presence in two
townships, Dunn and Cayuga, which the Six Nations surrendered in 1831
and 1834, at least in part to secure some income.[83] The 'intruders exceed
calculations,' reported Indian superintendent Samuel Peters Jarvis. The
townships held 'one hundred settlers, who had possession of the lands for
five or six years without paying anything, and occupying 10,000 acres.
During that period all the most valuable timber had been cut down and
sold.' This timber was to have been sold for the benefit of the Six Nations.[84]

THE CROWN FORCES SIX NATIONS LAND CESSIONS

The Upper Canadian government, then, had a straightforward message for the Six Nations Confederacy: it was unable to protect their lands from the squatters' depredations. There was one solution: if the Indians would surrender most of their lands, the depredations would cease. That is what was proposed to the Indians in 1841:

The Lieutenant-Governor has directed me to inform the deputation of Chiefs from the Grand River that he has considered their speech to him [protesting settler occupation and depredations on their lands]. [He] is of the opinion that very great difficulty will be found in any medium course between the expulsion of all the intruders or non-interference as experience has shown that with all the anxiety to do justice, and with all the care exercised to prevent injury to the Indian interests, the interference of the Indians themselves, continually, has created new difficulties, to which there seems to be no end ...

[He] is of the opinion that there can be no remedy formed for the continuance of the unsatisfactory and embarrassing state of affairs, while the lands remain the general property under circumstances which it is no reproach to the Indians to say that they cannot manage the estate for general interests of the tribes.

The Lieutenant-governor therefore, considers that it would be very much for the benefit of the interest of the Indians if they surrendered into the hands of the Government the whole tract, with the exception of such part of it which they may choose to occupy as a concentrated body ... and the Lieutenant-Governor strongly recommends that this course be adopted by them, that they immediately select a tract of sufficient extent to give each head of the family or grown up man a farm of one hundred or two hundred acres ... together with a further quantity to be reserved for firewood and other contingencies; and the Indians then remove to this tract and live together as a concentrated body upon the farm assigned to them, and that the residue of the tract be surrendered to be disposed of for the exclusive benefit of the Indians. The Lieutenant-Governor is also of the opinion that when the Indians are thus settled together, there will be no difficulty in keeping away any intruders, or summarily punishing them should they persevere in committing trespass on their tract of land.[85]

The reaction of the Six Nations' chiefs to this document was one of incredulity: it was a transparent ruse for a land grab – withdrawing legal protection from the Indians in order to force them to sell their lands. There was great dissatisfaction at Grand River, prompting Jarvis to send another letter on 15 January.[86] This letter went much farther. Jarvis blamed the squatter problem on the Six Nations:

From a careful inquiry into the nature of the claims of the white man, to the lands in their occupation, it is but too plainly apparent that they have been invited by the great majority of the Indians and that the latter have received large sums of money which they are wholly incapable of ever refunding. So far, indeed from the repeated remonstrances and calls upon them for protection, they find every measure proposed thwarted by the conduct of the Indians themselves, by the repeated pretended sales of their public property, and that, too, not only within the last year, but if I am correctly informed, within the last fortnight by some of the Chiefs and Indians who have been the most urgent in their remonstrances.[87]

This accusation is dishonest. Squatters were not living on the Six Nations' Grand River lands because they had paid high prices for them. Mrs Hill and her children had not become rich off their 999-year lease to Wilkes. The charge that the Six Nations' chiefs were, at the same time, selling their land and protesting the sale of Indian land to the government is without documentation. Indeed, even Jarvis appears to qualify his citation to an unnamed informant. The Six Nations' council had brought the issue of the removal of squatters to the attention of the government since the turn of the century: witness their remonstrance of 1809 in which they had carefully listed, by name, a number of squatters and demanded their removal.[88]

The real issue, however, is found in Jarvis's next sentence: 'Under such circumstances it cannot be expected, nor would it in any manner tend to the interests of the Indians, that upward of 2,000 white persons nearly equal in number to the Indians upon the Grand River, should be utterly removed from their homes, for which in some instances they have paid so dearly to individual Indians; neither justice nor policy, or a due regard to the Indians interests, requires, or will permit of such a measure nor can any such be expected or approved of by me or recommended to the government.' The colonial government was not about to evict 2000 squatters.

Finally, Jarvis interjected himself into Confederacy politics, embracing one of the Six Nations' factions, the 'industrious and worthy' remnants of Brant's faction, while criticizing the other:

The above plan proposed [regarding the Six Nations' land cession] meets with the approbation of the most intelligent and industrious and worthy of the Indians ... Those who are opposed to it must therefore reflect that any private division in the Council from what ever cause proceeding, cannot prevent the Government from interfering in seconding the wishes of the Industrious and from promoting the wealth of the Nations as a body.

In case any further division should take place in Council and by declining amicably to meet their views of Government, the Indians should continue to thwart the measure devised as most conducive to their interests, I am apprehensive that the Government will be compelled, however, reluctantly, to take into their own hands the exclusive management of their affairs, and as Chief Superintendent it will be my duty immediately upon by return, to recommend such a course, to prevent the public property of the Six Nations from being sacrificed to the avarice and rapacity of individuals.

Jarvis's reference to the 'avarice and rapacity' of some traditional Six Nations chiefs (those in the opposing faction) is beyond comment – a year earlier, after all, the Executive Council had awarded some Six Nations' lands to Wilkes, who was avaricious and rapacious – but this language cannot have been lightly chosen. Jarvis's determination to protect the 'public property' of the Six Nations from their traditional chiefs can be taken only as a political statement.

On 18 January, three days after Jarvis's letter, the chiefs assembled and surrendered their lands. They kept only the 20,000 acres Jarvis suggested, approximately 100 acres per person, plus the improved lands individual members of the Six Nations actually occupied, totaling about 55,000 acres.[89] We know nothing about the actual deliberations that led to this process, but the outlines are clear. Since at least the time of Brant's original land sales, the Six Nations had been divided into at least two factions. 'The Indians of the Six Nations have been long divided into parties,' Lieutent Governor Sir John Colborne reported in the 1830s, 'one of which was in the interest of the Brants, and another supported by the chiefs opposed to them.'[90] Jarvis threw his support behind one faction, threatening the other. It is not difficult to explain the viewpoint of the Six Nations' chiefs who wanted to hold on to their lands: attachment to land had deep roots in Six Nations culture. Those who wanted to sell may have been motivated by individual gain from land sales, as well as from a feeling that the annuity money would benefit the Six Nations, the same kind of ideology that may have moved Brant in his land sales.[91]

This land surrender did not stop squatters. Although a much denser concentration of Indians on far less land restricted the squatters' opportunities, their claims for Indian lands were still going to Upper Canadian courts at the time an 1858 report on Indian affairs was published.[92] The crown was now committed to an assimilationist policy that involved the protection of Indians on their remaining lands: authorities were more willing to defend the remaining reserve lands from squatters as an element of the permanent resolution of the 'Indian problem.' Yet the legal process ground on slowly.[93] A special act provided for trials of squatters by land commissioners with an appeal to the Court of Chancery. The Chancery Court repeatedly held against the squatters,[94] but the government still treated them as entitled to some measure of special consideration for all the labours they had expended to develop the country: £8,000 in Six Nations annuity moneys were paid individual squatters for their 'improvements' on the 55,000 acres retained by the Indians.[95] While the squatter problem existed on lands other than Indian ones – tenacious squatters occupied any lands they could find – the government used the squatter issue to force the cession of the Grand River lands.

THE GRAND RIVER SIX NATIONS: LIFE, LAND, AND THE LAW, 1784–1860

What underlay the dispossession of the Six Nations from most of their Grand River lands? It seems fair to say that, in part, the issue was racism and ethnocentrism, forces at work in the expansion of the British empire and the formation of colonial settler states. There can be no question that many officials were both contumacious and ignorant of Indians in the mid-nineteenth century. Their attitudes took a number of forms. On the simplest level, settlers believed that they could make productive use of lands that Indians wasted. But that may cast their dispossession of Indians in too neutral a light. The idea that the Six Nations' laziness and chicanery in land deals were responsible for the squatters is rooted in mythology and in misrepresentation of the actions of the 2000 Indians living there. Most basic to this was the idea that the Indians were 'improvident,' relying on government annuities for survival because they had an aversion to labour[96]: 'This reliance has doubtless had the effect of encouraging their natural indolence and improvidence; of keeping them a distinct people; of fostering their natural pride and consequent aversion to labour; and of creating an undue feeling of dependence upon the protection and bounty of the Crown.'[97]

The logic following from this was that the Indians could not make actual use of the lands reserved for them but preferred to get money without work by leasing or selling this land to settlers. A detailed inventory of Indian improvements to the Six Nations' lands disproves the view of them as 'indolent': they had considerable properties by contemporary standards. A government report done in 1843 found 397 houses (primarily built of logs) and 55 barns on 6908 acres of improved land.[98] Indians owned 85 wagons, 127 sleighs, and 153 plows. Stock included 350 horses,

561 oxen, 790 cows, and 2070 hogs.[99] The Six Nations' Grand River lands were composed of isolated homesteads, often small farms, spread out along country roads.[100] There were two small settlements: a Mohawk village of about twenty-four houses, two miles east of Brantford, and a Tuscarora village of about thirty houses, eleven miles east of Brantford, near the Six Nations' council house.[101]

The Six Nations at Grand River, in common with the other First Nations in Upper Canada, had repeatedly complained for over forty years to crown authorities about settler depredations on their lands. Other than the use of direct violence against settlers, an option never accepted by Six Nations leadership, there were no means available to exclude squatters who engaged in questionable legal arrangements with individual Indians.

Besides the Hagar case, which ended disastrously for the Six Nations, there was only one other documented case of direct Six Nations action to enforce their land rights against squatters. John W. Hill, a Mohawk chief, destroyed the nets of squatters in an effort to drive them away from an Indian fishing ground. The squatters, like Hagar, sued Hill and he lost; he was ordered to pay costs and a fine. Bankrupted by the judgment, Hill borrowed Six Nations money, but he was then unable to repay the debt. He appealed to Superintendent Jarvis to be advanced money from the annuities due him, his relatives, and their families in an effort to pay the debt.[102] There is no record that Jarvis advanced the money. Hill was impoverished for his effort to exclude trespassers from a Mohawk fishing ground.

Jarvis summarized the complaints of the Six Nations in the 1840 report: 'The evils complained of, are: First, the unauthorized destruction of Game within the Indian reserves by the surrounding inhabitants. Secondly, the cutting and lawless removal of Timber; and, Thirdly, the illegal occupation of lands by trespassers, under pretended sales or licenses from some individual Indians, or under no title whatever.'[103] He went on to state that the crown was not going to take any action to support the Indians in any of these areas.[104]

Taking these complaints in order gives some insight into changes in the way of life of the Six Nations as their lands became more affected by settlement. There can be no question that the game was decimated by the 1840s, yet hunting was still an activity of great importance to the Indians. Jarvis, together with the other Indian agents, believed that the hunt was primarily of symbolic importance: 'As to the destruction of Game within their hunting grounds, encircled as they are by agricultural settlements of the European race, it is hardly worth the inquiry; for if the whole people within the several reservations had to depend upon this source of subsistence, they would speedily become extinct. It continues just plentiful enough to keep alive their ancient propensities, and furnish a pretext for continuing the habits of savage life.'[105] Following the logic of his argument, Jarvis believed that the ultimate destruction of the game would benefit the Indians by eliminating this 'pretext,' a view that ignored the cultural linkages between hunting and traditional life. Men hunted in extended family bands, often taking male children out of school for weeks. About two-thirds of Six Nations men engaged in an extensive fall hunt of two weeks to three months. The most common hunting grounds were in the townships of Norwich, Zorra, Denham, Wendham, Blenheim, and along the Chippewa Creek, but, when unable to find game there, they went far distant.[106] The fact that these hunts continued long after the game had disappeared troubled authorities, who saw Indian hunting as wasteful and also as a continuation of primitive traditions.

But there was a more pragmatic and legalistic rationale for Jarvis's views. Even the most severe penal sanctions, he believed, would not stop the settlers from killing game on Indian reserves, a simple extension of the view that the law could not stop squatters. Moreover, he had a measure of juridical equality in mind: as long as Indians were allowed by law, through their treaty rights, to hunt in settled lands, 'it would be unfair to make the killing of game by white people on Indian reservations penal.'[107] Such logic does not follow from the jurisprudence of treaty law: the Indians had surrendered many of their traditional land rights but retained the right to use the land for hunting and fishing. On their reserves, they retained all hunting and fishing rights.[108] Jarvis's real point was not legal but political: even if Indians had different legal rights than settlers, it was not politically prudent to enforce them.

Customary land tenure at Grand River divided much of the land into individual holdings. Although these holdings were unrecorded, all recognized their boundaries and the terms upon which the land was held. Individual Indians could sell their lands and improvements to other Indians, but not to settlers. Improvements could be sold to settlers, under both tribal and Canadian law. Temporary use of Indian lands could be rented or leased to settlers under Six Nations customary law, but not under Canadian law. The ruse of Wilkes to gain effective title through a 999-year lease was not of his invention but rather was a common frontier device to circumvent Canadian laws prohibiting the 'purchase' of Indian land. Still, all such leases were illegal as well. Illustrating the parallel operation of two legal systems, these leasing arrangements also attempted to circumvent Six Nations law permitting an individual lease for a temporary use of Indian land but forbidding its sale.[109]

Following their own law, the Six Nations made a great deal of money leasing different kinds of land use rights to local farmers. This was not an alternative to Indian farming: contemporary accounts claim that most Six Nations families farmed small plots of land. Rather, settlers used the land much more extensively than the Six Nations did, and individual Indians leased surplus lands to settlers. Similarly, in an age with a high death rate from all sorts of causes, Indian widows often leased their lands to non-Indian farmers. Sometimes this was because settlers paid higher prices, but it is also likely that there was no market in leases to Indians: Indians had farm land and did not need to lease it.

While individual Indians appear to have leased land to squatters for timber-cutting, squatters used the pretense of timber leases to engage in rapacious lumbering practices that violated the terms of the leases: 'The timber thus cut is taken generally by speculators from the United States, to which country it is conveyed. It is generally cut under some pretended license from a Chief or other individual Indian, having no authority whatever to confer it; the extent to which this illegal traffic has been carried on, on the Grand River, may be conceived when it is stated, that the tolls of that navigation are very materially increased by this transport.'[110]

These depredations on Indian lands were accompanied by increasing Six Nations involvement in Canadian politics, capped by the election of John Brant to the House of Assembly in 1832.[111] There is no historical documentation on Brant's motivations for seeking a seat in the assembly, but he was elected with the support of settlers on the Six Nations' lands, especially Warner Nelles, an election official.[112] The creation of a new riding, Haldimand County, with about 1000 electors living mostly on the Six Nations' lands, may have prompted Brant to move into electoral politics to protect the interests of the Six Nations within the larger Canadian society, a rationale that would have been consistent with his father's politics.

His election was challenged on the basis that the majority of votes for him were cast by persons, primarily squatters but also including Indians, who were not landowners and therefore had no right to the franchise; Brant himself met the property qualification but few other Indians did.[113] He was disqualified and his opponent seated.[114] The affair left the Six Nations bitter, for it denied them not only the franchise but also ownership of their lands.[115] The underlying issue was a crown attack on their communal ownership of lands: if Indians took title to their farms in fee simple, they would have the right to vote. The dishonesty here was that, even if individual Indians did take personal allotments, these were still held in trust by the government and did not satisfy the property qualification for voting. Almost irrelevant in this context, but illustrating that juridical equality was largely conceded in Canada, no one contested the right of Indians, as a general class of persons, to vote, nor the right of Brant to hold political office. By this time a handful of Six Nations Indians were qualified electors, having qualified the same way as white men: they purchased land outright from the crown.[116]

Besides the repeated protests of the Six Nations over both their own land rights and the unwillingness of the government to control squatters, the most documented issue arousing Six Nations grievances against the government in the 1830s was the Grand River Navigation Company. Through a complex chain of events, the Indian Department joined local settlers in a scheme to develop the valley by opening of a system of locks on the Grand River. This navigation system would bring settlers to the district and boost the economy but also displace Indians from their lands. To add insult to injury, the Indian Department financed the company with the Six Nations' annuity money but without consulting the chiefs, forcing the Indians to pay for a scheme to increase settler pressure on their lands.[117] The Six Nations repeatedly protested the whole enterprise: it would ruin their fishery, flood their lands, and move more settlers into the valley. They raised an obvious political issue: given that the Six Nations owned a controlling interest in the company (80 per cent of the stock by 1840), why did they not have control of the board of directors?[118] By the late 1840s the company, which had never been profitable, was bankrupt, costing the Six Nations virtually all of their annuity money.

Underlying the issue of Six Nations land rights was their assertion of national sovereignty. In this regard, the distribution of 'presents' was a unique feature of British-Indian relations in Canada that assumed both legal and symbolic dimensions. In elaborate annual ceremonies, Indian agents personally distributed goods to Indians. These trade goods including cloth, blankets, knives, and cooking implements were useful and valuable in frontier commerce. The ceremony involved the gathering of an entire Indian nation for a number of days of feasting, speeches, and meetings, a celebration that, with the use of alcohol, became increasingly wild. British authorities after the 1830s were determined to end the distribution of presents, both because of their discomfort with the annual ceremonies and because these ceremonies highlighted the nations' unique political status in Canada and encouraged dependency.[119]

Not surprisingly, the First Nations saw the issue differently: 'Father, these "presents" (since we are taught to call them by that name), are not in fact presents. They are a sacred debt contracted by the Government, under the promise made by the Kings of France to our forefathers, to indemnify them for the lands they had given up, confirmed by the Kings of England since the cession of the country, and, up to this time, punctually paid and acquitted.'[120]

For the First Nations, both the event of the distribution of presents and the value of the goods themselves represented British deference to their sovereignty and nationhood, an annual recognition of the valuable services rendered by the Indians and an acknowledgment of their distinct status in Canadian society.

The symbolism of the distribution of 'presents' as a recognition of their national status as allies of the crown had great meaning to the Six Nations. Some glimpse of this can be seen in the Six Nations' role in the 1837–38 uprising in western Upper Canada.

Despite their strained relations with white settlers and the Upper Canadian government, the Six Nations remained loyal at the time of the rebellion. William Johnson Kerr, a mixed blood, was ordered to mobilize Six Nations warriors to cut off the westward retreat of rebels following a skirmish at Short Hills, south of St Catharines. The warriors turned out in force. One hundred went west through settlements south and west of Brantford to convey the message that the Indians were on the march, a powerful symbolic threat to the settlers, many of whom may have been sympathetic to the rebels. Kerr then went south along the Grand River with 150 warriors, doubling the force by the time he reached its mouth. This rapid mobilization of 400 warriors – representing the Six Nations' total military capacity – in support of the crown was an indication of how deep both the warrior role and political support for the crown was in Six Nations culture. Kerr reported that 'he found it impossible to restrain the Indians or keep them back.'[121] Although this large Indian militia did not catch any of the rebels, they flushed them from the woods so they could be captured by other troops.

A few months earlier at Scotland (west of Toronto), the main force of rebels had been met by a force of 450 militia and 100 warriors daubed in war paint. While some local news reports claimed that the warriors had been sent out to scalp and murder the rebels, all of the evidence is that the Six Nations conducted themselves as soldiers.[122] Still, their presence in war paint conveyed a powerful image of their continued military position on the frontier, as well as feeding the settlers' fears of massacre at the hands of 'savages.'[123]

Yet, for the Six Nations, the events of 1837–8 were only a short interlude in what was otherwise a mundane, and often difficult, existence. Most Indians lived the life of simple farmers, eking out a small cash income from crops and land rentals or providing day labour or small services to settlers. They lived in scattered one-room log houses, possessing a few farm animals. Small-scale hunting and fishing was important through the 1850s: long after it ceased to have economic utility, it was important for traditional reasons. Unemployment and alcohol abuse were common, and many Indians lived in poverty. Criminal court records from the 1870s on show a disproportionate share of Indians arrested and jailed on a wide range of petty criminal charges, mostly related to drinking and assaults or petty property crimes.

The Bagot commission's investigation of Indian Department operations, reflecting the ethnocentrism of the times, was disapproving of the way all Indians – including the Six Nations – spent their days:

One of the peculiarities of the Indians, in their native state, is their proud aversion to labour; hence in the early stages of civilization, they are accustomed to impose upon the women the greater part of the labour in the field and household ... A systematic division of the day and the hours of labour is not yet practiced among them. The Indian seldom leaves home in the morning before eight or nine o'clock, when the sun being risen the air begins to grown warm; he then in some settlements goes to chapel, in others to his field, where he continues at work during the heat of the day, for six or seven hours, leave off at about four P.M. The rest of the day is spent in idleness in the village, or in fishing and fowling ... At times he will stay at home all day, or sleep during the heat of the day.[124]

CONCLUSION

The Six Nations defended both their land title and their sovereignty in a lengthy and complex series of disputes with the colonial government. These disputes continue to this day. For any number of reasons, some Six Nations chose to admit settlers to their lands, while other lands filled with squatters after the 1790s. The Six Nations, like any other landholders, had authority, under the common law, to eject squatters forcibly – trespassers – from their territory. But such action in the context of a hostile legal system might have constituted assault and been punished under colonial law. In any case, the Indians did not exercise this right.

British and Upper Canadian authorities, who had both the power and the legal authority to eject squatters from Six Nations lands, did not do so.

At first, they deferred to the Six Nations' claims of sovereignty, but, by the early 1800s, they were refusing to honour the requests of the chiefs that certain squatters be removed. By the 1820s Canadian authorities were permitting squatter occupation of the Grand River lands as one element of a strategy to force the Six Nations to cede their lands to the crown, in turn promoting a policy of forced assimilation. Frontier settlers became masters of legal strategies to maintain their precarious status, inventing documents to provide some claim of right. Ironically, in the legal chaos that followed, even such a claim became irrelevant, with mere occupation of the land sufficient to accord a substantial legal claim.

The Six Nations repeatedly protested squatter encroachments upon their lands. Despite the close proximity of the squatters and the level of provocation, there were only a few violent interracial incidents during the entire period. This testifies both to the continued strength of Six Nations law and to the Indians' commitment to lawful solutions to their land disputes with both local settlers and the government. The Six Nations were determined to hold the British authorities to the terms of the treaties, a lesson learned from close proximity to the United States with its major Indian uprising in the War of 1812, but also deeply rooted in a long-standing alliance with the crown. Notwithstanding considerable difficulties with colonial authorities, the Six Nations, in their own culture, never lost their unique status as 'allies' of Britain.

The relationship between the Six Nations Confederacy and the British and Canadian governments has a clear legal history that was understood as such by both sides from the late 1780s. It is a complex history but it is evident that colonial authorities denied their legal obligations to the Six Nations, creating, in the process, disorderly conditions that stand in sharp contrast to the image of an orderly Canadian frontier. The crown, then, took legal advantage of this disorder.[125] With no recognition of their legal rights, the Six Nations were forced to accept repeated reductions of their lands, the last occurring as their reserves were occupied by as many settlers as Indians. While the process took a different form in other Indian land cessions, similar dishonesty and coercion was employed.[126]

3

'The Common Law Is Not Part Savage and Part Civilized': Chief Justice John Beverley Robinson and Native Rights

If the Six Nations' struggle over their land and their sovereignty represents one of the foundational conflicts defining the legal relationship between Indians and Canada, John Beverley Robinson, Canada's most eminent jurist in the first half of the nineteenth century, made more of a contribution towards defining the formal legal context within which this conflict occurred than any other Canadian judge. Here, our attention turns to the poor fit between Indian people and the formalities of Upper Canadian law in the early to mid-nineteenth century, as revealed in the decisions of the colony's leading jurist.

Born in Quebec in 1791, Robinson was chief justice of Upper Canada from 1829 to 1862, following service as solicitor general and attorney general, a fifty-year legal career that began in 1812 at the age of twenty-one.[1] In these various official capacities he participated in the legislative and executive branches of government and was a leading member of the 'family compact' that ruled Upper Canada.[2] Conscious of Canada's place in the British empire, Robinson effectively cultivated his official links to London, a relationship that earned him appointment as chief justice of Mauritius in 1822. Although he declined the appointment because he thought his future would be brighter in Canada, it is clear that Robinson saw himself as a common law judge within a British and colonial context.[3] There is not a single piece of evidence to suggest that Robinson, whose legal mind dominated Upper Canadian jurisprudence in the middle of the nineteenth century, had any consciousness at all of the legal issues presented by the presence of the colony's 12,000 native people.[4]

Robinson was the son of a Virginia planter who had fought for Britain in the American Revolutionary War, and, after the conflict ended, relocated with his regiment to New Brunswick before eventually settling in Kingston, Upper Canada. Loyalists such as Robinson Sr fashioned Upper Canada in their own image. At the centre of the colony's jurisprudence was not mere legal conservatism but a profound loyalty to the crown, an unwavering belief in crown-centred public order, and a strong legal defence of the crown's prerogatives.[5] This cluster of intellectual traits was consistent with prevailing models of legal education. The death of his father when John was seven years old left his family impoverished and John was sent to live at an Anglican school where loyalty to God and the crown was at the heart of his education.

Apprenticed to a lawyer, Robinson quickly made his mark with his appointment, in 1812, at such a youthful age, as acting attorney general. Ever ambitious, he left this position after the War of 1812 to pursue a formal legal education at Lincoln's Inn, one of the London Inns of Court that controlled entry into the British legal profession.[6] This education consisted of dull recitations at formal dinners, exercises in finding the proper rule of law to apply in each case presented.[7] The leading text of the time, Blackstone's *Commentaries*, sought to record hundreds of years of English common law and in so doing make it easy for any lawyer to 'find' the law.[8] Colonial lawyers had access to few cases and legal treatises. The modern case-reporting systems did not exist, and so a lawyer could not readily do his own legal research. But Osgoode Hall, where Robinson later worked, had a substantial law library which would have included British and later, as these countries produced a legal literature, Canadian and American cases and treatises.[9] A problem with importing the English system of formal law and legal reasoning to the colonies should be obvious: Indians and Indian rights do not loom large in Blackstone.[10]

English law was often not a good fit to frontier conditions and Canadian judges, conservative as they were, soon began to construct their own common law. Robinson was well educated for his time and his decisions reflect more than his legal education. They reflect 'polyjuralism,' a willingness to borrow legal ideas from other jurisdictions, including even the United States, and indicate, for example, a familiarity with French law.[11] Yet, in common with most other Upper Canadian judges, Robinson did not often cite American cases. American law, at this time, was undergoing a period of significant change as American judges instrumentally adapted the English common law to American economic conditions, providing an 'Americanization' of the common law.[12] Many of the problems faced by American judges, especially in relation to frontier economic relationships, were similar to those in Canada. While it cannot be said that Canadian judges followed American law in these matters, they were influenced by it.[13]

None of this polyjurality is found in Indian law cases. Robinson, like most Upper Canadian lawyers, merely brought the general principles of English law to Canada and attempted to apply them to Indians. Tribal sovereignty and land rights were not to be found in the English common law. The earliest Indian law cases provide a unique opportunity to study Robinson's conservative common-law methodology.

Robinson's thirteen reported Indian law opinions span twenty-seven years, from *Doe Ex. Dem Jackson* v. *Wilkes* in 1835 to *Regina* v. *The Great Western Railway Company* in 1862.[14] Although two generations of judges had already served in Upper Canada and a court system had been in place since the mid-1780s, only one Indian law case, *Regina* v. *Phelps*, had been reported before Robinson's chief justiceship.[15] (There were, of course, unreported criminal and, perhaps, civil cases.) The legal status of Indians and Indian lands was not established in Upper Canadian courts. Rather, since the Royal Proclamation of 1763 this matter had been left to executive and legislative political processes. Thus, Robinson's thirteen reported cases are foundational in the case law – and therefore the common law – of Indian rights in Canada. It must reflect his perception of his role as chief justice that, through all these cases, Robinson never explicitly defined the legal position of Indians in Ontario. As a result, twenty-three years after his death, in the most important nineteenth-century Canadian Indian case, *St. Catherine's Milling and Lumber Company* v. *The Queen*, Robinson's opinions were cited by both sides: for the proposition that Indians had no title to their land, as well as for the proposition that they did have such title.[16] Robinson authored a large number of Indian law cases: no nineteenth-century judge in North America wrote more published opinions on Indian law than Robinson.[17] At the same time, however, he went out of his way to craft narrow judgments, basing many of his holdings on legal issues or procedural technicalities having nothing to do with native rights.

Legal formalism, the construction of elaborate opinions carefully following precedent, is one manifestation of judicial conservatism. R.C.B. Risk, a careful observer of late-nineteenth-century Ontario law, notes the impact of this formalism on the courts' decision-making process: 'In

Ontario the courts seemed to assume that the common law was composed of rules firmly settled by authority, primarily English authority. It was almost never expressly justified, beyond the justification implicit in its mere existence and the internal authority of courts in a hierarchy ... The process of making decisions seemed usually to be simply finding facts and applying rules. If the law was obscure or uncertain, the court simply had to look harder to find it.'[18] Moreover, this judicial conservatism occurred in a context where the highest appeal was to the Privy Council, an arrangement that put all colonial law under the direct review of British judges.

The implications of all of this for Indian rights are clear: there was no legal precedent, and so judges resorted to some mixture of general common law principles and legislative policy.[19] Further, since Indian matters were not of great legislative importance, legislative policy itself was weakly developed until after the dominion's 1876 consolidation of the Indian acts.[20] The result was a jurisprudential void that bound conservative judges to a body of law that did not give direction.

Jurisprudence, in itself, does not explain the course of Indian law in Upper Canada, for the legal decision-making process was the product of a narrow circle of judges who were also among the political, economic, and social leaders of the colony. The highest levels of nineteenth-century legal policy making in Upper Canada were occupied by only a few people who exercised great, often unchallenged, influence for long periods of time.[21] Native rights were of small concern in this political environment. More difficult to assess in the judicial decision-making process is the role of the judges' own investments in land speculation and their legal representation of land speculators as private clients for lucrative fees.[22]

THE INDIAN LAW CASES OF JOHN BEVERLEY ROBINSON

Robinson's Indian law opinions are not consistent, nor is there a logical chain of development within them over time. In *Regina* v. *Baby* he ruled that 'Indian lands' were crown lands and, therefore, could not be alienated without the consent of the crown, a legal position derived from the Royal Proclamation and reflecting government policy.[23] This formulation of the issue of Indian title made any Indian legal status irrelevant: it was crown land. Robinson had to express a direct view of the legal status of native people four years later in *Totten* v. *Watson*, a case involving the alienation of land granted to an Indian chief in fee simple.[24] His opinion again turned on his view of crown prerogatives, this time cast in racial and paternalistic terms: 'We should find it not difficult to suppose that the legislature might possibly have intended to protect the Indians to that extent, for they are a helpless race, much exposed, from their want of education and acquaintance with business, and the intemperate habits of many of them, to be taken advantage of in their dealings with white people.'[25] Robinson inferred a distinct status to the Indian land at issue because the crown's land grant – to the Six Nations Confederacy – must carry with it the crown's judgment that the Indians in question were distinct from the majority of the Indians in Ontario and intelligent enough to manage their own affairs. Similarly, in *Sheldon ex rel. Doe* v. *Ramsay*, it mattered to Robinson that the Six Nations Confederacy did not appear in law as either a person or a corporation and thus could not hold title to land under English or Canadian law.[26]

Robinson avoided taking on these important legal issues in a direct way. His reference to the 'possible intent of the legislature' in protecting Indians was probably dishonest even in his own frame of reference: with his forty years of experience in government, he well knew what the Indian policy of the legislature was. He was both denying the importance of policy in coming to a holding that put Indian lands up for sale, and boldly asserting that the courts were not obligated to defer to legislative policy in determining Indian rights under the law. Twelve years before, in *Bown* v. *West*, Robinson, in the tradition of social jurisprudence, had begun his lengthy opinion with a discussion of the government's Indian policy, the same Indian policy that he now professed ignorance of.[27]

The extent of Robinson's familiarity with issues of Indian law prior to his appointment to the bench is not known but Indian issues, especially those involving Six Nations lands, had been important in Upper Canadian government during the nearly twenty years that Robinson had been politically active as solicitor general, attorney general, and member of the Legislative Assembly prior to his 1829 judicial appointment.[28] As attorney general he had taken the position that Indians were fully amenable to the criminal laws of Canada.[29] He had represented clients with interests in Six Nations lands, probably in common with every other lawyer in the province. He was paid £699 for his legal work on behalf of William Dickson's interest in block 1, a tract of 94,035 acres of Six Nations land.[30] Robinson also, as a private lawyer, took a leading role in the canal-building boom occurring in Upper Canada after the 1820s, a role that must have involved the securing of complex land titles. There is no evidence that any of these titles directly involved Indian lands then under dispute.[31] Indeed, Robinson's personal papers contain almost nothing about Indian matters.

Robinson's first Indian title case was *Doe Ex. Dem. Jackson* v. *Wilkes*, an 1835 case involving two competing claims to the title of a lot at Brantford, one through the commissioner of crown lands and one through the Six Nations' Haldimand grant.[32] Since Jackson had taken the land under a crown title, that might have ended the matter without any need for the court to pass judgment on the nature of the Six Nations' land title.[33] Robinson, however, directly considered the legality of the Haldimand grant. He must have done so with the intention of using his judicial office to settle the legal chaos occurring in a substantial portion of Upper Canada over the issue of the legal title to Six Nations lands. His view had two components, one now familiar in Canadian Indian law, one idiosyncratic. Robinson's position on the title of the Six Nations was that they held a political, but not legal, right to their land.[34] Haldimand's grant had not been made under seal as governor, but under a military seal. In Robinson's view, this was a fatal defect because 'no grant of the King is pleadable unless under the great seal,' a position he supported by citing English common law.[35] Robinson applied this principle to a declaration by Henry Goulburn, under-secretary of state for the colonies, who had admitted in 1816 that 'the grant on the Grand River which was, after the peace of 1783, made to the Five Nations and their posterity forever, is a grant as full and as binding upon the government as any other made to individual settlers.'[36] Holding that Goulburn's statement was only a statement of a political right meant that *all* Upper Canada land grants were political rather than legal. This obviously was not the case: most of Haldimand's land grants had gone to Loyalists whose legal title was not in question. Haldimand's authority had been both political and military, and it had been exercised during and immediately after a state of war.

This holding, besides denying legal title to the Six Nations over lands that they had the political right to occupy, ruled on the legal status of the Six Nations as Indian nations. The attorney general, representing Jackson (and thus defending the title granted by the commissioner of crown lands), also argued that the Haldimand grant was defective for want of a grantor.[37] This position challenged, not only the Six Nations' land title, but the legal status of the nations themselves. Since there was no such thing as an Indian nation or tribe recognized as a legal entity under the common law, a grant of land to an Indian nation was legally defective because such a grantee did not exist in the eyes of the law.[38] Robinson, ingeniously in his own mind, resolved this issue by holding that the 'Indians were by this grant made a corporate body and enabled to take and hold a corporate capacity, although no corporate name was expressly given to them.'[39] This interpretation denied any legal status to the Six Nations as Indian nations. Rather, they held the legal status 'constructive corporations.'

This extraordinary legal reasoning cannot have been unintentional. For example, Robinson's judgment came after the American cases *Cherokee Nation* v. *Georgia* and *Worcester* v. *Georgia* by four and three years respectively.[40] Robinson, with access to a law library that included American reports of the period, must been aware that those cases recognized Indian tribes as 'domestic dependent nations,' legal as well as political entities.[41] He was apparently attempting to define a legal status of Indians in Canada that rejected the American view of the Indians as possessing some type of sovereignty in their capacity as 'domestic dependent nations.' The legal status accorded Indians in these American decisions is a far cry from Robinson's 'constructive corporations.'

Doe ex dem Jackson v. *Wilkes* has the markings of a test case. Jackson had hired a great deal of expensive legal talent to defend his claim to a lot consisting of a fraction of an acre. William Henry Draper, Jackson's lawyer, was also the attorney general and had worked closely with Robinson on a wide variety of issues, beginning with Draper's first position as a young lawyer in Robinson's office in 1829 when Robinson himself was attorney general.[42] John Wilkes was a land speculator with extensive holdings of formerly Indian lands.[43] The significance of the case was far-reaching: Six Nations land titles were held not legal in Upper Canadian courts. Only those holding land titles from the commissioner of crown lands had legal titles, a holding consistent with the Royal Proclamation.

Robinson did not write again about Indian matters for five years and was then presented with a very different legal issue. In *Little et al* v. *Keating*, an 1840 Walpole Island case, a squatter by the name of Shepherd Collock was convicted by the commissioner of crown lands, on the complaint of two Indian chiefs, of possessing 'a portion of Crown lands.'[44] Little pretended to be living in Collock's house under a lease, but this was apparently a fraud: not only was Little Collock's son-in-law, but Collock was still living in the house. While the evidence showed that Collock had occupied this land since 1816 and that the whole of Walpole Island had been set aside for the Indians, Chief Justice Robinson, after granting a new trial on appeal, held that the conviction was defective in that the commissioner had no general jurisdiction over Crown lands and so needed to formally aver in his charges that the lands in question were Indian lands.[45] Since a common law rule required strict construction of any penal statute, the court could 'intend nothing in favour of convictions' and the conviction was reversed on this ground alone. Moreover, under the 1839 Indian Act, these Indian lands referred only to 'lands in which the title of the aboriginal inhabitants has never been extinguished,' which Robinson read as applying only to 'such lands as some tribe or tribes actually occupy or claim to.'

The opinion was equally technical in other areas, denying that it could 'tell judicially whether Walpole Island be land occupied and claimed by Indians or not' when the court both knew that it was and had the opportunity, at a new trial, to remedy the small defect in the original conviction by simply finding the lands to be Indian lands. The Court of Queen's Bench also found that the evidence of Collock's occupation of the lands, on the 'complaint of the Indian Chiefs, naming no one and not saying whether upon oath or not,' was defective. This ruling, completely consistent with judicial formalism, held the commissioner of crown lands to formal rules of evidence, refusing to modify them for frontier conditions. The commissioner doubtless knew the name of the complainant, as well as that Collock's occupation of Indian lands was open and well known, but had not adequately put this in the record.[46]

As an aside, Robinson, who had until recently held power in three branches of government, was troubled by the 'apparent impropriety' of the Indian agent acting in a double capacity in judicially giving the order to remove the occupant of the land and then, as a trustee for the crown, taking possession of the land.[47] These legal formalisms approached the absurd in frontier conditions: in a country with few legal officials, every Indian agent would either need a second official to act as a receiver or get a local law enforcement official, likely in sympathy with local squatters, to make the ejection. Furthermore, it was a selective brand of judicial formalism: Robinson did not apply it in all areas.

Since Walpole Island was unceded Indian lands, this case was the only case Robinson decided where the Royal Proclamation clearly applied.[48] Since the Royal Proclamation had the force of law, even without the provisions of the 1839 Indian Act, no whites could occupy Walpole Island lands. Thus, Robinson's narrow construction of the later statute is unsatisfactory in judicially enforcing the Royal Proclamation. He was legally obligated to give full weight to all the pre-existing provisions of the proclamation. Not only did Robinson personally not do so, but there is no evidence that the issue was ever raised in court by either party. This omission may indicate that the Royal Proclamation was not seen by lawyers and judges of the day as protecting any Indian rights independent of the early Upper Canadian Indian acts. Yet these acts were much narrower in scope than the Royal Proclamation. The result here is again anomalous: it could not have been foreseen in 1763 that the intent of the Royal Proclamation could be defeated by the technical requirements of the rules of evidence: how does one prove that undefined lands are 'Indian lands' in a common law court with very precise rules of evidence and equally precise rules governing land title? Robinson went to great lengths to defeat the efforts of the crown to protect Indian land rights on Walpole Island.

There is an historical context to this case that raises significant questions about Robinson's underlying motivations. At this time Walpole Island was almost entirely occupied by squatters, and so the impact of this decision was to leave Collock in illegal possession of land, on an island set aside as Indian lands, in open defiance of the crown and its Indian agent, J.W. Keating. Keating, appointed Indian agent in 1838, had done what Indian agents at the Six Nations' lands had said was impossible. Under an 1839 'Act for the Protection of the Lands of the Crown' empowering Indian agents to expel squatters from Indian reserves, Keating, working in cooperation with the chiefs, began to expel squatters.[49] Squatters swore out complaints against Keating and he was twice arrested and taken to court, where he used his own funds to defend himself.[50]

This result can be read in several ways. On the one hand, it surely cannot be denied that formal legal principles might well lead the court to put the commissioner of crown lands on notice that he owed a higher level of due process to squatters. Robinson's decision went out of its way to put technical impediments in the path of the commissioner's ejectment of the squatters, impediments that made no sense under frontier conditions and were not consistently applied in other areas of crown jurisdiction. In doing so, the court impaired not only tribal interests in protecting their diminishing reserved lands but also crown Indian policy aimed at the stabilization of Indian/white relations and the protection of Indian lands from squatters. Robinson cannot have been deferring to crown policy, nor can he have been ignorant of it.

But, on the other hand, the case can be analysed for its underlying policy. In particular, Robinson's protection of squatter interests requires explanation. His personal views on squatters are known and probably represented the views of the rest of the political elite:

I have no sympathy with the genus squatter ... If I were like Louis Napoleon legislating for a country I would allow no pre-emption right to be [given those] who have gone upon land to which they well knew they had no ... claim ... but would give them plainly to understand that so far from the impudent act of trespass giving them a claim they might be satisfied that whatever others persons might get a grant of land, they simply never should on any terms.

I think the favor that has always been shown to squatters has a democratizing tendency.[51]

Squatters impeded the orderly development of a crown lands policy, as well as carrying political and social ideas not consistent with conservative government. Squatters were also often aliens, meaning Americans, bearing disloyal and republican ideas.[52] Yet squatters represented economic development and constituted a powerful political-interest group, and so they posed a difficult problem for Robinson as a judge. Robinson, as a land speculator, had interests in common with squatters: squatters forced the abandonment of lands by Indians, opening them up to legal sale and ownership which raised the value of land. There is also a window here into the legal strategies of the squatters. Collock appears to have invented a scenario involving Indian agent Keating's 'trespassing' on the 'innocent' Little family, indicating the kinds of legal strategies that squatters may have frequently employed.

In *Bown* v. *West*, another Grand River case, a squatter again used ingenious arguments to gain title to Indian lands. In this instance, Robinson began by relying on *Jackson* v. *Wilkes* as precedent, making *Bown* v. *West* the first Indian law case in Ontario that turns on the precedent of Upper Canadian case law.

West, the assignee of Isaac Davids, or Duncan, a Mohawk living on the Six Nations' Grand River lands, bargained with Bown for a parcel of land with improvements that Bown subsequently purchased. Bown later found out that he had been swindled, misled about the quantity of the land he was purchasing.[53] While Duncan had improved 34 acres of land, West sold Bown a parcel of about 134 acres. Duncan had, perhaps legally, assigned to a non-Indian whatever interest he had in several buildings and improvements on 34 acres of cleared land that he 'owned' according to the customary law of the Six Nations. Bown, who entered into a contract to buy this interest in the land and the tavern located on it, got into a dispute over the value of the property after finding that part of Duncan's property rights was unclear under Six Nations law.[54] Bown may or may not have known the true extent of the lands, but he was the initiator of the transaction and was fully aware of the deficiency in the underlying Six Nations' title: he was evidently speculating that, once he was a squatter under a valid claim, he could ultimately gain a crown title.[55] Thus, as in the previous case, Bown had a legal strategy to gain an equitable claim to

Indian lands in spite of laws preventing such actions. When the matter became too complex, however, Bown feigned innocence and rescinded the contract.[56] The complexity of squatter schemes to gain possession of Indian lands can be seen in each of these cases and must represent the range of devices employed in gaining control of Indian lands.

Bown v. *West* brought out the best lawyers in Upper Canada, who again denied a settler claim on Indian lands but, at the same time, were troubled by the magnitude of the problem.[57] While the court's holding was straightforward – no contract for exchange of Indian lands was valid – the complexity of the landholding arrangements in effect at the Six Nations Confederacy at mid-century was almost beyond the capacity of the law to adjudicate. Chief Justice Robinson, for example, pointed out that the crown, while recognizing that Indian title could not be acquired by settlers, often protected the settlers' property rights in improvements built upon Indian lands under traditional doctrines of equity. Robinson further recognized that some interests of squatters were so substantial that a court of equity could hardly refuse to acknowledge them.[58] Yet he did not recognize any equitable right on the part of Bown, and no reported case ever granted a squatter an equitable title in Indian lands.

Squatters did get equitable rights recognized against the crown, but not in Robinson's court. When William Blake was chancellor of Upper Canada, administering the equity court, he and Robinson were in open disagreement on the issue of the equitable rights of squatters, and squatters could prevail against the crown in his court.[59] Such rights, however, were more often recognized by political authorities and crown land officials who, after the crown took Indian title, granted a great deal of land to squatters who had improved it. This recognition came so frequently that false claims of 'improvements' became a common fraud, perpetrated on the government by squatters who hastily threw up a shabby building or two and quickly fenced some land.[60]

In *Bown* v. *West*, Robinson described Indian interests in a completely different way, for the first time incorporating a language – and a policy – of dependency that invoked a new role for the government and the courts in Indian matters: 'The government, we know, always made it their care to protect the Indians, so far as they could, in the enjoyment of their property, and to guard them against being imposed upon and dispossessed by the white inhabitants.'[61]

The Six Nations' lands issue was taken up once more by Chief Justice Robinson in *Doe d. Sheldon* v. *Ramsay et al*, arguably his most important Indian law opinion.[62] Like many of the other land-tenure cases, the basic legal issues belie the chaos of land title in Upper Canada. Two groups of landowners disputed title of a large tract of Six Nations lands. The plaintiff, Sheldon, claimed title under an 1820 sale from the commissioner of forfeited estates; the latter had seized the lands through legal process from Benajah Mallory, who had, under English law, forfeited his lands through his treason in fighting for the United States in 1813. Mallory's title derived from a 999-year lease signed in 1805 by Joseph Brant. Sheldon then brought an action for ejectment of squatters inhabiting those lands.[63] The squatters argued that Sheldon had no legal title because Mallory could not forfeit lands he did not own. Because settlers could not acquire a title from Indians, the original lease from Brant was unlawful.

The largest part of the opinion is spent on an unrelated issue: the land was so poorly described in the forfeiture sale that it was not clear what lands were being conveyed. The parcel was variously described as 60 acres and as 420 acres, delineated by a hut and a marked tree that no longer existed, and defined by a surveyor's description that was factually impossible.[64] Based on this conflicting testimony, believed 'unreasonable and inadmissible' by Chief Justice Robinson, a jury had awarded Sheldon the large parcel of land he claimed, almost three miles along the south bank of the Grand River.[65] In the context of Upper Canadian politics of the time, it is not unlikely that the jury, composed of local landholders whose lands were defined by comparable surveys, was sympathetic to Sheldon, the landowner, construing his title against the crown as extensively as possible.[66] Robinson then turned to the question of Brant's land tenure as the legal key to defeating Sheldon's title, challenging the legality of the Haldimand grant as not being under the proper seal.[67] While this position was derived directly from *Jackson* v. *Wilkes*, Robinson departed from his position that Haldimand's grant had constructively incorporated the Six Nations.[68] In fact, he reversed himself completely: even if Haldimand had a legal right to grant crown land to the Six Nations, the grant was defective for 'want of a grantee or grantees. It grants nothing to any person or persons by name, and in their natural capacity.'[69]

Robinson held further that Brant had no legal authority to sell lands occupied by the Six Nations because the confederacy did not own those lands in fee simple: 'We cannot recognize any peculiar law of real property applying to the Indians – the common law is not part savage and part civilized. The Indians, like other inhabitants of the country, can only convey such lands as they legally hold, and they must convey such lands as they legally hold, and they must convey by deed executed by themselves, or by some person holding proper authority.'[70] It followed that 'no legal estate in any land was created by Captain Brant's lease' and that Mallory had no interest which could be forfeited to the crown.[71] This holding, however, had nothing to do with the nature of Indian title. Rather, it turned on Robinson's interpretation of legal defects in Haldimand's land grant, a technical problem deriving from the common law of property.

Judge Robert Easton Burns wrote a concurring opinion that, while not extending beyond Robinson's regarding the land dispute, went further in denying the sovereignty of the Six Nations:

It can never be pretended that these Indians while situated within the limits of this province, as a British province at least, were recognized as a separate and independent nation, governed by laws of their own, distinct from the general law of the land, having a right to deal with the soil as they pleased; but they were considered as a distinct race of people, consisting of tribes associated together distinct from the general mass of inhabitants, it is true, but yet as British subjects, and under the control of and subject to the general law of England ...

Whether the Indian tribes of this continent acknowledge such absolute authority [of a chief to sell land], and whether it would require to be delegated by a council, I do not know; but whatever may be the Indian laws or customs in this respect, I take it to be clear that the property in the lands which were confessedly at one time in the crown, must be dealt with and disposed of according to the general law of the country ...[72]

Illustrating the centrality of land litigation in Upper Canadian law, Justice William Henry Draper, having taken part in the case while a member of the bar (and simultaneously serving as attorney general), gave no judgment. He had represented Wilkes in *Doe ex dem. Jackson* v. *Wilkes* and had, in that case, argued for the legal recognition of the Six Nations' title through the Haldimand grant.[73] He only took that view as an advocate: as a judge he never supported any view that the Six Nations had either political sovereignty or a title to their lands. Because he had argued that position as an attorney, however, he must have understood the underlying law.[74]

The three judges on this court appreciated the complexity of Indian title. Burns's concurrence, at a time when concurring opinions were rare, must have meaning. While not disagreeing with Robinson, he made a point to state even more sharply his view that the Six Nations' lands were subject to Canadian land law, just as all other lands were. But he also denied Six Nations sovereignty, an issue never directly addressed by any other Upper Canadian judge, and not directly at issue in the case. Burns's discussion of the point may mean that the sovereignty claim was understood to be behind the more narrow property issue. It may also have been in reference to the use of sovereignty language in American cases at the time.

An explanation suggests itself for Robinson's change of opinion on the question of the corporate status of the Six Nations. By 1852 he had been dealing with Indian matters for twenty-three years. Yet no distinct legal status of Indians had found a place in Canadian law. Robinson may have intended *Sheldon* v. *Ramsay* to settle that question in Canadian law in a way distinct from American law in that it would encourage the full amalgamation of Indians into Canadian society. Robinson did not invent the idea of an Indian nation as some kind of constructive corporation. Ten years prior to *Wilkes*, Parliamentary Undersecretary Robert John Wilmot-Horton rendered a legal opinion to Lord Bathurst on the Indian claim to the Seigneurie of Sillery, a former French land grant in Quebec. Horton held, among other issues, that 'the present claimants have no corporate character, in which they could maintain an action for the recovery of the lands.'[75]

Indian nations as legal entities had both brought lawsuits and been held to hold lands under English law since *The Mohegan Indians* v. *Connecticut* as well as under American law.[76] Once Robinson decided that the Six Nations were not a constructive corporation, however, he left them with no legal status at all under the common law as applied in Canada. This put Robinson at least partially at odds with the Colonial Office, which recognized that Canadian Indians had a political status as Indian nations.[77] Access of Indian nations to British and colonial courts to redress their legal grievances was a critical element of the colonial policy of 'liberal treatment' of Indians. While all individuals in Canada – including Indians – had access to Canadian courts, no Indian nation was a party in a nineteenth-century case.

Robinson made one more attempt to assign some kind of common law legal category to the Indian nations. In *Regina* v. *McCormick*, five years later (1859), he was still uncertain about the Six Nations' corporate status.[78] Though his original view was that Haldimand might have constructively incorporated the Six Nations by granting the nation land, this would not have applied to aboriginal legal rights generally, which pre-existed the Haldimand grant. The Indians in *McCormick* were not a party in the case but were involved because the Ojibwa were the original owners of Point Pelee island in Lake Erie. In 1789 Thomas McKee took possession of the land in question as a squatter without legal title, and in 1823 his family sold the land to William McCormick. When McCormick died he left the land to his children. After sixty years of unchallenged occupation, the crown sought to recover the unsurrendered land.[79]

Robinson began his analysis by posing two questions that the crown needed to answer to recover the lands: first, whether the crown had ever exercised any act of ownership over the island; second, whether the crown had acquired the island by purchase from 'the aboriginal tribe to which it had belonged.'[80] This second question recognizes both that some aboriginal nation originally owned the island and that the nation owned the island not as a constructive corporation but as an Indian nation.[81]

The first question was answered by the common law doctrine that adverse possession had to be open and adverse, that is, against the will of the lawful owner, by a party claiming title. An unknown trespasser could not meet the requirements of this narrow rule.[82] Since these lands were unsurveyed, occupied by the original Indian inhabitants whose 'title' had not been extinguished, adverse possession did not apply. It was not 'open' in the sense that the crown was aware of the occupation. Robinson had now twice acknowledged that aboriginal inhabitants had title as Indian nations.

But here Robinson's analytical framework broke down and he never answered the second point of his own question. Instead of moving on to how the crown had acquired Indian title to this land, Robinson held that adverse possession could not run against an Indian nation because 'the Indians could not have adopted any legal proceedings for dispossessing trespassers, either as holding in a corporate capacity or otherwise,' meaning in any other legal capacity, including as individuals.[83]

This analysis is important for three reasons: First, if the issue of adverse possession was even possible against an Indian nation, it meant that the Indian nation owned the land: adverse possession only runs against an owner. Second, the standard for adverse possession against an Indian nation was different than that against the crown because, even if an Indian nation knew of the open occupancy of their lands, they were not, in Robinson's view, in a legal position to dispossess settlers under existing law. While no statute enabled an Indian nation to eject squatters (as it did commissioners of crown lands), Indians could take such action as a common law right following lawful possession that did not require a specific statutory foundation. The Indians 'owned' their lands but apparently lacked the same legal rights as other Upper Canadians to protect them.

The whole idea of Indian nations having the legal right to dispossess trespassers from their lands had to be based on a legal foundation that put Indians within the law as legal actors. Individual Indians, as legal persons, had full access to criminal and civil courts in Upper Canada, but as a practical matter they lacked the economic and social means to bring a civil case to court.[84] It is also likely that cultural differences kept Indians from using the British colonial courts as a dispute-settlement mechanism, a process that had no parallel in tribal society. No case decided by Robinson actually had an Indian as a party.[85]

Third, Robinson was back to 'holding in a corporate capacity or otherwise' as a description of the legal ways members of an Indian nation might hold property.[86] Thus, if a tribe was not some kind of public 'corporation,' it was something else. Exactly what it might be was specified only once in Robinson's original posing of the issue. After a reference to 'aboriginal Indian tribe,' Robinson described the land as occupied by 'Indians,' a term that included both individuals and collective entities.[87] This puts Robinson further from resolving the legal status of Indian title in 1859 than he was fifteen years earlier. Justice Burns perhaps intended to correct Robinson's lack of clarity by writing a concurring opinion that posed the question as to whether adverse possession applied to the unsurveyed public lands of the province, but his opinion answered the first half of Robinson's issue without addressing Indian title.[88]

Regina v. *Baby* is among the first Ontario cases in which an Indian appeared in civil court as a witness against a white man, testifying for the crown against Baby, a land speculator charged with purchasing Indian lands in violation of the first Upper Canadian Indian Act (1839).[89] *Baby* is also among the few cases where Indians appeared in court, arguing their tribal position in a legal matter. The tribe's ownership of the land, however, was not defended by Baby against the crown, and it was not at issue. The case, tried in 1854 at Sandwich, concerned Indian lands in the Detroit area.[90] These lands, like Walpole Island, had been extensively occupied by aggressive American squatters since before the turn of the century. Many of the lands had been sold by Indians directly to settlers, leading to confusion of land titles similar to the situation at Grand River. Joseph Brant had made common cause with Sarah Ainse, an Oneida, who held a substantial block of land opposite Detroit.[91] The Baby family was of old French-Canadian stock, well connected in Upper Canadian politics.[92] The land in question had been in settler hands since the 1790s, for a steam-mill built by a Mr Hands had been there as long as Alexander Clark, a fifty-four-year-old Indian witness, could remember.[93] The Indians held a council and decided to take possession of this land and sell it in order to use the money to make improvements in their village.[94] After they asked their Indian agent, Colonel Bruce, for permission to sell the land but 'could get no satisfaction,' the tribe went ahead and sold the land to Baby anyway for £250, the purchaser specifically agreeing to take all risks of the bargain and bear all expenses.[95] Quite reasonably, the Indians sold title to land they had already lost the use of. Baby gambled that he could ultimately gain crown title to the land.

Baby then took advantage of the state of frontier land dealings and claimed title to a larger tract than the Indians had actually sold. When he approached the crown authorities to negotiate a sale of the lands he pretended to represent the nation's interest, concealing his own contract for ownership of the land.[96] The tribe, realizing this betrayal, then rescinded the agreement, testifying for the crown at trial.

Baby, a wealthy man capable of hiring the best legal counsel, used every argument at his disposal but was convicted in a jury trial. On appeal, he raised the same arguments. First, he denied that the lands were Indian lands, implicitly challenging the crown to prove the Indians had title but also arguing that Indian lands were only those lands physically occupied by Indians. He had purchased a mill on lands long abandoned by the tribe.[97] The Court of Queen's Bench, with Chief Justice Robinson again writing the opinion, avoided the title issues, focusing instead on the statute's prohibition of the act of contracting or bargaining with Indians over land – a phrase governing *any* lands, regardless of title. Second, relying on the chaotic state of lands on the frontier, Baby made a number of technical arguments alleging a discrepancy between the lands he was charged with bargaining for in the indictment and those lands described by the evidence at trial.[98] This argument challenged the capacity of the crown to sustain such convictions with Indian witnesses who, while they were allowed to give evidence, were not likely to describe lands in the same terms as described in court documents. Since the court focused on the illegality of the bargaining process, the precise description of the lands was irrelevant.

Finally, the defendant argued that he lacked the criminal intent to violate the law. Baby did not intend to alienate Indian lands in violation of the statute. Rather, he intended to seek crown approval for his transaction, describing it at merely 'conditional.' The court rejected this argument as running against the public policy designed to protect the Indians from unscrupulous land speculators, a rare statement of Indian policy for Upper Canada courts.[99] Moreover, Robinson interjected a view of Indian title into Baby's *mens rea*: Baby 'knew that the Indians had not the legal title, which was vested in the Crown ...'[100]

Contrasted with *Little* v. *Keating, Baby* goes to great lengths to give effect to the Indian Act of 1839. While Robinson gave the crown nothing in *Little* v. *Keating*, a civil case with a lower standard of proof, he was willing to uphold the conviction of Baby of a criminal offence in spite of numerous technical defects in the trial. The Little family consisted of a pretty rough brand of squatter, but Baby was a member of the richest and most powerful political family on the Detroit frontier. The differences between these two judgments may be idiosyncratic, but one possibility is that over time Robinson became dismayed at the level of fraud and dishonesty in frontier land dealings and, convinced that the continuation of these practices destabilized frontier settlement, abandoned the strict legal formalist approach he had adopted in *Little*.[101]

The law protecting the alienation of Indian lands did not cover the few cases where individual Indians had acquired a legal title to their land in fee simple. *Totten* v. *Watson* is apparently the first case in which Ontario courts dealt directly with the legal doctrine of Indian title, an issue that could be avoided in the trespassing cases because the law of trespassing covered lands 'occupied' by Indians.[102] The land title here was distinct from other cases because 1200 acres had been patented to Captain John Deserontyon, a Mohawk chief, in 1801.[103] He had left the land to three sons and one of them, William John, had sold 100 acres of his inheritance to Cuthbertson, a cousin, in 1842 and the same land to William Totten in 1856. As if this does not exhibit enough of the confusion involved in Upper Canadian lands in the mid-nineteenth century, squatters also lived on the same land but had sold their rights earlier to Totten who, prior to purchasing the land from William John, was already clearing and farming it. Totten's title was challenged under the same statute applied in *Baby* that forbade the sale of land by Indians.[104]

The Court of Queen's Bench, again in an opinion written by Chief Justice Robinson, had no difficulty distinguishing patented lands held by Indians from lands traditionally occupied by Indians. The distinction was crown title: Indians were 'merely permitted' to occupy and enjoy their traditional lands 'at the pleasure of the Crown.' Though the law had never attempted to interfere with the disposition of lands granted to individual Indians by the crown, the court noted that 'very few such grants have been made.'[105] In acknowledging the full property rights of individual Indians in patented lands, Robinson dismissed, without any legal analysis or cited precedent, any Indian property right in their traditional lands, an issue that was not being litigated in *Totten*. This position was consistently held by Ontario courts and was the basis for the province's argument in *St. Catherine's Milling*, but it was not a part of the holding in *Totten* since the court did not decide that issue.

This is not the end of *Totten* for Robinson acknowledged that it was possible that the Indian Act (1839) forbade even the sale of patented Indian lands. The context of the act made it appear to Robinson that it referred only to unpatented Indian lands, but he conceded that the level of Indian dependency was so great that the Legislative Assembly might have intended an even more paternalistic policy. Robinson never came to a consistent position, however, interpreting the Indian Act liberally in favour of government policy. He always balanced government policy against the wide range of private interests involved.

The common element of all these cases is that they involved settlers claiming recognition of land rights derived from Indian title. None of these cases directly involved Indians as parties. Indian rights, while lost or diminished in most of these cases, were not directly decided but were dismissed in dicta. Two of the cases, both actions by crown commissioners to eject squatters, were initially brought by officials acting in response to Indian complainants: *Little* v. *Keating* and *Regina* v. *Baby*. The courts often defended Indian lands against the alienation by individual settlers, although several squatters, for equitable reasons, were allowed to prevail against the crown over lands that had recently been in Indian hands. With the exception of one case, *Little* v. *Keating*, decided against the crown on technical grounds, the opinions were not overly technical, relying instead on broad statements of crown Indian and lands policy.[106]

Regina v. *The Great Western Railway* involved Indian lands at Sarnia sold by the crown lands commissioner for the benefit of the tribe. The railroad then built a roadbed along the river front, blocking off parts of the settlement from the water.[107] Robinson used the case to permit common-law trust doctrine to extend to surrendered Indian lands.[108] The lands in *Great Western Railway*, involving a right-of-way through downtown Sarnia, had been surrendered by the Indians to the crown under a written instrument containing the 'trust or condition expressed in their deed, that it was to be disposed of for their benefit.'[109] Thus, a trust agreement had been created by a written deed between the government and the Indians. The crown itself acknowledged the existence of this trust relationship, leaving it impossible for the court to find that such an agreement did not exist. As early as 1844, the Bagot commission's report had recognized that certain

Indian lands were taken in trust by the government, a distinction that implied that others were not held in trust.[110] While Robinson's narrow construction of the trust concept in relation to Indian lands would have had limited applicability, the use of this concept in defining the legal status of Indian lands soon became much more general, with the crown itself employing it to describe its management of Indian lands.[111] Robinson did not adapt the common law of trusts to fit Indian lands. Rather, he deferred to the crown's existing usage of the concept, contributing nothing himself to the application of the doctrine.[112]

THE INDIAN LAW OPINIONS OF ROBINSON'S COLLEAGUES

Any analysis of the Indian law jurisprudence of a particular judge requires an understanding of its context. The immediate context is the legal work of Robinson's brother judges.

Judges James Macaulay, William Henry Draper, and William Hume Blake were unquestionably Robinson's intellectual equals and none of them would have deferred to Robinson on a point of law. Blake and Robinson, for example, openly disagreed on the legal status of squatters. This disagreement was as much political as legal, but it also reflected the distinct function of the Chancery Court, a court of equity, much more willing to interpret the law in view of frontier conditions. Robinson, judge of a common law court, was more bound by the common law.[113]

Examination of these other Indian law cases illustrates Robinson's domination of the court on Indian issues. While Robinson authored thirteen reported opinions during the years 1829–64, all of the other judges together authored only seven.[114] Only Blake and Draper wrote two each. James Esten, Macaulay, and John Spragge each wrote only one opinion. In 1839 Macaulay, while a judge, authored the first of the general reports on Indians in Upper Canada, a report that can properly be taken to represent his official views on a variety of Indian law matters.

The Macaulay report of 1839 was the most extensive judicial statement on the position of Indians in Canada, running over four hundred manuscript pages.[115] Unfortunately, the document is so shallow and unimaginative that it had little significance. Macaulay's view centred on the duty of Canada's Indian 'citizens' to settle on individual plots of farm land and work hard; if they did so, the report maintained, they were certain, like the Irish, to better their lives.[116] In Macaulay's view, the Indians' collective ownership of property made it impossible for them either to advance socially or economically or to understand the notions of individual responsibility that underlay English law. The full extension of Canadian law to Indians to protect their individual property completed Macaulay's reasoning.[117] These views may have been representative of those of the other judges and members of the ruling elite as well. Macaulay was not selected for this task because he was idiosyncratic: he functioned at the centre of Upper Canadian law and politics for decades.[118]

The Queen v. *Hagar* involved the attempt of a notorious squatter on Six Nations lands to circumvent the terms of the Indian Act of 1839 by making a verbal lease with Mary Martin, an Indian woman, to farm her lands.[119] Brought into court, Hagar disingenuously claimed that the Indian Act forbade only 'legal leases' for Indian lands, not informal, verbal leases. Judge Draper found, however, that the Indian Act broadly forbade leasing 'in any manner or form, or upon any terms whatsoever.' Thus, the fact that Hagar's lease was illegal was irrelevant under the act.[120] This opinion supported the government's Indian policy.

Draper's other opinion, in *Owens* v. *Thomas*, involved a contract entered into by a blind, illiterate Indian, who required an interpreter, that turned entirely on matters of contract law.[121] Owens had paid $140 for a pair of horses, owing a balance of $130. Tracy, the seller of the horses, came to Owens afterwards with a paper for him to sign. When Owens asked what is was, Tracy responded that it was of no consequence. After Owens put his mark on it, he found out it was a chattel mortgage, and Tracy seized the horse. Incredibly, Owens lost at trial and appealed, a sad commentary on the state of local justice in rural Ontario. Draper found that the common law required that contracts be read to blind or illiterate persons and voided the contract, handing a victory to the only Indian litigant in any of these cases.[122] That Owens lost in the lower court may illustrate the common wisdom that an Indian could not get justice against a settler in crown courts, but the reality is that almost no cases involved Indians civilly suing non-Indians. Owens did, lost in the trial court, and then won on appeal.

There were no dissents against any of Robinson's opinions and only twice did a brother judge write a concurring opinion. These two opinions, both by Robert Easton Burns, in *Sheldon* v. *Ramsay*, and *Regina* v. *McCormick*, seem to indicate that Burns was more hostile to the Indians' legal position than Robinson was, although this difference is relative since neither directly acknowledged either Indian title or Indian sovereignty.[123] This can be inferred only from *McCormick*, where Robinson engaged in some small analysis of Indian title while Burns turned the entire case on a construction of crown lands acts that had nothing to do with Indian title.[124] In *Sheldon* v. *Ramsay*, however, Burns engaged in a three-page review of the legal status of Indians under Upper Canadian law that denied, not only land title, but any legal recognition of Indians as nations or governments, including Robinson's view that Haldimand had 'incorporated' the Six Nations.[125]

This concurrence is the most extensive discussion of the status of Indians by a Canadian court prior to *St. Catherine's Milling*. It is also the only Canadian analysis of this period that implicitly refutes, without citing it, John Marshall's analysis in the Cherokee cases. The fact that Burns's analysis of Indian title disagreed with Robinson's in these two cases nine years apart indicates the consistency of Burns's views, as well as that there was an open disagreement at the time over the role of the courts in determining the legal status of the Indian nations. Burns would have used the Court of Queen's Bench in a more active way to create a jurisprudence denying Indian rights.

ROBINSON'S NATIVE RIGHTS JURISPRUDENCE: A SUMMARY

Robinson's conservatism in Indian law matters was not based on precedent: he rarely cited other cases in his opinions. Often he made reference without citation to well-understood common law principles, but there is no sense that Robinson made much use of a law library in writing his Indian law opinions. His 'polyjurality' was not found in native law cases: he never cited Quebec or American cases, and he never made reference to Quebec, American, or even British colonial history, a history that he was familiar with.[126]

Considering Robinson's long legal service in Upper Canada, he must have had personal views on Indian matters that he brought with him to his judgeship. Yet his voluminous personal papers cast only a few hints of these views. In 1824, in his official capacity as attorney general, he had written Wilmot Horton, under-secretary of state for colonies: 'To talk of treaties with the Mohawk Indians, residing in the heart of one of the most populous districts in Upper Canada, upon lands purchased for them and given to them by the British Government, is much the same, in my humble opinion, as to talk of making a treaty of alliance with the Jews in Duke Street or with the French emigrants who have settled in England ... I can find no justification for the supposition that any Indians in the Province are exempt from the general law – or ever were.'[127]

On a personal level, Robinson's family was deeply involved both in land speculation and in business. Robinson himself was close to his brothers Peter and William. Peter was a businessman, land speculator, fur trader, and politician, who served as a crown lands commissioner. He died with an estate of 7592 acres of land, but he was also short on his accounts of crown lands by £11,000, a fortune. His brother John and friends made up the loss.[128] William Robinson had followed Peter into business and government, serving in the House of Assembly and on the Legislative Council. He also was financially involved, with John, in the Welland Canal. Under consideration for a patronage post as assistant commissioner of public works in 1850, he was instead appointed a commissioner to negotiate a treaty with the Indians of northern Ontario.[129] He then negotiated the two 'Robinson Treaties' of 1850 with the Ojibwa north of Lake Huron and east of Lake Superior. Although John was instrumental in getting this political appointment for his brother, there is no evidence that he had anything to do with the treaties, nor is there any idea of his views on the legal status of Indian treaties.[130]

Sitting as chief justice during the time of three commissions appointed to investigate Indian affairs in Upper Canada, 1839, 1840, and 1844, and during the time of the passage of the first of the Indian Acts, Robinson's tenure as judge coincided with the emergence of a formal Upper Canadian Indian policy and, ten years later, with the transfer of authority in Indian affairs from the Colonial Office to the colony. Given that a substantial portion of Robinson's jurisprudence expressed deference to the authority of the crown as represented by local political authorities, it seems logical to assume that Robinson as judge would defer to political authorities in Indian matters. This would have been consistent with English jurisprudence, which was marked by a broad deferral to parliament in developing policy areas, a deference partially necessitated by the structural difficulties of ordered change in a precedent-based jurisprudence: if judges could not broadly interpret the common law to take account of social and political change, then they deferred to a legislative body which could do so by statute.

Yet Robinson did not give this deference to the legislature in Indian matters. As often as he supported the Legislative Assembly on matters of Indian policy, he substituted his own policy judgment, even if it undermined a crown policy. The most dramatic of Robinson's departures from government policy was in his attempt, followed by no other judge, to deny any legal meaning at all to the Haldimand grant, an analysis that was never adopted.[131] While colonial authorities were unsure of the precise nature of the legal title transferred by Haldimand to the Six Nations, the central fact that Haldimand had, in the name of the crown, granted a huge tract of land to Britain's Six Nations allies for them to 'hold forever' was never denied. For Robinson, however, this Six Nations title was such an impediment to the growth of Upper Canada that he attempted to construct a legal doctrine denying that Six Nations title had ever existed in law as distinguished from politics.

While, in general, Robinson deferred to the crown on lands policy, he did not consistently do so. In his view, there should have been no distinction between Indian lands and crown lands, and his technical interpretations of the Indian Act of 1839 resulted in less protection for Indian lands. *Little* v. *Keating* was the first time Robinson passed on any provision of the Indian Act. There, Robinson, on narrow, technical grounds, held the ejectment of a squatter from Indian lands on Walpole Island by crown commissioners unlawful, insisting on a completely unrealistic level of procedure and the proof of land occupancy for frontier conditions.[132] Twenty years later, Robinson was still limiting the authority of crown lands commissioners over Indian lands. *Vanvleck et al.* v. *Stewart et al.* involved the sale of pine saw logs cut by the Six Nations Indians on their Grand River lands. Robinson held that Indians could cut and sell saw logs without the approval of the crown lands commissioner.[133] While this might be read as Robinson favouring some small measure of autonomy for the Six Nations over their own resources, the narrower point is that he refused to uphold the authority of the commissioner under the earliest Indian Act, the same statute interpreted in *Little* v. *Keating* twenty years before.[134] Robinson also limited the authority of the crown lands commissioners in *Jones* v. *Bain*, another a case involving the cutting and sale of Six Nations timber.[135] Only in one of the four lands commissioners' cases to come before his court did the crown prevail, *Regina* v. *Baby*.[136]

Robinson directly referred to the government's Indian policy in only two opinions and on one of those occasions he pretended not to know what it was. These short references indicate that he was, in fact, aware of the nature of that policy.[137] While an interpretation of the Indian Act of 1839 in accordance with government policy was directly at stake in *Totten*, Robinson's broadest discussion of the government's Indian policy was in *Bown* v. *West*. The context of Robinson's discussion of the government's Indian policy is of as much interest here as the substance:

The government, we know, always made it their care to protect the Indians, so far as they could, in the enjoyment of their property, and to guard them against being imposed upon and dispossessed by the white inhabitants. What particular regulations have been made with a view, was not in evidence in this cause; but we cannot be supposed to ignorant of the general policy of the government, in regard to the Indians, so far as it has been made manifest from time to time by orders of council and proclamations, of which all people were expected and required to take notice. In the second year of Queen Victoria, a statute was passed, (ch.15,) the object of which was to prevent trespasses upon lands reserved for the Indians; it has no provisions which can affect the case before us.[138]

This broad statement of policy, in Robinson's view, stemmed from a statute, the Indian Act, that was not relevant to the case at hand. *Bown* involved another squatter attempt to gain possession of Indian lands that could not be directly purchased because of the Indian Act of 1839. Duncan, a Mohawk living on Six Nations lands, could sell his improvements (his house, barn, outbuildings, and cleared land) but not the land itself. These improvements were 'owned' by him according to the customary law of the Six Nations even though he did not 'own' the land, which remained, according to Six Nations customary law, the property of the confederacy.[139] While Robinson's interpretation of the Indian Act was consistent with the policy of the government, it was also a paternalistic reading vis-à-vis the Six Nations, denying any effect to their customary law and any recognition of the property rights of individual Indians.

These views reflected a colonial mindset that denied native people a place in the larger society. They were also consistent with Robinson's rigid adherence to conservative views of social order. There was no room for Indians in that social order: they could remain physically outside it, beyond the frontier, or they could assimilate. At the same time, the parallel idea of two sets of laws, one for Indians and one for Euro-Canadians, amounted to lawlessness in Robinson's mind. Moreover, the uncertain legal status of Indian lands and the related squatter problem threatened the stability of the social order. The squatters' ruthless treatment of Indians was not condemned by Canadian courts in the nineteenth century for political reasons, although Robinson himself disdained all squatters, linking them to the republican rabble that challenged the rule of the family compact.[140]

CONCLUSION

Robinson's jurisprudence of Indian law was a jurisprudence of the orderly colonial development of the Upper Canadian frontier. No particular principles unique to native people applied to this jurisprudence, although individual Indians had the juridical rights of citizens and spe-

cific statutory provisions were generally deferred to. Robinson, for all his
'polyjurality,' never defined a legal status for an Indian nation, clumsily
persisting for fifteen years in a discussion of their 'corporate' status that
led nowhere. He acknowledged that the crown held Indian lands 'in
trust' only after the crown admitted it, never in his own analysis applying
that concept to Indian nations.

His Indian law opinions, like his other opinions, are not easily categorized. While many scholars of early- to mid-nineteenth-century American
and Canadian legal history have emphasized the instrumentalism of
much of the jurisprudence, this is less evident in Upper Canada than in
the United States.[141] Another view, focusing on Upper Canadian jurisprudence, emphasizes its conservatism and devotion to the narrow precedent of English law as well as the high value placed on the rule of law.[142]
Robinson's failure to lend strong judicial support to a legislative policy to
evict squatters from Indian lands reveals an instrumental policy designed
to open up Indian lands for settlement, even at the expense of his cher-
ished values of law and order. Lawless squatters, people personally
loathed by Robinson, most often prevailed against the crown in his judgments. But they also prevailed against Indian lands, forcing their sale and
impoverishing Indians. Robinson's Indian law opinions are inconsistent
in a broad doctrinal sense, failing to disclose any consistent view of
Indian rights, but for the most part they leave the Indians without any
place at all in the social order of Upper Canada. That result is consistent
with an instrumentalist jurisprudence denying Indian rights. Robinson's
opinions themselves, however, failed to create any kind of legal discourse
of aboriginal rights, a discourse that he could easily have derived from
his studies of the common law.

There is a changing tone to his judgments over time. In the 1830s and
1840s Robinson's opinions added to the chaos and disorder of Indian policy. Not only did he deny that the Six Nations had any land rights whatever, but he also often refused to support crown measures to expel
squatters. By the 1850s and 1860s he was more willing to defer to crown
policy in determining Indian rights, upholding the 1839 Indian Act's
measures against squatters. What had happened in the meantime, of
course, was that the Indians in Ontario had been deprived of their lands
and stripped of much their power.

Two kinds of cases predominated in Robinson's Indian law opinions:
four cases involved crown efforts to evict squatters at the request of
Indian nations. The squatters won three of these cases. The Indian legal
interest here was unambiguous: in causing these evictions, the crown was

carrying out a legal obligation – arising from both the Royal Proclamation and the Indian Act of 1839 – that it most often denied. Native people were insistent in demanding the evictions, for the physical and cultural integrity of their reserves was at stake, but they were not parties. The right of the crown to evict squatters from reserves was not a legal issue, and so these cases generally turned on procedural rules. Five cases involved conflicting land titles: settlers holding land titles derived from transactions with Indians faced, in civil actions, other whites holding land titles directly from the crown. The Indian interest here was either non-existent or, at a minimum, less direct than in the former cases, but it was these cases that led to the most complex opinions.[143] Litigants often lied about the nature of their Indian titles, a legal process permeated with fraud. Nevertheless, in these cases the legality of Indian title was often directly at issue, with the legal rights of the First Nations unrepresented. No Indian nation or individual Indian appears as a party in any of the Robinson cases; however individual Indians were parties in a number of criminal cases, as well as in a few civil cases that were not appealed.[144]

Robinson had a close relationship with the major political, social, and economic events in Upper Canadian history for fifty years. Not only did he serve the crown in every legal capacity possible, but he sat in the Legislative Assembly and Executive Council and was speaker of the Legislative Council. When the rebellion of 1837 threatened Toronto, Chief Justice Robinson, who was worried about the Walpole Island Indian agent having official roles in both the administrative and judicial branches, turned out with a gun to defend the government.[145] As a private lawyer (a capacity he never engaged in without simultaneously holding high government office), he represented both canal-building interests and large land speculators. As a judge he rode circuit to every corner of Upper Canada, spending weeks on dirt roads travelling through small villages. He was widely read and functioned at the social and political centre of Upper Canadian society, and his large house near Osgoode Hall served as a gathering place. It can only be concluded that Robinson was as knowledgeable about Indian matters as anyone in Upper Canada's political elite. Yet none of this knowledge ever emerges directly in his opinions.

The impact of United States Indian law on Robinson was nil. There can be no question that Robinson was familiar with the Indian law decisions of John Marshall and James Kent. Yet his reasoning lacked any of the elaborate common-law legal reasoning of aboriginal rights evident in dozens of American cases of the same period.[146] These opinions, including a number from neighboring New York State, would have been available at the Osgoode Hall library. By the 1830s and 1840s American treatises, including those by Robinson's counterpart, Chancellor James Kent of New York, and Justice Joseph Story, contained lengthy and detailed analyses of the common law of aboriginal rights.[147] The neighboring state of New York, in particular, produced a number of decisions on the legal rights of Six Nations under American law.[148] As early as 1810, Kent had held in *Jackson v. Wood* that 'it is a fact too notorious to admit of discussion or to require proof, that the Oneida Indians still reside within this state, as a distinct and independent tribe, and upon lands which they have never alienated, but hold and enjoy as the original proprietors of the soil.'[149] Marshall, Story, and Kent boldly waded into the complex arena of early-nineteenth-century land rights, federalism, and sovereignty with their Indian law jurisprudence.[150]

Robinson's 'polyjuralism' in economic and business matters did include regular reference to American cases, and thus his blindness to Indian law cases must have been intentional. This is not to assert that Robinson should have followed Marshall's or Kent's reasoning: the American cases have their own historical and jurisprudential problems. Rather, it is enough to assert that there was an elaborate common law of aboriginal rights that Robinson could have addressed in Upper Canadian terms. American cases, for example, took the Royal Proclamation as a source of aboriginal rights and Robinson should have done so as well, even if he had created his own interpretative framework. Robinson never cited it.

The avoidance of the American cases cannot be explained only in terms of conservative politics: there was plenty of American authority for Robinson's conservative positions. The Supreme courts of Georgia, Alabama, and Tennessee authored elaborate opinions denying, even ridiculing, the idea of any aboriginal right to land and sovereignty.[151] John Marshall in *Johnson v. McIntosh*, for example, was often cited in British colonial jurisprudence for the proposition that native people had lost their lands by conquest.[152] The American cases carried with them a jurisprudential attitude towards the legal position of Indians in colonial society: the legal position of native people was complex and based on both inherent aboriginal rights and a lengthy British colonial history of dealing with those rights. Robinson's jurisprudence lacked this orientation, and so he did not feel he needed to address the complexity of those questions. For him, the position of Indians was a simple one, analysed on the same basis as that of all citizens. The lengthy British legal history of dealings with aboriginal people, including the Royal Proclamation, was irrelevant in his mind; he never discussed this history in his opinions. His judgments, in fact, fail to cover the basic common law ground of native rights, a jurisprudence developed in dozens of American cases by the 1850s. What difference incorporating a common law discourse of aboriginal rights into early- to mid-nineteenth-century jurisprudence would have made we cannot say. But the decision of Robinson, and Canadian judges generally, to avoid creating a nineteenth-century common law of aboriginal rights clearly structured the twentieth-century legal discourse on this subject.

Robinson's definition of the tribes as 'constructive corporations' for land-tenure purposes was an attempt to deny any distinct legal status for Indians in Canada, and it stood in sharp contrast to Marshall's approach in the United States. Unable to persuade any other judges to his position, he denied that native people needed any legal status at all beyond the common law rights of ordinary British subjects. The crown accorded the First Nations a political status, and it administered an Indian policy and a lands policy towards any object it saw fit.

Robinson's care and deference for the rights of squatters under Canadian law went hand in hand with his complete disregard for the rights of Indians, rights that native people held under an existing common law that Robinson refused to cite. This reflected more than just the racism and ethnocentrism of the European settlers of the day. At the core of Robinson's jurisprudence was the rejection of any aboriginal right that would impede the orderly settlement of Upper Canada.

The seeds of this new jurisprudence exist within broader Canadian legal history as well. Just as John Beverley Robinson was convinced that 'the common law is not part savage and part civilized,' Quebec Judge Samuel Monk, three years after Robinson's death, not only cited the Royal Proclamation for the proposition that Indians retained their own law but also remarked that the common law could no more be carried to Rat River in a knapsack than the Cree law of divorce could be carried to Lower Canada in a canoe.[153] The common law never was 'part savage and part civilized.' Rather, there were (and are) two laws, two legal orders, two systems of jurisprudence, existing side by side.

4

'The Migration of These Simple People from Equity to Law': Native Rights in Ontario Courts

While the Six Nations' various land disputes posed important legal issues in early Upper Canada, and the jurisprudence of John Beverley Robinson and his colleagues dominated the colonial definition of the place of Indians in English and Canadian law, there were still other contested legal domains. Canadian law had recognized from the early nineteenth century that native people had access to civil and criminal courts, both as plaintiffs and defendants, but this simple statement of juridical equality did not reflect the reality of native legal status.

More than any other single issue, the failure of colonial government to deal effectively, or even honestly, with the squatter problem reveals the gap between the juridical ideal and the reality of colonial law. Still, the fact is that Upper Canada produced more nineteenth-century cases in native law than any other Canadian jurisdiction and more than any comparable American jurisdiction.[1] These cases, involving either Indian people or title to Indian lands, can be understood only in their political, economic, and social context, but they also have a jurisprudential logic of their own, one that reflects the opinions of a colonial judiciary trained in the English common law tradition. This rich legal tradition, as has been seen, takes strange meanings in a colonial context. It is not based on precedent nor often even on crown policy: squatters fared far better in court than they did in royal commission reports or in the House of Assembly.[2]

A search of the indexes to Ontario's seven major reporting systems reveals fifty-two reported nineteenth-century cases concerning Indian rights in some form, four of which were appealed to a higher Ontario court and led to a second reported opinion in the same case.[3] Three of these cases were appealed to the Supreme Court of Canada and two of these were further appealed to the Privy Council. Two more cases, both between the province of Ontario and the dominion of Canada, were filed as original cases in the Supreme Court of Canada. Thus, a total of sixty-three Ontario cases involving Indians and Indian rights were reported in the nineteenth century. Reporting systems were commercial enterprises published for sale to the legal profession. The selection of cases for inclusion was not random but based primarily on the commercial importance of the case to the profession. There can be no question that important Indian rights cases were omitted: two of the most important nineteenth-century Ontario Indian cases were not reported. *Attorney General of Ontario* v. *Francis et al.* was the first major case calling for an application of the *St. Catherine's Milling* decision. It was unreported until published nearly a hundred years later in *Canadian Native Law Cases* from notes found in the files of a lawyer.[4] *Caldwell* v. *Fraser* further applied *St. Catherine's Milling* in a 'learned and elaborate' judgment that has been quoted and discussed in a legal treatise but has never been reported.[5]

There is no simple way of determining how many equally important cases went unreported: such cases lie in hundreds of obscure records in provincial archives.[6] Courts were held in dozens of rural locations, some very remote. Judges, lawyers, and clerks travelled long distances to bring Anglo-Canadian justice to the farthest corners of Upper Canada.[7] Their records were kept in bench books, large volumes in which were entered detailed notations of each case before the court. Judges, even in capital cases, kept their own notes on the evidence. The range of reported cases represents the types of native legal issues brought before the courts, but they do not constitute all the cases. Criminal cases, most of the cases involving native people, constitute only a small portion of the reported cases, a problem that we return to in the next chapter.

These sixty-five cases (including *Francis* and *Caldwell*) represent one record of the legal status of native people in nineteenth-century Ontario. Analysis of these cases reveals a great deal about the role of the law in structuring the place of Indians in Canada. This is true because of the historical importance of Ontario as the political centre of English-speaking Canada even if we acknowledge that substantially independent legal histories exist for British Columbia and the Maritime provinces.[8] Quebec had its own legal tradition, as well as its own legal history of Indian rights, but this tradition was largely irrelevant in English Canada.

INDIAN TITLE BEFORE *ST. CATHERINE'S MILLING*

The largest number of the reported cases were concerned with Indian land title which had in some manner been acquired by settlers. There is no question what kinds of interests were at stake: land was the economic foundation of early-nineteenth-century Ontario society and the value of settler claims on Indian lands was enormous.[9] Strictly speaking, these were not 'Indian title' cases because no actual Indian title was at stake. In the majority of these cases, no Indians were even parties, their title having been long ago alienated by competing colonial interests. Most arose either from the Six Nations' Grand River lands (and are therefore not aboriginal title cases) or during the tenure of John Beverley Robinson as chief justice; they form the basis of Indian law in Upper Canada and have already been considered in that context. Laws for nineteenth-century Ontario Indians, meant either the legal basis for settler claims to their lands or the reason for their being locked in a jail cell for violation of some crime under Canadian law, most often an offence unknown to Indian tradition.[10]

The designs of settlers on Indian lands lay behind the original colonial Indian policy, the extension of English law to the frontier under the Royal Proclamation of 1763.[11] Among other provisions, the proclamation forbade the alienation of Indian lands except by the crown. The major impetus for the Royal Proclamation was that the uncontrolled land-grabbing practices of settlers provoked Indian wars and destabilized the frontier, alienating the Indian nations at a time when the British needed them as allies.[12] There were also humanistic concerns: such settler practices were immoral and injurious to the Indian nations, causing drunkenness, disease, and impoverishment. The Royal Proclamation remained the law of Canada after the American revolution, the legal foundation of British and later Canadian Indian policy.[13]

While the legal issue posed in each of these land-rights cases differs, the Royal Proclamation established a process for the alienation of Indian lands that denied frontier settlers direct access to Indian lands. Rather, only the crown could acquire Indian lands through negotiation and purchase in a treaty process. Moreover, the nature of the treaty process itself was detailed in the proclamation, with the governor or commander-in-chief empowered to call a public meeting of the Indian nation for the purchase of its lands.[14] No official could negotiate an Indian land cession at an ordinary tribal council or with isolated individuals or bands, measures designed to reduce the likelihood of fraud or confusion in land dealings.

But the protections of the Royal Proclamation were illusory in actual practice: most of the Indian lands in settled Canada were lost. Herman Merivale, assistant secretary of state in the Colonial Office after 1847, cited Canada's Indians as 'a remarkable instance of the mischievous manner in which even the best intentions towards the Indians have been carried into execution. After declaring in the most solemn language the perpetuity of the cession of the lands, it [the Royal Proclamation] ends with the saving clause, "unless the Indians shall be inclined to part with them." By virtue of this provision, every art has been introduced to obtain their consent to the usurpations made upon them; bit by bit they have been deprived of their magnificent hunting-grounds.'[15] This 'saving clause' allowed the crown great latitude in 'negotiating' with weak and dislocated Indian nations, even when the legal procedures specified in the Royal Proclamation were followed – and they not always were.[16]

An elaborate series of 'land surrenders' followed in Upper Canada in the early 1800s, spreading to the north shore of Lake Superior by the Robinson Treaties of 1850.[17] Once the land was acquired by the crown, it could be allocated to individual settlers. While some lands were 'reserved' for Indians, a legal status still the subject of litigation because the crown claims actual ownership, these reserves were also subject to acquisition and sale by the crown, often with the proceeds to be used for the benefit of the Indians.[18] Even Indian 'reserves' became populated by settlers.

In theory, these 'orderly' procedures should have led to a stable process of settler acquisition of Indian lands, but that was not the case. In fact, nearly twenty reported cases indicate that the process was chaotic. Assuming that these cases are representative of the range of problems that arose, the land-alienation process was fraught with confusion and corruption. Further, given the difficulty of access to the courts and the large proportion of unreported cases, there must have been many more such land problems. While these cases raised the issue of 'Indian title,' they did not involve indigenous people directly but rather resolved competing settler claims for land that was formerly held by Indians.

At the outset, one legal principle was established: Canadian law, rather than First Nations law, governed Indian lands. The Six Nations Confederacy enlisted the best Upper Canadian lawyers of the day in defence of their lands and consistently lost. For example, *The King* v. *Epaphrus Lord Phelps* pitted the Mohawk against the crown in a dispute over which law governed Mohawk lands, Canadian or Six Nations; the answer, Canadian.[19] Yet the Six Nations were unique only in the strength and consistency with which they put forward their legal position in Upper

Canadian courts. While Indians had full legal access to the courts, the reality was that justice was so often denied that a report of the Aborigines' Protection Society confused the reality with the law. Concerned about the 'neglect of a means of securing justice to Indians in courts of law,' the group charged in an 1839 report that the Indians were 'disabled by the colonial laws to appear in courts of justice either singly or as tribes.'[20]

The government of Canada, officially at least, shared these concerns. In its detailed reserve-by-reserve report on Indian affairs in Canada in 1844, the Bagot commission concluded that the provincial government had failed to protect the Indians from the massive theft of their lands and the result was great poverty on the reserves.[21] As noted, the Colonial Office, fearful of the power of local settlers on the local government, held direct control over Indian affairs until it passed this authority to the Upper Canada government in 1860.[22] Its policy was paternalistic, based on legislation, dubbed 'Indian Acts,' designed to protect and support the Indians until they could be assimilated: a policy of 'liberal treatment.'[23]

The Bagot commission, as we have seen, came on the heels of a policy of relocation recommended by Sir Francis Bond Head, appointed lieutenant governor of Upper Canada in 1835. Head had a considerable interest in Indian affairs and issued a memorandum on the subject on 20 November 1836. This followed an inspection tour in which Head somewhat romantically (and perhaps metaphorically) claimed that he had 'entered every shanty or cottage, being desirous to judge with my own eyes of the actual situation of that portion of the Indian population which is undergoing the operation of being civilized.'[24]

In direct language more like that of the Aborigines' Protection Society than that of colonial administrators, Head decried the way that settlers treated Indians:

The fate of the red inhabitants of America, the real proprietors of its soil, is, without exception, the most sinful story recorded in the history of the human race ...

So long as we were obtaining possession of their country by open violence, the fatal result of the unequal contest was but too clearly understood ...

Whenever and wherever the two races come into contact with each other, it is sure to prove fatal to the red man ... If we stretch forth the hand of friendship, the liquid fire it offers him to drink proves still more destructive than our wrath. And, lastly, if we attempt to Christianize the Indians, and for that sacred object congregate them in villages of substantial log-houses, lovely and beautiful as such a theory appears, it is an undeniable fact, to which unhesitatingly I add my humble testimony, that, as soon as the hunting season commences, the men (from warm clothes and warm housing having lost their hardihood) perish or rather rot in numbers by consumption ... in short, our philanthropy, like our friendship, has failed in its professions.[25]

Farming had been a complete failure; congregating Indians for purposes of civilization had created more vices than it had eradicated. Head concluded that the 'greatest kindness we can perform towards these intelligent, simple minded people, is to remove and fortify them as much as possible from all communication with the settlers.'[26] He recommended nothing less than the American policy of Indian removal, the creation of Indian reserves far west and north of European settlement. Manitoulin Island, together with several other islands in Lake Huron, was where Head proposed resettling the Indians, far from the colonized areas of Upper Canada.[27]

There was a legal policy implicit in this removal strategy. Head opposed the extension of English law to Indians. Using an analogy, he argued that applying law to Indians necessarily created injustice because the laws Europeans lived under were unsuited to native people. A sound Indian policy, he said, involves 'moral considerations and elastic adaptations which are totally incompatible with the straight Railroad habits of a Public Accountant ... if the Two parties are brought into Contact, either the Accountant must abandon his Principles or the poor Indian must be made the Victim of the Four Rules of Arithmetic. The Migration of these simple People from Equity to Law would be productive of the most serious Evils to them as well as to the government.'[28] Head's intent is clear: he favoured a paternalistic policy of government protection of Indians that was inconsistent with the legal recognition of any Indian rights. This policy of 'equity' would, in Head's view, be defeated by law: the recognition of the legal rights of native people would interfere with the government's ability to care for them in a paternalistic fashion.

The accountant and the arithmetic in the metaphor was a thinly disguised lawyer with his laws, who either had to abandon his legal principles or make the poor Indian the victim of the formal requirements of law: a comment on the immutable quality of judicial formalism. This position was a direct refutation of the native policies of the Colonial Office, which urged the extension of English law to indigenous peoples. Head's views on Indian relocation, presumably rooted in 'equity' because there was no basis in the common law to remove a population from its land, were rejected by the Bagot commission. The full extension of

English and Canadian law to Indians, however, was another matter. It was held out as a juridical ideal throughout the nineteenth century but never followed in law or policy. Instead, a system of 'legal dualism' prevailed.[29]

THE LEGAL STRUCTURING OF DEPENDENCY: INDIAN SALE OF TIMBER, FIREWOOD, AND FARM PRODUCE

Prior to 1837 there were no laws protecting Indian lands per se from trespass or the alienation of those lands to settlers. Rather, general laws applicable to crown lands were used for what protection Indian lands received. Beginning in 1837, then continuing in succeeding years, the Legislative Assembly passed specific laws designed to punish depredations on 'Indian lands.' Two acts of 10 August 1850 are among the Ontario forerunners of the dominion's 1878 Indian Act, the consolidated legislation governing the legal status of Indians in Canada. Both aimed at protecting Indian lands from 'trespass and injury.'[30] The same laws that forbade Indians to make any agreements alienating their lands with frontier settlers also forbade them to make such agreements regarding the timber, stone, hay, and soil on those lands. The laws were aimed at preventing the wholesale butchery of the forests at the hands of timber merchants. The courts initially attempted to apply the law in the same way but were soon caught up in the contradictions of the government's policy of treating the Indians as dependants: such a literal interpretation of the law destroyed any possibility of Indians contributing to their own livelihood, further reducing them to dependency. The fact that the courts came to treat these natural resources differently than land reveals that they had the interpretive capacity to do so.

Of particular interest is the case of *Feagan* v. *McLean*. Feagan had been arrested by an Indian commissioner and criminally charged with trespass for purchasing cordwood from John Peters, an Indian on the Grand River reserve who had cut the wood from land he legally occupied.[31] J. Martin, representing the crown in the prosecution of the case, argued that 'Indians on reserve lands have no interest in the soil. They have the right of occupation and cultivation, and of clearing their land for cultivation, and of taking their necessary firewood; but not the right of cutting and selling the timber without regard to cultivation.'[32]

After the case was removed from Division Court to the Court of Queen's Bench by certiorari as a special case, the court in two different and inconsistent opinions ruled against the crown. Judge John Wilson appears to have been troubled by the precise limits of the whole question of Indian title, ruling that, since nothing in the statutes forbade Indians from cutting and selling their timber, they must have the right to do so, a judgment that implicitly found some Indian property right in this timber. This reading of the opinion is consistent with Wilson's remarkable opening assertion that 'the land either belongs to or is held by the Crown in trust for the Indians.'[33] At this time, few legal minds in Ontario held to the view that unsurrendered Indian land was held in trust for the Indians. Applying trust doctrine to Indian lands gave the Indians an actionable property right against the crown.[34] Otherwise, Indians were 'mere occupants' of their lands at the pleasure of the crown.[35]

Judge Joseph Morrison concurred in the result but used reasoning that did not challenge the Indian Department nor concede any Indian rights to the land. Rather, Morrison held that the evidence did not show that the cordwood was not cut in clearing the land. In this reasoning the Indian right of occupancy included the common law right to clear the land for agricultural purposes. If the wood had been cut for such purpose, it could be legally sold. Morrison endorsed the paternalism of the Indian Department by calling for more regulations to protect the Indians from 'any evil disposed person who may prompt and induce an Indian so to destroy the property belonging to the whole tribe,' apparently to make it easier to distinguish between firewood cut for sale to settlers and firewood cut in furtherance of occupancy.[36]

A later case reveals that the Indian Department did not give up on the issue. Good, a white man married to an Indian woman and farming on the Grand River reserve, was convicted and fined $20 by a magistrate (in order to facilitate enforcement, the Indian Acts provided that all Indian agents were magistrates) of selling his own hay without permission of the Indian Department.[37] Good appealed, arguing, among other things, that the statute could mean only 'natural hay' that was the wild produce of the land and not domesticated hay that he had sown and grown with his own labour. The court held, following a simple rule of statutory construction, that the word 'hay' meant its common meaning which is both wild and domesticated grasses dried and prepared for feed.[38] The conviction was then reversed on a technicality concerning the way in which costs were assigned.[39] This result technically upheld the Indian Act but not the conviction entered by the Indian agent. The court's refusal to distinguish between natural hay and domestic hay left Indian farmers with no legal right to sell their produce without a permit from the Indian agent. This law interfered with the assimilationist policy of making Indians self-supporting as small farmers who subsisted by raising a wide variety of crops and animals for market.

A parallel case, also leading to reversal on a technicality, is *Regina* v. *Fearman*.[40] In violation of the Indian Act, an unnamed Indian woman had sold a quantity of wood without licence. The wood had been seized and held by the Indian Department on the property of one Johnson. Fearman and others entered Johnson's property and took the wood in question. They were convicted of larceny but appealed, arguing that the wood had not been legally seized and therefore was not legally in the custody of the Indian Department. At issue was a statutory requirement that such a seizure of wood be ordered by a justice of the peace upon a written affidavit, a requirement that in this instance the Indian Department had neglected to meet. The appellate court, citing the principle of strict construction of a penal statute, reversed Fearman's conviction, although the facts clearly showed that he had stolen and sold wood that belonged to the Six Nations.[41]

What is clear from both Fearman's theft of Indian Department wood and other cases is that the Six Nations at Grand River resisted the department's control over their resources by violating the law. Another example of such resistance is James Hunter. Arrested and jailed for selling cordwood, Hunter was convicted and jailed by the Indian agent acting as magistrate, but he responded by bringing charges against the agent.[42] The case illustrates a great deal of tension between the agents' exercise of their legal powers and the Indians. Hunter had been tried by the Indian superintendent and sentenced to pay a fine of $15 plus costs of $6.75 or thirty days in jail on default.[43] After serving seven days in jail Hunter was freed on a writ of habeas corpus, alleging wrongful imprisonment. He then charged the Indian superintendent, J.P. Gilkison, with assaulting and imprisoning him without legal authority.[44] The Queen's Bench Division took little note of Hunter's argument, finding that the Indian agent had the authority of a magistrate and had acted within his power.[45]

THE LEGAL STATUS OF INDIAN PEOPLE

Though the collective property rights of Indians did not fare well in nineteenth-century Ontario courts, those same courts were protective of the juridical rights of individual Indians. In this regard, the judiciary reflected the government's Indian policy. Indians and their little remaining 'property' were to be paternalistically protected by the colonial government, but individual Indians were entitled to the same legal rights as people of European descent. This policy, British in its origin, is the most important legal difference between nineteenth-century Canadian and American Indian law.[46]

The policy did not extend to the recognition of Indian nations. As early as 1839 Justice James Macaulay had stated that the Indian had 'no claims to separate nationality such as would except him from being amenable to the laws of the land.'[47] Similarly, Chief Justice Robinson never recognized any legal status for Indian nations. This stated a de facto policy that can be traced back to the beginnings of a British court system in Upper Canada in the 1790s.[48]

Mid-nineteenth-century provincial Indian Acts, consolidated from earlier laws in 1857, took direct aim at the legal rights of individual Indians and changed existing policy by declaring the Indians a 'class incapable *in many respects* of managing their own affairs.'[49] In fact, Indians were not allowed to manage their own affairs in any area. The report of special commissioners appointed to investigate Indian Affairs in Canada in 1856 declared that the legal status of Indians, formerly the same as that of non-Indians, had changed with the adoption of these early Indian Acts.[50] However, while new restrictions on the rights of individual Indians had some impact, it seems that at least some Upper Canadian courts continued to follow their pre-existing practice of according full legal rights to Indians and did not cite the Indian Acts to deny to individual Indians any right that the courts had previously recognized. In doing so, the courts followed the common law in continuing to recognize that Indians had full rights as individuals. Doubtlessly, most of the loss of Indian rights occurred de facto at the reserve level where Indian agents were magistrates, issuing judgments from which few Indians could afford to appeal.

Yet, as clear as this legal policy was to the judges, it also seems evident that the framework of legality in Indian/white relations did not extend beyond the courts to the social and political culture. In its 1839 *Report on the Indians of Upper Canada*, a committee of the British parliament recommended that full legal rights be extended to the Indians of Canada. Since it is incredible that parliament was unaware that the Indians had already had such rights for over forty years, the likeliest hypothesis is that the committee meant legal rights in fact instead of legal rights in theory.[51] While property qualifications kept almost all Indians from voting, they also kept many settlers from voting. Indians could not acquire individual title to their reserve lands, but they could save their money and buy land on the open market, like any other person. Social, economic, and political, rather than legal forces, kept Indians from equality.[52]

Yet this lack of political power had effects in a wide variety of legal matters. Indians, for example, were not eligible to sit on a coroner's inquest or any other jury. In 1838 a French settler killed an Indian with several blows 'at a village of Christian Indians on the River Credit. The coroner was sent for, but he was unable to allow any of the Indians to be put on the jury.'[53] This result kept Indians from participating in the legal process of determining whether the killing was justified or whether it was murder. There was no legal disability at that time for Indians sitting on juries. Rather, as in the case of John Brant's election to the Legislative Assembly, jurors had to be voters and to be voters they had to meet property qualifications that could not be met with communally held property.

Parliament was not the only body confused about the actual legal status of Indians in Canada. The Aborigines' Protection Society published a journal, *Aborigines' Friend*, which regularly reported on Canadian Indian matters. The organization also published numerous pamphlets and an annual report, with a network of correspondents from all of the colonies. Its views centred on the recognition of full legal rights for native people:

The political organization of the natives and their admission to equal privileges with the whites, is more important to their civilization than may at first appear ... it is a question to which we have not yet obtained a satisfactory answer, whether the aboriginal inhabitants, domiciliated and settled on reserves, can exercise the elective franchise. Had they been represented in the colonial legislature the encroachments on their land, from which they have in so many cases suffered, would not have been made. See Mr. Buller's report from which it appears that there were recently 3,000,000 of acres of fertile land which had been got from the natives by the government, and were sold at an advantageous price on account of the improvements made by them upon it. It appears, also, from the report of the Commissioners of Inquiry upon the Indians of Canada that they are disabled by the colonial laws to appear in courts of justice, singly or as tribes, which alone would go far from preventing them from ever becoming civilized.[54]

It appears that Indians were always competent witnesses in Upper Canadian trials: the issue never had the legal significance in Canada that it did in Australia and India.[55] The matter was raised in *Regina* v. *Pah-Mah-Gay* by the lawyer for the defendant, a Potawatomi Indian sentenced to death at Sandwich in 1859 for shooting his brother in the back while drunk.[56] Pah-Mah-Gay's attorney argued on appeal that Esh-quay-gon-abi, a young Potawatomi, was not a competent witness because, not being Christian, he had not been sworn to testify under oath. No one had raised this issue at trial. This put the crown in the position of defending the veracity of its only witness, whose testimony was essential to support the murder conviction and death sentence passed on Pah-Mah-Gay. The High Court relied on several English precedents holding that a Christian oath was not necessary; all that was required was an affirmation that the witness knew of his obligation to speak the truth.[57] The conviction was upheld.

In dicta the court stated that it was swayed by the strong precedent of English cases and would have ordinarily concluded the testimony was not admissible.[58] It is also possible that the fact that it was the crown arguing for accepting Esh-quay-gonabi's testimony may have influenced the court. The court's deference to the precedent of English cases was a disingenuous deference to legal formalism: Indians had been testifying as witnesses in Upper Canada for at least fifty years but the issue had never reached an appellate court.[59] Meanwhile, colonial courts in Australia and India had grappled with the issue, and colonial legislatures had by statute nullified the common law rule forbidding the practice. The reason Canada was different may stem from the fur trade: Indians had to be able to function as legal actors in a market economy in order to carry on that trade.

There is no question that Canadian courts had avoided the issue until 1861 by finding ways to admit Indian testimony: by this time dozens of Indians had been convicted of crimes in cases in which the trial judge admitted Indian testimony.[60] Yet there is no legal record of issues that are not raised, and so this can only be surmised. Many cases involved non-Indian witnesses. Other cases, involving Indians in an ongoing relationship with Canadian society, must have involved Indians who were either Christian or who had taken the oath as if they were. But it seems more likely that many, if not most, Upper Canadian Indians were simply administered the oath and that they then gave evidence. Many of the Six Nations Indians, for example, following the example of Joseph Brant, were deeply committed to their traditional religion, yet they deferred to the symbolic power of Christian religion on some occasions because it was both polite and politic to do so.[61]

While Indians were liable in civil actions for debt, a protective statute forbade any person to 'obtain any judgment for any debt or pretended debt' except in special circumstances, an effort to block settlers from cheating Indians.[62] This statute was repealed in 1869 and tested in *McKinnon* v. *Van Every*.[63] A county court judge had held for a settler plaintiff attempting to collect a debt incurred by an Indian prior to 1869, arguing that the repeal of the statute had changed the law and made the Indian retroactively liable for debt . On appeal the judgment was reversed. The court relied on technical rules of statutory construction in refusing to give retroactive application to a statute, but it also upheld the public policy behind the law.[64] The repeal of this statute left Indians subject to actions for debt with substantial exceptions for personal property on reserves.[65]

It was also evident that Indians could make wills distributing their personal property, subject to the Indian Act. In *Johnson* v. *Jones* the will of Catherine Keshegoo, an Indian living at Grand River, was challenged by her half-brother and next of kin.[66] She had left a substantial estate consisting of $400 in promissory notes and $414 in household furniture to another person, James Johnson. Her brother relied on section 20 of the Indian Act, which provided that, if an Indian male died holding a location ticket (meaning an Indian agent's designation of a place of habitation on a reserve), his lot and goods went to the next of kin.[67] Such provision did not apply to the will of Catherine Keshegoo because she was not an Indian male. The Chancery Court held that Indians were citizens with all the rights of other citizens except when those rights were restricted by statute.[68] By this logic, Catherine Keshegoo could leave her personal property to anyone she wished. However, her location could not be bequeathed because Indians had no property right in their reserve lands. The assignment of locations was a matter for the Indian agent, subject to the statute.[69] The allocation of lands of an Indian reserve, however, followed tribal law and was not determined by the Indian agent, who merely administered those allocations.

In his ruling, the judge cited *Regina ex. rel Gibb* v. *White*, among other cases, for the proposition that Indians had the same rights as other Canadians.[70] Thomas B. White, a Wyandotte, had been elected reeve of Anderson Township, Essex County. Although receiving monies as an enrolled member of the tribe, White made a good living as a trader and owned patented lands in fee simple. Dallas Norvell, the loser in the election, challenged the result, arguing that White had never been enfranchised or exempted from any of the disabilities of an Indian created by the various Upper Canadian Indian Acts.[71]

The opinion of Judge Dalton of Essex County Court in chambers was straightforward, beginning with a comparison of the legal status of Indians in the United States and Canada. While Indians in the United States were 'aliens' and not citizens, it was so obvious that Indians were full citizens of Canada that 'authorities are needless for such a proposition.' Some provisions of the Indian Act protected the rights of reserve Indians, but any Indian who left the reserve and patented lands worth in excess of $100 was not an Indian within the meaning of these provisions and enjoyed the full benefit of the law. The part of the act providing for the enfranchisement of Indians referred to Indians who lived on reserves and thus were still subject to the protection of the government, but not to Indians like White, who had entered into the mainstream of Canadian life. The only restrictions applying to such Indians dealt with the disposition of lands acquired from the tribe, the sale of spirituous liquors, and holding in pawn anything pledged to purchase such liquors. No provision of law was necessary to provide for White's right to hold elective office: he was under the same law as any other citizen.[72] While this distinction may not have been either obvious or intended by legislators, the court construed the common law to protect the civil rights of Indians as individuals.

Another Indian, George W. Hill of Grand River, also functioned in settler society until he was arrested in 1907 for practising medicine without a licence.[73] Hill made the opposite argument of White, alleging that as an Indian enrolled on a reserve he was subject to federal law and not Ontario law and thus was not amenable to Ontario police regulations.[74] The judges spent a considerable amount of time on the case. First, they looked to both the Indian Act (which was silent on the practice of medicine) and to the relevant Ontario statute (which was also silent on the matter). The Court of Appeal, avoiding difficult questions pertaining to the application of Ontario statutes to the activities of reserve Indians, held that the Indian Act did not limit the activities of Indians. Therefore, when an Indian chose to leave the reserve and engage in a wider sphere of activities, he put himself under the same regulations as anyone else.[75] The court withheld judgment on whether Ontario law could prevent an Indian from practising medicine on his reserve.[76] The underlying issue here was one of Canadian federalism: the British North America Act, which had created the dominion of Canada, specifically relegated jurisdiction over 'Indians and Indian lands' to the national government.[77]

With the exception of some confusion over the reach of Ontario police regulations into Indian reserves,[78] there was no question that Ontario Indians were full citizens when it came to Ontario law, limited only by the provisions of the Indian Act. By and large, Ontario courts did not challenge the scope of the Indian Act, and, at least with regard to the status of individual Indians, there were no significant legal challenges to federal power. At the same time, Ontario courts did not take account either of the unique status of Indians within the province or of the racism and crime that Indians suffered at the hands of local settlers. Such conditions created serious problems for any Indians attempting to assert their legal rights in local courts. For many Indians, simple evidentiary problems must have prevented them from getting legal redress for their injuries. Owens, the illiterate and blind Indian sold a horse by Thomas, his white neighbour, had no evidentiary problem but still lost before a local jury on an egregious fact pattern: blind men cannot execute binding contracts in foreign languages without having the contract read.[79] How many Ontario Indians could afford an appeal from a local court judgment? How many petty injustices against Indians left a trail of facts as clear as these?

THE INDIAN FAMILY AND THE LAW

Matters involving Indian families were not often taken to the Ontario courts. The one case that was reported, *Robb* v. *Robb*, testing the legality of a marriage under First Nations law, was treated with exceptional hostility and revealed the extent of judicial formalism in Ontario law.[80] John Robb of Kingston had died, leaving his estate to his son, William Robb, or his son's heirs. Since William had died, his daughter, Sarah Jane Robb, stepped forward to claim the estate but was sued by John Robb's wife, who claimed that Sarah was illegitimate and therefore not entitled to her father's inheritance. The facts showed as plain a case as could be made out for a marriage under Indian law. William, in 1869, had journeyed to Vancouver Island and had married an Indian woman named Supul-Catle, daughter of Wah-Kus, chief of the Comox. Wah-Kus had given a feast in honour of the couple and presents had been exchanged, indicating an acceptance by all parties of family obligations. The couple lived in Wah-Kus's home for ten years until the death of Supul-Catle. Robb then took his daughter back to Kingston, introducing her as his child and raising her in his parents' house. He claimed that he had been legally married to the child's mother.[81]

Judge Thomas Robertson, of the Ontario Court of Common Pleas, rejected these facts as proof that a legal marriage existed.[82] In doing so, he did not follow Canada's leading case on the legal status of Indian marriages, *Connolly* v. *Woolrich* (considered in chapter 9), which, on similar facts, had upheld the legality of such marriages.[83] For Robertson, the two cases were distinguished by geography: Connolly, a trader whose 'moral character was beyond reproach,' would have had to travel '3,000 to 4,000 miles in canoes, or on foot, to get married by a priest or magistrate,' while

Robb was within the jurisdiction of British Columbia, presumably within reach of its authorities, and therefore could have contracted a marriage under British Columbia law if he had so desired.[84] Moreover, Robertson was concerned both that the Comox were pagans and that they practised plural marriage, facts that reduced his willingness to accord tribal marriages any legal status under Ontario law.[85] Yet, though rejecting any recognition of a marriage under Comox law or custom, Robertson ruled the marriage legal under a common law maxim that 'when a doubt exists as to the legality of a marriage, courts are bound to decide in favour of the alleged marriage.'[86] In this reasoning, the facts that distinguished the two marriages, simple geography, also provided Judge Robertson with a basis for believing that a legal marriage might have occurred: Robb had access to British Columbia magistrates and clergy.[87] While the courts of Quebec recognized marriages under Indian law, Ontario courts rejected this view. Robb's marriage was valid only because there was a legal presumption that he had contracted a legal marriage under British Columbia law.[88]

THE LEGAL STATUS OF INDIANS UNDER CIVIL LAW AND THE INDIAN ACT

The dearth of civil actions involving Indians reported in Ontario law is an indication that Indians were functioning outside the settler economy. It seems, however, that Indians were always fully cognizable in civil actions. C.R. Ogden, attorney general of Lower Canada, was directly asked by the government in 1839 whether Indians could make civil contracts, and he responded in the affirmative.[89]

One unreported case from Rice Lake might indicate why civil actions involving Indians were rare. Roach, a trader, had allowed individual Indians to run up a bill for £700 by pressing upon them every kind of trade good imaginable. The amount was so absurd that he was not able to take the case to court on grounds of equity. Undaunted, he obtained the signatures of almost every member of the tribe on a confession of judgment. Using these documents he obtained judgments against the individuals and then executions against their personal property.

The Indian agent intervened, but it was the avariciousness of Roach that undermined his case. He had obtained judgments and executions against infants and others who had not signed the documents. The court stated, in setting aside these executions, that it was this latter oversight that determined the outcome of the case: 'There was no law which protected Indians any more than the white man from the effects of their obligations.'[90] Upon an investigation of the matter it turned out that many Indians had not signed such confessions of judgment at all; that others had signed what they thought was a petition to the crown asking for money; and that others had signed under a variety of misrepresentations. The fact that an Ontario sheriff and clerk sanctioned the issuance of executions of judgment against infants testifies to the quality of local justice in rural Ontario, with judges far removed from the cases that they passed judgment on.

There was another side to the range of civil issues involving Indians that came before Ontario courts. Most legal matters between Indians were resolved through their own law, generally without the knowledge of Canadian authorities. Both the report of the parliamentary committee of 1839 and the Aborigines' Protection Society advocated that Indian 'laws and usages should be carefully collected, and observed by our courts,'[91] but this would have required Canadian courts to defer to Indian law in tribal matters. Such an idea could never have been considered by colonial officials in Canada. In none of the nineteenth-century Upper Canadian cases did a court defer to native law.

After the 1857 adoption of Ontario's Indian Act, the basis of Indian law in Ontario (and later Canada) became statutory rather than common law. The 1856 report of the special commissioners on Indian Affairs noted both the 'peculiar' legal status of Indians and the changes in that status that had occurred since the Macaulay report of 1839 and the report of 1844.[92] The Indian Acts 'acknowledged the inferiority of Indians in regard to their legal rights and liabilities as compared with Her Majesty's other subjects.'[93] This policy went against seventy years of common law decisions and policies. For example, the Indian Act instituted a procedure to 'gradually enfranchise' Indians, at a time when Ontario Indians were free to vote on the same basis as whites – as long as they met property qualifications that could not be met through communal ownership of land. Defeating this policy and working to the opposite effect was the special status of reserve Indians. Indians were legal minors, protected against their own inexperience in the making of contracts; Indian property, held by the Crown, was immune to any kind of civil seizure; and Indians were exempt from taxation and assessments on their lands under the terms of various treaties.[94]

Indians did not any longer hold the same legal status as whites. But neither had they moved from equity to law. Rather, Indian legal status under the 1857 Indian Act had changed to a form of dependency controlled by the Indian Department bureaucracy.[95] The act created a system of legal dualism, with Indians subject to distinct laws and holding different legal rights than non-Indians. The assimilationist vision of the progression from 'equity to law' model had been abandoned, and in its place government had substituted a legal model of Indian as child, a ward of the government to be maintained in this distinct legal status until, at some unknown point in the future, he was ready to assume the same legal rights as other citizens.[96] That said, however, John Borrows makes clear that there is another history of the Indian Act, a history of Indians ignoring and resisting it.[97]

5

'Entirely Independent in Their Villages': Criminal Law and Indians in Upper Canada

For Indians, full access to the 'privileges of British law' more often meant the opposite of legal protection of their land rights: they went to prison. Indians were frequently convicted of crimes in nineteenth-century Ontario. Although their numbers were under-represented in criminal arrests through the 1870s, the pace apparently increased towards the end of the century. The range and type of these convictions will be dealt with in more detail in chapter 7.

Early trials of Indian offenders were most often not reported but remain only in the docket books of local courts and the circuit reports of King's Bench judges on assizes. The very existence of these trials early in the century, however, establishes that at least some Canadian authorities presumed that they had criminal jurisdiction over Indians. The actual situation was confused, with the authorities through the 1820s taking inconsistent positions. While various kinds of land-title cases constitute most of the reported cases, criminal law cases came to be the dominant Indian cases by the middle of the nineteenth century. These criminal cases are absent from the published reports because Indians lacked the funds to appeal their criminal convictions: they just went to jail.

ENGLISH CRIMINAL LAW AND INDIANS

The origin of colonial criminal jurisdiction over native offenders can be analysed on several levels that reflect different sets of social relationships on the frontier. It seems clear that one set of rules prevailed for crimes occurring within the reach of British authority, another for crimes between Indians in their own lands. The simplest explanation is that the common law followed the flag: since there was no law exempting Indians from criminal jurisdiction, they were as subject to the law as anyone else – almost. One set of court records, for the Court of Oyer and Terminer and General Gaol Delivery presided over by Judge William Dummer Powell, reveals that the full majesty of English law was taken to the far corners of the Upper Canadian frontier as early as 1792 and applied to Indians.[1] In a court session held that September at L'Assomption, near Detroit, a grand jury investigated four homicides involving Indians.[2] An Indian man, Wawanisse, had been killed at Michilimackinac by parties unknown; Pierre Crocher had been killed at Detroit by Guillet, an Indian; Chabouguoy and Cawguochish, two Indian men, were indicted for the murder of David Lynd, alias Jacquo, at Rivière à la Tranche; and Louis Roy was charged with killing Francis Lalonde at Saginaw. Although arrest warrants were issued for all the alleged perpetrators of these crimes, only Roy could be found.[3] Of the four cases, three were inter-se, involving only Indians, reflecting the high Indian population of the district. Most important, from the standpoint of criminal jurisdiction, is that the court made no legal distinctions based upon the respective races of the alleged perpetrators, perfunctorily issuing arrest warrants for Chabouguoy and Cawguochish. It is also significant that formal legal process was begun even though adequate information, and available defendants and witnesses, existed only in one of the four cases: Louis Roy was tried for the killing of Francis Lalonde. Lalonde, Roy, and Antoine Prevost, evidently drunk, 'were diverting themselves by throwing sticks, stones, and mud at each other.' Roy threw a rock towards Lalonde, inviting him to catch it. Instead, he was struck in the side and soon died. The jury, following careful and highly technical instructions of the judge on four kinds of deaths under the common law, found Roy not guilty of murder, instead holding the death an 'excusable homicide by misfortune.'[4] Powell later tried an Ojibwa, Mishinaway, for murder on a return visit in September 1795. Although no record at all of the case exists, it appears that he was successfully defended by Walter Roe, an attorney paid for by the Indian Department.[5]

But 'following the flag' was not simply a matter of drawing political boundary lines across the continent: it meant that settlers were protected by the criminal law, but only within the actual range of settlement. In 1795 Isaac Brant, son of Joseph, shot and killed Lowell, another early killing of a settler by an Indian in Upper Canada. The case never went before a magistrate but the government prepared to initiate legal proceedings. At the same time it was not clear that the Mohawk would peacefully give up Isaac Brant, raising the possibility of armed resistance. There was an exchange of letters within the government in contemplation of what action to take, but the government was unwilling to challenge Joseph Brant.[6] Judge William Dummer Powell was sent to see Joseph, who equivocated, taking the position that English law did not reach the Six Nations territory but also expressing the hope that the young men would follow it. To this astute and perhaps duplicitous political position he added that it would take the militia to enforce English laws in Indian territory and that he doubted that the militia would act against him. Powell was of the opinion that the Indian nations were 'entirely independent in their villages,' a legal argument never advanced again in Upper Canada but one that must have had some weight given his position. Finally, Powell characterized the murder victim as a 'white vagabond' and said that the case was not worth further trouble. British authorities were unwilling to challenge the Six Nations and did not proceed with the case.[7]

This murder case unhappily turned into another: Joseph Brant himself killed Isaac Brant in self-defence as the young man attacked his father in a drunken rage. No charges were brought against Joseph. Rather, in an action that proves that tribal law was still functioning among the Six Nations at Grand River in murder cases at the time,[8] he turned himself over to the tribal council for their adjudication. The council found that Brant had acted in self defence. Two other relations of Brant murdered a settler at Grand River in 1791. There was a jurisdictional struggle, with the British insisting that the two be turned over to crown authorities for trial and the Six Nations refusing. Colonel Andrew Gordon cut off delivery of presents and provisions for a time to force the Indians to turn over the accused, but authorities in Quebec resumed the trade.[9]

Ogetonicut, an Ojibwa, was the first Indian in Upper Canada to face a trial for killing a settler (although not, as we have seen, the first Indian tried for murder). At the frontier near Lake Scugog in 1803, Samuel Cozens, a settler, killed Whistling Duck. Ogetonicut followed tribal law in killing John Sharp, a trader, to avenge his 'brother.'[10] Since no Canadian authorities functioned in the area and the land was unsurrendered to the crown, the crime went unnoticed for several months until Ogetonicut travelled to York to trade, was recognized as Sharp's killer, and arrested. A number of stories exist about the broader circumstances of the killing, but they commonly reveal that Sharp was an illegal trader who had given the Ojibwa liquor in exchange for furs. It was in the dispute that followed that Sharp was killed and his camp looted.[11]

A new administration in Upper Canada headed by Peter Hunter feared that the lives of frontier settlers would be in jeopardy unless an example were made of Ogetonicut. It was decided that he be tried for murder near where the crime occurred so that the Indians there would see the power and majesty of British justice. The *Speedy*, a Provincial Marine naval vessel, was ordered to take the trial party to Newcastle, where a courthouse had been built and where the trial would be conducted as near Lake Scugog as English law could reach. On the way, the ship went down in a storm, losing all on board including Judge Thomas Cochran; Robert Isaac Dey Gray, solicitor general; Angus Macdonnell, a lawyer and member of the House of Assembly; James Ruggles, a justice of the peace; George Cowan, Indian agent; John Fisk, a constable; and Ogetonicut.[12]

While this case never reached a trial court, its course reveals a great deal about Upper Canadian law in relation to Indians at the turn of the century. Fundamental to the imposition of English law on the Indians was the idea that Canadian authorities would protect Indians from settlers. Yet, although Ogetonicut had waited a year before avenging the death of his brother, no effort was made to try Cozens.[13] To deprive the Indians of their traditional law under such circumstances was one-sided: exposing the Indian nations to the depredations of frontier settlers while according them no means of self-protection. Sir William Johnson, while head of the Indian Department, had promised Pontiac and other chiefs that he would punish settlers who injured Indians in return for the Indians agreeing not to retaliate for such attacks themselves.[14] Upper Canadian authorities consistently failed to do so: there appear to have been a number of indiscriminate killings of Indians by frontier settlers in the twenty-five years preceding 1804.[15] In two separate incidents, Mississauga chiefs had been killed by off-duty British soldiers, who escaped punishment; Chief Snake was murdered by five soldiers in Kingston in 1792; Chief Wabakinine and his wife were killed at York in 1796, beaten to death by soldiers.[16] These killings all stemmed from drunken altercations before witnesses. The killers of Chief Snake were acquitted. No indictment was brought in the killing of Chief Wabakinine.[17] It is impossible to believe that the killings of these two chiefs did not have a profound effect on the Mississauga living along the northern shores of Lake Ontario: they could not have had any confidence in British justice.

Another case, that of Angelique Pilotte, a native woman who was probably Ojibwa, stemmed from an infanticide at Drummond Island in 1817. Secretly pregnant and probably afraid of losing her job as a maid, she buried her newborn child in a field. Suspected by her employer, she was turned over to local justices of the peace who ordered her transported to Niagara for trial. A month later, Justice William Campbell, seeing that she was without counsel, appointed Bartholomew Beardsley to represent her. Witnesses were transported from Drummond Island for the trial. Infanticide carried special rules, including a presumption that a baby concealed at birth was murdered. Angelique's detailed confession did not help matters and she was convicted by a jury with a strong recommendation of mercy. Campbell pronounced the death sentence, the only punishment for murder at that time.[18]

In her clemency petition Beardsley raised several issues, including the fact that First Nations birthing practices were different from English customs: babies were delivered in secret. Therefore, it was unfair to apply a common-law legal presumption to an Indian who concealed a birth. Settlers at Niagara also wrote petitions and her sentence was commuted to one year in jail.[19] John Applegarth, one of the jurors, wrote the *Niagara Spectator* a lengthy letter on the case. In his view the jury recommended mercy because 'she was a savage and had no knowledge of the usages of the Christians ... and her whole trial rested neither on the letter nor spirit of any British law.' He went on to blame her employers for not obtaining proper counsel for her.[20] It is impossible to say what influenced the colonial secretary to commute the sentence, but such reprieves were common throughout English law.

It is difficult to establish precisely when colonial authorities took criminal jurisdiction over intra-Indian crimes because, as in the numerous cases of settlers killing Indians, so many killings produced no legal response. In 1821 a grand jury submitted a report to Chief Justice Powell in the case of François, a Huron charged with killing a native woman on the Anderdon reserve near Lake Huron. The jury was unsure, not only whether Canadian law had jurisdiction over such a crime, but also whether it was 'equitable' to charge natives 'asserting the character of a free and Sovereign Power within their own lands.'[21] Considerations of equity, treaty rights, and public policy were as important as the narrow question of the limits of Canadian criminal jurisdiction.

All of these issues came together in the Shawanakiskie case. Shawanakiskie, an Ottawa, killed an Indian woman on the streets of Amherstburg in the fall of 1821. He was locked in jail and tried in October 1822 at Sandwich before Justice William Campbell. Shawanakiskie's lawyer argued that he had avenged the murder of a parent, a justifiable killing under tribal law, and that treaties guaranteed Indians the right to their own laws. This argument raised the issue of the treaty-based sovereignty of Indian nations as well as considerations of equity, namely, the unfairness of executing an Indian acting within a distinct cultural system and unfamiliar with Canadian law. Although Justice Campbell instructed the jury that 'there were no common law grounds doubting a lack of jurisdiction' and convicted Shawanakiskie, he delayed the execution to permit Lieutenant Governor Sir Peregrine Maitland to ascertain what authority existed for the trial of tribal Indians.[22] The process that followed reveals considerable doubt about Canadian jurisdiction over Indians in the 1820s.

Maitland referred the question to Chief Justice Powell, who gave an inconclusive reply although he had personally tried Indians for murder as early as 1794.[23] Powell noted that 'no instance of an Indictment against an Indian for homicide of an Indian has ever occurred before me, nor any heard of by me until the Assizes at Sandwich for 1821.' In that year another Indian had been indicted and tried but acquitted for lack of evidence. Powell's legal position, however, was more complex than this, as can be seen by the language of his 1821 jury charge:

There is in the Sheriff's Report a case on which I have some hesitation to direct the course of the Jury – that of homicide of an Indian by an Indian. On similar occasions the enquiry has been abstracted on the representation of a Treaty between the King's Governor and the Commanders in Chief with the Indian Tribes, stipulating that all white criminals taking refuge amongst them should be given up to our criminal justice, on the other hand that Indian Blood should be accounted for amongst themselves when spilled by an Indian.

These people are ignorant of our Law, and we of their habits, which perhaps supply the place of what we call Law. We know that our own law on matters of homicide makes wide discrimination, for the highest character of crime to absolute justification – but we are ignorant of the opinions and habits of the red man in this respect ... Such considerations have led to discountenance such prosecutions in our courts.[24]

Powell, in an earlier period, had taken a stronger position on this issue than his 1821 report admits. Indians had been regularly tried in Ontario courts, including before Powell. But there was no consistent policy on extending criminal jurisdiction over Indians. Other cases had been resolved by simply not prosecuting for reasons of equity or local policy. Obviously, as long as Indians were not prosecuted for such reasons, the larger question of Indian sovereignty and treaty rights did not need to be decided.[25]

The matter was then submitted to the colonial secretary, Lord Bathurst, who referred it in turn to Robert Peel, the home secretary, the official responsible for criminal law in England. Peel sent the issue back to Canada, requesting from Maitland any information he had about the treaty recognition of Indian law. Maitland took two years to answer the question but finally concluded that 'after the most diligent Search ... there appears to exist no treaty that can give colour to the idea that an Indian is not to be considered as amenable to the law for offences committed against another Indian within His Majesty's Dominions.' This position was also the position of the Upper Canadian government, which may have been at odds with the judges on this matter. John Beverley Robinson, as attorney general, advised in 1827 that 'the Governor has no power to exempt the Mohawk Indians inhabiting the Province from the operations of the laws Civil and Criminal.'[26] The Home Department issued a warrant for Shawanakiskie's execution but, in an action customary in Indian murder convictions, included a proviso that the lieutenant governor could commute the sentence, in this case to transportation for life. There is no evidence of the final disposition of Shawanakiskie, but it is likely that he was executed at Sandwich in 1826.[27] Although this case supports the proposition that Canadian law applied to all inter-se Indian killings, the actual facts narrow its impact: Shawanakiskie's actual crime occurred in the streets of Amherstberg and thus involved an Indian acting in settled territory under Canadian jurisdiction.[28]

The practice of not prosecuting inter-se Indian offences must have been deeply rooted in Upper Canada, for even an opinion from the Colonial Office did not resolve the issue. Almost twenty years later, it received attention in the 1839 and 1844 reports on Indian affairs. Judge Macaulay, in his 1839 report, devoted several paragraphs to the legal status of Indians in Upper Canada. While stating that the 'resident Tribes are peculiarly situated,' he went on to note that 'it would be difficult to point out any tenable ground on which a claim to an exempt or distinctive character could be rested. The Six Nations have, I believe, asserted the highest pretensions to separate nationality, but in the Courts of Justice they have been always held amenable to, and entitled to the protection of the Laws of the land.'[29]

Macaulay reported that Indians had been tried on criminal charges for homicides committed against both settlers and each other in different parts of the province. He personally recalled a trial before him of a Six

Nations Indian at Niagara on charges of stealing one or two blankets from an Indian woman. The victim had turned to British justice and sworn out a complaint before a justice of the peace. The defendant's lawyer argued that the court lacked jurisdiction because the

matter was only cognizable among the Indians themselves, according to their own usages and customs: but I had to refuse the plea, not being able to point out any legal authority by which the protection of the Criminal Law could be refused to the Indians inhabiting the county of Haldimand ... and I observed, that however important it was that a sound distinction should be exercised by local magistrates in cases not of an aggravated character, I could not but admit that, in my opinion, the Indians were responsible for crime.

Macaulay remarked that he had also convicted a Delaware Indian of a larceny committed in Carradoc Township.[30] This evidently did not resolve the issue, for a year later the superintendent of Indian affairs asked C.R. Ogden, attorney general of Canada, for an opinion on the legal status of Indians. Ogden's response was simple: 'The Indians have legal capacity, either as plaintiffs or defendants.'[31]

Through all of this jurisdictional confusion, involving some of the most prominent judges in Upper Canada, there was no mention of two British statutes that, in a modern context, have been interpreted as extending British criminal jurisdiction into Indian territory, although the matter is in doubt.[32] The Act of 1803 was passed in reaction to frontier lawlessness:

Whereas crimes and offences have been committed in the Indian Territories, and other parts of America, not within the limits of the Provinces of Lower or Upper Canada, or either of them, or of the jurisdiction of any of the Courts established in those Provinces, or within the limits of any civil Government of the United States of America and are therefore not cognizable by any jurisdiction whatever, and by reason thereof great crimes and offences have gone and may hereafter go unpunished, and greatly increase: For the remedy whereof be it enacted that, from and after the passing of this Act, all offences committed within any of the Indian Territories, or parts of the said Provinces of Lower or Upper Canada, or of any civil Government of the United States of America, shall be deemed to be offences of the same nature, and shall be tried in the same manner and subject to the same punishment, as if the same had been committed within the Provinces of Lower or Upper Canada.[33]

The 1821 Act used the same general language but referred more specifically to 'animosities and feuds' arising from the fur trade, and it extended the jurisdiction of Canadian courts to the lands of the Hudson's Bay Company.[34]

There can be only one reason why Upper Canadian legal authorities did not refer to these acts in their discussions of the general application of English law to the Indian nations in Upper Canada. These acts cannot have been thought to apply to Indians within Upper and Lower Canada, an interpretation confirmed by ambiguous statutory language. In any case, William Dummer Powell had taken jurisdiction over Indians accused of crimes before the passage of the 1803 act. The actual legal basis for this assertion of criminal jurisdiction over Indians was parallel to the crown's assertion of civil jurisdiction. Under British colonial law, the denial of any special legal status to Indians made them citizens subject to the same law as any other citizens of Canada once British sovereignty was asserted. This interpretation denied tribal sovereignty and was based on racist and colonial views of tribal law.

The assertion of British criminal jurisdiction over the Indian nations reversed a long-standing policy recognizing First Nations law in intra-tribal matters. In 1774 Major Thomas Gage, commander in chief, instructed Guy Johnson, superintendent of Indian affairs, of this policy: 'I imagine there must be some mistake in what you mention respecting the Indians of Canada being subject for the future in all things to the laws of England, Indians are commonly left to their own usage's and customs in most things; perhaps they may have been informed that in cases of murder, or robbery they would be tried agreeable to English law. You will know before this reaches you, that the French laws in most instances are to have force in Canada, but I don't imagine the Indians are much interested in this matter.'[35]

The confusion over this policy in the 1820s and 1830s reveals that the policy was one of political expediency, and in fact it was abandoned without any specific statutory measures. Judges, in the far reaches of their jurisdictions, had a great deal of freedom within the common law to dispose of Indian cases without entering convictions. Evidence in such cases was often inadequate. Witnesses were often unavailable. Defendants could not be located. Complainants were persuaded to drop the charges. When the matter was referred to England, the colonial secretary deferred to the home secretary, reflecting the division of their respective authorities between colonial matters and matters of criminal law. The home secretary decided the issue as though it were an internal issue of English criminal law, the same way he would have rendered an opinion on an issue referred to him from any part of England.

More troubling for the courts was the question of *mens rea*, the problem of punishing natives for offences when they lacked any wrongful intent because they were either following First Nations law or were ignorant of British law.[36] *Regina* v. *Machekequonabe*, discussed in chapter 10, is among the best-known native-law cases in the common law world, holding an Ojibwa criminally responsible for a manslaughter in killing a 'wendigo,' an evil spirit clothed in human flesh.[37] The young man was on sentry duty to protect his village from the wendigo and lacked any criminal intent. Again, British sovereignty took preference over considerations of justice.[38]

The broader issue in *Machekequonabe* is the unanswered question in Shawanakiskie, the legal status of Indian sovereignty and the continuing survival of First Nations law in maintaining social control and punishing crime. The Delaware at Muncey Reserve denied, in an 1820 council, that they were subject to English law: 'We do not consider ourselves subject to the Laws of White People. When any bad thing is committed by us we have a mode of our own of punishing the person who is guilty, or of compromising the matter.'[39]

In 1842 Mississauga Chief Peter Jones (Kahkewaquoanaby), an advocate of extending English law to Indians as a means of assimilation, complained that 'Magistrates will not act in Indians cases' and that at the Credit River Reserve natives followed 'a code of several Rules & regulations among themselves.'[40] Since this reserve was near Toronto, it is clear that Canadian law was slow to penetrate Indian communities. The Six Nations were also resistant to the imposition of Canadian law within their communities and maintained their own laws.[41]

LAWS REGULATING THE SALE OF LIQUOR TO INDIANS

Selling liquor to Indians was a frontier folk crime, widely engaged in and often, but ineffectively, prosecuted. The scope of this prohibition was broader than the rest of the Gradual Civilization Act of 1857, covering all Indians regardless of their physical location or legal status. Thus, even Thomas White, voter, reeve of Anderson Township, landowner, and Wyandotte Indian, could not either purchase or be sold alcohol although he could legally have become prime minister.[42] After criminal cases and squatter land-title problems, more reported Ontario cases deal with this issue than any other issue of Indian law, a glaring example of the reality of nineteenth-century Indian life. These cases put the smallest details of Indian existence under the hand of the criminal law. Though liquor laws regulated Indians and settlers equally, their focus was the perceived social disorganization of Indian society. These cases also illustrate that nineteenth-century Indian law was far more concerned with the forced assimilation of Indians than with the protection of Indian rights.

Typical of the cases is *Regina* v. *McAuley*, an 1887 case challenging the scope of the magisterial authority of an Indian agent.[43] Agent Duncan McPhee of Rama reserve convicted Alexander McAuley, a hotel keeper, of selling beer and whisky to four Indians on the testimony of Simeon Rocky-Mountain, an Indian. The testimony showed, not only that McAuley's wife had served the liquor, but that McAuley had been away from his hotel for five months, including the time when the liquor was sold, working at a lumber camp in another county.[44] This fact was not of concern to either agent McPhee or the Court of Common Pleas, who followed the common law rule that the act of the wife was that of the husband.[45] McAuley was convicted and fined $50 or ninety days in jail. Failing to pay the fine, he was arrested on a warrant and taken to jail.[46]

The court was concerned, however, with the precise limits of the powers of an Indian agent. Those powers appeared to be quite broad under the statute, giving Indian agents the same powers as police magistrates over 'any infraction' brought under the Indian Act.[47] The court decided that it was obvious that police magistrates must have authority within some prescribed jurisdiction and set out to enquire what area McPhee's powers were limited to. This enquiry must have been a bit disingenuous given that McPhee had tried McAuley on the Rama reserve for a sale that had occurred in Rama Township, adjacent the reserve. The court found that McPhee was the Indian agent at Rama and had a magistrate's powers there and in Ontario County, consistent with the intent and scope of the Indian Act. However, the court also found McPhee the 'agent for the Chippewa Indians at Rama' and that the indictment was defective because it did not allege that the Indians involved were Chippewa.[48] McAuley's conviction was reversed. Such a limitation of McPhee's powers is pure nonsense under the Indian Act, since Indians often moved freely from one reserve to another and the agent's task was broadly defined as a general supervision of Indian activity in his area. There is no question that Mrs McAuley was in the business of selling liquor to Indians. Legally requiring each Indian agent to aver that the specific Indians involved in each case were under his jurisdiction limited his powers.

This interpretation of the act in *McAuley* seems dishonest in view of *Regina* v. *Green*, a case arising a year later.[49] Green, an Indian, was convicted in Brantford's police magistrate's court of selling liquor to an Indian and sentenced to four months in jail at hard labour. On appeal he argued that he had been charged with selling liquor on 27 September but convicted of selling liquor on 29 September. The Indian Act, in recognition of the rough quality of rural or frontier justice, contained a provision that 'no conviction ... shall be quashed for want of form ... and no warrant of commitment shall be held void of reason of any defect therein ... if there is a good and valid conviction to sustain the same.'[50] The conviction was upheld, the judge holding that where an offence is legally proved to have occurred in an area over which the convicting magistrate has jurisdiction, the conviction must be upheld.[51] Consistent with the Ontario courts' lack of concern with legal technicalities is *Regina* v. *Murdock*.[52] There, a defective conviction for selling liquor to Indians was amended on appeal, the defect being corrected so that the conviction could be upheld. The Indian agent, acting as a police magistrate, had neglected to assert that the person to whom the liquor was sold was an Indian, clearly a substantial issue, more egregious than failing to note the tribe of the Indians as in *McAuley.* The appellate court, noting the record silent on this issue, found that the sale had occurred on the Grand River reserve, and that the law prohibited the sale of liquor 'to a person' on an Indian reserve as well as to Indians, again an interpretation supporting a broad Indian Act.[53]

Not withstanding *Murdock*, the courts' hostility to the criminal jurisdiction of Indian agents acting as police magistrates under federal authority surfaced again in *Regina* v. *MacKenzie*.[54] J.P. Gilkinson, Indian agent at Grand River reserve, had tried James MacKenzie for selling liquor to Andrew Statts, an Indian, in the town of Brantford. MacKenzie had refused to appear before Gilkinson, alleging that he was prejudiced against him, but was represented by his lawyer. Gilkinson insisted on proceeding with the trial and MacKenzie's lawyer withdrew from the proceedings. Upon completion of the taking of evidence, Gilkinson declared the case closed, with no evidence being offered for the defence. Three days later, in the presence of MacKenzie and his lawyer, the judgment was read, finding MacKenzie guilty and fining him $50 or three months in jail in default of payment. MacKenzie appealed, alleging eight errors in the trial.[55]

His conviction was reversed on two grounds. The first was that his sentence to jail in default of fine was unlawful, since the statute provided for fine *and* imprisonment, a defect that could easily have been corrected on appeal. Second, the Court of Common Pleas found that the evidence did not establish that the liquor was not made use of under the sanction of a medical man or minister of religion, legal uses under the statute.[56] This issue, a part of the burden of proof, had not been raised at the trial and was both a defence to the charge and also an error of the type that appellate courts might correct from the record on appeal.[57] MacKenzie, for example, had also alleged that nothing in the record showed Statts to be an Indian, an equally important element of the prosecution's burden, but the appellate court was not moved by this argument. Young, a tavern keeper in the village of Caledonia charged both with selling liquor without a licence and with selling liquor to Indians, had lost a similar appeal the same year, arguing the technicality that it had not been proven that he did not have a licence.[58] The appellate court held that the burden was on Young to prove he was licensed.[59]

Nineteenth-century Ontario jails were filled with Indians charged with being intoxicated. The settlers who sold them liquor did considerably better in court. Appellate courts showed an inconsistency in their tolerance of technical defects in such convictions, but they appear to have had some reservations about the police magistrate's powers of Indian agents which led them to overturn some of their convictions on minor technical grounds. The message to the Indian agents was to restrict their power to Indians and to Indian reserves and to be cautious about extending their jurisdiction to local settlers.

FISH AND GAME LAWS

The only major area of Indian activity for which there are no reported nineteenth-century Ontario cases is the criminal prosecution of fish and game laws. There appear to have been a substantial number of prosecutions, but none led to reported cases, doubtless reflecting the lack of the individual Indian defendant's ability to finance appeals. The records of the Ontario attorney general indicate that Ontario denied Indians any special right to hunt and fish, holding Indians to the same fish and game laws as settlers. William McKirdy, a trader at Nipigon Lake, wrote the attorney general an 1892 letter directly posing this question. McKirdy pointed out that Indians in his region had 'no means of living except from fishing and hunting and serious results will follow from applying Ontario fish and game laws.'[60]

The province's answer was deliberately evasive. J.M. Gibson, provincial secretary, wrote that although Ontario laws did apply, the laws specifically provided that 'Indians or settlers in unorganized districts' could kill game for food or necessities of life but not for sale or traffic.'[61] That was exactly the point: McKirdy wrote back immediately that hunting was of no use unless the Indians could sell their furs.[62] The province's position was disingenuous, and in fact the Indians' legal right to hunt and fish was not clearly extinguished in the nineteenth century.[63] Rather, there was a dishonest pattern of selective enforcement.

The actual legal situation was complicated. Indians held both treaty and common law rights to hunt and fish.[64] The Robinson-Huron and Robinson-Superior treaties specifically allowed 'the said Chiefs and their Tribes the full and free privilege to hunt over the territory now ceded by them and to fish in the waters thereof, as they have heretofore been in the habit of doing'[65] Treaty 3, in common with many other treaties, guaranteed Indians the right to hunt and fish.[66] These guarantees might be made either directly, in the text of a treaty, or indirectly, with the Indians ceding some rights and, through not ceding hunting and fishing rights by treaty, implicitly retaining them. Ontario later argued that this promise was subject to future governmental regulations, but such regulations were not understood by Indians at the time and were not part of the discussions at treaty.[67] Indians had no choice in the matter: they often had to hunt and fish for their livelihood.

The Indians, therefore, hunted and fished anyway, risking the punishment of the law. Thomas Fox was arrested in 1909 for being illegally in possession of ten beaver pelts. He received a jail sentence, but the magistrate suspended it because Fox had no ability to pay. Since the statute did not provide for a suspended sentence, the attorney general was asked for a ruling. The magistrate 'has no power to suspend sentence,' held the attorney general, but, recognizing the hopelessness of the situation, he added that 'it might be better to let the matter stand.'[68]

A year later W.F. Langworthy, crown attorney at Port Arthur, wrote for instructions on the same issue. Two Indians had been arrested for shooting a moose near Sturgeon Lake and were defended in court by their Indian agent. Even though the shooting occurred off the reserve, the agent argued that the Robinson-Superior Treaty gave the Indians the right to hunt. The attorney general again replied that the position of the province was that Indians were subject to the same fish and game laws as others, denying any legal impact of the Robinson Treaties on Ontario law.[69]

The arrogance of the Ontario government caused much suffering among the Indians in northern and western Ontario. It also caused at least one death. In the fall of 1914 Peter Hunter, an Ojibwa from Sioux

Lookout, met with George Fanning, an Ontario fish and game officer, who had received a report that Hunter and another Indian were hunting moose out of season and selling the meat at night in Sioux Lookout. Threatened with jail, he had agreed to return to his home at Wako and stop hunting. Three weeks later Fanning heard that Hunter, on the way to Wako, had shot two large moose, leaving the meat for settlers and Indians to see, saying that he would get even with the game warden. The next fall Hunter returned to Sioux Lookout and started selling moose again. He was arrested by Fanning and taken before a police magistrate. Sentenced to a fine of $20 and costs or thirty days in jail, he was taken to jail in Port Arthur because he had no money. After serving his sentence he was discharged in the middle of winter and froze to death. Fanning, asked to file a report on the incident, had no regrets: 'sending him to jail done him no harm ... but it did the Indians around here considerable good.'[70] Ontario's construction of the application of its fish and game laws to Indians was simply wrong, an injustice still not corrected.[71]

CONCLUSION

English and Canadian criminal law implicitly recognized First Nations jurisdiction over inter-se crimes, a measure of their inherent sovereignty. There was never a specific change in law or policy extending criminal law to Indians. Rather, these matters were handled on a case-by-case basis, deferring to local conditions. It was well into the nineteenth century before Indians were routinely brought under Canadian criminal law. By the end of the century, Indians were being jailed in large numbers, reflecting both high levels of conduct that was criminal under Canadian law and also local racism in law enforcement. Today, Indian people continue to be arrested and jailed in disproportionate numbers.

It cannot be said that the courts blindly followed the policies set out by the executive branch. For example, an Indian Department policy of prohibiting the sale of liquor to Indians was not given full effect by the courts when it would have been quite simple to do so. Similarly, Indian Department paternalism in controlling Indian resources was deemed inappropriate by the courts, and judges weakened the capacity of the Indian Department to control Indian wood and hay. Perhaps in both these areas, liquor-law enforcement and the control of Indian resources, local settler interests conflicted with provincial policies and the Ontario courts were responsive to local interests.

In the north, the continued criminal prosecution of Indians for following traditional hunting, fishing, and trapping practices, protected by treaty but now 'illegal' because of the imposition of provincial laws governing natural resources, is a continuing source of conflict. For many Indians, hunting and fishing in the face of arrest and prosecution is a simple assertion of their treaty rights.

6

'A More Than Usually Degraded Indian Type': *St. Catherine's Milling* and Indian Title Cases

If John Beverley Robinson's Indian law opinions fairly represent the Canadian jurisprudence of the first half of the nineteenth century, *St. Catherine's Milling* represents the jurisprudence of the end of the century. Indeed, *Attorney General of Ontario* v. *St. Catherine's Milling and Lumber Company* is a foundational case in Canadian law, defining the nature of aboriginal land rights.[1] Ontario lawyers and judges determined both the argument and disposition of the case from beginning to end, with their arguments prevailing both in the fledgling Supreme Court of Canada and in the Privy Council. The case represented a significant political and constitutional victory for Ontario and the provinces, weakening the power of the federal government. The First Nations, none of whom were a party to the case, were even greater losers, denied the ownership of their lands although left with some poorly defined 'usufructuary' rights. Unlike the earlier Canadian Indian cases, racist language was used in the opinions. Finally, because the case went to the Privy Council at the height of Victorian-era imperialism, it became one of the most significant cases on native rights in the common law world.[2]

St. Catherine's Milling is a peculiar kind of Indian law case in that it had little to do with a hundred-year history of pre-existing Indian law, taking almost nothing, for example, from Robinson's opinions and ignoring existing Canadian cases. While it was perhaps understandable that opposing counsel could disagree about the meaning of every single precedent, the ignorance of the legal status of Indians and Indian lands shown by the dozen Canadian judges on three courts who passed on the case is remarkable. As a landmark, the case brought together for the first time in Canada in one pile of papers the history of the taking of Indian lands in British North America.

INDIAN LAND TITLE IN NINETEENTH-CENTURY ONTARIO LAW

At the core of this dispute was the control of Ontario's vast northern lands. Under the British North America Act that created Canada, Indian lands (and Indians) were under dominion jurisdiction. Crown lands within the existing provinces, including Ontario in this case, were under provincial ownership.[3] This division, between Indians and Indian lands under crown control on the one hand, and provincial control of most other crown lands on the other hand, was at the core of the federalist arrangement that was to be the political foundation of Canada. The legal question of who held the underlying title to Indian lands was unclear, disputed by both sides. The first of the cases that hinted of the difficulties involved in this power-sharing was *Bown* v. *West*.[4] The case, as we have seen, involved a suit for breach of a contract to sell Indian lands at Grand River. The Court of Chancery denied relief on the ground that Indian lands were vested in the crown and therefore could not be contracted for sale. This holding was in reality narrower than it appeared, for the Six Nations at Grand River had received their lands as a grant from the crown and were not traditional occupants; thus, *Bown* ruled only on crown land grants to Indian nations and not on the larger question of aboriginal title.[5]

Church v. *Fenton* was the most important Indian land title case prior to *St. Catherine's Milling* but, given the unique legal history of Six Nations land title, it was not directly relevant to the larger question of Indian title generally.[6] The lands involved were Indian lands, surrendered to the crown in 1854 and held by the Indian Department as 'Indian lands' under control of the provincial government. That government sold the land to settlers, to be paid for in ten annual instalments beginning in 1857. Upon completion of the instalments, patents were issued, dated 14 June 1869. The next year the land was sold for taxes due for the years 1863–9. The owner of the land argued that, until the land was patented, it was still 'Indian lands' under crown jurisdiction and not subject to provincial taxes. This issue was a significant one since crown lands (and Indian lands) were commonly sold in instalments with a substantial proportion of the frontier tax base at issue.

Much Indian land was disposed of in this fashion, the proceeds being held 'for the benefit of the Indians.' The practice was popular with government officials because it held out the prospect of paying for the dominion's expensive Indian policy. Ultimately, most of the Indian lands in Upper Canada were sold to settlers, for example, with the Six Nations Grand River lands being reduced to less than 10 per cent of their original size.[7] This policy was of great benefit to local settlers and to the province. Not only was land made available to settlers, but it became productive and taxable. The loss of their lands led to the increasing poverty of the Indians, however, depriving the tribes of any economic base.

The Ontario Court of Common Pleas decision in *Fenton* is illuminating, for it took a long detour into the nature of Indian title not necessary to support its judgment. Judge Gwynne, who was to be on the Supreme Court of Canada at the time of *St. Catherine's Milling*, held that the lands were subject to taxation and tax sale by broadly interpreting a pre-Confederation statute making assigned crown lands subject to local taxation to include assigned Indian lands. He claimed that Indian lands were a subcategory of crown land, sold in the same way, and therefore subject to the act.[8] Indian title was dealt with by asserting that the Crown had a 'right by conquest' over Indian lands but had 'waived' that right and chosen to extinguish Indian title by 'treaty of surrender.'[9] The court went on to describe this arrangement as the basis of the 'expression' to the effect that certain lands are vested in the crown 'in trust' for Indians. The legal basis of the trust arrangement was doubted by the court, but it held that it did not matter in the outcome of this particular case.[10] While this assertion was not challenged, it came to provide much of the basis of Ontario's case in *St. Catherine's Milling*: Indian lands were indistinguishable from crown lands generally. *Church* did not decide any questions of Indian title and turned much more on matters of frontier tax policy under Canadian federalism. The case was appealed to the Ontario Court of Appeal and ultimately to the Supreme Court of Canada, but the appeal was dismissed.[11]

Adding to this confused state of jurisprudence regarding Indian land rights in Ontario were several cases holding that the crown held reserve lands 'in trust' for Indian tribes following surrender.[12] As early as 1844 the Bagot commission report had recognized that certain Indian lands were taken in trust by the government, a distinction that clearly implied that others were not held in trust.[13] The idea that the crown held Indian lands in trust acknowledged some kind of legally actionable property right in those lands. This probably accounts for Chief Justice Robinson's initial refusal to apply trust doctrine to Indian lands in his 1852 decision in *Doe d. Sheldon* v. *Ramsay*.[14] Robinson had denied that any kind of legal right in Six Nations lands had been conveyed by the Haldimand deed. Rather, it was only 'a declaration by the government that it would abstain from granting those lands to others, and would reserve them to be occupied by the Indians of the Six Nations.'[15]

Yet, ten years later, as we have seen, Robinson extended trust doctrine to surrendered Indian lands in *Regina* v. *The Great Western Railway Company*.[16] The difference in Robinson's analysis may not have seemed significant even to him at the time. While the Grand River lands in *Sheldon* v. *Ramsay* were unsurrendered Six Nations lands, the lands in *Great Western Railway*, involving a right-of-way through downtown Sarnia, were surrendered by the Indians to the crown through a written instrument containing the 'trust or condition expressed in their deed, that it was to be disposed of for their benefit.'[17] Thus, a trust agreement had been made by a written deed between the government and the Indians. The crown itself acknowledged the existence of this trust relationship, leaving it impossible for the court to find such an agreement did not exist. While a narrow construction along the lines of Robinson's decision in *Great Western Railway* might have had limited applicability, the general use of the concept 'trust' soon became much more general in Indian affairs, with the crown itself using it to describe its management of Indian lands. The careful management and sale of Indian lands for their benefit was consistent with a policy of 'liberal' treatment of Indians.

By the time of *Mutchmore* v. *Davis* in 1868, the crown had conceded that it held the Grand River reserve in trust for the Six Nations, a conclusion that Upper Canadian courts had also reached.[18] In this case, involving conflicting settler titles to Six Nations lands, Chancellor Phillip Vankoughnet matter of factly stated that 'these lands were dealt with by the Crown in the way it considered most for the benefit of the Indians, for and towards whom it assumed the duty of trustee and guardian.'[19] While Robinson had narrowly found a trust relationship based on a written deed, Vankoughnet found it in the nature of the relationship that the crown had assumed toward the Six Nations Confederacy, a duty involving considerable management of tribal moneys and lands. The trust relationship still required the existence of some legal relationship between the crown and First Nations, a circumstance that did not apply to the unsurrendered lands of western tribes. And, in the final analysis, all of these statements about the trust relationship (including a similar statement in *Fegan* v. *McLean*)[20] were only dicta and not a part of the holding of the cases, describing a de facto legal relationship that the crown acknowledged. Therefore, none of these cases had any impact in *St. Catherine's Milling* because nothing in trust doctrine reached the issue of legal title to unsurrendered Indian lands. No Ontario court had directly passed on that question. The law lords in the Privy Council assumed that some kind of trust relationship existed between the crown and the tribes but that this legal relationship did not represent the full extent of the crown's title to the land.[21]

One of the two stated aims of the 1856 report on Indian affairs in Canada was to suggest 'the best mode of so managing the Indian property as to secure its full benefit to the Indians, without impeding the Settlement of the Country,' a statement that both embodies trust doctrine and recognizes that Indians held property recognized under British law.[22] Other language in the report refers to the legal protection of the 'Indian estate,' another term that must mean a recognition of Indian property rights.[23] While this language does not prove that the Indian tribes had recognized property rights in their lands, it does convey a legal uncertainty about the status of Indian lands.

INDIAN TITLE UNDER FIRST NATIONS LAW

Whether or not there was precedent on the Indian title question in English and Canadian law, the term 'ownership' was repeatedly used in connection with Indian title from coast to coast in nineteenth-century Canada. We know this from a number of sources, including Indian statements at the time, the research of ethnographers in the late nineteenth and early twentieth centuries, and Indian actions that were consistent with the practice of land ownership.

In 1929 anthropologist Diamond Jenness asked Parry Island Ojibwa about their land tenure:

The entire band owned all the hunting territory, and likewise all the fishing places and maple groves; for the land was not subdivided, except temporarily, among the different families.[24]

It is quite clear ... that in pre-European times, and for a short period afterwards, the eastern Algonkians, including the Ojibwa, recognized ownership of land by the band alone ... Today ... they still claim that the entire band owns all the territory, both the reserve on the island that the Government has set aside for its use and the wooded districts on the opposite mainland not developed yet by European settlers.[25]

On the opposite side of the continent, Governor James Douglas of Vancouver Island justified his purchase of land from the Indians there by saying that the Indians believed that they owned it and were prepared to use force to defend their lands.[26]

The lands involved in *St. Catherine's Milling* were part of the territory covered by Treaty 3, which, along with Treaties 1 and 2, had been negotiated in the early 1870s with the Indians of northwestern Ontario and Manitoba. These lands occupied a key position in the country's efforts to open the west, and it was for this reason that the negotiation of Treaties 1, 2, and 3 was the first important act of the dominion government in Indian affairs. Extensive preparations were made for the treaties, with commissioners and soldiers sent out from Ottawa and the east. In the Treaty 3 negotiations, begun in 1872, the commissioners invited the Saulteaux chiefs to express their views. They remained silent. After a time, they stated that there was 'a cloud before them that made things dark and they did not wish to commence proceedings till the cloud was dispersed.'[27] The commissioners enquired what the problem was and were told that four of the Saulteaux were in jail. A number of Swampy Cree had signed contracts as boatmen with the Hudson's Bay Company but had deserted. Brought before a local magistrate, they were fined but sent to prison for forty days in default of payment. Though most had been released, four were still imprisoned. The commissioners insisted that they could not entertain a demand to release prisoners from jail as a matter of right because 'every subject of the Queen, whether Indian, half-breed, or white, was equal in the eye of the law; that every offender against the law must be punished, whatever race he belonged to.' When the Indians did not accept the logic of this position, the commissioners yielded and discharged the four Indians because 'the Queen desired that every Indian participate in the negotiations,' at the same time insisting that 'henceforth every offender against the law must be punished.'[28]

From this beginning, Canadian law was at the heart of the dominion's Indian policy in the west, an extension of the Upper Canadian Indian policy of eighty years before. The commissioners insisted that the Indian nations select their representatives for the treaty negotiations and then present them so that their names could be recorded. The Indians, for their part, expressed their belief that they had a right to large reserves, including a right to dispose of these tracts of forest, adjacent waters, and underlying mineral rights.[29] The sovereign demeanour of the western Indians offended the commissioners, but it would have been recognized by the early Upper Canadian officials who had been frustrated in their negotiations with the Six Nations. The Saulteaux of Treaty 3 knew that their land was invaluable, both for its mineral and forest wealth and because Canada needed a route to the west. Ma-we-do-pe-nais, a Saulteaux from Fort Francis, set out the Indian view: 'All this is our property where you have come ... This is what we think, that the Great Spirit has planted us on this ground where we are, as you were where you came from. We think where we are is our property. The sound of the rustling of the gold is under my feet where I stand; we have a rich country; it is the Great Spirit who gave us this; where we stand upon is the Indians' property and belongs to them.'[30]

The first negotiations ended when Indians made demands that Canada's negotiators were unprepared to meet. The Saulteaux wanted more money, compensation for roads already constructed and for wood taken for steamboats. The nature of their demands makes it clear that the Saulteaux did not see the treaty in terms of selling their lands. Rather, they saw the treaty process as protecting their rights by limiting and clearly defining the scope of crown encroachments.[31]

The negotiations were resumed the next year, 1873, with the crown offering substantially better terms. The Saulteaux had rejected an annuity offer of three dollars per person; pointing out that the Americans were paying $14 south of the border. After prolonged correspondence with Ottawa, the treaty commissioners were authorized to raise their offer. This correspondence reveals the government's sense of urgency in inducing the Saulteaux to sign; various negotiating strategies were discussed, including the offer of much larger annuities to the headmen. Treaty 3 (also known as the Northwest Angle Treaty) was finally signed for a 'present' of $12 per person and an annuity of $15, along with other benefits – without higher payments to headmen.[32] The strong position taken by the Saulteaux was known throughout western Canada and influenced the demands of Indians in the remainder of the numbered treaties.

ST. CATHERINE'S MILLING IN ONTARIO'S CHANCERY COURT

The historical context of *St. Catherine's Milling* is thoroughly documented, but its legal meaning is often distorted.[33] This, the most extensively litigated Indian law case in Ontario prior to *Bear Island*, involved Indian title only in an obscure way: Ontario and the dominion each claimed title to Indian lands. These respective claims were based on different theories of the alienation of Indian title. Upon Confederation, title to crown lands within existing provinces remained with the respective provinces, while the dominion retained crown lands in the territories. While responsibility for Indian lands went to the dominion government, actual title remained in the crown (and therefore in the province), creating a conflict between the dominion and the provinces.

St Catherine's Milling and Lumber Company was an Ottawa corporation that took a timber lease from the dominion government on an extensive tract of pine lands at Wabigoon Lake near Dryden in northwestern Ontario. The dominion government claimed that it had taken the lands from the Saulteaux Ojibwa through their land surrender in Treaty 3.[34] In this view, the lands in question were Indian lands until ceded to the dominion government by treaty, a position grounded in the logic of the Royal Proclamation. Ontario claimed that the lands were crown lands because Indians held no title in their land, only a lesser right to occupy and use the lands. According to its reasoning, the dominion government had negotiated a treaty for political purposes, to ensure good relations with the Indians, and had not, through any treaty, acquired a proprietary interest in the land. It followed that St Catherine's Milling and Lumber Company had no lawful lease and no right to take timber on crown lands that had been passed to Ontario at Confederation.[35]

Ontario had an advantage in having recently won a decade-long battle against the dominion over its western and northern boundaries, defining the limits of the province west to what is the current Manitoba/Ontario boundary and including most of the Treaty 3 lands.[36] At Confederation, the western and northern boundaries of Ontario were not agreed on, and so the dispute was submitted to arbitration in 1874; the resulting decision in 1878 was in favour of Ontario. The dominion did not accept the arbitration decision and Ontario appealed the decision to the Privy council, winning in 1884 a judgment substantially upholding the arbitration award.[37] This litigation had given the province and its lawyers a ten-year head start in collecting documents and building arguments about Ontario's claims to western lands.[38]

Ontario had another advantage in bringing the case in its own courts, in the Chancery Division before John Alexander Boyd, whose decision and its underlying reasoning was substantially upheld (with some significant changes) all the way to the Privy Council. Showing that this was no ordinary case, Oliver Mowat, premier and attorney general of Ontario from 1872 to 1896, personally represented the province.[39] Ontario's legal position was straightforward: Indians had no legal title to their land but only what political right the crown, for liberal, humanitarian reasons, permitted. At stake was more than ownership of millions of acres of crown land. The whole structure of Canadian federalism was in the process of development. Ontario, leading the provinces, favoured a weak dominion government; the dominion sought a much stronger central government.[40]

The idea that Ontario's ownership depended on Indian title had not even occurred to the province until a campaign speech that Prime Minister Sir John A. Macdonald delivered in Toronto in 1882. Macdonald claimed that Ontario's boundary claims were irrelevant because the dominion had actual ownership of all lands regardless of the province they were located in: the dominion took title from the Indians through its purchase of the lands in Treaty 3. Therefore: 'Even if all the territory Mr. Mowat asks for were awarded to Ontario, there is not one stick of timber, one acre of land, or one lump of lead, iron, or gold that does not belong to the Dominion.'[41] It is not clear when or why Macdonald determined to argue this position, sure to be politically controversial as well as legally difficult. Macdonald was arguing, for the first time in Canadian history, that Indians 'owned' their traditional lands, that they held title to their property under Anglo-Canadian law.

Macdonald's argument made Ontario's victory in the boundary dispute meaningless and caught the province by surprise; virtually none of the papers in the extensive documents Ontario collected in the boundary dispute deals with Indian title.[42] Ontario had been anxious to litigate the boundary dispute but only on the basis of historical and geographical materials supporting its strong legal position under the BNA Act. It had not taken Indian title seriously and was unprepared to litigate the issue. This can be best seen in correspondence between Walter Cassells, the lawyer entrusted to manage the *St. Catherine's Milling* case, and Oliver Mowat. Mowat deferred to the legal opinion of David Mills, a lawyer and politician, who played a leading role in the boundary dispute. Mills's actual expertise in Indian title did not stem from the boundary dispute but rather from his years as minister of the interior in the Liberal government of Alexander Mackenzie (1873–8), when Indian affairs were among his responsibilities and complex matters of Indian title in British Columbia were on his desk.[43] At that time, Mills had taken the position that British Columbia Indians held an aboriginal title.[44]

Cassells was neither familiar with the Indian title issue nor at all certain that the case would actually turn on Indian title.[45] The allocation of powers to the provinces and the dominion ultimately rested on a judicial interpretation of the meaning of the BNA Act, an interpretation that might rest on other grounds, perhaps highly technical rules of statutory interpretation. It was only in February 1885 (the case was tried beginning on 18 May) that it became clear that the dominion intended to rely on Indian title in its case, yet there was still no guarantee that the court would actually decide it on those grounds.[46] The case bogged down procedurally over the question of admissions, a formal agreement between the parties of basic facts not at issue in order to facilitate court proceedings. Apparently Mowat wanted to admit that, under the Royal Proclamation of 1763, the tribes had owned their lands prior to Treaty 3, a position that Cassells would not agree to and one that would have made Boyd's opinion impossible.[47]

Owing to the formalities of the rules of evidence at the time, without admissions the trial would have bogged down in technicalities that might have kept either side from getting a legal judgment in its favour on the question of ownership of the lands.[48] For example, Ontario might have had difficulty even proving that St Catherine's Milling had taken timber from provincial lands at Lake Wabigoon. Both sides, however, wanted to use the admissions process to gain advantage, dragging out the agreement. As late as 8 May, ten days before the case was argued, Mowat wrote D'Alton McCarthy, the Conservative member of parliament from Barrie who represented the St Catherine's Milling and Lumber Company, proposing an admission that no land surrenders had occurred in any other provinces, a point that presumably would underscore Ontario's argument that the Indians did not own their lands.[49] McCarthy would not agree to this, but by now it had occurred to him that, by agreeing that any government documents could be taken judicial notice of, he had unintentionally given Ontario a substantial advantage both because of the large collection of documents it had at its disposal and because Ontario was freely citing documents that McCarthy was unfamiliar with.[50]

Chancellor John Alexander Boyd had been president of the Chancery Division of the High Court of Ontario for four years at the time he heard *St. Catherine's Milling*. Prior to that he had spent twenty-two years as a partner (with Walter Cassells) in one of Toronto's elite law firms, that of Edward Blake, a leading Liberal politician and member of one of Ontario's most distinguished families who ultimately would argue the *St. Catherine's* case before the Privy Council.[51] Boyd was well schooled in the technical intricacies of the law, a conservative jurist who could be depended on to write nicely crafted opinions. He appears to have had no knowledge of either Indians or Indian law prior to the case, although he was evidently familiar with the Indians in the vicinity of his summer house on Georgian Bay.[52]

The case moved with great rapidity through the courts, being first argued in Chancery Division on 18 May 1885 and decided on 10 June, argued in the Ontario Court of Appeal in December 1885, and in the Supreme Court of Canada in November of 1886. Perhaps more important than the reported opinions are the respective arguments of both Ontario and the dominion about the nature of Indian title. These arguments represent the best legal analysis on issues of Indian rights available in Canada at the time. The factums of both sides argued in the Supreme Court of Canada survive, together with a printed appendix of the primary historical documents cited.[53] While there is no complete record of the arguments in the two Ontario courts that had earlier ruled on the case, the Supreme Court record doubtless represents a polished version of Ontario's original arguments. The dominion's argument was apparently not firmly established until the Supreme Court session: having lost in the Ontario courts, the dominion had considerably more incentive to re-think its case than the province did. The dominion case that there was an Indian title to unsurrendered lands had become much stronger and more thoroughly researched by the time the case reached the Supreme Court.

The Ontario argument was essentially the work of David Mills. As noted, Mills had paid particular attention to the condition of Indians in British Columbia, where the province did not recognize Indian title and was rapidly alienating Indian land.[54] Mills clearly thought that the Indians had some 'right or title' to their lands that had to be legally extinguished before settlement could begin.[55] In 1881 Mills had asserted in parliament that 'both the British Parliament and the American Supreme Court have always recognized a title in the Indians – not a political sovereignty over the country, but a personal right of property in the soil. That title in all other British colonies had been always considered as existing before the Crown undertook to deal with the lands for the purpose of sale or disposal to other parties.'[56] As Mills, a staunch provincial rightist in parliament, came to represent Ontario's interests in expanding to the west, his position on Indian title shifted; he now denied that the government's acknowledgement of Indian land title meant that the land actually *belonged* to the Indians. Rather, this recognition of title was a mere political expediency, designed to maintain good relations with Indians.[57]

The main thrust of the Ontario argument was far removed from the legal and historical nature of Indian title. It focused on the intent of the BNA Act, arguing that its reference to 'Indian lands' meant only Indian reserves and not all of the unoccupied land in Canada. Most of the efforts of judges concentrated on this issue and the interpretation of the statute dominates the reported opinions.

The legal and historical nature of Indian title, however, was a critical element of the Ontario case, playing a complex role in its structure. The argument about the nature of 'Indian title,' in some respects, was little more than the fodder of an exercise in judicial formalism, at times hardly even relevant to the case in the minds of the judges. In this context, it is a misnomer to refer to the case by its popular name, the 'Indian title' case: Indian titles were not at issue except to the extent that some provincial or dominion legal right might derive from that Indian title. Yet, even if Indian title was fodder, it was a special kind of fodder for it brought into the common law the full range of nineteenth-century ideas concerning Indian land ownership. In light of the legal maxim that the holding in a case cannot be separated from its facts, St. Cathe-rine's Milling arguably turns on issues other than Indian title and thus is an inappropriate case as judicial precedent on Indian title questions. A detailed look at the four opinions and the arguments of both sides in the Supreme Court will put the Indian title argument in the context of the rest of the case.

At trial in Chancery Division, Mowat's argument had centred on Indian title, arguing that Ontario Indians had only a moral claim to the land, one that was not recognized in law.[58] He cited two Ontario cases, *Bown* v. *West* and *Church* v. *Fenton*, for that proposition, along with the American case, *Johnson* v. *McIntosh*, and the American commentator Chancellor Kent.[59] The Ontario land surrenders, which had been numerous and had involved complex and direct negotiations between the crown and the various tribes in Ontario, were dismissed as 'only out of endeavour to satisfy the Indians'; no property right had been involved.[60] To underscore this point, Mowat argued that British Columbia had never recognized any Indian land title, implicitly denying that Ontario had an entirely different legal and political history.[61]

D'Alton McCarthy, appeared for the St Catherine's Milling and Lumber Company, although he in fact represented the dominion.[62] In arguing for the dominion's title to the land, he drew on American cases both for the legal proposition that the Indians had some form of title and for the political proposition that Indian matters, in a federal system, not only fell to the national government, but also represented a broad federal power, not the narrow authority over small reserves that Ontario would have recognized. While McCarthy cited *Cherokee Nation* v. *Georgia* and *Worcester* v. *Georgia* (collectively referred to as the 'Cherokee cases') as well as a number of other American cases and commentators, he failed to refer to their context, a complex dispute between the states and the national government over both the alienation of Indian lands and political control over Indian affairs.[63]

Chancellor Boyd's opinion was delivered on 10 June, three weeks after the case was argued. He relied entirely on the research and argument of Ontario in his judgment. This is not surprising given the opinion's forty-one pages, quickly written during a period when Boyd was sitting in other cases. He began by noting that the lands in Canada had been vested in the crown by conquest and that the public lands in Ontario were transferred by statute from the crown to the province in 1837.[64] Then Boyd turned to the Indian title issues that underlay Ontario's claim. Characterizing the Indians as 'heathens and barbarians,' Boyd denied that 'any legal ownership of the land was ever attributed to them,' citing a 1675 New York opinion of a 'multitude of counsellors.'[65] He then cited *Johnson* v. *McIntosh* as supporting the proposition that Indians had no legal ownership of the land.[66] Given both the complexity and the weight of the historical evidence, Boyd's use of precedent for the proposition that the Indians had no title in their unsurrendered lands is simply wrong. Moreover, his citation of Chief Justice John Marshall's opinion in *Johnson* v. *McIntosh* is misleading, for, while that opinion does subscribe to a conquest-based theory of the extinguishment of Indian title, it also holds that the Indians have a substantial property right in their lands which can be surrendered only to the government of the United States and not to private parties.[67] This construction would have supported the St Catherine's Milling and Lumber Company's view of the case.[68] Boyd ignored Chief Justice Marshall's opinions in the Cherokee cases, precedent enormously damaging to his view of Indians as 'barbarians' without legal rights to their lands.

Boyd then offered his analysis of Canadian Indian policy. Referring to a 'benevolent policy' for the 'liberal treatment of Indians' (whom he also referred to as 'rude red-men'), Boyd recited a short history of British paternalism, which was designed to open up the frontier to settlers while at the same time protecting the Indians and avoiding a 'collision' between the two groups.[69] While the Indians were given various 'guarantees' to protect their 'territories,' only those reserves that were formally surrendered by treaty were 'reserves' held for the Indians by the crown. These reserves, in Boyd's analysis, were the 'Indian lands' placed under dominion control by the BNA Act. All other lands were crown lands belonging to Ontario.[70] This was a narrow holding, avoiding most of the complexity of the law of Indian title. On the other hand, Boyd grounded his holding in an explicit statement of Canadian Indian policy, the first Canadian judge to do so in the context of a judicial opinion.

Boyd's treatment of the Saulteaux reflects the racism of late-nineteenth-century Indian policy and requires comment. His characterization of Indians as 'barbarians' was an instance of dehumanizing and racist language that had not previously found its way into Canadian judicial opinions and that therefore must reflect a change of altitude among Canada's educated class about matters of race. Boyd was also writing in the context of the Northwest Rebellion of 1885 and his passions may have been inflamed by the war, even though the Saulteaux themselves had had nothing to do with the rebellion. Whatever the reason for his views, Boyd gratuitously referred to the Saulteaux as 'a more than usually degraded Indian type' while giving no indication of what, in his view, made these Indians more 'degraded' than others or what legal purpose was served by his description.[71] The logic of his language, in the context of this case, is that 'degraded' peoples could not hold title to land.

The making of Treaty 3 had revealed a politically articulate Indian nation with a strong tradition of land tenure and a well-organized social order.[72] Only one witness was called at the trial, Alexander Morris, who had negotiated Treaty 3 and who put the treaty in evidence.[73] Unfortunately, none of Morris's testimony was relevant to the outcome of the case. Morris could have testified that the Saulteaux of the Treaty 3 area believed that they owned their lands and that the treaty-making process itself showed that the Indians were treated as owners of the land. Moreover, Boyd's assumption that the Saulteaux were 'nomadic' and failed to make use of their lands could have been refuted by testimony on their extensive agricultural economy and well-established hunting, trapping, and fishing territories.[74] The lawyer with the most to gain in presenting the Indians' position on their land ownership was McCarthy and he did not do so. The image of McCarthy calling as witnesses dozens of Indian chiefs would clearly have changed the tenor of the case.[75] Finally, the Saulteaux were not even parties in the case: the dominion was no more interested in boldly advocating the idea of 'Indian title' than Ontario was: it was merely a legal argument.

ST. CATHERINE'S MILLING IN THE ONTARIO COURT OF APPEAL

The Ontario Court of Appeal, hearing the appeal over three days beginning on 1 December 1885 and deciding it four months later on 20 April 1886, dealt much less with the legal issue of Indian title than it did with the question of the meaning of the BNA Act in allocating powers between the dominion and provincial governments. Its judgment therefore gives us some idea of what Boyd's opinion might have looked like if he had avoided deciding the case on the Indian title issue. Still, the fact that the Court of Appeal took so much more time with the case than Boyd, wrote a much shorter opinion,[76] and changed the legal foundation of his lower court decision – distancing itself from his views on Indian title – must indicate a conscious legal (or political) decision to take the approach it did in the face of an obvious appeal to the Privy Council. Be this as it may, the Court of Appeal was in line with Cassells in seeing *St. Catherine's Milling* not as a broad Indian title case but as a much narrower case centring on the legal interpretation of the terminology and meaning of the BNA Act.

The opinion of Chief Justice John Hagarty, upholding Ontario's claim to the land in dispute, turns on his interpretation of the intent of the BNA Act and not on his view of Indian title. In fact, Hagarty admitted the difficulty of the question of Indian title, did not accept Boyd's view, and believed that Treaty 3 actually extinguished Indian land rights. This view necessarily admits that the Indians still held some form of property right prior to the treaty.[77] Judge Featherston Osler, without writing a separate opinion, concerned with Judge Hagarty.

Judge George Burton, underscoring the deliberate effort of the court to base its opinion on grounds distinct from those of Chancellor Boyd, wrote a separate concurring opinion supporting Boyd's analysis. In the veiled language of an era when judges did not criticize each other, Burton began his comments by denying the entire logic of Hagarty's opinion. He pointed out that 'once we understand the facts, [the case] does not present any very formidable difficulties.'[78] The implication of this carefully constructed sentence is that Hagarty had wasted his time on a 'formidably difficult' construction of language that would have been unnecessary had he 'understood the facts'. What facts Hagarty did not understand were made clear in Burton's next sentence. Calling the contention that the Indians had title to the land a 'startling one' that had never before been argued in a British court of justice, he dismissed the American cases without referring to their arguments in any detail.[79] While generally endorsing the views of Boyd in his own analysis of the law of Indian title, Burton went beyond the chancellor and offered a strong defence of the prerogatives of the province. He claimed both that the province had control over the Indian tribes and that, in negotiating the Confederation agreement, the delegates of the provinces would never have yielded control over the vast lands of Canada to the dominion.[80]

Judge Christopher Patterson similarly accepted Boyd's construction of the BNA Act, but, like Hagarty, he did not agree with Boyd on the question of Indian title. Patterson recognized that the relationship between the Indians and Europeans was 'peculiar' and that the Indians had some type of sovereignty over the land, which included some right to sell or transfer it.[81] His views were essentially those of the American justice Joseph Story, whose treatise on the United States constitution was cited as 'answering the contention that the lands belonged to the Indians in any sense which deprived them of the character of lands belonging to the province,' a clear recognition that the Indians had a distinct property right in their lands although one that was somehow shared with the province.[82]

THE APPEAL IN THE SUPREME COURT OF CANADA

The differences in the judgments of the Chancery Division and the court of appeal might have led the Supreme Court of Canada to write a masterful opinion setting out the rights of Indians to a permanent place in their country, but in fact the court missed its opportunity. This is not surprising in view of the troubled history of the new court, created in 1875. By the mid-1880s, the court had not yet defined a role for itself between powerful provincial appellate courts and the Privy Council. Indeed, the Supreme Court held such low status that qualified judges were reluctant to serve on it,[83] and *St. Catherine's Milling* was the first important case the court decided.

The dominion had the right to by-pass the court, appealing directly to the Privy Council where the case inevitably was headed, but it chose the intermediate appeal to the Supreme Court instead, evidently on the belief that its case in the Privy Council might be strengthened by a Supreme Court victory.[84] The appeal was heard beginning on 19 November 1886 and decided seven months later, on 20 June 1887. A complete outline of the respective cases made by Ontario and by the St Catherine's Milling and Lumber Company (representing the interests of the dominion government) can be gleaned both from their printed factums and from the brief summary printed in the reported opinion. The factums are tedious documents, laden with technical formalities rather than good legal argument. Ontario's factum is surprisingly short and weak, given both what was at stake and the eminence of the lawyers that produced it. Signed by Oliver Mowat and E.F.B. Johnson, it runs fourteen pages, nearly half of which consists of strings of citations. It is little more than a bald-faced assertion of the Ontario view of the points in dispute, with no real argument of the complexities of Indian title raised by the company's attorneys.[85]

The appellants' seventy-nine-page brief is much more complete, indicating a complete reworking of their losing argument in the Ontario courts and reflecting the complexity of Indian title in the crown case.[86] McCarthy had finally done his homework, meeting Ontario's research into the primary documents on Indian title with his own research. The major thrust of his argument was that the legal rights of Indians to their lands had always been recognized in North America in a variety of ways. Rather than just asserting this, the brief contained excerpts from dozens of treaties and cases – largely American – showing the nature and extent of Indian title.[87] McCarthy's confidence in his case was evidently raised by this new research and, in spite of his losses in the courts below, he was confident of victory.

Yet, for all its research, McCarthy's brief is a model of ineffective legal writing, a long listing of citations – more than a hundred – for the proposition that the American colonies recognized some Indian title to their land.[88] This evidence was primarily in the form of colonial treaties and land grants, not nineteenth-century cases which might have been more persuasive as legal precedent. Dozens of American state court cases had dealt with the question of Indian rights.[89] By and large, all of the views denying any Indian title had been rejected in the United States, either by the state courts themselves or, following the 'Cherokee cases,' by federal courts rejecting state claims to Indian lands. Some of these cases turned on theories of Indian rights in a federal system that were important in the dominion's claim of jurisdiction over Indian lands. The 'Cherokee cases' involved an expansive Georgia claim to Cherokee lands based on Georgia's views of its state sovereignty over lands within its borders.[90] Georgia, and the neighboring states of Alabama and Tennessee, had, in the early 1830s, made detailed and sophisticated arguments of the nature of the state's extinguishment of Indian title that were now rejected by the United States Supreme Court.[91]

A 279-page 'Joint Appendix' was prepared and printed on the order of Justice Fournier. It appeared on 6 October 1886, about six weeks before the case was heard.[92] This document, containing all of the historical references of both parties, must have been prepared with great haste and showed the intent of the court to consider the primary documents in its deliberations. About fifty of its pages dealt with the American colonies, the remainder covering British relations with Indians in the various Canadian provinces, the history of Indian title in Canada.

Chief Justice Sir William Ritchie's opinion went immediately to the issue of land title. He held that the Indians had a legal right of occupancy, the crown a legal title in the land, a decision primarily based on American cases which had been presented by McCarthy for the dominion.[93] While this decision did not follow Chancellor Boyd's position (which was also the Ontario position) completely denying an Indian property right in the land, it had the same legal effect since it left the crown with ultimate title and Ontario taking that title under the BNA Act.[94] Ritchie's twenty-three-page opinion ended on that note, with the chief justice acknowledging that the case had been so 'fully and ably dealt with by the learned Chancellor ... I feel I can add nothing to what has already been said by him.'[95] His judgment, however, had departed from Boyd's view of Indian title, and so this compliment was legally meaningless. The shifting of the dominion's position to reflect American cases had also shifted the legal foundation of the case.

Justice Samuel Strong, dissenting, did a careful analysis of the nature of Indian title in a thirty-six-page opinion relying heavily on American cases.[96] He construed the question at hand narrowly, whether 'lands reserved for Indians' in the BNA Act included the lands surrendered by the Ojibwa in Treaty 3.[97] His survey of the different types of traditional land-tenure arrangements that might be accorded the Indians all had one common element: lands held traditionally were 'lands reserved for the Indians' with the Indians having definite property rights. Influenced by American law, Strong found an unwritten common law that 'these territorial rights of the Indians were strictly legal rights' which had to be taken account of in the distribution of property between the dominion and the provinces upon Confederation.[98] He also held, again influenced by American precedent, that unsurrendered Indian lands were the property of the crown but were lands reserved for Indians which passed to the dominion on Confederation rather than to Ontario.[99]

Justice John Gwynne, in a lengthy opinion, agreed with Strong.[100] Justices William Henry, Fournier, and Henri-Elzear Taschereau agreed with Ritchie in short opinions, with Henry again complimenting the work of Boyd, saying he 'entirely approved' of his opinion.[101] Fournier, who had ordered the printing of the appendix, was the only justice who wrote no opinion at all, concurring with the judgment of Ritchie.[102] Ontario had won 4–2 in the Supreme Court.

THE APPEAL TO THE PRIVY COUNCIL

By now both positions had been argued and judges had written opinions on both sides. The inevitable appeal to the Privy Council to decide the question of Ontario's control of crown lands was to prove anti-climatic, leading to a short opinion more focused on the intention of the BNA Act than on Indian title.[103] But neither side took the result for granted. McCarthy, in spite of his three losses in courts below, came to believe that the law was on the dominion's side and that he would win.[104] Ontario had prevailed upon Edward Blake, perhaps the best lawyer in Canada, to argue its position. The case was argued on 20 July 1888. Ontario won again, and the legal views of Chancellor Boyd were substantially vindicated.

The Privy Council, however, did not accept his view that Indians had no property right in their lands. Without conceding that Boyd was wrong, Blake had effectively conceded this point, sensing that it was unacceptable to the law lords. Instead, he adopted a middle view which he characterized as following from the general run of United States decisions: Indians in Ontario – and Canada – had a legal right of occupancy but not ownership of their lands.[105] This usufructuary right was a significant right and more of an Indian interest in their traditional lands than Ontario had argued for. But the important issue was the province's ownership of Indian lands through crown title. Blake recognized that even the 'middle position' supported this result: if the crown had any legal right to Indian lands, Ontario took it under the BNA Act. Undeveloped lands within the boundaries of provinces belonged to the provinces, not to the national government.

AFTERMATH

While *St. Catherine's Milling* decided the broad question of Ontario's ownership of crown lands within the province, it left unresolved a whole range of complex questions regarding Indian reserves in Ontario. Several important cases followed in the wake of *St. Catherine's Milling* but added little doctrinally. Rather, these cases continued Ontario's aggressive policy of asserting provincial claims over Indian lands. Neither the interests of the Indians nor those of the dominion government fared very well. In *Attorney General of Ontario* v. *Francis* another dominion timber lease was at issue, also in the far northwest of Ontario.[106] These lands, however, had been made part of an Indian reserve in the Robinson-Huron Treaty of 1850.[107] The Canadian government had the lands surveyed in 1884 and in July 1886 the timber was sold for 'the benefit of the Indians,' with the money to be held in trust.[108] However, Ontario had also sold the same timber in 1872. The Ontario timber leases were 'widely advertised' but the Dominion government neither objected nor made any claim that an Indian reserve was contained on the lands.[109]

As if this confusion and ineptness of both governments in managing Indian lands was not sufficient, a heavy measure of arrogance emerged as the two parties continued their dispute over basic issues of federalism. When the dominion government learned by accident of the Ontario sale, Lawrence Vankoughnet, a veteran official of the Indian Department, travelled from Ottawa to Toronto expressly to resolve the matter. At the end of his interview with Ontario's deputy commissioner of crown lands, he was left with the impression that Ontario would 'settle with the purchasers of its licenses,' and the Indian Department proceeded with the sale of the federal licences. Ontario, however, did not do so, pitting two sets of licensees against each other. The attorney-general of Ontario sued in Chancery to eject the federal licensees.[110]

The dominion government had no evidence of the existence of an Indian reserve of its own creation, a commentary on the state of its administration of Indian affairs. In presenting its case, it called on Mongowin, chief of the Ojibwa band that lived on the lost reserve. Mongowin knew his heritage intimately and testified that his father, Shewanakishick, had called a council at Whitefish Lake to ask the band if he should agree to the reserve granted in the treaty. Mongowin then testified to the boundaries of the reserve described at that council: 'following the road' around the reserve beginning with Nebenenekahming, 'place of the high cranberries,' and ending, after passing nine further places, with Muckohdehwaugohming, Black Lake.[111] Several other Ojibwa witnesses confirmed this account. The court found, based on the Indians' testimony, that the reserve existed. Remaining was the task of setting its boundaries: a simple matter since the Ojibwa description closely matched a recent dominion survey.[112]

Ontario then argued that surrendered Indian lands, being no longer 'Indian lands or lands reserved for Indians,' reverted to the province under the BNA Act. Judge Ferguson rejected this argument, holding that the dominion's sale of timber was an administrative act done for the benefit of the band.[113] Indian lands had often been sold or leased 'for the benefit of the Indians.' Ontario's argument attempting to deny that practice would have had the effect of shifting much Indian land – and assets – to provincial administration. Because the lands in question were 'Indian lands,' the dominion prevailed. The opinion was handed down within a month of the Privy Council's decision in *St. Catherine's Milling.* The court had withheld its judgment pending a decision of the Privy Council, but it later found that the decision had no bearing on the case: 'lands reserved for Indians' were under dominion jurisdiction under the BNA Act.[114]

Ontario was not yet finished with its expansive claims to lands reserved for Indians prior to Confederation. The province sought control over its lands and resources in a way that ignored Indian rights.[115] *Ontario Mining Company* v. *Seybold et al.* involved another northwest Ontario Indian reserve.[116] The case was decided by Chancellor Boyd and contains many elements of his original *St. Catherine's Milling* opinion. At stake was provincial title to another tract of Indian lands that the dominion had secured through Treaty 3. In negotiating that treaty the dominion had granted the Indians a number of reserves, including Sultana Island in Lake of the Woods. In 1886, however, the Saulteaux had surrendered Sultana Island to the dominion; the land was to be sold 'for the benefit of the Indians,' with the money received from the sale to be held in trust. The dominion sold the mineral rich land to Ontario Mining Company. The province of Ontario, following the Privy Council decision in *St. Catherine's Milling*, disputed this title, arguing that, since the dominion did not have title to Treaty 3 lands, it could not transfer any title to Ontario Mining Company.[117]

While some legal elements of this case were similar to those in *St. Catherine's Milling*, not just land title was at issue. Ontario conceded dominion authority over Indian affairs, but its argument also limited the dominion government's capacity to conduct Indian affairs by denying its power to act unilaterally in the granting of reserves to Indians. The treaty-making process, Ontario maintained, required the consent of the provinces. Underlying this argument was likely the belief that provincial involvement in treaty negotiations could serve to protect local interests by ensuring that Indians received the most worthless and out of the way lands.

Boyd conceded that the dominion had a right to grant reserves to the Indians, as well as to sell those lands and hold money in trust for the Indians. This power was limited by its purpose, however: if the land ever stopped being used to benefit Indians, it reverted to the province because it was the province that held title to the land.[118] Mineral rights were a different matter. They were not included because the Indians had only an occupancy right that they had conveyed to the dominion government. The Indians had no interest in minerals; therefore, ownership of the minerals remained with the crown and had been passed to Ontario at Confederation.[119] On appeal to Ontario Divisional Court, Boyd's judgment was upheld in a three-page opinion which once again complimented his reasoning.[120] Afterwards, the Supreme Court of Canada also upheld Boyd, an action that increased the wealth of the provinces at the expense of both the Indians and the dominion.[121] The case followed *St. Catherine's Milling* to the Privy Council, where the dominion once again lost.[122] The dominion government was forced to negotiate an agreement with Ontario in order to gain access to any land for purposes of Indian reserves.[123] Without the consent of Ontario, Indians had no right even to the land under the shacks they lived in.

The dominion government's power to sell or lease Indian lands and to use the proceeds to benefit the tribes, a process that had been common in Canada since the early nineteenth century, was also challenged successfully. The Rat Portage Saulteaux had yielded up six hundred acres of land on Sultana Island so that the dominion could sell or lease the land for the benefit of the tribe. *Caldwell* v. *Fraser* involved a lawsuit between two parties, one holding a lease under dominion title, the other under Ontario title.[124] The case arose at the same time as *Seybold* but involved different parties.[125] In an unreported opinion, published in a treatise on mining law, Judge John Edward Rose held that the dominion had no right at all to sell or lease lands for the benefit of the Indians. Once the Indians were finished with a reserve the land reverted to the province.

The process of adjudication of these cases left all sides dissatisfied and contributed to a feeling among government officials that the courts should be kept out of Indian policy. The underlying message was that the provinces and the dominion needed to negotiate these jurisdictional differences and not rely on litigation. This point was made in a letter from the Ontario treasurer to Prime Minister Wilfrid Laurier, written while *Ontario Mining* was being litigated: 'Every now and again questions are arising where doubts as to jurisdiction exist, and it seems to me that instead of depending upon the slow, inconvenient and expensive process of leaving the determination to the courts ... much might be accomplished by an effort to arrive at an understanding as to what jurisdiction should be.'[126] It is no accident that few major Indian title cases were decided by Canadian courts until the 1960s.[127] Substantial issues of Indian rights existed, but the courts deferred Indian legal rights to political policy makers, depriving Indians of their legal rights in Canadian society as well as access to the law as an institution capable of defending their rights.

CONCLUSION

St. Catherine's Milling symbolizes the legal and political domination of Ontario in nineteenth-century Indian law. The case remains important in modern title cases, including *Calder*, *Delgamuukw*, and *Bear Island*.[128] Yet almost no part of its analysis, taken element by element, is still good law.[129]

Initially, as we have seen, *St. Catherine's* was not even an 'Indian title' case: its legal roots derived from the Ontario boundary issue. While Prime Minister Macdonald first denied Ontario's title, neither side saw their legal dispute over the control of western resources turning on Indian title until the late winter of 1886, a few months before the issue came to trial. Until that point, Ontario's lawyers were preparing a case based on the legal interpretation of the phrase 'lands reserved for Indians' in the BNA Act. This issue, in fact, decided the case in one court, the Ontario Court of Appeal, and influenced it in both the Supreme Court of Canada and the Privy Council; 'Indian title' was a secondary issue in the case, arguably unnecessary in deciding it. A broader issue was the place of Indians and Indian reserves in Canadian federalism. Douglas Sanders notes that Indian reserves were the main institution that a weak dominion government inherited from the provinces.[130] Yet the dominion took control over Indian reserves without taking control of 'Indian lands.' These were crown lands, held by the provinces.

While the holding that Indian title is 'usufructuary' is still the law of Canada, this holding itself reflects the underlying racism of the case, expressly seen in Boyd's opinion. Indians, in nineteenth-century colonial thought, could not hold the same kind of title that Europeans held: rather, they held some kind of lesser title, if any at all.[131] Furthermore, the 'Indian title' was decided by the courts without any representation of the Indian nations. This was true in spite of the fact that the Six Nations Confederacy had been contesting a version of the land-title issue for a hundred years. Treaty 3 Saulteaux thought and acted as if they owned their lands, to the point of upsetting Canadian officials with their 'arrogance.' Ontario's victory gave the province power over these Indians in ways that paralleled its struggle with the Six Nations Confederacy in the early nineteenth century.

7

'Canadian Courts Are Open to Enforce Their Contracts': Canadian Law and the Legal Culture of Ontario Indians

Nineteenth-century Ontario Indians were legal actors who actively used both their traditional law and Canadian law to protect their interests. By the 1880s, when as many as one-fourth of the Six Nations Indians at Grand River at some point in their lives were being jailed for petty offences, the same Indians were using Canadian, British, and international law to bring a claim against the dominion government for the loss of some of their lands in 1832 to the Grand River Navigation Company. This would be one of the first successful land claims won by an Indian nation against the Canadian government.[1]

The Grand Council of the League of the Iroquois, the traditional government of the Six Nations Confederacy, regularly included in its meetings the adjudication of disputes, handing down judgments that were legally binding under tribal law.[2] The Six Nations were more organized than other Indian nations, but none of these legal processes was unique to them. Indians throughout Ontario were legally active, constructing their own legal relationships with each other, local settlers, and provincial and federal institutions. First Nations legal actions demonstrated a shrewd understanding of the legal complexities of their position in relation to Canada, as well as a great deal of legal imagination.

THE SIX NATIONS AT GRAND RIVER IN THE LATE NINETEENTH CENTURY

Of the legal histories of all native peoples, that of the Six Nations is the most carefully preserved, including dozens of recorded cases. These cases, dealing primarily with constitutional law, land law, Indian citizenship, and inheritance, reveal a fully functioning Six Nations legal system. While matters of criminal law were not officially decided, the Grand Council exercised its powers over various forms of misconduct, using the nations' 'forest bailiff' to eject individuals from lands occupied without legal right, to investigate the unlawful taking of wood from neighbours' lands, and, in one instance, to eject a young man guilty of adultery from his father's house.[3] Clearly, the Six Nations were exercising jurisdiction over many of the same issues that the crown was trying in its own district courts.

Nonetheless, there was direct competition between the courts. For example, Jonas Baptiste brought an action in the Grand Council for improvements to lands that he had lost title to for failing to make payments. When the Grand Council ruled against Baptiste, he threatened to bring the suit in Ontario district court. He was expressly forbidden to do so by the council, but he defiantly brought the lawsuit anyway. Dismissed for jurisdictional reasons and ordered to pay costs, Baptiste applied to the Six Nations for assistance. The Grand Council refused, an action that meant that he went to jail.[4] The council's action in forbidding access to Ontario courts was doubtlessly an attempt to protect its own jurisdiction in intra-Indian matters.

This act was in defiance of an order-in-council of 1890 in which the dominion government had stated that Canadian courts were 'open to enforce their [Six Nations] contracts, or to afford redress for injuries to their persons or property, not only as between them and the white people, but in relation to each other.'[5] The Six Nations, however, did not accept this statement of their legal rights and few Indian civil cases went to provincial courts. Their legal dispute with the dominion, still unresolved, intensified in the early twentieth century as both dominion and Ontario officials attempted to exercise jurisdiction over members of the Six Nations. In *Council* v. *Estate of Jasper Jones, Sophie General and Department of Indian Affairs* the Grand Council held that it and not the Department of Indian Affairs had jurisdiction over inheritances on the Grand River reserve.[6] Shortly thereafter, in *Sero* v. *Gault*, a Mohawk woman whose net had been seized by Thomas Gault, an Ontario fishery inspector, sued in district court to recover her net, arguing that no Ontario warden had authority on an Indian reserve.[7] Although this was not a Grand River case, the Six Nations mobilized behind the treaty-based defence.[8] Losing in Ontario courts, they took the case to the League of Nations.[9] This early-twentieth-century action, asserting the Six Nations' sovereignty in an international legal forum, outraged and embarrassed the Canadian government.

The cases also reflect an evolving Six Nations law. For example, in 1885 William Jamieson sued the Grand Council for damages when stray dogs killed some of his sheep.[10] The council refused to pay, citing the lack of a tribal statute, but referred the matter to the fire-keepers, traditional Onondaga chiefs charged with guarding the wampum belts, for a final decision.[11] They decided that the nation should not pay damages in such cases.

Like the Grand Council of the Six Nations, the Grand General Council of Ontario Indians frequently addressed legal issues in the late nineteenth century. For instance, at an 1883 meeting in Hagersville involving 109 delegates from 21 reserves,[12] the council specifically addressed three legal issues. Most important, the delegates objected to a section of the Indian Act that denied Indians government-interest moneys while in custody for criminal offences. To the delegates, this was a 'great injustice' since Indians were 'doubly punished for crime.' First, they paid the same penalty as a non-Indian, then the Indian Department denied them their interest money.[13]

A discussion of enfranchisement followed with most delegates favouring full political rights for Indians. A minority, however, was opposed, believing that full enfranchisement would be used to break up the reserves.[14] Delegates also believed that Indians should be able to make a will bequeathing property without the interference of the Indian agent who, under the Indian Act, had to approve such inheritances.[15] This meeting shows that Indians were political actors actively concerned with reforming the Indian Act in the general direction of increasing the rights of individual Indians, but with some internal disagreement. Whole bands met in council, voted to request enfranchisement, and petitioned the Ontario government.[16] The Cape Croker band petitioned for enfranchisement but also went farther, asking that their chief get control of tribal money from a corrupt Indian agent. The band further demanded removal of John McIver, their Indian agent, for corruption and incompetence, citing eleven reasons.[17] The Indian nations, like the dominion and Ontario governments, could cite the law to protect their interests although they often lacked the power to put the law in motion.

THE LEGAL HISTORY OF THE CHIPPEWA AT CAPE CROKER

John Borrows, a member of the Nawash band at Cape Croker, has written his people's legal history using a variety of sources which include both oral history and his own experience as a status Indian. This history is remarkable in that it clearly reveals a range of alternative understandings of Indian history that are culturally specific, unique to each First Nation. Kegedonce, Borrow's great-great-great-grandfather, begins the legal history by choosing to move with some of his people to Canada from the United States during the War of 1812 and to fight with the British against the Americans in order to advance the cause of self-determination for his people. Later, he also chose to accept the Christian religion in an effort to increase the power of Indians to deal with the powerful pressures of white society.[18]

His son, Peter Kegedonce Jones, was in school in 1836 when the nation relinquished 1,500,000 acres of land through Treaty 45 1/2, reserving 450,000 acres and moving to Nawash, now called Owen Sound. In 1854 the government proposed Treaty 72, ceding 500,000 additional acres of Nawash and Saugeen land. In a process fraught with irregularities and false promises, this land was surrendered. The Indians were guaranteed a large reserve, with huge money payments, and sold the land in a treaty process that did not include time for adequate consultation between the two bands. Finally, in Treaty 82 in 1857, Peter Jones surrendered the entire area, removing the Nawash to the Cape Croker reserve. Again, this land was ceded under great pressure, with a good amount of alcohol used to induce cession. Both of these cessions involved considerations of sovereignty, of removing the Nawash to the security of a reserve away from the destructive influence of settlers and alcohol.[19] Peter Jones' wife, Margret McLeod, played a major role in the preservation of the Ojibwa language and culture, and she also exercised political leadership within the band.[20]

Charles Kegedonce Jones, the first child born after the Nawash band's resettlement at Cape Croker, served thirty-five years as both a traditional and elected chief, leading the tribe under Indian Act jurisdiction. Because there was no game at the reserve, the family lived each winter in a camp in the forest and there, at the age of ten, Charles had his first success at hunting, bringing home a bear. He later attended boarding school, where he learned mathematics and carpentry. Records of the tribal council for the years between 1890 and 1920 show a determined effort to maintain self-government, in the face of an Indian Act that even denied that an Indian was a person. The tribal council used every means at its disposal to promote the band's sovereignty, notwithstanding continuing diminutions of its rights. A 1902 memo, for example, protested a reduction in the band's fishing territory: 'The band solemnly protests against diminution or curtailment of their rights and privileges enjoyed and that the reasons assigned for reducing the area are considered to be insufficient, unacceptable and unjustifiable, and the Band looks for speedy restoration of their undoubted rights with as little delay as possible.'[21]

Working with the Grand Council of Ontario Indians, Jones and other chiefs frequently met with the Canadian government, representing First Nations positions on a variety of issues. The council fought for Indian rights and increased self-government and, in general, carried on self-government in spite of the limiting provisions of the Indian Act. Similarly, the council advanced Indian economic interests by advocating hunting and fishing rights, an approach that included asserting those rights by ignoring Canadian restrictions.[22]

This legal history has much more detail than is presented here, but it is a history of continuous struggle for tribal sovereignty against great odds. In every sphere of activity, the Nawash band used what means were available to increase its powers. These means included both taking what advantage the band could of Canadian law and repeatedly violating provisions of the Indian Act, or hunting and fishing regulations, that were deemed in contravention of Ojibwa law. In this story, legal history is an interaction of Ojibwa and Canadian law, not a one-dimensional process of the Ojibwa giving way to Canadian power.

THE MANITOULIN INCIDENT OF 1863

On at least one occasion, Ontario Indians violently resisted Canadian authority. In 1863, Indians on Manitoulin Island, believing that they owned fishing rights in Lake Huron, objected to a fishery operating on unceded tribal lands.[23] The Indian Department requested a fishery inspector, the only government official in the area, to warn the Indians to leave the fishery alone. The inspector, William Gibbard, got into a shouting match and left the settlement. The Indians, determined to drive the settlers from their land, landed at the fishery and threatened the fishermen at knife-point. Reinforcements from a nearby ship drove them off, but fifty Indians returned the next day and forced the abandonment of the fishery.[24] The Indian Department dealt with this violation of Canadian law by using a legal model: Gibbard recruited thirteen armed police officers from Toronto and Barrie and returned to Wikwemikong, on Manitoulin Island, to arrest the offenders.[25] The Indians resisted, with some verbally harassing the police while others returned with guns. A shouting and pushing match ensued.[26] The small police party was inadequate to the task.

A compromise was worked out. The Indians would not appear before any Ontario court, in accord with their position that the province had no jurisdiction over them. But they would agree to appear before a government hearing, consistent with their position 'as allies of her majesty.' Gibbard then proceeded towards Sault Ste Marie and, at Bruce Mines, broke his agreement and arrested Oswa-ane-mekee, described as 'one of the law-makers of Wikwemikong' and took him to court. There, a Toronto lawyer on vacation represented Oswa-ane-mekee and had the charges dropped. Gibbard made additional accusations, and Oswa-ane-mekee was recharged, but he was then bailed out by his attorney. Gibbard was murdered by parties unknown on his way back to Collingwood, and the charges were not pursued.[27] Significant here is the legal structuring of "Manitoulin Incident": the Indians believed that they were sovereign, that they owned their fishery and had a right to protect it. The Ontario government sent a large party of the police to arrest what amounted to an entire Indian band on petty criminal charges.

INDIANS AND THE LAW IN TURN-OF-THE-CENTURY NORTHERN ONTARIO

There was nothing unusual about the legal history of the Indians of Nawash, Grand River, and Manitoulin. Indians everywhere asserted their legal rights in a wide variety of ways. In the Robinson Treaty of 1850 Chief Michel Dokis, for example, negotiated a reserve for his Ojibwa band on the French River that included sixty-one square miles of good timber.[28] Any legal alienation of the Dokis band's lands required their consent. This was not an issue until the 1880s when logging companies approached Chief Dokis and the Indian Department to lease timber rights to the reserve. The band refused to sell their timber. The Indian Department thought of changing the law so that the timber reserves of 'unreasonable' Indians could be sold without their consent, but such an action would expose the fiction of Indian consent and possibly bring about a popular reaction.[29] The department tried to bribe the band to agree to a surrender of its timber by arranging a surrender vote and writing to every male member of the nation a letter promising payment of a large amount of money. But Chief Dokis was a strong leader and he prevailed: the band voted against surrender.[30] It continued to do so until 1908, finally voting eleven to six to surrender the timber. The election was not a fair one: the Indian Department called it without sufficient notice to enable Chief Dokis to organize his resistance, also arranging a large quantity of liquor for a feast the day before. Even having lost the timber, the band benefited from the chief's determination: instead of the few thousand dollars first offered in 1881, the timber sold for $1.1 million: $600 per person per year instead of the original $4. The Dokis band became the richest, per capita, in Canada.[31]

The complaint of H.P. Blackwood, president of the Minaki Campers Association at Lake Minaki, near Kenora, must reflect the frustration of late-nineteenth-century Canadians who could not stop the Indians from carrying on their own lives, even as increased settlement put them under close scrutiny. Winnipeg residents had built many summer homes on Lake Minaki but Indians, often under the influence of alcohol, camped on beaches nearby and engaged in 'dreadful behaviour.' Thefts occurred and, according to Blackwood, 'ladies are complaining that it is not safe to stay at the lake.'[32] The Indian Department sent a special agent to investigate Blackwood's charges and the agent identified a saloon keeper as the source of the liquor. The department, however, was not able to stop the liquor trade or restrict the activities of the Indians.[33]

This case is not the only evidence of local officials refusing to arrest Indians, as much because the exercise was pointless as out of any concern with the underlying social or economic issues. In one instance, the Indian Department complained to the attorney general of Ontario about the lock-up at Fort Frances. Not only had 'six or seven' Indians escaped but the local authorities, knowing where the escapees were, failed to rearrest them.[34] The Indians had served one to two days in jail at the time of the escape, and so local officials probably thought that that was sufficient for the purposes of justice. The situation at Kenora was arguably even worse: that jail was so full that Indians tried and sentenced for liquor offences had to be released with a suspended sentence. Again the Indian Department intervened, requesting that the Ontario attorney general see to it that sufficient jail 'accommodation' be available to 'receive Indian prisoners.'[35]

The same issue arose at Little Current, where the local authorities refused the Indian constable admission of Indian prisoners to the jail. The Manitowaning reserve had no jail of its own, a situation that necessitated either taking prisoners to the next jail, twenty-three miles away, or releasing them.[36] Local authorities claimed that the village lacked the funds for a full-time jailer, but the Indian agent claimed this excuse was false.[37] Rather, it seemed that the town did not want the trouble of a jail filled with Indians. All of these cases suggest some of the limits of criminal law in locking up Indian defendants. The Indian Department must have been concerned with how Canadian law appeared to the Indians under such circumstances, straining its legitimacy.

In 1898 William Young, police magistrate at Rat Portage (later Kenora), went with a constable to investigate complaints of trouble with Indians and theft at lumber camps in the Lake of the Woods area.[38] Young complained that 'rather a dishonest set of Indians lived in this locality,' stealing many provisions from the lumber companies. The Indians 'took to the woods' when Young arrived and were there safe from arrest. The magistrate left an arrest warrant with the foreman of one of the lumber camps. He was quite proud of his initiative, writing that an arrest 'will be easily done as they will have no suspicion of his being authorized to arrest anyone.' Young went on to remark that 'the Indians must be made to understand that acts of this kind will bring punishment on them.'[39] No further record of this case remains, hence we cannot know if the arrest warrant was executed. In any case, this report provides insight into the quality of criminal justice being rendered Indians in northwestern Ontario. A logging company employee was legally empowered to arrest Indians for allegedly stealing company property. The capacity of Indians to 'take to the woods' was not without limits as the changing economy required increasing contact with settlers.[40]

While these Ojibwa and Saulteaux did not leave a legal record comparable to that of the Six Nations, they had functioning political and legal cultures, aspects of which are known from *Machekequonabe*, a case that documents the defence of their communities against a wendigo (see chapter 11). On another front, complaints of theft by Indians were frequent but it is impossible to ascertain the extent of such activity. In any event, theft is one survival mechanism of starving people. Further, property, as well as theft, has social and political meanings in a context where Indian land had been stolen – or taken away according to legal processes that had no parallel, or legitimacy, in native society.[41]

The picture of Indian life by the end of the nineteenth century in Ontario is a dismal one. Gradually, Indians had retreated to their reserves, becoming increasingly invisible.[42] Racism ran rampant in rural villages, as it did in federal government policy. The Reverend J. Cadot, a Roman Catholic missionary, complained of conditions at Wiarton, reporting that Indians resented the affront of discrimination in the inns and barbershops in the village, discrimination that forced them to eat at separate tables not properly cleaned or to be waited on in remote sections of inns.[43] This kind of treatment occasionally reached embarrassing proportions. When Peter Whiteduck and Jocko, two Indians, escaped in 1916 from jail at Pembroke, a community of several thousand in the Ottawa valley, killing a jailer in the process, their reserve was occupied by a large force of vigilantes. Men were not permitted to leave their homes to report to work, houses were illegally searched and the occupants abused. Following an investigation, the attorney general of Ontario complained that local authorities had abused their powers, reporting that no white community could ever be treated that way.[44] In the end, Jocko was shot dead by a legal posse under questionable circumstances and Whiteduck returned to jail. There, he wrote several sad letters on toilet paper asking his friends to help him escape to the woods. The letters were seized by his jailer and used in court as evidence of his dangerousness. In truth, they testify more to Whiteduck's despair, isolation, and loneliness.[45]

The *Bear Island* case of 1984 brought public attention to the legal history of the Temagami Ojibwa.[46] Their story is an amazing one, not because it is unique, but because it illustrates the complex legal and political histories that every Indian band has. Nebenegwune, headman of the band, was not present at the signing of the Robinson Treaty at Sault Ste Marie.[47] During the late nineteenth century the band zealously guarded their independence, trading in furs for their livelihood in complete isolation from Ontario law. The killing of Chief Cana Chintz by his brother Syagquasay led to a maze of jurisdictional confusion between Quebec and Ontario, with the band finally punishing the crime under its own law.[48] The Temagami tried hard to negotiate a favourable accommodation between itself and the provincial government. This was necessitated by the legal confusion generated by *St. Catherine's Milling*, because, under that ruling, crown land that the dominion provided as a reserve belonged to Ontario and so the province had to agree to any settlement. Ontario and dominion negotiators were not able to agree on the Temagami claims, leaving Ontario, in 1929, to demand that the Indians pay rent on the land their Bear Island homes were built on.[49] In *Bear Island*, the trial court judge did not accept the oral history presented in support of the band's claim, holding instead that the Temagami were represented by Tawgaiwene, a neighbouring chief, at the Robinson-Huron treaties and had, therefore, sold their lands at that treaty.[50] Today, Ontario, though conceding some Temagami settlement rights to a few hundred acres, still refuses to recognize anything more than the band's limited usufructuary right to the rest of its land. The band, in turn, has an unbroken history of asserting their rights to both land and sovereignty against both Ontario and the dominion.

The evidence of Temagami legal tradition – legal precedent in tribal law – was viewed by the Ontario court in 1984 through the formalistic framework of Canadian law. The question of the legal status of Nebegwune as headman in 1850 turned on the law of evidence, with the court applying a 'balance of probabilities' test to its own culture-bound and subjective reading of Temagami history.[51] A sounder approach to this question would have it turn on Temagami history and traditional law.

THE JAILING OF INDIANS IN LATE-NINETEENTH-CENTURY BRANTFORD

The one kind of law that Indians did not lack access to was the criminal law: thousands of criminal cases were brought against Ontario Indians in the nineteenth century. The run of cases from Grand River, suggests that there was a great deal of legal activity there.[52] The register of the Brantford jail provides a detailed (but not complete) listing of the Indians charged with criminal offences.[53] An examination of the number and types of criminal charges brought against these Indians demonstrates the reach of one form of Canadian legal activity involving Indians. To be sure, civil law might be a better measure of the legal integration of Indians into late-nineteenth-century Ontario because it reflects both individual choice to use the law as well as the institutional capacity to do so, the resources to get a case into court. As noted earlier, however, civil cases involving Indians are rare, reflecting Indian poverty and isolation, and also difficult to access because civil court records do not uniformly record race and most southern Ontario Indians had Christian names.

By and large, criminal cases did not consist of disputes between Indians taken to the courts by the Indians themselves; rather, these cases were brought by Canadian officials, either Indian agents or police officers, applying either general Canadian criminal law or offences under the Indian Act particular to Indians. The law involved might be called 'imposed law' because it was external to native society, part of an attempt of Euro-Canadians to enforce their standards of behaviour on Indian people through their domination of legal institutions.[54]

The whole question of the character of law and order on the Six Nations' Grand River lands is inseparable from the squatter and land-title issues. Chaos in land tenure destabilized social relations, both among natives and between natives and whites. The refusal of the crown to evict squatters had both an immediate and a symbolic effect on the local legal culture. By definition, the enforcement of law then became problematic, a choice made by crown officials depending on local political conditions.

Clouded land titles not only created an environment of official lawlessness but also, in themselves, provoked disputes. Squatters had no easy way to take trespassing, assault, and theft charges to the courts when their lack of legal title undermined the legality of their claims.

The accounts of the Grand River area as a lawless place in the nineteenth century need to be understood in this political context.[55] Indeed, such 'lawlessness' was one of the reasons that colonial authorities forced the Six Nations to cede most of their lands. In 1817 a Gore District grand jury condemned the Grand River settlement of the Six Nations as a 'frequent scene of riot and tumult ... out of the reach of the law.' Peter Lossing and others petitioned the Legislative Council about 'frequent depredations of the Six Nations Indians against each other and neighboring settlers, and the repeated instances of horrid murder ... among themselves.' The petitioners called on the government to intervene in the interests of social order, blaming a 'laxity in the Indians' former modes of regulating and punishing offenders' as well as alcoholism.[56]

The George Powlis Murder Case

The murder trial of George Powlis in 1839 provides one view of the underside of Grand River Indian life. Powlis, a grandson of Joseph Brant, was arrested, together with his brother and father, for the murder of Susannah Doxtater, a Mohawk, whose naked body was found strangled in an area called 'Vinegar Hill,' a 'place of resort for dissolute people' at the eastern edge of Brantford, between the city and the Mohawk village.[57] Investigation showed that she had not been killed where her body was found but nearby, with the tracks of four men and one woman leading from that site to the other.[58]

The evidence against the Powlises was circumstantial, but substantial. Distinctive sleigh tracks led from Joseph's house to the murder site. All three defendants had been in Brantford on the day of the murder, with testimony establishing that Joseph and Paul had left George off at Vinegar Hill on their way home. George had bought a ring and chestnuts at Brantford: the ring was found at the murder site, with chestnut shells also found on the snow. The jury acquitted Joseph and Paul but convicted George of murder, and Judge Levius Sherwood sentenced him to death. Powlis, supported by fourteen chiefs of the Six Nations, petitioned for clemency.[59]

The Executive Council, the body responsible for reviewing clemency petitions, deferred to a report of Sherwood that the conviction was based entirely on circumstantial evidence which, although sufficient to establish guilt in the minds of the jury, left the judge himself, although he had passed the death sentence, troubled by doubt. Solicitor General William Draper, however, urged that a 'murder committed by an Indian should be visited with a punishment calculated to produce a deep impression on the minds of those of his own race' and recommended transportation for a term of fourteen years. Powlis wound up with a sentence of seven years in Kingston Penitentiary, partly on the grounds that protracted imprisonment was felt more severely by Indians. The Six Nations continued petitioning for Powlis's release, as did Samuel Peters Jarvis, chief superintendent of Indian Affairs. Chief Justice John Beverley Robinson discussed the case with Sherwood, who also then supported a pardon. Eventually, Powlis was pardoned in spite of the opposition of Civil Secretary Thomas William Clinton Murdoch, who believed that 'it is with these people [Indians] more than others, that it is necessary to discourage the ideas that such crimes may be committed with impunity or atoned for by light punishment.'[60]

Six Nations Indians in the Brantford Jail

The Brantford jail register records a great deal of data for each person lodged there, including race, occupation, residence, offence, sentence, number of previous arrests, and discharge date. Brant County, with Brantford (population 12,000) the major city, was, in the early 1880s, a prosperous agricultural county of 34,000 people, including about 3000 members of the Six Nations. Most of the rich Grand River lands had been surrendered and, by 1880, the Six Nations' lands were largely limited to Tuscarora Township, whose 2891 inhabitants included 2509 Indians.[61] There, the Six Nations lived as small farmers and labourers, in a dispersed Indian community beginning on the outskirts of Brantford. A post office, store, and mission were located at Ohsweken, the only settlement. Initially, the Indians kept to themselves, applying their own law to minor offences and civil matters, but Canadian authorities came increasingly to intervene in traditional matters.[62] A published account of the operation of Six Nations law on the Grand River reserve shows that traditional law was commonly used throughout the nineteenth century.[63]

Six Nations Indians went to jail in great numbers after 1873 (when jail records are first available).[64] Over time, there was a change in the pattern of jailings. Initially, Indians were jailed at roughly their proportion of the population but, by the end of the century, they were jailed at a disproportionate rate, which remains the situation for native people in modern Canada.[65] For example, for the last eight months of 1873 (no records for the first four months exist), 27 out of 359 people lodged in jail were Indians – 7.5 per cent.[66] Indians represented about 9 per cent of the total population, and so these data indicate that they were being arrested roughly in proportion to their share of the population. In 1874 Indians accounted for 57 jailings out of 519, or about 11 per cent; and in 1880 their share of jailings was 49 out of a total of 210, or 23 per cent. At the end of the century (there is a large gap in the records), comparable data indicate a continuation of this disproportionate pattern: from October 1899 through September 1900, there were 37 Indians among a jail population of 176 – 21 per cent. For the next year, October 1900 through September 1901, 41 Indians were jailed, representing 20 per cent of the jail's population of 203.[67] By these data Six Nations Indians were being jailed at more than twice their proportion of the population.

An examination of the pattern of Indian jailings reveals some details of the economy and society of the Six Nations Indians at Grand River, as well as providing an indication of the scope of the imposition of Canadian law on Indians. Most Indians were jailed for drunkenness, often after failing to pay small fines. Ellen Doxtader, a 'housekeeper,' was jailed for twenty days after failing to pay a $5 fine for being 'drunk and disorderly.' Mary English, whose occupation was listed as 'prostitute,' served the same sentence also for failing to pay a $5 fine, after being charged with being 'drunk and disorderly.' John Whiskey and Joseph Hill, both labourers, on failing to pay the $5 fine, served the same sentence on the same charge.[68]

There is little change in this record over time: the number of arrests increases, the standard sentence for 'drunk and disorderly' rises from twenty to thirty days, and the number of previous arrests keeps on increasing. Julia Good, a housekeeper, forty nine years old, spent Christmas of 1899, 1900, and 1901 in the Brantford jail on separate charges. She served thirty days for assault in November 1899, her thirty-first jailing. In December she served fourteen days for vagrancy. By December 1901, her record showed thirty-eight previous arrests. At that time, she was sentenced to thirty days in jail for being 'drunk,' an old woman jailed nine times in two years.[69]

James Hill, a farmer sentenced to thirty days or a $5 fine for drunkenness, paid his fine.[70] The jail records show, however, that only a few Indians ever paid their fines, probably reflecting the poverty of the Six Nations Indians. In a cash-poor society, even $5 fines most often meant a month in jail. Richard Marade, a twenty-seven-year-old labourer, was sentenced to ninety days in jail for assault or a fine of $18. The fine was paid after he had served fourteen days in jail, apparently reflecting the amount of time it took friends or relatives to raise the money.[71]

Besides the run of drinking and minor assault arrests, a large number of jailings involved petty property crimes, theft, vandalism, or trespassing. It is difficult to characterize the meaning of these jailings. On the one hand, they might well suggest a considerable amount of effort on the part of the Indian agent to use the law to force Indians to adopt Euro-Canadian values, emphasizing individual property instead of communal property. Arrests under the Indian Act for resource-disposition offences – selling timber and hay without the agent's permission – were in this category. The prison records do not record sufficient information in most cases to ascertain the kinds of property interests involved.

Of particular interest is the fact that property offences were the most likely to result in acquittals, a rare event in drunk and disorderly arrests. Aurelia Sero, aged fourteen, was held for one day on a charge of 'destroying property' but acquitted. James Hill, Peter Davis, and Henry Hill, boys aged ten to thirteen, were arrested for stealing property from a railroad and held two days before being acquitted. Lucy Sero, a servant aged seventy, was arrested for 'obtaining goods under false pretenses' and discharged. Meshak Green, a twenty-two-year-old labourer, was discharged after two days on the same charge. William King, jailed for 'horse-stealing,' was discharged after four days. Emily Carver was arrested twice, once for 'theft' and once for 'destroying property' only to have both charges dropped.[72] Well over half of all persons jailed for property crimes were discharged without being convicted, usually after one to four days in jail, suggesting that the crown could not secure convictions in those cases. This must mean that, unlike in drunk and disorderly cases where a police officer was the complaining witness, the prosecution was unable to get the testimony of complaining witnesses in property crime cases. Some of these property offences may have been brought by the crown with the crown as a victim, probably upon the action of the Indian agent acting on various sorts of information that was not legal evidence. The fact that most of the charges were dropped in a few days may have been of no concern: the majesty and power of the government was established merely by arresting Indians for property offences and locking them in jail.

Felony charges against Indians were rare. Of these, about half were for a single crime, horse-stealing, probably the most common nineteenth-century rural crime since horses were the major property of value that could easily be removed from a farm. Four Indian men were convicted of horse-stealing. They received long sentences: John Everett and Peter Green, both illiterate labourers twenty-one years old, drew four-year sentences. George Green, twenty years old, received a one-year sentence, and Peter English was sentenced to six months. English, listed as an eighteen-year-old farmer, drew another three-year sentence for horse-stealing the next year.[73] The fact that all four young men were listed as 'unable to read' in jail records at a time when most Indians were described as 'literate' indicates that even the most basic formal education was not reaching all segments of the Grand River population. Because distances to schools at Grand River were not great by nineteenth- century rural standards, it is likely that those Indians who avoided schools did so for cultural and political reasons.

Serious crimes of violence were rarer still. Ed Wilson, a twenty-two-year-old carpenter, received a five-year sentence for rape, the only rape conviction reported in the five years sampled, although several other rape charges were dismissed.[74] There appear to have been three homicides involving Six Nations Indians at Grand River between 1873 and 1901, a far cry from a racist image of Indian violence stemming from drinking and fighting. One of these, Ben Carrier, a twenty-eight-year-old labourer convicted of killing his wife, was hanged.[75] John Yellow, convicted of manslaughter for a drunken killing, received a ten-year sentence.[76] Saddest of all was the case of Margaret Wabaneeb. She killed her daughter, Margaret Fox, by hitting her in the head with an axe while visiting her in the Brantford jail. Fox had been convicted of vagrancy and was serving a thirty-day sentence. Wabaneeb was let out on bail and ultimately acquitted of manslaughter charges, probably reflecting the hopelessness of convicting an eight-five-year-old woman of such a crime.[77]

Most of the convictions were the result of summary trials for misdemeanours before police magistrates. The Indian agent at the Grand River reserve was legally empowered to act as a police magistrate and we know from several appellate cases that he aggressively did so.[78] If we extrapolate from the 1873–80 and 1899–1901 data to estimate the arrests in the missing volume of the Brantford jail records (and assume that the pattern between volumes one and three is stable), it appears that about 1000 Six Nations Indians were jailed during this twenty-eight-year period.[79] This is a staggering proportion of a population of 3000. While some of the jailings involved recidivists, with Julia Good's thirty-nine arrests holding the record, most offenders are listed as never having been previously jailed. After Julia Good, the leading recidivist was Joseph John, who in 1900 had twenty-four arrests; however, Good and John were the only Indians with very high numbers of jailings booked into the Brantford jail between 1899 and 1901. No others had more than five arrests, with eight out of ten of those jailed never having been jailed before. This suggests that jailings were widespread at Grand River, involving a substantial proportion of the total population: at least 500 adult males, adjusting for recidivism over the twenty-five-year period.[80] Even though Julia Good was jailed the most, few of those jailed were women.

This evidence also suggests that the stereotype of the handful of Indians repeatedly arrested for drunkenness does not describe the situation at Grand River and Brantford. The fact that two Indians, Julia Good and Joseph John, appear to fit that pattern shows that local authorities were willing to arrest Indians repeatedly for drunkenness. It also shows that no other Indians fit that pattern: otherwise, they presumably would have been repeatedly arrested as well. Most arrests were for drunk and disorderly behaviour, generally involving one incident, sometimes two, at most three to five. Only in a few cases were there repeated incidents of disorderly conduct.

However, the widespread distribution of jailings resulted in the coercive impact of Canadian criminal law being employed against a large proportion of Grand River Indians. The social and cultural meaning of being jailed in nineteenth-century Ontario must have been far different for Indians than for Euro-Canadians. Jail as a social institution was (and is) foreign to tribal society: the putting of human beings, free by nature, in small cages seemed cruel to native people.[81] Through this process Canadian law was imposed on the Six Nations people and the open use of tribal law to resolve disputes and maintain social control was impaired, a deliberate, colonial interference with Six Nations life and culture.

CONCLUSION

Many strands of Indian legal history come together in a review of the criminal record. On one level, the government promised a simple relationship: Canada's courts were open to Indians for all purposes. But this simple statement of juridical equality denied a much more complex reality. Indians were involved in a challenging system of legal relationships with the government, involving two forms of law, native and non-native. Beyond this, each First Nation, as John Borrows has shown us, has its own legal history, its own unique record of legal relations with the government. Thus, it is not simply a meeting of two sets of laws that makes this history so complex: it is a meeting of two sets of laws in a wide variety of distinct legal contexts.

Part of this history – but only a part – is a history of imprisonment and oppression. Indians were jailed in numbers far greater than their proportion of the population in Ontario in the last third of the nineteenth century. While the Six Nations' Grand River lands were seen as 'lawless' almost from the beginning of settlement, it was the complete occupation of Ontario by settlers that finally allowed colonial criminal law to reach Indian criminal activity in practice rather than merely in theory, as had previously been the case. The imposition of Canadian criminal law on native people generally resulted from Indian trips to Brantford, when Indians put themselves under the watchful eyes of city police and town constables.

There is no question that the Brantford pattern was repeated in off-reserve cities and towns all over Ontario. Indian poverty and drinking-related behaviour, coupled with Euro-Canadian racism, produced high arrest rates. There has been no comprehensive collection of this data, although the general pattern is undeniable. The local arrest data, however, do not represent the full exposure of Indians to Canadian jails. The Indian agents were also magistrates and had the power to fine and jail native people. Few records of the legal proceedings of magistrates' courts remain: most of these jailings were unrecorded.

But there is also a legal history here that is completely invisible: how many Indians went out in late nineteenth-century Ontario to assert their traditional hunting and fishing rights – and to bring back meat and fish to feed impoverished Indian communities? Indian nations employed a wide variety of tactics to protect tribal interests in the face of the awesome legal power Canada exercised under the Indian Act. While this is a complex and largely unwritten legal history, the unfolding legal events of the late twentieth century testify to the continuity of First Nations assertions of sovereignty. If prison is a metaphor for one kind of First Nation legal history, then the exercise of sovereignty through countless fishing and hunting expeditions is the metaphor for another. There were thousands of such stories in the late nineteenth century.

8

'The Indians Are a Perseverant Race':
Indian Law in Quebec and Atlantic Canada

Canadian Indian law was Ontarian, the product of Ontario judges. At Confederation in 1867 Ontario Indian law, both common law and statutory, became the basis for dominion Indian law. After *St. Catherine's Milling* was decided in favour of Ontario, an anomaly existed in the legal status of Indian reserves in northern and western Ontario: while the dominion government was responsible for Indian affairs, the province of Ontario had title to crown lands. In the meantime, many Indian reserves had already been allocated and were occupied by Indians. The Indian reserve arbitration cases were a process to settle the dispute between the dominion and Ontario over the allocation of these reserve lands. Similarly, the dominion's Indian Acts and Indian policies after 1867 reflected Ontario Indian law and policy.

All that said, we will now focus on the development of nineteenth-century Indian law in the rest of Canada. This time-frame limits the earliest part of of our discussion to eastern Canada. British Columbia was not colonized until the 1850s and 1860s, a British colony with a history distinct from that of the rest of Canada and having more in common with the history of Australia and New Zealand. The prairie northwest was colonized by Canadians after Confederation, bringing dominion, not provincial, Indian law to the prairies. These developments in other parts of Canada are treated in the following chapters.

The civil law system of Quebec was thrown into disarray by the conquest of Quebec, the rise of an English-speaking merchant class in Montreal, and the division of Quebec into Upper and Lower Canada, weakening any role that the Quebec legal tradition might play in a Canadian law of native rights.[1] While the Maritime colonies did not produce significant numbers of cases on Indian matters during the nineteenth century, Quebec did, although at only about one-third the level of Ontario. Quebec has a rich and unique legal history, with French civil law surviving over more than two hundred years of colonization. Yet French civil law, like the English common law, did not have a place for the recognition of the rights of native people. It was simply another regime of colonial law. An analysis of the Quebec cases, therefore, reveals that, while French civil law was recognized under the British regime, it was not significant in matters of Indian law. British and English-speaking Canadian judges in Quebec cited some of the language of the civil code, but their results came from a common-law interpretative framework. French-speaking judges did not come to different results.

QUEBEC INDIAN LAW

Quebec law was not often cited in Ontario, even though the two provinces were merged as Canada West and Canada East from 1841 to 1867. Its lack of influence is not surprising given Quebec's civil law foundation, but this does not account for the development of Indian law in Quebec. Nor does the idea that Quebec's law was civil law fully or accurately represent the state of legal affairs there. Montreal, the commercial capital of Canada, had a large English-speaking business community from the late eighteenth century. William Dummer Powell, for example, practised law there in the 1780s and, although fluent in the French language, rarely resorted to the civil law.[2] Civil law was generally limited to matters of private law within the French-speaking population. Not only did British criminal law and other areas of public law apply, but English speakers used the common law in all areas of their lives, with perhaps only the law of real property retaining a civil law core. Though matters dealing with Indians transcended a public/private distinction, they turned on the same colonial policy in Quebec that was applied in Ontario, often interpreted by British or English-speaking Canadian judges well versed in common law but ignorant of civil law.

Just as pre-conquest Quebec Indian law was irrelevant in Canada, matters of French Indian policy mattered little. Indeed, a major reason for the Royal Proclamation of 1763 was not only to block further American settler forays into Indian lands but also to assert a British Indian policy over formerly French lands beyond the frontier.[3] France had a different policy than Britain, recognizing some measure of Indian sovereignty and not generally attempting to bring Indians within the reach of French law. This distinction also reflected different social and demographic realities of the two colonial systems.[4] The French economy was built more on the fur trade than on settlement, and so policies that strengthened native society on the frontier were intended to promote the fur trade. Settlement was primarily limited to an area along the St Lawrence River and its tributaries, occupied in the 1760s by no more than 60,000 settlers at a time when the settler population of British North America from Newfoundland to Georgia was in excess of a million, often extending hundreds of miles inland. There was not the level of Indian and settler conflict that the British faced in its American colonies. Indians living or working among the French were, however, subject to French law, although there was no French pretension of extending their laws beyond the frontier.[5] The French never made treaties with Indians or directly recognized native sovereignty, but neither did the French believe that their trading centres incorporated native people into the French legal and political community. Native people were sovereign as long as they remained in native communities.[6] Indeed, it is not even clear that France claimed title to Indian lands by discovery.[7]

Like the English colonial authorities, Quebec authorities took criminal jurisdiction of Indians when they were present in French settlements. There were, for example, about two hundred criminal cases involving Indians in Montreal courts between 1670 and 1760. Most of these led to no formal action beyond the immediate arrest and detention. Although Indians were fully subject to French law within the settlements, they were rarely formally prosecuted for their offences, mostly involving drinking and assault. French authorities did not concern themselves with offences occurring in the Indian settlements surrounding Montreal.[8] Even in interracial murder cases, the French were reluctant to punish Indians. Indians treated Montreal authorities with contempt and particularly objected to the imprisonment of native people.[9]

The Huron and Mohawk Land Disputes with the Jesuits

The first native law cases in Canada involved the 1760s land claims of the Huron at Sillery and Lorette, and the Mohawk at Caughnawaga, both brought soon after the British seizure of Quebec. The cases, unrelated except that in both Indian nations challenged the Roman Catholic

Church's usurpation of Indian land grants under French rule, did not turn on property law or Indian title as much as on the legal construction of the French law of crown land grants.[10]

Both of these cases involved lands granted to Indians in the mid-1600s by French authorities but then turned over to the Jesuits to administer for the Indians' benefit. The settlements became refuges for displaced Indians from several nations.[11] At the heart of the cases were claims of aboriginal title on the part of the Mohawk, who argued that they possessed the land prior to its alienation by French authorities.[12]

The Mohawk at Caughnawaga produced a record of litigation of Indian land claims that was unprecedented in the eighteenth century. At their insistence the boundaries of their lands were surveyed in 1762. This survey reduced some of the Jesuit lands and the Jesuits carried the matter in 1766 to the Court of Common Pleas at Montreal, where they lost. Appealing to the Superior Court at Quebec in August 1768, the lower judgment was 'totally reversed' and the lands restored to the Jesuits. In 1797 the Mohawk appealed directly to Lord Dorcester, governor of Quebec, who instructed the solicitor general to institute an action against the Jesuits for the recovery of the Indian lands. In 1798 the crown brought suit on behalf of the Indians for recovery of the land, but the suit was dismissed in 1799 with costs to the crown. The Six Nations, who took up the Mohawk cause as part of their broader land disputes with British authorities, sent a delegation to London in 1807 to protest the loss of their lands, and a second report on the situation was ordered by Lord Castlereagh, the secretary of war. In 1830 another Six Nations delegation appealed to the Colonial Office, which commissioned a report on the issue.[13]

The report was adamantly against making any concessions on these lands to the Six Nations for two reasons. First, the matter had been fully litigated three times in a colonial court, and therefore any further action would make a mockery of colonial law. Second, the Colonial Office wanted to discourage Indians coming to London to present grievances, by-passing local colonial authorities.[14] The report rejected the implicit rationale of Indian claims to this land: local settlers had no recollection of any Indian occupation of the lands. Their occupants had always been Jesuits.[15] With the dispute already eighty years old, the commissioner of the Jesuits' estates condescendingly commented: 'But the Indians are a perseverant race, and have not failed to reiterate their applications to every successive Governor since the conquest [of Quebec], notwithstanding that their pretensions have always been rejected as frivolous.'[16]

The Colonial Office, nonetheless, probably not committed to defending the Jesuits' property rights under Quebec law, requested that local authorities see if they could come to some solution to the case without regard to the law in order to satisfy the Indian nations. Local authorities were not inclined to do so, apparently believing both that nothing short of restoring the land would satisfy the Indians and also that such an extra-legal solution would undermine colonial land titles.[17] In the end, therefore, whatever the Indian's title, it lost to the Jesuits' title.[18]

Judge Samuel Monk and the Estate of William Connolly

The boldest and most creative common law decision on Indian rights in nineteenth-century Canada was authored by Judge Samuel Monk, a Canadian-trained, English-speaking jurist from a distinguished Halifax family of lawyers and judges who had been made a judge of the Lower Canada Superior Court in Montreal. in 1859.[19] There is a family connection in Monk's background that provides a context to his powerful opinion.[20] George Henry Monk, patriarch of the family, had been appointed Indian commissioner of Nova Scotia in 1783, serving on and off in the post for more than twenty years and continuing as a 'volunteer' after he was appointed to the bench and the British had stopped paying a salary for an Indian commissioner.[21] Though he displayed a general humanistic concern for his Mi'kmaq charges, Commissioner Monk, more than sixty years before Samuel Monk's appointment to the bench, was unable to keep squatters from taking Mi'kmaq lands.

The case, *Connolly* v. *Woolrich and Johnson et al.*, involved the estate of William Connolly, a wealthy Hudson's Bay Company trader, who at his death in 1849 left two families in a legal dispute that stands as a metaphor for race relations in mid-nineteenth century Canada.[22] In 1803 at Rivière-aux-Rats in the Athabaska country, Connolly, at the age of seventeen, had married 'in the manner of the country' (by common law), Susanne Pas-de-nom, a daughter of a Cree chief. For twenty-eight years she had lived with him in dozens of locations in the northwest from Fort William to the Rocky Mountains, bearing him six children. When he retired in 1831 he took her back to Montreal, but suddenly, in 1832, he married Julia Woolrich, a long-standing family friend, in a Roman Catholic ceremony. They had two children and lived an upper-class life in Montreal until Connolly's death, all the time supporting Susanne in a nunnery in Manitoba. When Connolly died he left a will leaving his entire estate to his wife, Julia, and their two children. Julia died in 1864, setting up a lawsuit between Connolly's children by Susanne and his children by Julia.[23] The lawsuit was carefully framed and brilliantly argued by what was probably the best legal talent then available in Montreal. Evidence of the social position of Connolly is that two of Monk's brother judges were called as witnesses in the case, one for each side. The estate was one of the largest ever probated in Quebec up to that time.[24]

The argument for Susanne's children was that their parents had a legal marriage under Cree law, as well as under existing English and French law; therefore, the second marriage was null and void. The opposing position ridiculed the idea of a marriage under First Nations law being recognized in Canada, dismissing Susanne as a concubine and the children as illegitimate. Dozens of witnesses were called to testify both to the general character of such marriages in the northwest and to the particular character of Connolly's marriage. The case and its appeal occupies 170 pages of two reports.

Judge Monk recognized not only the marriage but the Cree law that governed it. In his judgment, Monk quoted the writings of ethnographers on the character of Indian marriages. As important, he was the first Canadian judge to quote Chief Justice John Marshall's *Worcester* v. *Georgia* opinion describing the Indians as 'a distinct people, divided into separate nations, independent of each other and of the rest of the world, having institutions of their own, and governing themselves by their own laws.'[25] In all, Monk's extended quotation from *Worcester* took up four pages of fine type, leading to a holding unprecedented in nineteenth-century Canadian law: 'I have no hesitation in saying that, adopting these views of the question under consideration ... the Indian political and territorial right, laws, and usage's remained in full force both at Athabaska and in the Hudson Bay region, previous to the Charter of 1670, and even after that date, as will appear hereafter.[26] Monk then set his sights higher, endeavouring to determine to what extent First Nations law survived the HBC Charter of 1670. He did not mince words: 'Apart from the immense and irresponsible powers conferred upon the Company, it has been contended that the grant in free and common soccage in fee simple of such extensive regions of territory in the actual possession of aboriginal and powerful nations, was not in the power of the crown, and was a violation of the plainest principles of public international law.'[27] This part of the exercise was unnecessary: Monk held that the Athabaska River flowed not into Hudson's Bay but into the Arctic Ocean; therefore, it was never within the territory granted to the company.[28] He then turned to the Royal Proclamation, quoting it at length and holding that: 'There is nothing to be found in this, or in any subsequent proclamation, abolishing or

changing the customs of the Indians or the laws of the French settlers ...
nothing which introduced the English common law into these territories.
When Connolly went to Athabaska, in 1803, he found the Indian usages
as they had existed for ages, unchanged by European power of Christian
legislation. He did not take English law with him.'[29]

This language, moving from English common law to American law to
international law to detailed analysis of the HBC's charter and the Royal
Proclamation (and also including the Treaty of Utrecht and references to
the colonial law of East India) was sweeping enough. Monk, however,
went further using metaphors that gently mocked the common law and
British sovereignty over First Nations:

The pretension of the Defendant, therefore, that, to the exclusion of the laws and
customs of the natives, the common law of England prevailed at Rat River in 1803,
or at any subsequent period, must be over-ruled, and in doing so the Court may
remark that it was not competent in any case for Mr. Connolly to carry with him
this common law of England to Rat River in his knapsack, and much less could he
bring back to Lower Canada the law of repudiation in a bark canoe. If he could in
this way carry the law of England there, he is bound by it, as I view the fact of this
case; and coming back to Canada, he cannot bring with him, or invoke the Cree
law of divorce at will.[30]

Judge Monk was treating with sarcasm the notion that the English
common law somehow 'followed the flag,' a fundamental principle of
colonial law. The only way it could have reached Rat River was if Connolly had 'carried it in his knapsack.' More important, Monk assigned the
same legitimacy to Cree law in this framework that he assigned to
English common law: Connolly had no more right to carry English common law to Rat River than he had to carry Cree law back to Quebec. Each
was the living embodiment of a particular culture, the law where it functioned. Monk's framing of the logic of this syllogism also made fun of the
legal opportunism of Connolly's Quebec heirs: on the one hand, they
wanted to apply the English common law of marriage to Rat River, but
they also wanted to apply the Cree law of divorce in Quebec to end Connolly's twenty-eight-year-old marriage without formal legal action.

While Monk could reasonably have ended his judgment with this argument and result, his lengthy opinion continued. He cited American, British, French, and canon law of marriage and divorce and of Indian rights,
describing the conditions of the frontier in great detail, before holding,
not just that Susanne's children had a right to inherit, but that the second

marriage was void, thereby making Julia's children, children of a Montreal Roman Catholic family of high social standing, illegitimate. Connolly's nephew, Judge Alwin, who testified on behalf of his own niece
and nephew, Connolly's children, must have been enraged.[31] The core of
the defence argument was that a Cree marriage could never be valid in
Canada because Cree law permitted polygamy and was therefore bar-
baric, beyond any recognition of the common law. Monk found polygamy an exception in Cree society and also irrelevant because it did not
apply in Connolly's case.[32] His judgment was bold, covering as much
common law ground as he could have covered, and giving as much recognition to Cree law as he possibly could have. Alexander Cross, lawyer
for Julia's children (and later judge of the same court), had squarely
placed the racist views of the day before Monk for his consideration,
arguing that the Cree were 'barbarians' with 'infidel laws' that should not
even be recognized between Crees in their own country.[33] Yet, in Monk's
court, these 'infidel laws' not only carried the day but left two children of
Quebec's elite as poverty-stricken bastards, an outrageous result by the
standards of Victorian Canada.

This judgment was affirmed on appeal two years later, with the appeal
court following Monk's reasoning. A further appeal was to be taken to
the Privy Council but the case was settled, probably on the lawyers'
advice that there was at least some chance that the Privy Council would
reverse the judgment.[34]

Twenty years later, in 1884, the Quebec Superior Court itself came to
the opposite result in *Fraser* v. *Pouliot*, a parallel, but unrelated, case.
Alexander Fraser was another fur trader who brought his fortune, and his
Indian family, back to Quebec. He had married Angelique Meadows 'in
the manner of the country' in the northwest about 1788. He gave their
children his name and took several of them to Quebec for baptism. In
1806 he retired to Rivière-du-Loup, building a small house near his own
manor house for Angelique and the children. He then engaged in two
prolonged affairs with house servants and fathered seven more children.
Upon his death in 1833 he, like Connolly, left two sets of children to contest the estate.[35]

This left the Quebec courts an issue similar to the one they had faced in
Connolly but with one important difference: Fraser had never even pre-
tended to marry his two servants, and thus the courts did not have to
chose between two sets of marriage laws. After Fraser's children by
Angelique won in the trial court, the case was appealed to the Quebec
Court of Queen's Bench. Judge Monk still sat on that court and had, in the

meantime, been joined by Alexander Cross, the losing attorney in the *Connolly* case. This time Monk wrote in dissent and Cross's views of Indian marriage law prevailed. Cross completely denied the legality of marriages under First Nations law, even between Indians. For him marriage had to be contracted 'in a Christian sense.'[36] Other issues turned on the law of trusts and estates and the case ultimately went first to the Quebec's Supreme Court and then to the Supreme Court of Canada, but Cross's denial of the legality of First Nations marriages prevailed.

Indian Lands in Quebec Courts in the Mid-Nineteenth Century

As broadly cast and creative as the judgment in *Connolly* was, the largest single number of Quebec cases, as in Upper Canada and the Maritimes, were actions either for the ejectment of squatters from Indian reserves or for punishing squatters who removed wood from reserves, parallel offences to those brought in Upper Canada under the protective legislation that was the forerunner of the Indian Act of 1876. These cases were interpreted in the same way in Quebec although there, unlike Ontario, the Indian Act was always upheld. In *Commissioner of Indian Lands for Lower Canada* v. *Payant dit St. Onge* [and] *Payant dit St. Onge* v. *On8anoron* the familiar issue of an Indian selling wood under a claim of Indian title in violation of the Indian Act came before the Quebec Superior Court in 1856.[37] While the Indian commissioner brought the complaint against St Onge, he was acting on the insistence of the chief of the reserve at Sault Saint-Louis. Payant, a settler, filed a counterclaim against On8anoron, a member of the nation who had leased him the right to cut wood. The nation had been agitated by the sale of their wood and both Payant and On8anoron acted according to On8anoron's customary right (referred to and implicitly recognized as 'common Indian right' by the court) under tribal law to enter on tribal common lands and remove wood. The court held that neither defendant had any legal right to 'sell or dispose' wood from these lands.[38] On8anoron had violated First Nations law and been brought into court by his nation, acting through the Indian commissioner because the Indian nation had no legal standing to bring its own action.

A more complex version of this same problem occurred in *Bastien* v. *Hoffman*.[39] Bastien, a Huron living at the Lorette reserve, sued Hoffman, demanding that she remove a mill flume damaging Bastien's lands and pay £75 in damages. Hoffman denied that an Indian could sue her, alleging that Indian property was vested by law in the commissioner of Indian lands and under First Nations law Bastien could not possess the neighbouring lands because he already had another habitation on the reserve. Hoffman further alleged that the land was the common property of the Huron, not Bastien, and that the chiefs and Indian commissioner had granted permission to contract the mill flume and dam.[40]

Judge Drummond did a parallel common-law and civil-law analysis of the property rights of the Huron at the Lorette reserve. Based on Huron law, each of the members of the nation were in civil law terms 'proprietors par indivis' or tenants in common of the whole tract. The property was managed by a chief under Huron law. Each member of the nation secured, from the chief, a right of possession of the land occupied by his family. The court then held that the rights of individual Indians were 'possessory not real. They import a defensive, not an aggressive power.'[41] In the interpretation of the court, while the possessory rights of Indians were to be defended, this did not create a right to litigate.

The court narrowly held that all legal actions on behalf of the Huron nation or its members had to be brought by the Indian commissioner under the Indian Act. But it went beyond this in denying a civil law right to bring such an action: even if all rights to legal actions on behalf of Indians had not been vested by the legislature in the Indian commissioner, members of the Huron nation, as tenants in common, 'did not possess one foot of property in which the whole nation' did not share; thus, no tenant could plead against another tenant for there was no right to bring the action under civil law.[42]

The only squatter to dispute his ejectment from a Quebec reserve was Morrison, a schoolmaster at Caughnawaga reserve, who was evicted from his lands there under the Indian Act in summary proceedings before an Indian commissioner.[43] Morrison challenged the proceedings, arguing that he had been convicted without evidence. The Superior Court granted certiorari and reviewed the record. It found that Morrison had confessed to having settled on Indian lands without leave, thus providing sufficient evidence to support the eviction. Judge MacKay, in his opinion, remarked that the records of lower magistrates had to be recognized 'otherwise there would be no end of things' and that 'the Court leans rather to support convictions.'[44] There was no room here for the kind of narrow technicalities that squatters often succeeded in using against Indian commissioners in Ontario, probably because the political interests of squatters never had the power in more settled Quebec that they had in Ontario.

In an age of a formal jurisprudence grounded in technicalities, the Quebec cases depended more on substance than on form. Even the major exception, *Ex parte Lefort* v. *Dugas et al.*, turns more broadly on the appropriate due process of an appeal of a criminal conviction under the Indian Act than on narrow technicalities. Moise Lefort was a constable at Caughnawaga. Pierre Montour, an Indian, testified that, after the bell for vespers rang, only he and Lefort were standing on the railroad platform. Lefort then invited Montour into his office and gave him two drinks from a bottle of whisky he kept in a cupboard.[45] Convicted of giving whisky to an Indian, Lefort appealed.

Among the issues was the scope of review on appeal of convictions under the Indian Act. The crown argued that the appellate court had only the right to review matters of law and could not hold a hearing to re-examine the evidence. Judge Davidson, of the Quebec Superior Court, held that he had the authority to retry the entire case. He did so and the evidence revealed starkly different facts. One Curotte testified that the two were never left alone on the railroad platform but that Montour had accompanied Curotte to his house and remained there. Two additional witnesses, including Montour's brother-in-law, testified that Montour had a capacity for telling falsehoods. Finally, Montour took the stand and denied that he had testified that Lefort had provided him with whisky. Davidson, left with no evidence supporting a conviction, acquitted Lefort.[46] Thus, this reversal of a conviction under the Indian Act did not turn on a technicality but rather on the entire substance of the case.

Ignace Kaneratahere and Thomas Tahantison, two Indians living on the Sault Saint-Louis Reserve, put up property (of which they were in possession of under tribal law) as security for Akwirente and others, appealing their conviction on riot charges. The Lower Canada Court of Queen's Bench held that since Indians did not hold title to their property in their own names they could not post property bond, citing the Indian Act provisions that all suits against Indians be brought through the Indian commissioner. Rather, Indians had title as 'possessors or occupants' only, not a title that could be mortgaged or given as security.[47] This ruling was upheld on appeal.[48]

Quebec courts, however, did see some of the same kinds of claims of settlers for Indian lands that dominated Ontario Indian cases. In *Commissioner of Indian Lands* v. *Jannel* a land purchase directly from the Abenaki was defended on the grounds that the lands in question were outside the boundaries of any Indian village.[49] The court rejected the claim, pointing out that the Indian Act made no such distinction: lands could not be acquired from Indians at all.[50]

Undoubtedly the most extensive Indian legal dispute in late-nineteenth-century Quebec, between the Mohawk and the Catholic Church, was not a reported case because it resulted in a series of criminal indictments that all led to either mistrials or minor convictions. The Mohawk at Kanesatake, next to the village of Oka, had refused to give up their legal rights to disputed lands that the Sulpicians, a Catholic order, had been awarded title to by the government in 1840.[51] Throughout the nineteenth century, Mohawks entered these lands to cut wood. The Sulpicians complained to the authorities and arrests were repeatedly made. In 1868 Chief Ocite led a large number of Mohawk to the Sulpician woodlands and awarded each a 'grant' of land.[52]

Joseph Onasakenrat, an educated Mohawk who had served as secretary of the Sulpician mission, became a chief in 1868. Aware of the disputes with the Jesuits in other parts of Quebec, he petititoned the government to recognize Mohawk land rights. The chiefs then wrote the secretary of state that 'in default of justice having been rendered us, the chiefs on behalf of the nation will adopt such means as will ensure the removal of these priests.'[53] The priests were visited by the chiefs and ordered to leave. The chiefs were then arrested for assault and held in prison until the priests did not appear for trial. Heated disputes continued until, in 1877, a large party of Mohawk attacked and burned the Sulpician mission. The police arrested forty-eight Mohawks, with fifteen ultimately tried. Five separate trials followed, with juries dividing along religious lines as Protestants refused to convict Indians for attacks on Roman Catholic Church property. All charges were dropped in 1881.[54] A cycle of recurring arrests and escalating violence dominated these decades at Kanesatake: between 1870 and 1873 alone, about one-third of the adult male Mohawks in the village were brought up on criminal charges for cutting wood without the permission of the Sulpicians.[55]

THE DENIAL OF INDIAN RIGHTS IN ATLANTIC CANADA

The Beothuk of Newfoundland

Atlantic Canada Provinces produced few Indian law cases, and Prince Edward Island and Newfoundland are the only Canadian jurisdictions without a single reported nineteenth-century Indian case.[56] This means that settlement proceeded without resort to law. In these circumstances there was a denial of native rights and a lack of accessibility to the courts by Indians.

The killing of the Beothuk in Newfoundland was known to colonial

The Cree chief Big Bear in leg irons at Fort Carlton immediately following the 1885 Metis rebellion. Big Bear's role in the events of 1885 reflected the complexity of his position as a Cree chief. Ultimately, he was sent to prison for treason, a punishment that broke his health.

Big Bear and Poundmaker during their trial at Regina in September 1885. Beverley Robertson, a Winnipeg lawyer hired by the government to defend the Indian defendants, is standing at the far right. Big Bear had been in custody two months by this time and was disoriented at the trial, unsure of what he was charged with. The others in the photograph include Horse Child, Big Bear's youngest son, at his side, and Chief Stewart of the Hamilton police, front centre. From the left in the back row are Constable R.Y. Black, Father Cochin, Superintendent R.B. Deane, and Father André.

Stony Mountain Penitentiary, Manitoba, in 1892. This prison opened in the late 1870s with the extension of Canadian authority to the prairies. Forty-eight Indians were sentenced here as a result of the 1885 trials, so many that the prisoners were put to work building a new wing. Indians suffered high rates of serious illness during these prison terms.

White Cap, a Sioux chief, was the only Indian charged with criminal offences after the North-West uprising who was acquitted in the Regina trials. Conflicting testimony put him manning the trenches at Batoche alongside the Metis, as well as participating in Metis council meetings – held in French, a language he could not speak. The jury acquitted him of treason-felony charges.

Negotiating Treaty 8, Fort Vermillion, Alberta, 1899. Here David Laird, lieutenant
governor of the North-West Territories, explains the terms of the treaty. The
Indian treaties were negotiated according to a clear system of rules, first specified
in the Royal Proclamation of 1763. The crown arrived at each treaty site well
prepared, with a treaty text that was often not well understood by the Indians.

Negotiating Treaty 9, Flying Post, Ontario, 1906. There were hundreds of treaty negotiations in Canada, spanning over two hundred years. Each of these negotiations was historically specific, involving First Nations with issues particular to that time and place.

The Indian Reserve Commission arrives at Kuper Island reserve, British Columbia, 1914. British Columbia Indians, living primarily in communities facing the
water, were given only small reserves, often only the size of the village. After
repeated protest, the crown and the British Columbia government agreed to
appoint a commission to survey each village site and make recommendations
regarding increasing the size of each reserve. The commission, like the Sproat
commission of thirty years earlier, was ineffective. This photograph shows a
clear view of the size of the Kuper Island reserve, typical of the geography of
native communities.

Nisga'a land-claims negotiating committee, British Columbia, 1913. The Nisga'a have carried on a land dispute with the government of British Columbia for well over a century. This photograph clearly shows the level of organization of the Nisga'a in pursuit of their land rights. British Columbia not only refused to negotiate, denying the legitimacy of the First Nations' claims, but also patronized its native citizens, arguing that outside agitators, often missionaries, were behind their protests. These men look capable of carrying on a debate about land rights on any terms.

A group of Indians dressed for a holiday in front of the fire hall on Main Street in Rat Portage (now Kenora), Ontario, 1899. Rat Portage, the heart of Treaty 3, was a frontier community at this time. Canadian law structured Indian / white relations on the frontier in many ways. Rat Portage was the scene of two wendigo trials, the enforcement of hunting and fishing regulations against Indians who often had little other means of livelihood, Indian labour issues in logging and commercial fishing camps, and even trouble with summer cottagers who feared their Indian neighbours.

The Six Nations' council house at Ohsweken was the political and spiritual centre of Indian life at Grand River. Throughout the nineteenth century (and continuing through the present time) Six Nations legal tradition was preserved with the Grand Council functioning as a judicial body, deciding cases according to traditional law.

Henry Dokis and family in the late nineteenth century. The Ojibwa at the Dokis reserve, on the French River in Ontario, recognized the value of their forests and protected them for future generations in the face of great opposition from the Indian Department, which repeatedly forced tribal votes on the issue of selling their timber, sometimes attempting to influence the voting process with economic inducements offered to poverty-stricken individual Indians. Canadian Indian policy was to sell Indian resources and take the money received 'in trust' to finance various expenses in the administration of Indian affairs, a circular policy that led to the loss of natural resources.

Indians skidding logs at Cape Croker. The struggle over control of natural resources was critical to native people in nineteenth-century Ontario. Most tribal resources were sold by the crown, often with considerable resistance, and often under circumstances of dubious legality. Native people worked extensively in logging, fishing, and other natural resources–based industries in Ontario.

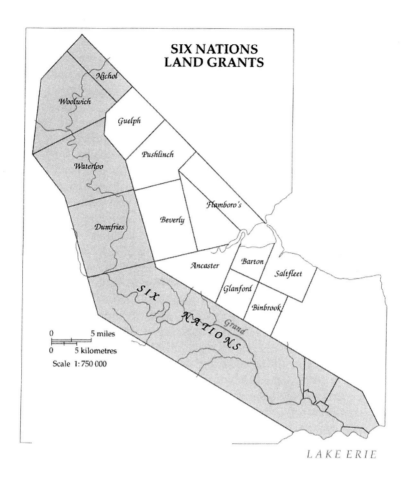

**SIX NATIONS
LAND GRANTS**

Nichol

Woolwich

Guelph

Puslinch

Waterloo

Hamboro's

Beverly

Dumfries

Ancaster

Barton

Saltfleet

Glanford

SIX

Binbrook

NATIONS

Grand

0   5 miles

0   5 kilometres

Scale 1:750 000

LAKE ERIE

Map A. Six Nations Land Grants. Purchased by the crown from the Mississauga
and granted to 'His Majesty's faithful allies,' this tract of land twelve miles wide
along the Grand River in Ontario has been the source of numerous legal disputes
between the Six Nations, the crown, and numerous non-native landholders.

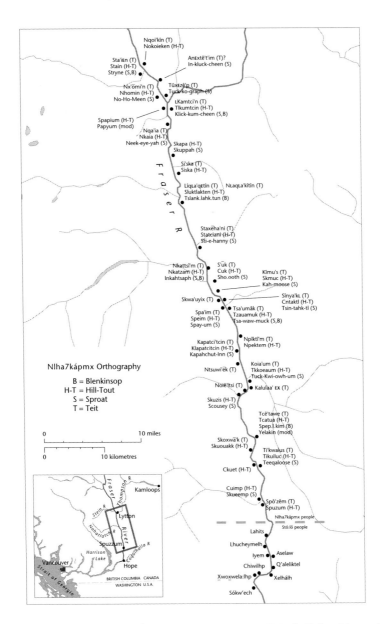

Nqoï'kín (T)
Nokoieken (H-T)

Sta'itn (T)
Stain (H-T)
Stryne (S,B)

Anextē't'im (T)?
In-kluck-cheen (S)

Nxʷōmi'n (T)
Nhomin (H-T)
No-Ho-Meen (S)

Tûχezē'n (T)
Tuck-ko-graph (S)

LKamtci'n (T)
Tlkumtcin (H-T)
Klick-kum-cheen (S,B)

Spapium (H-T)
Papyum (mod)

Nqa'ia (T)
Nkaia (H-T)
Neek-eye-yah (S)

Skapa (H-T)
Skuppah (S)

Si'ska (T)
Siska (H-T)

Liqla'qɛtīn (T)
Sluktlakten (H-T)
Tslank.lahk.tun (B)

NLaqLa'kītin (T)

Staxēha'ni (T)
Statciani (H-T)
Sti-e-hanny (S)

Nkattsi'm (T)
Nkatzam (H-T)
Inkahtsaph (S,B)

S'ūk (T)
Cuk (H-T)
Sho.ooth (S)

Kīmu's (T)
Skmuc (H-T)
Kah-moose (S)

Skwa'uyix (T)

Sinya'kL (T)
Cntaktl (H-T)
Tsin-tahk-tl (S)

Tsa'umák (T)
Tzauamuk (H-T)
Tsa-waw-muck (S,B)

Spa'im (T)
Speim (H-T)
Spay-um (S)

Npīktī'm (T)
Npektem (H-T)

Kapatci'tcin (T)
Klapatcitcin (H-T)
Kapahchut-Inn (S)

Koia'um (T)
Tkkoeaum (H-T)
Tuck-Kwi-owh-um (S)

Ntsuwi'ek (T)

Noïē'ltsi (T)

Kalulaa' ɛX (T)

Skuzis (H-T)
Scousey (S)

Tcē'tawe (T)
Tcatua (H-T)
Spep.l.kim (B)
Yelakin (mod)

Skoxwa'k (T)
Skuouakk (H-T)

Ti'kwaLus (T)
Tikuiluc (H-T)
Teeqaloose (S)

Ckuet (H-T)

Cuimp (H-T)
Skueemp (S)

Spö'zēm (T)
Spuzum (H-T)

Nlha7kápmx people
Stó:lō people

Lahits

Lhucheymelh

Iyem

Aselaw

Chiwilhp

Q'aleliktel

Xwoxwela:lhp

Xelhálh

Sókw'ech

Nlha7kápmx Orthography

B = Blenkinsop
H-T = Hill-Tout
S = Sproat
T = Teit

0   10 miles

0   10 kilometres

Fraser R

Thompson R
Fraser R
Stein R
Nahatlatch R
Coquihalla R

Kamloops

Lytton

Spuzzum

Harrison Lake

Vancouver

Hope

Strait of Georgia

BRITISH COLUMBIA CANADA
WASHINGTON U.S.A.

Map B. Winter villages in the Fraser River Canyon, British Columbia, early
nineteenth century. Apparently, there were at least forty Nlha7kápmx and Sto:lo
villages along this thirty-seven-mile section of the Fraser River. Extensive cultural
exchanges occurred here as interior and coastal peoples met for fishing, trading,
and ceremonial purposes.

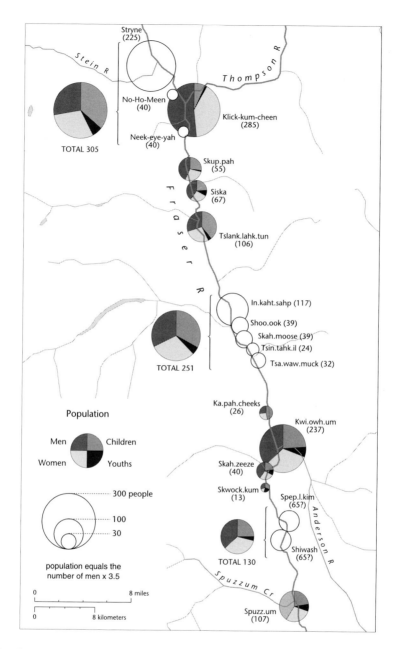

Stryne
(225)

Stein R

Thompson R

No-Ho-Meen
(40)

Klick-kum-cheen
(285)

Neek-eye-yah
(40)

TOTAL 305

Skup.pah
(55)

Siska
(67)

Fraser R

Tslank.lahk.tun
(106)

In.kaht.sahp (117)

Shoo.ook (39)

Skah.moose (39)

Tsin.tahk.il (24)

Tsa.waw.muck (32)

TOTAL 251

Ka.pah.cheeks
(26)

Kwi.owh.um
(237)

Population

Men   Children

Women   Youths

Skah.zeeze
(40)

Skwock.kum
(13)

Spep.l.kim
(65?)

Anderson R

Shiwash
(65?)

TOTAL 130

300 people

100

30

population equals the
number of men x 3.5

0   8 miles

0   8 kilometers

Spuzzum Cr

Spuzz.um
(107)

Map C. Native population in the Fraser River Canyon, 1878. This map shows the changes in native occupation of the same section of the canyon as depicted in Map B. About ten villages hold a population estimated at 1622, a fraction of the earlier population.

Map D. The Gitksan and Wet'suwet'en territories contested in *Delgamuukw* v. *British Columbia*, one of the most complex legal cases in Canadian history. British Columbia took most of its aboriginal lands without treaties. The Gitksan and Wet'suwet'en, in common with other First Nations in British Columbia, continued their traditional use of these lands and, in the face of increasing government pressure on their resources, brought a land-claim case in provincial courts.

reformers in the early nineteenth century and was cited by the parliamentary select committee in 1837 as evidence of the uncontrolled aggression of colonists against native people.[57] In a sense, this is the shortest legal history of native people in any of the colonies that became Canada: because the Beothuk all apparently died, either of disease or murder, they did not appear in the courts at all.[58] There was only one attempt to prosecute colonists for murdering Beothuk. In 1822 two furriers, James Carey and Stephen Adams, killed a Beothuk man and woman at Badger Bay. The case went to a jury trial, with the two admitting the killing but claiming self-defence. Their story is incredible. Upon sighting two figures in the distance, they fired warning shots to see if the Indians were 'friend or foe.' When the Indians did not flee, the two approached them. The Beothuk, armed with knives, continued a threatening advance – on two armed men – who finally shot them at a distance of five paces. Obviously such an advance would have been sheer suicide, raising a question about the honesty of this self-serving account. Carey is reported to have boasted about the killings. There was no direct evidence, however, to contradict the testimony of the furriers. The jury acquitted.[59]

The full story of what happened between the settlers and the Beothuk on the north coast of Newfoundland is still unknown. At the most basic level there was a cycle of attack and retaliation over the settlers' occupation of the fishing grounds. Governor Hugh Palliser summed up the situation in a report to the secretary of state in 1766: 'The barbarous system of killing prevails amongst our People towards the native Indians ... whom our People always kill, when they can meet them.'[60] As the conflict escalated, armed settler parties made forays into the interior, killing Beothuk in their camps. Colonial authorities, aware of the situation, refused to take action, either to impose the control of law over the settlers or to protect the Beothuk.[61] John Reeves, law adviser to the Board of Trade, was dispatched to Newfoundland in 1791 to help set up a court system. He took a special interest in the uncontrolled killings of Beothuk and believed that the cause was a failure of law: since the settlers lived beyond the protection of English law, they had no recourse but to resort to methods of self-help. Reeves believed that the enforcement of existing laws would ameliorate the situation, although he conceded that it would be difficult in the far reaches of the colony.[62]

The evidence is that the Beothuk kept up a pattern of stealing and molesting the settlers' fishing camps well into the early 1820s, very near the point of their complete disappearance. This can be read in several ways: on the one hand, as starving people, they may have had no choice but to steal. But much of the theft involved items that they could not use and, like their vandalism, has an appearance of being designed to assert their sovereignty over traditional fishing lands.[63]

The killing of the Beothuk was accompanied by disease and starvation, and in 1829 Shawnadithit, the last known Beothuk, captured in 1822, died in St John's. At that time there were probably other Beothuk in the forests in the centre of the island, perhaps also dying of disease and starvation. Modern oral history reveals, however, that they did not all die but, sensibly in the face of genocide, fled to the Montagnais nation of Labrador or were gradually adopted into Mi'kmaq communities on Newfoundland.[64] The land claims of the descendants of the Beothuk are still denied on the basis that, since all of the Beothuk were killed, there is no one left to make such a claim.[65]

The Mi'kmaq of Nova Scotia

The situation in Nova Scotia was very different. Not only was the province much more settled, Indian rights there were recognized in New England treaties (predating the American revolution) and had evolved from a more developed New England legal order. Furthermore, Nova Scotia was a small province, with well-developed legal institutions: provincial courts had been functioning there since the early eighteenth century.[66]

Yet this colonial legal culture did not reach Indians. Judge Brenton Halliburton wrote in 1823 that Indians 'never litigate or are in any [instance] impleaded. They have a code of traditionary and customary laws among themselves.'[67] Indian lands were not taken by treaty as they were in Upper Canada. Maritime treaties, many of which predated the procedures set out in the Royal Proclamation of 1763, were agreements providing for peace and friendship but not land cession.[68] Until a reserve policy was developed, lands were simply occupied by the crown or by settlers. Nova Scotia courts were beyond the reach of Indians. The Indian law cases that did arise date to the late nineteenth century, after most Indian land had been alienated by squatters. This failure to enforce the law in protection of Indian lands left local squatters free to take what lands they wanted.

There is an extensive history of this failure to protect Mi'kmaq lands on their reserves. Much as in Upper Canada, Nova Scotia, with an Indian population of about 1400 in the 1840s, had centred its Indian policy on a reserve system.[69] But, as events on the Wagamacook reserve illustrate, there was little or no enforcement of laws protecting Mi'kmaq lands. Sometime between 1830 and 1832 a number of Scottish settlers moved onto these lands, cleared forests, built houses and barns, and began farming. They were informed that they were trespassing on Mi'kmaq lands and the local sheriff served an eviction notice. Refusing to leave, they petitioned the Legislative Assembly, pleading ignorance and arguing that they were an asset to the Indians. The assembly's Indian committee refused the petition and published a notice on all reserves (indicating the problem was widespread) ordering all trespassers to leave by 1 July 1837.[70]

The committee's report is revealing in its openness in describing Nova Scotia's squatter problem in the 1830s:

It appears to be only necessary to carry out the measures of the Government to the contemplated extent to prevent the Indians from entertaining a suspicion that any British subject can trespass upon their reserves with impunity. The case is embarrassed with the circumstance that the persons who have trespassed upon these reserves are poor and ignorant people who have more probably taken up their position and made improvements on their reserves under an impression that they would be treated with as much lenity and forbearance as persons who have taken unauthorized possession of the Waste lands of the Crown in various parts of the Province. The trespassers upon the Indian reserves can hardly be supposed capable of accurately considering that the good faith of the government towards the Indians renders it impossible to extend the same kindness and tenderness to them as it might were the trespasses commited upon unreserved Crown lands.[71]

The Indian committee responded to two competing policies, one of keeping good faith with the Indians in enforcing its agreements with them, the other of 'leniency and forbearance' in dealing with squatters. The conclusion of its report urged that trespassers be evicted, with those who had made substantial improvements allowed to rent the lands for a short period of time so that their removal could be accomplished with 'as little loss as possible.' But the report was ignored and, in 1845, another report revealed that all of the reserves on Cape Breton except two had been violated. This time the recommendation was that 'no lenient measures will make an impression on these people (that is the trespassers.)' The committee urged ejectment, adding that 'to this end the most uncompromising proceedings alone will succeed.'[72]

The failure of these 'uncompromising proceedings' was evident by 1849. H.W. Crawley, the Indian commissioner for Cape Breton, reported that: 'under present circumstances no adequate protection can be obtained for the Indian property. It would be in vain to seek a verdict from any jury in this Island against the trespassers on the reserves; nor perhaps would a member of the Bar be found willingly and effectually to advocate the cause of the Indians, inasmuch as he would thereby injure his own prospects, by damaging his popularity.'[73]

Thirty years later this same situation was revealed in a case in which the crown was still attempting to eject trespassers from Cape Breton reserves. *McLean* v. *McIsaac* was a lawsuit filed by squatter David McLean against the Indian commissioner, Donald McIsaac, who had been trying to remove MacLean and his son from the Whycocomagh reserve. McLean's occupation had been quite open: he had cleared the land, erected fences, and cut hay for 'over twenty years.'[74]

The Mi'kmaq at the Whycocomagh reserve had repeatedly demanded that the Indian commissioner remove McLean, but no action was taken until 1879. The Reverend Donald McIsaac, the newly appointed Indian commissioner, received instructions from the Indian Department to notify McLean that if he was 'found trespassing upon the Indian reserve ... by cutting wood, scantling, timber, etc., or removing or making hay, or removing the same off the reserve, or otherwise encroaching on the vested rights of the Indians or the Indian Department,' proceedings would be taken to enforce penalties under section 16 of the Indian Act. McLean responded by letter claiming that he had occupied the land for twenty-five years and asking for compensation for his improvements.[75]

McIsaac, in response to continuing Indian protests, ordered McLean's hay cut and seized. McLean, however, continued his occupation of the lands and, in 1882, together with his son, was arrested on a warrant issued by McIsaac. He was tried by a stipendiary magistrate and committed to jail in default of payment of a fine of $20, hardly a punishment calculated to deter squatters. McLean then sued McIsaac for assault, false imprisonment, and trespass. Although Justice McDonald at Port Hood instructed the jury to the contrary, the jury returned a verdict in favour of McLean. McIsaac appealed to the Nova Scotia Supreme Court, where he won. McLean could not hold land against the crown by adverse possession. The 'right of the Indian agent to enter upon and take the hay from these reserves for the benefit of the Indians' was so obvious that the court held that it was unnecessary to discuss the issue.[76]

The position of the Mi'kmaq was entirely presented through the Indian commissioner. The commissioner had no inclination at all to eject McLean from tribal lands until repeatedly prodded by the Mi'kmaq. McLean's open occupation of tribal lands dated back twenty or more years before 1879. He was confident enough of his legal position to demand payment for improvements from the Indian Department and to sue McIsaac for damages, convincing a local jury to hold in his favour. Throughout these proceedings, from 1879 to 1885, he delayed his ejectment, which may well have been his objective. In the meantime, the Indian Department allowed him to purchase some reserve lands that he had improved by his labour.[77]

In the area of fishing rights, the Mi'kmaq fared as poorly as they did with their land rights. Although the Mi'kmaq Treaty of 1752 contains an express right to sell fish, the kind of commercial language the Supreme Court of Canada was evidently looking for in *Van der Peet*, the Mi'kmaq were, for a wide variety of reasons, pushed out of the fishing industry in Nova Scotia, and their treaty rights were ignored.[78] These treaty rights endured in the minds and hearts of the Mi'kmaq, unrecognized by Canadian law until the Supreme Court of Canada recognized them in 1985 in *James Matthew Simon* v. *The Queen*.[79]

New Brunswick

New Brunswick, like Upper Canada, was a Loyalist colony, dating from the resettlement of Americans following the revolution: it was separated from Nova Scotia in 1784. However, unlike Upper Canada, which was forced by the Six Nations to pay a great deal of attention to Indian policy, New Brunswick never developed parallel policies. Yet the basic humanity of Indians was recognized and land set aside for them.[80] Thus whereas, the early killings of Indians by settlers in Upper Canada went unpunished, the first criminal trial at Fredericton was of two Loyalists who had shot an Indian whom they claimed was stealing hogs, and the result was that one of the men, a military veteran, was hanged for murder, evidently as a demonstration of the impartiality of British justice.[81] Judge Brenton Halliburton, of the Nova Scotia Supreme Court, later wrote that 'whenever English soldiers or hunters shot an Indian they 'boast of having killed a black duck.'[82]

Since New Brunswick, like Nova Scotia, had no land-cession treaties, Indian lands were reserved only as requested by Indians. The province did not make provision for a reserve policy, did not even have an Indian Department, and left local reserves under part-time Indian commissioners without adequate powers.[83] The colonial government did not even engage in the pretext of defending Indian reserves: most of the reserves were occupied by squatters. Historian George F.G. Stanley noted that

New Brunswick Indians were 'pretty much ignored' and that there was 'no body of provincial jurisprudence dealing with aboriginal rights.'[84]

Protests reached the Colonial Office, which ordered the province to submit a report on the condition of Indians, including their land entitlements. After ignoring this request for three years, Indian Commissioner Moses Perley visited all of the reserves in 1841.[85] His report did not focus on the failure of the New Brunswick government to protect Indian lands. Instead, in eight pathetic pages, it lamented 'the calamitous fate which so often befalls uncivilized men when brought into contact with the natives of Europe' Perley also decried the fate of 'the degraded Indians at Bathurst' and the 'frightful decrease in numbers' of the children at Cascopediac. The report then made a number of recommendations towards the settlement and assimilation of the Indians, first calling for 'compact settlements, not very remote from older Settlements' a policy that would have permitted precisely what the government was doing: selling off Indian lands to settlers and leaving the Indians with small plots, concentrated on a handful of reserves so they could be protected, educated, and assimilated. Perley was amazed by the brazen attitude of many of the squatters. All of the land at Indian Point reserve, for example, had been 'pounced upon' by squatters, leaving the Indians on three acres surrounded by a strong picket fence.[86] All of these actions had occurred in complete disregard for the law.

The history of the loss of Indian lands on the Little South West reserve illustrates the failure of the provincial government to protect Indian lands. By the time of the Perley report, this 10,000-acre reserve had already been occupied by squatters: they had built dozens of homes and cleared hundreds of acres of land. About fifty Mi'kmaq remained, in complete poverty. Chief Barnaby Julian had received nearly £2,000 for a confusing array of deeds, rents, and leases, but his family had squandered the money, with none of it going to any of the other members of the band.[87] Some of the most valuable Little South West lands were sold at auction in 1849, the proceeds targetted 'for the benefit of the Indians.' But the remaining lands were in an ambiguous situation, with some of them still occupied by squatters. These people remained in occupation of their lands until the 1890s, when an Indian agent was appointed to resolve the land-title problems on reserve and former reserve lands. The situation was in chaos: some purchasers at the 1849 auction had still not paid in full: they were given six months to pay, at 6 per cent interest dating back to the original purchase. Others had been squatters throughout the entire period. They were ordered to pay $2 an acre for the land or to remove themselves. Many still did nothing. Two different groups of Mi'kmaq also filed claims on the lands. The crown negotiated a land surrender with one of these groups that was contested into the late twentieth century.[88] Over the next ten years, twenty-eight more plots of land were sold, with the price down to 80 cents an acre.[89] It took the full century to end the squatting at Little South West Reserve. The squatters were never removed but ultimately obtained title to their lands at bargain prices.

New Brunswick also refused to protect Indian lands in other ways, as evidenced in *Doe d. Burk* v. *Cormier*. The Cormiers had mortgaged their farm to Burk, who sought to foreclose. The land was on the Buctouche Indian reserve, but the Cormiers, who had purchased directly from the Indians 'the same as others had done,' had failed to secure title from the dominion. The Supreme Court of New Brunswick, ignoring the entire issue of Indian title as well as Canadian Indian policy, upheld the foreclosure, an incredible result for the end of the nineteenth century.[90]

Sir John Allen, chief justice of New Brunswick, disagreed on appeal, holding that the province, following *St. Catherine's Milling*, owned all Indian lands. Therefore, the Cormiers did not hold legal title to the land they had mortgaged, and those lands therefore could not be either mortgaged or foreclosed. The province had, in this view, the sole right to administer and alienate Indian lands.[91] Once again, white settlers' occupation had gone on for decades undisturbed by either New Brunswick or Canadian authorities.

In another case, *Ex parte Goodine*, the New Brunswick Supreme Court, in a narrow holding reminiscent of Ontario courts, overturned a conviction under the Indian Act on dubious technical grounds. Peter Goodine had been convicted before a police magistrate in Fredericton for selling intoxicants to an Indian woman. He was fined $50 plus costs and ordered to spend two months in jail on default of payment. The court construed language in the Indian Act that provided for imprisonment for default of payment of the fine to apply only to the commander of a steamer or vessel because that was the language in the clause most immediately preceding the provision.[92] This formalistic interpretation ignored the intent of the act: limiting the sentencing provision to sea captains made no sense at all in relation to Indian policy.

As distinct as Newfoundland, Nova Scotia, and New Brunswick were in local matters, Indians in all of these jurisdictions did not have access to local courts to protect their lands. Moreover, in common with Upper Canada, and throughout colonial law generally, the reverse was not true: Indians were subject to colonial laws when they committed crimes. Peter

Paul, a Mi'kmaq, killed his mother-in-law at Hammond Plains in 1829, shooting her point-blank during a quarrel. Judge Brenton Halliburton referred the case to the Colonial Office, which, just as with the Shawanak-iskie case occurring in Upper Canada in the same decade, held that British law reached Indians, recommending, in this case, a two-year sentence.[93] Ten years later in Prince Edward Island another murder occurred, again involving two Mi'kmaq. Tom Williams had murdered Joe Louis, evidently after an argument about Louis injuring Williams's son many years earlier. Although the jury recommended mercy, the judge sentenced Williams to hang. The lieutenant governor reprieved him, believing that Williams had no comprehension of the crime but had engaged in 'the savage virtue of revenge.' Williams was banished.[94]

In other criminal matters, there is an under-representation of Indians in the official records. While the case files are filled with prosecutions of settlers for drinking, assault, and petty theft, few Indians were tried for such offences. Of 2435 jail committals in Halifax between 1854 and 1860, 16 involved eight different Indians. Of 807 drunkenness charges brought in Saint John in 1871, 12 involved Indians. Only one Indian was charged with larceny. Four Indians are recorded as imprisoned in the Saint John and Dorchester penitentiaries between 1844 and 1873: one for insanity (a civil matter), the other three for perjury, larceny, and assault respectively. There are two possible explanations. One is that Indians were very law-abiding and did not commit many crimes. But this flies in the face of evidence that there was considerable drinking and fighting among Indians. The other explanation is a kind of reverse discrimination: in intra-Indian criminal matters short of murder, colonial authorities did not ordinarily prosecute.[95]

CONCLUSION

Distinct regional histories have been set out in this chapter. Quebec had its own legal history, as complex as Upper Canada's. There were many possibilities in the unique colonial situation of Quebec that might have made important differences in Canadian Indian law, but they did not. The English conquest of Quebec brought English public law to Quebec. The legal history of French Quebec included a unique history of Indian/French relations, but this was substantially lost to English Canada.

Judge Samuel Monk's bold opinion in *Connolly* v. *Woolrich* derived from his reading of the common law and had nothing to do with his status as a Quebec judge. Still, the opinion might have been followed, but it was not. It stands as the most remarkable nineteenth-century example of the potential of the common law to create a multicultural legal order that respected indigenous rights. Judge Monk read Cree law as seriously as it deserved to be read, a legal tradition to be given effect, along with the common law, in governing a marriage that bridged two legal traditions.

The legal history of aboriginal rights in Atlantic Canada was one that paralleled that of Ontario. While squatters in New Brunswick, Nova Scotia, and Ontario faced different colonial regimes that had their own unique local practices, none of these regimes could politically afford to resist the push of squatters for more land.[96] This inability of local colonial authorities to protect Indian rights effectively was, in itself, one of the major problems in nineteenth-century colonial administration and an issue at the heart of the parliamentary inquiry of 1837. But, politically, Indian matters in Atlantic Canada were not as important as those in Ontario and, as a result, Indian lands were less protected there and Indian rights perhaps more egregiously ignored.

The precise details of the Beothuk tragedy are disputed, but what is clear is that it occurred under a colonial legal order that did not intervene to protect native people. It is an event in Canadian legal history cited in the parliamentary subcommittee report of 1837 as an example of the brutality of colonial policy towards Indians in Atlantic Canada. While recent work challenges the 'genocide' thesis which was accepted in that report and widely embraced thereafter, there is no denying that uncontrolled extra-legal violence directed against the Beothuk was one of the causes of their extermination.

9

'Can We Be Free under the Law of Queen Victoria on Top of Our Land?': Indians and the Law in British Columbia

The legal history of the First Nations in British Columbia has become synonymous with their struggles for recognition of their sovereignty, land title, and fishing rights. This long conflict has been brought to the consideration of the Supreme Court of Canada in *R. v. White and Bob, Calder* v. *Attorney-General of British Columbia, Guerin* v. *R., Regina* v. *Sparrow, Delgamuukw* v. *British Columbia*, and the *Van der Peet* trilogy.[1] These are among the most important indigenous rights cases in recent Canadian history, cases that each turn on some discussion of the legal history of Indians in colonial British Columbia. They have done much to change, not only the substance of Canadian Indian law, but the basic methodology of how Indian law should be practised. It was the traditional Nisga'a, Gitksan, and Wet'suwet'en chiefs who brought the actions in *Calder* and *Delgamuukw* and determined the basic legal strategies of those cases.[2] These strategies, in turn, were not products of the 1970s and 1980s but were deeply rooted in the legal history of a century of Indian resistance to British Columbia's expropriation of their lands and natural resources.[3]

At the time British Columbia joined Confederation in 1871, article 13 of the Terms of Union provided that 'a policy as liberal as that hitherto pursued by the British Columbia Government shall be continued by the Dominion Government.'[4] This statement was not merely of somewhat dubious meaning, it was also the product of political chicanery. While the 'liberal treatment of Indians' in the rest of Canada resulted in a policy of the treaty-based acquisition of Indian lands prior to settlement, British

Columbia had, after the initial Vancouver Island treaties, refused to recognize Indian title and made no further treaties. The dominion government and the Indians of British Columbia both immediately recognized
the conceit. The dominion noted that Indian land policy in British Columbia was 'not as liberal as' the one the dominion was currently pursuing in
Manitoba and the Northwest Territories: in fact, it was a good deal less
liberal. But this did not matter, for the terms of the agreement only bound
Ottawa not to reduce the already small British Columbia reserves. Indians complained that their lands were being taken without compensation
while Indians in Canada sold their lands through treaties for substantial
annuities. British Columbia reserves averaged ten acres per person, while
those in the rest of Canada were much larger.[5] Since most British Columbia reserves had not been surveyed by the time of Confederation, survey
parties often met hostile Indians, who were aware that one function of the
surveys was to reduce the size of the reserves.[6] This Indian resistance was
accompanied by a demand for 'British justice,' for the legal recognition of
their land titles under British and Canadian law. Richard Wilson, a Tsimshian chief, was among a group of Indian leaders who came to see British
Columbia Premier William Smithe in Victoria in 1887: 'What we want is
to be free as well as the whites ... Can we be free under the law of Queen
Victoria on top of our land?'[7]

British Columbia's legal history is distinct from that of Ontario and
Canada, expressing a different colonial approach to indigenous legal
rights. When British Columbia joined Confederation in 1871, two incompatible legal conceptions of the 'liberal' treatment of Indians merged
within the same country, exposing the underside of the word 'liberal' in
defining the treatment of Indians in Canada. The province, until the
1990s, never recognized Indian title, denying any aboriginal right to
lands.[8] Most of the land in British Columbia was never alienated from the
First Nations by treaty but was taken after the Indians had been removed
to small reserves representing little more than occupied village and fishing sites.[9] The First Nations legal history of this process is exactly the
opposite: from the beginning, Indians asserted that they owned their
lands and objected to their confinement to small reserves. Both of these
histories have now come together in ongoing negotiations for a treaty
process in British Columbia.[10]

A 1913 photograph captioned 'Members of the Land Committee of the
Nishga Tribe' reveals a solemn group of twenty-nine Nisga'a men,
dressed in what must have been Sunday suits, posed in front of a land
office.[11] While the men are unidentified as individuals, they could not

have had more than rudimentary education and probably were mostly employed as fishermen or workers in salmon canneries. It was forty years after British Columbia had joined the dominion of Canada, hardly fifty years since British Columbia was made a colony – perhaps within the living memory of some of the men on the land committee. The photograph stands as eloquent testimony to the origin of the Indian land-title issue in British Columbia: the First Nations never wavered in their insistence that they owned their lands. The Nisga'a, the plaintiffs in *Calder*, and the Gitksan and Wet'suwet'en, the plaintiffs in *Delgamuukw*, were engaged in a legal struggle with British Columbia over their lands and their fisheries from the origin of the colony.

Governor James Douglas's first report on the situation in British Columbia made this point:

Indians at Hills Bar threatened to 'make a clean sweep of the miners assembled there.' The quarrel arose out of a series of provocations on both sides, and from the jealousy of the savages who naturally feel annoyed at the large quantities of gold taken from their country by white miners. [I informed the Indians that] 'The laws would protect the rights of the Indian, no less than those of the white men.' I also appointed Mr. George Perrier as Justice of the Peace for the District of Hills Bar, and directed the Indians to apply to him for redress whenever any of them suffer wrong at the hands of white men, and also cautioned them against taking the law into their own hands, and seeking justice according to their own barbarous customs.

I also appointed Indian magistrates, who are to bring forward when required, any man of their several Indian nations who may be charged with offences against the laws of the country; an arrangement which will prevent much evil; but without the exercise of unceasing vigilance on the part of the Government Indian troubles will sooner or later occur.

The recent defeat of Colonel Steptoe's detachments in the US has greatly increased the natural audacity of the savage and the difficulty of managing them.[12]

Nor was Douglas the only colonial official who noted the Indians' strong sense of their legal right to their lands. F.W. Chesson, secretary of the Aborigines' Protection Society, wrote the Colonial Office at the same time:

But there is another aspect of the question which is of equal importance. The Indians, being a strikingly acute and intelligent race of men, are keenly sensitive in regard to their own rights as the aborigines of the country, and are equally alive to the value of the gold discoveries; no better proof of which could be furnished than the zest and activity with which large numbers of them have engaged in gold digging.

As therefore, the Indians possess an intelligent knowledge of their own rights, and appear to be determined to maintain them by all the means in their power, there can be no doubt that it is essential to the preservation of peace in BC that the natives should not only be protected against wanton outrages on the part of the white population, but that the English Government should be prepared to deal with their claims in a broad spirit of justice and liberality. It is certain that the Indians regard their rights as natives as giving them a greater title to enjoy the riches of the country than can possibly be possessed either by the English Government or by foreign adventurers. The recognition of native rights has latterly been a prominent feature in the aboriginal policy of both England and the US. Whenever this principle has been honestly acted upon, peace and amity have characterized the relations of the two races, but whenever a contrary policy has been carried out, wars of extermination have taken place ... We would beg therefore most respectfully to suggest that the native title should be recognized in British Columbia and that some reasonable adjustment of their claims should be made by the British Government.

It would seem that a Treaty should be promptly made between the delegates of British authority and the chiefs and their people, as loyal, just, and pacific as that between William Penn and the Indians, but that more stringent laws should be made to ensure its provisions being maintained with better faith than that was carried out on the part of the whites. No nominal protector of aborigines, no annuity to a petted chief, no elevation of one chief above another, will answer the purpose. Nothing short of justice in rendering payment for that which it may be necessary for us to acquire, and was framed and administered in the spirit of justice and equality, can really avail.[13]

The impetus for recognition of Indian title in both of these arguments was the view that the Indians had a legal system that included the ownership of the land. A colonial recognition of that regime would avoid repeated difficulties, perhaps even warfare.

While disputes over fishing rights are common to indigenous people in all parts of Canada, the salmon fishery in British Columbia is so rich and Indians are so dependent on fishing that much of the dispute over land rights there is interrelated with the issue of fishing rights. It was fishing rights that were most valuable to many of the First Nations: traditional fishing locations were owned by individual bands. Indian settlements typically occupied only a small area, backed by a thick forest, but faced the water. The water provided both transportation and sustenance. Traditional fishing rights take many forms, but often cover a wide region of specific locations, fished seasonally. Salmon, the most valuable fish, migrated with the seasons. There were also lesser fisheries, some fished regularly, but some only if the salmon failed. Therefore, each band had a number of traditional fishing grounds. In this context, locating Indians on small reserves had a completely different meaning than it did on the prairies, as long as their traditional access to fishing sites was not restricted. Gold mining, of course, occupied the same inland rivers that were regularly fished. The colonial authorities also recognized the value of the fishery and quickly moved to sell licences to canneries.[14]

TRADITIONAL LAW AND THE VANCOUVER ISLAND TREATIES

The Indian nations of British Columbia were numerous and powerful with a strong legal tradition that included rights to the land, rights that they each had a long history of asserting against other Indian nations.[15] The fur trade had increased the value of these land rights, with fur-trapping sites also owned by particular Indian nations and family-based bands within those nations, ownership rights that all parties recognized and transgressed only under the explicit threat of traditional legal sanctions. By the time of the colonization of Vancouver Island in 1849, Indian nations had a long tradition of incorporating trade with Europeans, mainly the Hudson's Bay Company, into their cultures on their own terms.[16]

The rich natural resources of British Columbia supported one of the largest indigenous populations in North America. These peoples were uncommonly diverse, speaking a number of languages and representing many cultures.[17] The Northwest Coast peoples – Tlingit, Tsimshian, Haida, Nootka, Kwagiulth, Bella Coola, Coast Salish – lived in villages composed of large wood-plank houses, facing the sea. In the front of these villages dozens of totem poles recorded the family histories of the people living there. While the villages were permanent, the people did not live the entire year in one location but engaged in annual movements to hunting, fishing, trapping, and trading locations. There were highly ritualized social exchanges between coastal peoples. Residents of Victoria were amazed in 1854 when 2000 Haida, perhaps 25 per cent of the nation, arrived in large canoes after traveling over 600 miles of rough seas to visit the Songhee, a Coast Salish settlement across Victoria Harbour, and see for themselves the beginnings of permanent European settlement.[18] They stayed for months, to the chagrin of the few settlers.

The Indian nations of the interior of British Columbia were even more diverse because the geography and natural resources were more varied, producing a broad range of cultural adaptations. Some of these nations were interior extensions of coastal peoples with similar cultures and long traditions of contact and trade: Interior Salish, Tlingit, and Tsimshian. Others were Athapaskan peoples: Carrier, Tahltan, Sekani; or Columbia Plateau peoples: Okanagan, Lillooet, Kootenay, and Shuswap.[19]

Governor James Douglas is one authority on the power of First Nations law at the beginning of the colonial period. His experience in the colony was unique among colonial governors: he had been an HBC officer in the northwest for thirty years.[20] Douglas was aware of some of native law, writing that Indians 'have distinct ideas of property in land, and mutually recognize their several exclusive possessory rights in certain districts.' Moreover, Douglas recognized that Indians were prepared to protect these rights under their own law and would 'feel a sense of injury' if they were deprived of their lands without some process of extinguishment.[21] As a representative of the HBC, Douglas purchased Indian lands. Because the HBC legally exercised British colonial authority on Vancouver Island, these early purchases, now called the 'Douglas treaties,' are recognized as treaty agreements under Canadian law.[22]

The context of the Douglas treaties has no relation to the more developed process of the early Ontario or later numbered plains treaties. The texts of the Vancouver Island treaties are exactly alike, verbatim copies of land-cession agreements between the British and the Maori in New Zealand.[23] Moreover, it seems that the Indians never signed under the text of the treaty. Rather, in the spring of 1850 they signed blank pages that, apparently more than a year later, were written out in boilerplate treaty language.[24] Douglas made these treaties under his authority as an official of the HBC and paid for the Indian lands involved with company money.[25] He never referred to the instruments as 'treaties,' calling them instead 'the contract or deed of conveyance.' This distinction is not of legal consequence. The instruments sent by the Colonial Office were in fact treaties although the specific word 'treaty' was never used in them. Such agreements are judged by their contents; a treaty is a type of contract between nations.[26]

Douglas's two periods of rule on Vancouver Island bridge two distinct colonial experiments. Initially, Great Britain colonized Vancouver Island through the HBC, in an effort to hold back American expansion.[27] Fort

Victoria, the first British settlement, was founded in 1843. Until that time the company had primarily limited its activities to the northern and central parts of present-day British Columbia, carrying on a lucrative trade through the Saskatchewan River to Hudson Bay. As a fur-trading enterprise, the HBC made little effort to develop the island, in sharp contrast to the rapid influx of American agricultural settlers into the Oregon country. The Colonial Office responded by making the island a colony in 1849. Richard Blanshard, a thirty-two-year-old barrister, was sent out from England to serve as governor but was in the impossible position of governing a territory entirely owned by the HBC.[28] After eighteen months he resigned and Douglas, the HBC's chief factor at Fort Victoria, was appointed to succeed him, thereby giving the company control over the political and economic direction of the colony.[29]

It was in this context that Douglas made the Vancouver Island treaties. Most of them were made before he was governor but in his capacity as chief factor of the HBC post at Fort Victoria. Between 1850 and 1854 Douglas made fourteen treaties with the Indians on Vancouver Island.[30] These agreements covered small tracts of land needed for settlement in the vicinity of Victoria, Nanaimo, and Fort Rupert. The process of making the treaties, as noted above, was faulty by any standard.[31] In all, Douglas paid $2130 for these lands. Since the land cessions were small, of lands directly needed for settlements, and the Indians perceived a benefit from controlled settlement, the Indian nations accepted the treaties as validly negotiated between their chiefs and the crown. Even the fact that the chiefs signed blank papers does not alter their validity, as long as the words that were eventually added fairly recorded their oral agreement. The legal reason for this is obvious: by those treaties, Douglas subjected the colonies of Vancouver Island and British Columbia to the same Indian land title that the Colonial Office claimed in Ontario and other parts of Canada.

The precise nature of that recognition is difficult to determine. On the occasion of a personal inspection of the Nanaimo coal mines, Douglas noted that the HBC had given instructions for him to secure 'undisputed legal possession' of the mines. The company, already holding an unlimited licence from the crown to most of western Canada, could purchase legal title only from the Indians. Douglas's response to his orders reveals that, as early as 1853, the Indians were contesting the ownership of these lands: 'I observe the request of the Governor and Committee [HBC] that I should take an early opportunity of extinguishing the Indian claim in the coal district, and I shall attend to their instructions as soon as I think it safe and prudent to renew the question of Indian rights, which always gives rise to troublesome excitements, and has on every occasion been productive of serious disturbances.'[32]

Puzzling by eastern standards and apparently inconsistent with the 'troublesome excitements' noted above, but making sense in the context of the fur economy, Douglas reported that numerous other Indian nations had expressed a wish to sell their lands on the same terms.[33] Douglas, however, refused to enter into more treaties. The Indian nations' motivations in offering these sales of relatively small areas of land are not difficult to discern: in the fur economy, any Indian nation with direct access to a post derived a trading benefit. It could control the access of other Indian nations to trade and earn a substantial income as middlemen. Many First Nations were enriched by the fur trade. With a clan-based band structure, this wealth concentrated in the hands of some families who, in turn, used that wealth to increase their power and prestige in such rites as the potlatch.

GOVERNOR JAMES DOUGLAS'S INDIAN POLICY

Not only were no treaties ever made by Douglas on the mainland, but he stopped making treaties on Vancouver Island even though the Colonial Office had ordered him as governor to deal fairly with the Indians and negotiate surrenders of their lands.[34] Douglas himself summarized his policy in a well-known exchange with the Colonial Office in the early 1860s, requesting £3,000 to purchase additional Indian lands: 'I made it a practice up to the year 1859, to purchase the native right in land, in every case, prior to the settlement of any district.'[35]

The colonial secretary responded, acknowledging the importance of purchasing 'the native title to the soil' but calling it a matter of 'purely colonial interest,' and also denying Douglas's request for funding from the Colonial Office for further land purchases.[36] Douglas stopped making treaties with the Indians, not because colonial policy regarding purchasing Indian title changed, but because he refused to appropriate funds for such purchases. At the same time the mainland colony of British Columbia was awash with gold and Douglas concentrated on constructing an extensive road system.[37] The Colonial Office not only knew that Douglas was proceeding with settlement without purchasing Indian title but, for the mainland colony, appointed an entire colonial administration even though it was fully aware that no provision had been made for the purchase of Indian lands.

What Douglas actually did is not clear to this day. Officially, he sent out surveyors charged to survey as Indian reserves exactly what lands each Indian band requested, opening the remainder of the land for settlement.[38] If any band had a complaint on the boundaries allotted to their reserve, the surveyor was to return and re-survey, giving the band whatever lands it wanted. On the surface this policy is difficult to fault: each band was given exactly the lands it wanted and all other lands were open to settlement. But, under closer examination, the policy was a fiction based on a misunderstanding of Indian land use.[39] Precisely how, for example, could Douglas survey all of the land a band wanted and still have land for settlement? And exactly how did the Indian nations end up with so little land, resulting in the land dispute that today divides British Columbia, if, in fact, they were entitled to all of the land they wanted?

The British Columbia Indians were numerous and well organized. They appreciated the value of their lands and believed that they owned them.[40] Under these conditions, Douglas did not want to engage in a treaty-making process and purchase Indian title. At the same time, taking Indian title by force was both militarily difficult and politically impossible: the Colonial Office would not stand for it. Douglas's solution solved the immediate problem of Indian title peacefully, without treaties or purchase of Indian lands.

Small Indian reserves, essentially villages, were established near every settlement, providing an economic base for an Indian community dependent on the settlement for sustenance. British Columbia Indians were to be Christianized, brought under the rule of law, and put to work in the new economy of the province. The Indians, using these villages as a base, were to participate in the colony on an equal basis with settlers, even to the extent of pre-empting crown lands for agriculture, mining, or other economic activity. This was the Douglas 'system.'[41]

The adoption of Douglas's 'system' was expedited by its economic and political context: the colony of British Columbia was formed in 1858 to enable the Colonial Office to assert control over a gold rush. The Fraser River valley produced large quantities of gold from the late 1850s, attracting many miners from the United States. The violence and disorder of the California gold rush of 1848, including the wholesale massacre of Indians there, was well known in Canada. Americans did not like living under foreign flags, once again raising a threat to British interests in the northwest. When the miners reached the gold fields they found Indians panning for gold. The resulting conflicts sorely tested the capacity of colonial law to control the frontier.

Miners above Yale were forced to flee by an Indian uprising in August 1858. The causes of this war, like that of any Indian war, are difficult to determine but war represents an assertion of Indian sovereignty: Indians wanted to control the mining activity and reap the profits. American miners had an anti-Indian demeanour, trampling on Indian lands and treating Indians with contempt. Other issues involved alcohol and the abuse of Indian women by miners. Miners at Yale raised a militia to proceed up the river. Peaceful Indian villages were attacked and burned, but the main force of Indians was intent on negotiating an agreement that respected their rights. Two militia officers who trampled an Indian flag of truce were killed. The final agreement included, among other things, a surveying of Indian lands to protect them from mining activity, a ban on the sale of alcohol to Indians, and the appointment of marshals and justices of the peace to keep order.[42] Colonial policy centred on the creation of a legal order in British Columbia powerful enough to control both American miners and Indians, and the legal rights of Indian settlements adjacent the mining camps were to be respected. This was only ten years after the California gold rush and colonial authorities were determined to avoid the lawlessness and disorder of the American model. The policy apparently worked. Miners quickly returned to the upper Fraser valley and the search for gold expanded to the far corners of the colony over the next twenty years. While the settlement of Vancouver Island occurred slowly and was primarily agricultural, southern British Columbia was rapidly settled by gold seekers. Indians worked a variety of jobs in the gold fields, including teamsters, bearers, and labourers. They also sold fish, game, and produce to feed the miners.[43]

LAW AND LEGAL CULTURE ON COLONIAL VANCOUVER ISLAND

Nowhere in colonial Canada was the contrast between a legal framework for colonization and the alternative – arbitrary rule by a powerful economic elite – more marked than at early Fort Victoria. Governor Blanshard, a young and inexperienced barrister, was helpless and impotent, as was the law he brought to the colony. James Douglas, his successor, understood that the rule of law was incompatible with the fur-trade enterprise: 'The interests of the Colony and Fur Trade will never harmonize; the former can flourish only through the protection of equal laws, the influence of free trade, the accession of respectable inhabitants; in short, by establishing a new order of things, while the fur trade must suffer by each innovation.'[44]

Given this context, it may be surprising that Douglas's early Indian policy relied on a legal framework for ordering Indian/settler relations. In his first address to the Vancouver Island Legislative Assembly, Douglas made reference to both the power of the Indian nations and his determination to treat them with 'justice and forbearance, and by rigidly protecting their civil and agrarian rights.'[45] Later, Douglas appointed Indian magistrates to 'bring forward any man of their several Indian nations who may be charged with offences against the laws of the country.'[46] He also ignored the common law rule against the admission of evidence from non-Christians, just as it was ignored in Ontario.[47]

Douglas appointed magistrates but, in common with other colonies at an early stage of development, these men were not lawyers. Because this led to an erratic quality in their decisions, Douglas put the system under his own control, creating a Court of Appeal and appointing his brother-in-law, David Cameron, a clerk with no legal education, to the position.[48] Douglas ordered a legal treatise from the Colonial Office: 'I would beg you to send at least twenty sets of that useful work, "Burn's Justice."'[49] So that there would never be a legal void in the colony of Vancouver Island, Douglas secured a legal opinion: 'According to the opinion of lawyers in general, the colonists of a territory circumstanced like British Columbia carry with them the law of England, so far as it is applicable to their circumstances.'[50]

This was the legal policy for any settled colony and local laws took account of the special circumstances. The first law for the new colony of British Columbia was Douglas' proclamation of 6 September 1858 prohibiting the sale of liquor to Indians and, in the event this prohibition was contravened, providing for a punishment of two to six months in jail and a fine of five to twenty pounds. This was soon followed by a law prohibiting the alienation of crown lands, referring to Indian lands.[51]

It is possible that Douglas's conversion to a legal framework for incorporating Indians into the colony was in response to pressure emanating from the Colonial Office. Major struggles earlier with indigenous people in New Zealand, Australia, and Canada over land rights and public pressure from such groups as the Aborigines' Protective Society had moved the Colonial Office to urge that native people be accorded 'legal rights.'[52] Colonial Secretary Sir Edward Bulwer Lytton set out for Douglas the official view of the civilization of Indians: 'The success that has attended your transactions with these Indian nations induces me to inquire if you think it might be feasible to settle them permanently in villages; with such settlement civilization at once begins. Law and Religion would become naturally introduced amongst the red men, and contribute to their own security against the aggressions of immigrants.'[53] Douglas responded with his 'system:' Indians should be settled in villages and 'should in all respects be treated as rational beings, capable of thinking and acting for themselves [and] should be placed under proper moral and religious training, and left under the protection of the laws, to provide for their own maintenance and support.'[54]

This approach was in sharp distinction to the Indian policies followed in eastern Canada, in Spanish missions in California, and in the United States.[55] In Douglas's view, these policies had led to dependency and disorder, a system of maintaining the Indians as a welfare class. Under the system Douglas proposed, Indians would be protected in their villages but would be forced to participate in the larger economy. This, of course, fundamentally reproduced the Hudson's Bay Company's relationship with the Indian nations, a relationship that had produced a great amount of disorganization and alcoholism in many bands. Douglas, as early as 1850, had established a Songhee village directly opposite Fort Victoria and observed the role that village played in frontier society.[56] He would certainly have seen that the neat plan of Lytton for settling the Indians in villages under the protection of British law would not work in practice.

Douglas, with thirty years' experience on the frontier, saw the Indian villages that surrounded colonial settlements in a different way. He was not particularly offended by the disorder that he saw there. Rather, that disorder served the economic interests of the HBC and the colony, and both had learned to tolerate it as long as it was disorder of a petty level, ordinary drinking and fighting, occurring under the watch and supervision of the company.

The HBC, while under the authority of British law, was a law unto itself. In most instances the law practised was the 'law of the country,' a law based primarily on the principle that any injury to the company met a greater injury in return.[57] Given that Douglas's magistrates lacked law books until near the end of the 1850s, it is not difficult to imagine what law the magistrates relied on. Long after extra-legal forms of vigilantism were rejected in colonial policy elsewhere in the world and replaced by the form of British law, vigilantism, primarily aimed at Indians, prevailed on Vancouver Island and in British Columbia. The Colonial Office was fully aware of this situation and sanctioned it.

In the first of what was to become a number of Indian killings of settlers on Vancouver Island and in British Columbia, James Skea, a shepherd, was found shot dead near his hut, with two guns and four blankets missing. Suspicion immediately focused on a group of Cowichan who had stopped by the sheep station that morning.[58] Douglas believed that immediate action was required 'as an example to others.' But he also wanted to avoid implicating the whole Cowichan nation in the crimes of individuals. Accordingly, he posted a large reward for the killers and sent a demand that they be immediately surrendered. When this did not occur, Douglas, in the winter of 1853, organized a flotilla of boats and a force of 130 men to approach the Cowichan, who Douglas now believed harboured the killers. Two hundred warriors were painted with war paint. Douglas met with the chiefs in a small tent and gave them presents and, in return, they surrendered Squ-eath, telling Douglas he was the guilty man.[59] The governor then delivered a speech about the rules that were to govern their future contact with settlers.

After a second man was hunted down at Nanaimo, a jury, composed of naval officers, was impanelled on the *Beaver*. 'As the prisoners admitted their guilt there could be only one verdict,' according to Douglas: death by hanging was the only punishment for murder at common law.[60] The execution took place immediately, 'in front of the whole Indian nation, the scene appearing to make a deep impression upon their minds.'[61] This is the first recorded trial of Indians on Vancouver Island under colour of British law, a trial that probably lasted only a few hours. Douglas did not take the defendants to Victoria for civilian trials. Rather, he used the opportunity to demonstrate British power. In a speech to the Cowichan, he informed them that 'the whole country was a possession of the British Crown, and that Her Majesty the Queen had given me a special charge, to treat them with justice and humanity ... I told them to apply to me for redress, if they met with any injury or injustice at the hands of the Colonists and not to retaliate ... above all things, I undertook to impress upon the minds of the chiefs, that they must respect Her Majesty's warrant and surrender any criminal belonging to their respective Indian nations, on demand of the Court Magistrate.'[62]

Douglas returned to Cowichan in 1856 with 437 officers and men to punish another 'outrage.' Chief Tathlasut, of the Somenos band, had shot Thomas Williams, an English settler, as an act of revenge for Williams's seduction of his intended bride. This action, resulting in the wounding of Williams, was again in accordance with Cowichan law. Douglas, how-ever, following HBC policy in always punishing Indians for shedding white blood, organized a punitive expedition. The men marched through miles of brush and approached the village. The Cowichan met them decked out in war paint and the two forces advanced until they were within arms length, the Indians refusing to give up the accused. Finally, British troops forcibly seized Tathlasut. The next morning he was tried on the spot by a court of six officers and six enlisted men. That evening he was hanged from a tree at the same spot where he had shot Williams. The Cowichan did not approve of the hanging and had yielded only to force.[63] Douglas was free to take Tathlasut to Victoria for trial before Judge David Cameron, but he preferred the immediate military trial and execution as an assertion of British sovereignty over the Cowichan and as a demonstration of the powerlessness of Cowichan law.[64]

There were other killings of settlers by Indians on Vancouver Island before the colony was merged into British Columbia in 1864, mostly in outlying areas and also dealt with as military actions. The Royal Navy and its gunboats were powerful instruments of British authority in the 1850s and 1860s. While many of the navy's punitive expeditions ended with something of the form of law in a quick trial and hanging on a 'portable gallows,' they bore little resemblance to British justice and were illegal under British law: the colony of Vancouver Island had a functioning court system with jurisdiction over these cases.

The first naval action was an attack on the Kwagiulth village of Newitty in 1850 led by Governor Blanshard. The events there are still the subject of dispute. Three sailors employed by the HBC deserted their ship, intending to make their way to California and the gold rush. The company put up a reward of thirty blankets for the recovery of each of the three men but, in the meantime, they had been killed by Taskshicoate, Tawankstalla, and Killonecaulla. It has been suggested either that the company, in an effort to discourage desertion, had offered the Indians a reward for the men 'dead or alive' or that the Indians honestly mistook the nature of the reward that was offered.[65]

Dr John Helmcken had taken up his duties as magistrate and justice of the peace at Fort Rupert on the north coast of Vancouver Island on 27 June 1850 and was the civil official responsible for the administration of justice in the district. This appointment illustrates how quickly colonial authorities established the rule of law in distant areas of settlement: the new governor had arrived from England only four months earlier. Helmcken was unable to find the killers of the HBC sailors; he believed that the Newitty were not the guilty parties and blamed the Fort Rupert Kwagiulth. As Helmcken communicated to Blanshard, there was not a great deal he could do under the circumstances. He could either offer a substantial reward and hope that someone turned over the guilty parties or mount a punitive expedition, which meant leaving a weak garrison at the fort facing danger from local Indians.[66] Governor Blanshard brought the British warship *Daedalus* to Fort Rupert and took charge of the matter. He instructed Helmcken to tell the Indians that 'the white man's blood never dries.' As HBC governor Sir John Pelly informed Earl Gray, 'It has been the uniform policy of the Hudson's Bay Company, never to suffer the blood of a white man to be shed by a savage with impunity.'[67]

Helmcken approached the Newitty and offered a reward of twenty blankets for the killers. They resisted, acknowledging the murder and offering to pay for the lives of the sailors in furs but refusing to hand over the guilty men. Guns were pointed at Helmcken and he retreated. The Indians' action reflected their sovereignty and law: they offered to pay with furs for the value of the sailors' lives. Blanshard, however, sent gunships. As the Newitty deserted and headed inland, the navy burned their village. Days later more boats were sent. A village at Bull Harbour was attacked by the navy, an action that met with some resistance. Again, the Newitty retreated into the forest, leaving one man killed and three wounded. They then decided to capture the killers and turn them over, but evidently the men were protected by their clans. Failing in the capture, the Newitty shot two of the three killers, killing a slave in the place of the third. The bodies of the men were desecrated and their remains turned over to the British.[68] While Helmcken had nominally been in charge of the early stages, by the end he was under the control of the governor acting through military authorities.

Fifteen years later navy captain Nicholas Turnour, commanding the warship *Clio*, landed at Fort Rupert to demand that three Kwakiulth who had killed a Newitty be handed over and that he be allowed to search the village for liquor. His party was met by Chief Jim with fifty warriors, while fifty more yelled encouragement from the village. Jim refused to give up the men unless the navy gave over two men as hostages, again applying Kwagiulth law. The navy gave an ultimatum requiring that the men be handed over within a short period or the village would be bombarded. Chief Jim also threatened to attack Fort Rupert and had raised four flags over the village as a sign of his people's sovereignty. Although the flags were brought down and a white flag sent up as a sign of peace, the Kwagiulth refused to hand over the three men. The *Clio* opened up its guns on the village, destroying all of the houses and sixty canoes.[69] Colonists in Victoria were upset over popular accounts of the action and the colonial legislature demanded a report on the ship's activities. The thrust of the complaint was not the extent of the navy's brutality but that these measures were being used beyond the control of civilian authorities and the law.[70]

More public concern was aroused by a murder case arising out of the Songee community at the outskirts of Victoria. Allache, a twenty-year-old Tsimshian, killed a black seaman after a drunken confrontation over the seaman's attentions to Allache's wife. Alfred Waddington wrote a lengthy editorial in the *Colonist* describing Allache's trial and execution as 'judicial murder,' unworthy of British justice. Not only had Allache been tried without a defence lawyer, with a Chinook interpreter who did not speak either 'good English or Tsimshian,' but ultimately he was hanged by a fellow prisoner, who had been convicted of selling liquor to Indians but pardoned on condition that he serve as hangman. The young man was hanged 'so that an example might be made' for other Indians. The following day, a white man received a four-year sentence for manslaughter for stabbing to death a helpless drunk by the side of the road.[71]

A series of Indian 'pirate' attacks beginning in 1859 brought about the familiar navy response but, again, with some attempt to involve civil authorities. The American brig the *Swiss Boy* was beached for repairs on Barkley Sound on the west coast of Vancouver Island. Local Indians, some Ohiet, some Sheshat, boarded and removed everything of value. The crew fled into the forest until rescued by Swell, a Makah chief. A navy investigation found the Indians ready to trade, their village full of goods removed from the *Swiss Boy*. The Indians informed navy officers that they considered the *Swiss Boy* their property because it had beached on their lands.[72]

The ignorance of the Makah in the ways of British law moved the colony to appoint an Indian agent, William Banfield, for the west coast of Vancouver Island. Banfield was to use his influence among the west coast Indians but he disappeared on 20 October 1862 and it was believed that he had drowned. Later, Klatsmick, an Ohiet chief, boasted that he had stabbed Banfield. Taken to Victoria for trial, Klatsmick was acquitted, the judge not accepting Indian testimony against him.[73]

The crew of the *Swiss Boy* fared better than that of the *Kingfisher* five years later, in 1864. That ship was attacked by ten Ahousats, plundered, and the entire crew killed and thrown overboard.[74] These events brought another navy attack: in the fall of 1864 nine villages on the west coast of Vancouver Island were destroyed, along with sixty canoes. Fifteen Indians were killed and a number taken to Victoria for trial for the *Swiss Boy* and *Kingfisher* piracies. The major offender, Chapchah, an Ahousat chief, who had lured the *Kingfisher* into the village by claiming that he had oil to trade, repeatedly escaped capture by leading his warriors into the dense forest behind the village. Chief Justice David Cameron dismissed the charges against the Indians, holding that the testimony of an Indian was inadmissible in British Columbia courts. Cameron's ruling was wrong: the Colonial Office had instructed Douglas as early as 1852 that Indian testimony could be accepted in court, sworn according to whatever form was locally appropriate.[75] Once again, the veneer of formal legal process was imposed after a military action, and again the legal process failed.

LAW AND LEGAL CULTURE IN MAINLAND
BRITISH COLUMBIA, 1858–90

Just as the colony of Vancouver Island was hastily created in 1850 to stave off American imperialist ambitions in the northwest, the colony of British Columbia, the mainland portion of the current province, was created in 1858 to put some order in the gold rush there and keep American prospectors from creating their own 'state.' James Douglas was appointed governor of the new colony as well, administering both simultaneously until he retired in 1864, the year that the two colonies were merged.[76] Chief Justice Cameron of Vancouver Island was never considered for a parallel post in British Columbia. Rather, Matthew Baillie Begbie was dispatched from London with a commission as judge of British Columbia.[77] Begbie's qualifications were typical of colonial judges: a London barrister trained at the Inns of Court, he had a small commercial practice and good connections.[78] There are indications that the Colonial Office did not think the posting an important one, for the initial offer to Begbie was an appointment as a magistrate. Begbie accepted the appointment as magistrate, but he wanted more money for expenses and a recognition of his claim on the post of chief justice when it was created. After some negotiations, he was appointed a judge rather than a magistrate at a salary of £1000 a year.[79] Beginning in March 1859 and during succeeding years, Begbie rode circuit as the only judge in British Columbia. Following British law, both in substance and procedure, Begbie rode to outlying districts periodically to 'deliver' the jails. These criminal trials would be followed by civil trials, held by a separate court but with Begbie the only judge.

Indians were everywhere in the gold rush. Not only did they occupy the prime gold fields, which were located on sand bars at river mouths that were also ancient fishing sites, but they engaged in the commerce of the gold rush. British Columbia Indians panned for gold, worked as teamsters, cargo carriers, and labourers, and sold meat, fish, vegetables, and baskets to the miners. This activity, in the context of an event as wild as the gold rush, created a number of violent situations leading to criminal trials of Indians.

Begbie's first case involved two Indians accused of killing an American miner at Yale. They were brought separately before him and the grand jury, composed of American miners. Begbie was convinced that the charges were false, and so he directed the grand jury to dismiss the case. The next case led Begbie to instruct the jury that bringing a case required hard evidence, not merely suspicion. This prisoner was discharged also. Begbie hired Martin, a French-speaking Carrier Indian who had served as interpreter, as his 'Indian servant,' also hiring seven Indian packers for the remainder of his circuit.[80] While on circuit Begbie was a representative of the crown and met with delegations of Indians. He learned Chinook, the local trade dialect, as well as the local Chilcotin and Shuswap languages.[81]

Like many judges in Upper Canada, Begbie appears to have accepted Indian testimony at face value without regard for the common law prohibition against accepting the testimony of non-Christians. William Marshall, a miner, was charged in 1860 with assaulting an Indian. Judge Begbie sat with a local magistrate and heard testimony against Marshall, all given by Indians. They convicted Marshall wholly on Indian evidence. A delegation of settlers called on Begbie to complain of the court's acceptance of Indian testimony, but to no avail. If Indians were to have a chance at equal justice, as Begbie saw it, they had to be able to have their evidence heard.[82] Begbie's method consisted of a generic oath affirming belief in a supreme being who punished falsehoods, and there is no indication that this mattered to Indians who did not have a parallel to the 'courtroom oath' in their societies: people were expected to be honest in their personal dealings.[83] Begbie authored a native evidence ordinance permitting the use of Indian testimony and this was adopted by the British Columbia legislature in 1865, legalizing a practice that he had followed for five years. He then redrafted the ordinance for the united colony in 1867.[84]

Begbie, in the colonial period, believed that Indians held title to their lands until such title was extinguished. He wrote Douglas in 1860 that 'I may also observe that the Indian Title is by no means extinguished. Separate provision must be made for it, and soon.'[85] Given his position as chief judicial officer in the colony, this legal view is significant. He was also sympathetic to First Nations law. He recognized the impulse for revenge, at the root of Anglo-Saxon law, in many of the killings before him and also in the practice of offering trade goods in payment for a killing, a practice for which he had some sympathy. Later, he ordered justices of the peace not to interfere with the traditional legal authority of the chiefs over drunken and disorderly members of their bands.[86]

The colonial law that Begbie applied was political law, with legal doctrine used for political ends. Just as he deferred to First Nations law for reasons of politics and expediency on some occasions, so did he defer to American law for the same reasons: it increased the legitimacy of British law among the miners, making it more flexible and less oppressive. On one occasion Begbie used an American criminal law text to define the difference between murder and manslaughter to a jury of American miners.[87] It did not matter to British colonial authorities whether an individual murderer was found guilty of murder or manslaughter, so long as British sovereignty prevailed.

Begbie's most famous Indian law decisions, both occurring late in his career, defended the rights of Indians as individuals and held portions of the Indian Act illegal, putting him and his vision of one frontier law at odds with the Canadian Indian policy of legal paternalism. The Indian Act of 1884 outlawed the Northwest Coast potlatch, which involved complex ceremonies that included the giving of gifts and other ritual exchanges. This repressive measure was thought necessary in order to speed the Indians' assimilation, as well as to break their resistance to the imposition of the Indian agent's authority. Indians were outraged by the 1884 act and openly ignored it. Hamasak, a Kwakiuth from Mamalil-likulla, twice openly tried to organize an inter-village potlatch and was arrested on 1 August 1889 by his Indian agent and two native police. He pleaded guilty and was sentenced to six months in jail by the Indian agent, who was acting in his capacity as justice of the peace.

Hamasak's friends applied to Chief Justice Begbie for a writ of habeas corpus. Begbie, in an unreported opinion, held the law void in that it did not properly define the term 'potlatch' and therefore was too vague to sustain a criminal conviction. Not leaving it at that, Begbie went on to discuss the meaning of the potlatch in Indian culture, intending to communicate his view on the inappropriateness of the Indian Act prohibiting such behaviour.[88] This directness was a deliberate affront to the Indian Department, but Begbie strongly believed that Indians should be under the same law as all other citizens. He was also not finished with the Indian Act on this issue. His only reported Indian rights case, *Ex Parte Ettamass*, involved an Indian who was being held in custody by an Indian agent in 1892 under the terms of the Indian Act's prohibition of various kinds of Indian ceremonies. Finding that Ettamass was not charged with any crime, Begbie granted a writ of habeas corpus, releasing him from custody.[89]

Begbie's disdain for the Indian Act does not just emerge from these two cases in which he limited its impact. He challenged the act directly in an 1885 case in which the dominion government sought to repossess part of the Songhees reserve in Victoria. Begbie, in common with the official view of British Columbia politicians, took the position that the Indians of British Columbia were distinct from those in the east: 'There every Indian man, woman and child and chief is fed by the elemosynary daily bounty of the state; here not one Indian or one Indian's father or [sic] has ever been so fed. All Indians in B.C. are entirely self supported and self-supporting; clearly, a code of laws [the Indian Act] which may suit a mass of state-fed hereditary paupers educated to habitual idleness, is not necessarily adapted for a race of laborious independent workers.'[90] While Indians all over Canada had to defy the Indian Act simply in order to get on with their lives, there were few officials with the courage to support them in that position. Begbie was ahead of his time and a thorn in the side of the Indian Department. His legal opinions were consistent with his view that Indians were subjects of British law who were entitled to be treated the same as any other subject, a view that explicitly rejected the paternalism and legal dualism underlying the logic of the Indian Act.

The Indian Department, however, was not easily defeated by an aged provincial judge, even one of Begbie's stature. In 1895 it amended the Indian Act again, carefully rewording it to meet Begbie's specific legal objections to it. The department also continued to be outraged by the Indians' defiance of government policy.[91] All of this defiance was linked in the view of the government, and it included the continued land claims of British Columbia Indians: the Nass valley – the Nisga'a lands – was 'one seething mass of disaffection and discontent owing to the potlatch.'[92] Over the succeeding fifty years, British Columbia Indians persisted in holding potlatches, both openly and clandestinely. The Indian Department brought scores of prosecutions, sending many Indians to jail.[93] It is impossible to say what the full impact of these prosecutions was. On the one hand, the Indians always defied the law.[94] But, on the other hand, the traditional cultures were hard hit by this kind of repression, along with the full impact of social and economic change on indigenous cultures.

THE EXECUTION OF INDIANS IN COLONIAL BRITISH COLUMBIA

Consistent with Begbie's 'liberal' view that Indians were equal under the

law was his role in the trial and execution of more than two dozen Indians. This was a disproportionate number of Indian executions for a small
population.[95] While Begbie's district included all of mainland British
Columbia, his effective area of control included only the lower Fraser
River valley.

The large number of executions belies the myth of the peaceful Canadian frontier: Begbie legally executed more Indians than were killed in
some wars, underscoring the broader meaning of Begbie's role in the colony. It was his job to assert British control of the unstable gold-rush frontier, a position that was more political than legal. He and Douglas were
the leading colonial officials in British Columbia, with both living in Victoria, outside the mainland colony. Begbie was a trusted adviser to Douglas, consulting with him on a regular basis about all of the political and
legal matters in both colonies.[96] While Douglas was the governor, British
power in the Fraser River valley was exerted through legal officials.
Judge Begbie had a considerable retinue: a sheriff and his deputies, local
magistrates appointed in each village, and the clerks who manned the
courts and land offices. Begbie handled this job masterfully. He had a
powerful judicial presence, using his court as a forum to educate and control the mining communities. Authoritarian and blustery, he once told a
jury that they deserved to be hanged for finding a murderer guilty of only
manslaughter.

There is no parallel to these executions anywhere in the hundred colonies that Britain founded, even in the penal colony of New South Wales;[97]
they make the founding of British Columbia a bloody colonial enterprise.
But this violent history was 'legal,' with each of the executions ordered by
a British judge.[98] In all, Begbie hanged twenty-six men; twenty-two Indians, one white, and three Chinese. During the same period, fifty-two men
were charged with murder: five were acquitted, nine found guilty of
manslaughter rather than murder, and eleven reprieved after conviction
and imposition of the death sentence, each on the motion Judge Begbie.[99]

This aggressive if not bloodthirsty execution policy on mainland British
Columbia followed, and may have been modelled after, a parallel policy
begun by Governor Douglas on Vancouver Island. It appears that seven
Indians were hanged there before the merger of the two colonies, from a
much smaller indigenous population.[100] Begbie was the only judge on the
mainland until Henry Crease was appointed as second judge in 1870.
Crease sentenced two more Indians to hang during the colonial period,
bringing the total to twenty-four.[101] After the appointment of Crease,
Begbie rode circuit less, conducting fewer trials, and the number of

Indian hangings decreased. By way of comparison, the number of executions of Indians in British Columbia in this ten-year period far exceeded the total of all executions in the rest of Canada.[102]

Although it is tedious and tragic to analyse the legal history of the twenty-four mainland British Columbia Indian hangings, these were significant legal events which structured the position of Indians in British Columbia.[103] Public hangings were symbolic displays of state power. The mode of execution was intended to have maximum impact on the people who watched it. Before the invention of the 'long drop' later in the nineteenth century, those who were hanged most often died by strangulation, after kicking around on the end of a rope for twenty minutes or more, losing control of bodily functions, bleeding, and making horrible noises.[104]

In this context, speculation about Judge Begbie's humanity or motivation seems irrelevant although, at the time, the popular image of him as a 'hanging judge' had wide currency in Canada. Among the stories told about him was that one day, when no hangman could be found, Begbie personally entered a cell, pinioned a man's hands behind him, took him out, and hanged him.[105] Yet in fact there is no evidence that Begbie ever witnessed one of the executions he ordered, even though all were public.[106] Begbie himself wrote that, on his appointment, 'I was informed in so many words that they wanted to send out a man who would not hesitate to try a criminal under a tree and hang him up to a branch of it, and that I was expected not to hesitate to do so.'[107]

The murder trials Begbie conducted, like all his trials, would have been rudimentary, occurring in hotel lobbies, halls, or whatever venue he could find. While the formalities of British law were loosely followed, the major protection available to the defendant was his right to a jury trial. Lawyers were rare on the frontier, and most often Begbie conducted the trial all by himself, presenting the case as the prosecutor, making sure that the defendant's defence was adequately offered, and passing sentence after the jury returned a verdict. Begbie, as judge, had complete control of the evidence because there was no one to object to whatever evidence was admitted (which is why it was not a problem for him to allow Indians to give evidence, whether it was legal under British law or not). At that time the defendant was never allowed to testify in his own defence, although he could provide unsworn statements to the judge. Miscommunication due to language differences was an insurmountable problem that Begbie did not adequately address. Often trials involved two untrained interpreters. One translated from the aboriginal language of the defendant to Chinook jargon, a simple trading language. Another translated from Chinook to English. Since neither language contained the legal concepts needed for an adequate defence, the defendant was doubly disadvantaged and little legal subtlety must have survived the double translation.[108]

Death by hanging was the only punishment prescribed by law for murder, and so, if the jury convicted the defendant, the judge had no choice but to impose the death sentence. The trial process was a short one, with few trials taking more than several hours.[109] The hanging took place in public within a few days at the same location. There was no formal appeal process, although the condemned could petition the Executive Council for a commutation of sentence. The sentencing judge made a recommendation to the council, which was usually followed.[110]

In sentencing Paskel, an Indian, to hang for the murder of a white man, Begbie proclaimed that 'the law for the savage as well as the Christian is death for death.' Paskel mounted the scaffold with James Barry, a white man sentenced to hang for an unrelated killing. Barry collapsed on the scaffold and had to be held up so he could be hanged. Paskel was defiant, boasting that he had killed ten white men. When they attempted to put a hood over Paskel, he insisted that they hood Barry first because, 'as an Indian, he had no idea of having anything done to him that was not also done to the King George man.'[111] Obviously, these hangings of Indians had a racial meaning that all present understood. This was the only way that British power could be brought to the hinterlands of British Columbia. Paskel, for his part, even on the day of his death, insisted on his equality with white men. He wanted to be hooded last so that he could see for himself that he was not being hanged differently.

The main policy goal of colonial law was to protect the lives and property of settlers from all forms of attack, Indian as well as white. A second goal was the socialization of Indians. Indian attacks on white people were feared for reasons that were both racist and also quite understandable given the brutal reality of frontier conditions. Most of the Indians who were executed had killed white settlers.

Kalabeen and Scothla, two brothers, were tried for killing Francois Caban at Hat Creek. The trial itself, typical of most trials of Indians, was unfair: the two were unrepresented and there was no evidence at all legally admissible against Scothla. Kalabeen had initially made a self-incriminating statement but apparently had done so without proper cautions. Nevertheless, Judge Begbie held that the caution had been given.[112] As in many intra-racial murders, there was no clear motive. Robbery was commonly put forward as a motive in such cases but in this instance it did not apply because the dead Coban had money in an inside pocket.[113] In any event, both Kalabeen and Scothla were convicted by a jury after a half-hour of deliberations. Begbie, asking the prisoners to make statements before sentencing, noted that 'I have never seen an instance where there seemed such an utter absence of all ideas of any moral guilt, or offence, in taking a human life,' adding that 'they seemed to think that shooting a man was no different than shooting a grouse.'[114]

In another case, Chak-Atum-Kah had killed Holmes, a white man. Holmes, who had an Indian wife, returned home to find her and their child dead of smallpox. 'Holmes cried for a while, then washed his face and lit his pipe. After smoking he went to his canoe and drank some whiskey.' As he did so Chak-Atum-Kah shot him.[115] This is the kind of killing that whites saw as without motive but, obviously, Chak-Atum-Kah had some reason for killing Holmes. He never offered any defence or explanation in court, and was ultimately hanged.

Most Indian killings were simply attributed to 'Indian savagery,' but in fact complex cultural motivation may have been at work. For example, two Indians were sentenced to death by Judge Begbie in 1861 for slitting the throat of a white man. One testified that 'his heart was bad, that his father was dead and his mother was dead, and there was no one to care for him, and he must kill a white man.' They then killed the first white man they met.[116] Chilpakin, a young man previously convicted and reprieved for a killing in 1866, was tried at Lillooet in 1868 for the murder of a Chinese man some years before. At the time of the killing, Chilpakin was probably only twelve or thirteen years old. Overcome by grief at the death of his sister, Chilpakin and his friend Tesch had decided to go out and kill a 'Chinaman.' The two had brutally assaulted Tien Fook, stabbing him in the neck, hitting him in the head with an ax, and cutting his stomach open.[117] This was precisely the kind of 'irrational' Indian violence that settlers feared. Indian defendants were most often stoic and silent in court, saying nothing about their crimes, nor offering a word in their own defence.

Another significant case involved the only vigilante lynching in British Columbia. Louie Sam, a fifteen-year-old Sto:lo boy, was lynched in 1884 by a party of Americans who had crossed into Canada. Louie Sam was accused of killing James Bell, a Washington dry goods merchant, in a $500 robbery on the American side of the border. The Sto:lo, rather than seek revenge, put their faith in the Canadian justice system, trusting Canadian authorities to punish the American offenders through the ordinary course of the law. The Canadian authorities promised the Sto:lo to secure justice in the case, but they failed to follow through. There was no political will to do so.[118]

British Columbia's legal history has become synonymous with the province's denial of Indian title and its refusal to negotiate with the Indian nations for a peaceful settlement of land disputes. This story began with James Douglas, who permitted the wholesale settlement of settlers on Indian lands in British Columbia during the Fraser valley gold rush. The great pains that Douglas and the Colonial Office took to extend British law there through Judge Begbie and their licensing of miners and the recording of mining claims shows that the colonial government had the capacity to assert control over the alienation of Indian lands. While in the rest of Canada a policy was followed requiring colonial authorities to purchase Indian lands through treaties, British Columbia authorities denied that the Indians had any ownership rights to their lands at all. Indians were settled on reserves consisting of small portions of their lands, often ten acres per person.[119] But even these small reserves were often either unsurveyed, or poorly surveyed, and settler encroachments were unpunished by local magistrates.

The origins of this British Columbia policy are still not fully known. Joseph Trutch, chief commissioner of lands and works until 1871, then lieutenant governor, was responsible for the merger of British Columbia Indian policy with dominion policy. Though his overt racism and hostility to Indian interests makes him a convenient person to blame for the policy, other British Columbia colonial administrators, beginning with Douglas, also failed to carry out specific Colonial Office directives to make arrangements to purchase Indian title.[120] Colonial Secretary Bulwer Lytton, while stating that the Colonial Office expected the Indians to be treated humanely and justly, expressly deferred to Douglas's judgment and experience.[121] What followed may be explained as a failure of the Colonial Office to provide adequate supervision of local officials, persons more responsive to settler demands than to Indian rights. This, in fact, was a problem in all of the colonial settler states, a major impediment to colonial self-rule.

Much of the puzzle in reading the inconsistencies between Douglas's language in dispatches to the Colonial Office and his deeds stems from his desire to placate the Colonial Office. Yet this does not explain everything. For example, Douglas's request for £3,000 from the Colonial Office to extinguish Indian land title revealed both a recognition that there was an Indian title and a desire to use that money to purchase it. Once the money was refused, putting the burden on the local treasury, Douglas apparently decided not to bother with further purchases because they were not politically necessary. This decision must have been discussed informally in ruling circles in Victoria, even though no records of these conversations exist. Here we can speculate that the California method of dealing with Indians during the gold rush there – occupying their land and forcing them to move into the hinterlands or to accept wage work in the gold fields – was familiar to all of the settlers in British Columbia, and probably known to Indians as well from contacts in Washington and Oregon.

Douglas's political objective was to secure British Columbia for the crown and to open it up to settlement without an Indian war. His policy of surveying small reserves and establishing the Indians there in proximity to the settler economy accomplished those goals more cheaply and efficiently than purchasing their lands through a system of treaties. This is perhaps why such a political uproar followed the publication of *Papers Relating to the Indian Land Question* in 1877. The language of those papers repeatedly acknowledges Indian title in ways that local political officials in British Columbia had no desire or ability to defend; in fact, they had tried to keep the papers secret.[122] It seems likely that a number of local politicians were ignorant of the content of the papers: legal matters in British Columbia had been entirely handled by a handful of men between the late 1850s and Confederation.[123]

The view of Ontario political leaders at Confederation was that Joseph Trutch and British Columbians had misled the dominion on the nature of the province's Indian policy. The well-known language of article 13, apparently the work of Trutch, was not debated at the time of Confederation, and therefore its origin and intention can only be speculated on. Yet the only interpretation possible is that Trutch dishonestly turned 'liberal treatment' around to its opposite meaning, guaranteeing British Columbia a policy as 'liberal' as previously employed, which is to say not liberal at all: no more and no less liberal than tiny reserves of ten acres per person, with no recognition of Indian title.[124]

The dominion, after an initial struggle with British Columbia over its Indian policy, abandoned the fight. Lord Dufferin, governor general of Canada, made an official tour of British Columbia in 1876. After numerous meetings with Indians, Dufferin finally addressed the issue of Indian title in his departing speech. He was direct:

Now we must all admit that the condition of the Indian question in British Columbia is not satisfactory. Most unfortunately, as I think, there has been an initial error ever since Sir James Douglas quitted office, in the Government of British Columbia neglecting to recognize what is known as the Indian title. In Canada this has always been done; no Government, whether provincial or central, has failed to acknowledge that the original title to the land existed in the Indian nations and communities that hunted or wandered over it. Before we touch an acre we make a treaty with the chiefs representing the bands we are dealing with, and having agreed upon and paid the stipulated price, oftentimes arrived at after a great deal of haggling and difficulty, we enter into possession, but not until then do we consider that we are entitled to deal with an acre.[125]

More important, perhaps without knowledge of the legal implications of his statement, the governor general asserted that an 'Indian title' to the land was of exactly the same character as a crown title: 'I consider that our Indian fellow-subjects are entitled to exactly the same civil rights under the law as are possessed by the white population, and that if an Indian can prove a prescriptive right of way to a fishing station, or a right of way of any other kind, that right should no more be ignored than if it was the case of a white man.'[126]

The deadlock between the province and the dominion over Indian lands was finally resolved: during the late 1870s an Indian land commission, the 'Sproat Commission,' composed of representatives of both the dominion and the province, weakly attempted to redefine reserve boundaries, travelling widely through the province and holding dozens of meetings on Indian reserves. No significant amounts of land were added to reserves: British Columbia held title to its crown lands and would not appropriate additional lands for reserves.[127] The Indian nations of British Columbia repeatedly objected to their treatment in meeting after meeting with the Indian land commissioners, pointing out that they had legal rights to their lands under British and Canadian law. The roots of present-day land-rights cases in British Columbia can be traced to these meetings.[128]

The meeting of the Sproat commission with the Nlha7kapmx (Thompson) at Lytton in 1879 provides a window into their process. Commissioner Gilbert Sproat found that the Nlha7kapmx had spent $500 making elaborate preparations to receive him. They had enacted a new code of laws and formed a new governmental structure, complete with an elected chief and thirteen counsellors. The Nlha7kapmx nation was prepared to administer its own laws, and sought to use its new political structure to negotiate an appropriate resolution of its land disputes with the Sproat commission. The reality, however, was that Sproat himself was at odds with the provincial government and, although his commission was a joint body intended to reconcile dominion and provincial interests, the dominion lacked the political will to back him. Provincial authorities, fearful of the potential of organized Indian nations in British Columbia, were enraged by the political and legal positions that the Nlha7kapmx took. Their legal initiatives were rejected, and there was no resolution of their land claims. They had been unilaterally deprived of their lands under conditions that violated established British colonial policies.[129]

According to Sproat, 'I am sorry to say that I found ... that many of these Nekla-Kap-a muk [Nlha7kapmx] tribes had much to complain of. Some of them had no land reserves at all; others had lost old village sites and fisheries; some had bits of land disproportionate to their requirements; others had land and no water for irrigating it. Places very dear to the Indians had been taken from them, and in several instances, they had been deprived of their cultivated fields without compensation.'[130]

Lytton was only one of many Indian communities Sproat visited. He believed that his decisions allocating additional land to Indians would support existing Canadian policy by resolving the British Columbia Indian land-title issue and, at the same time, would put the Indian nations on a sound economic basis as functioning communities with a sufficient land base. Sproat spent the summer of 1878 in Nlha7kapmx villages, beginning at Spuzzum. Sproat found 107 people in Spuzzum, where there had been 400 'a short time before.' In the eighty miles between Spuzzum and the Stein River, there were only 1622 impoverished Indians, less than a quarter the number of fifty years before, in seventeen small reserves spread along the river, some only two or three acres in size. The Indians importuned him to visit their villages, pointing out that they were 'quiet and obedient to the law' but that settlers had secured most of their land.[131] Sproat was not able to give them any additional land.

Still, the British Columbia Indians did not give up hope. William, 'Chief of the Williams Lake Indians,' wrote to the *Daily British Colonist* that 'justice is no use to the dead Indian.' He went on to report that he had heard that Sproat was coming but that he was slow to arrive at Williams Lake because he had no horse. 'Her majesty,' wrote William, 'ought to give him a horse and let justice come fast to the starving Indians. Land, land, a little of our own land is all that we ask from her Majesty.'[132] But British Columbia authorities remained unmoved in their refusal to recognize Indian land rights.

CONCLUSION

Given the political state of Indian affairs in British Columbia, it should not be surprising that the province's courts did not produce any Indian law decisions during this period. This fact is stunning, however, in the context of the British empire at that time. Indians were recognized as persons under the British law applied in colonial British Columbia and British justice was well organized both on Vancouver Island and on the mainland. Magistrates were operating in all the settlements on Vancouver Island by 1852 and Judge Begbie had brought British law to the mining settlements of the mainland in 1859. Yet while Begbie received 'delegations' of Indian chiefs in the Fraser River valley in the early 1860s, that contact did not translate into Indian access to the courts. In any case, Indians did not believe that British Columbia courts would resolve their grievances against settlers, particularly over matters of land title. The legislature, for its part, was hostile to Indians. The first session of the post-Confederation legislature passed a law denying Indian people the right to vote or hold public office. As in Ontario and Quebec, Indians who met the ordinary qualifications of voting could vote until the passage of the statutory limitations on Indian rights included in the Indian Act of Canada.[133]

The hostility of the British Columbia government to native rights was evident when a delegation of Tsimshian and Nisga'a traveled to Victoria in 1887 to meet with Premier William Smithe and other officials. The Indians had one demand: they wanted a treaty. Smithe treated them with contempt, asking a rhetorical question: 'What do you mean by a treaty?' When John Wesley of the Nass valley roughly defined a treaty as 'after a certain amount of land is cut out for the Indians, outside of that we want a law such as the law of England and the Dominion Government which made a treaty with the Indians,' Smithe continued his game, asking another rhetorical question: 'Where did you hear that?' Wesley responded, 'It is in the law books.' Smithe countered with: 'Who told you so?' In the end, Smithe wanted to see the law book that Wesley referred to and Wesley promised to produce it. But Smithe had the last word, as colonial authorities did on all matters of law: 'There is no such law either English or Dominion that I know of; and the Indians, or their friends, have been misled on that point.'[134] A hundred years later it is difficult to know what late-nineteenth-century 'law book' Wesley was referring to. He might have had in mind the *St. Catherine's Milling* opinion (bound in a reporter), the recently published *Papers Relating to the Indian Land Question*, or, as Hamar Foster suggests, Alexander Morris's recently published *The Treaties of Canada with the Indians of Manitoba and the North-West Territories.*[135]

The Nisga'a worked for twenty years to prepare an Indian title case for the Privy Council in England. By May 1910, lawyers for the dominion and British Columbia had agreed on ten questions to be referred to crown authorities, but provincial authorities, obviously fearing they would lose, refused to let the three questions dealing with Indian land title to be referred to the Privy Council.[136] The case did not proceed.

In the context of contemporary racism and rapid settlement in the 1870s, 1880s, and 1890s, it is not difficult to imagine what the legal landscape of British Columbia looked like to Indians. The evidence is that, as in Upper Canada, legal chaos prevailed. Indians who brought actions against settlers for trampling on their cultivated areas could not secure convictions, while settlers who brought similar cases against Indians were likely to get convictions. Magistrates claimed that they lacked the power to eject squatters from encroaching on Indian reserves. Local land offices regularly granted settlers pre-emption certificates to Indian lands. Indians, under colonial law, lost their ability to pre-empt land without the special approval of the premier, an approval that was rarely granted.[137] Indian lands, on the other hand, even if not pre-empted by settlers, were taken away by government surveyors insensitive to Indian uses of potato fields, fishing grounds, graveyards, and traditional village sites. Indian hunting and fishing rights, reserved by the Vancouver Island treaties, were also illegally extinguished. By the late 1870s and 1880s, Indian hunters and fishermen were being regularly arrested and prosecuted for violating provincial hunting and fishing laws.[138] The idea of Indian equality in British Columbia law was a deliberate fiction, designed to justify the colony's land policies. The only real access Indians had to colonial courts was as defendants in the criminal courts, and that was not to advance Indian rights but to punish them for a full range of offences against settlers.

Nonetheless, The First Nations continuously invoked the idea of law, of British justice, to redress their grievances against the colonial government. They believed that British law protected their sovereignty and land title and argued those points. While they were joined in this by sympathizers (often missionaries), and while the provincial government blamed those sympathizers for the activism of the Indians, this view ignores the capacity of the Indian nations to understand and make use of the law and legal language to defend their interests. Premier Smithe, for example, refused to see the two missionaries who accompanied the Tsimshian and

Nisga'a delegations in 1887, but the Indians were as able to make legal argument as Smithe was: neither could cite the precise legal treatises as their authorities, but both knew how to use legal argument to make their cases.

Although the legal history of Indian title in British Columbia demonstrates conclusively that British and colonial authorities recognized Indian title through the 1850s and 1860s, British Columbia courts still refuse to recognize Indian title. Among the legal arguments they use is one that is purely disingenuous: even if Indian title was recognized in the 1850s and 1860s, the province argues, it was extinguished in fact in the 1870s and afterwards because the province ignored Indian title, repeatedly acting in ways inconsistent with provincial recognition of that title. Yet the reverse side of that argument must be true also: even when the province insisted that the Indians had no title to their lands, the Indians acted as though they did, repeatedly refusing to accept the province's version of the law. Chief Justice Allan McEachern's judgment in *Delgamuukw*, not only a wholesale denial of Indian rights but one based on a version the facts that ignored indigenous oral history, simply continued the tradition of provincial intransigence.

10

'The Enforcement of the Extreme Penalty': Canadian Law and the Ojibwa-Cree Spirit World

A series of 'wendigo' killings – a 'wendigo' was an evil spirit clothed in human flesh – brought to the attention of Canadian law around the turn of the twentieth century represent the extension of Canadian law to the heart of traditional Indian culture. These killings, however, also represent the extent to which some of the First Nations defied or ignored that law. Only one of the cases, *Regina* v. *Machekequonabe*, led to a reported opinion. That opinion is one of the best-known indigenous law cases in the common law world, often cited for the proposition that the criminal law universally applies even when the indigenous people involved had never been exposed to the common law and were completely ignorant of it, surely a profoundly unjust circumstance in which to inflict severe punishment.[1] Nonetheless, this was a foundational principle of British colonial law, extended around the world to indigenous peoples who had no knowledge of the existence of that law, let alone any comprehension of its principles.[2] Machekequonabe, an Ojibwa, was found guilty of manslaughter in an 1896 trial for kiliing what he believed to be a wendigo.[3] At least six other wendigo killings were processed by Canadian law in the dozen years following *Machekequonabe,* and others had previously come to the attention of Canadian authorities. Furthermore, in additional cases it seems that Indians, in order to protect their religious and cultural beliefs from Canadian law, carefully distorted the facts of homicide cases to conceal that they were wendigo killings.

THE WENDIGO IN OJIBWA AND CREE SOCIETY

There is an extensive anthropological literature on the wendigo,[4] and on wendigo killings, in Canada.[5] The wendigo lived in the cultural worlds of the Algonquian-speaking Indians of the north, most commonly in the Ojibwa and Cree nations. They were cannibal spirits that could inhabit the bodies of living people, causing them to kill even members of their family.[6] In appearance,

'the windigo [sic] is a particularly abhorrent creature. He has a frightening and menacing mouth, wholly devoid of lips. He has tremendous, jagged teeth through which his breath flows with a sinister hissing, making a loud and eerie noise, audible for miles.

His eyes are protuberant, something like those of an owl except that they are much bigger and roll in blood. His feet are almost a yard in length, with long, pointed heels and only one toe, the great toe. His hands are hideous with claw-like fingers and fingernails ...

His strength is prodigious. With one mighty stroke of his hand, he can disembowel a man or a dog. He rips off the surface of the earth as he wanders about, snapping off the tops of trees ...

He seeks out victims, trailing them hauntingly and relentlessly, waiting until darkness before seizing and eating them. Whenever a hunter disappears, failing to return from the forest, the Indians invariably account for this misfortune by explaining that a windigo has devoured him. [He has] a heart of ice, [and] a body swelled to the size of a pine tree and as hard as stone, impenetrable by a bullet or arrow and insensitive to cold.[7]

With such powers, the wendigo was a real threat, not only on his (or her) own terms as a large, dangerous figure in the woods, but also because he could inhabit living persons, turning a loved one into a killer and cannibal. This was especially dangerous given the dispersal of these Indians into small hunting and fishing bands for much of the year, isolated from each other and at the mercy of the elements.[8] Since wendigos could not easily be discovered or killed, a rich tradition of sorcery developed that matched the graphic detail of the wendigo legends themselves.

This sorcery tradition merged with the traditional law of the Ojibwa. Diamond Jenness describes the place of the wendigo in Ojibwa law at the Parry Sound reserve. Although disputes between families or clans might be settled by the heads of household or band leaders in council, many crimes, especially homicides, occurred in secret. In this situation, individuals might fear to inform or take action lest they be subject to sorcery later. Fear of sorcery was always present in the minds of the Ojibwa. If a man discovered or suspected that another hunter was trespassing on his hunting grounds, he would not visit the trespasser's camp and demand redress, because the wrongdoer might take offence and through witchcraft cause him to break through the ice or meet with some other misfortune. Instead, he would himself employ witchcraft against his adversary or engage a medicine man for the same purpose. Murder by violence was probably rare, but these Ojibwa attributed many deaths to sorcery, which was murder in another form; and murder called for a compensating life unless the deed were compensated with goods or hunting territory. A convicted sorcerer might be killed at sight by the relatives of his victim, although the executioner still ran the risk of possible vengeance. The chief and council could assume responsibility for the killing, legitimizing it under Ojibwa law. They investigated serious cases of theft and alleged murder, summoned the accused man before them, and sanctioned the death penalty or a fixed amount of indemnity. If the culprit belonged to another band, they conducted the negotiations with envoys who came to settle the issue.[9]

Wendigo mythology was similarly incorporated into Ojibwa law, with a well-established traditional legal order, inseparable from religion, existing to resolve disputes and punish killers. Jenness gives one account of a probable wendigo killing, although he does not identify it as such. A man had camped in the forest with his wife and baby while on a long and unsuccessful hunt. While he was away, his wife had killed their baby by putting it in a pot of boiling water. She then went to rejoin her people, trying to cover her trail. Her husband followed her, finding her in the wigwam of her people, sitting with the women on one side while the men sat on the other. 'Here is the murderer,' he cried, 'she has killed our baby.' Her eldest brother exclaimed, 'Has she killed the baby?' Upon affirming it was true, he seized his war club and struck his sister dead. He then ordered a younger sister to live with the man in her sister's place.[10] The brother's action, carried out in the open in front of the men of the band, was legal, for it carried an official sanction, an execution within the family. He would not be subject to retaliation because the only source of retaliation would have been the aggrieved relatives of his sister, and all of them had been present at the killing. This closed the matter. If she had been of another band, a much more complex process would have occurred, with envoys of one band negotiating with the other, attempting to get their sanction for the killing. If this was not done they ran the risk of beginning a cycle of revenge as her relatives avenged her death. Since most wendigo killings were carried out in secret, it was not easy to identify and punish the offenders.[11]

This execution account contains much more detail, but is not very different from the wendigo execution described by George Nelson among the Cree in 1823. The members of a hunting band observed a person in their band become a wendigo. He recognized some of the signs himself and asked that they kill him upon their first recognition of wendigo symptoms. The others left his brother behind to kill him but, because it was so hard to kill a wendigo, hid nearby to provide support. Although his brother shot him in the heart, there was no blood. The others attacked him and bound him, burning his body on a large pile of dry wood.[12] This incident highlighted a common feature of such killings: the decision to kill a wendigo was usually left to the members of the hunting band, who designated a person, usually a close relative, to carry out the execution. Reliance on a relative for the execution, as among the Ojibwa, eliminated the danger of retaliation and revenge.

Wendigo stories fascinated Euro-Canadians in the north and entered dozens of journals and logbooks. Morton I. Teicher carefully (but surely not exhaustively) lists seventy accounts, including thirty-six in the nineteenth century and ten in the twentieth: thirty among the Ojibwa, fifteen among the Saulteaux (a western branch of the Ojibwa), and nine among the Cree.[13] The people who wrote these accounts – traders, missionaries, ethnographers, officials, and travellers – lacked an understanding of the place of the wendigo in Indian society. The wendigo stories were recorded as intriguing windows into Indian life, complete with images of savagery, primitive religious beliefs, and cannibalism.

The problem with this view is that wendigos were real to Indian hunters. Although there were many dangers in the great north woods, the danger of a hunter being killed by a wendigo was particularly frightening. Not only was it a horrible death but, because Indian people lived in a rich spirit world, the dead spirit of one killed by a wendigo was not at rest. It was a killer spirit, roaming the evil world of the wendigo. Euro-Canadians dismissed this as superstition. Teicher, using a culturally biased psychological framework, termed it a 'psychosis.'[14]

The first outsiders to encounter cases of wendigo killings were HBC traders. By the mid-nineteenth century a number of these cases had surfaced and were being described in a common language that showed some degree of knowledge of indigenous tradition. While the HBC had political and legal sovereignty over its lands, it did not have any authority over crimes among Indians.[15] There were, however, exceptions. The Cree religious leader Abishabis (Small Eyes) led a messianic revival in northern Manitoba in the early 1840s. This revival, a mixture of Christianity and Cree religion, was so strong that some of its adherents did not hunt for either furs or food, leading to starvation.[16] HBC traders opposed the revival because it cut into their business. By 1843 the movement was in decline and Abishabis murdered an Indian family at York Factory, returning to Fort Severn. There he was put in irons by John Cromartie, the local HBC trader, on the complaint of local Indians that Abishabis was threatening them and they were afraid to go out hunting while he was near. He was allowed to escape in the hope that he would leave the area, but he did not, so he was put back in chains on 28 August. Two days later three Cree 'resolved to mete out their own justice' and dragged him out of confinement, killed him with an axe, burning his body 'to secure themselves against being haunted by a wendigo.'[17] It appears that Cromartie was in collusion with the Cree: Indians did not routinely break into HBC posts to release and kill prisoners.

MACHEKEQUONABE'S CASE

This case arose at Sabascon, a small reserve northeast of Lake of the Woods, among Ojibwa with little previous contact with Canadian society.[18] We know more about this case than most others because it is one of three wendigo cases that left a full transcript.[19] The trial was held at Rat Portage (now Kenora) on 3 December 1896. The entire case was based on the testimony of one man, Wasawpscopinesse, and, judging from the length of the transcript, took only a few hours.[20] The killing had occurred on the night of 11 or 12 June 1896.

A wendigo had been repeatedly seen around the camp for months, driving the people there to an increasing state of alarm. Prosecutor H. Langford examined Wasawpscopinesse on the meaning of the wendigo and the impact of his appearance on the community. Wasawpscopinesse's testimony was given through an interpreter, but still reflects his reluctance to describe the wendigo:

Langford: 'Do they believe there is more than one [wendigo]?'
Wasawpscopinesse: 'I do not know.' ...
Langford: 'What form has it?' A. 'I do not know, I never saw one. It is in the form of a man.' ...
Langford: 'You never saw a wendigo?' A. 'No.'

Langford: 'Did you know anybody who did?' A. 'Our forefathers have seen them.' ...

Langford: 'How can you tell a wendigo from a man?' A. 'I could not tell, because I have never seen any.'

Langford: 'How could you tell if you had seen one?' A. 'Sometimes it is a man that goes to work and eats other men.'

Wasawpscopinesse's testimony then went on to describe the wendigo's profound effect on the community:

Last spring it was seen around there [the camp] quite a few times. We hid every-thing, took the canoes up and hid them. Quite a while afterwards he was seen again. He was around the camp quite a long while; we were having a dance one night, and we saw him coming towards the school-house. One man followed and fired at him with shot. He shot at him twice. There was some blood on the left side of his track, in the leaves. We went the next morning and seen the blood. They fol-lowed the trail quite a piece. About half a day; they would lose it for about three steps, and then find it again. [The footsteps] were two spans long of the fingers. It was in bare feet.[21]

This testimony establishes that the community believed that it was threatened by a wendigo. Beyond this, more can be gleaned. First, it seems that Wasawpscopinesse was a reluctant witness, saying as little as he could about the community's belief in wendigos. His descriptions are sparse, even evasive. Second, part of his testimony described the shooting in the left side of a wendigo the night before Machekequonabe shot any-one. The next morning, members of the band – experienced trackers – had followed meticulously described wendigo tracks. It is impossible to say how this occurred, but it was honestly believed by Wasawpscopinesse and everyone else in the community.

Responding to this threat, the band took action. That night Macheke-quonabe was one of eight Indians placed on sentry duty around their community. These sentries, including Wasawpscopinesse and Peskawa-keequic, spaced themselves 'quite a piece' apart, at regular intervals around the community. The man who was shot, 'a tall Indian with a blan-ket over him,' 'started to run,' with both Machekequonabe and Wasawpsecopinesse chasing after him. Machekequonabe called out to him three times, but the figure did not respond. Wasawpsecopinesse con-tinued: 'I saw a flash of the gun ... He gave a war whoop, the one who was shot ... He did not fall right away, but made a circle going around back.' Machekequonabe cried on learning that he had shot his foster father, Peskawakeequic, another of the sentries.[22]

The Indian Department, perhaps surprisingly sensitive to the underlying legal issues in the case, had retained a lawyer to represent Machekequonabe, A.S. Wink of Port Arthur. Wink mounted a dull, unimaginative defence. His first questions of Wasawpscopinesse were aimed at determining whether he was a pagan or a Christian. When Langford objected that the religion of the witness did not make any difference, Wink argued that he intended to show that 'this is a form of insanity to which the whole tribe is subjected.' The judge intervened, correcting the lawyer: 'This is not insanity at all, it is superstitious belief.'[23] Wink then proceeded on his apparent belief that two shots, not one, had been fired, confusing the events of the night before with the killing at hand. Finally, he established that Machekequonabe was a pagan, a 'good Indian,' and remorseful about the killing, all facts that were legally irrelevant.[24] After Wink ceased questioning, the trial judge asked whether the tribe was a large one (another irrelevant fact), receiving an affirmative answer.[25]

We know more about Wink's defence because of documents in the case file. Two pages of handwritten notes refer to cases establishing the common law defences of mistake of fact and justification. Since these defences would apply to Machekequonabe, it appears likely that the handwriting is Wink's. The notes also accompany correspondence between Wink and the Indian Department concerning his bill and so probably were intended to show the amount of work he did in preparation for his defence. The mistake of fact and justification defences were not raised at the trial, although they were appropriate defences under the common law. In a letter to Oliver Mowat, then minister of justice in the federal government, Wink stated that he raised a kind of insanity argument with Judge John Rose, following the presentation of evidence but before the case was submitted to the jury, and that the judge would not accept it.[26] Wink's failure to raise the other issues cannot be accounted for, although, with an unsympathetic judge, it might well not have mattered.[27]

The trial court rejected the defendant's defences and convicted him of manslaughter, sparing him the death penalty for intentional murder.[28] Judge Rose, in a common practice of the day, led the jury to their verdict by asking them a series of questions. This one-sided colloquy began with Rose's assertion that 'I think we may take it for granted that the prisoner did kill the Indian' and extended through 'his appearance in the box indicates not only sanity, but intelligence.' Rose concluded: 'I think I must direct you, as a matter of law, that there is no justification here for the killing, and culpable homicide without justification is manslaughter...'[29] Rose balanced the harshness of his judgment with a lenient sentence, six months in jail.[30]

The Indian Department, recognizing that the case had important implications in Indian administration, financed an appeal.[31] In divisional court Machekequonabe's new lawyer, J.K. Kerr, argued the common law defence of reasonable mistake of fact.[32] The court refused to look beyond the narrow question of whether there was adequate evidence to support the jury verdict, ignoring the question of law posed by the defense, an issue that the judge withheld from the jury in his instructions. The verdict was upheld in a seven line opinion.[33] This opinion is among the shortest of any in an Ontario criminal appeal of that time: the court did not address the important underlying issues of Indian policy or criminal law. Many Canadians, while defending broad criminal jurisdiction over Indians, were troubled by the case's failure to take any cognizance of the subjective fear of an Ojibwa band of the wendigo. The transcript paints a vivid picture of a community of Indians apprehending real danger. The intricate cultural world of the Ojibwa found no recognition in Ontario courts.

A string of wendigo cases followed in central Canada leading to parallel results, although none ever again went up on appeal. What were the goals of Canadian justice in such cases? There is direct evidence on this point in the case of *Rex* v. *Tushwegeh*, another Ojibwa murder case from northwestern Ontario.[34] Tushwegeh, for unknown reasons but with facts quite indicative of a wendigo killing, strangled Geeshingoose, his brother-in-law, in their camp at Cat Lake. Upon hearing of the crime, a police constable was sent to Cat Lake to gather evidence. Although he completed his investigation, this constable died of natural causes before his evidence could be given, raising the issue of whether another officer should be sent to reinvestigate the case in another attempt to try Tushwegeh. Ontario Department of Justice officials were reluctant to proceed with 'such a doubtful case,' now two years old.

The Indian Department, however, took a different view and, through the Canadian Department of Justice, prevailed on Ontario officials. It was 'important that this Indian be put on trial even though prospects of seeing conviction are extremely weak, as it is necessary that the Indians should understand they are within reach of the strong arm of the law.'[35] Tushwegeh was brought out of the wilderness in November of 1905, too late in the year to call witnesses so that a trial could be held. He was held in jail all winter and tried at Kenora in the summer of 1906. He was acquitted, for the evidence was inadequate. Nevertheless, the criminal law had served its purpose: Tushwegeh, although acquitted, had served as much time in jail as Machekequonabe had been sentenced to. It had extended the power of the Canadian state to the farthest reaches of the country.[36] The law could be used to control and socialize Indians, a powerful instrument to force assimilation. This goal was perhaps more important than the promotion of justice through convictions and prison sentences: the First Nations must defer to the power of Canadian law.[37]

PAYOO AND NAPAYSOOSEE

The Queen v. *Payoo and Napaysoosee* was tried twice, once at Fort Saskatchewan and again at Edmonton, about 1900. Although the case went unreported, one of the lawyers thought it of ethnographic interest and preserved a record.[38]

A band of thirty-two Cree was camped near Little Slave Lake in northern Alberta in the winter of 1898–9. Moostoos, one of the adult men, convinced the others that he was about to become a wendigo and would first kill his children and then 'clean out' everybody else unless his friends killed him first. Eliza, the first witness called, gave a graphic account of the killing. She testified that, while praying, Napaysoosee, Chuckachuck, and herself held one of Moostoos's legs while Mayasksaysis held the other. Moostoos, during this time, was saying: 'You will all die tonight if you don't kill me first.' Payoo then struck Moostoos with an axe. Eliza, perhaps incredibly, remembered nothing else, no other details at all.[39]

Most of the band was called to testify, providing a view of the group mentality behind the killing, although a view that was distorted by the band in order to protect some of their people. Entominahoo, a medicine man and the leader of the band,[40] testified that Chuckachuck killed Moostoos, and that Napaysoosee gave him a second blow, followed by Payoo, not immediately but after a little time. Then, because wendigos often rise after death, they staked his body down with trap chains and moved their camp far out of the area.[41] Marie added that Chuckachuck struck Moostoos with an axe as well, although he was already dead.[42] Napaysoosee testified that Moostoos had refused to eat that day and acted like he had never acted before. He got worse as the day progressed, threatening people and biting them. Napaysoosee claimed to have struck him in the side with an axe, although not hard, and only after 'his brother in law' had hit him in the head.[43] He put the band's actions in a self-defence context: 'The reason we struck him was because he had threatened to kill us all. It was to save our lives. We were all foolish with fear.' Later, he cut off Moostoos's head so that he couldn't come back. Napaysoosee also differed in his account of the actual killing, saying that Chuckachuck had been handed the axe by Eliza, but that he did not see which of them actually struck Moostoos in the head.[44]

Payoo confirmed Napaysoosee's account, denying that he had struck Moostoos with an axe, and accusing the others of lying: 'They are lying when they say I struck the first blow. They are all related to one another, and I am alone among them. When I went in he was dead and no one was holding him.' Payoo further claimed that he recognized the axe as Eliza's and the knife as Napaysoosee's. He also claimed that Napaysoosee, Chuckachuck, Entominahoo, and Mihkooshtikwahnis were all medicine men and that 'the medicine men always help one another. It is a rule of their order.'[45] Kunuksoos, father-in-law of Moostoos, testified that 'Chuckachuck struck first. Napaysoosee second. Payoo third blow. The first blow killed him, but he was moving until after the third.'[46]

Napasoosee was recalled and repeated his claim that Chuckachuck had given Moostoos the first blow and that Moostoos had 'never moved' after that blow. Then, according to Napasoosee, Chuckachuck taunted him: 'You are a coward if you do not strike him, we will all be killed.' Chuckachuck gave him a knife and somebody else gave him an axe. Napasoosee then hit Moostoos with the axe and drove the knife into his bowels.[47] Payoo, also recalled, claimed that he was outside the house while the first two blows were struck and had no idea who struck them. When he entered the house he was handed weapons and told to strike Moostoos. 'I took an axe and struck. I thought on the body but it seems it was on the head. I felt afraid. I was thinking about my children.'[48]

After four hours of deliberation the jury convicted Napasoosee of manslaughter but acquitted Payoo.[49] The case is important because it is one of the rare cases involving Indians where there was a substantial difference in the testimony: different people within the band constructed mutually exclusive versions of the facts, which necessarily means that some people lied. Most of the evidence pointed to Chuckachuck as the killer for he seems to have struck Moostoos in the head with an axe before any of the others, leaving him unconscious, perhaps even dead. For reasons that cannot be determined, Chuckachuck was not even charged. Entominahoo, a medicine man, was present throughout the killing and was probably in control of the actions of Chuckachuck and Napaysoosee, but he, too, was not charged.

The jury sorted out the partially contradictory testimony of nine people and, for reasons that are not clear, decided that the testimony of Payoo and Chuckachuck was more credible than that of Napaysoosee. According to all the testimony, the central motivation behind the crime was self-defence. However, it was not a reasonable exercise of self-defence under Canadian law because the cultural world of the Cree was not legally recognized. Judge Charles Rouleau, deciding that some punishment was necessary, sentenced Napaysoosee to two months' imprisonment. Fifteen years before, this same judge had brought in death sentences at Battleford for murder, but in the context of the Northwest Rebellion.[50]

Napaysoosee's punishment seems unfair: the killing of Moostoos was done by the entire band, probably decided on by Entominahoo, and carried out with Chuckachuck, Napaysoosee, and Payoo each striking blows with an axe, while at least four others held Moostoos, a strong man, down. It seems that the band had manufactured a story that, while partially accurate in describing the wendigo killing, protected the core of their leadership, deflecting responsibility to Payoo and Napaysoosee, less important individuals. The contradictions in testimony follow from keeping so many people in agreement on the details of a false story, as well as from the reluctance of Napaysoosee and Payoo to volunteer themselves for imprisonment. Most often these schemes probably worked because, as can be seen here, Canadian law was often satisfied with any reasonable explanation that satisfied the symbolic functions of justice, providing some punishment and advancing Canadian hegemony over First Nations law.[51]

JACK AND JOSEPH FIDDLER

The most detailed trial transcript of a wendigo case involved Joseph Fiddler, a leader of the Sucker band of the Saulteaux on the Upper Bay River in northeastern Manitoba. Fiddler was tried at Norway House in 1906, convicted of murder, and sentenced to death for the killing of Wasakapequay, an old woman who had been delirious for days, to prevent her from becoming a wendigo.[52] The case received a considerable amount of attention at the time, ending in a popular letter-writing campaign to spare Fiddler's life.[53] His sentence was commuted to life just before he died in Stony Mountain Prison after serving eighteen months.[54] Tragically, his death occurred just as the government decided to pardon him and send him home.[55]

Fiddler's case came to the attention of the North-West Mounted Police (NWMP) in much the same way other wendigo killings did. The killings were important events in Saulteaux life and people talked about them. William Campbell, an HBC trader at Island Lake, stopped in at Norway House on the way back to his post from a visit to Winnipeg. Trading stories with Sergeant Daisy Smith of the NWMP, he revealed that he had heard of killings among the Sucker band seven years before. Perhaps unintended by Campbell, Smith reported the talk to his superiors: 'At Sandy Lake, about three days travel from Island Lake, there is a band of pagan Indians and it is generally believed that these people are in the habit of killing one another whenever one gets delirious through fever or other causes. They are very superstitious and ... they kill through superstitious belief not through malice. But from the information I have obtained, I cannot get but one case that there is proof of, and that Mr. Campbell gave me, but it transpired seven years ago.'[56] Headquarters ordered Smith to 'have a patrol made to Sandy Lake ... and fully investigate the rumor as to the alleged homicides amongst the Indians.'[57]

A patrol led by Constable O'Neil, after a stay at Island Lake, moved on to Narrows Lake, where they found Robert and Adam Fiddler, sons of Jack. They agreed that the band would come to hold a council with the officer as soon as the ice melted, making canoe travel possible.[58] The Sucker band was delayed, but members of the Crane band arrived. They were questioned by O'Neil, and one of them, Norman Rae, admitted that Jack and Joseph Fiddler had killed a wendigo the previous fall. Although part of the Sucker band came in the next day, Jack and Joseph were not with them, inducing the Mounties to follow the band members back to their camp on Caribou Lake. There they found Jack Fiddler and others building birchbark canoes. The policemen waited for two days until Joseph came and then called both men into the NWMP camp, 'explaining to them the crime they had committed, and that they must come ... to Norway House.' They were also cautioned not to speak to anyone about the murder.'[59] After the band discussed the option of killing the policemen, they agreed to let Jack and Joseph go to Norway House. The group (now including Angus Rae, son-in-law of Jack Fiddler, who, the Mounties had discovered, was a witness to the killing) left later that day.[60]

They returned to Sandy Lake to hold the long-delayed council. The policemen informed the Indians gathered there that they must follow Canadian law. Sucker bandmen cried openly when they were told that Jack and Joseph Fiddler were being taken to Norway House for trial. However, the NWMP's goals were much broader. Robert Fiddler was told that he would have to get rid of two of his three wives. The Indians raised a question about being forced to trade with the HBC but stopped talking when the policemen asked for the names of the traders who had threatened them. Finally, the band expressed their desire for a treaty, a reflection, perhaps, of the hardships they were then facing as a result of declining fur prices and the increasing scarcity of game. The NWMP promised that they would report this matter to Ottawa.[61] Then the policemen left for Norway House, with the two Fiddlers and two Raes in custody.

There, after a brief preliminary examination based on the testimony of Angus Rae, the two were held over for trial on murder charges.[62] This decision was troubling because the band had no exposure to Canadian law. The summer passed without any action on the part of Canadian authorities to arrange the trial. This may have been due to confusion on how to proceed, for on 15 September NWMP Superintendent C.E. Saunders wrote to the assistant commissioner in Regina urging that the charges be dropped and the Fiddlers sent home. Saunders based this assessment on his judgment that there was a 'lack of evidence'; however, since Rae's eyewitness testimony was sufficient, it appears that Saunders's position was inspired more by humanitarian or policy considerations. A practical concern was that unless the men were released by mid-September, they would be unable to return home because of winter.[63] Still, there was no decision from Regina, and on 30 September Jack Fiddler fled into the woods. He was found a few hours later, having hanged himself.[64]

The trial of Joseph Fiddler began a week later. Following a custom later common to Canadian justice, the court travelled to Norway House to conduct the trial. Dating back to the *Speedy* incident, this was designed to impress the Indians of the frontier with the majesty of Canadian law, an advantage thought to be lost by the more efficient option of taking the Indian defendant to a court far out of his home country. The trial process was unfair. Commissioner Aylesworth Bowen Perry of the NWMP, the man who had made all of the policy decisions leading to the arrest and indictment, served as judge, in his capacity as a stipendiary magistrate of the North-West Territories. The crown prosecutor, D.W. McKerchar, was a Liberal; he faced no opposing counsel because Canadian law did not require a defence counsel, even for an Indian who did not speak English and was charged with a capital offence. The Indian Department sent an 'observer,' C. Crompton Calverley. Canadian authorities, who had provided a lawyer for Machekequonabe only six years before, may have already intended a more severe outcome. Other policemen served as court functionaries, and a jury was found in the vicinity of Norway House.[65]

The first witness, NWMP constable William J. Cashman, testified to the circumstances of the arrest but was then asked if any white people lived among the Sucker band to instruct them in the law. Cashman responded that, although none lived in the immediate area, two whites, a trader and a mission schoolteacher, lived at Island Lake, two hundred miles away by river.[66]

Norman Rae (Pesequan) however, provided the core of the government's case. The woman killed was Wahsakapeequay, the daughter-in-law of Joseph Fiddler, the wife of his son, Thomas. Wahsakapeequay was delirious and, at some point, was laid out on a cotton cloth, held down by John and Norman Rae, and strangled with a cord by Jack and Joseph.[67] Prosecutor McKerchar asked Rae whether this execution carried out a law of the band: he answered that it did.[68]

Angus Rae followed Norman to the stand. After giving the same version of the killing, McKerchar's questions ventured farther into Saulteaux culture. Angus was asked if he had objected to the killing. When he responded in the negative, he was asked if a member of the band was bound to obey the 'ogema,' or leader, Jack Fiddler. 'Yes,' responded Angus, 'If the ogema tells me to do a thing I must do it.' When pressed if something would happen to him if he refused, Angus testified that harm would come to him, although he did not know from what source or what kind of harm.[69] Angus also provided the motivation for the killing, testifying that people who died delusionally came back as wendigos, killing and eating people, and so had to be killed to prevent this transformation.[70]

Then, perhaps by surprise, Angus Rae disclosed a history of wendigo killings in the Sucker band. There had been others: David Meekis, also delerious, had been killed and his body burned by Joseph Fiddler, James Meekis, Joseph Meekis, and Elias Rae.[71] Years before Angus had seen Askamekeseecowiniew burned as well, killed by James Meekis, Lucas Meekis, Joseph Meekis, and John Rae.[72] When asked if the ogema, Jack Fiddler, had given any reason for killing these people, Angus Rae responded that 'when they are sick and so long in misery they put them out of their misery.'[73]

McKerchar continued to follow the same line of questioning but did not shake Angus Rae on this point. Finally, he asked directly: 'Did you ever hear the ogema say that anyone who died out of his mind turned into a cannibal?' Rae responded, 'Yes, that is what the ogema says.'[74] Rae was reluctant to state that the band was afraid that the woman would come back as a cannibal and kill people and only did so after prompting by the crown attorney.

At the very end of Angus Rae's, testimony the crown attorney asked him if others were sick at this time. Incredibly, Rae testified that a man, Menewaseum, had been sick shortly after the woman. As Angus Rae walked past a wigwam he was handed a piece of string and told to pull it. 'Only then I knew that I had strangled a man.' Jack Fiddler was holding the other end of the string, but Angus did not know that until Joseph Fiddler told him.[75] Here it has to be obvious that Angus Rae's testimony cannot be true. The physical act of strangulation takes a number of minutes, requires great force, and provokes a strong response from the victim. The walls of a wigwam are not thick or soundproof: you cannot be ignorant of the struggle of a strangling man inside a wigwam, nor of the identity of another man holding another end of a rope only a few feet away. Even crown prosecutor McKerchar was skeptical, asking, 'Why, when you were asked before did you not tell us about this other man being killed this way?' Angus Rae responded, again incredibly, that he was 'leaving this till last because they were Crane tribes.'[76]

The other killings had nothing to do with Fiddler's trial and were prejudicial to his case. Beyond this, they raise important ethnographic questions about the motivation of Angus Rae and Indian witnesses in such cases generally. It is impossible to know Rae's motivations for testifying against Fiddler. He may have been afraid, but he may also have perceived that he had something to gain in terms of band leadershp. He also faced potential murder charges: the promise that he would be sent home if he cooperated may explain his testimony. While parts of his testimony were probably true, other parts were false. As in the other wendigo cases, his testimony reveals that many people in the band were involved in the killings.

The trial consumed all of one day, ending with the testimony of an Ojibwa missionary, the Reverend Paul Paupanakiss, who testified that he knew nothing about the wendigo phenomenon, testimony that must also have been false. At six, the court adjourned for dinner, and then at seven Joseph Fiddler was asked if he wanted to take the stand. He declined but asked that Crompton Calverley speak for him. Calverley gave a short speech defending Fiddler's actions on the ground that they followed tribal custom. Prosecutor McKerchar spoke briefly to the jury, asking for a conviction.[77]

Commissioner Perry then instructed the jury that, if they believed the evidence in the case that Mrs Thomas Fiddler was killed by the accused, then they must find Joseph Fiddler guilty of murder. Once this guilt of murder was established, it was up to the accused to reduce the crime to justifiable homicide or manslaughter. Like Judge Rose, Perry interjected his own views into the charge:

Was he justified in killing her because she might have turned into a cannibal? This might possibly be urged as a defence. The tribe was ignorant of the law of the land. We questioned both witnesses as to that and the impression left on my mind is that they do know what the law forbids ... As to the question of pagan belief, if you find that the accused is justified in killing because of his pagan belief where will it land us if we accept such a belief. What the law forbids no pagan belief can justify. The law says: 'Thou shalt not kill.'[78]

Perhaps more disturbingly, Perry, in his charge to the jury, denied that Joseph Fiddler had been acting according to Saulteaux law, a critical issue in the case. 'To my mind the evidence is not clear on the customs of the Sucker tribe.'[79] Perry cited the testimony of the Reverend Paupanakiss denying knowledge of the custom of killing wendigos, as well as Angus Rae's testimony that he knew only what Jack Fiddler had told him about wendigos.[80] If this evidence of customary law was deficient it was because Fiddler did not offer a defence, something he could have done only with a lawyer. The effort of the crown to deny that any customary law existed relative to wendigos was a part of the Crown's purpose to get a death sentence for the Fiddlers by denying the existence of any mitigating factors.

The jury was confused and came back asking for two legal definitions: guilt of manslaughter and death from the result of self-defence. Self-defence was defined as resulting from an immediate danger, manslaughter as a killing from a loss of self-control. The jury also wanted to ask more questions of the Raes concerning how the woman got into the wigwam, but the judge denied this request. The jury reported that it was deadlocked, but it was ordered to retire again to consider the verdict. The jury then convicted of murder, with a recommendation of mercy.[81] Under existing Canadian law, the death penalty was the only punishment for murder, and so Perry sentenced Fiddler to death.[82]

This result can be analysed in narrow legal terms as well as in broader political ones. From a strictly legal standpoint, as long as the burden fell to the defendant to prove some mitigation or defence after the crown had proven an intentional killing, Fiddler's failure to offer a defence was necessarily fatal. Perry's statement of the law in this respect was correct, although, given that he knew the defendant did not have a lawyer, he had more of a duty to charge the jury on both manslaughter and on self-defence and common law justification. His charges were inadequate in the context and determined the outcome of the jury's deliberations.

In terms of the Indian policy of the Canadian government, this was a period of a 'get tough' policy aimed at Indians who followed traditional law in violation of Canadian law. The Indian Department was embarrassed by the continued adherence of Indians to traditional customs into the twentieth century and was rethinking the policy of 'lenience' which had produced short sentences in earlier cases of this type. The government of Canada wanted to make an example out of Joseph Fiddler.[83]

But it did not want to hang him. Commissioner Perry, two weeks after obtaining Fiddler's conviction, wrote to the minister of justice in Ottawa urging a commutation of his sentence. Perry gave Ottawa a view of Saulteaux customary law opposite to that he had given the jury: 'He believed, however, that insane persons were dangerous to the well being of his tribe and that unless they were strangled they would turn into cannibals ... It is clear that it has been the custom of the tribe from time immemorial to put to death members of their band, and other bands, who were thought by them to be insane or incurable.'[84]

Joseph was transferred to the infirmary of the Stony Mountain Prison in January 1908. NWMP Inspector Pelletier and Constable Cashman took Angus Rae back to the Sucker band, arriving at Narrows Lake in February. Pelletier used the occasion to lecture the Saulteaux, using a HBC trader as an interpreter. He spoke for about two hours, explaining the law. He characterized the Sucker band as 'the worst band in the district, murderers, liars, and very crooked.'[85] He threatened to appoint a new chief if the band did not change its ways. He reminded them that just because they lived in isolation did not mean that the government did not hear what was going on.[86] Angus Rae, who had spent eight months imprisoned with the Fiddlers, lived in fear. He dug a cellar under his lodging so that he could escape if the police ever came after him again.[87]

There followed a popular effort to free Fiddler, led by HBC traders and others at Norway House, including three of the six jurors.[88] The government was divided on the issue, with the Indian Department urging Fiddler's release. However, the Department of Justice, while favouring eventual release, took the position that he needed to serve more time. Perry was particularly adamant that Fiddler not be released too soon; in this, he was probably motivated by the belief that if Indians were released from prison after serving only short terms, others in their tribes would not acquire sufficient fear of Canadian law.[89] Fiddler plead for his own life with a petition to the minister of justice: 'I desire to ask you not to look upon me as a common murderer. I was the Chief of my tribe, we had much sickness, and the sick ones were getting bad spirits and their friends were afraid of them ... If you let me go back to my place I will teach my family and people the white man's law. I am sick now and can't walk, but I think I will live if you let me go home. I will tell them how the white man lives. I wish you to consider that I am a poor Indian and don't know anything.'[90]

Fiddler, a chief, was reduced through his imprisonment to depression and to begging for his freedom. The government's lack of decision on the issue led to a tragic conclusion. The season for travel was ending, and the government was aware that Fiddler was very sick. On 4 September the governor general ordered his immediate release from Stony Mountain Prison, but Fiddler had died on 1 September.[91]

PAUL SABOURIN

In wendigo cases, it appears that Indians generally did not talk to the police about the crimes. When they did, various levels of distortion permeated their stories. The case of Paul Sabourin, a Slave Indian from the North-West Territories, illustrates this.

The facts are deceptively simple, belying the cultural complexity of these cases. In the encampment of a hunting band in the spring of 1899, four men and four women were in a tent when Joseph Sabourin told Charles Martel to go out and shoot a sick dog. Martel answered that he would do it but needed to find his shoes first. Paul Sabourin then said, 'I will shoot the dog myself if you don't do it.' He went outside and the others heard a shot. Paul came back into the tent, took a blanket, and lay down. The others went outside and found Josephine Laudry shot in the back of the head. According to the testimony of Michel Lefoin, another Slave Indian in the camp, Sabourin never spoke to anyone in the band about the killing, and no one had any idea why he did it.[92]

The testimony of Lefoin, followed by Charles Martel, provide a great deal of detail about the event but no direct evidence of the reasons for the killing. Both testified that Paul Sabourin was given to preaching the word of God but only occasionally and in generalities. The victim had stopped sleeping in a tent and, incredibly, was sleeping outside – impossible in March and April in the North-west Territories – again with no reason given. She had previously been sleeping in a second tent with her husband and two other couples but had moved outside. Her husband and another man were away hunting when she was killed.[93]

Sabourin was represented by a lawyer, H.C. Taylor, appointed by the court to defend him. Taylor cross-examined both witnesses but appears to have lacked any theory of a defence. The jury, after a short deliberation, convicted Sabourin of murder. Asked if he had anything to say before sentence was passed, he admitted the killing but claimed that he 'had not my mind to myself.'[94] He was sentenced to death by Judge Charles-Borromée Rouleau, the same judge who had presided at the Battleford trials and the trials of the killers of Moostoos. Both Judge Rouleau and the crown prosecutor, N.D. Beck, urged that the sentence be commuted to life because of the mental condition of the prisoner.[95] Others petitioned for commutation as well and Sabourin's sentence was commuted to life.[96] He died of consumption in Stony Mountain Prison on 20 November 1902.[97]

The Indian Department interceded with the Department of Justice on Sabourin's behalf and arranged the commutation for explicitly stated policy grounds. Rarely do we have such an explicit statement of policy underlying a criminal case. James Smart, deputy superintendent of Indian affairs, wrote the minister of justice:

I have the honour to draw attention to the fact that the accused was from Great Slave Lake, a section of the country inhabited by Indians with whom no Treaty has as yet been made and which is not yet in touch with civilization, and that he can therefore hardly be regarded otherwise than as an untutored savage ...

I submit for your consideration the impossibility of judging only by the white man's methods, the conduct of a savage governed by superstitions and whose habits are entirely opposed to those of civilization ... the enforcement of the extreme penalty might create an impression, amongst the Indians with whom the accused is connected, that contact with civilization imperiled their existence. Such an impression would defeat the object, recognized by the Indian Act and the provision made by Parliament from time to time for the Indians, namely gradually to inculcate in them habits of thought similar to those of the white population in this country. As a first step in this direction it may be necessary in the most remote future to negotiate a Treaty with the Indians of Great Slave Lake; and it would be unfortunate if these people were found then to hold the view that the white man's justice was without mercy and without consideration of their ignorance and general condition ...

... I have the honour to ask your consideration of the question whether the interests of justice would not be best served by treatment of an Indian unacquainted with civilization in a manner no more severe than would be accorded a child below the age of fourteen years, concerning whom there is a prima facie presumption that he does not understand the nature and consequences of his act. Even the most highly educated Indian until enfranchised is subject to civil disabilities though capable of crime. Whatever his actual age he is still an infant in the eyes of the law; and in view of the wide distinction between him and an Indian of the class of the accused it appears to be a matter fairly open to question whether the latter should be considered more responsible for his actions than a child of the age mentioned.[98]

Smart's policy statement demonstrates, in the negotiating of Treaty 8, it was necessary to convey an impression of the humanity of Canadian justice. The statement is also noteworthy for its direct assertion that an Indian was a child and should be punished as such. While this view underlay much of Canadian Indian policy, it was never explicitly stated in a criminal context. In any event, Indians were not, in fact, punished as children: by 1900 there were many Indians in Stony Mountain Prison.

The testimony of the two witnesses in this case is unbelievable and it is obvious that they were covering up a series of events that had occurred in the band. It is impossible that no one in the band had 'any idea' why Sabourin shot Josephine Laudry. Obviously, it could have been for a number of reasons, including some kind of sexual jealousy, as well as insanity. Superimposed on this case, however, are facts that make it look like a wendigo killing that was deliberately covered up. Josephine was isolated from the rest of the group, sleeping outside near the campfire rather than in either of two tents. The original order to shoot the 'sick dog' came not from Paul Sabourin, but from his brother Joseph Sabourin. The 'sick dog' then disappears from the testimony. Finally, the complete denial of any knowledge of any reason for the crime reveals a cover-up. A fight or sexual jealousy would have been easy to testify to had they occurred. Paul Sabourin would not defend himself beyond the statement that 'he was not in his own mind' when he did it. A more reasonable explanation is that the group decided to kill the woman as a wendigo and, for whatever reason, Paul was selected, or agreed, to take responsibility for the deed in order to protect others, including his brother Joseph.

CONCLUSION

The wendigo trials partly can be understood as an exercise in legal imperialism, the extent to which Canadian authorities would go to impose their law on the First Nations. These trials occurred at the margins of

Canadian political and legal authority. All of these bands, however, had been in a trading relationship with the HBC for over a hundred years. The power of Canadian authorities could not be more strongly expressed than with the death penalty, almost always reprieved in intra-Indian cases.

Yet such an analysis alone is unsatisfactory. The wendigo trials also provide a window into the legal world of Cree, Saulteaux, and Ojibwa communities on the frontier at the turn of the century. Traditional law and traditional sorcery were still intact in Indian communities. They were closely interlinked in the world-views of the Indians of the great north woods. Premature and violent death was common and the line between a murder and a death by 'natural causes' was not obvious in Ojibwa and Cree culture. The traditional legal orders of these societies provided mechanisms designed to let small hunting bands make difficult legal decisions involving life and death.

The fact that the wendigo killings were legal under First Nations law undoubtedly made it easier for the NWMP to 'solve' the crimes: they simply arrested the band members who were responsible for carrying out traditional law in the execution of wendigos. While, as in the case of the Fiddlers, this might involve actual band leaders, more often it appears to have involved the young men selected by band leadership to carry out the killings. The killings came to the attention of authorities because they were not hidden. They were common knowledge and people talked about them. Word passed from band to band until it reached the authorities probably, as in the Fiddler case, through traders. Once the police went to remote communities, always accompanied by interpreters, to ask about those killings, they often found witnesses. The NWMP carried a great deal of coercive power with them, including the power to arrest even the witnesses and take them from their communities to far-off guardhouses for months at a time.

The power of the police, however, had its limits. It seems likely that most of the witnesses' stories were partial truths, manufactured with a definite goal in mind. Some of these stories were also probably false. Often the stories seemed designed to protect some people at the expense of others, perhaps reflecting family loyalties or band hierarchy. Often, too, witnesses seemed intent on defending the wendigo tradition and tribal culture. Traditional healers or medicine men were deeply involved in these events, and their involvement did not often emerge at trial.

Protecting that culture took the full energy of traditionalists because there were few areas of First Nations law more at odds with Canadian law than the wendigo killings. Not only were these killings beyond the reach of Canadian law, but the traditional reasons for them defied the moral sensibilities of Euro-Canadians. A world of evil spirits in the forest that would kill you if you did not kill them first made complete sense to Ojibwa and Cree Indians; it made no sense at all to whites.

Canadian law might have accommodated the tribes by attempting to incorporate the honestly held beliefs of Indians into the traditional common law defences. However, this was beyond colonial jurisprudence.[99] The wendigo killings raised policy issues that Canadian authorities did not want raised. It might have been argued that to recognize a wendigo killing as the reasonable exercise of self-defence would have encouraged the continuation of the practice rather than have permitted justice in individual cases. Nothing in Canadian Indian law was concerned with justice in individual cases: greater policy goals coloured the issue. The royal prerogative of the pardon or commutation was not unaffected by the scope of this policy, but it was more removed from it. By the late nineteenth century, most convicted murderers were having their sentences commuted, and there was no reason why Indians should be any different. There were important cultural differences, however, in the meaning of imprisonment. There was no parallel in Indian society for transportation to Stony Mountain Prison and being locked up in a small cell. Many Indians died in prison, even during short sentences. Few lived long lives after release. For them, even a short prison term was often a death sentence.

11

'No Recognized Law': Canadian Law and the Prairie Indians

The settlement of the prairies occurred after Confederation, and therefore only in the prairie provinces (and, later, in the north) was there a 'Canadian' Indian policy as opposed to the various colonial policies of Ontario, Quebec, Atlantic Canada, and British Columbia. The dominion Indian policy applied on the prairies was Ontarian: the tribes were to cede their lands to Canada through treaties, be settled on small reserves, and find a place in the broader Canadian society as small farmers.[1] This Indian policy, a political matter, was to be implemented within a legal framework. The law was to precede settlement, with the North-West Mounted Police, led by officers who were appointed as stipendiary magistrates (even though only a few were lawyers), central to this process.[2] The process was begun with Treaty 1, the 'Stone Fort' Treaty negotiated at Lake Winnipeg. Alexander Morris, lieutenant governor of Manitoba and the North-West Territories and former chief justice of Manitoba, was sent farther west to negotiate treaties 4, 5, and 6, complex and detailed legal documents in which the Indian nations sold their lands to the Canadian government.[3] David Laird succeeded Morris as lieutenant govenor of the North-West Territories and negotiated Treaty 7.[4]

This treaty-making process degenerated into oppression, land theft, and starvation. The Northwest Rebellion of 1885 included isolated acts of violence by Indians on the North Saskatchewan River, that, in the racially charged environment of the time, led to the myth that there was also an Indian rebellion.[5] The Indians bore the brunt of the repression that followed. Dozens of warriors and a handful of Metis were tried on various charges, including Cree chief One Arrow on a charge of treason. His indictment was read in a Regina courtroom in both English and Cree. In English it read that he, 'together with divers and other evil disposed persons ... armed and arrayed in a warlike manner, that is to say with guns, rifles, pistols, bayonets and other weapons, being then wickedly and feloniously assembled and gathered together against our said Lady the Queen, most wickedly and felonious did levy and make war against our said Lady the Queen ... and against the peace of our said Lady the Queen, her Crown and dignity.' One Arrow heard the indictment translated into Cree as an accusation that he had 'knocked off the Queen's bonnet' and 'stabbed her in the behind with his sword.' First confused, then enraged, he demanded to know if the interpreter was drunk. He had never even met the Queen.[6]

This literal translation of the indictments was evidently the practice in all of the trials. Big Bear, a Cree chief, was confused by the reading of his indictment and denied its charges: 'These people all lie. They are saying that I tried to steal the Great Mother's hat, how could I do that? She lives very far across the Great Water, and how could I go there to steal her hat? I didn't want her hat, and didn't know that she had one.'[7]

These incidents describe as well as any other both the comedy and tragedy of the imposition of British and Canadian law on the prairie Indian nations. The Canadian law of treason had no meaning at all for speakers of the Cree language and could not be translated. A crown, after all, really is only a hat. Why does a hat need land? How can a hat own the land? And why would a powerful Cree chief stab a lady he had never met in the behind with a bayonet? Moreover, even if all of this had made sense to Cree, Assiniboine, and Dakota held in irons, the English law of treason punishes only those who owe allegiance to the English crown and instead intentionally turn against it.[8]

The 'sale' of Hudson's Bay Company rights in western Canada to the dominion in 1869 for £300,000 had brought two fully functioning legal systems together on the Canadian prairies, Anglo-Canadian and native. Unlike the situation in Ontario in the 1780s, when the Six Nations were unable to understand their inferior legal status because nothing in their experience or history prepared them for it, the native people on the prairies were alert to the Canadian history of dishonesty and avariciousness in their dealings with Indians. The 'sale' of HBC lands to Canada infuriated the native people living there: it was they, not the company, who owned those lands.[9] Native people were explicit about their ownership of the land. The immediate impetus for a hurried signing of Treaty 6 was Chief Poundmaker's blocking of progress on telegraph lines near Battleford: lines could not be strung across Cree lands without a treaty.[10] The impending pressure of settlement and plans for a trans-Canada railroad were much of the impetus for Treaty 7.[11]

This aspect of the treaty process, the treaties' recognition of aboriginal rights, is central to any modern Canadian understanding of Indian law. It is important to recognize that Indian nations had clear reasons for negotiating treaties with the crown and brought their own agendas to the treaty negotiations. Not all of these reasons were legal reasons, but many were. Poundmaker's insistence that the telegraph not cross Cree lands without a treaty involves, for example, a demand that the crown acknowledge both Cree ownership of the land and their sovereignty as a nation by a payment for crossing the land with telegraph wires. The ceremonial and political functions of the treaty-making process were also important to native people, a recognition of their status as nations.[12]

THE NWMP AND THE MYTH OF THE LEGALLY STRUCTURED FRONTIER

The North-West Mounted Police was created in 1873, before the signing of treaties 3 through 7, and were a key element of the Dominion government's strategy of settling the frontier in an orderly way. While the contribution of the NWMP to the Canadian national culture is enormous, with the familiar red uniform of the 'Mounties' recognized around the world, it is important to dissect the legal portions of the NWMP's mythology, the myth that the Canadian frontier was peaceably settled because the NWMP was there, providing law and order.[13]

Any legal history involving the NWMP needs to begin with a recognition that the force was far more than a national police force, directed from Ottawa expressly so that it was not responsive to local pressures from settlers or Indians. It was a self-contained legal institution organized on a quasi-military model: Mounties arrested, prosecuted, judged, and jailed offenders under their jurisdiction. The commissioner and assistant commissioners were appointed stipendiary magistrates, with full judicial power extending even to capital crimes. Inspectors and captains were appointed justices of the peace, with authority to try minor crimes summarily.[14] This legal function was not incidental to the force but was rather at its core. Although military experience dominated, some NWMP officers were legally trained. James F. Macleod, assistant commissioner in the early 1870s and then its second commissioner from 1876 to 1880, articled in the law offices of Alexander Campbell, a member of John A. Macdonald's cabinet and former law partner of the prime minister.[15]

A popular explanation for this extra-ordinary delegation of judicial power over a civilian population is that it reflected a Canadian determination to avoid the American experience of trouble with Indians caused by settlers; another explanation holds that the NWMP was created to push American hunters, trappers, and whisky traders back across the border, thereby fending off the continued American threat to Canadian sovereignty in the west. A Canadian-centred explanation, however, more reflects what actually occurred on the frontier. The dominion government, taken unaware by the objections of the Saulteaux to Treaty 3 (and also familiar with United States Indian wars), both feared and perhaps even expected that the plains Indians would resist settlement. Accordingly, it created the NWMP both to protect settlers and to implement the Ontarian Indian policy of settling the Indians as farmers on small reserves.[16] Any kind of military force could have asserted Canadian sovereignty in the west, as had already been proved in the suppression of the Red River resistance of 1869–70. But only a federal police force could bring the Indians and Metis within the reach of Canadian law.[17] In any case, the question of the origins of the force is irrelevant: the issue here is the legal impact of the NWMP on the Indian nations.

The most salient single fact in NWMP history is the story of its immediately favourable reception by the western tribes. This appears to have been because the tribes, each for its own reason weary of the chaotic state of social relations on the frontier, embraced a conception of the NWMP as the immediate representative of the Queen, led by highly visible officers who were 'in charge' and able to make decisions and take limited, but appropriate, actions consistent with those decisions. These officers led their own parties of armed, red coated 'warriors', who roamed the prairies, carrying out the Queen's business. This structure was familiar to the tribes, and was compatible with their own traditional forms of meeting and face-to-face negotiation.[18]

The Hudson's Bay Company, although by the nineteenth century operating a substantial legal system, recognized tribal law and applied its legal order only to employees, other settlers, or Indians within the sphere of company operations, that is, the small communities around trading posts or engaged in trading activity.[19] Indian law had been recognized by HBC authorities for several hundred years.[20]

Indian society in the west had been destablized by both the fur trade and the beginnings of settlement. The largest Indian nation in Canada, the Cree, had been a primary beneficiary of the fur trade. Initially woodland Indians occupying the northern forests, the Cree lived around the southern shores of Hudson Bay. This put them in an immediate position to serve as fur trappers and also as middlemen in the fur trade. The trade enriched the Cree, giving them access to trade goods of various kinds, including guns. A rapid expansion of Cree population brought thousands of Cree west and south, out onto the prairies. Here they clashed with the Blackfoot Confederacy, traditional occupants of much of the southern Canadian plains. The Saulteaux Ojibwa, allies of the Cree in the fur trade, also moved west to the prairies from the woodlands around Lake of the Woods. Various Sioux peoples, involved in repeated wars with the United States, moved north in large numbers, beginning with the Minnesota Uprising of 1863. These shifting native populations destablized the existing indigenous social order on the plains. The use of weapons in tribal warfare transformed Indian warfare from quasi-legal and highly symbolic international exchanges with few casualties to highly destructive enterprises that decimated some tribes. Simultaneously, the whisky trade undermined the traditional authority of the chiefs.

In these circumstances, the NWMP's arrival held out the promise of greater social stability on the plains. In the plains Indians' world-view, the Mounties were the representatives of another powerful nation, long represented in the west by the Hudson's Bay Company. The NWMP cultivated the good will that it found among the Indian nations. NWMP officials were deferential to the chiefs and worked through traditional tribal structures in doing their work. Narrow law-enforcement concerns gave way to policy considerations favouring good relations between the Mounties and the tribes. For example, cattlemen in southern Alberta in the 1870s were told that it was impossible for the force to patrol herds to protect against occasional Indian cattle stealing. Obviously, this reflected the policy choice that it was not worth using limited NWMP resources in a kind of enforcement activity that threatened to incur the hostilities of the tribes. Intra-Indian offences were punished only when some member of the band complained, and then only when the chiefs yielded up the offenders.[21] Annual Indian arrests, even in the late 1870s, were measured by the fingers on one hand.[22]

The Northwest Rebellion was a watershed in NWMP/Indian relations that exposed the weaknesses in the dominion's prairie Indian policy. The Indian Department had determined that its Indian policy was too expensive and only created Indian dependency, and so it decided to cut rations to starvation levels to force Indians to work as small farmers. The plan was cruel and unworkable. In legal terms it put a law-enforcement burden on the NWMP that the Mounties could not bear: they had to police starving Indians. As resentment levels rose, altercations between reserve Indians and Indian Department officials increased. Grown Indian men were forced to beg petty Indian Department officials for extra food for starving and sick children. The latters' refusal was not infrequently met with violence as individual Indians took law into their own hands, striking officials or stealing food. Yayakootyawapos, the father-in-law of Big Bear, served two months in the guardhouse at Fort Battleford for striking a distribution officer at Fort Pitt.[23] This was no way to treat Cree elders and the injury must have run deep.

By the early 1880s the arrest and punishment of Indian offenders rose to far higher levels than than those of the 1870s; there were now forty to fifty arrests a year, still a low level given the size of the population but high compared to the small statistics of the earlier decade. Policing cattle theft, impossible in the 1870s, became standard police procedure in the 1880s, leading to a single arrest of eighteen Blood warriors in one sweep.[24] The significance of this large increase in arrests and imprisonment of Indians is not measured in simple numbers: imprisonment was an enormously powerful symbol of the meaning of police power. Prison destroyed the spirits of plains Indians, culturally so accustomed to the openness of the prairie and the sky.

Throughout the century, the evidence is that tribal law enforcement was predominant in intra-Indian affairs. Within the band of the Cree chief Foremost Man, only two nineteenth-century intra-Indian offences were reported to the NWMP for settlement, both assaults.[25] In two famous incidents, Indians who killed NWMP officers were protected by their tribes for lengthy periods of time while pursued fruitlessly by the NWMP.

Almighty Voice, a Cree warrior in the Mannechinas Hills, north of the Saskatchewan River, shot a settler's cow in 1895. Evidently a Mountie told him that they were going to hang him, and he escaped from custody. NWMP Sergeant Colebrook was sent to arrest Almighty Voice. Warned to keep back, he was shot to death at a distance of fifteen feet. There followed an extensive NWMP effort to capture Almighty Voice. The thick police file on the search reports many false leads, including a report of his suicide. These leads appear to have come from Cree helping him avoid capture. He stayed at large a year and a half before being surrounded. Almighty Voice held off the police for several days, killing another

Mountie. He was finally killed in a barrage of cannon fire, but only after keeping the police awake with his death song.[26]

Almighty Voice was the grandson of One Arrow, arrested in 1880, also for shooting cattle. His father, John Sounding Sky, had served six months in jail for stealing a coat and money.[27] The activity of his family, coupled with evidence of both material support and actual assistance at evading the police, makes it clear that Cree warrior culture was prepared to resort to means illegal under Canadian law in the interests of survival.

The Blood warrior Charcoal engaged in a parallel series of killings in southern Alberta in the early 1890s. Charcoal's actions were more individualistic and less tribally supported than Almighty Voice's: distressed by his young wife's action in running off with a rival, he resolved to commit suicide and, to this end, he killed in order to secure a spirit to guide him through the spirit world. Although his actions divided the tribe, Charcoal had substantial support and successfully evaded capture for months. Ultimately he killed a Mountie and was later betrayed by his own brother. He was captured, tried, and hanged for murder at Fort Mcleod.[28]

Almighty Voice and Charcoal were famous cases that left lengthy archival records because they were so rare. The NWMP put massive resources into such manhunts to make the point that individual Indians should expect to be dealt with severely by crown authorities if they chose to kill settlers or to defy Canadian law. The new wing built (partially by Indian prisoner labour) at Stony Mountain Prison in Manitoba after the 1885 trials was kept filled with Indians after the early 1890s, mostly on charges of cattle theft. Sentences were generally short, a year or two, but the warriors who returned from Stony Mountain were sick and rarely resisted again.[29]

THE NORTHWEST REBELLION TRIALS

The Northwest Rebellion looms large in western Canadian history. Wars are not ordinarily the subject of legal history, but Canadian authorities insisted, for political reasons, on treating the rebellion as an internal act of treason, trying dozens of Indians for criminal offences that were mostly coincidental. Ultimately, eight were hanged for murder and more than forty sentenced to Stony Mountain Prison. Prime Minister John A. Macdonald used the rebellion as a pretext to crush Indian complaints concerning their reserves, living conditions, and Canadian settlement on their lands. 'The execution of the Indians ... ought to convince the Red man that the White man governs.'[30] While the rebellion in fact was a Metis affair, few Metis were tried, although Louis Riel, the rebellion's leader, was executed for treason.[31]

The Metis rebellion coincided with isolated Indian violence stemming from the settler occupation of native lands, impoverishment, and starvation.[32] A small number of Indians were in the Metis trenches at the Battle of Batoche, the most important military engagement of the rebellion. Nine settlers were killed at Frog Lake by Cree warriors over resentment at their mistreatment by Indian Department employees on that reserve.[33] These same Cree warriors then besieged Fort Pitt. In a complex series of events, some coincidental, some following from misunderstanding and confusion, a number of other impoverished Indians proceeded to Battleford to request food, convincing local inhabitants that they were being attacked. In all this confusion several other whites were killed.[34]

The most famous Indian criminal trials in Canada – still legendary among native people – were those of Poundmaker and Big Bear for treason. The very definition of treason, and the reason it is such an infamous crime at common law, requires the specific intent to betray one's own country.[35] Not only was the entire conception of the offence foreign to the Cree, Dakota, and Assiniboine warriors who rose against the Canadian state, but the whole question of how and when the Indian nations were incorporated into Canada was unraised and unanswered.[36] The inability of the Cree language to accommodate a translation of the treason charge rendered it impossible for the Indians to defend themselves. Even the crown recognized this, choosing to charge Indians with the reduced offence of 'treason-felony' instead of high treason (the charge against Riel) 'because the Indians have an indefinite notion of the allegiance which they owe to their Sovereign.'[37] F.B. Robertson, a Winnipeg attorney, was retained by the government to defend all of the Indians in the Regina trials.[38] He did not raise a defence based on Indian allegiance to the crown; instead, as in any ordinary criminal case, he focused on challenging the crown's evidence in rigorous cross-examination. The substantive law of treason was a part of his defence in another, more minor, way: he argued the evidentiary point that the *mens rea*, the specific intent to commit treason, could not be proven by inference from mere presence, but this was consistently overruled by the judge.[39] Obviously, such an evidentiary ruling permitted juries to find Indians physically present near a battle guilty of treason by inference.

The rebellion trials occurred in two stages. Riel and the alleged leaders of the rebellion, including Poundmaker, Big Bear, and One Arrow, were tried for treason at Regina. Only Riel was charged with high treason, carrying the death penalty. All of the other defendants were charged with treason-felony, a lesser charge. Later, a larger number of Indians were tried at Battleford for ordinary criminal offences occurring at Frog Lake and Battleford during the rebellion, although additional Indians were tried for treason in the second set of trials as well. Only two Metis, Riel and Mangus Burston, were tried for treason, along with two whites.[40] Nearly a hundred Indians were in custody and charged with individual criminal offences, with sixty ultimately convicted. Indians drew the brunt of the legal repression of the Northwest Rebellion.

These trials can be analysed on several levels. The political decision to try Indians and as well as Metis for the rebellion showed that the crown intended to stage these trials with the intent of breaking the back of Indian resistance to the federal government's Indian policy. The trials were show trials, designed to convince the Indians of the futility of further resistance and also to remove dozens of Indian leaders, almost all Cree, to prison until they were no longer a threat to Canadian officials. But prison sentences were death sentences to many Indians: One Arrow and Poundmaker, vigorous middle-aged men, were sick and dying old men after serving only a few months of their three year sentences. Big Bear, at sixty, was already old for an Indian, and with his health broken in prison, he died shortly after his release.[41]

In legal terms, the quality of justice rendered was a travesty. The evidence against most of the Indians, usually dubious eyewitness testimony of victims, was weak. It is clear, too, that the interpreters did not do an adequate job and that appointed lawyers did not conduct vigorous defences. The judges, for their part, conducted the trials in a partisan way. Judge Charles-Borromeé Rouleau of Battleford, who had just had his own house looted and burned in the rebellion, sat in judgment of Indians accused of looting and burning Battleford. Judge Hugh Richardson, who presided in Regina, insisted on a definition of treason that included merely being present at some identifiable point in the rebellion among persons engaged in the rebellion.[42] Juries, all-white and all-male in the 1880s west, seeking revenge for settlers killed in the rebellion and anxious to open up Saskatchewan to settlement by repressing the Indian threat, rotely returned 'guilty' verdicts no matter what the evidence.[43]

Cultural factors influenced individual members of Indian tribes in ways incomprehensible to either Canadian juries or Canadian law. Even at the time, for example, it was recognized that Big Bear, a Cree chief, had opposed the war. But his band had engaged in killing settlers and burn-ing Frog Lake and Big Bear had remained with his band. Robertson, in his summation to the jury, sought to educate them in the role of an Indian chief: 'The Indian looks to his own little band; apart from them he can do nothing; apart from them he cannot live; he must remain with his band; he cannot get away from them; he is not free if he sees mischief being done, he is not free to say, I will move away from here, I will go among other people who won't do these things; he cannot do that, and what else has my learned friend, Mr. Scott, to rest upon here in making a case against Big Bear, except that he was with his band?'[44]

While Robertson was overstating the control that a band had over an ordinary Indian warrior who was free to leave, he understated the responsibility of a chief. A chief was responsible for his band and was obligated to stay with them, even on a course where they refused to fol-low his leadership. Big Bear remained with his people to offer them what guidance he could.[45] One Arrow was convicted on even less evidence than Big Bear. One person saw him at Batoche carrying a rifle and speak-ing to Riel. Robertson pointed out that all Indians routinely carried rifles and that no one had any idea what he had said to Riel.[46]

The Sioux chief White Cap was acquitted on treason-felony charges on evidence not much different than that involving One Arrow. White Cap had left his reserve near Saskatoon for Batoche, where one witness, a mes-senger, swore that he saw him manning a gun in the rifle pits. Robertson viewed that testimony as incredible, attacking the witness for his positive identification of White Cap 'out of a hundred and fifty other Indians in the excitement of the moment.' Another witness put White Cap in a meeting of Riel's Metis council. Robertson pointed out that White Cap spoke only Dakota while the council meetings were held in French and Cree. More important Robertson angrily sparred with Judge Richardson over his jury instructions on the law of treason, obtaining an instruction that raised the standard from mere presence to 'aiding and abetting or encouraging rebellion or the prosecution of the unlawful design.' Robert-son then attacked the Regina jury for so quickly convicting his clients in all of the previous cases. This time, however, the jury acquitted White Cap in fifteen minutes.[47]

Given that the testimony in this case put White Cap in a rifle pit where his 'aiding and abetting' was clear, it would seem that the key to acquittal was not the judge's instruction. White Cap did have the testimony of a wit-ness, Dr Gerald Willoughby, who testified to White Cap's honesty and peaceful behaviour. By the time of the Battle of Batoche, White Cap claimed to have fled to Saskatoon, where he complained to Willoughby that he had been forced to join the Metis council. This added something of a defence of duress to White Cap's story. These two stories are inconsistent, but the jury did not believe that the crown's witnesses were telling the truth when they placed White Cap in the trenches at the Battle of Batoche.[48]

Besides One Arrow, Poundmaker, Big Bear, and White Cap, two groups of Indians were tried for treason-felony at Regina. Nine Cree were charged with offences at Frog Lake, Fort Pitt, and Frenchman's Butte. These cases were all based on the testimony of witnesses to the events, and, although there were often the same kind of identification problems as those attending the White Cap case, the juries convicted. The next day, Robertson defended four Sioux and one Cree charged with treason-felony for participating in events at Duck Lake and Batoche. The cases were so weak that Robertson did not even bother a summation argument, but again convictions were returned.[49] In all, eighteen Indians were tried at Regina for treason-felony, leading to seventeen convictions, with prison sentences of two or three years.[50]

All of these cases tried at Regina are overshadowed by the trials and hangings at Battleford. According to one observer, Father Alexis Andre, Judge Rouleau, was 'a vindictive man and a servile instrument in the hands of the government.'[51] Underlying these mass trials was the crown's clear desire to hang a large number of Indians before Indian witnesses in order to impress upon native people the seriousness of Canadian justice and put an end to the large-scale resistance disrupting the reserves. Assistant Commissioner of Indian Affairs Hayter Reed put it matter of factly: 'I am desirous of having the Indians witness it – No sound thrashing having been given them I think a sight of this sort will cause them to meditate for many a day.'[52]

Among the Cree at Frog Lake sentenced to death, only Wandering Spirit plead guilty. Bad Arrow, Miserable Man, Walking the Sky, Little Bear, and Iron Body were convicted individually of the various killings. Itka and Man Without Blood, both Assiniboines, plead guilty to two unrelated killings in the Battleford area. Louison Mongrain, a Frog Lake Cree, was sentenced to death for killing a NWMP corporal at Fort Pitt. Charlebois and Dressy Man were sentenced to death for killing a wendigo in an unrelated event in the Cree camp after the Frog Lake killings. Bright Eyes was convicted of manslaughter in the same killing and received a twenty-year sentence.[53] Unlike at Regina, no defence lawyer was assigned at Battleford. This meant much more perfunctory trials with a number of murder trials occurring in one day.

Mongrain, Charlebois, and Dressy Man had their sentences commuted, but the first eight were hanged at Battleford on 26 November. Hundreds of witnesses were admitted to the fort and more waited outside. The warriors sang their death chants and then were led out to a gallows outfitted with eight ropes. The condemned were given ten minutes for final statements. Except for Wandering Spirit the men were defiant. They smiled, sang, and shouted sharp war cries. Little Bear told the Indians to remember how the whites had treated him, and he urged his companions to have contempt for the punishment the government was about to inflict on them. Black caps were drawn over their faces and the execution was quickly carried out. The men were buried on the fort grounds.[54]

The rest of Rouleau's sentences for ordinary theft were more severe than those received for treason in Regina, averaging six years for horse theft. Two Indians who plead guilty to arson at Frog Lake received ten-year sentences. Another received a fourteen-year sentence for burning the Frog Lake church. In all, Rouleau tried more than thirty Indians for these property offences in addition to the twelve murder cases.[55]

CREE LAW AND TREATY 6

The immediate context of Cree participation in the Northwest Rebellion was Indian dissatisfaction with Treaty 6. The 'numbered treaties,' Treaties 1 through 7, negotiated with western Indians beginning in Manitoba in 1871, were intended to open up the west for settlement.[56] They continued an Ontarian Indian policy: Indian lands were to be purchased, with the tribes moving to small reserves to take up the life of small farmers.[57] The tribes, however, had a different understanding of the treaties. Since a treaty is an international agreement, somewhat analogous to a contract, the very validity of the agreement turns on both parties having an identical understanding of the nature and substance of the agreement.[58]

As we have seen, the opening of the northwest to settlement followed its 1869 'sale' to the crown by the HBC for £300,000. The Indian nations, never having accepted the company's 'ownership' of their lands, knew of this sale, setting an underlying tone of resentment in the treaty negotiations.[59] The scale of the land cessions was unprecedented in Canadian treaty history. In 1871 and 1872 the crown in Treaties 1 and 2 purchased land needed for immediate settlement in southern Manitoba.[60] Treaties 3, 4, 5, 6, and 7 involved huge tracts of lands, not yet settled, where native people pursued a traditional lifestyle, albeit one modified by changing economic and environmental realities, especially the decline of the fur trade and the great buffalo herds.[61]

There are substantial oral histories that reveal the Indian understanding of these treaties. Most of these oral histories can be corroborated. For example, since they had shared the prairies with Euro-Canadian fur traders for two hundred years, native people must have seen the treaties as recognizing that pre-existing relationship. The concept of selling their land cannot have been known to the Indians, who never held private property. Similarly, the idea of settling on reserves was impossible to Indians who covered hundreds of miles each season searching for buffalo or returning to winter shelter. There is a complexity to Indian views of agriculture, although such economic activity did not originally exist on the prairies west of Winnipeg (outside of some limited farming around HBC posts). Prairie Indians were aware of farming as the basis of the Canadian economy and saw it as one solution to their impoverishment.[62]

The Indian nations understood the treaties as peace and friendship agreements, with specific cessions of some land-use rights on their part in return for payments in cash and goods from the crown. Treaties 3, 4, 6, and 7, for example, secured railroad, road, and telegraph routes across the prairies. Treaty 6 elders invariably remember that the crown bought the rights to the top six inches of soil for farming, promising that the nations could continue to use all of the land not suitable for farming. It was assumed in 1876 that very little of the plains could be successfully farmed. The First Nations expected the land to serve a number of different users, for different purposes. Such arrangements were familiar to them and traditionally had been regulated through First Nations law, generally without any conflict. For example, the family and clan trapping, hunting, and fishing territories in the north had existed for generations.

The context of the treaties, the treaty-making meetings, reinforced this view. Treaty commissioners, high-ranking politicians, were preceded by parties of Mounties. The tribes were called together from across the region and had been meeting among themselves for days. The negotiations were delayed in Treaty 6 while the tribes engaged in a sacred peace-pipe ceremony, purifying the words that were exchanged in the treaty-making process. These words, of course, were translated from English to Indian languages and back. It is still not clear how words representing complex legal terms were translated, but it is clear that they were not translated well. For example, there are several words for 'land' in Cree depending on the context. The belief of modern Cree that the nation sold only the top six inches of their lands at Treaty 6 may stem from a mistranslation of the kind of 'land' that they were negotiating for.[63]

One famous mistranslation from Treaty 6 became important following Big Bear's treason trial in 1885. Big Bear had apparently expressed a fear of being hanged at the time of the negotiation of Treaty 6 in 1876. This was translated as a desire on his part to exempt Indians from Canadian law by providing that Indians could not be hanged for their violations of law. In fact, however, Big Bear spoke of 'having a rope around his neck' like a wild horse, captured and no longer free. The interpreter confused 'ay-saka-pay-kinit' (lead by the neck) with 'ay-hah-kotit' (hang by the neck).[64] This point, if properly understood, would have put directly on the table one of the major unresolved issues of Treaty 6. The Indians did not realize that they would be confined to their reservations; instead, they believed that they would be allowed to continue their traditional hunting patterns, with the reserves serving as a base. The only possible conclusion one can reach is that the crown's negotiators were deliberately vague on this point because they wanted to keep the Indians negotiating and induce them to sign the treaty.

This view is reinforced by two famous clauses in Treaty 6, both originating with the Indians: one provided for a 'medicine chest' to be kept by the agents, and the other provided that the crown 'render assistance in time of need.' The British Colonial Office as well as Canadian authorities had boilerplate treaty language and all of the numbered treaties are similar in provisions. Thus, the final language of the treaties reflected, not a negotiated agreement between the crown and the Indian nations, but the efforts of crown negotiators to induce Indians to sign a prepared text. The price of these provisions was negotiable: Indians in Treaty 3 had held out for higher payments, a fact known to the signers of later treaties. But in Treaty 6 the tribes had specific concerns not addressed by money alone. Disease and starvation were common, caused by white settlements, social dislocations, and the scarcity of buffalo. The tribes sought specific provisions to alleviate these hardships. What resulted was the 'medicine chest' and 'assistance in time of famine' clauses.[65] The meaning of these clauses is still at issue. The crown reads these terms literally and narrowly; the tribes read them broadly and in an 1879 context. In their view, for example, a 'medicine chest' can refer only to adequate medical assistance in modern terms. The complete destruction of tribal economies created a permanent famine, requiring permanent 'assistance in time of famine.' Much of the underlying tension leading to the Northwest Rebellion reflected the government's refusal, in violation of the treaty, to provide adequate relief from starvation.

In Treaty 7, the 'Blackfoot Treaty' of 1877, a similar story of mistranslation is reported. Language that took the treaty commissioners a long time to speak was translated into a few sentences by interpreters, about one-sixth of the commissioner's language in one account. English terms critical to the meaning of the treaty – crown, Canada, land, reserve, sovereignty – had no meaning in the Blackfoot language. Indeed, there is not even a word for 'treaty.' To this day fluently bilingual speakers of Blackfoot and English cannot adequately translate the treaty from English to Blackfoot.[66]

Explicit references to Canadian law were made in several places in the treaties. Indians agreed to be subject to Canadian law and to assist Canadian law-enforcement officials in carrying out the law by yielding up offenders. Liquor was outlawed in native communities, and the crown pledged to enforce those prohibition laws. The right of Indians to hunt and fish was recognized but made subject to 'such regulations as may from time to time be made by Her Majesty's Government of the Dominion of Canada.'[67] Other laws were proposed and discussed in the various councils but not included in the treaties. The Cree at Fort Carlton, for example, proposed a 'strong law, prohibiting the free use of poison [strychnine]. It has almost exterminated the animals of our country, and often makes us bad friends with our white neighbors. We further request, that a law be made, equally applicable to the Half-breed and Indian, punishing all parties who set fire to our forest and plain.'[68]

The legal status of Indian treaties was not an issue in nineteenth-century courts outside the St Catherine's Milling case.[69] Yet there is no question that the treaties were seen as legal documents by Indians at the time. The sacred pipe ceremony bound the participants to speak the truth and carry out their agreements. The tribes ceded up certain rights to their lands in return for payments, in cash and goods, from the government. Treaty Commissioner Alexander Morris who, with commissioners Adams Archibald and Wemyss Simpson, had negotiated Treaties 4, 5, and 6, was a lawyer and former chief justice of Manitoba.[70] NWMP Superintendent James Macleod, who together with Lieutenant Governor David Laird, had negotiated Treaty 7, which was based on the earlier treaties, was also a lawyer. British courts and American courts had held treaties to be legal documents, with their terms enforceable in court.[71]

It is impossible to say what the Indian understanding of these treaties was. Parts of the evidence are contradictory. For example, the Indians at Fort Carlton, according to official documents, discussed leasing their land to whites for four years rather than selling it. This discussion itself would indicate that the tribes understood that they were selling the land. But that assumes that Indians knew what a lease was. Other Indians counselled against selling the land, again a discussion that would indicate that the tribes knew that they were discussing a land sale. The final language – the Indians 'hereby cede, release, surrender and yield up to the Government ... forever, all their rights, titles and privileges whatsoever, to the lands' – seems unambiguous but it is boilerplate language, inserted in all the treaties, and it is not clear how it was translated.[72]

Since the treaty process was controlled by dominion authorities, an unknown number of bands refused to enter into treaty. Big Bear's band is the best known of these, but it is still not clear what proportion of the tribes actually signed treaties. It was in the interests of the crown to exaggerate the representation of the bands. Various bands had been fragmented for any number of reasons, and it is not clear whether they were represented at treaty. It is also not clear that people signing for some bands had authority to do so, or, if they held some legitimate authority, that they held the authority to make the kinds of cessions that were allegedly made. The crown's fiction that Indian land was being voluntarily ceded inherently recognized the opposite: that the tribes were free not to participate in the treaty process and to decline to cede their lands. Big Bear's opposition is the most thoroughly documented.

He and his followers objected to both the process and the substance of treaty making. As a young man he had had a dream about being trapped by the Queen's presents. These presents were offered to plains Indians with the promise that the government would treat them justly, but they also obligated the Indians to participate in a formal relationship with the crown. 'When we set a fox trap we scatter pieces of meat all around but when the fox gets into the trap we knock him on the head. We want no baits! Let your Chiefs come like men and talk to us.'[73] Yellow Sky, an Ojibwa, allied with Big Bear, refused to take treaty as well, explaining his reasons to Indian Agent M.G. Dickieson. As Dickieson wrote: 'After some time a spokesman rose and said they desired to be independent ... that they did not wish to take anything from the Government, or to come under the law. He said I was not to think it was because they were unfriendly to the Government or to the white man that they do not join with the other Indians but they wished to remain as they were. They had likewise been told that by holding out, 'better terms' would be granted to them.'[74]

This account delegitimizes the idea of tribal independence as an option. Local officials appear to have treated all Indian objections to treaty as negotiating ploys, merely designed to get more money. Yet it is hard to believe that Big Bear's underlying motives were merely to secure money.[75] Rather, the evidence consistently supports the view that he and his people believed that they had a choice to take or not take treaty. From the standpoint of the law, it is clear that they had such a choice. Ultimately, Big Bear's band took treaty six years later, in December 1882. They were starving, and signing the treaty gave them a right to government relief.[76]

The earlier plains treaties were suggested by the Indians in response to the pressure of white settlement. It now seems evident that the motivation of the tribes in initiating the process was to implement a political and legal framework for the protection of their rights. These treaties were interrelated for both Canadians and Indians: in each treaty, the treaty commissioners followed similar instructions from Ottawa, and the Indians present knew of the terms of previous treaties. Alexander Morris led the commissioners at Treaties 3, 4, 5, and 6, creating a continuity in the negotiations. But each treaty process was distinct, involving different considerations on the parts of Indian and government alike.[77]

The treaty documents are remarkable for they reveal a detailed negotiating process with a clear Indian agenda. They also reveal two distinct sets of negotiations and understandings: while the formal, written treaties outline a broad understanding, they also include some specific rights guaranteed Indians. At the same time, the negotiations reveal a number of verbal promises and understandings that were clearly understood by the Indians to be a part of the broad treaty agreement. In retrospect there can be no question that the Indian nations, unschooled in European international law and accustomed to a tradition where agreements between the Indian nations were verbal, took these verbal agreements as part of the treaty. Within six months of the signing of Treaty 1, Lieutenant Governor Archibald wrote Ottawa that 'It is impossible to be too particular in carrying out the terms of the agreements made with these people. They recollect with astonishing accuracy every stipulation made at the Treaty, and if we expect our relations with them to be of the kind which is desirable to maintain we must fulfill our obligations with scrupulous fidelity.[78] Indian complaints about Crown violations of treaty provisions were continuous and angry from within a few months of their signing. These involved both promises written into the treaties, as well as 'outside' or verbal promises made in the treaty context. If the dispute about the meaning of 'maintaining a school on each reserve,'[79] a measure both favoured by the tribes and consistent with the government's own Indian policy, is any indication, the crown's actions show bad faith and fraud from the outset.

In 1873 Treaty Commissioner J. Provencher requested from Ottawa an appropriation to build a school at Brokenhead reserve. Deputy Superintendent General of Indian Affairs Lawrence Vankoughnet responded: 'According to the terms of Treaty 1 a school is to be maintained on each Reserve thereby made – of which there is one – whenever the Indians on the Reserve should desire it ... Mr. Provencher states that the Indians of Brokenhead desire an appropriation towards the erection of a school house. No stipulation is made in the Treaty that an appropriation shall be provided for such effect.'[80] In Vankoughnet's view, the phrase 'maintaining a school' meant an annual appropriation of $300 for the operation of each school. While Provencher, a good bureaucrat, did not want to challenge directly his superior's legal interpretation of the meaning of this treaty provision, he dutifully pointed out the problem this raised: The Indians' request was 'just one more instance of the misunderstanding that took place at the time of the making of the Treaty. By the obligation of "maintaining a school" assumed by the government, the Indians misunderstood that all the expenses connected with the school would be supported by the Government.'[81] This exchange is revealing on a number of levels. In terms of simple legal interpretation, it seems obvious that the crown's narrow interpretation of the plain meaning of the phrase 'maintaining a school' is both dishonest and intended to injure the Indians, not only in a 1990s context but also in the context of 1873. If the crown refused to build the schools referred to by treaty, who would build them?

But more important, the exchange occurred in early 1876, more than six months before Treaty 3, containing the same language, was signed on 3 October 1876. The Treaty commissioners at Treaty 3 knew that the phrase 'maintaining a school' was being interpreted by the crown and the tribes in an inconsistent way and used it anyway, knowing that it would mislead the Indians. The Treaty 3 Indians were deliberately misled, and deceit on this point was practised again in all of the succeeding prairie treaties.

Such basic illegality goes to the heart of the treaty-making process. What was the crown's ultimate 'policy' towards the Indians as revealed by this fraud? Stealing even a basic education from children cuts against any serious policy of assimilation, even in the terms of 1870s Canadian policy. The crown's policy was evidently to buy Indian land as cheaply as possible without regard to the social costs that beset tribes forced onto reserves with no source of income. This attitude was communicated to the treaty commissioners, who understood their role as simply getting the tribes to sign treaties, no matter what had to be promised in order to accomplish this end.

If promises directly written into the treaties in plain language fared this poorly, the 'outside' promises made at the time must have been calculated to mislead the Indians about the extent of their benefits under the treaties and to induce them to sign. The treaty reports, prepared for publication by Alexander Morris himself, show extensive outside promises and the intentional use of ambivalent language.[82] These self-serving accounts are only one side of a complex and disputed negotiation process and do not reveal the full extent of the promises made to Indians.[83]

Dissecting the substance of the miscommunications is less important than recognizing that the misunderstanding was known at the time and was intentional, perhaps even unavoidable, and at the heart of the treaty process. The range of issues involved goes well beyond the narrow, technical interpretation of a simple concept like 'maintaining a school.' There seems to be no question, for example, that the difficult and complex issues of native self-government, the recognition of Indian law, the nature of the title to the land that was ceded, the function and ownership of the reserves, and the promised level of crown economic support for impoverished aboriginal communities were all understood in different ways by the crown and the Indian tribes.[84] To call this 'misunderstanding' is to put a neutral cast on the process: the crown, as drafter of the treaties and the imposer of its legal order on the plains Indians, was responsible for the clarity of the meaning of the treaties and deliberately misled the Indians in order to persuade them to sign.

TREATIES, BUFFALO, AND THE LOSS OF THE COMMONS

The signing of the plains treaties occurred in the context of social and ecological changes on the frontier that would permanently alter their economies and social orders. Unrestricted organized buffalo hunts by American and Metis hunters had reduced both the size and the distribution of the herds. As a result, the traditional hunting cycles of the plains Indians were no longer possible: tribes had to range farther and farther in search of buffalo. Not only did this change existing land use patterns, but it may have exacerbated tribal conflict between the Cree and the Blackfoot Confederacy as the Cree were forced to hunt farther south and west of their traditional ranges. Even with increased hunting ranges, hunger and starvation became serious matters for the plains Indians.[85] This was an unprecedented situation for cultures used to the wealth of large buffalo herds.[86]

White and Metis hunting on the plains was beyond the control of the tribes: the hunters could not be stopped by Indians without the intervention of Canadian authorities. The Dakota had attempted to stop the well-organized Metis hunting parties, but had been defeated in the 1851 Battle of Grand Coteau, a victory that marks one 'beginning' of the Metis nation.[87] Plains Indians took a number of steps to control access to their lands and to regulate hunting practices. As early as 1858 the Plains Cree, in council, 'determined that in consequence of promises often made and broken by the white men and half-breeds, and the rapid destruction by them of the buffalo they fed on, they would not permit either white men or half-breeds to hunt in their country or travel through it, except for the purpose of trading for their dried meat, pemmican, skins and robes.'[88]

Just as the direct pressure of white settlement had forced many (but not all) of the eastern Indians to treaty, so the tragedy of the loss of the commons did much to force the plains Indians to enter into treaty with the Canadian government. Chief Sweet Grass of the Plains Cree put it simplest: 'Our country is no longer able to support us.'[89] Some idea of the state of Indian society on the prairies soon after Canada negotiated its agreement with the Hudson's Bay Company can be gleaned from the full context of Sweet Grass's words.

Sweet Grass, on his own volition, went in to the HBC's Edmonton House on 13 April 1871, accompanied by a few warriors. Meeting there with W.J. Christie, the chief factor, Sweet Grass asked whether his land had already been sold and what the intention of the Canadian government was towards his people. He had heard about negotiations in Treaty 3, (which, at this point, had failed because the Saulteaux had angrily refused the commissioner's terms) more than a thousand miles to the east, and wanted to know when he would be offered a treaty. Sweet Grass referred to an epidemic that had raged through the country in the past summer, the starvation and poverty of Indians, and the diminution of the buffalo. He asked for presents at once.[90]

Christie had no governmental authority at all, but he promised that Canada would deal 'liberally' with Sweet Grass's people, as it had done in previous Indian treaties. Christie then, on his own authority, gave presents to Sweet Grass and 'otherwise satisfied them,' convinced that 'they would have proceeded to acts of violence, and once that had commenced, there would have been the beginning of an Indian war, which it is difficult to say when it would have ended.'[91] He agreed to take a message from Sweet Grass to the lieutenant governor of Manitoba.

The message was simple in its terms. Beginning with a strong statement that the Cree 'don't want to sell our lands; it is our property, and no one has a right to sell them,' Sweet Grass went on:

Our country is getting ruined of fur-bearing animals, hitherto our sole support, and now we are poor and want help – we want you to pity us. We want cattle, tools, agricultural implements, and assistance in everything when we come to settle – our country is no longer able to support us.

Make provision for us against years of starvation. We had great starvation the past winter, and the small-pox took away many of our people, the old, young, and children.

We want you to stop the Americans from coming to trade on our lands, and giving firewater, ammunition and arms to our enemies the Blackfeet.

We made a peace this winter with the Blackfeet, Our young men are foolish, it may not last long.

We invite you to come and see us and to speak with us.[92]

While it is doubtful that most of the Cree accepted the necessity of changing their lifestyle as early as 1871, Sweet Grass's words make it clear that some of them took this view, a view that partially coincided with dominion policy at the same time. The end of the plains economy supported by the buffalo commons fit two dominion objectives: farmers could not occupy plains ranged by buffalo, and Indians could not carry out their nomadic hunting activities on a plains devoid of game.

In the late nineteenth century, the dominion considered legislation to limit the buffalo hunt and to use the NWMP to enforce these conservation laws. Given the extent of the hunt and the depth to which the hunting culture and economy permeated plains life, the idea of a law-enforcement effort to save the buffalo may have been unrealistic. But this was also a culture committed to the idea of a policed transition to an orderly frontier and the very basis of the treaty process was that the Canadian government was both willing and able to enforce treaty terms. The elders of Treaty 7 remember that the government committed itself to protect the buffalo.[93]

In any case, by 1874 the Canadian government was aware of the severity of the problem: the buffalo were fast disappearing and the plains Indians were dependent on the buffalo for food and shelter. The loss of the buffalo would leave many thousands of Indians with no means of sustenance.[94] The dominion government recognized that it had a choice in the matter, with some Liberal and Conservative members of Parliament believing that the government had a treaty obligation to preserve the buffalo.[95] This view, in itself, presumes a liberal policy of interpreting treaties in favour of Indians, since no treaty had any express provision regarding the preservation of game.

The Department of Justice, in charge of all government legislation, prepared an extensive report on the protection of buffalo. Because the matter was of local, rather than national, concern, the report was referred to the North-West Territorial Council. A subcommittee of that council did its own investigation of the problem, taking evidence from witnesses. There was no shortage of ideas, nor was there disagreement about the seriousness of the problem. Witnesses suggested the introduction of a hunting season for Metis and whites (but not for Indians), as well as severe punishment for those who killed buffalo without using at least half of the meat, another measure aimed at white and Metis hunting practices that took skins and tongues but left the meat to rot. An export duty on hides and pemmican was directed at the Americans at the heart of the trade.[96]

Ottawa transferred the whole matter to the Territorial Council, which ultimately passed a watered-down ordinance in November of 1877. The act forbade the use of 'buffalo pounds' and the running of buffalo off cliffs. Slaughter for amusement or to 'secure their tongues, choice cuts or peltries' was prohibited. A closed season on cows ran from 15 November through 14 August, and no calves under two years old were to be killed. Indians were subject to the law but granted certain concessions during winter months. Severe penalties were provided, with half of the fine going to the informer.[97]

The ordinance was repealed a year later, a monument to the ineffectiveness of the Territorial Council, Ottawa's lack of interest, and Indian distrust of Canadian law.[98] Indians, especially at the making of Treaty 4 and Treaty 6, called for a law to protect the buffalo. Yet other Indians did not accept any legal regulation of their hunts. Sitting Bull, then in exile in Canada, asked rhetorically, 'When ... did the Almighty give the Canadian government the right to keep the Indians from killing the buffalo?'[99] It should not be surprising that internal differences on such matters existed within Indian tribes: the idea of relying on Canadian law to protect age-old hunting activities was foreign to Indian culture.

The underlying issue was probably not the potential effectiveness of such laws in preserving buffalo. Rather, it was a vision of a social order under the control of Canadian police. NWMP Commissioner George A. French had testified before the Territorial Council subcommittee urging the adoption of sweeping laws to protect the buffalo and never indicated any sense that the NWMP could not carry out this law-enforcement task.[100] If the NWMP was effective enough to police western settlement, the policing of the buffalo hunt should have been no problem.

The commissioners at Treaty 4 reported that 'many of the bands have no desire to settle and commence farming, and will not turn their attention to agriculture until they are forced to do so on account of the failure of their present means of subsistence by the extermination of the buffalo.'[101] Unsettling within this whole context is the possibility that the dominion government deliberately failed to take action because it understood that the buffalo hunt was vital to the plains tribes and thus the destruction of the buffalo would force the Indians onto reserves. There is no question that American authorities deliberately failed to protect the buffalo for these reasons.[102] Ottawa's two-year delay was critical in the repeal of the 1877 ordinance. Similarly, Ottawa's deference to the new North-West Territorial Council because 'it could probably devise a cheaper and better plan than this parliament' was as disingenuous as the Territorial Council's abandonment of a duty on pemmican and hides because the matter properly belonged to the dominion government.[103] The Territorial Council was directly appointed by Ottawa and worked under dominion authority. As in so many critical matters in Indian policy, there is no direct evidence that the dominion government intended to wait idle while the buffalo were exterminated. Yet there can be no doubt that Canadian authorities were aware of the American policy of extermination of the buffalo.

Indian problems on the international border turned on the migration of the buffalo herds, as tribes moved back and forth across a border that was meaningless to their traditional hunting patterns. While a tribe was on either side of the border, it engaged in all kinds of political relationships with the respective governments of Canada and the United States. This included accepting 'presents' and other forms of aid from both sides, a practice that American and Canadian authorities found dishonest, evidence of the bad character of Indian people, but that was completely consistent with the tribes' own view of their nation-to-nation relationships with the two countries. This international problem would also disappear with the end of the buffalo.

The preservation of the buffalo, on the other hand, would have kept the Indians eating well for a number of years while a gradual policy of settling the reserves was implemented. Feeding the Indians was an expensive proposition, far more costly than the police efforts that might have prolonged the great buffalo herds. Game-law enforcement was not impossible in the mid-1870s, although it is not clear whether the buffalo could have been adequately protected. The important point, however, is that such enforcement was not even attempted.

The Indian Act does not loom large in Canadian legal history, yet it consigned Indian nations and Indian people to a legal never-never land. Parliament's passage of the Indian Acts of 1869 and 1876 institutionalized the colonial Ontario Indian policy in all of Canada, but these measures were primarily aimed at the plains Indians. At its legal core, the Indian Act was inconsistent with the ongoing treaty-making process. If Indians were legally children in the eyes of the law, dependents without the capacity to negotiate contracts, then they could not sell their land to anyone, not even the crown. If the crown was their legal guardian, then it was a conflict of interest for it to sell their lands to itself at any price. To sell Indian lands to itself at very low prices was not only a violation of fiduciary duty but fraud. The crown's legal view of this matter denied any actual Indian ownership of the land, recognizing the treaties as merely political documents.

It seems unlikely that any of the Indians in the numbered treaties had knowledge of the Indian Act, much less of their inferior status under it, during the negotiations. Indeed, the Indian Act did not even exist until just before the time of the negotiations for Treaty 6.[104] While there is no evidence that the Indians of Treaty 6 were aware of either the Indian Act or any legal meanings it might have, the same cannot be said of the crown. Deputy Superintendent General of Indian Affairs Vankoughnet acknowledged in a memorandum on 22 August, the day before Treaty 6 was signed, that 'the legal status of the Indians of Canada is that of minors, with the Government as their guardians.'[105]

Minors, of course, cannot sign either political or legal documents, and so the resulting treaties, whether political or legal documents, were invalid according to this logic: the crown wanted to have it both ways. The illegality and illogic of the crown's position raises a number of questions. At its basest, the Crown policy behind treaty negotiations appears simply to have been to pacify children, a treacherous and hypocritical betrayal of principle, even by the standards of the day. It is impossible to believe that Vankoughnet's official statement of policy was either new or unknown to the treaty commissioners. Even if the statement, made only one day before the signing of Treaty 6, was unknown to treaty commissioners at the time, the same treaty-making process continued through

Treaties 7 and 8, when the Commissioners would have been aware that they were conducting a solemn political and legal negotiation with 'children.' The point is obvious: the Indian Act was patently inconsistent with both the political and the legal components of the treaty process. Politically, the tribes would never accept the status of children. Legally, children could not negotiate anything.

Few of the provisions of either the 1869 or the 1876 Indian Act were new. The act originated in Upper Canada in the 1830s with individual laws protecting Indians from the depredations of whites. The first of these forbade whites to purchase, lease, or otherwise contract to buy Indian lands. Later acts prohibited whites from making any contracts at all with Indians or from foreclosing on Indian property.[106] While these acts forbade whites only from engaging in legal transactions with Indians, their effect was to make it impossible for Indians to engage in many forms of commerce. An Indian farmer, for example, could not mortgage his buildings to borrow money to make improvements. He could not sell the hay or produce of his farm without the approval of the Indian agent, a requirement that interfered with the operation of the government's policy of promoting Indian self-sufficiency.[107]

This paternalism worked in two opposing ways. On the one hand, the Indian Acts criminalized a good deal of the routine actions of rural whites living in the area of Indian reserves. Purchasing or leasing Indian lands or buying hay, firewood, lumber, or produce from individual Indians were against the law, punishable by either imprisonment or fine. Not only was this substantive law broad and general, but it carried with it summary procedures before a special court: the Indian agent was designated a magistrate for offences under the act. Local whites regularly violated these laws.

On the other hand, the Indian Act made Indians a special class of persons, legal dependents on the crown, children in the eyes of the law. They could not vote, buy or use alcohol, sell the produce from their own farms, enter into contracts for any purpose, mortgage their property, or sell or lease their lands. Although Indians were subject to the penal provisions of the Indian Act in the same way that all residents of Canada were, these social disabilities were more often civil in nature. Agreements made contrary to the Indian Act were unenforceable in court.

The acts, then, not merely consisted of civil disabilities and criminal penalties but also created a top-down and autocratic legal order on the reserves. This organization of the rule of law into what amounted to an administrative order on the reserves paralleled the function of the

NWMP as both a law-enforcement and a judicial agency. This prompted one Anglican missionary in the northwest to comment as follows: 'There seemed to be no recognized law except the decision of a Magistrate, and no one could tell what this would be or the code that might rule him. There was, in fact, no law, although there was supposed to be a Government. We were not in Ontario, or Quebec, or Manitoba. We were in an undefined territory, subject to the man who happened to be in office, and he was a great distance from his superiors and found no difficulty in shielding himself behind his own reports.'[108]

The scope of the Indian Act was enormous: thousands of adult Indians, with strong cultural ideals of autonomy and freedom within their own societies, were put under this legal order, with many of the details of their daily lives under the control of Indian agents, a range of lower-level reserve officials, or police. It is impossible to document the precise level of resistance. Starving Indians resisted in a number of ways. There are a number of documented assaults on Indian agents and employees of the Indian Department. Big Bear's father-in-law, Yayakootyawapos, had returned in 1884 empty-handed from a long hunt in the dead of winter. He went to the reserve farmer, Delaney, an Indian Department employee, to beg food for his family. Delaney brusquely turned him down and ordered him out of the ration house. Yayakootyawapos refused to leave and Delaney grabbed him by the arm. Yayakootyawapos produced a knife. Delaney ran out of the building, locking Yayakootyawapos inside. The NWMP came shortly, arrested Yayakootyawapos, and had him sentenced to two years in the guardhouse at Battleford.[109] His trial would have consisted of a hearing of a few minutes' duration, with Delaney probably serving as the only witness. This harsh sentence represents the use of criminal law to defend the agent-dominated social order on the reserves. Evidently, this was not the limit of such prosecutions. When Crow Collar, a Sarcee, broke the scales in the ration house in a dispute over the distribution of food, he was defended by his chief, Bull's Head. NWMP Assistant Superintendent John McIllree threatened to arrest Bull's Head for his actions, evidently on the theory that the chief was responsible.[110]

The Department of Indian Affairs was authorized under the Indian Act in 1895 to create school-attendance regulations by order-in-council, with criminal penalties for parents who refused to send their children to boarding schools. But even this new use of law to coerce assimilation was balanced against the reality of tribal power on the plains: the issuance of orders-in-council was delayed because officials were fearful that it would 'irritate the Indians.'[111] Thus, it was not only the NWMP that was selective in deciding when to use formal legal mechanisms in controlling Indians: such 'benevolent despotism' performed important functions in making the legal order flexible and able to adapt to circumstances that made enforcement poor policy.

THE PASS SYSTEM

The Indian Act turned out not to offer Canadian authorities enough control over prairie Indians. After the 1885 rebellion a pass system was introduced, confining Indians to reserves unless they procured a 'pass' from the Indian agent stating their place of travel as well as the reason for and duration of their visit. This pass system was completely extra-legal and recognized as such by all crown officials at the time. The adoption of the pass system on the prairies was the product of Department of the Interior policy, but without resort to the necessary legislation that would have extended the Indian Act. The fact that it was not even necessary to have legislation to cover such a wholesale and widespread illegality reflects the extra-legal quality of law on the prairies. The NWMP opposed the pass system, but also apparently informally tried to enforce it – at least until 1892 – insofar as enforcement was possible given that the system had no validity in law.[112]

While the intent of dominion authorities was to force plains Indians to reserves, nothing in the text of the treaties bound the Indians to live there. The language of the treaty negotiations, in fact, expresses the opposite intent: the Indians were determined to carry on their traditional ways as much as possible and would have refused to sign any agreement in effect imprisoning themselves on reserves. It was the Northwest Rebellion of 1885, however, that gave Canadian authorities their immediate pretext to force the Indians back to the reserves as a matter of military necessity. General Frederick Middleton wrote Lieutenant Governor Edgar Dewdney early in the uprising requesting that he issue an order that Indians and Metis return to their reserves or be treated as rebels. Dewdney did so, even though it is not clear that many Indians were, in fact, off their reserves.[113] Immediately after the war ended, Dewdney reminded an Indian agent that the order was due only to the exigencies of war and that there 'exists no law by which Indians can be punished for being off their Reserves.'[114]

The Indian Department, however, took matters into its own hands. On 16 August 1885 Hayter Reed, assistant Indian commissioner for the

North-West Territories, issued an order that Indians in the Battleford area not be allowed to leave their reserves without passes: 'I am adopting a system of keeping the Indians on their respective Reserves and not allowing any [to] leave them without passes – I know this is hardly supported by any legal enactment but we must do many things which can only be supported by common sense and by what may be for the general good. I get the Police to send out daily and send any Indians without passes back to their reserves.'[115]

Although little is known about the actual use of passes, the policy was soon general throughout the prairies. The Indian Department had pass forms commercially printed. Reed sent three books of printed passes to the Indian agent at Peace Hills in October, with instructions that he distribute the forms to his agency farmers. These printed pass forms were in use until at least 1918.[116] The pass system was unique to the prairie reserves.

Sam Steele, NWMP commander, reported on the difficulties of enforcing the pass system:

I have the honour to report for your information that as usual immediately after treaty payment there are a great many Indians moving about visiting other reserves, etc., and probably with the view to keeping them on their Reserves, the Agent at the Blood Reserve has refused them passes, the Piegans who have been met off their Reserve have all been provided with passes.

I doubt the possibility of keeping the Indians at home by such coercive measures as stopping their rations or refusing a pass, they will go in spite of all their Agent can do and if they have to start on a long journey without any rations the chances of their killing cattle is very greatly increased. There is an order throughout the district to turn back any Indians without a pass but a difficulty arises in the fact that few of our men can speak sufficient Blackfoot to make themselves understood and the Indians when it suits their purpose can be very obtuse: they are aware too that we have no legal right to turn them back.[117]

Reed's response was to caution the Indian agents not to allow Indians to leave their reserves.[118]

Steele's choice of language is significant. An Indian's assertion of his treaty right to travel amounts to being 'very obtuse.' It does not require much to imagine hundreds of confrontations between Indians travelling off their reserves and the NWMP insisting that they return. Language of treaty rights and knowledge of the law must have informed individual Indian's discussions with the Mounties. Treaty negotiations make it clear that the tribes were concerned about carrying on their traditional way of life and did not want to be forced to live on the reserves. They were assured that the lands were 'reserved' for their exclusive use but that they did not have to live there. The traditional right to 'pursue their hunting and fishing' activities, which required extensive travel 'throughout the lands surrendered,' was specifically protected by treaty.[119]

The enforcement of extra-legal 'laws' was clearly troublesome to NWMP officers. Indians off the reserve without passes could either be ordered or escorted back or, if they were in local towns, charged with vagrancy, the criminal offence of existing without lawful means of support.[120] No record exists of the numbers of Indians either charged with vagrancy in western towns or forced back to the reserve under threat of prosecution and jail. There was no offence of vagrancy in the Indian Acts. Such a provision would have been redundant: Indians, subject to the civil and criminal laws of Canada, were subject to the laws of vagrancy on the same terms as whites. Most likely the threat of imprisonment for vagrancy was used to get Indians to move on out of town, since few western towns wanted to fill their jails with visiting Indians.

Nor are there any records of the internal administrative process of granting or denying passes. Magnus Begg, agent at the Blackfoot reserve, reported: 'Some Indians have asked me lately for passes to Red Deer to pick berries, but I would not grant them. If I hear of any number going North I will notify the Police to look after them.'[121] Agents were warned, by circular from the Indian Department headquarters in Regina, to monitor 'the arrival of any strange Indians, even though from other agencies under pass ... and their business ascertained.' Another circular limited passes to one every three months. Still another circular warned of the problem of Indians visiting the industrial schools without passes. Indian children were isolated in these schools and it is significant that the efforts of family and friends to visit them amounted to an administrative problem.[122]

These circulars indicate that official lawlessness was structured and institutionalized, but they do not reveal the extent of the actual use of the pass system. The administration of the Indian Act in the northwest must be understood in the context of the structured illegality of the administration of the pass system by both Indian agents and the NWMP, although the NWMP apparently abandoned enforcing the system. These officials were law-enforcement officers and magistrates, yet they participated for a time in the administration of illegal rules confining Indians to small reserves. This demonstration of official lawlessness symbolizes the nature of the rule of law on Indian reserves on the prairies: it was, at least in part, lawless.

Perhaps the most infamous provisions of the Indian Act were those that prohibited Indian dancing.[123] Indian Department officials were only partially aware of the place of ceremony in native life, but they did understand that it was at the heart of tribal culture. This culture was to be broken. It not only symbolized values primitive and un-Christian, considered inappropriate in a modern Canada, but was a direct threat to Canadian domination of the Indian tribes and to an assimilationist Indian policy. The Indian agents could never understand the complexity of what went on in Indian ceremonies, but it bound the people and tribes together in a unique world.[124]

Two amendments to the Indian Act were aimed at the repression of Indian ceremonies. The first, passed on 19 April 1884, was aimed at the potlatches of the Northwest Coast tribes:

Every Indian or other person who engages in or assists in celebrating the Indian festival known as the Potlatch or in the Indian dance known as the Tamanawas is guilty of a misdemeanour, and shall be liable to imprisonment for the term of not more than six nor less than two months in any gaol or other place of confinement; and any Indian or other person who encourages, either directly or indirectly an Indian or Indians to get up such a festival or dance, or to celebrate the same, or who shall assist in the celebration of same is guilty of a like offense, and shall be liable to the same punishment.[125]

This act was not aimed at the plains Indians. The NWMP had serious questions about its legality, as did Judge Matthew Begbie of the British Columbia Supreme Court. Begbie struck down the law in the first case to come before the courts.[126] Eleven years later, a time span indicating that the government was not in any hurry, a revision was passed narrowing the scope of the law to specific kinds of ceremonies:

Every Indian or other person who engages in, or assists in celebrating or encourages either directly or indirectly another to celebrate, any Indian festival, dance or other ceremony of which the giving away or paying or giving back of money, goods, or articles of any sort forms a part, or is a feature, whether such gift of money, goods or articles takes place before, at, or after the celebration of the same, and every Indian or other person who engages or assists in any celebration or dance of which the wounding or mutilation of the dead or living body of any human being or animal forms a part or is a feature, is guilty of an indictable offence.[127]

Once again, the act was aimed at Northwest Coast Indians and the law was meant to satisfy difficulties with the ambiguity of the 1885 act. The two dances referred to were the potlatch and Hamat'sa rituals. But the language would also have included two common plains rituals, the sun dance and the thirst dance, which involved the piercing of human flesh, several ceremonies in which dog flesh was consumed, and other dances involving the giving away of property.[128]

It is difficult to determine the impact of these laws on the daily religious and ceremonial life of plains Indians. The Cree Chief, Piapot, was arrested twice, once in the late 1890s and again in 1901. Piapot agreed to include a traditional piercing ritual in his annual rain dance, a version of the sun dance. The Indian agent heard of the event and had Piapot arrested and imprisoned in Regina. Through a visitor the chief learned that a sign on his cell indicated that he was imprisoned for being drunk. The chief, who did not drink, became enraged.[129] In 1901 he was arrested for participating in a give-away dance, along with five other band members. The others were released but Piapot, who had allegedly incited the others to resist arrest, was given two months in jail. This imprisonment of an old chief was designed to have a repressive impact on the tribe.[130]

Within the context of the Indian Department's assault on tribal life, these laws were probably not significant on the plains in terms of the actual use of the criminal sanction. Only a handful of Indians actually went to jail on such charges, either real or fictitious. But these laws were important as part of the machinery of repression. Children were removed to schools, tribes were broken up as families were scattered on small plots of land, and language was repressed as children were forced to speak only English in school.

The more important role played by the laws regulating these ceremonies was symbolic. The ceremonies indicated how distinct plains Indian culture was from Euro-Canadian culture. Since government policy was based first on repression, then on forced assimilation, the rich ceremonial life of the tribes was a serious threat to both policies. Large gatherings of warriors for sun dances left the Indians there free to engage in any kind of discussions and actions.

There is no assessment of the effectiveness of these laws in repressing prairie Indian culture. Most ceremonial activity went underground, some to the far corners of reserves in secret. Some ceremonies occurred in the open in disguised form: traditional ceremonies took over official holidays, even Christian religious holidays. Many Indian agents simply ignored the laws, either because they came to believe that Indians had a right to their own cultural and religious activities, or because the tension and difficulty of their position made it politic to do so. The NWMP never enthusiastically investigated such offences because they did not see them as criminal. For the NWMP, the greater problem was Indian defiance of official authority: Piapot was punished more for resisting authority than for holding a thirst dance.

While the attack on tribal culture through outlawing traditional ceremonies has received most attention because of its ethnocentrism and legal absurdity, it was compulsory residential schooling that represented the major thrust of the government's assimilationist policy. Adult Indians would always harbor their cultural traditions. Children, however, could be resocialized. The compulsory residential school policy, also a legal policy, provided for in the Indian Act, was at the centre of this plan. Similar to the pattern of resistance to the legal repression of tribal customs, Indians found a number of ways to resist the residential-school movement, from keeping their children at home to the children's own defiance of the overbearing school regimes.[131]

CONCLUSION

The dominion of Canada imposed an undemocratic and authoritarian legal order in the North-West Territories in the 1870s. The objects of that legal order were two groups without voices in Canadian society: American hunters, traders, and settlers, and Indians. Both groups, with little relationship to each other, stood in the way of the peaceful settlement of farmers on the Canadian prairies and of the expansion of the Canadian state to the Pacific.

The NWMP, at best, constituted a liberal, authoritarian, and paternalistic legal institution, officered by eastern Canadian and British gentlemen under strict orders to protect the interests of the Queen's Indian 'children' from avaricious settlers and Americans. At worst, the NWMP was a racist and paramilitary organization charged with the task of quieting the Indians with the most judicious use of violence possible under the circumstances. In either model, NWMP officers served as police, prosecutor, judge, jury, and executioner, imposing a form of Canadian law unrecognizable in Ontario or Quebec on the Indians and Metis of the prairies. Indian accommodation of the NWMP stemmed more from the force's political role than from its legal function: it was easy to meet with the NWMP and negotiate small solutions to immediate problems. The force had a quasi-military structure that was understandable to the tribes, much more familiar than the faceless bureaucrats of the Indian Department.

Lieutenant Governor Edgar Dewdney and the North-West Territorial Council had extensive legal powers but exercised those powers in a disreputable manner, reckless of native interests and life. Two examples clearly establish this. Legislation to protect the buffalo was within their range of authority and was requested by the tribes. There is no question that such legislation would have involved some difficult enforcement issues, but that was also true of legislation against American whisky traders or Indian cattle thieves, enforcement activities that the NWMP was clearly able to carry out.[132] The council's legislative effort to protect the buffalo was belated, inadequate, and short-lived. Similarly, this council directly administered Indian affairs in the north-west. Treaty 6 guaranteed the Indians crown assistance in time of starvation. Local Indian Department authorities were given direct orders to starve able-bodied Indian men and issue inadequate rations for Indian women and children. This forced adult Indian warriors to stand idly by and watch their families starve. Indians used a number of adaptive strategies to circumvent this abuse of authority, including both covert and overt resistance.

The social order of the Cree, Saulteaux, Blood, Blackfoot, and Dakota, survived tenaciously through the early reserve process. The traditional legal authority of the chiefs kept peace among the tribes but was tested by the hardships imposed by reserve life. The traditional divisions between peace chiefs and war chiefs gave way to different kinds of social divisions, with traditionalists and young men testing existing authority structures. Many of the chiefs, including Poundmaker, Big Bear, and Piapot, exercised great leadership ability in keeping the diverse elements of their bands together. The upheaval around the 1885 rebellion further divided a number of bands.

The illegality of the treaty process still pervades the legal culture of the plains tribes. The sense of dishonesty and betrayal was immediate, brought out in the open in the discussions at treaty, and then repeated over the succeeding months and years as it became increasingly obvious that the crown would not keep its treaty agreements. This was not an option open to the tribes, who approached treaty with pure heart after purification rituals obligating them to speak true words. There was no tradition of dishonesty or of the manipulation of the meaning of words in aboriginal meetings. There were no bureaucrats or courts to decide the legal meaning of plain words like 'maintaining a school.'

Conclusion

The legal history of Indians in Canada is detailed and historically and culturally specific to hundreds of communities representing dozens of First Nations. Each of these communities has legal stories that need to be told because they are at the core of any understanding of the legal history of the First Nations in Canada.

In 1990 a group of natives blocked the tracks of the Canadian National Railway at Long Lake 58, a 537-acre reserve occupied by eight hundred Ojibwa in northwestern Ontario. There was a legal issue underlying the many grievances of the people of Long Lake 58. The Canadian government maintains that they ceded their lands to Canada at the 1850 Robinson-Superior Treaty. The community argues both that it was not represented at that treaty, negotiated hundreds of miles away, and that the treaty covered only the area drained by Lake Superior while Long Lake 58 lies within the Hudson Bay watershed. These lands were not ceded until Treaty 9 in 1905, another treaty that Long Lake 58 people were not represented at. And, no matter who owns these lands, they have been ruined by clear-cutting and the lakes have been fished out and polluted. The community is impoverished.[1]

In blocking the CNR tracks, the people of Long Lake 58 adopted a 'reverse' legal strategy. Stated by Francis Abraham, a seventy year old mother of fifteen, 'Where did the MNR [Ministry of Natural Resources] get the right to tell us what we can do and what we can't do on our own land? How come we have to do a land claim while the others who came and took our land never have to prove anything.'[2] In this view, it is the Canadian government that should bear the burden of proving its claim to the Long Lake 58 community's traditional lands, rather than the community bearing the legal burden of 'proving' its traditional ownership. This legal strategy defies the whole common-law centred logic of the law of aboriginal rights in Canada. If Canada, in fact, has some legal basis for its claims on Indian lands, then why is the government not suing the First Nations and proving its legal title in court? And which nation's laws should govern the dispute?

When Ontario Provincial Police officers announced that the Ojibwa were 'trespassing' and threatened arrest, the community was defiant: it was the CNR and the government that were trespassing on Ojibwa land. Ultimately, after their legal point was made and they were permitted to occupy a camp within the CNR 'why,' a railway junction, the people of Long Lake 58 removed their blockade from the tracks.[3]

The Cree and Dene of northern Saskatchewan have a clear memory of Treaty 10 promises in 1906. They were promised the right to carry on their traditional hunting, fishing, and trapping-based way of life, along with reserves and economic support. In their view, the government tricked them, taking advantage of their trust, their poverty, and their inability to understand English. One ninety-seven-year-old elder recalled, 'I was there when the treaty was signed and there were discussions for a week and we were told, "We're coming to you to sign the treaty, not to harm you in any way. By signing this treaty we are agreeing to help and take care of you people. We are in no way going to harm the way you live."'[4] Yet in the years that followed, their forests were clear-cut, and large-scale uranium mining raped and polluted the lands and waters.

A few hundred miles to the west, the Lubicon Lake Cree of northern Alberta have lost their oil-rich lands, ceded in Treaty 8. In May 1899 David Laird, lieutenant governor of the North-west Territories, headed north from Edmonton with thirteen wagons. At Lessor Slave Lake his party signed Treaty 8 with Cree chiefs representing the bands present.[5] At the time, the treaty commissioners understood that a number of bands were still living a traditional life in the forest and knew nothing of the treaty proceedings. An effort was made to find a few of these bands and treaty adhesions were signed, but the commissioners returned home at the end of July, fully aware that they had not reached all of the bands, including the Lubicon Lake band.[6] The Lubicon Cree never signed a treaty and still claim their lands and the underlying mineral rights.

These legal disputes are unresolved. While all the issues are unique, none is unusual: they represent the broad range of legal disputes that currently exist between Canada and the First Nations. But the disputes are not just nation to nation. Every Indian person lives in the shadow of this legal history, and the stories of injustices are part of their oral traditions. A Cree law student at the University of Saskatchewan stated the reason for his absence from classes: 'I am not going to be in class next week. I am going moose hunting. I am not getting a license either.' The Indians of northern Saskatchewan do not recognize the termination of their hunting, fishing, and trapping rights through the 1930 Natural Resource Transfer Agreements.[7] They believe those rights are entrenched in their treaty and cannot be unilaterally abrogated. This student, by hunting, asserts both his people's sovereignty and his land rights. As a law student, he is getting a legal education that includes both his traditional law as well as the law of Canada. In order to live his life he must reconcile these two laws.

These kinds of cases define modern First Nations legal culture. An understanding of law and legal rights is foundational to the current position of First Nations within Canada, part of the definition of being a native person. But this legal understanding starts with the idea that Canadian law is often, to be blunt, illegal.[8] There is, for example, a substantial literature on the legal construction of treaty language that requires that such language be construed 'liberally' in favour of the tribes, interpreting words not in a technical manner, but in the way they would have been ordinarily understood naturally by the Indians.[9] The common law logic of this position denies the Canadian government the benefit of the miscommunication, procedural irregularities, confusion, and fraud that it introduced into the treaty process and affirms the broad principles of the Royal Proclamation.[10] The First Nations' legal history is replete with examples of illegality in Canada's treatment of Indians.

Modern First Nations legal culture takes this alleged illegality as the starting point for continued legal dealings with Canada. In effect, law has become simply another arena for political struggle. Since the courts are Canadian, interpreting Canadian and common law, they are important arenas for presenting and debating aboriginal-rights issues, but their decisions resolve little. Every victory is narrow, giving one Indian community or First Nation some right they believe they were entitled to all along. In one case, Regent, Conrad, Georges, and Hugues Sioui, in the exercise of traditional Huron cultural rites guaranteed under a treaty, made camp in the forest of Quebec.[11] They were in violation of Canadian law and, following a Canadian practice of nearly two hundred years' standing, were promptly arrested for the trivial offence of 'camping without a permit.' The Sioui brothers, in one of the most important treaty rights cases in Canada, went to the Supreme Court of Canada where they won the right to camp, cut down trees for small fires, and practise certain religious rites on crown land as provided for in a 1760 treaty.[12] This victory, while significant, won the Siouis no right that their people had not had for generations. Yet they could have lost: every defeat underscores the illegality of the whole history of dispossession and impoverishment.

Medig'm Gyamk, chairman of the chiefs' governance working group in *Delgamuukw*, the Gitksan and Wet'suwet'en lawsuit against British Columbia over ownership of their traditional lands, made precisely this point (ironically, given the Supreme Court of Canada's subsequent reversal) when summing up his reaction to Judge Allan McEachern's opinion in *Delgamuukw*[13]: 'It doesn't matter what the judge said.' In his view, either the opinion would be overturned on appeal or the Gitksan and Wet'suwet'en would succeed eventually in another arena.[14] Satsan, speaker from the Office of Hereditary Chiefs, elaborated this position: while their strategy did not include losing the decision, their main objective was to bring forward their claim and show both the integrity of their law and the illegality of the crown's claim to their lands. 'What's important here is for people to appreciate that we are doing a lot of other things than going to court; although we spent a lot of time in preparation for this case, we also spent a lot of time working among ourselves....We're already winning. It doesn't matter what the court says, we're already winning as a people.'[15]

In any case, it went without saying that the Gitksan and Wet'suwet'en would continue their legal struggle in the courts as well as in the public arena. There is a long view of legal history in Indian rights cases. After Judge McEachern's decision was rendered, in March 1990, Wigetimstochol, a Wet'suwet'en hereditary chief, used two hunting and fishing stories to make the same point. 'The grizzly bear doubles back and sneaks up on you,' he said, remembering a lesson he had taught children. And, in the spring, as they had for millennia, the Wet'suwet'en went fishing. 'I told them [the Department of Fisheries] we don't need any permits ... Do you give the grizzly bear a permit to go fishing? ... So, therefore, you don't need to give me a permit. I go fishing when I need to go fishing.'[16]

Just as the Supreme Court of British Columbia was dismissive of Gitksan and Wet'suwet'en law,[17] so traditional chiefs marvelled at the common law method of reasoning used by the court and compared it unfavourably to their own legal culture: 'That's really funny. Look at that.

They can change the law any time they want. Where our laws have remained unchanged for centuries.'[18] While the common law is variable, drawing its decisions from abstract principles that are in turn derived deductively from a vast legal tradition and applied on a case-by-case basis, Gitksan and Wet'suwet'en law was memorized by each generation, handed down as stories from elders.[19]

This legal history shows that there is a broad common law of First Nations/Canadian relations, grounded more in actual human practice than it is in the case law. The lived legal histories of aboriginal people are a part of the common law. This lived legal history itself bestows substantial land rights, a good measure of sovereignty, and a broad range of other rights, including cultural, hunting, fishing, and trapping rights.[20] Indians, as legal actors, not only make legal history but, in effect, make law too.[21] In this sense, legal history is a lived history.[22] The dispute over aboriginal hunting and fishing rights now spreads across Canada. If one read only the statutory law, it would be clear that aboriginal rights to hunt and fish are often limited. The case law testifies to the instability of that law, to its disputed legitimacy. The existing hunting and fishing practices of Indian people tells us much more than the cases do about the extent of their legal dispute with Canada, its seriousness, and of the traditional reasons for hunting and fishing without licences. *Sparrow, Van der Peet, Gladstone,* and *N.T.C. Smokehouse* also show us the extent to which any Indian fisherman can make constitutional law.[23]

The law and legal institutions have been an important arena of political and social struggle, structuring and then containing disputes and violence that might have erupted elsewhere. The nineteenth-century policy of sending law ahead of settlement, in this sense, worked. The corollary of this has been that First Nations nationalism and identity have found effective expression in First Nations and Canadian law. The Indian nations have been strengthened by these legal conflicts. Internal solidarity in poverty-stricken tribes has repeatedly been bolstered by the experience of promoting a land claim, resisting some government injustice, or just going fishing together without the required permits. Chief Clinton Rickard, a Tuscarora who fought Six Nations struggles on both sides of the border in the early twentieth century, made it clear how important it was for the Six Nations to take their case against Canada outside the jurisdiction of Canadian law and, using international law, to the League of Nations. He had little money and, while in an Ontario jail on trumped-up criminal charges, his crops, his sole source of income as a small farmer, rotted.[24] Most of these legal struggles have been lost but, while winning is clearly better than losing, it appears not to have mattered much in terms of the First Nations' understanding of their law and legal rights. Fundamentally, the asserting of Indian legal claims against Canada is not about winning or losing. It is about building nationhood.

This said, it is important not to romanticize Indian poverty, the disorganization of Indian communities, or the human costs of waging and losing these struggles. Any history of Indian Canada must recognize the debilitating effect of recurring social disorganization on these communities.[25] Generations have been lost to poverty, alcohol and drugs, sexual abuse, and despair. And we cannot forget that the most visible symbol of Canadian law in most aboriginal communities is the RCMP and the regular criminal-court proceedings held in schools and community halls, proceedings originally brought to native communities in the colonial era in order to impress them with the power of the King's law.[26] Canada's Indians go to jail in numbers that approach the highest arrest and incarceration rates in the world.[27] Being jailed is an important part of the personal legal histories of a high proportion of Indian people. Many assertions of Indian rights are also violations of penal laws, and many Indian rights cases, including those of Ronald Sparrow, Dorothy Van der Peet, the Sioui brothers, and the 'trespassers' blocking the CNR tracks at Long Lake 58, are violations of the penal code.

There are several implications to these broad conclusions. One is that the 'existing aboriginal rights' language of the Constitution Act itself needs to be understood historically, in light of continued First Nations assertions of those rights. Whatever legal rights Indian people have asserted and re-asserted under their traditional laws are obviously 'existing.' But, even without this constitutional language, the 'middle ground' of the meeting of European and indigenous legal traditions in North America is a common law that both recognizes legal traditions and incorporates elements of their common understanding into modern Canadian law.[28] Since indigenous law, unlike the common law, is not a written law, the lived tradition of native rights must find recognition in modern Canadian law. The common law at its roots is simply the lived legal tradition of the English people, applied on a case-by-case basis by judges educated in that tradition, later recorded, and continuously evolving to meet changing needs and values.

Modern Canadian law and legal history must include indigenous legal history, the lived legal history of Indian people. This tradition includes both First Nations traditional law as well as First Nations oral history, their memory of legal encounters, such as the treaties, that now are recalled inconsistently by two sides. What is needed is a new common law that recognizes indigenous law and legal tradition as well as Anglo- and Franco-Canadian law and legal tradition. To create such a common law will require great creativity and legal imagination, but the quality of Canadian scholarship, perhaps best indicated by the rich discourse on *Delgamuukw*, clearly indicates that this capacity exists.[29]

Yet that alone is not enough. Canadian legal history tells a complex story of Canadian/First Nations relations. It is not necessary to pass moral judgment on preceding generations in order to recognize that a continuing relationship between the First Nations and Canada requires being honest about what has occurred in the past. For example, we can begin with Francis Abraham's question posed at Long Lake 58: 'How come those who took the land never have to prove anything?' Or, perhaps put more technically, why is the burden of proof in a land claim on the Indians? What was it that the Indians understood that they were giving up in each of the various treaties? How in legal terms did the Indians understand the nature of the entire treaty transactions? Were they 'selling,' 'ceding,' or 'lending' or 'leasing' their lands and resource use rights? Were they relinquishing their sovereignty or negotiating peace and friendship agreements? What oral promises were made 'on the side' in order to induce the chiefs' signatures? Were Indians promised the right to hunt and fish and trap on their traditional lands forever? What was the legal object of the Indian Act, especially after any idea of 'gradual civilization' had ended? What damage has the Indian Act regime done Indian communities? And exactly how did Canada get legal title to the Gitksan and Wet'suwet'en lands? Did the crown force the cession of Six Nations and Mi'kmaq lands? If the executions of Indians after the Northwest Rebellion were intended to quiet Indian resistance to forced relocation to small reserves, does this not suggest a different reading of the government's NWMP-based 'send the law ahead of settlement' policy? If Judge Samuel Monk's common law reasoning, which incorporated two legal traditions into one Canadian law, had been the legal norm since the 1860s, would Indian/Canadian relations have been different? We can be certain that the law of Canada would be different.

Some of these questions are rhetorical, many of them bridge legal history with traditional history, but Canada has to accept that this history of 'liberal treatment,' even if it was well intended and avoided overt warfare, did not lead to a result that anybody in the late twentieth century can take much satisfaction in. The questions posed above are important legal questions that are today understood in many different ways by the

First Nations and by Canadian law. And they are properly legal questions, even though they may also be political questions. The federal government's current Indian policy is in shambles. However, perhaps because this policy is so obviously in disarray, there are numerous initiatives on the table. British Columbia has negotiated a treaty with the Nisga'a.[30] The Gitksan and Wet'suwet'en, following the Supreme Court's judgment in *Delgamuukw*, are in a position to negotiate a similar treaty if they choose to re-enter negotiations.[31] Saskatchewan is engaged in talks on the possible reopening of negotiations for all of the province's treaties. The Cree of Quebec have clearly established that their claim to sovereignty and nationhood is at least as strong as (if not stronger than) Quebec's, and they have indicated that they will not separate from Canada but assert their sovereignty to build a new relationship with Canada. This assertion makes the further point that the Canadian nation is a union of many, not just two, founding peoples, placing indigenous peoples in the centre of discussions of Canadian unity.[32] Many First Nations have been working for many years on detailed land claims that have yet to be filed (or have only recently been filed, beginning a lengthy period of negotiation and/or litigation).[33] Indeed, some of the best legal history currently being done in Canada is unpublished research by scholars working on these claims for First Nations. The Supreme Court decision in *Delgamuukw* no doubt will encourage more First Nations to come to Canadian courts, bringing not only their legal claims but also their law into the process.

To a certain extent, we have to recognize here that some of the 'ought' elements of the previous discussion – how various aboriginal rights 'ought' to have been recognized by Canadian courts – to an extent, can also be understood as in the process of happening: Indian/Canadian relations already *are* different because North Americans for two hundred years, in both the United States and Canada, *have* had the benefit of a new common law of Indian/white relations that already has reshaped the formal law that structures the relationship between the two societies. Brian Slattery, Jeremy Webber, and others have shown us that the law has been changed by the meeting of Euro-Canadian and native cultures across the vastness of North America.[34] In addition, the First Nations have long both believed in and argued 'law' that has not been explicitly recognized by Canadian courts. And, as long as this law shapes the way the First Nations see themselves in relationship to Canada and is brought to the courts, in case after case, it exists as Canadian law, whether the courts recognize it or not.[35]

It seems appropriate to end by returning to the cultural complexity of the task of understanding and writing this kind of legal history. Lord Dalhousie observed First Nations law in action and recognized the powerful place it held in their cultures. Yet his advice that Indian law be respected was not followed. It should be obvious, in a multicultural country occupying First Nations traditional lands, that native law must be incorporated into Canadian law, creating a new common law of all the peoples of Canada. Law, however, is not just rules and institutions but also a powerful cultural force. The law must be fair and reflect the most important human values of any society, a complex task in a multicultural nation. Looking at 'existing aboriginal rights' through the long view of legal history reminds us that the First Nations have always been in Canada and have always had distinct legal and political cultures. This history has been structured, for better or worse, by Canadian law. The Canadian legal order cannot be understood in relation to the First Nations in any simple or one-dimensional way. In the past, there was a complex interaction occurring across Canada, in different ways among different First Nations. Much of what happened is unknown or known only through oral tradition. Yet we do know a great deal about this legal history and can reconstruct much of it from a wide variety of sources. In drawing our interpretations, we remain prisoners of our culture – and of our law. But simply beginning to try to understand the meanings of this law, of this legal interaction, and the legal relationship that evolved is critical to fashioning a Canadian law that respects the First Nations and their law.

Notes

INTRODUCTION

1 'Despatch, Lord Dalhousie to Mr Secretary Huskisson, Quebec, Nov. 22, 1827,'
  *British Parliamentary Papers, Correspondence and Other Papers Relating to Aborigi-
  nal Tribes in British Possessions, 1834,* reprinted in Irish University Press Series
  of British Parliamentary Papers, *Anthropology: Aborigines,* vols. 3, 5. Lord Dalhousie served in Canada from 1819 through 1828.
2 Ovide Mercredi, former national chief of the Assembly of First Nations, and
  Mary Ellen Turpel, a First Nations lawyer and law professor, have called the
  situation of First Nations people in Canada a 'national disgrace' and of 'inesti-
  mable social cost.' See *In the Rapids: Navigating the Future of First Nations* (Toronto: Penguin Books 1994), 229. Tony Hall describes the unsettled state of
  relations between the First Nations and Canada in 'Treaties, Trains, and Troubled National Dreams: Reflections on the Indian Summer in Northern Ontario,
  1990,' in Louis A. Knafla and Susan W.S. Binnie, *Law, Society, and the State:
  Essays in Modern Legal History* (Toronto: University of Toronto Press 1995),
  290–320.
3 J.R. Miller, *Skyscrapers Hide the Heavens: A History of Indian-White Relations in
  Canada* (Toronto: University of Toronto Press 1989), and Olive Patricia Dickason, *Canada's First Nations: A History of Founding Peoples from Earliest Times*
  (Toronto: McClelland and Stewart 1992), provide introductions to this voluminous literature.
4 For introduction to the range of these land claims, the legal issues they raise,

and the historical research that supports them, see Ken Coates, ed., *Aboriginal Land Claims in Canada* (Toronto: Copp Clark Pitman 1992); Robert Paine, ed., *Advocacy and Anthropology* (St John's: Institute of Social and Economic Research, Memorial University of Newfoundland 1985); Noel Dyck and James B. Waldram, eds., *Anthropology, Public Policy, and Native Peoples in Canada* (Montreal: McGill-Queen's University Press 1993); and Frank Tough and Arthur J. Ray, eds., *Advocacy and Claims Research*, a special issue of *Native Studies Review*, vol. 6, no. 2 (1990). Dozens of First Nations employ historians and anthropologists to research land claims and most of this research is unpublished. As well, because many of the claims are still in process, some of the research is kept secret since, in an adversarial setting, an Indian nation may not want to alert the crown to the nature of particular claims.

5 *Calder v. Attorney General of British Columbia*, [1973] S.C.R. 313; *Guerin v. The Queen*, [1984] 2 S.C.R. 335; *Attorney General for Ontario v. Bear Island Foundation et al.* (1984) 49 O.R. (2d) 353; (1989) 68 O.R. (2d.) 294; (1991) 2 S.C.R. 570; *R. v. Sioui* [1990] 1 S.C.R. 1025; *R. v. Sparrow*, [1990] 1 S.C.R. 1075; *R. v. Badger* [1996] 1 S.C.R. 771; *R. v. Van der Peet*, S.C.C. No. 23803, [1996] S.C.J. No. 77; *Delgamuukw v. The Queen*, (1990) 48 B.C. 211; [1993] 5 W.W.R. 97; reversed S.C.C. file no. 23799, 11 Dec. 1997 (unreported.)

6 Antonia Mills, *Eagle Down Is Our Law* (Vancouver: University of British Columbia Press 1984), 10–14, makes it clear that Wet'suwit'en chiefs determined the essential course of their nation's legal argument in *Delgamuukw*. John Borrows, in 'A Genealogy of Law: Inherent Sovereignty and First Nations Self-Government,' *Osgoode Hall Law Journal* vol. 30, no. 2 (1992), 291, writes the legal history of First Nations self-government through the history of his own family, members of the Nawash First Nation of southern Ontario.

7 There are a number of studies of native political action in Canada, including Michael Asch, *Home and Native Land: Aboriginal Rights and the Canadian Constitution* (Toronto: Methuen 1984). The armed stand-off at Oka in the summer of 1990 brought Canadian native issues to the attention of the world through elaborate media coverage and is the subject of several books. See, for example, Geoffrey York and Loreen Pindera, *People of the Pines: The Warriors and the Legacy of Oka* (Toronto: Little, Brown 1991), and Alan Borovoy, *Uncivil Obedience: The Tales and Tactics of a Democratic Agitator* (Toronto: Key/Porter Books 1991). See also Geoffrey York, *The Dispossessed* (London: Vintage 1990), Boyce Richardson, *People of Terra Nullius: Betrayal and Rebirth in Aboriginal Canada* (Vancouver: Douglas and McIntyre 1993); Boyce Richardson, ed. *Drumbeat: Anger and Renewal in Indian Country* (Toronto: Summerhill Press and the Assembly of First Nations 1989); Rick Hornung, *Inside the Mohawk Civil War*, (Toronto: Stoddart 1991); and Tony Hall, 'Treaties, Trains, and Troubled National

Dreams.' Stephen Cornell, *The Return of the Native: American Indian Political Resurgence* (New York: Oxford University Press 1988), details this process for the United States and it is surely related to the parallel resurgence in Canada. The rebirth of indigenous nationalism in the United States and Canada is also connected to parallel developments around the world. There is a voluminous literature on these developments on a country-by-country basis. See Marc Miller (and the staff of *Cultural Survival*), *State of the Peoples: A Global Human Rights Report on Societies in Danger* (Boston: Beacon Press 1993).

8 Hamar Foster, 'Canadian Indians, Time, and the Law,' *Western Legal History* vol. 7, no. 1 (winter/spring 1994), 107–11. Douglas Sanders has observed that counsel for the province hardly seemed to take the *Calder* case seriously: 'The Nishga Case,' *British Columbia Studies* vol. 19 (1973), 3, 15.

9 *Delgamuukw et al* v. *the Queen*. *Delgamuukw* and Judge Alan McEachern's opinion have produced a large volume of scholarly literature, almost all of it critical. See Frank Cassidy, *Aboriginal Title in British Columbia: Delgamuukw v. The Queen* (Lantzville, B.C.: Oolichan Books 1992); Antonia Mills, *Eagle Down Is Our Law*; and a special issue of *B.C. Studies* (1992) 3–65. A map of the *Delgamuukw* land claim is printed in Donald Kerr and Deryk W. Holdsworth, eds, *Historical Atlas of Canada*, vol. 3 (Toronto: University of Toronto Press 1990), plate 2.

10 *Delgamuukw* v. *The Queen* (Smithers Registry ed., a bound volume printed and sold by the court and in wide circulation. The published opinion is four hundred pages long, not the kind of opinion that can easily be photocopied from an official report.) 1 While *Bear Island*, (1984) 49 O.R. (2d) 353; (1989) 68 O.R. (2d.) 294; (1991) 2 S.C.R. 570, an Ontario case involving the land claims of the Temagami Ojibwa, pales by comparison, that trial took 119 days over two years. The testimony filled 68 volumes, backed by 3000 exhibits, filling an entire courtroom. See Tony Hall, 'Where Justice Lies: Aboriginal Rights and Wrongs in Temagami,' in Matt Bray and Ashley Thomson, *Temagami: A Debate on Wilderness* (Toronto: Dundurn Press 1990), 223–55, 228.

11 *Delgamuukw, also know as Earl Muldoe, suing on his own behalf and on behalf of all the members of the Houses of Delgamuukw and Haaxw (and others suing on their own behalf and on behalf of thirty-eight Gitksan Houses and twelve Wet'suwet'en Houses as shown in Schedule 1 v. Her Majesty the Queen in Right of the Province of British Columbia and the Attorney General of Canada* ([1997] 3 S.C.R. 1010 at numbered paragraphs 89–169).

12 It is not clear what effect this will have on the use of historical evidence in native-rights cases. Merely allowing the use of oral history as independent evidence still leaves the courts free to weigh that evidence against more traditional forms of written historical evidence. Peggy J. Blair, 'Prosecuting the

Fishery: The Supreme Court of Canada and the Onus of Proof in Aboriginal
Fishing Cases,' *Dalhousie Law Journal*, vol. 20, no. 1 (1997), 17, 50, reports:
'However, in virtually all cases in which oral history has been successfully
used in the context of litigation the aboriginal perspective has been supported
by documents written by Europeans. The author has been unable to locate a
single case in which oral history in itself, without some kind of documentary
support – a contradiction in terms – has been sufficient to make out an aboriginal right.'

13 S. 35 (1): 'The existing aboriginal and treaty rights of the aboriginal peoples of
Canada are hereby recognized and affirmed.' There is a substantial literature
on the meaning of this section. See Noel Lyon, 'Constitutional Issues in Native
Law,' in Bradford Morse, *Aboriginal Peoples and the Law: Indian, Metis, and Inuit
Rights in Canada* (Ottawa: Carleton University Press 1985), 408–51; Kent
McNeil, 'The Constitutional Rights of the Aboriginal Peoples of Canada,'
Supreme Court Law Review, vol. 4 (1982), 218 (part 1), 255 (part 2); William Pent-
ney, 'The Rights of the Aboriginal Peoples of Canada in the Constitution Act
1982 Part II–Section 35: The Substantive Guarantee,' *University of British
Columbia Law Review*, vol. 22 (1988), 207; Brian Slattery, 'The Constitutional
Guarantee of Aboriginal and Treaty Rights,' *Queen's Law Journal*, vol. 8 (1983),
232.

14 Antonia Mills, *Eagle Down Is Our Law*, 180–1; Michael Asch and Patrick Macklem, 'Aboriginal Rights and Canadian Sovereignty: An Essay on R. v. Sparrow,' *Alberta Law Review*, vol. 29 (1991), 492.

15 These are the first two steps of the three-step *Sparrow* test, elaborated and
applied in *R. v. Van der Peet v. the Queen*, (1996) 137 D.L.R. (4th) 289, 310–38. It
takes the court ten pages (310–20) to describe the test for determining an 'existing Aboriginal right,' the first step of the three-step *Sparrow* test. The third step
of the test, applied only if there is an existing aboriginal right and it has not
been extinguished, requires the crown to justify its infringement of the aboriginal right (336–8), effectively balancing existing aboriginal rights against a
wide range of other social interests. Kent McNeil, 'How Can Infringements of
the Constitutional Rights of Aboriginal Peoples Be Justified?' *Constitutional
Forum*, vol. 8, no. 2 (1997), 33, argues that it is improper to balance the constitu-
tionally protected rights of aboriginal peoples against other non-constitutional
interests.

16 (1996), 133 D.L.R. (4th) 324; (1996), 137 D.L.R. (4th) 289; Catherine Bell, 'R. v.
Badger: One Step Forward and Two Steps Back?' *Constitutional Forum*, vol. 8,
no. 2 (1997), 21; L.I. Rotman, 'Hunting for Answers in a Strange Kettle of Fish:
Unilateralism, Paternalism and Fiduciary Rhetoric in Badger and Van der
Peet,' ibid., 40; John Borrows, 'The Trickster: Integral to a Distinctive Culture,'

ibid., 27; Russel Barsh and James Youngblood Henderson, 'The Supreme Court's *Van der Peet* Trilogy: Naive Imperialism and Ropes of Sand,' *McGill Law Journal*, vol. 42 (1997), 993; Chilwin Clhienhan Cheng, 'Touring the Museum: A Comment on R. v. Van der Peet,' *University of Toronto Faculty of Law Review*, vol. 55, no. 2 (1997), 419; Anna Zalewski, 'From Sparrow to Van der Peet: The Evolution of a Definition of Aboriginal Rights,' ibid., 435.

17 Bradford Morse, 'Permafrost Rights: Aboriginal Self-Government and the Supreme Court in R. v. Pamajewon,' *McGill Law Journal*, vol. 42 (1997), 1011, 1030–42.

18 Mary Ellen Turpel, 'Aboriginal Peoples and the Canadian Charter: Interpretive Monopolies, Cultural Differences,' *Canadian Human Rights Yearbook*. 1989–90, reprinted in Richard F. Devlin, *First Nations Issues* (Toronto: Edmond Montgomery Publications 1991), 40–73, 62.

19 John Borrows, 'With or Without You: First Nations Law (in Canada),' *McGill Law Journal*, vol. 41 (1996), 630, and 'A Genealogy of Law: Inherent Sovereignty and First Nations Self-Government,' *Osgoode Hall Law Journal*, vol. 30 (1992), 291; 'Constitutional Law from a First Nation Perspective: Self-Government and the Royal Proclamation,' *University of British Columbia Law Review*, vol. 28 (1994), 1.

20 (1996), 137 D.L.R (4th) 289; (1996) 137 D.L.R. (4th) 649; (1996), 137 D.L.R. (4th) 528; Russel Barsh and James Youngblood Henderson, 'The Supreme Court's *Van der Peet* Trilogy.'

21 Hamar Foster, 'Canadian Indians, Time, and the Law,' 69–112, 105. By way of example, the Supreme Court of Canada in *R. v. Pamajewon* (1996) 2 S.C.R. 821 held that gambling was not an aboriginal right because it was not 'truly aboriginal.' Bradford Morse, 'Permafrost Rights: Aboriginal Self-Government and the Supreme Court in R. v. Pamajewon.' Morse's title, of course, refers sarcastically to the court's application of a 'frozen rights' standard to Ojibwa aboriginal rights to self-government: if these rights did not exist in nineteenth-century Ojibwa society, then they are not 'aboriginal.'

22 (1990), 56 C.C.C. (3d) 263 at 276.

23 (1996), 137 D.L.R. (4th) 289, 325–7.

24 Ibid. at 327–66.

25 Diane Newell, *Tangled Webs of History: Indians and the Law in Canada's Pacific Coast Fisheries* (Toronto: University of Toronto Press 1993), shows how complex aboriginal fishing rights were along the Pacific Coast (at 40–5). While the particular rights involved varied considerably from culture to culture, various kinds of ownership of sites were common, along with complex exchanges in return for fishing rights. In this context, any discussion of 'commercial fishing' rights limited to late-twentieth-century notions of the meaning of 'commer-

cial' denies that various exchange rights in the nineteenth century were the equivalent of 'commercial' in twentieth-century terms. But the problem is broader: 'existing aboriginal rights' have to be interpreted in relationship to economic concepts like 'commercial,' which do not define the nature of aboriginal exchanges of fish and other goods. If 'commercial' has any reference to money or modern economic transactions, aboriginal exchanges cannot meet the definition. Peggy J. Blair, 'Prosecuting the Fishery,' 17, 50.

26 Noel Lyon, 'Constitutional Issues in Native Law,' in Bradford Morse, *Aboriginal Peoples and the Law*, 408–51, 419.

27 (1996), 137 D.L.R. (4th) 289. Aboriginal rights that were extinguished prior to the adoption of the constitution are not protected, but determining whether such rights were, in fact, extinguished also requires a complex historical analysis. Russel Barsh and James Youngblood Henderson, 'The Supreme Court's Van der Peet Trilogy, 1005–6, argue that this framework is too factually complex and specific to each of 600 First Nations even to be law.

28 James [Sakej] Youngblood Henderson, 'Empowering Treaty Federalism,' *Saskatchewan Law Review*, vol. 58 (1994), 241–329, 242.

29 Graham Parker, 'Canadian Legal Culture,' in Louis Knafla, ed. *Law and Justice in a New Land: Essays in Western Canadian Legal History* (Toronto: Carswell 1986), 3–29. The model was explicitly at the root of nineteenth-century Ontario Indian law and is central to Chancellor John Alexander Boyd's opinion in *St. Catherine's Milling*. (1885) 10 O.R. 196, 203–16.

30 The impoverished condition of native people in the United States and Canada is the subject of an immense literature. Canada recently struck a royal commission on aboriginal peoples, which issued a voluminous report that was devastatingly critical of government policies: *Royal Commission on Aboriginal Peoples: Report* (Ottawa: Canadian Government Printing Office 1996). This is not to deny that there are differences between the two countries. One is that the United States government would not commission such a report on its Indian policies. Perhaps another difference is that their limited sovereignty has been effectively used by some Indian nations in the United States to build vital economies, often based on gambling. The Mashantucket Pequot of Connecticut, a small nation, operate the second-largest casino in the world, which grosses $1 billion a year, supports a vast network of tribal businesses and cultural institutions and events, and makes cash payments to each member. *New York Times*, 1 September 1997, 1.

31 Bob Freedman, 'The Space for Aboriginal Self Government in British Columbia: The Effect of the Decision of the British Columbia Court of Appeal in Delgamuukw v. British Columbia,' *University of British Columbia Law Review*, vol. 28 (1994), 49, 70–3.

32 David H. Flaherty, ed., *Essays in the History of Canadian Law*, 2 vols. (Toronto: Osgoode Society and University of Toronto Press 1981 and 1983), provides a good introduction to current scholarship in Canadian legal history. See also Louis A. Knafla, *Law and Justice in a New Land*; Peter Waite, Sandra Oxner, and Thomas Barnes, *Law in a Colonial Society: The Nova Scotia Experience* (Toronto: Carswell 1984); and Canadian Law and History Conference, *Papers*, 3 vols., Carleton University, Ottawa, 8–10 June 1987. Analytical works on the state of Canadian legal historiography are M.H. Ogilvie, 'Recent Developments in Canadian Law: Legal History,' *Ottawa Law Review*, vol. 19 (1987), 225, and B. Wright, 'Toward a New Canadian Legal History,' *Osgoode Hall Law Journal*, vol. 22 (1984), 349.

33 For a review of this literature, see Ogilvie, 'Recent Developments,' at 251–3.

34 Hamar Foster, 'The Queen's Law Is Better than Yours: International Homicide in Early British Columbia,' in Jim Phillips, Tina Loo, and Susan Lewthwaite, *Essays in the History of Canadian Law*, vol. 5, *Crime and Criminal Justice* (Toronto: Osgoode Society and University of Toronto Press 1994), 41–111; 'The Saanichton Bay Marina Case: Imperial Law, Colonial History and Competing Theories of Aboriginal Title,' *University of British Columbia Law Review*, vol. 23 (1989), 629; 'Forgotten Arguments: Aboriginal Title and Sovereignty in Canada Jurisdiction Act Cases,' *Manitoba Law Journal*, vol. 21 (1992), 343–89; 'Law Enforcement in Nineteenth-Century British Columbia: A Brief and Comparative Overview,' *B.C. Studies*, vol. 63 (autumn 1984), 3–28; 'Sins Against the Great Spirit: The Law, The Hudson's Bay Company, and the Mackenzie's River Murders, 1835–1839,' *Criminal Justice History: An International Annual*, vol. 10 (1989); 'Long Distance Justice: The Criminal Jurisdiction of Canadian Courts West of the Canadas, 1763–1859,' *American Journal of Legal History*, vol. 34 (1990), 1, 2; Hamar Foster, 'Letting Go the Bone: The Idea of Indian Title in British Columbia, 1849–1927,' in Hamar Foster and John McLaren, eds., *Essays in the History of Canadian Law, Volume VI: British Columbia and the Yukon* (Toronto: Osgoode Society for Canadian Legal History 1995), 29–85; 'How Not to Draft Legislation: Indian Land Claims, Government Intransigence, and How Premier Walkem nearly sold the farm in 1874,' *The Advocate*, vol. 49 (1991), 411–20.

35 Louis A. Knafla, *Law and Justice in a New Land*, contains three essays on Canadian Indian policy. None of the other works cited contains any reference to the legal history of native people. The development of historical work in native legal history over the last decade, however, is fairly reflected in the fact that Louis A. Knafla and Susan W.S. Binnie, *Law, Society, and the State: Essays in Modern Legal History* (Toronto: University of Toronto Press 1995), contains a fine essay that locates a current Ojibwa protest in its historical context. See Anthony Hall, 'Treaties, Trains, and Troubled National Dreams.' The volumes

in the Osgoode Society's continuing series *Essays in the History of Canadian Law* each contain important essays on native legal history, exemplified by Hamar Foster's two essays (cited above in note 34). The literature on Canadian Indian policy is voluminous, including dozens of monographs published by the Treaties and Historical Research Centre of the Department of Indian and Northern Affairs. In addition to this work there are dozens of published studies. See, for example, E. Brian Titley, *A Narrow Vision: Duncan Campbell Scott and the Administration of Indian Affairs in Canada*, (Vancouver: University of British Columbia Press 1986). Moving legal histories of native people and their relationship to Canadian society are contained in both *Bear Island* and *Delgamuukw*.

36 George. F.G. Stanley, 'As Long as the Sun Shines and the Water Flows: An Historical Comment,' in Ian A.L. Getty and Antoine S. Lussier, *As Long As the Sun Shines and Water Flows: A Reader in Canadian Native Studies* (Vancouver: University of British Columbia Press 1985), 1–26, 1. Scholars are just beginning to use oral tradition effectively in analysing legal events. See Julie Cruikshank, 'Discovery of Gold on the Klondike: Perspectives from Oral Tradition,' in Jennifer S.H. Brown and Elizabeth Vibert, *Reading Beyond Words: Contexts for Native History* (Peterborough, Ont.: Broadview Press 1996), 433–53. Oral history as evidence has often (but not always) fared badly in Canadian courts: it was, for example, completely disregarded in *Delgamuukw*. Robin Ridington, 'Fieldwork in Courtroom 53: Witness to *Delgamuukw v. B.C*,' *B.C. Studies*, vol. 95 (autumn 1992), 12–24.

37 Robert Williams, *The American Indian in Western Legal Thought: The Discourses of Conquest* (New York: Oxford University Press 1990).

38 Diamond Jenness, *Indians of Canada*, 7th ed. Toronto: University of Toronto Press 1984; originally published 1932), declared that 'doubtless the tribes will disappear' (at 264). Jenness wrote in another age, but it is also fair to say that his views represented the scholarly thinking of that age. For a critical assessment of his career, see Peter Kulchysky, 'Anthropology in the Service of the State: Diamond Jenness and Canadian Indian Policy,' *Journal of Canadian Studies*, vol. 28 (1993), 21–50.

39 Diamond Jenness, *Indians of Canada*, 257. Jenness, as an anthropologist, noted the nature of First Nations law in the communities he studied. This is reflected in his discussion of First Nations law at 125–6. See chapter 10 for a discussion of his observations on Ojibwa law and the wendigo killings. See also Sidney L. Harring 'The Rich Men of the Country: Canadian Law in the Land of the Copper Inuit, 1914–1930,' *Ottawa Law Review*, vol. 21, no. 1 (1989), 35–8, for a discussion of his work on Copper Inuit law.

40 For an introduction to this literature, see J.R. Miller, *Skyscrapers Hide the Heavens*, and Olive Dickason, *Canada's First Nations*, secondary works that both

make extensive use of this scholarship. See also Bruce G. Trigger, 'The Historians' Indian: Native Americans in Canadian Historical Writing from Charlevoix to the Present,' *Canadian Historical Review*, vol. 67 (1986), 315–42; and James W. St.G. Walker, 'The Indian in Canadian Historical Writing, 1972–1982,' in Ian Getty and Antoine Lussier, *As Long As the Sun Shines and Water Flows*. This anthology and J.R. Miller's *Sweet Promises: A Reader on Indian-White Relations in Canada* (Toronto: University of Toronto Press, 1991) contain a number of important articles exemplifying the new historiography.

41 Olive Patricia Dickason, *Canada's First Nations*, 63–7. See also Russel Barsh and James Youngblood Henderson, 'The Supreme Court's Van der Peet Trilogy,' 1005.

42 The following is a representative listing of the range of anthropological studies that include consideration of First Nations law. Recognizing that the border between the United States and Canada was open well into the nineteenth century, a few of these studies consider Indian nations that existed on both sides of the border or represent the legal traditions of interrelated peoples. Julius Lips, 'Naskapi Law' *Transactions of the American Philosophical Society*, vol. 37, no. 4 (1947); John A. Noon, 'Law and Government of the Grand River Iroquois' (New York: Viking Fund Publications in Anthropology, no. 12, 1949); William B. Newell, *Crime and Justice among the Iroquois Nations* (Montreal: Caughnawaga Historical Society 1965); A. Irving Hallowell, 'Aggression in Saulteaux Society,' in *Culture and Experience* (Philadelphia: University of Pennsylvania Press 1955), 277–90; James A. Teit, 'The Shuswap' (New York, 1909), 560–62; Cornelius Osgood, 'Ethnography of the Tainana,' *Yale University Publications in Anthropology*, vol. 16 (1937), 138–41; Walter Klein, 'The Sinkiaetk of Southern Okanagon,' *General Series in Anthropology*, vol. 6 (1938); Helen Codere, *Fighting with Property: A Study of Kwakiutl Potlatching and Warfare* (Seattle: University of Washington Press 1950); Wilson Duff, ed., *Histories, Territories, and Laws of the Kitwancool*. Anthropology in British Columbia memoir no. 5 (Victoria, B.C.: Provincial Museum 1959); John J. Honigman, *The Kaska Indians: An Ethnographic Reconstruction* (New Haven: Yale University Publications in Anthropology, no. 51 [1954]), 88–99, 142–65; Franz Boas, *Kwakiutl Ethnography* (Chicago: University of Chicago Press 1966), 116–119; Wilson D. Wallis, 'The Canadian Dakota,' *Anthropological Papers of American Museum of Natural History*, vol. 41 (1947), 19–24; J.W. Powell, 'Wyandot Government,' in Albert Cocuorek and John J. Wigmore, *Sources of Ancient and Primitive Law* (Boston: Little, Brown 1915), 279–91; Pliny Earl Goddard, 'The Beaver Indians,' *Anthropological Papers of the American Museum of Natural History*, vol. 10 (1916), 244–9; John Provinse, 'The Underlying Sanctions of Plains Indian Culture,' in Fred Eggan, *Social Anthropology* (Chicago: University of Chicago Press 1954), 341–74; William Christie MacLeod,

'Police and Punishment Among Native Americans on the Plains,' *Journal of Criminal Law, Criminology and Police Science*, vol. 28 (May/June 1937), 181–201, and 'Law, Procedure, and Punishment in Early Bureaucracies,' ibid., vol. 25 (1934), 225–44; Norman D. Humphrey, 'Police and Tribal Welfare in Plains Indian Cultures,' ibid., vol. 33 (1942), 147–61; Garrick Bailey, 'Social Control on the Plains,' in W. Raymond Wood and Margot Liberty, *Anthropology on the Great Plains* (Lincoln: University of Nebraska Press 1980); David Mandelbaum, 'The Plains Cree,' *Anthropological Papers of the American Museum of Natural History* vol. 27 (1940), 230–3; M. Rossignol, 'Property Concepts among the Cree of the Rocks,' *Primitive Man: Quarterly Bulletin of the Catholic Anthropological Conference*, vol. 12, no. 3 (July 1939), 61–70; Regina Flannery, 'The Gros Ventres of Montana,' *Catholic University of America, Anthropological Series* (1953), 42–51, 183–90; Bruce Graham Trigger, 'Order and Freedom in Huron Society,' *Anthropologica*, vol. 5 (1968), 151–69; Elisabeth Tooker, 'An Ethnography of the Huron Indians, 1615–1649,' *Smithsonian Institution, Bureau of American Ethnology Bulletin*, vol. 190 (1964), 52–7; 117–20; Cornelius Osgood, 'Contributions to the Ethnography of the Kutchin,' *Yale University Publications in Anthropology*, vol. 14 (1936), 114–15; 124–5; 132–3; Margaret Carswell, 'Social Controls among the Native Peoples of the Northwest Territories in the Pre-Contact Period,' *Alberta Law Review*, vol. 22 (1984), 303–8; Ruth Landes, 'Ojibwa Sociology,' *Columbia University Contributions to Anthropology*, vol. 24 (1937), 1–3, 50–1. There is a much larger literature on United States Indian nations that is also relevant, beginning with Karl Llewellyn and E. A. Hoebbel's classic, *The Cheyenne Way* (Norman: University of Oklahoma Press 1941). It is the leaving out of these legal traditions from the Canadian constitutional discourse that leads Mary Ellen Turpel to conclude 'that the Charter does not extend to them.' Mary Ellen Turpel, 'Aboriginal Peoples and the Canadian Charter: Interpretive Monopolies, Cultural Differences,' in Richard Devlin, *First Nations Issues*, 40–73, 62.

43 John Borrows, in 'With or Without You,' and 'A Genealogy of Law,' has written on some of this history and eloquently shows how it can be recorded for the benefit of all of the peoples of Canada.

44 Antonia Mills, *Eagle Down Is Our Law*, represents scholarship on Witsuwit'en law done at the direction of traditional chiefs, plaintiffs in *Delgamuukw*. While the case was lost, Medig'm Gyamk, one of the chiefs, had the last word on the judge's decision: 'It doesn't matter what the judge said.' See Frank Cassidy, *Aboriginal Title in British Columbia*, 303–9.

45 Arthur J. Ray, *Indians in the Fur Trade: Their Role as Hunters, Trappers, and Middlemen in the Lands Southwest of Hudson Bay, 1660–1870* (Toronto: University of Toronto Press 1974); Bruce M. White, 'A Skilled Game of Exchange: Ojibwa Fur Trade Protocol,' *Minnesota History* (summer 1987) 229–40.

46 D. Bruce Johnson, 'The Formation and Protection of Property Rights among the Southern Kwakiutl Indians,' *Journal of Legal Studies*, vol. 15 (January 1986), 41–67.

47 Jeremy Webber, 'Relations of Force and Relations of Justice: The Emergence of Normative Community between Colonists and Aboriginal Peoples,' *Osgoode Hall Law Journal*, vol. 33 (1995), 624; Richard White: *The Middle Ground: Indians, Empires, and Republics in the Great Lakes Region, 1650–1815* (Cambridge: Cambridge University Press 1991).

48 John Phillip Reid, 'Restraints of Vengeance: Retaliation in Kind and the Use of Indian Law in the Old Oregon Country,' *Oregon Historical Quarterly*, vol. 95 (spring 1994), 48–91; 'Principles of Vengeance: Fur Trappers, Indians, and Retaliation for Homicide in the Transboundary North American West,' *Western Historical Quarterly*, vol. 24 (February 1993), 21–43; 'Certainty of Vengeance: The Hudson's Bay Company and Retaliation in Kind against Indian Offenders in New Caledonia,' *Montana: The Magazine of Western History*, vol. 43 (winter 1993), 4–17.

49 This model is developed in two anthologies: W.J. Mommsen and J.A. De Moor, *European Expansion and the Law: The Encounter of European and Indigenous Law in 19th and 20th Century Africa and Asia* (Oxford: Berg Publishers 1992); and S.B. Burman and B.E.Harrell-Bond, eds., *The Imposition of Law* (London: Academic Press 1979). Cole Harris, 'Strategies of Power in the Cordilleran Fur Trade,' in *The Resettlement of British Columbia: Essays on Colonialism and Georgraphical Change* (Vancouver: University of British Colombia Press 1997), 31–67, applies a version of this model to British Columbia.

50 These reports are discussed in chapters 1, 2, 4, and 8.

51 Patrick Macklem, 'First Nations Self-Government and the Borders of the Canadian Legal Imagination,' *McGill Law Review*, vol. 36 (1991), 383; Bruce Clark, *Native Liberty: Crown Sovereignty: The Existing Aboriginal Right of Self-Government in Canada* (Montreal: McGill-Queen's University Press 1990). See also the work of John Borrows on First Nations' sovereignty cited in note 19.

52 Kent McNeil, *Common Law Aboriginal Title* (Oxford: Oxford University Press 1989); 'The Meaning of Aboriginal Title,' in Michael Asch, *Aboriginal and Treaty Rights in Canada* (Vancouver: University of British Columbia Press 1997).

53 Darlene Johnston, *The Taking of Indian Lands: Consent or Coercion?* (Saskatoon: University of Saskatchewan, Native Law Centre 1989).

54 Robert G. Moore, *The Historical Development of the Indian Act* (Ottawa, Department of Indian and Northern Affairs 1978), part 1, 'The Pre-Confederation Period,' 1–51. See also John S. Milloy, 'The Early Indian Acts: Developmental Strategy and Constitutional Change,' in Ian Getty and Antoine Lussier, *As*

Long As the Sun Shines, 56–64, and Richard Bartlett, *Indian Act of Canada,* 2nd ed. (Saskatoon: University of Saskatchewan, Native Law Centre 1992).

55 *Regina* v. *St. Catherine's Milling and Lumber Company,* (1885) 10 O.R. 196, 215–16.

56 Richard Cartwright, Jr. to Isaac Todd, October 1792, quoted in Jane Errington, *The Lion, the Eagle, and Upper Canada* (Montreal: McGill-Queen's University Press 1987), 22.

57 Ibid.

58 Patricia A. Bowles, 'Cultural Renewal: First Nations and the Challenge to State Superiority,' in Bruce Hodgins, Shawn Heard, and John S. Milloy, *Co-Existence: Studies in Ontario–First Nations Relations* (Peterborough, Ont.: Frost Centre for Canadian Heritage and Development, Trent University 1992), 132–50, 134.

59 *St. Catherine's Milling,* (1885) 10 O.R. 196, 211, 215.

60 R.C. Macleod, *The North-West Mounted Police and Law Enforcement, 1873–1905* (Toronto: University of Toronto Press 1976), 3.

61 Louis Knafla made these remarks at the 'Canada's Legal History: Past, Present, Future' conference at the Faculty of Law, University of Manitoba, Winnipeg, on 2 October 1997. He illustrated his point with the example that his own personal library of Canadian legal history included nine shelves of regional histories and only one shelf of national legal histories. The point proved quite controversial as some historians present argued that Canadian legal history, in fact, *was* a regional history and not a national history.

CHAPTER 1

1 John F. Leslie, *Commissions of Inquiry into Indian Affairs in the Canadas, 1828–1858: Evolving a Corporate Memory for the Indian Department* (Department of Indian Affairs and Northern Development, Ottawa, 1985), 9–10; David T. McNab, 'Herman Merivale and the British Empire, 1806–1874' (Ph.D. dissertation, University of Lancaster, 1978). Merivale was assistant undersecretary of state at the Colonial Office after 1847, during the period when control of Indian affairs was turned over to Canadian authorities. There is an extensive literature on the Colonial Office and native policy in Australia and New Zealand. See Henry Reynolds, *The Law of the Land* (Ringwood, Victoria: Penguin Books 1987); James Belich, *The New Zealand Wars and the Victorian Interpretation of Racial Conflict.* (Auckland: Auckland University Press 1986).

2 This period was before 'the great race' for colonies in Africa and Asia in the mid- to late-nineteenth century which added dozens of colonies to the empire. Most of India, also a colony in this period, was ruled 'indirectly' through

indigenous political institutions, an administrative method that put much less of a burden on the Colonial Office because it was freed of responsibility for the oversight of ordinary administrative matters. At the same time, this method caused considerable difficulties of its own. Vasudha Dhagamwar, *Law, Power, and Justice: Protection of Personal Rights under the Indian Penal Code* (Bombay: Tripathi 1974), 3–60; David Arnold, *Police, Power, and Colonial Rule: Madras, 1859–1947* (Delhi: Oxford University Press 1986), 7–35.

3 John J. Tobias, 'Protection, Civilization, Assimilation: An Outline History of Canada's Indian Policy,' and John S. Milloy, 'The Early Indian Acts: Developmental Strategy and Constitutional Change,' in Ian Getty and Antoine Lussier, *As Long As the Sun Shines and the Water Flows: A Reader on Canadian Native Studies* (Vancouver: University of British Columbia Press, 1983), 29–55, 56–64.

4 *Report on the Indians of Upper Canada, 1839*, Great Britain, Parliament, House of Commons, 'Subcommittee appointed to make a comprehensive inquiry into the state of the Aborigines of British North America,' 29.

5 Maitland to Bathurst, 18 January 1826, Colonial Office Papers, 42/377, 10, Quoted in Gerald M. Craig, *Upper Canada: The Formative Years*, (Toronto: McClelland and Stewart 1963), 124–5.

6 Jane Errington, *The Lion, the Eagle, and Upper Canada: A Developing Colonial Ideology* (Montreal: McGill-Queens University Press 1987), 32.

7 Robert Fraser, 'All the Privileges which Englishmen Possess: Order, Rights, and Constitutionalism in Upper Canada,' in *Provincial Justice: Upper Canadian Legal Portraits* (Toronto: Osgoode Society and University of Toronto Press, 1992), xxi–xcii. See also more general works in Upper Canadian political culture: S.J.R. Noel, *Patrons, Clients, and Brokers: Ontario Society and Politics, 1791–1896* (Toronto: University of Toronto Press 1990); David Mills, *The Idea of Loyalty in Upper Canada, 1784–1850* (Montreal: McGill-Queen's University Press 1988); S.F. Wise, *God's Peculiar Peoples: Essays on Political Culture in Nineteenth Century Canada*, B. McKillop and Paul Romney, eds. (Ottawa: Carleton University Press 1993); Jane Errington, *The Lion, the Eagle, and Upper Canada*.

8 Robert Fraser, 'All the Privileges which Englishmen Possess.' See, more generally, Jane Errington, *The Lion, the Eagle, and Upper Canada*, and David M.L. Farr, *The Colonial Office and Canada, 1867–1887* (Toronto: University of Toronto Press 1955).

9 Allan Greer and Ian Radforth, eds., *Colonial Leviathan: State Formation in Mid-Nineteenth Century Canada* (Toronto: University of Toronto Press 1992).

10 Most of the published historical research on Canadian Indian policy concerns these Indian Acts, and therefore my study focuses on the judicial, rather than the legislative, embodiment of Indian policy. It is important to note, however, that just as the judge-made law of Indian affairs in Canada largely originated

in Ontario, so did the Indian Acts of Ontario become the basis for the domin-
ion Indian Acts. Robert G. Moore, *The Historical Development of the Indian Act*
(Ottawa: Department of Indian and Northern Affairs 1978), part 1, 'The Pre-
Confederation Period,' 1–51. See also John S. Milloy, 'The Early Indian Acts.'

11 Canada, Legislative Assembly, *Report on the Affairs of the Indians in Canada*
1844, Journal of the Legislative Assembly, Appendix EEE, 1844–5 (more commonly referred to as the 'Bagot Commission'): 'The records of the Courts of
Justice furnish undoubted evidence that the Indians are amenable to, and
enjoy the protection of, both the civil and criminal laws of the Province.' (note
on p. 4 [report unpaginated]).

12 John Phillip Reid, 'Principles of Vengeance: Fur Trappers, Indians, and Retaliation for Homicide in the Transboundary North American West,' *Western Historical Quarterly*, vol. 24 (February 1993), 21–43; 'Certainty of Vengeance: The
Hudson's Bay Company and Retaliation in Kind Against Indian Offenders in
New Caledonia,' *Montana: The Magazine of Western History*, vol. 43 (winter,
1993), 4–17.

13 Tony Hall, 'Native Limited Identities and Newcomer Metropolitanism in
Upper Canada, 1814–1867' in David Keene and Colin Read, *Old Ontario* (Toronto: Dundurn Press 1990), 148–73.

14 Patrick Brode, *Sir John Beverley Robinson: Bone and Sinew of the Compact*. (Toronto: University of Toronto Press 1984), 98. The British barrister John Walpole
Willis, Robinson's rival for influence in the legal world of Upper Canada,
served a brief term beginning in 1827 on the Court of King's Bench in Upper
Canada before gaining a judicial appointment in Victoria, Australia. Judge Matthew Baillie Begbie, the dominant legal figure in nineteenth-century British
Columbia, in 1870 applied for a transfer to the Straits Settlements. David R. Williams, *The Man for a New Country* (Sydney, B.C.: Gray's Publishing 1977), 161.

15 William R. Riddell, *Michigan under British Rule: Law and Law Courts, 1760–1796*
(Lansing: Michigan Historical Commission 1926).

16 Ibid. William Riddell, *The Life of William Dummer Powell* (Lansing: Michigan
Historical Commission 1926), 60–77, describes the journey. Obviously, these
judges did not go beyond the range of Euro-Canadian settlement, and so Indians, living in the portions of Upper Canada that stretched towards the Manitoba border, were beyond the range of Canadian law. The area beyond the St
Clair River is now part of the United States, but it was occupied by British
authorities until after the War of 1812.

17 For a complete history of residential schools and their role in Indian assimilation, see J.R. Miller, *Shingwauk's Vision: A History of Native Residential Schools*
(Toronto: University of Toronto Press 1996). On the role of missionaries in the
process of Indian assimilation, see Elizabeth Graham, *Medicine Man and Mis-*

sionary: Missionaries as Agents of Change among the Indians of Southern Ontario, 1784–1867 (Toronto: Peter Martin Associates 1975). Education and religion, of course, often went hand in hand in schools operated by religious denominations.

18 W.J. Mommsen and J.A. De Moor, *European Expansion and Law: The Encounter of European and Indigenous Law in 19th and 20th Century Africa and Asia* (Oxford: Berg Publishers 1992), 15–38.

19 Great Britain, House of Commons, Committee on Aborigines in British Settlements, *Report on the Indians of Upper Canada, Parliamentary Papers*, 26 June 1837 (extract), in Kenneth Bell and William P. Morrell, *Select Documents on British Colonial Policy, 1830–1860*, 545–52. See also 'Native and Frontier Policy,' 449–596; and British Parliamentary Papers, Irish Universities Press Series, *Anthropology: Aborigines* (Shannon: Irish Universities Press 1968), 3 vols., a collection including (in volume 1) the full report of the select committee 'Appointed to Consider what Measures ought to be adopted with regard to the Native Inhabitants of Countries where British Settlements are made, and to the Neighbouring Tribes, in order to secure to them the due observance of Justice and the protection of their Rights; to promote the spread of Civilization among them, and to lead them to the peaceful and voluntary reception of the Christian Religion,' (hereafter *Report of the Select Committee*). Numerous supporting documents and supplemental reports follow the official report. Papers on Canada are included in vol. 3: 1–147.

20 Klaus Eugen Knorr, *British Colonial Theories, 1570–1850* (Toronto: University of Toronto Press 1944), 376–79.

21 *Report on the Indians of Upper Canada*, 1839.

22 J.R. Miller, *Skyscrapers Hide the Heavens*, 59–98; Richard White, *The Middle Ground: Indians, Empires, and Republic in the Great Lakes Region, 1650–1815* (Cambridge: Cambridge University Press 1991).

23 Quebec was divided in 1791 into Lower Canada and Upper Canada and, from 1840 to 1867, was administered with Upper Canada as a single colony, the province of Canada. Even in the 1840–67 period, however, the two Canadas were largely administered separately and maintained separate legal systems.

24 This parallels the situation in the various American colonies of the previous century. In the absence of strong considerations of imperial policy, local concerns dominated Indian policy. Both sides in *St. Catherine's Milling* argued opposing views of the legal recognition of Indian title in the other colonies, producing a huge volume of colonial documents for the Supreme Court's consideration on the matter but also revealing that there was no agreement at all about what these policies were. 'Supplemental Authorities,' a 400-page volume of documents agreed to by both sides, included in the original case file,

St. Catherine's Milling and Lumber Company, National Archives Canada, RG 125, vol. 58, file 648, pts. 1 and 2.

25 See James Belich, *The New Zealand Wars*, and Jan Critchett, *A Distant Field of Murder* (Melbourne: Melbourne University Press 1990); C.D. Rowley, *The Destruction of Aboriginal Society* (Ringwood, Victoria: Penguin Books 1972); M.F. Christie, *Aborigines in Colonial Victoria, 1835–1886*, (Sydney: Sydney University Press 1979); R.H.W. Reece, *Aborigines and Colonists: Aborigines and Colonial Society in New South Wales in the 1830s and 1840s* (Sydney: Sydney University Press 1974); Roger Milliss, *Waterloo Creek: The Australia Day Massacre of 1838, George Gipps, and the British Conquest of New South Wales*, (Ringwood, Victoria: McPhee Gribble 1992). Violence against indigenous peoples is a major theme of the *Report of the Select Committee*.

26 The *Report of the Select Committee* began with a colony by colony survey, starting with Newfoundland, which was held out as an example of perhaps the worst of the colonial atrocities against indigenous people. It pointed out that 'it was considered a meritorious act to kill an Indian,' ahistorically quoting Cotton Mather, one of the Puritan founders of Massachusetts Colony two hundred years before. It then went on to report that the last two natives of Newfoundland, a man and a woman, were shot by two Englishmen in 1823 (at 6). This reference to the disappearance of the native people of Newfoundland, coupled with Mather's quote, linked the American policy of genocide and removal with Canadian practice, a view of Canadian Indian policy at odds with that prevalent in Canada. British consciousness of the issue of genocide in relation to indigenous populations is significant, relating Canadian policy, unfairly exemplified by Newfoundland, to parallel developments in other colonies. Modern research contests this view of the disappearance of the Beothuk. Ingeborg Marshall, *A History and Ethnography of the Beothuk* (Montreal: McGill-Queen's University Press 1996.) The Beothuk disappearance is discussed in more detail in chapter 8. Tasmania's aboriginal population was not exterminated but removed to island reserves, where much of the population died, though some Tasmanian aborigines certainly survived on the mainland. Henry Reynolds, *Fate of a Free People* (Sydney: Allen and Unwin 1995).

27 L.F.S. Upton, *Micmacs and Colonists: Indian-White relations in the Maritimes, 1713–1867* (Vancouver: University of British Columbia Press 1979), 89, 102–4.

28 Klaus Eugen Knorr, *British Colonial Theories, 1570–1850* (Toronto: University of Toronto Press 1944), 350–88.

29 W.P. Morrell, *British Colonial Policy in the Age of Peel and Russell* (London: Frank Cass 1966). It is important to note here that New South Wales and Cape Colony had a profound influence on colonial policy in this period and engaged in a good deal of uncontrolled violence against their native inhabitants.

30 Paul Knaplund, *Sir James Stephen and the British Colonial System, 1813–1847* (Madison: University of Wisconsin Press 1953), 12–17.

31 Ibid., 14.

32 'Minute of July 22, 1839,' Public Record Office MSS, CO, 201: 286, quoted in ibid., 21.

33 'Minute, 15 Sept. 1841,' quoted in W.P. Morrell, *British Colonial Policy in the Age of Peel and Russell*, 40.

34 (1823) 8 Wheaton 543, 21 U.S. 240. Stephen was mistaken about the location of the land: the actual land in question was in the state of Illinois, formerly a part of Ohio Territory.

35 Memorandum, Stephen to the parliamentary undersecretary, Vernon Smith, 28 July 1839, quoted in W.P. Morrell, *British Colonial Policy*, 90. *Johnson* v. *McIntosh*, 21 U.S. (8 Wheat.) 543 (1823) adopts a conquest theory of the acquisition of Indian title that is abandoned (or at least retreated from) ten years later in *Cherokee Nation* v. *Georgia* 30 U.S. (5 Pet.) 1 (1831) and *Worcester* v. *Georgia* 31 U.S. (6 Pet.) 515 (1832). It seems highly likely that if Stephen, writing in 1839, had access to *Johnson* v. *MacIntosh*, he also had access to the later cases as well. Marshall's analysis of Indian sovereignty in those cases had no place in British colonial law. There is no evidence of any discussion of Marshall's later cases in any official British or Canadian context until *St. Catherine's Milling* reached the Supreme Court of Canada and the Privy Council in 1887 and 1888 respectively, forty years later.

36 The New Zealand/British Columbia connection is well known because the models for Governor James Douglas's Vancouver Island treaties were New Zealand land cessions. Hamar Foster, 'The Saanichton Bay Marina Case: Imperial Law, Colonial History and Competing Theories of Aboriginal Title,' *University of British Columbia Law Review*, vol. 23 (1989), 629–50 at 634–6. See also the discussion in chapter 9. The underlying ideas behind New Zealand native policy, however, were drawn from the British experience with native land cessions in British North America. At the same time, it is important to note that Great Britain did not claim sovereignty over New Zealand until after the Treaty of Waitangi, a fact that raises important legal distinctions between the position of the Maori and the Indians of Canada.

37 W.P. Morrell, *British Colonial Policy*, 90. The events in New Zealand were complex, but this purchase of lands was specifically done under the direction of the Colonial Office. Stephen's legal interpretation of the land title of Indians in the United States, counterpoising it to Canadian law, and his insistence that lands in New Zealand be purchased 'from the Maori' by treaty, would follow only from his interpretation that Indians in Canada had some kind of right to their lands; otherwise there was no need to purchase it. The New Zealand

treaties soon became the basis for the Vancouver Island treaties, and so the process came full circle from Upper Canada to the Colonial Office to New Zealand and then back to the Colonial Office and to Vancouver Island. I.W. Kawarhu, *Waitangi: Maori and Pakeha Perspectives of the Treaty of Waitangi* (Auckland: Oxford University Press 1989); Paul McHugh, *The Maori Magna Carta: New Zealand Law and the Treaty of Waitangi* (Auckland: Oxford University Press 1991); William Renwick, *Sovereignty and Indigenous Rights: The Treaty of Waitangi in International Contexts* (Wellington, Victoria University of Wellington Press 1991); Peter Spiller *et al. A New Zealand Legal History* (Wellington: Bookers 1995), 'The Law and the Maori,' 123–73. On the Vancouver Island treaties' New Zealand origins, see Wilson Duff, 'The Vancouver Island Treaties,' *B.C. Studies*, vol. 3 (fall 1969), 3–57, 7–8.

38 Quoted from the *Southern Cross*, 15 June 1858, in M.P.K Sorrenson, 'Treaties in British Colonial Policy: Precedents for Waitangi,' in William Renwick, *Sovereignty and Indigenous Rights*, 15–29 at 22.

39 'Speech of His Excellency in Council on the Second Reading of the Bill for appointing Commissioners to Enquire into claims to grants of land in New Zealand, 9 July 1840,' CO 209/6:270, quoted in Paul McHugh, *The Maori Magna Carta*, 108.

40 *R. v. Symonds* (1847), [1840–1932] NZPC Cases 387 at 390. Only *Johnson v. McIntosh* was cited and not the later, and more important, Cherokee cases.

41 Treaty of Waitangi, Article II.

42 House of Commons, *British Parliamentary Papers*, 'Report of the Select Committee on New Zealand together with the Minutes of the Evidence, Appendix and Index, 1844,' reprinted in British Parliamentary Papers, Irish Universities Press Series, *Anthropology/Aborigines*, vol. 1 (Shannon, Ireland: Irish Universities Press 1968).

43 (1847), [1840–1932] NZPC Cases 387 at 390. Quoted in Hamar Foster, 'The Saanichton Bay Marina Case,' 635–6.

44 There is a substantial literature on John Marshall's Indian law jurisprudence. See Philip P. Frickey, 'Marshalling Past and Present: Colonialism, Constitutionalism, and Interpretation in Federal Indian Law,' *Harvard Law Review*, vol. 107 (1993), 381–440; G. Edward White, *The Marshall Court and Cultural Change, 1815–1835* (New York: Macmillan 1988), chapter 10. 'Natural Law and Racial Minorities,' and John Hurley, 'Aboriginal Rights, the Constitution and the Marshall Court,' *Revue Juridique Themis*, vol. 17 (1982–83), 401.

45 *Worcester v. Georgia* 31 U.S. (6 Pet.)(1832) 515: 'The very fact of repeated treaties with them recognizes it [their title to self-government]; and the settled doctrine of the law of nations is, that a weaker power does not surrender its independence – its right to self-government, by associating with a stronger,

and taking its protection. A weak state, in order to provide for its safety, may place itself under the protection of one more powerful, without stripping itself of the right of government, and ceasing to be a state. Examples of this kind are not wanting in Europe.'

46 Stephen to Vernon Smith, 28 July 1839, CO 209 4:343, quoted in Paul McHugh, *The Maori Magna Carta*, 47.

47 All of the reports on the mismanagement of indigenous lands in these colonies went across Stephen's desk at the Colonial Office.

48 Keith Sinclair, 'The Aborigines' Protection Society and New Zealand: A Study in Nineteenth Century Opinion,' (M.A. thesis, 1946, Victoria University of Wellington, New Zealand), 12–36.

49 *Report of the Select Committee*, 1–87.

50 The eighty-seven-page final report is divided by colonies. Newfoundland was covered in half of a page, the rest of Canada ('North American Indians') in just under three pages. 'New Holland' and 'Van Diemen's Land,' modern-day New South Wales and Tasmania, received five pages; 'Islands in the Pacific,' chiefly New Zealand, eleven pages; South Africa, forty-four pages, fully half of the report. Thus, it is apparent how much indigenous issues in southern Africa dominated the report.

51 *Report of the Select Committee*, 87.

52 Ibid., 3–9. The report and its appendices run more than 1000 pages in three volumes.

53 L.F.S. Upton, *Micmacs and Colonists*, 89, 102–4.

54 *Report of the Select Committee*, 6, 7.

55 *British Parliamentary Papers*, Irish University Press Series, *Anthropology/Aborigines*, vol. 3, *Correspondence and Other Papers Relative to the Aboriginal Tribes in British Possessions*, 'Report of H.C. Darling, 24 July 1828,' 25–6. Papers on Canada run from pages 1 through 147.

56 The Seigniory of La Prairie was conceded to the Jesuits in 1647. In 1680 the adjoining Seigniory of Sault St Louis was conceded to the Jesuits in two grants 'pour contribuer a la conversion, instruction et subsistence des Iroquois.' The Iroquois moved from La Prairie to St Louis, but both seigniories continued under Jesuit administration until 1762 when Sault St Louis was vested in the Iroquois. Ibid., 66–7. The Huron claim dated from 1651 when Hurons at Sillery, near Quebec, received a grant as 'a settlement of Indians.' Ibid., 82, 106–13. A history of the establishment of these reserves is George F.G. Stanley, 'The First Indian "Reserves" in Canada,' *Revue d'histoire de l'Amérique Francaise*, vol. 4 (1973) 178–210.

57 'Despatch, Sir James Kempt to Sir George Murray, Quebec, 4 January, 1830,' Irish Universities Press, *Anthropology/Aborigines*, 3, 66–9. The Hurons had been

removed to Sillery and Lorette and were not original inhabitants of those lands.

58 Of the more than sixty pages of documents on these cases published in the *Correspondence and Other Papers Relative to the Aboriginal Tribes in British Possessions*, none included the actual decisions of the judges. However, for the purposes of the *Report of the Select Committee*, this is irrelevant: the Indians could not have defended their title under any conditions both because the substance of colonial law did not include Indian rights and because colonial legal institutions were de facto inaccessible to Indian tribes. In the end, the Indians lost their lands to the Jesuits.

59 *Report of the Select Committee*, 78–80.

60 Ibid., 80.

61 Ibid.

62 M.P.K. Sorrenson, 'Treaties in British Colonial Policy: Precedents for Waitangi,' in William Renwick, *Sovereignty and Indigenous Rights*, 15–29; Paul McHugh, *The Maori Magna Carta*, 63. This process is documented in a number of secondary accounts. An index and the full text of these treaties can be found in *Indian Treaties and Surrenders*, vols. 1 and 2, (Saskatoon: Fifth House Publishers 1992); originally published 1891. There were a number of irregularities in these treaties, including missed native groups. *Attorney General for Ontario* v. *Bear Island Foundation et al.* (1984) 49 O.R. (2d) 353; (1989) 68 O.R. (2d.) 294; (1991) 2 S.C.R. 570 concerns one of these missed groups, as does the Lubicon Lake Cree land claim. Darlene Abreu Ferreira, 'Oil and Lubicons Don't Mix: A Land Claim in Northern Alberta in Historical Perspective,' *Canadian Journal of Native Studies*, vol. 12, no. 1 (1992) 1–35.

64 Paul McHugh, 'The Aboriginal Rights of the New Zealand Maori at Common Law' (Ph.D. dissertation, University of Cambridge, 1987), chapters 2 and 4.

65 It is important to note that the treaty policy of the eighteenth and nineteenth centuries was the result of the high level of warfare in seventeenth-century New England and Virginia, which killed a large proportion of both settler populations. Russell Bourne, *The Red King's Rebellion: Racial Politics in New England, 1675–1678* (Oxford: Oxford University Press 1990); Kenneth M. Morrison, *The Embattled Northeast* (Berkeley: University of California Press 1984); Patrick M. Malone, *The Skulking Way of War: Technology and Tactics among the New England Indians* (Lanham, Md.: Madison Books 1993); Helen C. Rountree, ed., *Powhatan Foreign Relations: 1500–1722* (Charlottesville: University Press of Virginia 1993); and Ian K. Steele, *Warpaths: Invasions of North America* (New York: Oxford University Press 1994).

66 Dorothy V. Jones, *License for Empire: Colonization by Treaty in Early America*, (Chicago: University of Chicago Press 1982). Indian lands in Newfoundland

and British Columbia (with the exception of the thirteen Vancouver Island treaties) were not acquired through this treaty process. Some of the land in southern Rupert's land was later acquired by treaty, but the treaty process was not uniformly used across the north. There were also a number of irregularities in the treaty process.

67 G.P. Gould and A.J. Semple, *Our Land, the Maritimes*, (Fredericton, N.B.: St Anne's Point Press 1980), 9–14. These treaties were directly confirmed by British authorities in Annapolis Royal, Nova Scotia, in 1728, and so were extended to Canada.

68 For a discussion of First Nations land rights in Atlantic Canada, see chapter 8.

69 See Robert J. Surtees, 'Indian Land Cessions in Ontario, 1763–1862: The Evolution of a System' (Ph.D. dissertation, Carleton University, 1983); Donald B. Smith, *Sacred Feathers: The Reverend Peter Jones (Kahkewaquonaby) and the Mississauga Indians* (Toronto: University of Toronto Press 1987), and 'The Dispossession of the Mississauga Indians: A Missing Chapter in the Early History of Upper Canada,' *Ontario History*, vol. 73 (1981), 67–87.

70 Tony Hall, 'Native Limited Identities.'

71 These breaches of the Royal Proclamation procedure are all reported in early treaties in southern Ontario. Donald B. Smith, 'The Dispossession of the Mississauga Indians'; I.V.B. Johnson, 'The Early Mississauga Treaty Process in Historical Perspective' (Ph.D. dissertation, University of Toronto 1986); David Shanahan, 'The Manitoulin Treaties, 1836–1862: The Indian Department and Indian Destiny,' *Ontario History*, vol. 86, no. 1 (1994), 13–31; David McNab, '"Water is Her Life Blood": The Waters of Bkejwanong and the Treaty-Making Process,' paper presented to the Laurier III Conference, 1994; *Report of the Select Committee*, 78–80; Peter Schmalz, *The Ojibwa of Southern Ontario* (Toronto: University of Toronto Press 1991), 120–46. The later treaties in northern Ontario have similar problems. See Leo G. Waisberg and Tim E. Holtzkamm, 'The Ojibway Understanding of Fishing Rights under Treaty 3: A Comment on Lise C. Hansen, 'Treaty Fishing Rights and the Development of Fisheries Legislation in Ontario: A Primer,' *Native Studies Review*, vol. 8 (1992), 47–55.

72 'T.A.R.R Interview with Elders Program,' in Richard Price, *The Spirit of the Alberta Indian Treaties* (Edmonton: Pica Pica Press 1987), 103–60; Treaty 7 Elders and Tribal Council, *The True Spirit and Original Intent of Treaty 7* (Montreal: McGill-Queen's University Press 1996). Indeed, this view is basic to First Nations modern understanding of the treaty process. See Ovide Mercredi and Mary Ellen Turpel, *In the Rapids* (Toronto: Penguin 1993), 'Mending Broken Treaty Promises,' 59–79. This issue is further discussed in chapter 12.

73 In researching the *St. Catherine's Milling* case, both sides by 1885 used the Nova Scotia experience to argue opposing views of the history of Indian lands

there, a short legal historical memory indeed on matters aboriginal. See the respective factums: *St. Catherine's Milling*, 'Appellants' Factum,' and 'Respondent's Factum,' printed copy in NAC RG 125, vol. 58, file 642, pt. 1.

74 R. O. MacFarlane, 'British Indian Policy in Nova Scotia to 1760,' *Canadian Historical Review*, vol. 19 (1938), 154–67; William C. Wicken, 'The Mi'kmaq and Wuastukwiuk Treaties,' *University of New Brunswick Law Journal*, vol. 43 (1994), 241.

75 G.P. Gould and A.J. Semple, *Our Land: The Maritimes*, chapter 2, 'Indian Land Loss in the Maritimes Provinces,' 29–70; Elizabeth Ann Hutton, 'Indian Affairs in Nova Scotia, 1760–1834,' *Nova Scotia Historical Society Collections* (1963), 33–54.

76 John F. Leslie, *Commissions of Inquiry into Indian Affairs*, 9–10.

77 On the failure of assimilation for different nations in Ontario, see Peter S. Schmalz, *The Ojibwa of Southern Ontario*; Charles Johnston, 'The Six Nations in the Grand River Valley, 1794–1847'; and Sally M. Weaver, 'The Iroquois: The Consolidation of the Grand River Reserve in the Mid-Nineteenth Century, 1847–1875,' both in Edward S. Rogers and Donald Smith, *Aboriginal Ontario: Historical Perspectives on the First Nations* (Toronto: Dundurn Press 1994). See also J.R. Miller, *Skyscrapers Hide the Heavens*, 99–115.

78 John Leslie, *Commissions of Inquiry*, 21.

79 W.R. Wrightman, *Forever on the Fringe: Six Studies in the Development of Manitoulin Island* (Toronto: University of Toronto Press 1982), 16–56, discusses the Manitoulin experiment, which was partially carried out.

80 John Leslie, *Commissions of Inquiry*, 51–9. The full Macaulay report is in National Archives of Canada, RG 10, vol. 718.

81 Ibid., 79–83. Province of Canada, *Journals of the Legislative Assembly*, 1847, Appendix T, Appendix no. l, 'Report of Committee No. 4, on Indian Department.' This report was not published until brought out as an appendix of the much longer report of the Bagot commission.

82 2 Vic, c. 15 (1839). J. Leslie, *Commissions of Inquiry*, 83.

83 2 Vic, c. 15 (1839).

84 J. Leslie, *Commissions of Inquiry*, 82–106. This report was published in the *Journals* of the Legislative Assembly in two instalments. The conclusions were published first in *Sessional Papers, 1844–45*, Appendix EEE. Three years later the first two sections of the report were published in *Journals of the Legislative Assembly*, 1847, Appendix T. The study, unlike Macaulay's and the Legislative Assembly's, reported in detail on conditions on many reserves in Upper Canada. John Leslie, 'The Bagot Commission: Developing a Corporate Memory for the Indian Department,' *Canadian Historical Association Papers* (1982), 31–52.

85 J. Leslie, *Commissions of Inquiry*, 104.

86 Statutes of Canada, 13–14 Vict. c. 74: 1410.

87 Richard Pennefather was the long-time private secretary to Governor Edmund Head and, in 1856, the newly appointed civil secretary. *Journals of the Legislative Assembly*. Appendix 21, 'Report of the Special Commissioners to Investigate Indian Affairs in Canada,' 1858.

88 *Royal Commission on Aboriginal Peoples: Report* (Ottawa: Canadian Government Printing Office 1996). This report represents the most extensive investigation ever into Indian affairs in Canada.

89 J. Leslie, *Commissions of Inquiry*, 140.

90 David T. McNab, 'Herman Merivale and the Colonial Office Indian Policy in the Mid-Nineteenth Century,' in Ian Getty and Antoine Lussier, *As Long As the Sun Shines and Water Flows*, 85–103.

91 Ibid., 185–91.

92 *Statutes of Canada*, 20 Vict., c. 26, 10 June 1857.

93 J.R. Miller, *Skyscrapers Hide the Heavens*, 110–14. For a complete history of the Indian Act see John Leslie and Ron Maguire, *The Historical Development of the Indian Act*, 2nd ed. (Treaties and Research Centre, Research Branch, Department of Indian and Northern Affairs, Ottawa 1978.)

94 J.R. Miller, *Skyscrapers Hide the Heavens*, 110–12; John S. Milloy, 'The Early Indian Acts,' 59.

95 Ibid.; Darlene Johnston, *The Taking of Indian Lands in Canada: Consent or Coercion* (University of Saskatchewan: Native Law Centre 1989), 55–61. The operation of these 1830s and 1840s acts in Upper Canada is discussed in detail in chapter 2.

96 John S. Milloy, 'The Early Indian Acts,' 58.

97 Ovide Mercredi and Mary Ellen Turpel, *In the Rapids*, 81–95.

98 Indian Act, s. 2 defines an 'Indian' as 'a person who pursuant to this Act is registered as an Indian or is entitled to be registered as an Indian.' Donna Lea Hawley, ed., *1990 Indian Act* (Toronto: Carswell 1990), 36. There are obviously many problems inherent in the act defining who is a Canadian Indian. Robert Allen Watt was appointed by Arrow Lakes Sinixt elders as 'guardian of a sacred burial site.' The Arrow Lakes people had died out in the 1950s but were related to other peoples on both sides of the border. Watt was an enrolled member of the Colville Confederated Tribes in Washington. After seven years of looking after the sacred site, he was deported as an illegal alien. Bruce Miller, 'The "Really Real" Border and the Divided Salish Community,' *BC Studies*, vol. 11 (winter 1996–7), 63–79, 66–7.

CHAPTER 2

1 'Amended Statement of Claim, Between the Six Nations of the Grand River Band of Indians and the Attorney General of Canada and Her Majesty the

Queen in Right of Ontario,' Ontario Court of Justice, General Division, Brantford, Ontario, file no. 406/95, 26 April 1995.

2 The 'squatter problem' at Sandwich (Windsor) was, in reality, a sovereignty problem. The squatters opposite Detroit were Americans, and squatter prosecutions were designed to force Americans back across the river to Detroit. Ernest J. Lajeunesse, *The Windsor Border Region: Canada's Southernmost Frontier* (Toronto: The Champlain Society 1960). American immigration was an important social and political issue in Upper Canada. Paul Romney, 'Reinventing Upper Canada: American Immigrants, Upper Canadian History, English Law, and the Alien Question,' in Roger Hall et al., eds., *Patterns of the Past: Interpreting Ontario History* (Toronto: Dundurn Press 1988). Loyalty to the crown was a major issue to Canadian authorities who were much troubled by Americans coming to Canada simply to take advantage of cheap land. Lillian F. Gates, *Land Policies of Upper Canada* (Toronto: University of Toronto Press 1968), 98–122. Sally Ainse, an Ojibwa and a friend of Joseph Brant, secured from Ojibwa chiefs a block of land opposite Detroit at the mouth of the Thames River, legally recorded it at Detroit, and began selling parcels from this tract. Squatters, however, also filled the tract. Upper Canadian authorities found that the Ojibwa chiefs had also sold the same land to the crown, and they held that the crown purchase had precedence. Isabel Thompson Kelsay, *Joseph Brant, 1743–1807: Man of Two Worlds* (Syracuse: Syracuse University Press 1984), 544–5.

3 Judge James Buchanan Macaulay, who regularly heard cases on the Niagara frontier, indicated familiarity with the Six Nations claim in his 1839 report on the Indian nations in Upper Canada, although he did not give it legal effect: 'The Six Nations have, I believe, asserted the highest pretensions to separate nationality, but in the Courts of Justice they have been always held amenable to, and entitled to the protection of the Laws of the land.' This clearly shows that the Six Nations Indians made this legal claim from colonial times.

4 Ontario's Loyalist beginnings partly explain the uniquely conservative and colonial character of nineteenth-century Ontario history. See E.A. Cruikshank, *The Settlement of United Empire Loyalists on the Upper St. Lawrence and the Bay of Quinte in 1784* (Toronto: Ontario Historical Society 1934); R. Louis Gentilcore and David Wood, 'A Military Colony in a Wilderness: The Upper Canada Frontier,' in J. David Wood, *Perspectives on Landscape and Settlement in Nineteenth Century Ontario* (Toronto: McClelland and Stewart 1975). The situation on the Niagara peninsula at the end of the eighteenth century is described by Wilbur H. Siebert, 'The Loyalists and Six Nations Indians in the Niagara Peninsula,' *Proceedings and Transactions* of the Royal Society of Canada, third series, volume 9 (June 1915), 79–128.

5 The movement of the Six Nations Confederacy into Canada following their
   military service in support of the crown in the Revolutionary War is the subject of a voluminous historical literature. Upstate New York had substantially
   remained in British hands through the war, owing in no small part to the loyalty of the Iroquois. Barbara Graymont, *The Iroquois in the American Revolution*
   (Syracuse: Syracuse University Press 1972).
6 *Doe Ex. Dem. Jackson* v. *Wilkes* (1835 U.C.K.B.) (O.S.) 142; *Little et al.* v. *Keating*
   (1842), 6 U.C.Q.B. (O.S.) 265; *Bown* v. *West* (1846), 2 U.C. Jur. 675; *Byrnes* v.
   Bown, (1850), U.C.Q.B. 181; *Doe d. Dickson et ux.* v. *Gross* (1852), 9. U.C.Q.B. 580;
   Doe d. Sheldon v. *Ramsay et al.* (1852), 9 U.C.Q.B. 105; *Young and Young* v. *Scobie*
   (1853), 10 U.C.Q.B. 372; *Jones* v. *Bain* (1854) 12 U.C.Q.B. 550; *Regina* v. *Baby*
   (1854), U.C.Q.B. 346; *Totten* v. *Watson* (1858) 15 U.C.Q.B. 392; *Regina* v. *McCormick* (1859), 18 U.C.Q.B. 131; *Vanvleck et al.* v. *Stewart et al.* (1860), 19 U.C.Q.B.
   489; *Regina* v. *The Great Western Railway Company* (1862), 21 U.C.Q.B. 555;
7 'Haldimand's Proclamation of October 25, 1784,' National Archives of Canada, Haldimand Papers, B222, 1061, reprinted in Charles Johnston, *The Valley
   of the Six Nations*, 50–1.
8 Charles M. Johnston, 'The Six Nations in the Grand River Valley, 1784–1847,'
   in Edward S. Rogers and Donald B. Smith, *Aboriginal Ontario: Historical Perspectives on the First Nations* (Toronto: Dundurn Press 1994), 167–81, and
   'Joseph Brant, The Grand River Lands and the Northwest Crisis,' *Ontario History*, vol. 55 (1963), 267–82; William L. Stone, *Life of Joseph Brant* (Albany, N.Y.:
   J. Munsell 1864), chapters 12–16. Maps of these lands, totaling 570,000 acres,
   are found in R. Louis Gentilcore and C. Grant Head, *Ontario's History in Maps*
   (Toronto: University of Toronto Press 1984), 84–5; Charles M. Johnston, *The
   Valley of the Six Nations* (Toronto: The Champlain Society 1964), is an extensive
   collection of primary documents on the legal history of the Six Nations. Isabel
   Thompson Kelsay, *Joseph Brant*, is the best biography of Brant, and includes a
   detailed analysis of his land dealings on the Six Nations Grand River lands .
   The British were apparently ignorant of the extent of the Six Nations tract.
   Although it was clearly twelve miles wide (six miles on each side of the Grand
   River), they did not know that the Grand River extended almost all the way
   across southern Ontario.
9 Donald Smith, 'The Dispossession of the Mississauga Indians: A Missing
   Chapter in the Early History of Upper Canada,' *Ontario History* vol. 73 (1981),
   67–87 at 72, and *Sacred Feathers: The Reverend Peter Jones (Kahkewaquonaby) and
   the Mississauga Indians* (Toronto: University of Toronto Press 1987), 25–7; Peter
   S. Schmalz, *The Ojibwa of Southern Ontario* (Toronto: University of Toronto
   Press 1991), chapter 6, 'The Surrenders,' at 120–46. Robert J. Surtees, 'Indian
   Land Cessions in Ontario, 1763–1862: The Evolution of a System' (Ph.D. dis-

sertation, Carleton University 1983), at chapters 1, 2, 3, provides a detailed history of these early land cessions.

10 This issue was not legally settled by a court of law until *Logan* v. *Attorney General of Canada*, (1959) O.W.N. 316, although the colonial government of Upper Canada consistently took the position that the Six Nations Iroquois were subject to the same laws governing land tenure as all other Indians in Canada. The Six Nations do not accept that judgment. See Malcolm Montgomery, 'The Legal Status of the Six Nations Indians in Canada,' *Ontario History*, vol. 55 (1963) 93–105, and Darlene Johnston, 'The Quest of the Six Nations Confederacy for Self-Determination,' *University of Toronto Faculty of Law Review*, vol. 44 (1986) 1–32; Donald J. Bourgeois, 'The Six Nations: A Neglected Aspect of Canadian Legal History,' *Canadian Journal of Native Studies*, vol. 6, no. 2 (1986), 253–70. Charles M. Johnston, *The Valley of the Six Nations*, reprints the documents underlying the Six Nations lands in chapter C, 'A Disputed Title,' 70–119. The Six Nations took their case to the League of Nations in the 1920s, embarrassing the Canadian government. E. Brian Titley, *A Narrow Vision: Duncan Campbell Scott and the Administration of Indian Affairs in Canada* (Vancouver: University of British Columbia Press 1986), chapter 7, 'The Six Nations' Status Case,' 110–34. Political issues of self government, although not land issues, were at the heart of another major Six Nations case, *Isaac* v. *Davey*, (1974) 51 D.L.R. (3d) 170; (1973) 38 D.L.R. (3d) 23 and (1977) D.L.R. (3d) 481. See also Peter Maxwell Jacobsen, 'Who Rules the Valley of the Six Nations? A Discussion of *Isaac* v. *Davey*,' *McGill Law Journal*, vol. 22 (1976), 130–47. At the trial court level in *Isaac* v. *Davey*, an Ontario judge held that the Six Nations Confederacy had been granted their land in fee simple. This was overturned on appeal.

11 The Mississauga treaty process was in violation of the terms of the Royal Proclamation and it is not clear that the Mississauga understood the nature of the transaction. See Donald Smith, *Sacred Feathers*, 27; and Peter Schmalz, *The Ojibwa of Southern Ontario*, 120–46.

12 It seems clear that British authorities of this era did not believe that Indians could hold land on the same legal footing as whites, a racially based distinction. There was also, at the same time, a politically based distinction that recognized that the Six Nations political system and the British colonial political system treated land holdings differently. British authorities had not clearly thought through this question, simply seeing this grant of land to the Six Nations as expedient.

13 Mabel Dunham, *Grand River* (Toronto: McClelland and Stewart 1945), presents a popular history of the settlement of the Grand River valley by both Indians and whites. The 'Report on the Affairs of Indians in Canada,' *Journals of the*

Legislative Assembly, vol. 6 (1847), gives the Six Nations population as 2223, the largest Indian population in Upper Canada. The total Indian population of Upper Canada is given as 8862. 'Report, 1847' (unpaginated). The Six Nations lands are mapped and the 1785 Six Nations census is reprinted in Louis Gentilcore, *The Historical Atlas of Canada*, vol. 2 (Toronto: University of Toronto Press 1993), plate 7.

14 Joseph Brant has been the subject of numerous books and articles, giving rise to a kind of 'great chief' view of Indian history. While not intending to deny the importance of Brant in the history of the Grand River Iroquois, such a view exaggerates his personal role in the development of the Grand River land problem. William L. Stone, *Life of Joseph Brant*; Harvey Chalmers, *Joseph Brant: Mohawk* (East Lansing: Michigan State University Press 1955); Isabel Thompson Kelsay, *Joseph Brant, 1743-1807*. Brant's most significant contributions to the on-going land conflict at Grand River are: first, he claimed a special status for the Six Nations, based on their role as 'allies of the Crown,' a position almost certainly shared by all of the Iroquois chiefs; second, and more complex, he was closely allied with a number of whites and invited them to move to Grand River with the nation, either giving them grants of land outright or selling them land. This latter action is more controversial, especially in that it personally enriched Brant.

15 'Report on the Affairs of the Indians in Canada,' section 3, appendix T. This report was made by commissioners Rawson W. Rawson, John Davidson, and William Hepburn, and was dated 22 January 1844. The report is unpaginated and contains 100 numbered appendices. It is cited hereafter as 'Report, 1844 (1847).' The first two sections of this same report are separately printed in *Journals of the Legislative Assembly*, 1844–5, vol. 4, appendix EEE. This is cited hereafter as 'Report, 1844 (1844-45).' It is impossible to speculate why the report was published in this fashion, although a simple explanation presents itself. Sections 1 and 2, involving the major policy conclusions of the study, were published immediately in the appropriate legislative assembly journals. Section 3 is much longer, running several hundred pages, and contains most of the evidence supporting the conclusions published in Sections 1 and 2. This suggests that the importance of Indian matters led officials to decide, at a much latter date, to publish the detailed evidence gathered in the report. Similarly, the 1840 'Report on Indian Affairs' in Canada was not published at all in the *Journals* until 1847, as appendix 1 of the 1844 report.

16 William L. Stone, *Life of Joseph Brant*, 399–403, contains extracts from a speech by Joseph Brant clearly setting out his views on the nature of his agreement with the British on the Six Nations' lands. The entire speech is reprinted in Charles M. Johnston, *The Valley of the Six Nations*, 81–4. Thirty-five Iroquois

chiefs had given Brant a signed power of attorney to sell their lands in a
lengthy document stating the history of their understanding of the land agreement they had with the British (ibid. at 79–81). Harvey Chalmers, *Joseph Brant:
Mohawk*, 284–95, presents another description of this disagreement.

17 Gilbert Patterson, 'Land Settlement in Upper Canada,' Archives of Ontario,
Sixteenth Report (1920), 222–3.

18 Isabel T. Kelsay, *Joseph Brant*, 561–3.

19 Ibid.; William L. Stone, *Life of Joseph Brant*, 397–8. It should be clear that not all
of the Six Nations took this view: some opposed selling any of their lands.

20 Ibid.

21 Sir John Colborne, lieutenant governor of Upper Canada, to Lord Goderich, 30
Nov. 1832, *Aboriginal Tribes, Parliamentary Papers*, 1834, no. 617, 142, cited in
Charles M. Johnston, *The Valley of the Six Nations*, 297.

22 Gilbert Patterson, 'Land Settlement in Upper Canada,' 223.

23 Simcoe's Patent of the Grand River Lands to the Six Nations, 14 Jan. 1793,
reprinted in Charles M. Johnston, *The Valley of the Six Nations*, 73–4.

24 Donald Smith, 'The Dispossession of the Mississauga Indians,' 72.

25 There can be no question that both Simcoe and Haldimand intended to satisfy
the Indians that they were being granted lands, that is, given their lands to
own. The Six Nations would not have settled for anything less. If they did not
actually intend to convey such title, but merely to give the impression that
they were, then they appear to have intended to perpetrate a fraud upon the
Six Nations. The alternative explanation is that this miscommunication was
unintentional, the result of the confused political and cultural context of the
agreement.

26 An exhaustive analysis might be made of these deeds from the standpoint of
the British law of property, but land grants in Upper Canada simply did not
conform to the precise legal requirements of England. Even the restriction
allowing land to be sold only to the crown had parallels in restrictive cove-
nants and in the law of primogeniture. Whether the ambiguities in these con-
veyances were deliberate or not, it seems that colonial authorities chose the
legal vehicles used, and so they must bear responsibility for the outcome.
The Six Nations' chiefs would clearly not have settled for a meaningless land
title.

27 Peter Russell to Prescott, reprinted in Charles Johnston, *The Valley of the Six
Nations*, 98.

28 'Brant's Power of Attorney to Sell Indian Lands, Nov. 2, 1796,' reprinted in
Charles Johnston, *The Valley of the Six Nations*, 79–80. See also R. Louis Gentilcore, *Historical Atlas of Canada*, vol. 2, plate 7.

29 William L. Stone, *Life of Joseph Brant*, 401. The government appointed three

commissioners to administer these sales and hold the money in trust for the Six Nations. These three commissioners did not competently administer the lands, and numerous title problems followed. Isabel T. Kelsay, *Joseph Brant*, 553–78.

30 Joseph Brant, in fact, had himself put on an official list of United Empire Loyalists. Isabel T. Kelsay, *Joseph Brant*, 646.

31 Ibid., 561–62.

32 This issue of Indian title under British law was not seriously addressed until 1885 in the *St. Catherine's Milling Company* case, and it is discussed fully in chapter 6. In this particular context, Lieutenant Governor John Graves Simcoe and Joseph Brant openly disagreed on the question of the Six Nation's title, and Simcoe referred the issue to Lord Dorchester, governor of British colonies in North America. Ibid., 561–7.

33 Alexander Stewart, a Toronto lawyer married to the daughter of Brant Johnson, half-breed son of Sir William Johnson, regularly served as Brant's lawyer, evidently at a high fee. Ibid., 530, 571, 589, 592.

34 'Memoir of William Dummer Powell, 1797,' in Charles Johnston, *The Valley of the Six Nations*, 89–90.

35 The politics of the reports is discussed in Anthony Hall, 'The Red Man's Burden: Land, Law and the Lord in the Indian Affairs of Upper Canada, 1761–1858' (Ph.D. dissertation, University of Toronto 1984), 303–6.

36 Still, even in the 1840s the term 'squatter' had an ambivalent meaning. Some of the histories of Ontario land settlement do not use the word while others use it extensively. For example, Gilbert C. Patterson, 'Land Settlement in Upper Canada, 1783–1840,' does not use the term at all; Lillian F. Gates, *Land Policies of Upper Canada*, uses it hundreds of times. It also had general use in Australia, generally in the same way that it was used in 1840s Upper Canada; see Brian H. Fletcher, *Landed Enterprise and Penal Society: A History of Farming and Grazing in New South Wales before 1821* (Sydney: Sydney University Press 1976). Here I use 'squatter' to refer to the specifically illegal occupation of frontier lands, while 'settler' refers to the general frontier population. Given the unclear nature of much land title on the frontier, however, this distinction is often meaningless.

37 R. Louis Gentilcore, ed., *Historical Atlas of Canada*, vol. 2, plate 10.

38 'Report of Committee no. 4, on Indian Department,' 1 Feb. 1840, also printed as appendix T, *Journals of the Legislative Assembly*, 1847. This quotation can be found within the unpaginated report on the fourth page of appendix 1, attached to appendix T.

39 I have avoided referring to the Grand River lands of the Six Nations as a 'reserve' because that term was not a part of the original grant of land. The Six

Nations did not understand their lands to be what later became 'Indian reserves.' While the term 'reserve' has a legal meaning, it also refers, more generally, to the various tribes 'reserving' a portion of their lands in the treaty process, that is, 'reserving' for themselves the lands that were not sold. Later, the Upper Canada government passed laws governing 'Indian reserves' that were applied to Grand River, and so in this work the term 'Grand River Reserve' appears whenever it is appropriate in that context. It needs to be emphasized, however, that the Six Nations themselves do not view their Grand River lands as a 'reserve.'

40 'Report of Committee no. 4, on Indian Department'; 'Report, 1844 (1847),' appendix 16, 'Report of Samuel P. Jarvis, Superintendent of Indian Affairs,' 17 April 1841, unpaginated.

41 Gilbert C. Patterson, 'Land Settlement in Upper Canada, 1783–1840,' 50–1.

42 'Resolutions of a Six Nations' Council at the Onondaga Village, March 1, 1809,' in Charles Johnston, *The Valley of the Six Nations*, 110–12

43 Ibid., 111.

44 'Proclamation on the Indian Lands, February 1, 1812,' ibid., 113–14.

45 'Leases of Isaac Whiting and Ezra Hawley,' ibid., 114–15.

46 Archives of Ontario, Macaulay Papers, Robinson to Macaulay, 20 July 1852, quoted in Lillian F. Gates, *Land Policies of Upper Canada*, 295.

47 *Journal of the Legislative Assembly*, 1854–5, vol. 13, appendix MM.

48 'Report, 1844 (1847),' appendix 16, 'Report of Samuel P. Jarvis, Superintendent of Indian Affairs, 17 April 1841.

49 Ibid.

50 Ibid.

51 Lillian F. Gates, *Land Policies of Upper Canada*, 7. Gilbert C. Patterson, *Land Settlement in Upper Canada*, takes the view that many of the squatters were innocent purchasers, ignorant of the legal status of their lands (at 233–4). The most difficult cases doubtless involved hard-working farmers who purchased lands initially alienated illegally by speculators, perhaps thirty or forty years before, land that might have changed hands five or six times or more. But the chaotic legal status of the Six Nations' Grand River lands was common knowledge: it was, for example, an issue in local elections.

52 Simcoe's Patent of the Grand River lands to the Six Nations, 14 Jan. 1793. It might be pointed out here that it is (and was then) a fundamental principle of the common law that ignorance or mistake of law is not a defence to a criminal charge. J.C. Smith and Brian Hogan, *Criminal Law*, 7th ed. (London: Butterworths 1995), 80–3.

53 Lillian F. Gates, *Land Policies of Upper Canada*, 7. See also Leo A. Johnson, 'The Settlement of the Western District,' in F.H. Armstrong *et al.*, eds., *Aspects of*

Nineteenth Century Ontario (Toronto: University of Toronto Press 1974), 19–35;
J. David Wood, ed., *Perspectives on Landscape and Settlement in Nineteenth Century Ontario* (Toronto: McClelland and Stewart 1975), includes several important essays on Ontario land policy, including his own, 'Introduction: A Context for Upper Canada and its Settlement,' xvii–xxviii, and Alan G. Brunger, 'Early Settlement in Contrasting Areas of Peterborough County Ontario,' 117–40. This process is described and displayed in map form in R. Louis Gentilcore and C. Grant Head, *Ontario's History in Maps* (Toronto: University of Toronto Press 1984), 25–110. Comparable to the rapid development of the American northwest at the same time, Upper Canada's white population grew from 10,000 in 1790 to 951,000 in 1851, essentially an agrarian population inhabiting a narrow strip of land along the north side of Lake Ontario, then expanding across the peninsula between Lake Erie and Lake Huron.

54 The Royal Proclamation of 1763, a major statement of Indian policy and the source of most British law on Indian policy, expressly forbade the tribes to sell their lands to whites, and expressly forbade whites to make direct land purchases from Indians. Joseph Brant deliberately ignored this law, but Indian Superintendent Sir William Claus restated it as the basis of Canadian land policy in a speech at the Six Nations Council, on 17 August 1803. At the same time, Claus sent a messenger to the chief justice of Upper Canada at Fort Erie. 'Speeches by Brant and Claus at Six Nations' Council, Fort George, August 17, 1803,' reprinted in Charles M. Johnston, *The Valley of the Six Nations*, 133–6. Obviously, the fact that Claus felt the need to send a messenger to remind the chief justice of the existence of this law means there was some confusion about it on the Niagara frontier in 1803. It is clear that Brant had both ignored and flouted the law, in the belief that the Six Nations were sovereign and could dispose of their lands as they saw fit. Canadian authorities were caught off-guard by these actions and equivocated in their response. Thus, Claus is taking this measure to make certain that all branches of the government are being consistent on the issue of the legal status of Six Nations lands.

55 Clark was a Queenston land speculator. Brant had been trying to sell these lands since 1795 but had not been able to get buyers with the money to pay the prices they had agreed on. Since block 4 was one of the blocks originally put up for sale in 1795, it seems highly likely that some agreement on its sale had been reached at that time. However, it was not recorded, and apparently, like many of the other blocks sold then, the speculators involved had defaulted on their payments. This would support the view that Joshua Cozens had bought the land at that time but had not been able to pay for it. Isabel T. Kelsay, *Joseph Brant*, 643.

56 Cozens's claim is quite specific on the details of the deed. He claimed that

Joshua Cozens, on 8 Oct. 1796, paid £500 to Brant in front of Judge Robert Kerr, of the Surrogate Court for the Home District, and Angus McDonnell, barrister, who both served as witnesses. Further, in June 1797 Cozens paid Brant another £500 for a receipt acknowledging the payment of the money. Upon receipt of a title from the government, Cozens was to pay Brant a further £1000. Cozens was allegedly in the secret service of Lieutenant Governor Simcoe, who was to receive two-sevenths of the value of the land. The remainder of the land was to be used to resettle Loyalists from New York, although Simcoe recommended selling the lands in Europe at great profit. *Journals of the Legislative Assembly*, 1836, appendix 37, 'Report on Petition of N. Cozens,' 'Affidavit of N. Cozens, July 1, 1834, 5–6,' reprinted in Charles Johnston, *The Valley of the Six Nations* 164–7.' The details of this affidavit are self-serving, but they were believed by many. The affidavit illustrates the chaos of the land transactions of the time.

57 Isabel T. Kelsay, *Joseph Brant*, 562, 570, 588, 595, 616, 621, 630, recognizes that Joshua Cozens probably made some kind of land purchase from Brant in 1795 or 1796. The sale has a complex legal history: it originated as an 'illegal' sale, made personally by Brant without the approval of British authorities, but it was later recognized. Brant, however, either did not keep or lost his records of the sale. Almost all of the purchasers of these lands defaulted on their payments and many of the lands were resold, often without proper documentation.

58 Gilbert C. Patterson, 'Land Settlement in Upper Canada, 1783-1840,' 228–9. Many of these details are set out by Nelson Cozens himself in his affidavit.

59 Ibid. See also *Report, 1844 (1847)*, appendix 16.

60 No records exist that would show exactly how Nelson Cozens financed his claim. Considering the value of a township of land in land-hungry Upper Canada, it was obviously worth a great deal to Cozens to keep alive his claim. Contingency arrangements for legal fees were unethical at the time, but it is not improbable that the promise of a share of the land financed legal work in support of Cozen's claim. Isabel T. Kelsay, *Joseph Brant*, 562, 570, 588, 595, 616, 621, 630.

61 *R. v. Hagar* (1857) 7 U.C.C.P. 380. This is the same James Hagar who had intruded on Onondaga lands in 1832 and was instrumental in forcing the Onondaga to sell. Mabel Dunham, *Grand River*, 182.

62 Ibid., 182.

63 Ibid., 381–2.

64 Ibid.

65 Perhaps the final irony is that Hager, after all this conflict, left his name on a modern town, Hagersville, on those same Onondaga lands.

66 (1850) 1 Gr. 392 (1850).

67 Ibid., 393.

68 Ibid., 405.

69 The issue of whether an Indian could testify in court was long resolved in Canada: Indians apparently had given evidence in Canadian courts from the eighteenth century. See the discussion in chapter 5.

70 Wilkes was involved in another court case, also concerning the ownership of Brantford lands. See *Doe D. Wilkes and Babcock*, (1852) 1 U.C.C.P. 388.

71 'Report, 1844 (1847),' appendix 16. Jarvis's report, originally dated 16 July 1839, runs to five pages of small type.

72 Ibid.

73 Ibid. In a petition dated 18 Aug. 1836, Cozens had petitioned the Colonial Office, resulting in a dispatch from the secretary of state for the colonies denying his claim. Upper Canada, *Journals of the Legislative Assembly*, 1836, appendix 37, 'Report on Petition of N. Cozens.' Reprinted in Charles M. Johnston, *The Valley of the Six Nations*, 164–6.

74 'Report of Commissioners, 1844,' appendix 16.

75 Ibid. This 'discovery' was of a natural mill site that obviously the Indians knew of but chose to use differently.

76 Charles M. Johnston, *Brant County: A History, 1784–1945* (Toronto: University of Toronto Press 1967), 27. James Wilkes remained a leading citizen of Brantford through the rest of his life.

77 The Six Nations surrendered the town site, consisting of 807 acres, to the crown on 19 April 1830. 'Report, 1844 (1844–45).' It would have been this surrender that encouraged Wilkes to pursue his land claims because the crown then had the authority to grant the land.

78 'Report of the Commissioners, 1844.' Johnston, *The Valley of the Six Nations*, 27, states that John Wilkes had purchased the family lands from John Hill. Jarvis's statement that it was Ester Hill, John Hill's widow, is contemporaneous. Since the transaction was illegal in any case, there is no record of it.

79 Ibid., appendix 1.

80 'Protection of Indian Reserves.'

81 Ibid., appendix 100. The recommendation that Indians be appointed to official positions analogous to the Cherokee Rangers and the favourable reference to American Indian policy are remarkable in the context of Canadian Indian policy in the 1840s. While judges and lawyers did not refer to American cases, administrators and politicians were aware of, and did refer, to United States Indian policy, almost always in unfavourable terms. Indeed, a hallmark of Canadian Indian policy was to be consciously better – more 'liberal' – than United States policy. The Cherokee Lighthorse, dating from 1798, and initially

paid by the War Department, did exercise an interracial law-enforcement function on the frontier. Of course, the Cherokee nation was overwhelmed with squatters at this same time and forceably removed to the west. William McLoughlin, *Cherokees and Missionaries, 1789–1839* (New Haven: Yale University Press 1984), 24, 239–99.

82 'Report of the Commissioners, 1844,' appendix 1.

83 The Cayugas surrendered 20,671 acres in 1831. In 1834, 50,212 acres in the Dunn Township was surrendered by several Six Nations tribes. Mabel Dunham, *Grand River*, 182–3.

84 'Report of the Commissioners, 1844,' appendix 16, 'Samuel P. Jarvis, Indian Office, Toronto, January 5, 1841.'

85 Ibid.

86 A. Leon Hatzen, *The True Story of Hiawatha* (Toronto: McClelland and Stewart 1925), 123–5.

87 'Report of the Commissioners,' 1844, appendix 16. 'Samuel P. Jarvis, Indian Office, Toronto, January 5, 1841.'

88 'Resolutions of a Six Nations' Council at the Onondaga Village, March 1, 1809,' in Charles Johnston, *The Valley of the Six Nations* 110–12.

89 'Report of the Commissioners, 1844,' appendix 16.

90 Sir John Colborne, lieutenant governor of Upper Canada, to Lord Goderich, cited in Charles M. Johnston, *The Valley of the Six Nations*, 297. The historical and anthropological literature on native/white relations is replete with studies of 'factionalism.' One view of this is that what is 'politics' for Europeans is 'factionalism' for native people. In any case, internal divisions were natural in a period of rapid social change as different strategies were discussed and acted on. Peter Whiteley, *Deliberate Acts: Changing Hopi Culture Through the Oraibi Split* (Tucson: University of Arizona Press 1988), and William G. McLoughlin, *Cherokees and Missionaries, 1789–1839*, are two studies of factionalism, respectively among the Hopi and the Cherokee.

91 Every treatment of Joseph Brant and Six Nations history has an explanation of his land transactions, and these various explanations are discussed herein. It seems impossible to say precisely why Brant made his land sales, but some combinations of the reasons scholars commonly put forth are adequate as explanations. Most troublesome to historians is Brant's balancing of his personal pecuniary interests, which were substantial, with his assessment that the Six Nations needed both white neighbours to aid in acculturation and the income from the sale of lands.

92 'Report of the Special Commissioners to Investigate Indian Affairs in Canada,' *Journals of the Legislative Assembly*, vol. 16, appendix 6, appendix no. 21, 1858 (hereafter, 'Report, 1858'), unpaginated.

93 Robert Surtees, *Indian Land Surrenders in Ontario, 1763–1867*. Once almost all Indian land had been surrendered and the Indians were confined to small reserves, the entire nature of the land-surrender system changed. Obviously, there was no reason for frontier whites to sense this change: squatting had always been illegal and the laws had always been ignored. Settlers probably anticipated that the reserves would again be available for settlement in a few years. The Maritime provinces moved much more reluctantly against squatters and the problem continued there until the end of the nineteenth century. See chapter 8.

94 'Report, 1858,' Act 2, Vic. c. 15.

95 Ibid.

96 The report is dishonest in its characterization of these payments to the Indians. Tribes that surrendered lands were most often granted 'presents' by treaty on an annual basis. These are contracts for payments for the Indians rights to the lands surrendered. Annuities were monies held in trust by the crown for reserve lands surrendered on the condition that the lands be sold to white settlers and the money held in trust for the benefit of the tribe. The Six Nations in 1840 had, in trust, £25,733 in money invested, bearing interest of £7629, and £19,198 in Grand River Navigation Company stock. All of the other tribes in Ontario had payable a total of £5,405 in annuities. 'Report, 1844 (1847),' appendix 1. Simple division reveals that this amounted to about £4 per year for every resident of the Six Nations (based on a population of about 2000) and just over £1 per year for each of the 4000 to 5000 other Indians covered by annuities, hardly enough to 'cause' improvidence.

97 'Report, 1844,' 6.

98 Of these scattered rural households, 50 held no improved land; 96, under 5 acres; 85, 5 to 10 acres; 67, from 10 to 20 acres; 68, from 20 to 50 acres; 28, from 50 to 100 acres; and 10, from 100 to 200 acres. 'Report on the Affairs of the Indians in Canada,' 20 March 1845, *Journals of the Legislative Assembly*, vol. 4, 1845, appendix EEE (hereafter, 'Report, 1845'), unpaginated. This is commonly referred to as the Bagot report.

99 Ibid.

100 Some elementary arithmetic reveals that Six Nations resources were not equally distributed, and that there were many Indians not engaging in farming. About 400 houses among 2000 people puts five persons in each house; 55 barns were not many barns for a population of this size, and 350 horses, 561 oxen, 790 cows, and 2,070 pigs were not much stock for farmers. The 6908 acres of improved land equals three and one-half acres per person, or about 16 acres per house, probably about as much land as could be worked with the technology of the day.

101 'Report, 1845.' On living conditions generally, see Charles M. Johnston, 'The Six Nations in the Grand River Valley,' 167–81, and Sally M. Weaver, 'The Iroquois: The Consolidation of the Grand River Reserve in the Mid-Nineteenth Century, 1847–1875,' 182–212, both in Edward S. Rogers and Donald B. Smith, *Aboriginal Ontario.*

102 National Archives of Canada, RG 1, E3, vol. 36, 176–8.

103 'Report, 1840,' published as appendix 1 of the 1844 Report, unpaginated.

104 Ibid.

105 Ibid.

106 'Report, 1845.' It is interesting to speculate whether this number of males is some measure of those who might be in the 'traditional' faction, with those who had given up an empty hunt being in the Brant, or more acculturated, faction. There is no evidence on this point, but it might be noted that the hunting season falls after the crops are in and so even prosperous farmers might have taken off and gone hunting.

107 Ibid.

108 Jarvis's legal position here is puzzling but it is possible that he actually saw the issue in this way, completely denying the legal basis of his opinion.

109 'Report, 1845'; John A. Noon, 'Law and Government of the Grand River Iroquois' (New York: Viking Fund Publications in Anthropology, no. 12, 1949). The law of property is discussed at 85–106.

110 'Report, 1840.'

111 William John Quinsey, *York, Grand River: Its Early History and Directory, 1834–1860* (York Grand River Historical Society 1991), 16–19.

112 Warner Nelles's father, Hendrick William Nelles, a Loyalist from the Mohawk valley, had been a captain in the Indian Department during the American revolution. The Six Nations had deeded the Nelles family 4254 acres of prime Grand River lands in 1787. Charles Johnston, *The Valley of the Six Nations*, 70–1. This deed of land, illegal under Canadian law at the time, was later confirmed by colonial authorities on the petition of Nelles's sons. Ibid., 116–17.

113 Ibid. It seems clear that most of the votes for Brant were cast by whites living on the Six Nations' Grand River lands, but evidently an unknown number of Indians voted as well. It is important to note that all parties conceded that Indians had the right to vote – provided they met property qualifications that could not be met through the communal ownership of land.

114 *Journals of the Legislative Assembly*, 1831, 3–29.

115 Mabel Dunham, *Grand River*, 180.

116 Fred Landon, *Western Ontario and the American Frontier* (Toronto: Ryerson Press 1941), 48. In 1821 Barnabas Bidwell and later his son, Marshall Bidwell,

were excluded from the House of Assembly for not having taken the proper oaths of allegiance. Landon concludes that 'probably a majority of the people in Upper Canada were legally disqualified from holding any public office and had no valid title to their property.'

117 B.E. Hill, 'The Grand River Navigation Company and the Six Nations Indians,' *Ontario History*, vol. 63 1 (1971), 31–40.

118 Ibid., 35–6.

119 'Report, 1844,' part I, contains a lengthy discussion of the issue of presents, including a consideration of the possibility of discontinuing them.

120 Memorial of the Seven Nations to the governor of Lower Canada, *Parliamentary Papers*, 17 June 1839, no. 323:62, quoted in 'Report, 1844.'

121 Colin Read, *The Rising in Western Upper Canada* (Toronto: University of Toronto Press 1982), 138–9; Colin Read and Ronald J. Stagg, *The Rebellion of 1837 in Upper Canada: A Collection of Documents*, (Toronto: The Champlain Society 1985).

122 'A Correspondent to the Rochester *Democrat*,' Brantford, 17 Dec. 1837, Archives of Ontario, Mackenzie-Lindsey Clippings, no. 6017, reprinted in Colin Read and Ronald J. Stagg, *The Rebellion of 1837 in Upper Canada*, 241–2. This report is as anti-British as it is racist and anti-Indian. A British officer is reported to have bragged that he offered the Indians one dollar for each scalp they took from a rebel.

123 Ibid., 99.

124 'Report, 1844 (1844–45),' section 2, (unpaginated). The investigation was launched in October 1842 and reported in January 1844. John Leslie, 'The Bagot Commission: Developing a Corporate Memory for the Indian Department,' *Canadian Historical Association Papers*, 1982, 31–52.

125 Under modern Canadian law, the government is responsible for enforcing its agreements with the First Nations. Accordingly, there is still an ongoing legal dispute with the Six Nations over many issues, including some of the breaches of treaty agreements discussed here. A comprehensive claim was filed in 1995: 'Amended Statement of Claim, Between the Six Nations of the Grand River Band of Indians and the Attorney General of Canada and Her Majesty the Queen in Right of Ontario,' Ontario Court of Justice, General Division, Brantford, Ontario, file no. 406/95, 26 April 1995.

126 On contemporary Upper Canada, for example, see John Borrows, 'A Genealogy of Law: Inherent Sovereignty and First Nations Self-Government,' *Osgoode Hall Law Journal*, vol. 30, no. 2 (1992), 291 at 324–8; W.R. Wightman, *Forever on the Fringe: Six Studies in the Development of Manitoulin Island* (Toronto: University of Toronto Press 1982), 53–5. These methods, as Borrows points out, were illegal at that time under Canadian law.

CHAPTER 3

1 There is an extensive biographical literature on the life and jurisprudence of
Robinson, perhaps more than for any other Canadian judge. None of these
works discuss his Indian law opinions, even though they constitute a unique
and distinct portion of his work. Patrick Brode, *Sir John Beverley Robinson: Bone
and Sinew of the Compact* (Toronto: Osgoode Society and University of Toronto
Press 1984); Terry Cook, 'John Beverley Robinson and the Conservative Blueprint for the Upper Canadian Community,' *Ontario History*, vol. 64 (1972), 79–
94; David Howes, 'Property, God, and Nature in the Thought of Sir John Beverley Robinson,' 30 *McGill Law Journal*, vol. 30 (1985) 365–414; C.W. Robinson,
Life of Sir John Beverley Robinson (London: Blackwood and Sons 1904); Robert E.
Saunders, 'Sir John Beverley Robinson,' *Dictionary of Canadian Biography* (here-
after DCB), vol. 9 (Toronto: University of Toronto Press 1976), 668–79; Donald
J. McMahon, 'Law and Public Authority: Sir John Beverley Robinson and the
Purposes of the Criminal Law,' *University of Toronto Faculty of Law Review*, vol.
46 (1988), 390–23; B.J. Hibbitts, 'Progress and Principle: The Legal Thought of
Sir John Beverley Robinson,' *McGill Law Journal*, vol. 34 (1989), 454; Peter
George and Philip Sworden, 'The Courts and the Development of Trade in
Upper Canada, 1830-1860,' *Business History Review*, vol. 60 (1986) 258–80.
2 The different branches of government were effectively merged in colonial government. Besides serving several terms in the Legislative Assembly, the chief
justice sat on the Executive Council and served as speaker of the Legislative
Council. Among the duties of the Executive Council was drafting new legislation; therefore, Robinson drafted laws that he later passed on as judge. Patrick
Brode, *Sir John Beverley Robinson*, 179–185. The 'family compact' refers to a
small ruling elite composed of a few families prominent in Upper Canada from
the 1820s to the 1840s. Although the validity of this conception of Upper Canada's ruling elite has been questioned, the term was used by reformers of the
time to characterize a definite group of men, including John Beverley Robinson
(ibid., 142–47). This use of the term family compact has provoked some disagreement among historians. See Robert Saunders, 'What Was The Family
Compact?' *Ontario History*, vol. 49 (1957), 173–8 ; and David W.L. Earl, ed., *The
Family Compact: Aristocracy or Oligarchy?* (Toronto: Copp Clark 1967). The separate colony of Upper Canada was merged into a united Province of Canada in
1841. However, in a federal arrangement and because of Quebec's civil law
system, Canada West and Canada East maintained separate legal systems.
Robinson's title, therefore, simply changed from chief justice of Upper Canada
to chief justice of Canada West. After Confederation, Canada East, which had
been Lower Canada, became Quebec and Canada West took the name Ontario.

3 Patrick Brode, *Sir John Beverley Robinson*, 98.

4 This would have represented less than 5 per cent of Ontario's 1840 population of about 250,000. By 1900, Ontario, typical of the growth of the white population of all of North America, had a population of 1,200,000, reducing the Indian proportion to about 2 per cent. The term 'Indians' appears twice in Patrick Brode, *Sir John Beverley Robinson*, both times referring to his service with Indian allies in the Detroit area in the War of 1812 (14, 16). Robinson was concerned with the rise of a population of blacks in Canada because he saw blacks as inclined towards criminal behaviour. He angered abolitionists in Canada by ordering the deportation of a black man who had killed a white planter pursuing him as he fled slavery in Missouri. Abolitionists applied for a writ of habeas corpus in a British court, which overruled Robinson; however, before the writ could be served in Canada, the Court of Common Pleas in Toronto ordered Anderson released on a technicality. Ibid., 265–67; R.C. Reinders, 'The John Anderson Case, 1860–1: A Study in Anglo-Canadian Imperial Relations,' *Canadian Historical Review*, vol. 56 (1975), 393; and Paul Finkelman, 'The Anderson Case and Rights in Canada and England,' in Louis Knafla and Susan W.S. Binnie, *Law, Society, and the State: Essays in Modern Legal History* (Toronto: University of Toronto Press 1995), 37–72.

5 David Howes, 'Property, God and Nature in the Thought of Sir John Beverley Robinson,' *McGill Law Journal*, vol. 30 (1985), 365–414,. See also more general works on Upper Canadian political culture: S.J.R. Noel, *Patrons, Clients, and Brokers: Ontario Society and Politics, 1791–1896* (Toronto: University of Toronto Press 1990); David Mills, *The Idea of Loyalty in Upper Canada, 1784–1850* (Montreal: McGill-Queen's University Press 1988); S.F. Wise *God's Peculiar Peoples: Essays on Political Culture in Nineteenth Century Canada*, A.B. McKillop and Paul Romney, eds. (Ottawa: Carleton University Press 1993); Jane Errington, *The Lion, the Eagle, and Upper Canada* (Montreal: McGill-Queens University Press 1987).

6 E.A. Cruikshank, 'John Beverley Robinson and the Trials for Treason in 1814,' *Ontario Historical Society Papers and Records*, vol. 25 (1929), 191–219.

7 G. Blaine Baker, 'Legal Education in Upper Canada,' in David H. Flaherty, ed., *Essays in the History of Canadian Law*, vol. 2 (Toronto: Osgoode Society and University of Toronto Press 1983), 49–142.

8 Sir William Blackstone's *Commentaries on the Laws of England* were originally published in Oxford in four volumes, beginning in 1765. These volumes were continuously reissued in popular editions and were the basis of legal study in the nineteenth century throughout the common law world. There is a voluminous literature on the impact of Blackstone's writing. John W. Cairns, 'Blackstone, An English Institutist: Legal Literature and the Rise of the Nation State,'

Oxford Journal of Legal Studies, vol. 4 (1984), 318; D.R. Nolan, 'Sir William Blackstone and the New American Republic: A Study of Intellectual Impact,' *New York University Law Review*, vol. 51 (1976), 731.

9 G. Blaine Baker, 'The Reconstitution of Upper Canadian Legal Thought in the Late Victorian Empire,' *Law and History Review*, vol. 3 (1985), 165.

10 William Blackstone, *Commentaries on the Laws of England*, 1st ed. (Oxford: 1765), vol. 1: 104–5. Blackstone distinguished colonies that were vacant when acquired from colonies that were settled, stating that the first could be acquired by mere occupancy but the second type acquired by conquest or cession.

11 David Howes, 'Property, God and Nature,' 372.

12 Morton Horwitz, *The Transformation of American Law* (Cambridge, Mass.: Harvard University Press 1977), 1–30.

13 Peter George and Philip Sworden, 'The Courts and the Development of Trade in Upper Canada, 1830–1860,' *Business History Review*, vol. 60 (1986), 258–80; R.C.B. Risk, 'The Law and the Economy in Mid-Nineteenth Century Ontario: A Perspective,' in David Flaherty, ed. *Essays in the History of Canadian Law*, vol. 1 (Toronto: Osgoode Society and University of Toronto Press,) 1981, 88–131, 112–125.

14 *Doe Ex. Dem. Jackson* v. *Wilkes* (1835 U.C.K.B.) (O.S.) 142; *Little et al.* v. *Keating*, (1842), 6 U.C.Q.B. (O.S.) 265; *Bown* v. *West* (1846), 2 U.C. Jur. 675; *Byrnes* v. *Bown*, (1850), U.C.Q.B. 181; *Doe d. Dickson et ux.* v. *Gross* (1852), 9. U.C.Q.B. 580; *Doe d. Sheldon* v. *Ramsay et al.* (1852), 9 U.C.Q.B. 105; *Young and Young* v. *Scobie* (1853), 10 U.C.Q.B. 372; *Jones* v. *Bain* (1854) 12 U.C.Q.B. 550; *Regina* v. *Baby* (1854), U.C.Q.B. 346; *Totten* v. *Watson* (1858) 15 U.C.Q.B. 392; *Regina* v. *McCormick* (1859), 18 U.C.Q.B. 131; *Vanvleck et al.* v. *Stewart et al* (1860), 19 U.C.Q.B. 489; *Regina* v. *The Great Western Railway Company* (1862), 21 U.C.Q.B. 555.

15 (1823) 1 Taylor 47.

16 13 S.C.R. 577 (SCC) (1887). D'Alton McCarthy, representing St. Catherine's and Lumber and Milling Company (and the dominion government) referred in the appellant's factum to *Bown* v. *West*, *Little* v. *Keating*, *Regina* v. *Baby*, *Vanvleck* v. *Stewart*, *Regina* v. *Strong*. at 64–70. Oliver Mowat, representing the province of Ontario, cited in the respondent's factum *Doe Sheldon* v. *Ramsay*, *Totten* v. *Watson*, and *Regina* v. *Baby* (at 12–13). The original case file is in National Archives of Canada, RG 125, file 648, pts. 1 and 2.

17 Sidney L. Harring, *Crow Dog's Case: American Indian Sovereignty, United States Law, and Indian Law in the Nineteenth Century* (Cambridge: Cambridge University Press 1994), analyses nineteenth-century United States federal and state Indian law cases. There were hundreds. Chief Justice John Marshall authored five opinions. Only a handful of long-serving federal district judges such as Matthew Deady of Portland, Oregon, and Isaac Parker of Fort Smith, Arkan-

sas, much later in the nineteenth century, equalled Marshall's record, far fewer cases than Robinson. While virtually every state supreme court also handed down opinions on Indian matters, state Indian law jurisprudence waned after the Civil War as federal power clearly pre-empted the states in jurisdiction over the Indian tribes.

18 R.C.B. Risk, '"This Nuisance of Litigation": The Origins of Workers' Compensation in Ontario,' in David H. Flaherty, ed. *Essays in the History of Canadian Law*, vol. 2, 418–91, 449.

19 Early Upper Canadian legislative policy is analysed in John F. Leslie, 'Commissions of Inquiry into Indian Affairs in the Canadas, 1828–1858: Evolving a Corporate Memory for the Indian Department' (Treaties and Historical Research Centre, Research Branch, Indian and Northern Affairs, Ottawa 1985); and John Leslie and Ron Maguire, *The Historical Development of the Indian Act*, 2nd ed. (Treaties and Historical Research Centre, Research Branch, Department of Indian and Northern Affairs, Ottawa 1978), 13–36.

20 All of Canada's Indian laws were consolidated in 1876 – nine years after Confederation – into a single 'Indian Act.' John Leslie and Ron Maguire, *The Historical Development of the Indian Act*, 52–70.

21 Robert Fraser, *Provincial Justice: Upper Canadian Legal Portraits* (Toronto: Osgoode Society/University of Toronto Press 1992), a collection of essays from the *DCB* on leading legal figures of the early nineteenth century, clearly illustrates the elitist and close-knit characteristics of law and policy makers in Upper Canada.

22 Robinson and his brothers had large landholdings in a number of locations throughout the province. One historian has suggested that these holdings might have played a part in his decision in *Patterson* v. *Bowes* (later *City of Toronto* v. *Bowes*), (1854) 4 Grants 170. Paul Romney, 'The Ten Thousand Pound Job: Political Corruption, Equitable Jurisdiction, and the Public Interest in Upper Canada, 1852–56,' in David Flaherty, ed. *Essays in the History of Canadian Law*, vol. 2, 143–99, 181–2.

23 (1854) 12 U.C.Q.B. 346, 353.

24 (1858) 15 U.C.Q.B. 392, 395–6.

25 Ibid. Robinson also referred to both native rights and government policy in *Bown* v. *West*, discussed herein.

26 (1852) 9 U.C.Q.B. 105.

27 (1846) 1 E & A 117, 118.

28 Robinson's voluminous personal papers, held in the Archives of Ontario, contain no references at all to Indians or Indian matters. This may not be that difficult to explain: Robinson probably did not give Indians or Indian issues much thought at all in any of his official or private legal activity. Paul Rom-

ney, *Mr. Attorney: The Attorney General for Ontario in Court, Cabinet, and Legisla-*
ture, 1791–1899 (Toronto: University of Toronto Press 1986), also gives no
information on Indian matters in the attorney general's office during Robinson's long tenure in that office. There is a substantial legal history of the Six
Nations' dispute with the crown over their land title and sovereignty. See Malcolm Montgomery, 'The Legal Status of the Six Nations Indians in Canada,'
Ontario History, vol. 55 (1963), 93–105, and Darlene Johnston, 'The Quest of the
Six Nations Confederacy for Self-Determination,' *University of Toronto Faculty*
of Law Review, vol. 44 (1986), 1–32; Donald J. Bourgeois, 'The Six Nations: A
Neglected Aspect of Canadian Legal History,' *Canadian Journal of Native Stud-*
ies vol. 6, no. 2 (1986), 253–70.

29 Mark D. Walters, 'The Extension of Colonial Criminal Jurisdiction over the
Aboriginal Peoples of Upper Canada: Reconsidering the Shawanakiskie Case
(1822–26),' *University of Toronto Law Journal*, vol. 46 (1996), 273, 305. This case is
discussed in Chapter 5.

30 Isabel Kelsay, 'Joseph Brant,' *D.C.B.*, vol. 5 (1983), 803–12, and *Joseph Brant,*
1746–1807: Man of Two Worlds (Syracuse: Syracuse University Press 1984).
Charles Johnston, *The Valley of the Six Nations*, (Toronto: University of Toronto
Press 1964), lvi; 'Daniel Penfield to Brant,' 27 April 1807, reprinted in ibid. at
149–50; also, 'William Dickson to Claus,' 1817, reprinted in ibid. at 152–3.
Archives of Ontario, J.B. Robinson Docket Book, 1817–1821. Patrick Brode, *Sir*
John Beverley Robinson, 103. Given the nature of his practice, his political connections, and the large number of Six Nations land cases, it is highly likely that
Robinson was involved in more of these cases as well. A search of his private
papers in the Ontario Archives reveals nothing of these matters. Throughout
Robinson's public career, until 1829 when he became a judge, he maintained a
lucrative private law practice, in common with other crown officials of the
day.

This case, involving block 1 of the original Brant grants, 94,035 acres, had a
complex legal history, marked by forgery and fraud and Robinson probably
earned his fee. The original purchaser, Philip Stedman, a land speculator, had
wound up in an American debtor's prison but had allegedly assigned his
interest in the land to a number of others with three different parties, all
American land speculators, coming forward. Daniel Penfield, the most aggressive of these purchasers, paid huge sums of money to the Six Nations representing amounts owed by Stedman under the terms of the grant. In the anti-
American climate that followed the War of 1812, Canadian authorities decided
that Penfield's deed was nothing but a 'clumsy forgery,' but considerable legal
activity led to a judgment in favor of William Dickson, who took title under a
deed from Stedman's widow. Dickson's lawyer in this matter was John Bever-

ley Robinson, then attorney general of Upper Canada. His legal fee of £699 underscores the complexity of the case and belies the 'clumsy forgery' which, presumably, would have been easily detected. The case, *William Dickson* v. *Daniel Penfield* (Hilary Term, 1818) is unreported. There was no regular reporting system in Upper Canada until the next decade.

31 Robinson's principal involvement was with the Welland Canal, which followed a route which by-passed the Six Nations Grand River lands. This project avoided using a government-surveyed route from Burlington Bay to the Grand River that did run through Six Nations lands. Patrick Brode, *Sir John Beverley Robinson*, 110–11, 114, 120–1, 180, 192. There is no evidence of Robinson's involvement in the Grand River Navigation scheme, which was on Six Nations lands and begun after he was chief justice.

32 (1835) 4 U.C.K.B. (O.S.) 142. The reported case locates the lot in Brampton, but this cannot be accounted for unless it is a reporter's error. Since the main issue in the case is Wilkes's title under the Haldemand grant, and since Wilkes was a major speculator and founder of Brantford, this seems the most reasonable conclusion. Brampton was not in the Haldimand grant by any definition of its boundaries. Jackson held title through letters patent from the crown. Wilkes held title through a deed from Joseph Brant and Haldimand's grant to the Six Nations.

33 Ibid., 144, 149. The Simcoe patent had confirmed the Haldimand grant but with a proviso that Grand River lands could only be sold to the crown. Since Jackson took title under a crown grant, and Wilkes did not, Jackson had clear title.

34 Ibid., 149.

35 Ibid., 147.

36 Ibid., 143. The term 'Five Nations,' as used here, includes the Oneida, Cayuga, Seneca, Onondaga, and Mohawk. The Tuscarora had joined the Confederacy by this time, making it the Six Nations.

37 Jackson's original lawyer was William Henry Draper, among the leading lawyers in Upper Canada, soon to enter politics at Robinson's request as Tory leader and later to sit with Robinson on the bench. Patrick Brode, *Sir John Beverley Robinson*, 228, and George Metcalf, 'William Henry Draper,' *D.C.B.* vol. 10 (1972) 253–9. The attorney general's role in this case may have been as a private lawyer representing Wilkes, since the attorney general had private clients and the crown was not a party to this case.

38 *Doe Ex. Dem. Jackson* v. *Wilkes* (1835), 4 U.C.K.B. (O.S.) 142, 145–6.

39 Ibid., 146.

40 (1831) 5 Peters 1; (1832) 6 Peters 515.

41 30 U.S. 1 (1831); 31 U.S. 515 (1832). There is no direct evidence that Robinson

knew of these American cases, for neither he nor any of his brother judges ever cited them during Robinson's time on the bench. We do know that American reporters were in the law libraries of Upper Canada and that, by the end of the 1830s, the Colonial Office took notice of these cases with regard to the legal position of the Maori of New Zealand. Robinson cited American cases in some private law matters, and so they came within his purview while doing legal research. This was an age when judges laboriously researched and authored their own opinions without the help of law clerks.

42 George Metcalf, 'William Henry Draper.'

43 F. Douglas Reville, *History of the County of Brant* (Brantford, Ont.: Hurley Printing 1967; originally published 1920), 69–104. George H. Wilkes, the oldest living Brantfordite and grandson of John, is interviewed at 100–3.

44 (1840) 6 U.C.Q.B.(O.S.) 265. Nin.Da.Waab.Jig, *Walpole Island: The Soul of Indian Territory*, (Walpole Island: Walpole Island Heritage Centre 1987), 32–3. Both commissioners of crown lands and Indian agents held commissions as justices of the peace, subject to statutory limitations on their exercise of this authority.

45 (1840) U.C.Q.B. (O.S.), 266, 269–70.

46 Ibid., 269. The Upper Canada court structure in the mid-nineteenth century was complex, involving a system of unrelated courts with narrow jurisdictions that loosely followed the British model. A complete history can be found in Margaret A. Banks, 'The Evolution of the Ontario Courts, 1788–1981,' in David H. Flaherty, ed. *Essays in the History of Canadian Law*, vol. 2, 492–572.

47 *Little et al* v. *Keating* (1842), 6 U.C.Q.B (O.S.) 265, 268. Robinson, appointed chief justice in 1829, simultaneously held the offices of president of the Executive Council and speaker of the Legislative Council, giving him an important post in each of the three branches of government. In 1832 he resigned as president of the Executive Council, but he continued to sit as speaker of the Legislative Council until he left for an extended trip to England in 1838. Although he never resigned that post, he never again actually sat as speaker. With the union of the Canadas in 1841, judges ceased holding office in other branches of government. Therefore, technically at the time of *Little* v. *Keating*, Robinson held office in two branches of government. While Robinson had voluntarily stepped down from his position on the Executive Council, he was politically active throughout the 1830s. C.W. Robinson, *Life of John Beverley Robinson*, 199–200, 237–55.

48 David T. McNab, '"Water Is Her Life Blood": The Waters of Bkejwanong and the Treaty-Making Process,' paper presented to the Laurier III Conference, Walpole Island, 1994. All of the other Indian land cases decided by Robinson involved ceded Indian lands. This was because legal cases tended to come from the settled areas of southern Ontario. There were still unceded Indian lands in the north.

49 An Act for the Protection of the Lands of the Crown in this Province from Trespass and Injury, R.S.U.C., (1839) III Victoria, c. 15. This, the first Upper Canadian law to protect Indians from white intruders, is the precursor of the Indian Act. Hereafter, it is referred to in the text as 'Indian Act [1839]' to distinguish it from the dominion's Indian Act of 1876. Colloquially, the act was referred to as the 'Indian Act' in the 1840s and 1850s.

50 Nin.Da.Waab.Jig, *Walpole Island: The Soul of Indian Territory*, 32–3.

51 Archives of Ontario, Macaulay Papers, Robinson to Macaulay, 20 July 1852, quoted in Lillian F. Gates, *Land Policies of Upper Canada*, (Toronto: University of Toronto Press 1968), 295.

52 Paul Romney, 'Re-inventing Upper Canada: American Immigrants, Upper Canadian History, English Law, and the Alien Question,' in R. Hall *et al.*, *Patterns of the Past: Interpreting Ontario History* (Toronto: Dundurn Press 1988), 78–107. Although this crisis peaked in the 1820s (with Robinson going to England to urge the disenfranchisement of Americans living in Canada), the issue, and the squatter problem, were important through the 1830s and 1840s.

53 *Bown* v. *West*, (1846) 1 E& A, 117, 120.

54 Duncan covenanted that 'he is the true owner of the improvements and buildings, according to the custom of the Indians by his own labour have made the same.' Ibid. at 132. Under Six Nations law, individual Indians owned their improvements and buildings but not the land. Thus, Duncan accurately represented that he was selling improvements that he 'owned' under tribal law. John A. Noon, *Law and Government of the Grand River Iroquois* (New York: Viking Fund Publications in Anthropology, no. 12, 1949). The Six Nations law of property is discussed at 85–106.

55 Robinson directly acknowledged this in his opinion: 'There is a good deal in the accounts given by some of the witnesses, to throw suspicion on the defendant's conduct in this transaction. After reading the evidence, I am not satisfied that it was perfectly upright, and that he was open and candid.' Ibid., 137.

56 (1846) 1 U.C. Jur. 639, 642–50.

57 (1846) 1 U.C. Jur. 639; appealed to the Upper Canada Executive Council, (1846) 1 E & A 117.

58 (1846) 1 E & A 117, 121.

59 Brode, *Sir John Beverley Robinson*, 259–60.

60 Lillian F. Gates, *Land Policies of Upper Canada*; Edgar Good, 'Crown-Dominated Colonization of Six Nations and Metis Land Reserves in Canada' (Ph.D. dissertation, University of Saskatchewan 1994).

61 *Bown* v. *West* (1846), 1 E. & A. 117, 118.

62 (1852) 9 U.C.Q.B. 105.

63 Ibid. Sheldon, seeming to cover his bases, complicated matters by sending an

agent to Mallory in the United States and getting William Mallory, an agent of Benajah, to assign him Mallory's interest in the lands. It must reveal something of Sheldon's lack of faith in Canadian legal process that he backed up his forfeiture deed, issued by the crown, with an assignment of the legal rights of a convicted traitor.

64 Here it might be pointed out that Robinson showed a good grasp of the practice of Canadian land law as he sorted out the facts of the case. The legal records were full of errors: for example, Joseph Brant was originally referred to as 'Jacob' Brant (ibid. at 110), an error corrected by Robinson, who inserted a parenthetical 'should be Joseph Brant.' The discussion at ibid., 106–27, contains a history of Mallory's tenure on this parcel of land. A map is included at 114. This chaotic history, like that of Cozens, must be typical of many of the tracts that Brant granted or 'leased' to whites.

65 Ibid., 119. Robinson went on to remark that it was 'not easy to understand' how the jury could come to such an unjust result.

66 Since substantial property qualifications were required before a citizen could vote or serve on juries, squatters interests were not represented on the jury.

67 (1852) 9 U.C.Q.B. 105, 122.

68 Robinson's reference to 'incorporation' had nothing to do with corporate law as it is now understood. Rather, Robinson used the term in its historical common-law meaning, simply a common status recognized by the crown, analogous to a municipal corporation. Since medieval times, the King of England has chosen to deal with some of his subjects in a collective character. Blackstone discussed these entities as 'incorporeal hereditaments,' with the hereditament referring to the right being held by some kind of public corporate body. Sir William Blackstone, *Commentaries on the Law of England*, vol. 2 (Oxford: 1783), 20–38. These corporate bodies were all public corporations – municipalities and local governments or boards, charitable organizations, religious organizations, service societies – and could only be created by the King. Sir Robert Chambers, *A Course of Lectures on the English Law, 1767–1773*, vol. 1 (Madison: University of Wisconsin Press 1986; originally published 1767–73), 293–301. The logic here is that Haldimand, representing the King in British North America, constructively incorporated the Six Nations when he granted them lands to hold collectively.

69 (1852) 9 U.C.Q.B. 105, 122.

70 *Doe d. Sheldon v. Ramsay*, (1852), 9 U.C.Q.B., 105, 123.

71 Ibid., 125.

72 Ibid., 133, 135. This language, in a concurring opinion, is not a part of the holding.

73 Ibid., 136. See *Doe ex dem. Jackson v. Wilkes* (1835) 4 U.C.K.B. (O.S.) 142, 144.

74 Chief Justice Robinson had also represented parties in disputes over Grand River lands but, presumably because he had never represented a party in this particular case, he did not disqualify himself.

75 'Letter,' R.W. Horton to J. Butterworth, Colonial Office, 18 March, 1825, in British Parliamentary Papers, Irish Universities Press Series, *Anthropology: Aborigines*, vol. 3, 'Correspondence and Other Papers in Relation to Aboriginal Tribes in British Possessions, 1834,' 63–4.

76 Public Record Office, PC 2/ 115/264; PC 2/ 116/340–41. Joseph Henry Smith, *Appeals to the Privy Council from the American Plantations* (New York: Octagon Books 1965). 422–42. Although arising in an American colony before the revolution, the case was decided by the Privy Council under British law. Because of the anomalous status of this case, an American case decided under British law before the existence of Canada, it may have been unknown to Robinson. Robinson must have known, however, that the Cherokee nation had standing to sue the State of Georgia, an issue decided by the United States Supreme Court in 1831. *Cherokee Nation* v. *Georgia* (30 U.S. 1 (1831) had denied the Cherokee the right to sue Georgia as a foreign nation in the United States Supreme Court, but it implicitly left open all other jurisdictional forums.

77 The Colonial Office of the 1830s and 1840s set a high priority on applying the full measure of British law to native people and their institutions, believing that this would bring potential conflicts between native people and colonial settlers into the courts and thereby reduce the likelihood of colonial wars. This ultimately became a substantial part of Canadian Indian policy. Paul Knaplund, *Sir James Stephen and the British Colonial System, 1813–1847* (Madison: University of Wisconsin Press 1953).

78 (1859), 18 U.C.Q.B. 131.

79 Ibid., 132.

80 Ibid., 133.

81 The whole logic of the fiction of 'constructive corporation' was that the crown, by granting lands to the Six Nations had, de facto, created such a legal entity. Indian nations generally, however, had not been so created. The Ojibwa at Pointe Pelee had owned their land since time immemorial.

82 Ibid., 134.

83 Ibid., 134.

84 There was no court holding that individual Indians had full access to the courts as British subjects, but it was settled law in Upper Canada. Justice James Macaulay stated this clearly in his 'Report on the Indians of Upper Canada,' National Archives of Canada, RG 10, vol. 718.

85 Of those decided by his colleagues on the bench, only *Owens* v. *Thomas* (1856) 6 U.C.C.P. 383 involved an Indian party. Owens, a blind and illiterate Indian,

had signed a contract with Tracy. Sued for breach of contract, he lost in the trial court, but, on appeal, the judge had held that a contract not read to a blind, illiterate person was not valid at common law. This holding per se has nothing to do with Indian law, yet an individual Indian did get justice against an unscrupulous horse trader.

86 *Regina* v. *McCormick* (1859), 18 U.C.Q.B. 131, 136. The term 'corporate' here might have another meaning, a general reference to members of an Indian tribe holding property collectively. Robinson's other references are to the tribe as a corporation, so I read it in that context. But Robinson also appears to have merged these two meanings in his analysis.

87 Only a legal officer with authority to represent the corporation can bring an action in the name of a corporation, a constructive person in the eyes of the law; therefore, an individual member of a tribe could not defend the tribe's land rights if the tribe was, in fact, a corporation. Perhaps if Robinson had decided that an Indian tribe was some kind of constructive 'partnership' the problem could have been satisfactorily resolved in his view: any of the partners could bring an action in the name of a partnership. The problem with this framework is, not only that it denied the Indian nations a status as nations, but that the Indian nations knew nothing about it and hence could not actually defend their rights under it.

88 Ibid., 137–9.

89 (1854), 12 U.C.Q.B. 346. Indians as witnesses are discussed at 347–9. Evidently Indians were often used as witnesses in criminal cases, especially those involving Indian defendants, even in the late eighteenth century, although the practice was of doubtful legality under the common law.

90 Sandwich was located near where Windsor now stands.

91 John Clarke, 'Sarah Ainse,' *D.C.B*, vol. 6 (1987), 7–8. Ainse, a successful trader, bought a block of 150 square miles at the mouth of the Thames River, up to the point of present-day Chatham. Ainse was probably born a Shawnee but apparently married into the Oneida nation.

92 Fred Landon, *Western Ontario and the American Frontier* (Toronto: The Ryerson Press 1941), 12–61. François Baby was the founder of a fur trade family dynasty in the Detroit area. He died in 1820, leaving six children. John Clarke, 'François Baby,' *D.C.B*, vol. 7 (1988), 41–6. His son, James Baby, moved to Toronto, built an estate, and served in a number of public offices, including the Executive Council in the 1820s, alongside Judge James Macaulay. He was also a friend of John Beverley Robinson. John Clarke, 'James Baby,' 21–2. James and his brother, also named François, other brothers, and their children were heavily involved in land speculation in western Upper Canada, and it is not clear which Baby was the defendant in this case.

93 James Baby had petitioned the Executive Council at York on 13 July 1799
   stating that he had a mill opposite Sandwich and requesting that he be
   granted a vacant lot adjacent to it. The grant was approved. Archives of
   Ontario, Microfilm of the Minutes of the Executive Council (Lands) at York,
   13 July 1799. E.A .Cruikshank, ed., *The Correspondence of the Hon. Peter Russell*,
   (Toronto: Ontario Historical Society 1932–6), vol. 1: 109; 'Minutes of the Executive Council re. Gaol and Court House for the Western District, December
   12, 1796,' in Ernest J. Lajeunesse, *The Windsor Border Region* (Toronto: The
   Champlain Society 1960), 194, 195. Although this is apparently the mill in
   question, the defendant in this case (whose first name is not mentioned) must
   have been one of James Baby's sons, since Baby would probably have been
   too elderly to engage physically in all of the lobbying in Toronto reported to
   have gone on here. A map showing the mill, adjacent an Indian reserve, is at
   ibid., 206.
94 *R. v. Baby* (1854), 12 U.C.Q.B. 346, 347.
95 Ibid., 348.
96 Ibid., 360–1.
97 Ibid., 350–3.
98 Ibid., 355, 356.
99 Ibid., 359. None of Robinson's reported Indian law cases involved criminal
   law. The summary convictions brought before him for various land-law violations are best described as quasi-criminal, parallel to modern regulatory
   statutes. Robinson can be called a conservative only on general policy matters of criminal law, committed to enforcing the law to secure his vision of
   social order in Upper Canada. Donald J. McMahon, 'Law and Public Authority.'
100 *R. v. Baby* (1854), 12 U.C.Q.B. 346, 356.
101 It is not inconsistent, for example, to recognize that, given the instability of
   land titles in the period before the 1830s, squatters were necessary to develop
   the frontier, and also to see the continuation of these competing claims on
   lands into the 1840s and 1850s as undermining further development.
102 (1858) 15 U.C.Q.B. 392.
103 M. Eleanor Herrington, 'Captain John Descrontyon and the Mohawk Settlement at Deseronto,' *Queen's Quarterly*, vol. 29 (1921), 165–80.
104 (1858) 15 U.C.Q.B., 392, 393–4.
105 Ibid., 396.
106 Not all cases decided against Indians involved questions of Indian law. In
   Doe D. Dickson Et Ux. v. Gross ((1852), 9 U.C.Q.B. 580) the estate of William
   Claus, deputy superintendent of Indian affairs and Six Nations trustee, came
   before Robinson on a technical matter of estate law. Included in Claus's

property, added in the last months of his life, was a tract of Six Nations land, surrendered to the crown with the intent that it be granted to Claus. The Six Nations contested this grant, seeking to have it invalidated. Isabel Kelsay, 'Tekarihogen (John Brant),' *D.C.B.* vol. 6 760–2 at 761. While Claus's heirs had quickly sold the tract, his heir at law attempted to intervene under a statute permitting the estates of certain crown servants, including trustees of Indian lands, to be sold when the testator died in debt to his trust accounts. Claus was inept as a trustee, and he had disposed of extensive Six Nations lands in trust without being able to account for the funds. The crown, however, had made no effort at all to collect monies from Claus's estate. Robinson refused to intervene, permitting Claus's heirs to sell the land. While it was incumbent on political authorities to take action against Claus's estate under the terms of the statute, still there was no legal protection of the Six Nations' lands from Claus' fraud.

107 (1862), 21 U.C.Q.B. 555.

108 Ibid., 555, 577. Trust doctrine is discussed in more detail in chapter 6.

109 Ibid., 577.

110 'Report of the Commissioners, 1844,' (1847) section 3. 'Lands: 1. Title to Lands': 'On many occasions large Tracts of Indian Lands have been surrendered to the Crown in trust, for the purpose of being sold for the benefit of the Tribe concerned.' This is the earliest official reference I can find to the existence of a trust relationship in Ontario Indian lands. The use of trust doctrine in relation to Indian lands in a government report of 1844 predates its appearance in judicial opinions by eight years.

111 Leonard Ian Rotman, *Parallel Paths: Fiduciary Doctrine and the Crown-Native Relationship in Canada* (Toronto: University of Toronto Press 1996). Fiduciary relationships, while similar to trust relationships, are cast in broader terms (at 1–2).

112 A final Robinson case only indirectly involved an interpretation of the law in relation to Indian rights. In *Byrnes* v. *Bown* (1850), 14 U.C.Q.B. 181, Robinson held that the Highway Act did not apply to every Indian trail. The case had nothing to do with Indian lands but rather involved the problem of trespass across settlers' fields, since some claimed a right, under the Highway Act, to follow every Indian trail.

113 Patrick Brode, *Sir John Beverley Robinson*, 148–50.

114 Five of these cases are discussed below. *Kerr* v. *Lefferty* (1859), 7 Gr. 412, authored by vice-chancellor Esten, and *McDiarmid* v. *McDiarmid* (1862) 9 Gr. 144, authored by vice-chancellor Spragge, both involved complex inheritances of lands formerly ceded by Indians, but all of the parties were white and the decisions turned on no questions of Indian law.

115 Macaulay, like Robinson and Draper, had also served on the Executive Council, resigning only after being appointed judge in 1829. In 1839 he was appointed by Governor George Arthur to write a report on the Indian Department. His report covered 446 manuscript pages but came to few conclusions. He was shortly appointed one of three commissioners for a second report on the Indian Department in 1839–40. He was reportedly 'more sensitive to social considerations than those of his fellow judges,' a position more evident by his support for equitable rights for squatters than for his defence of the legal rights of the Indian tribes. Gordon Dodds, 'Sir James Buchanan Macaulay,' D.C.B. vol. 8 (1985) 511–13. His 1839 report did, however, conclude that Indians had full rights as Canadian citizens. John F. Leslie, 'Commissions of Inquiry into Indian Affairs in the Canadas,' 49–73. The 'Macaulay Report' is at the National Archives of Canada, RG 10, vol. 718 (vol. 719 is a typed version).

116 John F. Leslie, 'Commissions of Inquiry into Indian Affairs,' 49–73.

117 'Macaulay Report,' 355–7.

118 Gordon Dodds, 'Sir James Buchanan Macaulay.'

119 (1857), 7 U.C.C.P. 380.

120 Ibid., 381–2. Draper 'retired' to the bench in 1847 after a tumultuous political career in the 1830s and 1840s, including long service as attorney general, effectively leader of the government, and as a member of the Legislative Assembly. He succeeded Robinson as chief justice. George Metcalf, 'William Henry Draper,' D.C.B, vol. 10: 253–9.

121 (1856), 6 U.C.C.P. 383.

122 Ibid., 384, 385, citing Throughgood's case (2 Cokes Rep. 9), Shuller's case (12 Coke's Rep. 90), and Shepherd's Touchstone, 56. This is the first common law citation in any of the Indian law cases considered here.

123 Burns served twice as a district judge, alternating with a partnership with Oliver Mowat and Philip Vankoughnet in one of Toronto's largest firms. In 1849 he was appointed a Queen's Bench judge, serving until his death in 1863. While 'liberal' in his views, he was not brilliant and was a man of 'plodding habits.' Brian H. Morrison, 'Robert Easton Burns,' D.C.B, vol. 9: 108–9. His law partner, Oliver Mowat, took a similar position in St. Catherine's Milling, denying any legal status to either Indians or Indian lands.

124 Regina v. McCormick, (1859), 18 U.C.Q.B. 131, 136.

125 Sheldon v. Ramsay (1852), 9 U.C.Q.B. 105, 133–6.

126 David Howes, 'Property, God and Nature' at 372.

127 National Archives of Canada, Q Sero, 337, pt. II, 367, 368, quoted by Judge Riddell in Sero v. Gault (1921), 50 O.L.R. 27, 31–3. Robinson was rendering a legal opinion on the status of the Six Nations' claim to own their lands in fee

simple. In a private letter to John Macaulay in 1834 Robinson commented on the legal claim of Nelson Cozens to a large tract of Six Nations lands, giving essentially the same view: 'The land in question must have been long since acquired from the Indians by other individuals with the sanction of the province ... If this purchase now spoken of was originally made without the privity and acquiescence of the government, I should say it would stand no chance of being recognized under any circumstances.' John Beverley Robinson to John Macaulay, 7 July 1834 in John Macaulay Family papers, Ontario Archives, microfilm. See also *Journals of the Legislative Assembly*, 1836, appendix 37, 'Report on Petition of N. Cozens,' 'Cozens Affidavit, July 1, 1834,' 5–6. Reprinted in Charles Johnson, *The Valley of the Six Nations*, 164–7.

128 Wendy Cameron, 'Peter Robinson,' *D.C.B.* vol. 8: 752–6; Brode, *Sir John Beverley Robinson*, 189.

129 Julia Jarvis, 'William Benjamin Robinson,' *D.C.B*, vol. 10: 622–3; Hugh G.J. Aitken, 'The Family Compact and the Welland Canal Company,' *Canadian Journal of Economics and Political Science*, vol. 18 (1952), 63–76.

130 The Robinson-Huron Treaty covered lands north and east of Lake Huron; the Robinson-Superior Treaty covered lands north of Lake Superior. Robert J. Surtees, 'The Robinson Treaties' (Treaty Research Report, Treaties and Historical Research Centre, Department of Indian and Northern Affairs, Ottawa 1986).

131 *Doe Dem. Sheldon* v. *Ramsay* (1852), 9 U.C.Q.B. 105. See the discussion of this case earlier in this chapter.

132 *Little* v. *Keating* (1842), 6 U.C.Q.B. (O.S.) 265, 270.

133 *Vanvleck et al* v. *Stewart et al* (1860), 19 U.C.R. 489, 490.

134 2 Vic., chapter 15. It is as likely that Robinson favoured the rapid sale of timber to fuel the economic expansion of Upper Canada. The process was primarily of benefit to the large lumber syndicates who sold most of the timber to the United States; it was likely of small profit to Indians who cut and sold tribal timber.

135 (1854), 12 U.C.Q.B. 550.

136 (1854), 12 U.C.Q.B. 392.

137 Indeed, even without these two references it is impossible, given Robinson's legal and political position in Upper Canada, that he was not fully aware of the crown's Indian policy. Until 1829, as attorney general, he had a responsibility to enforce it.

138 *Bown* v. *West*, (1846), 1 E & A. 117, 118.

139 Ibid., 132.

140 Years of political tension led to rebellion in 1837. Aileen Dunham, *Political Unrest in Upper Canada, 1815–1836* (Toronto: University of Toronto Press 1927).

141 This is a very complex comparison. Morton J. Horwitz, *The Transformation of*

American Law (Cambridge, Mass.: Harvard University Press 1977), 1–30, and J. Willard Hurst, *Law and the Conditions of Freedom*, (Madison: University of Wisconsin Press 1956), 3–32. R.C.B. Risk, 'The Law and the Economy in Mid-Nineteenth-Century Ontario: A Perspective,' in David Flaherty, ed., *Essays in the History of Canadian Law*, vol. 1: 88–131, found that, with nominal differences, these models applied to Ontario as well as the United States.

142 G. Blaine Baker, 'So Elegant a Web: Providential Order and the Rule of Secular Law in Early Nineteenth Century Upper Canada'; T. Cook, 'John Beverley Robinson and the Conservative Blueprint for the Upper Canadian Community;' and David Howes, 'Property, God, and Nature.'

143 The indirect Indian interest here was their interest in selling their lands to whomever they pleased, a common law right that followed the ownership of land. The terms of the Royal Proclamation, however, made it clear that Indians, whatever their property right in land, were statutorily forbidden to sell or lease it to settlers. Thus, Indian title itself was not directly at issue in these cases.

144 During the entire period Robinson sat on the bench, he rode circuit and presided over criminal and civil trials. There is no record that he ever presided in a trial involving an Indian defendant, although, on purely statistical grounds, it is highly likely he did so because of the sheer numbers of cases he would have tried over his years on the bench. Early Upper Canadian trial records exist largely in the judge's bench books, large, bound volumes in which each judge recorded his notes on every trial. Constance Backhouse, *Petticoats and Prejudice: Women and the Law in Nineteenth Century Canada*, (Toronto: Osgoode Society and Women's Press 1991), provides an account of Robinson's conduct of a rape trial in Toronto in 1859 (at 92–7).

145 T. Cook, 'John Beverley Robinson and the Conservative Blueprint for the Upper Canadian Community,' 340.

146 Virtually every state supreme court in the United States issued at least several Indian law opinions by the 1840s because it was not yet clear that federal law pre-empted state law in Indian matters. Even the United States Supreme Court's 'Cherokee cases' did not fully settle the matter. Both because the Indian tribes were so numerous, and because federalism was such a significant legal and political issue, American Indian law produced a large number of important and lengthy decisions. Still, no state produced as many opinions as Ontario, and no single judge produced as many as Robinson. Sidney L. Harring, *Crow Dog's Case: American Indian Sovereignty, Tribal Law, and United States Law in the Nineteenth Century*, (Cambridge, U.K.: Cambridge University Press 1994), 25–56.

147 Chancellor James Kent, *Commentaries on American Law*, 4th ed., privately printed in New York in 1840, refers to Indians in two sections, in volume 1, at

257–8, and in volume 3 at 377–400. Justice Joseph Story, *Commentaries on the Constitution of the United States*, 1st ed., 1833, volume 3 at 540–3, also discusses the legal status of Indians and Indian lands under the constitution. Perhaps more important, both of these treatises discuss the legal status of Indians at common law and include numerous citations to English as well as American law. Both were available for most of Robinson's term as chief justice.

148 Gerald Gunther, 'Governmental Power and New York Indian Lands – A Reassessment of a Persistent Problem of Federal-State Relations,' *Buffalo Law Review*, vol. 8 (1958), 3–11. Not all of the early New York cases were favourable to the rights of Indians since judges there faced some of the same political pressure for the opening up of Indian lands that Robinson faced. Other cases turned on issues of state/federal relations that were irrelevant in Canada. Thus, it is important to recognize that Robinson's failure to cite American cases cannot be dismissed as his avoidance of cases that might have supported results different than Robinson wanted to reach.

149 (1810) 7 Johnson's Reports 290, 295 (N.Y.S.C.)

150 J. Burke, 'The Cherokee Cases: A Study in Law, Politics, and Morality,' *Stanford Law Review*, vol. 21 (1969), 500–31; G. Edward White, *The Marshall Court and Cultural Change, 1815–35* (New York: Macmillan 1988), chapter 10, 'Natural Law and Racial Minorities: The Court's Response to Slaves and Indians.'

151 *State* v. *George Tassels*, 1 Dud. 229 (1830); *Caldwell* v. *State*, 6 Peter 327 (1832); *State* v. *Foreman*, 8 Yerg. 256 (1835). *Caldwell* and *Foreman* each run over one hundred printed pages, making them the most lengthy of all nineteenth-century opinions.

152 21 U.S. 543 (1823) Marshall's 'conquest' language did not reappear in his later Indian law cases. Native people in Canada, of course, were not conquered by European armies but rather entered into profitable economic and political relationships with European nations.

153 *Connolly* v. *Woodrich* (1867) 17 R.J.R.Q. 75, 91. Judge Samuel Monk's remarkable and carefully written opinion has not received the attention it deserves. Constance Backhouse gives it a central place in her important analysis of the legal history of women in Canada, *Petticoats and Prejudice*, 9–20, but the case has not been important in aboriginal rights law. Mark Walters, 'British Imperial Constitutional Law and Aboriginal Rights: A Comment on *Delgamuukw* v. *British Columbia*,' (1996) *Queen's Law Journal*, vol. 17 (1996), 350, 378–85. properly puts the Monk case in its place as a major statement of Indian rights under mid-nineteenth-century Canadian law. Perhaps more important in the terms of this article, Monk had access to virtually the same common law jurisprudence that Robinson did and produced an opinion that recognized a broad range of aboriginal rights.

CHAPTER 4

1 Two simple comparisons should illustrate this point. New York, the United States' most populous state and one with a native population comparable to Ontario, produced thirteen reported native law cases before 1900. Quebec, the only other province with a sizable number of cases, produced only twelve cases.

2 'British precedent dominated legal reasoning in Upper Canada, but Robinson relied on precedent only when it served his purposes.' Patrick Brode, *Sir John Beverley Robinson: Bone and Sinew of the Compact* (Toronto: University of Toronto Press 1984), 104. Obviously, the selective use of precedent led to the same problems for native people under British law as the use of precedent: Native rights were never litigated in England, and hence there was no precedent.

3 The reports searched were the Upper Canada Reporter (U.C.R.), Upper Canada Common Pleas Reports (U.C.C.P), Ontario Weekly Reports (O.W.R.), Ontario Practice Reports (O.P.R.), Ontario Appeals Reports (O.A.R.), Ontario Reports (O.R.), and Grants Chancery Reports (Gr.). Brian Slattery, *Canadian Native Law Cases* (C.N.L.C.) (Saskatoon: Native Law Centre, University of Saskatchewan, 1980), vols. 1 through 3 reprints most of these cases but not all of them. The figure cited here represents the total number of reported opinions delivered by Ontario courts, and thus several cases are counted two or three times, having produced reported opinions by both a trial and one or more appellate courts. *St. Catherine's Milling*, discussed in chapter 6, was appealed from the Supreme Court of Canada to the Privy Council, producing four reported opinions.

4 2 C.N.L.C. 6. The case was found in Archives of Ontario. Aemilius Irving Papers, box 42, file 42, item 9. Irving, a prominent Ontario lawyer, represented the province in the case.

5 Delivered 31 Jan. 1898 by Judge Rose of the Ontario Court of Queen's Bench, and discussed in William David McPherson and John Murray Clark, *The Law of Mines in Canada* (Toronto: Carswell 1898), 15–16.

6 The Archives of Ontario is still collecting original court records from nineteenth century Ontario, records that have been inaccessible to modern scholars, often for a century or more.

7 There is a substantial legal history of the early judges of Upper Canada. See Patrick Brode, *Sir John Beverley Robinson*; William Renwick Riddell, *The Life of William Dummer Powell: First Judge at Detroit and Fifth Chief Justice of Upper Canada*, (Lansing: Michigan Historical Commission 1924); David B. Read, *The Lives of the Judges of Upper Canada and Ontario from 1791 to the Present Time* (Toronto: Rowsell and Hutchinson 1888); Robert Fraser, *Provincial Justice: Upper Canadian Legal Portraits* (Toronto: Osgoode Society and University of Toronto Press 1992).

8 British Columbia, a colony with little relationship to Canada before confederation, has a unique Native history that is well documented, including its own
   legal history. See *Papers Connected with the Indian Land Question, 1850–1875*
   (Victoria: Queen's Printer 1987; originally published 1875); Paul Tennant,
   *Aboriginal Peoples and Politics: The Indian Land Question in British Columbia,
   1849–1989* (Vancouver: University of British Columbia Press, 1990); Robin
   Fisher, *Contact and Conflict: Indian-European Relations in British Columbia, 1774–
   1890* (Vancouver: University of British Columbia Press 1977); Douglas Cole
   and Ira Chaikin, *Iron Hand upon the People: The Law against the Potlatch on the
   Northwest Coast.* (Seattle: University of Washington Press 1990); David Ricardo
   Williams, *The Man for a New Country: Sir Matthew Baillie Begbie* (Sydney, B.C.:
   Gray Publishers 1977). For the Maritimes, see L.F. S. Upton, *Micmacs and Colonists: Indian-White Relations in the Maritimes, 1713–1867* (Vancouver: University
   of British Columbia Press 1979), and Judith Fingard, 'The New England Company and the New Brunswick Indians, 1786–1826: A Comment on the Colonial
   Perversion of British Benevolence,' *Acadiensis* vol. 1 (1972), 29–42. Native people in Quebec and French Canada have a legal history that is distinct, and this
   history is considered in chapter 8.
9 About half of the reported cases concerns some kind of land issue. Most unreported cases were criminal cases.
10 The 1844 'Report on the Affairs of the Indians in Canada,' gave the whole
   Indian population of Ontario and Quebec at 43,000, with 28,000 living in
   Ontario (*Journals of the Legislative Assembly,* 1844–45, appendices EEE and T).
   Completely inconsistent is a report of 13,107 Indians in Ontario at Confedera-
   tion. The same report lists an Indian population of 26,706. See 'Indians of
   Ontario,' (Ottawa: Department of Citizenship and Immigration, Indian Affairs
   Branch 1962), 42.
11 Kenneth M. Narvey, 'The Royal Proclamation of 7 October 1763, the Common
   Law, and Native Rights to Land within the Territory Granted to the Hudson's
   Bay Company,' *Saskatchewan Law Review,* vol. 38 (1973–4), 123; Robert Clinton,
   'The Proclamation of 1763: Colonial Prelude to Two Centuries of Federal-State
   Conflict over the Management of Indian Affairs,' *Boston University Law Review,*
   vol. 69 (1989), 329; Brian Slattery, 'The Land Rights of Indigenous Canadian
   Peoples, As Affected by the Crown's Acquisition of Their Territories,' (Ph.D.
   dissertation, Oxford University 1979); J. Stagg, *Anglo-Indian Relations in North
   America to 1763 and an Analysis of the Royal Proclamation of 7 October 1763*
   (Ottawa: Department of Indian Affairs and Northern Development 1981). The
   full text of the proclamation is reprinted in A.L. Getty and Antoine S. Lussier,
   As Long As the Sun Shines and Water Flows: A Reader in Canadian Native Studies
   (Vancouver: University of British Columbia Press 1983), 29–37.

12 J.R. Miller, *Skyscrapers Hide the Heavens: A History of Indian White Relations in Canada* (Toronto: University of Toronto Press 1989), 59–80.

13 David W. Elliot, 'Aboriginal Title,' in Bradford Morse, ed., *Aboriginal Peoples and the Law: Indian, Metis, and Inuit Rights in Canada* (Ottawa: Carleton University Press 1985), 56. The respective courts in *St. Catherine's Milling* spent a considerable amount of time analysing the legal force of the Royal Proclamation. See 6.

14 These provisions are found in the Royal Proclamation as reprinted in A.L. Getty and Antoine Lussier *As Long As the Sun Shines*, 29–38 at 35. The original is unpaginated.

15 Herman Merivale, *Lectures on Colonization and Colonies* (New York: 1967), quoted in David T. McNab, 'Herman Merivale and Colonial Office Indian Policy in the Mid-Nineteenth Century,' in Ian A.L. Getty and Antoine S. Lussier, *As Long As the Sun Shines*, 85–103, 91–2.

16 David Shanahan, 'The Manitoulin Treaties, 1836 and 1862: The Indian Department and Indian Destiny,' *Ontario History*, vol. 86 (1994), 13–31.

17 Robert J. Surtees, 'Indian Land Cessions in Upper Canada, 1815–1830,' in A.L. Getty and Antoine Lussier, *As Long As the Sun Shines*, 65–84; Alexander Morris, *The Treaties of Canada with the Indians of Manitoba and the Northwest Territories*, (Saskatoon: Fifth House Publishers 1991; originally published 1880), 16–21. Surtees's work is based on his comprehensive history of the alienation of Indian land in Ontario, 'Indian Land Cessions in Ontario, 1763–1862: The Evolution of a System,' (Ph.D. dissertation, Carleton University 1983).

18 Robert J. Surtees, 'The Development of an Indian Reserve Policy in Canada,' *Ontario History*, vol. 61 (1969), 87–98. An exhaustive legal analysis of the legal status of Indian reserve lands is Richard Bartlett, *Indian Reserves and Aboriginal Lands in Canada: A Homeland: A Study in Law and History* (Saskatoon: University of Saskatchewan Native Law Centre 1990). On the scope of these fiduciary relationships, see Leonard Ian Rotman, *Parallel Paths: Fiduciary Doctrine and the Crown-Native Relationship in Canada* (Toronto: University of Toronto Press 1996).

19 (1823) 1 Taylor 47. The case is discussed in detail in William Renwick Riddell, 'The Sad Tale of an Indian Wife,' *Journal of the American Academy of Criminal Law and Criminology*, vol. 13 (1992), 82–9. This issue was not settled by *Phelps* and went through the Ontario courts to the Supreme Court of Canada in the 1970s in *Isaac v. Davey* (1973), 38 D.L.R. (3rd) 23 Ont. H.C.) ; (1974) 51 D.L.R. (3rd) 170 (Ont.C.A.); *Davey v. Isaac* (1977) 77 D.L.R.(3rd) 481 (S.C.C.). To the Six Nations, these issues are still unresolved.

20 Aborigines' Protection Society, *Report* (London: Aborigines' Protection Society 1839).

21 'Report on the Affairs of the Indians in Canada,' published in two parts in appendix EEE (sections 1 and 2) and appendix T (section 3), *Journals of the Legislative Assembly*, 1844–5 and 1847, respectively (unpaginated). The work of this commission is discussed in John Leslie, 'The Bagot Commission: Developing a Corporate Memory for the Indian Department,' *Canadian Historical Association Papers* (1982), 31–52.

22 David T. McNab, 'Herman Merivale and the Colonial Office Indian Policy; Douglas Leighton, 'The Compact Tory as Bureaucrat: Samuel Peters Jarvis and the Indian Department, 1837–1845,' *Ontario History*, vol. 73 (1981), 40–53; and Anthony J. Hall, 'The Red Man's Burden: Land, Law and the Lord in the Indian Affairs of Upper Canada, 1761–1858,' (Ph.D. dissertation, University of Toronto, 1984); J.R. Miller, *Skyscrapers Hide the Heavens*, 110–12.

23 Just as the judge-made law of Indian affairs in Canada largely originated in Ontario, so did the 'Indian Acts' of Ontario become the basis for the dominion Indian Acts. John Leslie and Ron Maguire, *The Historical Development of the Indian Act* (Ottawa: Department of Indian and Northern Affairs 1978), part 1, 'The Pre-Confederation Period,' 1–51. See also John S. Milloy, 'The Early Indian Acts: Developmental Strategy and Constitutional Change,' in Ian Getty and Antoine Lussier, *As Long As the Sun Shines*, 56–64.

24 'Memorandum on the Aborigines of North America,' Dispatch no. 95, published as appendix A of Francis Bond Head, *A Narrative*, (London: John Murray 1839), 1. Although found beginning at p. 489, the memorandum retains its original pagination.

25 Ibid., 2, 3.

26 Ibid., 4.

27 Ibid., 5. W.R. Wrightman, *Forever on the Fringe: Six Studies in the Development of Manitoulin Island* (Toronto: University of Toronto Press 1982), 20–56; David Shanahan, 'The Manitoulin Treaties, 1836 and 1862'; Ruth Bleasdale, 'Manitowaning: An Experiment in Indian Settlement,' *Ontario Historical Society Proceedings*, vol. 66 (1975), 147–57.

28 Head to Lord Glenelg, secretary of state for colonies, 4 April 1837 quoted in James Clifton, 'A Place of Refuge for All Time: Migration of the American Potawatomi into Upper Canada, 1830–1850' (Ottawa: National Museum of Man, Canadian Ethnology service paper no. 26, 1975), 55.

29 Judge Allan MacEachern's rejection of the capability of law to resolve British Columbia Indian land claims in *Delgamuukw* represents the same paradigm: any dispute between non-native Canadian citizens properly brought to the courts is subject to a decision based on existing law. Yet the law of native rights is a 'novel' concept, interesting theoretically but not involving justiciable legal rights. See the discussion of *Delgamuukw* in introduction.

30 John Leslie and Ron Maguire, *The Historical Development of the Indian Act*, 23.

31 *Fegan v. McLean* 29 U.C.R. 202 (1869)

32 Ibid., 203.

33 Ibid., 204. Admittedly, this statement is highly ambiguous: the words 'belongs to' might refer to either the crown or the Indians. A trust relationship binds the trustee, that is, the crown, to hold and manage the lands for the benefit of the Indian tribes, and creates a legal cause of action against the crown should it fail to carry out its legal duty. Trust doctrine derived, not from the political relationship of Indians to the crown, but from contract: the Indian land surrenders specifically provided that the crown would sell tribal lands and use the proceeds 'for the benefit of the tribe.' Thus, trust doctrine did not reach unsurrendered lands, including the lands at question in this case, unsurrendered Six Nations lands.

34 *Guerin v. the Queen* [1984] 2 S.C.R. 335 holds the crown liable to the Musqueam band for violating its fiduciary duty in leasing tribal lands for a golf course at below-market rates. While holding that the crown was not a trustee for the band, the court held that it was in a trust-like relationship.

35 *Feagan v. McLean*, 204. This issue was to be fully argued in *St. Catherines Milling* fifteen years later, discussed in chapter 6.

36 Ibid., 205–6. This case expanded on a much simpler case, *Vanvleck et al. v. Stewart et. al.* (1860) 19 U.C.Q.B. 489, decided nine years earlier, which also involved the Six Nations' Grand River lands.

37 *Regina v. Good* (1889) 17 O.R. 725. The reported case contains no indication whether the magistrate in this case was the Indian agent.

38 Ibid., 726–7.

39 Ibid., 727–8.

40 (1886) 10 O.R. 660.

41 Ibid., 663, 665–8.

42 *Hunter v. Gilkison* (1885) 7 O.R. 735.

43 Ibid., 736.

44 Ibid., 737, 735.

45 Ibid., 741–5.

46 The 'Friends of the Indian,' an influential American Indian reform organization, was actively arguing for the full extension of American criminal and civil law to Indians in the 1880s and 1890s, citing Canadian precedent for this policy. William T. Hagan, *The Indian Rights Association: The Herbert Welsh Years, 1882–1904* (Tucson: University of Arizona Press 1985). American Indians, as an attribute of their sovereignty, retain the right to use their own civil and criminal law to resolve disputes on their own lands. Sidney L. Harring, *Crow Dog's Case: American Indian Sovereignty, United States Law, and Indian Law*

in the Nineteenth Century (Cambridge, U.K.: Cambridge University Press 1994).

47 Duncan C. Scott, 'Indian Affairs, 1867–1912,' in Adam Shortt and A.G. Doughty, *Canada and Its Provinces*, vol. 7, *The Dominion*, (Toronto: Glasgow, Brook 1914), 351.

48 David B. Read, *The Lives of the Judges of Upper Canada and Ontario*, 5–16, is an early history of the development of British courts in Upper Canada.

49 'Report of the Special Commissioners to Investigate Indian Affairs in Canada, Province of Canada,' *Journals of the Legislative Assembly*, 1858, appendix 16, 'Position of the Native Tribes in the Eye of the Law.' Emphasis added.

50 Ibid.

51 Great Britain, House of Commons, 'Report on the Indians of Upper Canada, 1839,' 39, 40, 41, 51, 52.

52 See the discussion that follows. The only major legal constraint upon Indians which narrowed their rights was their disqualification as witnesses, unless they could take a Christian oath. This was eliminated by judicial interpretation (not by statute) in 1861 and seems to have been ignored in most cases.

53 John Beecham, 'Essay on Colonization,' referred to in Benjamin Slight, *Indian Researches* (Montreal: J.E. Miller 1844).

54 'Canada West and the Hudson's Bay Company,' Aborigines' Protection Society, *Report*, 1856, appendix, F, 14.

55 The accepted common law view of the time was that the testimony of non-Christians was inadmissible because it was not properly under oath. It was the mid-nineteenth century before the evidence of natives was admitted in Australia and India. A major legal issue concerning native people in nineteenth-century Australia was the admission of aboriginal testimony in court. This question raises a number of practical and theoretical considerations, involving magistrates and judges, appellate courts, the legislatures, and the Colonial Office. Not only were the rights of aboriginals as citizens at stake, but so also was the capacity of local government to try cases where aboriginals were witnesses, whether against whites or aboriginals. A wide variety of issues and interests were tied up in the narrow question of the admissibility of aboriginal testimony in Australian courts. As important as this issue was, it was beyond the scope of the formal workings of Australian law-making: all measures to permit the admission of aboriginal evidence were rejected in New South Wales until 1876, and were then only accepted after the issue became the admission of the evidence of atheists.

Given that aborigines became British citizens with settlement, it should have followed that their testimony would automatically have been accepted in British courts. In the way, however, was a racist and ethnocentric 1744 Indian case, *Omichund* v. *Barker*, holding that 'nothing but a belief in God and that he will reward and punish us according to our deserts is necessary to qualify a man to take the oath ... Infidels cannot be a witness' (1744) Willes 538, 549. Although aborigines were British citizens, they needed to have some recognized belief in a particular kind of god: only a god who would reward and punish. Without much inquiry, Australian courts held that aboriginal religion was not adequate to this test, although some non-Christian religious belief was. *R.* v. *Billy,* 27 Nov. 1840. House of Commons, *Parliamentary Papers,* 1844, 82–3. This case is unreported. See, generally David Kotthoff, 'The History of the Admission of Aboriginal Evidence into the Courts of New South Wales, 1788–1876' (LL.B. thesis, Australian National University 1974).

56 (1861) 20 U.C.Q.B. 195

57 Ibid., 196. The court cited *Omichund* v. *Barker* (1744 Willes 538), discussed in note 55. This case created a great deal of turmoil in colonial legal systems: there could have been no criminal law enforcement in any country in the British empire without the full acceptance of the testimony of native witnesses. By the 1820s and 1830s colonial dispatches contained dozens of references to the problem of admitting native testimony, and many colonies had resolved the issue statutorily, by permitting alternatives to the oath. David Kotthoff, 'The History of the Admission of Aboriginal Evidence.'

58 (1861) 20 U.C.Q.B., 197.

59 Indeed, the practice was simply taken for granted in Canada. William Dummer Powell permitted Indian testimony on the Detroit frontier after being appointed a judge there in 1796. At about the same time, several murder cases were pursued in the York and Kingston areas involving Indian witnesses. While there were numerous problems with these cases, including the loss of an entire court party in a shipwreck, they were partially built on Indian testimony and no one attempted to disqualify the Indian witnesses. These cases are discussed in chapter 5.

60 Australian colonial courts, for example, had faced this issue repeatedly since the 1820s, with a much smaller population and a native population that was much less integrated with the white population than was the case in Upper Canada. David Kotthoff, 'History of the Admission of Aboriginal Evidence.' The issue was finally resolved in *R.* v. *Billy.* The complete absence of the issue in Upper Canada must mean that it was not a problem, an indication that Indian testimony was being admitted. Here it might be pointed out that the crown itself had an interest in admitting Indian testimony because of the crown's prosecution of criminal cases. Individual settlers, involved in civil disputes with Indians or engaged in depredations against Indians that might bring about crown reaction, had an interest against admitting Indian testi-

mony. Because the colonial government was relatively strong in Upper Canada, Indian evidence was freely admitted.

61 Isabel T. Kelsay, *Joseph Brant., 1743–1807: Man of Two Worlds* (Syracuse: Syracuse University Press 1984). John Borrows makes this same point for the Ojibwa. See 'A Genealogy of Law: Inherent Sovereignty and First Nations Self Government,' *Osgoode Hall Law Journal*, vol. 30, no. 2 (1992), 291, 304–12.

62 Con. Stat. Can., chap. 9.

63 (1870) 5 P.R. 284

64 Ibid., 287.

65 *Avery v. Cayuga* (1913) 28 O.R. 517.

66 (1895) 26 O.R. 109.

67 Ibid., 112.

68 Ibid., 113–14.

69 Ibid., 111–12.

70 (1870) 5 P.R. 315.

71 Ibid., 316.

72 Ibid., 318. John Brant had been excluded from the Legislative Assembly in 1832 not because he was an Indian but because he did not own sufficient property in fee simple to meet the legal qualification to hold office.

73 *Rex v. Hill* (1907) 15 O.R. 406.

74 Ibid., 407–8.

75 Ibid., 410.

76 Ibid., 414.

77 BNA Act, s. 24. For a complete text and analysis of the British North America Act, see W.H. McConnell, *Commentary on the British North America Act* (Toronto: Macmillan 1987). Indians and Indian lands are discussed at 222–7.

78 *Re John Milloy and the Municipal Council of the Township of Onondaga* (1884) 6 O.R. 573 involved the reach of a municipal dog-control statute extending into the Six Nations' Grand River lands. The court held that statute valid, but only outside Six Nations lands.

79 *Owens v. Thomas* (1856), 6 U.C.C.P. 383

80 (1891) 20 O.R. 591.

81 Ibid., 592–3.

82 Ibid., 595–6.

83 (1867) 11 L.C.Jur. 197. This case is discussed in Constance Backhouse, *Petticoats and Prejudice: Women and Law in Nineteenth Century Canada* (Toronto: Osgoode Society and Women's Press 1991), 9–28. Connolly, while in the employ of the Hudson's Bay Company, had married an Indian woman according to tribal custom and brought his family back to Montreal. Later, he

abandoned his wife and, without bothering to obtain a divorce, married another woman. Upon Connolly's death, his Indian wife sued for a share in his estate. The Quebec court held that the marriage under tribal law was legal under Quebec law. This case is discussed in chapter 8.

84 Judge Robertson's gratuitous comment on Connolly's moral character in view of his close knowledge of the facts of the case, which centred on Connolly's abandonment of his Indian wife and their children, can be understood only as a reflection of his racism. He would surely have seen Connolly's actions as morally reprehensible according to the values of Victorian Ontario if he had abandoned his white wife and their family. Moreover, Robertson was wildly ignorant of both Canadian geography and Canadian history. By the mid-nineteenth century, missionaries of many denominations were attending to the Indians of the northwest and no place in Athabasca was more than 1000 miles from a clergyman, far less in many cases.

85 (1891) 20 O.R. 591, 596–7.

86 Ibid., 597.

87 Ibid., 599.

88 Ontario was not unique in refusing to recognize Indian marriages under customary law. This legal recognition of Indian marriages did not extend to plural marriages in the west which were prosecuted under Canadian law by the end of the nineteenth century. Bears Shin-Bone, a Blood Indian, was jailed on bigamy charges in 1899. *The Queen v. Bears Shin Bone* [1898–1901], 4 Terr. L.R. 173 (1900).

89 'Report, 1844 (1847),' appendix 99.

90 Ibid., appendix 16.

91 Great Britain, Parliament, *Report of the Subcommittee on Native People in North America*, vol. 38 (1839), 12.

92 'Report of the Special Commissioners Appointed on the 8th of September, 1856, to Investigate Indian Affairs in Canada,' appendix 20 *Journals of the Legislative Assembly*, 1858, vol. 16, unpaginated but three pages before section 3.

93 Ibid.

94 Ibid.

95 John S. Milloy, 'The Early Indian Acts: Developmental Strategy and Constitutional Change,' in Ian Getty and Antoine Lussier, *As Long As the Sun Shines*, 56–64.

96 John L. Tobias, 'Protection, Civilization, Assimilation: An Outline History of Canada's Indian Policy,' in J.R. Miller, *Sweet Promises*, (Toronto: University of Toronto Press 1991), 127–44.

97 John Borrows, 'A Genealogy of Law.'

CHAPTER 5

1 Alexander Fraser, 'Records of the Early Courts of Justice in Upper Canada,'
   Bureau of Archives for the Province of Ontario, *Fourteenth Annual Report*, 1917,
   180–1, Court of Oyer and Terminer, Province of Upper Canada, District of
   Hesse, 3 Sept. 1792. This report reprints a number of bench books of local
   judges. At the time, the Detroit area was among the most settled parts of
   Upper Canada, with the current boundary between Canada and the United
   States still not recognized. William Renwick Riddell, *The Life of William Dum-
   mer Powell: First Judge at Detroit and Fifth Chief Justice of Upper Canada* (Lansing:
   Michigan Historical Commission 1924).

2 Great Britain had a functioning legal presence in Detroit as early as 1760 and
   did not abandon Detroit following the American revolution, remaining until
   1815. William Renwick Riddell, *Michigan under British Rule: Law and Law
   Courts, 1760–1796*, (Lansing: Michigan Historical Commission 1926). Fred
   Landon, *Western Ontario and the American Frontier* (Toronto: Ryerson Press
   1941), 1–45.

3 Alexander Fraser, 'Records of the Early Courts of Justice in Upper Canada'
   180–1. These same trials are discussed in William Renwick Riddell, *Michigan
   Under British Rule*, 333–63.

4 Alexander Fraser, 'Records of the Early Courts of Justice in Upper Canada,'
   181–5. Riddell, *Michigan Under British Rule*, 328–46, contains a transcript of this
   trial.

5 William Renwick Riddell, *Michigan under British Rule*, 356, 460.

6 Brendan O'Brien, *Speedy Justice* (Toronto: Osgoode Society/University of Toronto Press 1992), 38; Isabel Kelsay, *Joseph Brant*, 529.

7 William Renwick Riddell, *The Life of William Dummer Powell*, 90. This result
   may appear inconsistent with Powell having already tried Mishinaway, and
   having indicted Chabouquoy and Cawquochish, all on murder charges, but
   Powell's logic focuses on the political sovereignty of Indians 'in their villages,'
   which is consistent with United States Indian law. The three Indians at Detroit
   (although this is not completely clear) were apparently functioning in white
   society, outside of their traditional villages. Powell and Brant already knew
   each other, having had dinner together in June of 1789 as Powell traveled
   through Niagara on his way to Detroit to assume his first judicial post. (at 66)

8 Isabel Kelsay, *Joseph Brant, 1743–1807: Man of Two Worlds* (Syracuse: Syracuse
   University Press 1984), 563–5.

9 Ibid., 529–30.

10 Brendan O'Brien, *Speedy Justice*, 54–62, is an exhaustive study of this case.
   O'Brien painstakingly puts together an account of this case even though no

legal records on the case exist. He acknowledges that it is not clear which Cozens killed Whistling Duck, but he believes that it was Samuel (at 56–8).

11 Ibid.

12 Ibid., 82–110.

13 Ibid., 62–4.

14 Ibid., 64.

15 Ibid., 42–4.

16 Ibid., 45–8. Wabakinine was severely beaten and died in a drunken altercation with soldiers over his sister. His wife was seriously injured in the melee and died several days later. This killing is also described in Donald B. Smith, *Sacred Feathers: The Reverend Peter Jones (Kahkewa-quonaby) and the Mississauga Indians* (Toronto: University of Toronto Press 1987), 28.

17 Brendan O'Brien, *Speedy Justice*, 43–9.

18 Constance Backhouse, *Petticoats and Prejudice: Women and Law in Nineteenth Century Canada* (Toronto: Osgoode Society and Women's Press 1991), 112–20.

19 Ibid., 121–4.

20 *Niagara Spectator*, 26 March 1818.

21 Quoted in Mark D. Walters, 'The Extension of Colonial Criminal Jurisdiction over the Aboriginal Peoples of Upper Canada: Reconsidering the Shawanakiskie Case (1822–26),' *University of Toronto Law Journal*, vol. 46 (1996), 273, 301.

22 Mark Walter's analysis of this case is extensively relied on in the discussion that follows. See also D. Carter-Edwards, 'Shawanakiskie,' in *D.C.B.*, vol. 5 (1983), 198.

23 Some basic documents in this case were published in A.G. Doughty and N. Story, eds, *Documents Relating to the Constitutional History of Canada, 1819–1828* (Ottawa: Public Archives of Canada, 1935).

24 Quoted in M. Walters, 'The Extension of Colonial Criminal Jurisdiction over the Aboriginal People,' 301.

25 Ibid. has a detailed discussion of the complexity of both Powell's and Campbell's position on this issue.

26 J.B. Robinson to J. Givens, superintendent of the Indian Department, 9 July 1827, quoted in ibid., 305.

27 Hamar Foster, 'Forgotten Arguments: Aboriginal Title and Sovereignty in Canada Jurisdiction Act Cases,' *Manitoba Law Journal*, vol. 21 (1992), 343–89, 378–9. On the same general issue, see also Hamar Foster, 'Long-Distance Justice: The Criminal Jurisdiction of Canadian Courts West of the Canadas, 1763–1859,' *American Journal of Legal History*, vol. 34, no. 1 (1990), 2. Without a reprieve, which would exist as a written record, the legal process resulting in execution would have gone forward. This same question was being resolved

in colonial Australia at about the same time. Barry Bridges, 'The Aborigines and the Law: New South Wales, 1788–1855,' *Teaching History*, vol. 4 (Dec. 1970), 40–70; 'The Extension of English Law to Aborigines for Offenses Inter Se, 1829–1842,' *Journal of the Royal Australian Historical Society*, vol. 59 (Dec. 1973), 264–9. The process in Australia was different, however: Chief Justice Sir Francis Forbes handed down a clear opinion holding that aborigines were fully responsible for their crimes under English law in *R. v. Congo Jack Murrell* (1836) 1 Legge (NSW) 72. Although the issue was brought to the government several times thereafter, Forbes's decision was always deferred to. It seems clear that, if Canadian authorities had chosen to do so, they could have resolved the issue without referring it to the Colonial Office.

28 Mark Walters, 'The Extension of Colonial Criminal Jurisdiction over the Aboriginal Peoples,' 306–11, clearly makes this point, disagreeing with my article "The Liberal Treatment of Indians": Native People in Nineteenth Century Ontario Law,' *Saskatchewan Law Review* vol. 56 (1992), 297, 304–5. I should say that Walters has convinced me that his interpretation of these cases is the better one.

29 Mr Justice Macaulay's report to Sir George Arthur, 1839, reprinted as appendix 99 of 'Report on the Indians of Canada,' 1844.

30 Ibid.

31 Memorandum of C.R. Ogden, Montreal, 9 May 1840, reprinted in ibid.

32 Hamar Foster, 'Forgotten Arguments,' 343–54. Foster disagrees with Bruce Clark, *Native Liberty, Crown Sovereignty* (Montreal: McGill-Queen's University Press 1990), 35. In reality, Canadian courts were simply unable to extend criminal jurisdiction to the frontier, whatever the statutes meant.

33 An Act for Extending the Jurisdiction of the Courts of Justice in the Provinces of Lower and Upper Canada, to the Trial and Punishment of Persons Guilty of Crimes and Offenses within Certain Parts of North American Adjoining to the Said Provinces, 43 Geo. II, c. 138 (1803). Quoted in Bruce Clark, *Native Liberty, Crown Sovereignty*, 126.

34 An Act for Regulating the Fur Trade, and Establishing a Criminal and Civil Jurisdiction within Certain Parts of North America, 1 and 2 Geo. IV, c. 66 (1821).

35 Gage papers, William L. Clements Library, University of Michigan, quoted in Bruce Clark, *Native Liberty, Crown Sovereignty*, 125.

36 Robert Seidman, 'Witch Murder and Mens Rea,' *Modern Law Review*, vol. 28 (1965), 46–61; 'Mens Rea and the Reasonable African,' *International and Comparative Law Quarterly*, vol. 15 (1966), 1135–64.

37 (1897) 28 O.R. 309. George Nelson, a fur trader, provides a classic account of the wendigo in Ojibwa life. See Jennifer S.H. Brown and Robert Brightman, *The Orders of the Dreamed: George Nelson On Cree and Northern Ojibway Religion*

and Myth, 1823 (Winnipeg: University of Manitoba Press 1988). A wendigo execution under tribal law is described at 92–3. These cases are fully discussed in chapter eleven.

38 This case is analysed in detail in chapter 10.
39 'Council with the Munsey Delaware of River Thames, 25 November 1820,' quoted in M. Walters, 'The Extension of Colonial Criminal Jurisdiction over the Aboriginal Peoples,' 287–8.
40 'Testimony before Commission on Indian Affairs, 13 October 1842,' 1. quoted, in M. Walters, 'The Extension of Colonial Criminal Juridiction over the Aboriginal Peoples,' 288.
41 John A. Noon, 'Law and Government of the Grand River Iroquois' (New York: Viking Fund Publications in Anthropology, no. 12, 1949).
42 (1870) 5 P.R. 80.
43 (1887) 14 O.R. 643
44 Ibid., 646.
45 Ibid., 649.
46 Ibid., 646.
47 Ibid., 651.
48 Ibid., 653–4.
49 (1888) 12 O.R. 373.
50 Ibid., 374–5.
51 Ibid., 376.
52 (1900) 27 O.R. 443.
53 Ibid., 444–5.
54 (1884) 6 O.R. 165.
55 Ibid., 166–7.
56 Ibid., 169.
57 *Regina* v. *White* 21 C.P. 354 at 356 was cited by the court for the proposition that under a few circumstances liquor could be legally provided to Indians.
58 *Regina* v. *Young* (1884) 7 O.R. 88
59 Ibid., 89.
60 Letter, William McKirdy to attorney general, Archives of Ontario, RG 8, Series, 1–1–D, no. 3257 (1892).
61 Telegram, Gibson to McKirdy, 4 July 1892, ibid.
62 Letter, William McKirdy to attorney general, ibid.
63 Roland Wright, 'The Public Right of Fishing, Government Fishing Policy, and Indian Fishing Rights in Upper Canada,' *Ontario History*, vol. 86, no. 4 (1994), 327–62. Although most of the Ontario treaties are silent on the subject of fishing rights, Wright believes that there was a common law right to fish in nineteenth-century Ontario that applied to all people, Indians and Europeans.

64 Ibid. Lise C. Hansen, 'Treaty Fishing Rights and the Development of Fisheries Legislation in Ontario: A Primer,' *Native Studies Review*, vol. 7 (1991), 1, presents the current Ontario government's view of the process, a position criticized by Leo G. Waisberg and Tim Holzkamm, 'The Ojibway Understanding of Fishing Rights under Treaty Three,' *Native Studies Review*, vol. 8 (1992), 47–55.

65 Alexander Morris, *The Treaties of Canada* (Toronto: Coles Publishing 1979; originally published 1880), 302–9.

66 Jean Friesen, 'Grant Me Wherewith to Make My Living,' in Kerry Abel and Jean Friesen, eds., *Aboriginal Resource Use in Canada: Historical and Legal Perspectives* (Winnipeg: University of Manitoba Press 1991), 141–55.

67 This is the core of the disagreement between Lise Hansen, 'Treaty Fishing Rights,' and Leo Waisberg and Tim Holzkamm, 'The Ojibway Understanding of Fishing Rights.'

68 Memorandum, attorney general to Cartwright, Archives of Ontario, RG 1, file 1799 (1907).

69 Letters, Langworthy to attorney general, and attorney general to Langworthy, Archives of Ontario, RG 4, (1910) file 898. The Robinson Treaties are discussed in chapter 7.

70 Archives of Ontario, RG 4, file 1572 (1916).

71 Douglas Sanders, 'Indian Hunting and Fishing Rights,' *Saskatchewan Law Review*, vol. 38 (1973–4), 45, and 'Hunting Rights – Provincial Laws – Application on Indian Reserves,' ibid., 234–42 ; Peter A. Cumming and Neil H. Mickenberg, *Native Rights in Canada*, 2nd ed. (Toronto: General Publishing 1972), chapter 20, 'The Law of Native Hunting and Fishing Rights,' and Donna Lea Hawley, *The Annotated Indian Act* (Saskatoon: Native Law Centre, University of Saskatchewan, 1990), 5–9.

CHAPTER 6

1 David W. Elliot, 'Aboriginal Title,' in Bradford Morse, *Aboriginal Peoples and the Law: Indian, Metis, and Inuit Rights in Canada* (Ottawa: Carleton University Press, 1985), esp. 57; Kent McNeil, *Common Law Aboriginal Title* (Oxford, U.K.: Clarendon Press 1989). See also *Calder* v. *Attorney General of British Columbia* (1973) S.C.R. 313, 320–3. The status of *St. Catherine's Milling* as a foundational case continues, with heavy reliance on it as precedent in both *Delgamuukw* and *Bear Island*, in spite of the fact that most of the important individual elements of the case either have been overruled or were simply always wrong. See Hamar Foster, 'It Goes Without Saying: Precedent and the Doctrine of Extinguishment by Implication in Delgamuukw et al v. The Queen,' *The*

Advocate, vol. 49 (1991), 341–57, and Douglas Sanders, 'The Nishga Case,' *B.C. Studies*, vol. 19 (autumn 1973), 3–20. *St. Catherines*, as the case was spelled in the Privy Council, was spelled *St. Catharines* in the Ontario courts. The Privy Council spelling is followed in scholarly accounts of the case to avoid the confusion of repeatedly changing the spellings, depending on which case is being referred to.

2 There is a vast literature on the common law of aboriginal title. See Brian Slattery, 'The Land Rights of Indigenous Canadian Peoples as Affected by the Crown's Acquisition of Their Territories' (Ph.D. dissertation, Oxford University 1979); Geoffrey Lester, 'The Territorial Rights of the Inuit of the Canadian Northwest Territories: A Legal Argument' (Ph.D. dissertation, Oxford University 1981).

3 BNA Act, s. 109. The discussion that follows treats in a few pages the law of aboriginal land rights in Canada, a legal issue of great complexity. See, for example, Brian Slattery, 'The Land Rights of Indigenous Canadian Peoples'; Bruce Clark, 'Indian Territory: Crown Rights Inchoate' (M.A. thesis, University of Western Ontario 1986); and Darlene Johnston, *The Taking of Indian Lands in Canada: Consent or Coercion*, (Saskatoon: University of Saskatchewan, Native Law Centre, 1990).

4 (1845) II Grants Chancery 639.

5 The legal status of the Six Nations Grand River lands is still at issue. See chapter 2.

6 (1878) 28 C.P. 384.

7 While most Indian lands were paternalistically 'sold' by the government for the 'benefit' of native people, Joseph Brant oversaw the sale of much of the Six Nations' Grand River lands to whites. Charles Johnston, *The Valley of the Six Nations* (Toronto: University of Toronto Press 1964).

8 *Church v. Fenton*, (1878) 28 C.P. 384, 395–401.

9 Ibid., 388. This apparently is the first time any Canadian judge asserted that Canadian Indians came under British jurisdiction by 'conquest,' an assertion of dubious historical validity turning on the conquest of French Quebec. See Mark Walters, 'British Imperial Constitutional Law and Aboriginal Rights: A Comment on *Delgamuukw v. British Columbia*,' *Queen's Law Journal*, vol. 17 (1996), 350 at 358–75.

10 Charles Johnston, *The Valley of the Six Nations*, 388.

11 (1879), 4 O.A.R. 159; (1880), 5 S.C.R. 239.

12 Trust doctrine is now regularly used in native law cases in Canada as well as other countries. Its history is analysed in L.I. Rotman, *Parallel Paths: Fiduciary Doctrine and the Crown-Native Relationship in Canada* (Toronto: University of Toronto Press 1996). See also *Guerin v. The Queen* [1984], 2 S.C.C. 335.

13 'Report of the Commissioners, 1844,' (1847) section 3, 'Lands: 1. Title to Lands.'
14 (1852) U.C.Q.B. 105, 122–3.
15 Ibid., 123.
16 (1862) 21 U.C.Q.B. 555, 577.
17 Ibid., 577.
18 (1868), 14 Gr. 346.
19 Ibid., 358.
20 (1869) 29 U.C.Q.B. 202, 204.
21 'In the Privy Council, *St. Catherine's Milling and Lumber Company v. The Queen*, argument of Mr. Blake, counsel for Ontario' (Toronto: The Budget 1888), 12.
22 *Journals* of the Legislative Assembly, 1858, appendix 16, 'Report of the Special Commissioners to Investigate Indian Affairs in Canada,' 'Introduction' (unpaginated). The other stated goal was to report 'on the best means of securing the progress and civilization of the Indian tribes.' Monies invested as annuities were also considered property.
23 Ibid.
24 Diamond Jenness, 'The Ojibwa Indians of Parry Island, Their Social and Religious Life,' (Ottawa: National Museum of Canada, bulletin no. 78, anthropological series no. 17, 1935), 4.
25 Ibid., 6. This analysis gives rise to a reverse version of the usufructuary position taken by Canadian courts. The Indian nations, in treaties with the British and Canadians, ceded land only for actual use by white settlers and reserved traditional Indian usages for themselves. This was easily possible since aboriginal and Euro-Canadian use of the land was most often for such different purposes.
26 Wilson Duff, 'The Vancouver Island Treaties,' *BC Studies*, vol. 3 (fall 1969), 3–57.
27 'Ontario v. Dominion of Canada,' National Archives of Canada, RG 175, Exchequer Court of Canada, Documents.
28 Ibid.
29 Wayne E. Daugherty, *Treaty Research Report: Treaty Three*, (Ottawa: Treaty Research Report, Treaties and Historical Research Centre, Indian and Northern Affairs Canada 1986). There is a large literature on Treaty 3, developed in the context of ongoing land claims. On water and fishing rights see Angela Emerson, 'Research Report on the Policy of the Government of Ontario Re. Headland to Headland Question, Treaty No. 3, 1873–78' (Toronto: Office of Indian Resource Policy, Ontario Ministry of Natural Resources 1978).
30 Alexander Morris, *The Treaties of Canada with the Indians of Manitoba and the*

North-West Territories (Saskatoon: Fifth House Publishers 1991; originally published 1880), 59, 62.

31 Wayne E. Daugherty, *Treaty Research Report: Treaty Three*, 20. See also J.E. Foster, 'The Saulteaux and the Numbered Treaties: An Aboriginal Rights Position,' in Richard Price, *The Spirit of the Alberta Indian Treaties* (Montreal: Institute for Research on Public Policy 1980), 161–80; and David McNab, 'The Administration of Treaty #3: The Location of the Boundaries of Treaty #3 Indian Reserves in Ontario,' in A. Getty and Antoine Lussier, *As Long As the Sun Shines and Water Flows,: A Reader in Canadian Native Studies*, 145–157, 146–7.

32 Wayne E. Daugherty, *Treaty Research Report: Treaty Three*, 21–53.

33 The context of the case is discussed in S. Barry Cottam, 'Indian Title as a Celestial Institution: David Mills and the St. Catherine's Milling Case' (at 247–66), and Anthony J. Hall, 'The St. Catherine's Milling and Lumber Company versus the Queen: Indian Land Rights as a Factor in Federal-Provincial Relations in Nineteenth-Century Canada' (at 267–86), both in Kerry Abel and Jean Friesen, *Aboriginal Resource Use in Canada: Historical and Legal Aspects* (Winnipeg: University of Manitoba Press 1991). See also Barry Cottam, 'An Historical Background of the St. Catherine's Milling and Lumber Company Case' (M.A. thesis, University of Western Ontario 1987); and Donald B. Smith, 'Aboriginal Rights a Century Ago,' *The Beaver* (February-March 1987), 4–15.

34 Alexander Morris, *The Treaties of Canada with the Indians of Manitoba and the North-West Territories*, 44–76; Wayne E. Daugherty, *Treaty Three*.

35 B. Cottam, 'Indian Title As a Celestial Institution,' 247–8.

36 J.C. Morrison, 'Oliver Mowat and the Development of Provincial Rights in Ontario: A Study in Dominion-Provincial Relations, 1867–1896,' in Ontario Department of Public Records and Archives, *Three History Theses* (1961).

37 Morris Zaslow, 'The Ontario Boundary Question,' in Ontario Historical Society, *Profiles of a Province* (Toronto: Ontario Historical Society 1967), 107–17. The official position of Ontario at the time was set out in David Mills, *A Report on the Boundaries of the Province of Ontario* (Toronto: Hunter, Rose 1873), prepared for the province, and was the basis for Ontario's argument in the arbitration commission. A large selection of papers on the issue is printed in Ontario Legislative Assembly, *Correspondence, Papers, and Documents Relating to the Northerly and Westerly Boundaries of the Province of Ontario* (Toronto: Blackett Robinson 1882).

38 Larry Lee Kulisek, *D'Alton McCarthy and the True Nationalization of Canada* (Ph.D. dissertation, Wayne State University, 1973), 53–81. By 1883 Ontario had had a team of lawyers at work on the boundary issue for eight years, producing five volumes of documents and maps. The dominion had virtually nothing beyond the report of an investigatory committee. The boundary dispute, how-

ever, did not turn on any issue of aboriginal title. Rather, it turned on historical boundaries extended westward in geographically imprecise terms.

39 A. Margaret Evans, 'Oliver Mowat: Nineteenth Century Ontario Liberal,' in
Donald Swainson, ed., *Oliver Mowat's Ontario* (Toronto: Macmillan 1972).
Mowat's role in the argument was symbolic, asserting the political importance
of the case.

40 Ibid.

41 Toronto *Mail*, 1 June 1882, quoted in C.R.W. Biggar, *Sir Oliver Mowat: A Biographical Sketch* (Toronto: Warwick Brothers and Rutter 1905), 460–1.

42 David Mills, *A Report on the Boundaries of the Province of Ontario*; (1873); Ontario
Legislative Assembly, *Correspondence, Papers, and Documents Relating to the
Northerly and Westerly Boundaries of the Province of Ontario.*

43 S. Barry Cottam, 'Indian Title As a Celestial Institution,' 251–3.

44 British Columbia, on joining Confederation, insisted that Indians there had no
aboriginal title to their lands. This is discussed in chapter 9.

45 Cottam, 'Indian Title as a Celestial Institution,' (at 256) sees Cassells as 'the
manager of the logistical problems involved in seeing the case through the
system.' Edward Blake, perhaps the best lawyer in Canada, had avoided dealing with any aspect of the Ontario boundary case because he saw it as a political liability to his career at the dominion level (at 249). Blake had preceded
Mowat as premier of Ontario, resigning to go into dominion politics. Joseph
Schull, *Edward Blake: The Man of the Other Way, 1833–1881* (Toronto: Macmillan
1975), 99. Ultimately, however, he argued *St. Catherine's Milling* 'brilliantly' in
the Privy Council for a princely fee of £6000. Anthony J. Hall, 'The St. Catherine's Milling and Lumber Company v. the Queen,' 275.

46 Cottam, 'Indian Title As a Celestial Institution,' 255.

47 Walter Cassels to Attorney General Mowat, 4 March 1885, Archives of
Ontario, MU 1469, Aemelius Irving Papers (hereafter Irving Papers). Cottam,
'Indian Title As a Celestial Institution,' (at 255), takes the opposite view of this
exchange. If Mowat was prepared to make such an admission, he evidently
did not believe that Ontario's case had anything to do with Indian title.

48 Through the process of 'admissions' the parties agree to certain facts, thereby
eliminating the need to prove those facts in a lengthy trial process. Given the
number of historical issues in dispute, it was of benefit to both sides to agree
to as many of these facts as possible so that the central issues of the case could
be directly addressed.

49 Mowat to McCarthy, 8 May 1885, Irving Papers.

50 'McCarthy to Mowat, 15 May 1885, Irving Papers; McCarthy to Mowat, 16
May 1885, ibid. This suggests that McCarthy was not well prepared for the
case. If he was as familiar with the primary documents as Cassels and Mowat,

he would not have been concerned about his unfamiliarity with the documents underlying the Ontario case.

51 John D. Blackwell, 'William Hume Blake and the Judicature Acts of 1849: The Process of Legal Reform at Mid-Century in Upper Canada,' in David H. Flaherty, ed., *Essays in the History of Canadian Law*, vol. 1: 132–74.

52 Donald B. Smith, 'Aboriginal Rights a Century Ago,' 8, suggests that Boyd's title to his summer home might have been clouded had Ontario lost the *St. Catherine's* case.

53 The original case file is held in the National Archives of Canada, RG 125, vol. 58, file 648, pts. 1 and 2.

54 British Columbia Indian land title has a legal history markedly different from that of Ontario, stemming from that province's distinct colonial status. Paul Tennant, *Aboriginal Peoples and Politics: The Indian Land Question in British Columbia, 1849–1989* (Vancouver: University of British Columbia Press 1990). See the discussion in chapter 9.

55 S. Barry Cottam, 'Indian Title As a 'Celestial Institution,' 250–2.

56 quoted in ibid., 252.

57 Ibid., 253. For a summary of different common-law legal approaches to aboriginal title, see Brian Slattery, *Ancestral Lands, Alien Laws: Judicial Perspectives on Aboriginal Title* (Saskatoon: University of Saskatchewan, Native Law Centre 1983).

58 (1885) 10 *Ontario Reports* 196, 199–201. The case was argued during the Northwest Rebellion of 1885, a Metis rising over land rights and other grievances. Obviously, this context might tend to undermine any idea that the Indians had extensive legal rights. See Donald Smith, 'Aboriginal Rights a Century Ago,' 9–10.

59 (1885) 10 *Ontario Reports* 196, 199. 8 Wheat. 543 (1824); Chancellor James Kent: *Kent's Commentaries*, 12th ed., vol. 1: 257.

60 (1885) 10 *Ontario Reports* 196, 200.

61 Ibid., 200. British Columbia *Sessional Papers* (1876), 'Papers Connected with the Indian Land Question' (Victoria, B.C.: Queen's Printer 1987; originally published 1875).

62 Larry Lee Kulisek, *D'Alton McCarthy*, 7–81. It seems that McCarthy collected substantial fees from both St. Catherine's Milling and Lumber Company and from the dominion, although, for political reasons, the dominion did not become a party to the case.

63 (1885) 10 *Ontario Reports* 196, 202. 5 Peter 1 (1831); 6 Peter 515 (1832); J. Burke, 'The Cherokee Cases: A Study in Law, Politics, and Morality,' *Stanford Law Review*, vol. 21 (1969), 500–31, and G. Edward White, *The Marshall Court and Cultural Change, 1815–1835* (New York: Macmillan 1988), esp. chapter 10. 'Nat-

356 Notes to pages 137–8

ural Law and Racial Minorities: The Court's Response to Slaves and Indians.' There are dozens of studies of the full context of the Cherokee cases. See, for example, William McLoughlin, *Cherokees and Missionaries, 1789–1839* (New Haven, Conn.: Yale University Press 1984), and *Cherokee Renascence, 1789–1733* (Princeton, N.J.: Princeton University Press 1986).

64 (1885) 10 *Ontario Reports* 196, 204–5. Act. 7 Will. IV, c. 118.

65 (1885) 10 *Ontario Reports* 196, 206. *Documents Relating to the Colonial History of the State of New York*, 486. The opinion itself was reprinted in Boyd's opinion, occupying more than two pages of fine print.

66 (1885) 10 *Ontario Reports* 196, 209. *Johnson* v. *MacIntosh* 8 Wheat. 595 (1823).

67 8 Wheat. 595 (1823). Chief Justice Marshall, author of the opinion, took a much more complex view of Indian political rights in the Cherokee cases and never again used conquest theory to justify denial of Indian rights. Marshall's analysis, however, was specifically in the context of political rights, although it seems logically to follow that 'domestic dependent nations' held some kind of legally recognized title to their lands.

68 Robert Williams, *The American Indian in Western Legal Thought* (New York: Oxford University Press 1990), part 3, 'The Norman Yoke: The American Indian and the Settling of the United States Colonizing Legal Theory,' 233–86, offers a detailed analysis of the late-seventeenth and early-eighteenth-century jurisprudence of Indian land rights.

69 These racist views of Indians were common among Canadians of the day. For an analysis of the Canadian Indian in nineteenth-century Canadian social thought, see Bruce Trigger, *Natives and Newcomers: Canada's Heroic Age Reconsidered* (Montreal: McGill-Queen's University Press 1985), chapter 1, 'The Indian Image in Canadian History,' 3–49.

70 (1885) 10 *Ontario Reports* 196, 218–20.

71 Ibid., 227. If Indians, like whites, held a title to their land, they held it whether degraded or not.

72 There is an extensive anthropological literature on the Saulteaux, a western branch of the Ojibwa, called Chippewa in the United States. Harold Hickerson, 'Land Tenure of the Rainy Lake Chippewa at the Beginning of the 19th Century,' *Smithsonian Contributions to Anthropology*, vol. 2, no. 4 (1967); Ruth Landes, *Ojibway Sociology*, Columbia Contributions to Anthropology, vol. 24 (New York, 1937).

73 (1885) 10 O.R. 196. His testimony was wasted because neither side apparently knew how to use his evidence. On the one hand, the making of Treaty 3 might have been used to prove that there was an aboriginal title and that had been sold to the crown. But that depended on some recognition that the Saulteaux had some kind of title to sell.

74 Donald B. Smith, 'Aboriginal Rights a Century Ago,' 4–15, 13–14. Leo Waisberg and Tim Holtzkamm, '"A Tendency to Discourage Them From Cultivat-
   ing": Ojibway Agriculture and Indian Affairs Administration in Northwestern
   Ontario,' *Ethnohistory*, vol. 40, no. 2 (spring 1993), 175–211.

75 To be fair to McCarthy, while the presence of Indian witnesses would have
   changed the tenor of the case, there is no evidence it would have changed the
   outcome.

76 The total opinion is twenty-four pages long as opposed to forty-one in Boyd's
   opinion. The majority opinion of Justice Hagarty, however, is only eleven
   pages long, one-fourth the length of Boyd's. Judge Burton's concurring opinion, really based on entirely different grounds than Hagarty's opinion, ran
   nine pages.

77 (1886) 13 O.R. 148, 154, 156–7.

78 Ibid., 159.

79 Ibid., 159.

80 Ibid., 163–4.

81 Ibid., 168–9.

82 Ibid., 172.

83 The Supreme Court of Canada did not fully emerge as an important appellate
   court until after 1949 when it became Canada's highest court of appeal, replac-
   ing the Privy Council. Before then it was a weak institution. David H. Flaherty, ed., *Essays in the History of Canadian Law*, vol. 1: 10. A complete history
   of the court is James Snell and Frederick Vaughan, *The Supreme Court of Canada: History of the Institution* (Toronto: Osgoode Society and University of Toronto Press 1985). This work does not see *St. Catherine's Milling* as an important
   case in the history of the Canadian Supreme Court.

84 Mowat favoured a direct appeal to the Privy Council and discussed that issue
   with McCarthy, who initially agreed because it would lead to a more speedy
   resolution of the case.

85 Respondents Factum printed copy in National Archives of Canada, RG 125,
   vol. 58, file 642, pt. 1.

86 The dominion government for political reasons chose to use the St Catherine's
   Milling Company as its proxy in the case, directly paying its lawyers, who
   argued the dominion's case. While it is commonly assumed that the St Catherine's Milling Company simply represented the dominion's position, this was
   denied by both parties, especially after the company and the dominion government wanted to distance themselves from a losing case. Barry Cottam, 'An
   Historical Background of the St Catherine's Milling and Lumber Company
   Case,' 59–61, 70–5; Appellants' Factum, printed copy in RG 125, vol. 58, file
   642, pt. 1.

87 Ibid. For example, American cases were often used ahistorically, with a number of cases from the period before the Cherokee cases cited with later cases. Some of the American cases from the earlier period did deny Indians any title to their lands, although later cases did not take this position.

88 See Appellants' Factum and 'Joint Appendix,' RG 125, vol. 58, file 642, part 1.

89 Sidney L. Harring, *Crow Dog's Case: American Indian Sovereignty, Tribal Law, and United States Law in the Nineteenth Century* (New York: Cambridge University Press 1994), chapter 2, 'Corn Tassel: State and Federal Conflict over Tribal Sovereignty,' 25–56.

90 Ibid. See also J. Burke, 'The Cherokee Cases: A Study in Law, Politics, and Morality,' and G. Edward White, *The Marshall Court and Cultural Change, 1815–1835*, esp. chapter 10, 'Natural Law and Racial Minorities: The Court's Response to Slaves and Indians.'

91 C. Peter McGrath, *Yazoo: The Case of Fletcher v. Peck.* (Providence, R.I.: Brown University Press 1966). *State* v. *George Tassells* 1 Dud. 229 (1830); *Caldwell* v. *State* 6 Peter 327 (1832); *State* v. *Foreman* 8 Yerg. 256 (1835). *Caldwell* runs 118 pages, with *Foreman* only a few pages less, making these the most elaborate judicial statements of Indian law in the United States.

92 'Joint Appendix,' RG 125, vol. 58, file 648, pt. 1. The order of Justice Fournier is printed at 277.

93 In the first paragraph of Ritchie's opinion, he cites Justice Joseph Story for this position on Indian title. (1887)13 S.C. 577, 578.

94 (1887) 13 S.C. 577, 599. Ritchie had formerly been chief justice of New Brunswick and had never written an opinion on native rights. The land rights of Indians in the Maritime provinces were as unclear as they were in Ontario, and the tribes there had been largely stripped of their lands. For a discussion of native rights in Atlantic Canada, see chapter 8.

95 (1887) 13 S.C. 577, 601.

96 Ibid., 608–13. The reliance on American precedent was common in nineteenth-century Canadian law. G. Blaine Baker, 'The Reconstruction of Upper Canadian Legal Thought in the Late-Victorian Empire,' *Law and History Review*, vol. 3 (1985), 219 at 236–9, 252–4.

97 (1887) 13 S.C. 577, 602; British North America Act, s. 91, ss. 24.

98 Ibid., 613.

99 Ibid., 637–8. David Elliot, 'Aboriginal Title,' argues (at 65) that 'on the point of Indian title there was no disagreement between the majority and minority views.' This position derives from their mutual reliance on American cases but ignores the deliberately ambiguous nature of the language and holding of the Cherokee cases, as well as the fact that Justice Joseph Story and Chief Justice John Marshall apparently disagreed on the question of Indian title. Moreover,

underlying both the American cases and *St. Catherine's Milling* are complex political and legal issues which had an impact on American Indian law and obviously underlay both the dominion and provincial positions in *St. Catherine's Milling.*

100 (1887) 13 S.C. 577, 651–76.

101 Ibid., 638–50, 639.

102 Ibid., 638.

103 (1888) 14 A.C. 46.

104 McCarthy to Macdonald, 7 Sept. 1888; McCarthy to Macdonald, 20 Aug. 1888, National Archives of Canada, Macdonald Papers, vol. 228.

105 15 A.C. (1888) 5. *In the Privy Council: The St. Catherine's Milling and Lumber Company v. The Queen: Argument of Mr. Blake, Counsel for Ontario.* This forty-nine-page pamphlet, apparently printed by Blake, publishes the text of his argument. Blake (at 5) took the position that while he was unable to make the concession that any view other than Boyd's was correct, he could proceed with the middle position 'on the assumption that it is the sound view of Indian title.'

106 2 C.N.L.C. 6. This case was not reported until found in the Ontario Archives in 1980.

107 Alexander Morris, *The Treaties of Canada*, at 16–21.

108 Ibid., 10.

109 Ibid., 11.

110 Ibid., 12–13. Vankoughnet's long career with the Indian Department is analysed in Douglas Leighton, 'A Victorian Civil Servant at Work: Lawrence Vankoughnet and the Canadian Indian Department, 1874–1893,' in A.L. Getty and Antoine S. Lussier, *As Long as the Sun Shines and the Water Flows*, 104–19.

111 Alexander Morris, *The Treaties of Canada*, 14–15.

112 Ibid., 17–18.

113 Ibid., 21–2.

114 Ibid., 22–5. The New Brunswick Supreme Court the same year handed down an opinion holding that title to Indian reserves, following *St. Catherine's Milling,* lay in the province and not in the dominion. *Doe D. Burk v. Cormier* (1890) 30 N.B.R. 142.

115 For a history of the Ontario/dominion dispute surrounding Treaty 3 lands, see Angela Emerson, 'Research Report on Police of the Government of Ontario Re. the Headland to Headland Question, Treaty No. 3, 1873–1978' (Office of Indian Resources Policy, Ontario Ministry of Natural Resources, Toronto 1978).

116 (1899) 31 O.R. 386

117 Ibid., 387–8. It appears that the dominion, in the 1870s, did not think that it had acquired title to these lands through Indian title. Rather, it took that argument from Ontario's claim, first raised in *St. Catherine's Milling*, that the opposite was the case.

118 Ibid., 397–98.

119 Ibid., 400.

120 (1900) 32 O.R. 30l.

121 (1903) 32 S.C.R. 1

122 (1902) 3 C.N.L.C. 203 (P.C.) Richard Bartlett, *Indian Reserves and Aboriginal Lands in Canada* (Saskatoon: Native Law Centre, University of Saskatchewan 1990), 66–7.

123 An 1894 agreement between Ontario and the dominion, providing for a joint commission to settle all land disputes pertaining to Indian reserve lands 'in order to avoid dissatisfaction or discontent among the Indians,' attempted to resolve this jurisdictional problem, but the issue is still problematic. *Province of Ontario v. The Dominion of Canada and the Province of Quebec* (1895) 25 S.C. 434–550. On Ontario's view of the effect of this agreement, see 'Re. The Indian Question, National Archives of Canada,' Office of the Attorney General of Ontario, 21 March 1910, RG 4, 4–32, (1910) file 587.

124 William David McPherson and John Murray Clark, *The Law of Mines in Canada* (Toronto: Carswell 1898), 15–23.

125 In ibid. McPherson and Clark, who reprint the judgment in its entirety (15–23), report that the decision was delivered on 31 Jan. 1898 and was 'on appeal.' *Seybold* followed almost a year later, argued on 26, 27 Oct. and 10 Nov. 1899 and decided on 2 Dec. 1899. However, Judge Rose sat in the northwest, in a district that included Sultana Island, while Chancellor Boyd sat in Toronto; thus, it appears that other lawsuits involving mining rights on the same island were filed in Toronto by the owners of the various mining claims.

126 Letter, Ontario secretary of the treasury to Wilfrid Laurier, re. Georgian Bay Islands, National Archives of Canada, RG 3, Series, 03–01–0–20, 26 Feb. 1900.

127 It is probably the range of legal disputes over tribal hunting and fishing rights that brought Indian rights back to the courts. Only in the 1970s did major issues of Indian title return to the court in *Calder et al.* v. *Attorney-General of British Columbia* (1973) D.L.R. (3d), 145. W.H. McConnell, 'The Calder Case in Historical Perspective,' *Saskatchewan Law Review*, vol. 38 (1974), 88.

128 *Calder* v. *Attorney General of British Columbia* (1973) 34 D.L.R.(3rd) 145 (S.C.C.); *Delgamuukw* v. *The Queen* (1991) D.L.R. (4th) 185 (B.C.S.C.).; *Attorney General of Ontario* v. *Bear Island Foundation et al.* (1984), 49 O.R. (2d) 574.

129 Hamar Foster, 'Forgotten Arguments: Aboriginal Title and Sovereignty in Canada Jurisdiction Act Cases,' *Manitoba Law Journal*, vol. 21 (1992), 343–5.

130 Douglas Sanders, 'Government Indian Agencies,' in Wilcomb Washburn, *Handbook of North American Indians 4: Indian-White Relations* (Washington, D.C.: Smithsonian Institution Press 1988), 279.

131 Kent McNeil: *Common Law Aboriginal Title*; Brian Slattery, 'Aboriginal Sovereignty and Imperial Claims,' *Osgoode Hall Law Journal*, vol. 29, no. 4 (1991), 681–703; Mark Walters, 'British Imperial Constitutional Law and Aboriginal Rights: A Comment on Delgamuukw v. British Columbia,' *Queen's Law Journal*, vol. 17 (1995), 350.

CHAPTER 7

1 Richard C. Daniel, 'A History of Native Claims Processes in Canada, 1867–1979' (Ottawa: Department of Indian and Northern Affairs, 1980), 122–30.

2 John A. Noon, *Law and Government of the Grand River Iroquois* (New York: Viking Fund 1949). An appendix, entitled 'A Casebook of Iroquois Law' and beginning at 116, reports more than a hundred cases. Noon based these reports on official records of the Grand Council that contain only the disposition of cases brought before the council. He then obtained the facts of each case by interviewing two chiefs in the 1930s who had sat on the council and could provide a factual statement of the issues in cases extending back to the 1870s (at 116). See also William B. Newell, *Crime and Justice among the Iroquois Nations* (Montreal: Caughnawaga Historical Society 1965).

3 John A. Noon, *Law and Government*. In this source, see 'Jonas Baptiste v. Council,' 117; Job 'Green v. Gus Green,' 118; 'In re Peter Williams,' 118; and 'Josiah Staats v. Simon Staats,' 119. The council did not concede that it lacked criminal jurisdiction; rather it simply did not actively assert it. In 'Council v. Estate of Jasper Jones, Sophie General and Department of Indian Affairs,' the council held that 'it is a tradition repeatedly confirmed by testimony of the chiefs that the Confederacy delegated to the Crown, and later to the Dominion government, full jurisdiction over only three matters. These are: rape, treason, and murder' (at 149). There is an oral tradition that some criminal matters were also decided under traditional law but that these matters were kept secret from Canadian authorities. The existence of a recorded adultery case would tend to confirm this.

4 Ibid., 117. Noon reports the legal issue in this case as 'Can a Six Nations Indian enter suit in the courts of the province of Ontario?' This statement was clearly not accurate in late-nineteenth-century Ontario law, but it reflects the issue as the chiefs who were Noon's informants saw it. Thus, while Ontario law clearly recognized the right of Indians to bring suit in Ontario courts, the Iroquois apparently were not clear that this was the case.

5 Order-in-Council, P.C. 2102, 12 Nov. 1890. Here it should be understood that this statement was completely unnecessary from a legal standpoint: this had been clearly the law since at least the 1840s. It seems that the dominion made the statement for the political reason of underscoring its control over the First Nations and the supremacy of Canadian law over the laws of the First Nations.

6 Ibid., 146 (1917).

7 (1921) 50 O.R. 27.

8 A general history of this lawsuit is in Malcolm Montgomery, 'The Legal Status of the Six Nations in Canada,' *Ontario History*, vol. 55 (1963), 93–105. The National Archives Canada contains extensive files on this case, including detailed arguments for and against Iroquois sovereignty. Attorney A.G. Chisholm, hired by the Six Nations, filed a 180-page brief with the court (missing from the files) arguing that Ontario lacked jurisdiction. See Darlene Johnston, 'The Quest of the Six Nations Confederacy for Self-Determination,' *University of Toronto Faculty of Law Review*, vol. 44 (1986), 1–32; and M. Jacobsen, 'Who Rules the Valley of the Six Nations? (A Discussion of Isaac v. Davey),' *McGill Law Journal*, vol. 22 (1976), 130–47. Charles M. Johnson, *The Valley of the Six Nations* (Toronto: University of Toronto Press 1964), reprints several hundred primary documents on the legal status of the Six Nations' Grand River lands.

9 Darlene Johnston, 'The Quest of the Six Nations Confederacy for Self–Determination.' See also Six Nations, 'Memorandum in Support of the Position That They Constitute an Independent State,' 22 Feb. 1924. A copy, document K–59, is held in Indian and Northern Affairs Canada, Claims and Historical Research Centre, Ottawa.

10 John A. Noon, *Law and Government*, 'William Jamieson vs. Council,' 118.

11 Ibid. The classic description of traditional Iroquois political organization is Lewis Henry Morgan, *League of the Ho-de-no-sau-nee or Iroquois* (New York: Dodd, Mead 1904). More modern interpretations of this political history (with particular reference to the Six Nations' relationship with the United States) are Oren Lyons et al., *Exiled in the Land of the Free: Democracy, Indian Nations and the U.S. Constitution* (Santa Fe:, N. Mex.: Clear Light Publishers 1992), and Bruce E. Johansen, *Forgotten Founders: How the American Indian Helped Shape Democracy* (Harvard: Harvard Common Press 1982).

12 *Minutes of the Grand General Council, New Credit Indian Reserve* (Hagersville, Ont., 1883).

13 Ibid., 17–18. The discussion refers to s. 82 of the Indian Act.

14 Ibid., 17–18.

15 Ibid., 15–16.

16 'Petition, Munsey Band of Indians to Attorney General of Ontario,' Ontario Archives, RG 4, file 1598 (1906).

17 Archives of Ontario, Reserve Records (7 July 1905). Peter S. Schmalz, *The Ojibwa of Southern Ontario* (Toronto: University of Toronto Press 1991), 217–18. Their memorandum, listing the reasons, is reprinted in John Borrows, 'A Genealogy of Law: Inherent Sovereignty and First Nations Self-Government,' *Osgoode Hall Law Journal*, vol. 30, no. 2 (1992), 345–6.

18 John Borrows, 'A Genealogy of Law: Inherent Sovereignty and First Nations Self-Government,' 290, 300–309. What follows is a brief summary of Professor Borrow's genealogy intended, not to appropriate any of his unique story, but to use this work to show how the legal histories of each First Nation can be written.

19 Ibid., 324–36

20 Ibid., 311–17

21 Archives of Ontario, Reserve Records (13 Aug. 1902), quoted in ibid., 351.

22 Ibid., 338–51.

23 Roland Wright, 'The Public Right of Fishing, Government Fishing Policy, and Indian Fishing Rights in Upper Canada,' *Ontario History*, vol. 86, no. 4 (1994), 337–62, 350–1.

24 Douglas Leighton, 'The Manitoulin Incident of 1863: An Indian-White Confrontation in the Province of Canada,' *Ontario History*, vol. 69 (1975), 113; W.R. Wightman, *Forever on the Fringe: Six Studies in the Development of Manitoulin Island* (Toronto: University of Toronto Press 1982), 49–54.

25 W.R. Wrightman, *Forever on the Fringe*, 51, reports a larger party of twenty-one special constables.

26 D. Leighton, *Manitoulin Incident*, 121–24.

27 W.R. Wrightman, *Forever on the Fringe*, 51

28 James T. Angus, 'How the Dokis Indians Protected Their Timber,' *Ontario History*, vol. 81, (1989), 181–200, 185.

29 Ibid., 186–7.

30 Ibid., 190.

31 Ibid., 196.

32 Letter, H.P. Blackwood to superintendent, Indian Department, National Archives of Canada, RG 4, file 4–32 (1913).

33 Ibid., Report, W.E. Bennett, Indian Department special agent, to superintendent.

34 Letter, superintendent of Indian affairs to attorney general 24 Sept. 1904, ibid., file 1324 (1904).

35 Letter, Mr Pedley, deputy superintendent of Indian affairs, to J.J. Foy attorney general, 2 May 1906, ibid., file 608 (1906).

36 Letter, Tom McLean, secretary, Department of Indian Affairs, to attorney general, 18 May 1907, ibid., file 865 (1908).

37 Letter, Mr Sims, Indian agent, to secretary, Department of Indian Affairs, 7 May 1908, ibid.

38 Report, William Young, police magistrate at Rat Portage, ibid., file 574 (1898).

39 Ibid.

40 Recall the case of Pierre Hunter, recounted in chapter 5, who froze to death after his jailing for shooting and selling moose. He escaped punishment for a year by retiring to his remote village but ultimately returned to Sioux Narrows to earn a livelihood.

41 See, for example, Eugene Genovese, *Roll, Jordan, Roll: The World the Slaves Made* (New York: Pantheon 1975), especially 'Roast Pig Is a Wonderful Delicacy, Especially When Stolen,' 599–613. On Ojibwa conceptions of property earlier in the nineteenth century, see Harold Hickerson, 'Land Tenure of the Rainy Lake Chippewa at the Beginning of the 19th Century,' *Smithsonian Contributions to Anthropology*, vol. 2 (1967), 41–63.

42 See, for example, Edward S. Rogers, 'The Algonquian Farmers of Southern Ontario, 1830–1915,' in Edward Rogers and Donald Smith, *Aboriginal Ontario, Historical Perspectives on the First Nations* (Toronto: Dundurn Press 1984), 122–66, and Peter S. Schmalz, *The Ojibwa of Southern Ontario*.

43 Letter, J. Cadot to attorney general, 9 Jan. 1908, Ontario Archives, RG 4, file 109 (1908). Wiarton is near the Cape Croker reserve on the Bruce peninsula. A history of Ojibwa life there is Peter S. Smaltz, *The Ojibwa of Southern Ontario*, chapter 8, 'Reserve Stagnation,' 180–226.

44 'Letter, attorney general to superintendant, Ontario Provincial Police,' RG 4, 1916.

45 Case file, 'Rex v. Peter Whiteduck,' Archives of Ontario, RG 22, series 392, box 134 (1916)

46 *Attorney General for Ontario* v. *Bear Island Foundation et al.* (1984) 49 O.R. (2d) 353 at 441–7. The judgment was appealed but lost in both the Supreme Court of Ontario [1989) 68 O.R. (2d.) 294] and the Supreme Court of Canada [(1991) 2 S.C.R. 570].

47 A number of other Ojibwa bands also argue that they were not represented at these treaty proceedings. Lise C. Hansen, 'The Anishinabek Land Claim and the Participation of the Indian People Living on the North Shore of Lake Superior in the Robinson Superior Treaty, 1850' (Research Report, Office of Indian Resource Policy, Ontario Ministry of Natural Resources, Toronto 1985). Robinson negotiated two treaties (the 'Robinson Treaties') on that occasion. This report refers to the first, no. 60, negotiated on 7 September with the Ojibwa on the north shore of Lake Superior. Two days later, on 9 September, Robinson

signed a second treaty, no. 61, with the Ojibwa living north and east of Lake Huron. The Temagami dispute is rooted in the second treaty. *Indian Treaties and Surrenders*, vol. 1 (Ottawa: Queen's Printer 1891), 147–52.

48 Bruce W. Hodgins, 'The Temagami Indians and Canadian Federalism, 1867–1943,' *Laurentian University Review*, vol. 11, no. 2 (1979), 71–95 at 72–3; and Bruce Hodgins and Jamie Benidickson, *The Temagami Experience: Recreation, Resources and Aboriginal Rights in the Northern Ontario Wilderness* (Toronto: University of Toronto Press 1989).

49 Bruce Hodgins, 'The Temagami Indians and Canadian Federalism,' 78–87.

50 *Attorney General for Ontario* v. *Bear Island Foundation et al*, (1984) 49 O.R. (2d) 353 at 441–7.

51 Kent McNeil, 'The Temagami Indian Land Claim: Loosening the Judicial Straight Jacket,' in Matt Bray and Ashley Thomson, *Temagami: A Wilderness Debate* (Toronto: Dundurn Press 1990), 189–93.

52 Paul Romney, *Mr. Attorney: The Attorney General for Ontario in Court, Cabinet, and Legislature, 1791–1899* (Toronto: Osgoode Society and University of Toronto Press 1986). The crown almost immediately refused to recognize any Indian legal title in this reserve (at 29–31). As early as 1797, six blocks of Iroquois land, ranging from 19,000 to 94,000 acres each, were sold to white speculators by the Indians, the sale being affirmed by the crown.

53 Brantford Jail Register, Ontario Archives, RG 21.

54 Susan Burman and B. Harrell-Bond, eds., *The Imposition of Law* (London: Academic Press 1979). Thomas Stone refers to this imposition of law as 'legal penetration' in his analysis of the imposition of Canadian law on the St Regis reserve in Quebec. See 'Legal Mobilization and Legal Penetration: The Department of Indian Affairs and the Canadian Party at St. Regis, 1876–1918,' *Ethnohistory*, vol. 22, no. 4 (1975), 375–408.

55 Sally M. Weaver, 'The Iroquois: The Consolidation of the Grand River Reserve in the Mid-Nineteenth Century, 1847–1875,' in Edward S. Rogers and Donald B. Smith, *Aboriginal Ontario*, 182–212, 205, reports that 'Six Nations people committed very few crimes.' This was clearly true in 1847, but Six Nations arrests were increasing from 1870 through the rest of the nineteenth century, producing a high arrest rate by 1900. The 'lawlessness' issue was largely political, used by politicians and settlers who wanted further encroachments on Six Nations lands.

56 'George Powlis,' *D.C.B.*, vol. 6 (1987), 198.

57 F. Douglas Reville, *History of the County of Brant*, (Brantford, Ont.: Hurley Printing 1967; originally published 1920), locates 'Vinegar Hill' in 1845 at Clarence St, the eastern boundary of Brantford. The Mohawk Village was located on the original site of Brant's Ford, also just east of the townsite (103, 97).

58 Ibid., 96–103. The clear implication here, protected by nineteenth-century con-
    ventions that did not openly discuss such crimes, is that Doxater was raped
    before she was brutally murdered. One witness thought that she had been
    'ravished.'

59 Ibid.

60 Ibid.

61 C.P. Mulvaney *et al.*, *The History of the County of Brant* (Toronto: Warner, Beers
    1883), 489–90, 247. See also C.M. Johnson, *Brant County: A History, 1784–1945*
    (Toronto: Oxford University Press 1967)

62 John A. Noon, *Law and Government*, and William B. Newell, *Crime and Justice
    Among the Iroquois Nations*.

63 Noon, *Law and Government*. See especially the case described in 'A Casebook of
    Iroquois Law,' at 116–84.

64 For an analysis of other events at Grand River in this period, see Sally Weaver,
    'The Iroquois: The Grand River Reserve in the Late Nineteenth and Early
    Twentieth Centuries, 1875–1945,' in Edward Rogers and Donald B. Smith,
    Aboriginal Ontario, 213–57. Weaver does not discuss these crime statistics.

65 Indians are arrested and jailed in Canada in numbers far greater than their
    share of the population; see Paul Havemann, *Law and Order for Canada's Indig-
    enous People* (Regina: Prairie Justice Research Centre, University of Regina
    1984). This situation is also true for the United States and Australia. Sidney L.
    Harring, 'Native American Crime in the United States: Patterns of Crime, Law
    Enforcement, and Economic Development,' in Lawrence French, ed., *Indians
    and Criminal Justice* (Montclair, N.J.: Allenheld-Osmun 1983); Elizabeth Egg-
    leston, *Fear, Favor, or Affection* (Canberra: Australian National University Press
    1976), and Kayleen Hazlehurst, *Ivory Scales: Black Australians and the Law*
    (Kensington: University of New South Wales Press 1987).

66 Brantford Jail Register, Ontario Archives, RG 21. The first volume available
    records all those lodged into the jail from April 1873 through the end of 1880.
    The second volume is missing. The third volume begins in October 1899. After
    that date the data is complete. I recorded all arrests for 1873, 1874, 1880, and
    1899–1901, believing that this would permit some analysis of changing arrest
    patterns over time.

67 This year is from 1 October through 30 September, to accommodate the fact
    that the volume begins with October data.

68 Brantford Jail Register, vol. l, July 1873.

69 Ibid., vol. 3, November 1899 through December 1901.

70 Ibid., vol. 3, January 1900.

71 Ibid., vol. 3, July 1900. I have no direct evidence on the reasons why Indians
    did not pay their fines. It is possible that there were other reasons besides pov-

erty: for example, there could be cultural reasons why families simply did not go to the jail to bail out their brothers and sisters, mothers, and fathers. Similarly, refusal to pay bail could have been an act of political defiance, a statement of the illegitimacy of white authority.

72 Ibid., vol. 3, July 1900 – January 1901.

73 Ibid., vol. 3, October 1899.

74 Ibid., vol. 3, October 1901.

75 Ibid., vol. 1 April, 1880. The case file is held in the Ontario Archives, RG 22, 392–0–278, box 7, 'Brant County.' This box contains ten Indian felony case files from the 1880s.

76 Ibid., vol. 1, September, 1880. The case file is held in the Ontario Archives, RG 22, 392–0–278, box 7.

77 Ibid., vol. 1, August 1880. The case file is held in Ontario Archives, RG 22, 392–0–278.

78 *Hunter* v. *Gilkinson*, (1885) 7 O.R. 735.

79 These data are based on the relatively consistent statistics of the 1870s and 1899–1901 – Indian jailings run between 37 and 51 a year, or about 1000 jailings over twenty-five years. Because the inmates are named in the jail records we can ascertain that most of these are not recidivists, although a few obviously were.

80 It is beyond the scope of this study to do a detailed analysis of Brantford jail statistics. The estimate makes the point that Indians were arrested in significant numbers.

81 A royal commission in Australia is currently investigating aboriginal deaths in custody. This commission has produced a large literature on the meaning of jail in native culture. See Royal Commission on Aboriginal Deaths in Custody, *National Report* (Canberra: Australian Government Publishing Service 1991).

CHAPTER 8

1 Pierre Tousignant, 'The Integration of the Province of Quebec into the British Empire, 1763–91,' *DCB*, vol. 4 (1979), xxxii–xcix.

2 William Renwick Riddell, *The Life of William Dummer Powell: First Judge at Detroit and Fifth Chief Justice of Upper Canada* (Lansing: Michigan Historical Commission 1924).

3 Pierre Tousignant, 'The Integration of the Province of Quebec into the British Empire,' xxxiv–xxxv. The upper Great Lakes area and the Mississippi valley were French at the time of the Royal Proclamation.

4 Olive Patricia Dickason, *Canada's First Nations: A History of Founding Peoples from Earliest Times* (Toronto: McClelland and Stewart, 1992), 165–67.

5 Cornelius Jaenen, 'French Sovereignty and Native Nationhood during the French Regime,' *Native Studies Review*, vol. 2, no. 1 (1986); W.J. Eccles, 'Sovereignty Association, 1500–1783,' *Canadian Historical Review*, vol. 65, no. 4 (1984,) 475–510; Olive Dickason, *Canada's First Nations*, 161–63; Ian K. Steele, *Warpaths: Invasions of North America* (New York: Oxford University Press 1994), 59–79.

6 John A. Dickinson, 'Native Sovereignty and French Justice in Early Canada,' in Jim Phillips, Tina Loo, and Susan Lewthwaite, *Essays in the History of Canadian Law*, vol. 5, *Crime and Criminal Justice* (Toronto: Osgoode Society and University of Toronto Press, 1995), 17–40.

7 Brian Slattery, 'Did France Claim Canada Upon "Discovery?"' in J.J. Bumsted, *Interpreting Canada's Past*, vol. 1, (Toronto: Oxford University Press 1986); W.J. Eccles, 'Sovereignty Association.'

8 Jan Grabowski, 'French Criminal Justice and Indians in Montreal, 1670–1760,' *Ethnohistory*, vol. 43, no. 3 (1996), 405–29, 407–11.

9 Ibid., 416–19.

10 There are other land disputes involving the French policy of giving Indian land to the Catholic Church to administer. The Oka/Kanasatake dispute stems from the same issue. John Thompson, 'A History of the Mohawks at Kanesatake and the Land Dispute to 1961,' in *Materials Relating to the History of the Land Dispute at Kanesatake*, (Claims and Historical Research Centre, Indian and Northern Affairs Canada, Ottawa 1993). On the modern dispute, see Geoffrey York and Loreen Pindera, *People of the Pines* (Toronto: Little, Brown 1991).

11 'Despatch, Sir James Kempt to Sir George Murray, Quebec, 4 January 1830,' British Parliamentary Papers, Irish Universities Press Series, *Anthropology: Aborigines, Papers Relative to the Aboriginal Tribes in British Possessions*, vol. 3: 66–9. The Huron were removed to Sillery and Lorette and were not original inhabitants of those lands (at 66–7). The Huron claim dated from 1651 when Huron at Sillery, near Quebec, received a grant as 'a settlement of Indians.' (at 82, 106–13). A history of the establishment of these reserves is George F.G. Stanley, 'The First Indian "Reserves" in Canada,' *Revue d'histoire de l'Amerique Francaise* vol. 4 (1973), 178–210.

12 'Despatch, Sir James Kempt to Sir George Murray.'

13 Ibid., 67–8.

14 Ibid., 69.

15 Ibid., 68, 70. Obviously, since the Iroquois claimed that they had traditionally owned the land, the recollection of local whites was completely irrelevant.

16 Ibid., 70, quoting J. Stewart, commissioner of Jesuit lands.

17 Ibid., 63–4.

18 The future of French civil law to accommodate Indian rights is still an issue for native people within Quebec, and, as Quebec nationalists pursue their goal of national sovereignty, Indians have raised the question of their own legal status in an independent Quebec.

19 Monk, as an English-speaking judge sitting at Montreal, would have applied the English common law and the relevant statutory law (British or Canadian) to public-law questions and the French civil law to areas of private law. Ordinarily, even private-law matters between English- speaking people were governed by common law, normally by an agreement between the parties.

20 George MacLean Rose, *A Cyclopaedia of Canadian Biography* (Toronto, 1888), 537, contains a short biographical sketch of Judge Monk. The account also refers to his 'vast legal knowledge' and 'high sense of justice' but most accounts of nineteenth-century judges contain similar superlatives.

21 L.F.S. Upton, *Micmacs and Colonists*: Indian-White Relations in the Maritimes, 1713–1867 (Vancouver: University of British Columbia Press 1984), 82–6, and 'Indian Policy in Colonial Nova Scotia, 1783–1871,' *Acadiensis*, vol. 5 (1975), 3–31; J. Bernard Gilpin, 'Indians of Nova Scotia,' *Nova Scotian Institute of Science Proceedings and Transactions*, vol. 4 (1875–8), reprinted in Harold F. McGee, Jr., *The Native Peoples of Atlantic Canada: A History of Indian-European Relations,* (Ottawa: Carleton University Press 1983), 102–19, 108.

22 (1867) 17 R.J.R.Q. 75.

23 Ibid., 76–7.

24 Constance Backhouse, *Petticoats and Prejudice: Women and Law in Nineteenth Century Canada.* (Toronto: Osgoode Society and Women's Press 1991), 9–20.

25 Ibid., 79–82 at 79.

26 Ibid., 82.

27 Ibid., 86.

28 Ibid., 89.

29 Ibid., 91.

30 Ibid., 91.

31 Ibid., 115.

32 Ibid., 105–08.

33 Ibid., George M. Rose, *A Cyclopaedia of Canadian Biography*, 166–7.

34 Constance Backhouse, *Petticoats and Prejudice*, 20.

35 Ibid., 22–3. *Fraser v. Pouliot et al.*, (1881) 7 Q.L.R. 149.

36 Ibid., 24.

37 (1856), 8 R.J.R.U. 29. 'On8anoron' is the spelling used in court records. The French used the symbol '8' to stand for one of the sounds of the Iroquois language in transcribing Iroquois words.

38 Ibid., 31–2.
39 (1867), 17 L.C.R. 238
40 Ibid., 238–40.
41 Ibid., 243–4.
42 Ibid., 244–5.
43 *Ex parte Morrison and de Lorimier* (1869), 19 R.J.R.Q. 404.
44 Ibid., 406. What is being referred to here are the handwritten notes of the trial, kept by each judge and, in the absence of an official stenographer, the only record of the evidence presented at trial.
45 (1887) 3 M.L.R. (S.C.)
46 Ibid., 244–5.
47 *Nianentsiasa v. Akwirente et al.* (no. 1) (1859), 3 L.C. Jur. 316.
48 *Nianentsiasa v. Akwirente et al.* (no. 2) (1860), 4 L.C.Jur. 367.
49 (1865), 18 R.J.R.Q. 187
50 Ibid.
51 This legal dispute is one of the best known in Canada. Geoffrey York and Loreen Pindera, *People of the Pines: The Warriors and the Legacy of Oka* (Toronto: Little, Brown 1991), 82–100, 89. See also Richard C. Daniel, 'The Oka Indians v. the Seminary of St. Sulpice,' in *A History of Native Claims Processes in Canada, 1867–1879*, (Ottawa: Department of Indian Affairs 1980).
52 John Thompson, 'A History of the Mohawks at Kanesatake,' 23–9, 27.
53 Ibid., 27–8.
54 Ibid., 29–31. See also Geoffrey York and Loreen Pindera, *People of the Pines*, 82–94.
55 Geoffrey York and Loreen Pindera, *People of the Pines*, 94.
56 See, generally, L.F.S. Upton: *Micmacs and Colonists*, and Harold Franklin McGee, Jr., *The Native Peoples of Atlantic Canada: A History of Indian-European Relations* (Ottawa: Carleton University Press 1983).
57 'Report of the Select Committee,' of British Parliamentary Papers, Irish University Press Series, *Anthropology: Aborigines, Papers Relative to the Aboriginal Tribes in British Possessions*, vol. 2: 6.
58 Ingeborg Marshall, *History and Ethnography of the Beothuk* (Montreal: McGill-Queen's University Press 1996); L.F.S. Upton, 'The Extermination of the Beothucks,' *Canadian Historical Review*, vol. 58 (1977), 33. While the view put forward by the parliamentary commission (and accepted by Upton) has been generally accepted for over a hundred and fifty years, Marshall suggests a more complex view of the extermination of the Beothuk. While some were massacred, he claimed that others carried out attacks on fishermen and trappers that led to a cycle of killing and retribution, while others died of starvation and disease. Marshall would agree that both the colonial and the

British government knew what was going on, but either failed to intervene or ineffectively intervened.

59 Ibid., 183–5.

60 Palliser to Grafton, 31 March 1766, quoted in L.F.S Upton, 'The Extermination of the Beothucks of Newfoundland,' 140.

61 I. Marshall, *Beothuk*, 112.

62 Ibid., 117–19. See also Christopher English, 'From Fishing Schooner to Colony: The Legal Development of Newfoundland, 1791–1832,' in Louis Knafla and Susan W.S. Binnie, *Law, Society, and the State: Essays in Modern Legal History* (Toronto: University of Toronto Press 1995), 73–98.

63 Marshall, *Beothuk*, 111–12.

64 Diamond Jenness, *Indians of Canada* (1932; rept. Toronto: University of Toronto Press 1984), 267.

65 In the written historical record, the basis for land claims against the crown, the Beothuk all died. Mi'Kmaq tradition is that survivors fled to neighbouring territory, or held out in isolation in the center of the Island. Marshall, *Beothuk*, 154–9. The burden of proof in a land-claims case, however, is on the native people who bring the claim. Thus, ironically, the more violent and disruptive the colonization process, the more inadequate and dishonest the official record, the more difficult job a First Nation has proving its claim.

66 Jim Phillips, '"Securing Obedience to Necessary Laws": The Criminal Law in Eighteenth Century Nova Scotia,' *Nova Scotia Historical Review*, vol. 12, no. 2 (1992), 87–124; Peter White, Sandra Oxner and Thomas Barnes, (eds.), *Law in a Colonial Society: The Nova Scotia Experience* (Toronto: The Carswell Company 1984); Philip Girard and Jim Phillips, eds., *Essays in the History of Canadian Law: The Nova Scotia Experience* (Toronto: Osgoode Society and University of Toronto Press 1990).

67 L.F.S. Upton, *Micmacs and Colonists*, 143.

68 William C. Wicken, 'The Mi'kmac and Wuasukwiuk Treaties,' *University of New Brunswick Law Journal*, vol. 43 (1994), 241–53; Adrian Tanner and Sakej Henderson, 'Aboriginal Land Claims in the Atlantic Provinces,' in Ken Coates, ed., *Aboriginal Land Claims in Canada* (Toronto: Copp Clark Pitman 1992), 131–60, 131–3; James Sakej Henderson, 'Micmac Tenure in Atlantic Canada,' *Dalhousie Law Journal*, vol. 18, no. 2 (1995), 196–294; Andrea Bear Nicholas, 'Mascarene's Treaty of 1725,' *University of New Brunswick Law Journal*, vol. 43 (1994), 3.

69 Elizabeth Ann Hutton, 'Indian Affairs in Nova Scotia, 1760–1834,' *Collections of the Nova Scotia Historical Society* (1963), 33–54; L.F. S. Upton, 'Indian Policy in Colonial Nova Scotia'; Richard H. Bartlett, *Indian Reserves in the Atlantic Provinces of Canada.* (Saskatoon: Native Law Centre, University of Saskatchewan, Studies in Aboriginal Rights, 9, 1986).

70 Harold Franklin McGee, Jr., 'White Encroachment on Micmac Reserve Lands In Nova Scotia, 1830–1867,' *Man in the Northeast*, vol. 8 (1974), 57–64, 57.

71 Provincial Archives of Nova Scotia, Manuscript Documents 430:187, quoted in ibid., 58.

72 *Journals of the Legislative Assembly* of Nova Scotia, 1845, quoted in ibid., 59.

73 Ibid., 1849, quoted in ibid.

74 (1885), 18 N.S.R. 304, 306.

75 Ibid., 306–7.

76 Ibid., 308–9.

77 Ibid., 308.

78 Bruce H. Wildsmith, 'The Mi'kmaq and the Fishery: Beyond Food Requirements,' *Dalhousie Law Journal* (1996) 116–40 at 117–19. The actual language of the Treaty of 1752 includes two clauses relevant to the sale of fish. Article 4 gives them 'free liberty of hunting and fishing as usual.' The second clause, also in article 4, is more complex, providing a 'Truck house' at the River Chibenaccadie, or any other place of their resort they shall have the same built and property Merchandize, lodged therein to be exchanged for what the Indians shall have to dispose of.' In the meantime, article 4 provided that Indians had 'free liberty to bring for Sale to Halifax or any other Settlement ... Skins, feathers, fowl, fish or any other thing they shall have to sell, where they shall have liberty to dispose thereof to the best advantage.'

79 [1985] 2 S.C.R. 387.

80 Judith Fingard, 'The New England Company and the New Brunswick Indians, 1786–1826: A Comment on the Colonial Perversion of British Benevolence,' *Acadiensis*, vol. 1, no. 2 (1972), 29–42.

81 L.F.S. Upton, *Micmacs and Colonists*, 145.

82 Ibid., 145. Nothing at all is known of whether and to what extent settlers killed Indians under such circumstances, but it is hard to imagine why Judge Halliburton would say this for nothing.

83 Ibid., 98–101; W.D. Hamilton and W.A. Spray, eds., *Source Materials Relating to the New Brunswick Indian* (Fredericton: Hamray Books 1976); G.P. Gould and A.J. Semple, *Our Land, the Maritimes* (Fredericton: St Anne's Point Press 1980).

84 George F. G. Stanley, 'As Long As the Sun Shines and the Water Flows: An Historical Comment,' in Ian A. L. Getty and Antoine S. Lussier, *As Long As the Sun Shines and the Water Flows: A Reader in Canadian Native Studies* (Vancouver: University of British Columbia Press 1993), 1–26, 7.

85 W.D. Hamilton, 'Indian Lands in New Brunswick: The Case of the Little South West Reserve,' *Acadiensis*, vol. 13 (1984), 3–28, 14.

86 Ibid., 16. M.H. Perley's 'Report on the Indians of New Brunswick,' *Journals* of

the *Legislative Assembly* of Nova Scotia, 1843, appendix 49, reprinted in Harold F. McGee, Jr., *The Native Peoples of Atlantic Canada: A History of Ethnic Interaction* (Toronto: McClelland and Stewart 1974), 81–9. Perley counted 935 Mi'Kmacs and 442 Malicetes, not including the Mi'kmaqs at Eel River and Dalhousie (at 82). See also W.A. Spray, 'Moses Henrey Perley,' *D.C.B.* vol. 9 (1976), 628–31.

87 Perley reported that the reserve was a personal fiefdom of the Julian family. It is not clear the extent to which this was true, but even he acknowledged that the situation at Little South West was unusual. Crown agents often derided the power of chiefs, accusing individual chiefs of personal corruption as part of a general assault on the Indian social order.

88 *The Queen* v. *Smith* [1983] 3 CNLR 161; (1981) 113 DLR (3d) 522 (Fed. CA.) re-litigated the Little South West Indian Reserve lands. The Supreme Court of Canada dismissed the case in a complicated holding, but noted that it was a case in which a non-Indian asserted a right of adverse possession dating from 1838.

89 W.D. Hamilton, 'Indian Lands in New Brunswick,' 19–28.

90 (1890), 30 N.B.R. 142, 142–5.

91 Ibid.

92 *Ex parte Goodine*, (1885), 25 N.B.R. 151, 151–4.

93 This case is discussed in L.F. S. Upton, *Micmacs and Colonists*, 147. The Shawanakiskie case is discussed in chapter six. See also Mark D. Walters, 'The Extension of Colonial Criminal Jurisdiction over the Aboriginal Peoples of Upper Canada: Reconsidering the Shawanakiskie Case (1822–26),' *University of Toronto Law Journal*, vol. 46 (1996), 273–310.

94 L.F. S. Upton, *Micmacs and Colonists*, 147.

95 Ibid., 146–7. These data, as well as the conclusion, are Upton's.

96 Richard H. Bartlett, *Indian Reserves and Aboriginal Lands in Canada: A Homeland: A Study in Law and History* (Saskatoon: Native Law Centre, University of Saskatchewan 1990), 7–23, surveys the colonial problem of local administration Canada-wide.

CHAPTER 9

1 (1964), 50 D.L.R. (2d) 613 (B.C.C.A.); [1973] S.C.R. 313; (1984) 2 S.C.R. 335, (1984) W.W.R. 481; (1990), 56 C.C.C. (3d) 263 (S.C.C.); (1991) D.L.R. (4th) 185 (B.C.S.C.), file no. 23799, Dec. 11, 1997, S.C.C. (unreported); [1996]137 D.L.R. (4th) 289 (S.C.C.). The *'Van der Peet* trilogy' includes *Van der Peet* and two other cases decided on the same day: *R.* v. *Gladstone* [1996] 137 D.L.R. (4th) 649 and *N.T.C. Smokehouse* v. *the Queen* [1996] 137 D.L.R. (4th) 528.

2 Antonia Mills, *Eagle Down Is Our Law* (Vancouver: University of British Columbia Press, 1984); Daniel Raunet, *Without Surrender, Without Consent: A History of the Nisga'a Land Claims* (Vancouver: Douglas and McIntyre 1996), 2nd ed.; Terry Glavin, *A Death Feast in Dimlahamid* (Vancouver: New Star Books 1990).

3 Christopher McKee, *Treaty Talks in British Columbia: Negotiating a Mutually Beneficial Future* (Vancouver: University of British Columbia Press 1996), 11–26.

4 Article 13, Terms of Union, 1871. The political process leading to this language is described in Robert E. Cail, *Land, Man, and the Law: The Disposal of Crown Lands in British Columbia, 1871–1913* (Vancouver: University of British Columbia Press 1974); Robin Fisher, *Contact and Conflict: Indian-European Relations in British Columbia, 1774–1890* (Vancouver: University of British Columbia Press 1977), and 'Joseph Trutch and Indian Land Policy,' *B.C. Studies* vol. 12 (winter 1971–2), 3–33; Paul Tennant, *Aboriginal People and Politics: The Indian Land Question in British Columbia, 1849–1989* (Vancouver: University of British Columbia Press 1990), 39–46; and Hamar Foster, 'Letting Go the Bone: The Idea of Indian Title in British Columbia, 1849–1927,' in Hamar Foster and John McLaren, *Essays in the History of Canadian Law, Volume VI: British Columbia and the Yukon* (Toronto: The Osgoode Society for Canadian Legal History 1995), 52–65.

5 Hamar Foster, 'Letting Go the Bone'; Daniel Raunet, *Without Surrender, Without Consent;* Terry Glavin, *A Death Feast in Dimlahamid;* Joane Drake-Terry, *The Same As Yesterday: The Lillooet Chronicle of the Theft of Their Lands and Resources* (Lillooet, B.C.: Lillooet Tribal Council 1989); Peter Carstens, *The Queen's People: A Study of Hegemony, Coercion, and Accommodation among the Okanagan of Canada* (Toronto: University of Toronto Press 1991).

6 Robert E. Cail, *Land, Man and the Law,* 185–9. The story of the First Nations' resistance to the surveying of their lands, as well as other manifestations of disapproval of British Columbia policy, emerges in each nation's history. This is evident, for example, in each of the histories cited in note 5. See also *British Columbia: Papers Relating to the Indian Land Question* (Victoria: British Columbia Archives 1987, reprint of original edition, 1877), 60, 61,117, 123, 128, 145–8, 151–5.

7 British Columbia Legislative Assembly, *Sessional Papers,* 1887, 259–60, quoted in P. Tennant, *Aboriginal People and Politics,* 57.

8 This position is clearly stated in each of the cases cited above. The full political history can be found in P. Tennant, *Aboriginal People and Politics.* Since *Delgamuukw,* British Columbia has been negotiating First Nations land rights in an on-again, off-again process. As of 15 Feb. 1996, the first of these agreements

was concluded with the Nisga, recognizing their right to 1930 square kilometers of lands in the Lower Nass valley, a payment of $191 million, various fishery, timber, and hunting rights, some measure of self-government, the return of some artifacts from museums, and other provisions. Daniel Raunet, *Without Surrender, Without Consent*, ix–xiv.

9 While most Indian lands in British Columbia are not covered by treaties, there are two distinct treaty relationships in British Columbia: first, the Vancouver Island Treaties, discussed later in this chapter, cover a small area on Vancouver Island (Wilson Duff, 'The Fort Victoria Treaties,' *BC Studies*, vol. 3 ([1969], 3–57). Second, Treaty 8 (1899), one of the 'numbered treaties' negotiated on the prairies, covers a large area of northeastern British Columbia (Richard Daniel, 'The Spirit and Terms of Treaty Eight,' in Richard Price, ed., *The Spirit of the Alberta Indian Treaties* [Edmonton: Pica Pica Press 1987], 47–100).

10 Christopher McKee, *Treaty Talks in British Columbia: Negotiating a Mutually Beneficial Future* (Vancouver: University of British Columbia Press 1996).

11 The photograph is published in Joane Drake-Terry, *The Same As Yesterday*, 176. *Nisga'a* is now the preferred spelling.

12 'Despatch from Governor Douglas to the Right Hon. Lord Stanley, June 15, 1858,' in *Papers Relative to the Affairs of British Columbia*, pts. 1–4 (London: George Edward Eyre, Her Majesty's Stationery Office 1859), 17 (hereafter cited as *Papers*). A copy of an unidentified press report on the defeat of American troops at the Snake River on 28 May 1858 was enclosed. Sir E.B. Lytton responded to Douglas's actions with approval (ibid., 47). This is not the only time that Douglas referred to the Indians as having a legal right to their land. Douglas wrote to Archibald Barclay, secretary, Hudson's Bay Company, 3 Sept. 1849: 'I would also strongly recommend, equally as a measure of justice, and from a regard to the future peace of the colony, that the Indians Fishere's ... should be reserved for their benefit and fully secured to them by law.' Quoted in Hamar Foster, 'The Saanichton Bay Marina Case: Imperial Law, Colonial History and Competing Theories of Aboriginal Title.'

13 'Letter, F.W. Hesson to Lytton, n.d., enclosed with despatch, Lytton to Douglas, Sept. 2, 1858,' *Papers Relative to the Affairs of British Columbia*, 1 56–8. *University of British Columbia Law Review*, vol. 23 (1989), 629.

14 Dianne Newell, *Tangled Webs of History: Indians and the Law in Canada's Pacific Coast Fisheries*, (Toronto: University of Toronto Press 1993), 46–65.

15 Anthropologists have long been interested in the complex native cultures of British Columbia and there is a substantial literature on these peoples. Wayne Suttles, *Handbook of North American Indians: volume 7 The Northwest Coast* (Washington, D.C.: Smithsonian Institution 1990), presents an introduction to this literature, but the volume devotes almost no attention to native law. The

ethnographic literature on the Indians of British Columbia, however, devotes
substantial attention to their traditional law. James Teit, *The Thompson Indians
of British Columbia* (New York, 1900), 270; James Teit, *The Shuswap,* (New York,
1909), 560–562; James Teit, *The Lillooet Indians* (New York, 1906), 236–46;
Verne F. Ray, 'The Sanpoil and Nespelem,' *University of Washington Publications in Anthropology,* vol. 5 (1932), 112–13; Walter Kline, et al., 'The Sinkaietk
or Southern Okanagon,' *General Series in Anthropology,* vol. 6 (Menasha, Wisconsin, 1938), 91–4; George A. Pettitt, 'The Quileute of La Push, 1775–1945,'
Anthropological Records, vol. 14, no. 1 (1950), 13–16; Marian Smith, *The Puyal-
lup-Nisqually* (New York: Columbia University Press 1940), 161–5; William
Christie MacLeod, 'Aspects of the Earlier Development of Law and Punishment,' *Journal of Criminal Law, Criminology, and Police Science*; Ralph Beals, 'Ethnology of the Nisean,' *University of California Publications in American
Archaeology and Ethnography,* vol. 31 (1933), 364–7; Helene Codere, *Fighting
with Property: A Study of Kwakiutl Potlatching and Warfare, 1792–1930* (Seattle:
University of Washington Press 1950); Franz Boas, *Kwakiutl Ethnography* (Chi-
cago: University of Chicago Press 1966) 116–19; John J. Honigman, *Culture and
Ethos in Kaska Society* (New Haven, Conn.: Yale University Publication in
Anthropology, no.40, 1949), 142–65; John J. Honigman, *The Kaska Indians,*
(New Haven: Yale University Publications in Anthropology, no. 51, 1954), 88–
99; Pliny Earle Goddard, 'The Beaver Indians,' *American Museum of Natural
History: Anthropological Papers,* vol. 10 (1916), 244–9; J. Alden Mason, 'The Ethnology of the Salinan Indians,' *University of California Publication in American
Archaeology and Ethnography,* no. 10, (1912), 173–5. There is also a large literature on Tlingit law and society, not cited here because the Tlingit are primarily
an Alaska tribe, although they are present in British Columbia and their legal
traditions are common to other Northwest Coast tribes. For an introduction to
this literature see Sidney L. Harring, *Crow Dog's Case* (Cambridge, U.K.: Cambridge University Press 1994), 220–30, and K. Oberg, 'Crime and Punishment
in Tlingit Society,' *American Anthropologist,* vol. 36 (1934), 145–56.
16 The fur trade literature is voluminous and has come to recognize a complex
Indian/Euro-Canadian interaction. Arthur J. Ray, *Indians in the Fur Trade: Their
Role As Hunters, Trappers, and Middlemen in the Lands Southwest of Hudson Bay,
1660–1870* (Toronto: University of Toronto Press 1974), is the seminal work,
although it does not cover any part of British Columbia. Shephard Krech III,
The Sub-Arctic Fur Trade: Native Social and Economic Adaptations (Vancouver:
University of British Columbia Press 1984), and J.C. Yerbury, *The Subarctic Indi-
ans and the Fur Trade, 1680–1860* (Vancouver: University of British Columbia
Press 1984), both deal with regions that include northern British Columbia.
17 Tennant lists thirty-one British Columbia tribal groups organized into 199

bands in 1987. Paul Tennant, *Aboriginal Peoples and Politics*, 5. The standard ethnographic work on the northwest coast region is Wayne Suttles, *Handbook of American Indians, volume 7, Northwest Coast.*

18 Hubert Howe Bancroft, *History of British Columbia, 1792–1887* (San Francisco: History Company 1887), 428.

19 These are mapped in Robin Fisher, *Contact and Conflict*, xvii. The names and tribal groupings that were given to these First Nations by colonial officials have been rejected by the First Nations, who prefer to use their traditional names.

20 Walter N. Sage, *Sir James Douglas and British Columbia.* (Toronto: University of Toronto Studies in History and Economics, vol. 6, 1930); Robert H. Coats and R.E. Gosnell, *Sir James Douglas*, (Toronto: Morang 1908); Derek Pethick, *James Douglas: Servant of Two Empires* (Vancouver: Mitchell Press, 1969); Clarence G. Karr, 'James Douglas: The Gold Governor in the Context of his Times,' in E. Blanche Norcross, *The Company on the Coast* (Nanaimo: Nanaimo Historical Society 1983), 56–78.

21 'Douglas to Newcastle, 25 March 1861,' *Papers on the Indian Land Question*, 19.

22 (1964) *Regina v. Bob and White* 50 D.L.R. (2d.) 613, 673–7. This citation is to the language that holds Douglas an agent of the crown in making the Fort Victoria treaties. The case interprets the legal history of these treaties in the context of the colonial history of Vancouver Island. *Saanichton Marina Ltd. v. Claxton* (1989) 36 B.C.L.R. (2d) 79, 57 D.L.R. (4th) 161 (B.C.C.A.), (sub nom Saanichton Marina Ltd. v. Tsawout Indian Band), aff'g in part (1987); 18 B.C.L.R. (2d) 217, 43 D.L.R. (4th) 481 (B.C.S.C.), discussed in Hamar Foster, 'The Saanichton Bay Marina Case.'

23 Douglas apparently wrote the HBC in London requesting a form for making such treaties after he had made them. In response, Archibald Barclay, the company secretary, sent a copy of a New Zealand 'contract or deed of conveyance' that Douglas recopied, in his own hand, on each of the succeeding Vancouver Island treaties, slightly changing the language to fit the specific requirements of each of the agreements. Douglas to Barclay, 16 May 1850, reprinted in Wilson Duff, 'The Fort Victoria Treaties,' *B.C. Studies*, vol. 3 (fall 1969), 3–57, 7–8. Hamar Foster, 'Letting Go the Bone,' 36–43, also analyses the New Zealand origins of the Victoria Island treaties, pointing out that there is an illogic in this borrowing: New Zealand authorities recognized Maori land rights and therefore needed a 'deed of conveyance' to purchase such title. Douglas and Vancouver Island colonial authorities did not recognize that Indians owned their lands and hence should not have needed any 'deed of conveyance.' Apparently, Douglas did not have this matter fully developed in his own mind. This is a much-debated matter among historians of early British Columbia.

24 Douglas's instructions to make treaties with the Indian tribes were sent from England by Lord Barclay in December 1849. Douglas made nine treaties that spring and wrote Barclay on 16 May 1850 explaining that he had obtained Indian signatures on blank paper and requesting 'a proper form by return post.'

25 Wilson Duff, 'The Fort Victoria Treaties.'

26 Mr Justice Norris, in *R. v. White and Bob* (at 666), specifically addressed this issue, concluding that whether or not a document is a 'treaty' does not depend on the simple use of that word. Rather, 'it embraces all such engagements made by persons in authority as may be brought within the term "the word of the white man" the sanctity of which was, at the time of British exploration and settlement, the most important means of obtaining the good-will and co-operation of the native tribes ... On such assurance the Indians relied.'

27 Derek Pethick: *James Douglas: Servant of Two Empires*; Robert Hamilton Coats and R.E. Gosnell, *Sir James Douglas*.

28 Walter Sage, *Sir James Douglas and British Columbia*, 148–70. Blanshard, although young, had already served the Colonial Office in the West Indies, British Honduras, and India, and he was probably seen as sufficiently experienced for a governorship in a small colony. Standards of colonial administration in this period were not high. There is no explanation of the Colonial Office's failure to perceive the problems in governing a colony entirely owned by the HBC, although the appointment of a person with colonial experience with no history of employment by the company was undoubtedly deliberate. As improbable as it may seem in hindsight, it may well be that the Colonial Office simply underestimated the determination of the HBC to resist the authority of the governor.

29 Because of the long distance between London and Fort Victoria, a long period elapsed between the actual making of an appointment and its effective date. Governor Blanshard, although appointed on 16 July 1849, actually arrived at Fort Victoria and read the proclamation of his appointment on 10 March 1850. Douglas made nine of the Fort Victoria treaties in the next two months in his capacity as chief factor, and without the assistance of Blanshard. Blanshard resigned and left the island on 1 Sept. 1851, leaving James Douglas as the head of a provisional government. Douglas was officially appointed governor in September 1851, serving as governor of Vancouver Island until 1858 when he was made governor of British Columbia, serving in both posts until he resigned in 1864.

30 The text of these treaties is reprinted in *Papers Connected with the Indian Land Question*, 5–11.

31 In spite of the fact that these treaties have questionable underpinnings, they

are important to the Indians of British Columbia because they implicitly recognize their sovereignty and land rights.

32 Douglas to Barclay, 3 Sept. 1853, quoted in Derick Pethick, *James Douglas*, 107.

33 Derick Pethick, *James Douglas*, 79.

34 Paul Tennant, *Aboriginal Peoples and Politics*, 17–25.

35 Douglas to Newcastle, 25 March 1861, *Papers on the Indian Land Question*, 19.

36 Newcastle to Douglas, 19 Oct. 1861, ibid., 20. This exchange is discussed in Paul Tennant, *Aboriginal People and Politics*, 17–25.

37 Ibid.

38 Ibid., 26–38. See also the accounts in Robin Fisher, *Contact and Conflict*, 150–7, and in Robert E. Cail, *Land, Man and the Law*.

39 Peter Carstens, *The Queen's People*, 54–9.

40 These aboriginal histories can be understood only in the context of the individual histories of each people. See Daniel Raunet, *Without Surrender, Without Consent*; Terry Glavin, *A Death Feast in Dimlahamid*; Joane Drake-Terry, *The Same As Yesterday: The Lillooet Chronicle of the Theft of Their Lands and Resources*; and Peter Carstens, *The Queen's People: A Study of Hegemony, Coercion, and Accomodation among the Okanagan of Canada*.

41 Tennant, *Aboriginal People and Politics*, 26–38.

42 F.W. Howay, *British Columbia from Earliest Times to the Present*, vol. 2 (Vancouver: S.J. Clarke 1914), 34–6; Tina Loo, *Making Law: Order and Authority in British Columbia, 1821–1871* (Toronto: University of Toronto Press 1994).

43 Robin Fisher, *Contact and Conflict*, chapter 5, 'Gold Miners and Settlers,' 95–118.

44 Douglas to Barclay, 16 May 1853, quoted in Pethick, ibid., 84.

45 Robert Coats and R.H. Gosnell, *Sir James Douglas*, 214.

46 Pethick, *James Douglas*, 150.

47 Ibid., 97.

48 Ibid., 113.

49 Despatch, Douglas to Lytton, 26 Oct. 1858, *Papers*, 2: 8. Twenty sets would appear to allow one for each magistrate, with a few extras for other officials. It should be noted that there were five magistrates functioning on Vancouver Island as early as 1852, possibly without law books. In 1858 Douglas was also governor of the mainland colony, which would have needed more magistrates than Vancouver Island. Evidently, there were few, if any, law books in the hands of these magistrates – none of whom was trained in the law. Therefore, it is impossible that they were applying formal law in their decisions prior to 1858. The corollary of this is that, after 1858, under Begbie's supervision, they may have been.

50 Despatch, Lytton to Douglas, 2 Sept. 1858, *Papers*, 1, 61. The general rule in

colonial law is that British law extended to the colonies 'so far as it is applicable to their circumstances,' and so this is simply a statement of existing law.

51 Despatch, Douglas to Lytton, 12 Oct. 1858, *Papers* , Part 2, 2.

52 Keith Sinclair, 'The Aborigines' Protection Society and New Zealand: A Study in Nineteenth Century Opinion,' M.A. thesis, 1946, Victoria University of Wellington, 1946). There is a detailed discussion of this movement in chapter 2.

53 30 Dec. 1858, *Papers on the Land Question*, 15.

54 Ibid., 14 March 1859, 16–17.

55 Robin Fisher, *Contact and Conflict*, 60–8; Paul Tennant, *Aboriginal People and Politics*, chapter three, 'The Douglas "System": Reserves, Pre-Emptions, and Assimilation,' 26–38.

56 Walter N. Sage, *Sir James Douglas and British Columbia*; Robert H. Coats and R.E. Gosnell, *Sir James Douglas*; Derek Pethick: *James Douglas: Servant of Two Empires*.

57 John Phillip Reid, 'Restraints of Vengeance: Retaliation-in-Kind and the Use of Indian Law in the Old Oregon Country,' *Oregon Historical Quarterly*, vol. 95, no. 1 (spring 1994), 48–91.

58 Douglas to Barclay, 5 Nov. 1852, quoted in Derek Pethick: *James Douglas: Servant of Two Empires*, 105.

59 Squ-eath means 'slave' in Cowichan, and so there is some evidence that the Cowichan surrendered a slave in place of the real murderer. Hamar Foster, 'Letting Go the Bone,' 45.

60 Barry Gough, *Gunboat Frontier: British Maritime Authority and Northwest Coast Indians, 1846–1890* (Vancouver: University of British Columbia Press 1984), 53–4. This was apparently the first trial of an Indian for a crime in the Vancouver Island colony. It is not clear what form of law Douglas used, but evidently it was a hybrid military version of the common law. Governor Blanshard had used the Royal Navy to fire upon Kwakiutl villages the year before in the Newitty affair, but these were military actions, not legal ones.

61 Ibid.

62 Barry Gough, 53–4.

63 Ibid., 61–4.

64 Cole Harris, 'Strategies of Power in the Cordilleran Fur Trade,' in *The Resettlement of British Columbia: Essays on Colonialism and Geographical Change* (Vancouver: University of British Columbia Press 1997), 65–6. Hamar Foster links these hangings with the treaty process on Vancouver Island. 'Letting Go the Bone,' 44–5.

65 Barry Gough, *Gunboat Frontier*, at 41, offers a third reason for the killing: that the men refused some 'extravagant demands' made by the Indians. See also Hubert Howe Bancroft, *History of British Columbia, 1792–1887*, 273–5.

66 Barry Gough, *Gunboat Frontier*, 41–2.

67 Pelly to Gray, 14 Jan. 1852, quoted in Barry Gough, *Gunboat Frontier*, 46.

68 Ibid., 43–5.

69 Ibid., 82–3.

70 Ibid., 83–4.

71 'Judicial Murder,' *British Colonist*, 27 Aug. 1860.

72 Barry Gough, *Gunboat Frontier*, 111–13.

73 Ibid., 113–14.

74 Ibid., 114–15.

75 Ibid., 118–21. It seems impossible that Cameron, who had doubtlessly tried many Indians in his courts in eleven years as chief justice of Vancouver Island, was wrong about the law on this issue. His counterpart on the mainland, Matthew Baillie Begbie, regularly accepted Indian testimony, as apparently did all of the other judges in British North America. That leaves this action inexplicable.

76 Jean Barman, *The West Beyond the West: A History of British Columbia* (Toronto: University of Toronto Press 1991); George Woodcock, *British Columbia: A History of the Province* (Vancouver: Douglas and McIntyre 1990); Margaret Ormsby, *British Columbia: A History* (Toronto: Macmillan of Canada 1958); E.O.S. Scholefield, *British Columbia: From Earliest Times to the Present*, (4 vols.) (Vancouver: S.J. Clarke 1914); Cole Harris, 'The Making of the Lower Mainland,' in *The Resettlement of British Columbia*, 68–102.

77 David R. Williams, *The Man for a New Country: Sir Matthew Baillie Begbie* (Sydney, B.C.: Gray's Publishing 1977). The entire discussion of Begbie's role in British Columbia history relies heavily on Williams's work.

78 Ibid., 16–27.

79 Ibid., 28–33.

80 Ibid., 45.

81 Ibid., 47

82 Ibid., 98.

83 Begbie to colonial secretary, 9 Nov. 1864, quoted in David R. Williams, *Man for a New Country*, 109.

84 Ibid., 109, 157. Although there was no reason for the ordinance in terms of Begbie's daily practice, it did bring the colony in line with the practice in other colonies, consistent with the framework of legality that the colonial office preferred. It was also doubtless in response to Judge Cameron's dismissal of the *Swiss Boy* and *Kingfisher* piracy cases. As a practical matter, the only remedy that a party in a legal case has to an erroneous ruling by a judge admitting evidence injurious to his case is an appeal. Appeals in criminal cases were limited everywhere under British law in the mid-nineteenth century; therefore, in

practice, the trial judge had enormous latitude in interpreting the law. No appeals at all were taken from any of Begbie's criminal cases until at least the late 1870s. In 1879 the Full Court, consisting of all of the Supreme Court judges, constituted a Court of Appeal. Before that time, very limited appeals might be heard by the original judge passing sentence (ibid. at 180).

85 Ibid., 105. By 1886 Begbie believed the opposite: that Indians had no title to their lands. See *A.G. and I.B. Nash* v. *John Tait (4 Metlatatla Indians)*, Begbie Bench Books, vol. 13, 28 Oct. 1886, British Columbia Archives.

86 David R. Williams. *Man for a New Country*, 107.

87 Ibid.

88 Ibid., 102. Bench Books, vol. 14 21 Aug. 1889. This case is discussed in Douglas Cole and Ira Chaikin, *An Iron Hand upon the People: The Law against the Potlatch on the Northwest Coast* (Vancouver: Douglas and McIntyre 1990), 34–6.

89 (1892) 2 BCR 232. Ibid., 118.

90 Bench Books, vol. 13, 17 Nov. 1885.

91 Douglas Cole and Ira Chaikin, *An Iron Hand Upon the People*, 42–6.

92 McCullagh to Vowell, 1 Feb. 1896, quoted in ibid., 46.

93 Douglas Cole and Ira Chaikin, *An Iron Hand upon the People*, contains accounts of many of these prosecutions. Daniel Raunet, *Without Surrender, Without Consent*, concludes that, although several Nisga'a were prosecuted for violation of the Indian Act for holding potlatches, others were able to continue the practices beyond the reach of the law (121–9 at 128–9).

94 Tina Loo, 'Dan Cramer's Potlatch: Law as Coercion, Symbol, and Rhetoric in British Columbia, 1884–1951,' *Canadian Historical Review*, vol. 73 (1992), 125–65.

95 David R. Williams, *The Man for a New Country*, 129–47. The white population of the merged colony of British Columbia in 1871 (including Vancouver Island), was 8576. There were 1548 Chinese and an estimated 25,661 Indians. Most of the Indians, however, lived beyond the reach of colonial courts. Assuming a Victoria population of about 3000 in the 1860s, and a loss in white population in the Fraser valley after the gold rush, this would provide a population of 20,000 at most under Begbie's effective jurisdiction, including no more than 9000 whites and no more than 9000 Indians living in villages accessible to British courts. Begbie himself estimated the white population of the colony of British Columbia (excluding Vancouver Island) at 2000 at the time of his first circuit in 1859, but excluding Indians and Chinese (at 153). Within these imprecise population parameters it is clear that twenty-nine executions occurred within a small population. These data are found in Jean Barman, *A History of British Columbia*, table 5, 363. The population of Victoria is found at 62.

96 David R. Williams, *The Man for a New Country*, 148–53.

97 The penal colonies in Australia probably had the highest levels of colonial executions, but these were not particularly matters of colonial law. British authorities were fearful of convict revolts and thus maintained a violent, quasi-military legal order. Since all of the convicts had been, in theory at least, spared the gallows when they were exiled to a penal colony, the penalty for major crimes in the penal colony was death. This legal order has nothing at all to do with the colonial legal order in British Columbia. British colonial regimes did not conduct extensive executions of native people in peace time, although executions often followed colonial wars.

98 Ironically, in 1870 Begbie had applied to the Colonial Office for a transfer to the Straits Settlements, again as chief justice. If that transfer had been granted Begbie might have presided over the trial of thirty Malays for the 1874 murder of J.W. Birch, first British resident in Perak, an important colonial trial leading to the hangings of two Malay chiefs. Begbie needs to be seen in this context as a colonial judge: he would have performed exactly the same political and legal role in Malaya.

99 David R. Williams, *The Man for a New Country*, 141–2. Williams erroneously reports the executions of four whites rather than one. The data are incomplete but substantially consistent. Hamar Foster reports slightly different data but involving a slighly shorter period and including both Vancouver Island and British Columbia. Examining Executive Council minutes for the period 1864–71, Foster found thirty-eight capital sentences considered, involving thirty-three Indians (one of them twice), three Chinese, one Kanaka (Hawaiian), and one not stated. Foster also notes that, inexplicably, at least three white men were convicted of murder and one, James Barry, was hanged in the same period, but there is no reference to them in Executive Council minutes. Foster's data finds twenty-six men hanged in this period, including twenty-three Indians. This is a large number of killings for a population of from 2000 to 4000 whites and an unknown number of Indians, and all the more so since only a few thousand were within the reach of the courts. Begbie's unique colonial court is just beginning to draw the attention of scholars. Hamar Foster, '"The Queen's Law is Better than Yours": International Homicide in Early British Columbia,' in Jim Phillips, Tina Loo, Susan Lewthwaite, *Essays in the History of Canadian Law*, vol. 5, *Crime and Criminal Justice* (Toronto: Osgoode Society and University of Toronto Press 1994), 41–111, 84. Tina Loo, *Making Law: Order and Authority in British Columbia*, 134–56, discusses only the Butte Inlet trials. It appears that Williams is wrong about the four white hangings – there was only one – but, otherwise, his account of the number of executions and Foster's are in general agreement. In any case, the over-representation of Indians in the execution statistics is still clear.

100 These Vancouver Island hangings are considered above. These hangings occurred before the period considered by Hamar Foster, '"The Queen's Law is Better than Yours."'

101 David R. Williams, *The Man for a New Country*, 140. Begbie hanged twenty-two Indians; Crease two.

102 Ibid., 142. These statistics are even more disproportionate when compared to the relevant populations. Canada had a population of over two million by 1867, while British Columbia's was only in the tens of thousands, most of them Indians living beyond the reach of Begbie's court. When the seven Vancouver Island executions are added, there were thirty-three Indian hangings in colonial British Columbia in less than twenty years.

103 These are, for example, most of the entire history of Indian executions in Canada. By contrast, seven Indians were executed for murder following the 1885 Northwest Rebelliion. In the entire nineteenth century, there appear to have been about ten additional Indian executions in the entire northwest – Manitoba, Saskatchewan, Alberta, Yukon, and the Northwest Territories.

104 V.A.C. Gatrell, *The Hanging Tree: Execution and the English People, 1770–1868* (Oxford: Oxford University Press 1994), 29–55, describes the slow death endured by most hanging victims. Peter Linebaugh, *The London Hanged: Crime and Civil Society in the Eighteenth Century* (Cambridge, U.K.: Cambridge University Press 1992); Steven Wilf, 'Imagining Justice: Aesthetics and Public Executions in Late Eighteenth-Century England,' vol. 5 (1993) *Yale Journal of Law and Humanties*, 51–78.

105 David R. Williams, *The Man for a New Country*, 131.

106 Ibid., 132.

107 Begbie to Douglas, 28 May 1862, quoted in ibid., 132.

108 Foster, '"The Queen's Law Is Better Than Yours,"' 67.

109 David R. Williams, *The Man for a New Country*, 136–7.

110 By the mid-nineteenth century well over half of imposed death sentences throughout the British Empire were being commuted. This liberal granting of commutations made sense in a society with dozens of offences carrying the mandatory death penalty. Rather than allow judges to exercise individual discretion in sentencing authority, this authority was centralized in the Home Office in England, in the Colonial Office for the colonies, and, after colonial self-government, in the respective ministries of the individual colonies.

111 David R. Williams, *The Man for a New Country*, 139. Somehow it is impossible to imagine formal 'cautions' being given Indians by frontier sheriffs.

112 Foster, 'The Queen's Law Is Better Than Yours,' 75–6.

113 Ibid., 75. It is difficult to imagine that robbers in the gold district would not

have checked for money inside clothing. Gold miners kept money in all sorts of places, but not uncommonly on their person.

114 Ibid., 76. Begbie made a similar statement after sentencing Klatssassin and others for the Butte Inlet killings.

115 Begbie to Seymour, 9 Nov. 1864, quoted in David R. Williams, *The Man for a New Country*, 116–17.

116 Ibid., 101.

117 Hamar Foster, '"The Queen's Law Is Better Than Yours,"' 76–7. Both death sentences were commuted because of the youth of the offenders.

118 Keith Thor Carlson, 'The Lynching of Louie Sam,' *BC Studies*, vol. 109 (spring 1996), 63–79.

119 Paul Tennant, *Aboriginal People and Politics*, 26–38.

120 Ibid., 39–45; Hamar Foster, 'Letting Go the Bone,' 53–6. An important parallel issue, made here only for contextual purposes, is that local British Columbia political leaders were hostile to the rights of Chinese immigrants, who had all legal privileges of citizenship. Patricia E. Roy, *A White Man's Province: British Columbia Politicians and Chinese and Japanese Immigrants, 1858–1914* (Vancouver: University of British Columbia Press 1989).

121 Lytton to Douglas, 31 July 1858, *Papers Relating to the Indian Land Question*, 12.

122 Paul Tennant, *Aboriginal People and Politics*, 47–50.

123 Hamar Foster, 'How Not to Draft Legislation: Indian Land Claims, Government Intransigence, and How Premier Walkem nearly sold the farm in 1874,' *The Advocate* 411–20.

124 Paul Tennant, *Aboriginal People and Politics*, 44; Hamar Foster, 'Letting Go the Bone,' 59–60. It seems that the only other possible interpretation is that the choice of wording was simply an accident, the inadvertent result of bad drafting. But the choice of words seems too precise for such an accident.

125 Molyneux St. John, *The Sea of Mountains: An Account of Lord Dufferin's Tour Through British Columbia in 1876* (London: Hurst and Blackett 1877), 223–4.

126 Ibid., 225–6.

127 Robin Fisher, *Contact and Conflict*, 188–9; 205–6; Hamar Foster, 'Indian Title in British Columbia,' 60–4.

128 Douglas Harris, 'The Nlha7kapmx Meeting in Lytton in 1879 and the Rule of Law,' *B.C. Studies*, vol. 108 (winter 1995–6), 5–28; Daniel Raunet, *Without Surrender, Without Consent*, 76–101.

129 Douglas Harris, 'The Nlha7kapmx Meeting in Lytton,' 5–10.

130 G.M. Sproat to superintendant-general, 6 Nov. 1878, quoted in Douglas Harris, 'The Nlha7kapmx Meeting at Lytton,' 22.

131 Cole Harris, 'The Fraser River Encountered,' in *The Resettlement of British Columbia*, 118–129. These villages are named and located in a map at 121.

132 *Daily British Colonist*, 7 Nov. 1879, quoted in Douglas Harris, 'The Nlha7kapmx Meeting at Lytton,' 24.
133 Joanne Drake-Terry, *The Same As Yesterday*, 103.
134 Daniel Raunet, *Without Surrender, Without Consent*, 95–6.
135 Hamar Foster, 'Letting Go the Bone,' 47–8.
136 Daniel Raunet, *Without Surrender, Without Consent*, 134–5.
137 Robin Fisher, *Contact and Conflict*, 170–1.
138 Daniel Raunet, *Without Surrender, Without Consent*, 115–18.

CHAPTER 10

1 Robert Seidman, 'Witch Murder and Mens Rea,' *Modern Law Review*, vol. 28 (1965), 46–61; 'Mens Rea and the Reasonable African,' *International and Comparative Law Quarterly*, vol. 15 (1966) 1135–1164 . Western criminal law is philosophically rooted in the rationality of punishing an evil mental state, most often put in terms of an intent to do an unlawful act. Obviously, the fiction that the common law applied to the farthest reaches of a remote country as soon as British political sovereignty 'took' that land potentially created millions of indigenous criminal offenders who had no culpable mental state at all, because they had no idea what kinds of conduct were unlawful. Indeed, they might never have heard of Britain, or of its law.
2 Sidney L. Harring, 'Please Send Six Copies of the Penal Code: British Colonial Law in Selangor, 1874–1880,' *International Journal of the Sociology of Law*, vol. 19 (1991), 193, provides an introduction to this literature, although there are hundreds of individual studies of the process of the imposition of British law in the colonies in the nineteenth and early twentieth centuries. See also S.B. Burman and B.E. Harrell-Bond, *The Imposition of Law* (London: Academic Press 1979); M.B. Hooker, *Legal Pluralism: An Introduction to Colonial and Neo-colonial Laws* (Oxford: Oxford University Press 1975); and Katherine Pettipas, *Severing the Ties That Bind: Government Repression of Indigenous Religious Ceremonies on the Prairies* (Winnipeg: University of Manitoba Press 1994), 17–41.
3 (1897) 28 O.R. 309. George Nelson, a fur trader, provides a classic account of the wendigo in Ojibwa and Cree life. Nelson served in the Ojibwa country from 1802 to 1804, 1804 to 1816, and 1818 to 1823, the last time keeping very extensive ethnographic notes on the Cree at Lac La Ronge, now in northeastern Saskatchewan. See Jennifer S.H. Brown and Robert Brightman, *The Orders of the Dreamed: George Nelson On Cree and Northern Ojibwa Religion and Myth, 1823* (Winnipeg: University of Manitoba Press 1988). A wendigo execution under traditional law is described at 92–3.

4 Wendigo is spelled in a variety of ways by different anthropologists. Throughout, I adopt the spelling 'wendigo,' used in *Machekequonabe*. It is also spelled
windigo, wintego, wihtigo, wetigo, windego, wendigo, wendago, windago,
wintigo, wintsigo, wehtigoo, windagoo, windikouk, weendigo, wentiko, wii-
tiko, whittico, weendegoag, weendago, and weetigo. Morton I. Teicher, 'Windigo Psychosis: A Study of a Relationship between Belief and Behavior among
the Indians of Northeastern Canada,' Proceedings of the Annual Meeting of
the American Ethnological Society, 1960, 2.
5 Morton I. Teicher, 'Windigo Psychosis,' is the most complete analysis of the
meaning of the windigo phenomenon in native society, and is accompanied
by a complete bibliography. See also Lou Marano, 'Windigo Psychosis: The
Anatomy of an Emic-Etic Confusion,' ' *Current Anthropology*, vol. 23, no. 4
(1982), 385–412; Leo G. Waisberg, 'Boreal Forest Subsistence and the Windigo:
Fluctuation of Animal Populations,' *Anthropologica*, vol. 17 (1975), 169–85;
Thomas H. Hay, 'The Windigo Psychosis: Psychodynamic, Cultural, and
Social Factors in Aberrant Behavior,' *American Anthropologist*, vol. 73 (1971),
1–22; Regina Flannery *et al.*, 'Witiko Accounts from the James Bay Cree,' *Arc-
tic Anthropology*, vol. 18, no. 1, (1982), 57–77; Jennifer Brown, 'The Cure and
Feeding of Windigos: A Critique,' *American Anthropologist*, vol. 73 (1971), 20–
2; D.H. Turner, 'Windigo Mythology and the Analysis of Cree Social Structure,' *Anthropologica*, vol. 19, no. 1 (1977), 63–73; Diamond Jenness, 'The
Ojibwa Indians of Parry Island, Their Social and Religious Life,' National
Museum of Canada, Bulletin no. 78, 1935. The repeated references to psycho-
analytical categories in analysing the wendigo phenonmenon stems from several factors, most commonly the frequency with which Indians became
afflicted with the belief that they were becoming wendigos, often taking some
form of mental illness. While this is related to the spiritual belief that wendigos are dangerous creatures that live in the forest, it is not the same thing. For
example, Machekequonabe killed in an ordinary case of self-defence and was
not afflicted with any form of mental disturbance. Mental disturbance takes
many forms and obviously takes distinct forms in different cultural contexts,
but the comparative study of mental disorder is not within the scope of this
study.
6 Morton I. Teicher, 'Windigo Psychosis,' 2.
7 Ibid., 3.
8 Ibid., 7–16.
9 Diamond Jenness, 'The Ojibwa Indians of Parry Island,' 3.
10 Ibid., 3. The killing has all of the earmarks of a wendigo killing: it was sudden,
with no apparant reason, with the body of a living person apparently inhabited by an evil spirit and with hints of cannibalism. While Jenness gives no

date for this killing, his informant's account, recorded in 1935, probably represented a late-nineteenth or early- twentieth-century event.

11   Ibid., 3.

12   Jennifer S.H. Brown and Robert Brightman, *The Orders of the Dreamed*, 92–3.

13   Morton I. Teicher's, methodology in 'Windigo Psychosis,' which can be deduced from his bibliography, was to read existing ethnographic accounts of native people. He cites about 150 of these in his bibliography, and presumably he did not cite many more in which he failed to find evidence of the wendigo phenomenon. These works are cited at 123–9. He also cites *Machekequonabe* by its case citation, showing that Teicher used legal records.

14   Teicher, 5–6.

15   Hamar Foster, 'Long Distance Justice: The Criminal Jurisdiction of Canadian Courts West of the Canadas, 1763–1859,' *The American Journal of Legal History*, vol. 34 (1990), 1–48; 'Sins against the Great Spirit: The Law, the Hudson's Bay Company, and the Mackenzie River Murders, 1835–1839,' *Criminal Justice History: An International Annual*, vol. 10 (1989), 23–76; and 'Killing Mr. John: Law and Jurisdiction at Fort Stikine, 1842–1846,' in John McLaren *et al.*, *Law for the Elephant, Law for the Beaver: Essays in the Legal History of the North American West* (Regina: Great Plains Research Centre, University of Regina 1992); Edward S. Rogers, 'Northern Algonquians and the Hudson's Bay Company, 1821–1890,' in Edward Rogers and Donald Smith, *Aboriginal Ontario: Historical Perspectives on the First Nations* (Toronto: Dundurn Press 1994), 307–43.

16   'Abishabis,' in *D.C.B.*, vol. 7 (1988), 3–4.

17   Ibid., 4.

18   There were, in 1900, five small reserves on Sabaskong Bay on the northeast end of Lake of the Woods and I assume that the killing occurred in this area. I have retained the spelling in the reported case. R. Louis Gentilcore, ed., *Historical Atlas of Canada*, vol. 2 (Toronto: University of Toronto Press 1993) plate 33, 'Native Reserves: Names and Descriptions.' Given this location, there is a likelihood that there was more contact with Canadian society than was acknowledged in the facts of the case: the Lake of the Woods area was developed, logging had occurred there, and the transcontinental railroad passed nearby. It may simply be that the defence alleged this to be a fact and the crown, believing it legally irrelevant, did not contest it. It is also possible that this particular band, even though in geographical proximity to whites, had avoided contact with Euro-Canadians as much as they could.

19   Here it is important to point out that, in the late twentieth century, legal scholars benefit from the fact that both sides of a dispute are represented and have the opportunity to present their respective arguments to the court. For Indians before the middle of the twentieth century, this was a rare phenonomenon,

and thus most 'Indian law' is based on a one-sided analysis of every case. This is not to suggest that the resulting state of Indian law would necessarily be different if the Indian position had had legal representation, because obviously considerations of politics and economics may well have determined the outcome of Indian cases. Clearly, however, if the native side had been represented, we would have at least a much greater understanding of the facts of Indian law cases as well as of the Indian perspective on the underlying legal issues.

20 *Queen* v. *Machweekequonabe* (*sic*), RG 13-C1, vol. 2089, National Archives of Canada. This file contains both a twelve-page official transcript as well as various legal documents.

21 Ibid., transcript, 2–3. Langford's questions are omitted.

22 *Regina* v. *Machekequonabe* 28 O.R. 309 (1896).

23 Transcript, 7, RG 13–C1, vol. 2089.

24 Ibid., 8.

25 Ibid., 8. It seems that this answer was wrong: the killing occurred on a small reserve. Although no population data appear in the transcript, given common band sizes of the time, it was likely less than a hundred people, of whom most were children.

26 Letter, Wink to Oliver Mowat, 9 Dec. 1896, in the original case file, RG 13-C1, vol. 2089: 'The prisoner should not be found guilty of manslaughter, contending that the shooting was due to misadventure, or that the act of shooting was done by the prisoner when labouring under such a disease of the mind and to such an extent as to render him incapable of appreciating the nature and quality of the act and of knowing that such act was wrong, or that he was labouring under a specific delusion, but in other respects sane, which caused him to believe in the existence of a state of things which, if it existed, would justify or excuse his act.'

27 Wink charged the Indian Department for his services at trial $201.25 with a two-page itemized bill. It was reduced to $75.

28 *R.* v. *Machekequonabe*, 310

29 Transcript, 10, 11, RG 13–C1, vol. 2089.

30 Ibid., 12.

31 There was apparently no Indian Department policy on the financing of criminal appeals of Indians, presumably because Indians were wards of the state and entitled to its protection. Indeed, the paucity of Indian criminal appeals necessarily proves that the Indian Department financed few of them: every criminal appeal leaves a record. This conviction could not have been appealed because of the sentence – six-month sentences for Indians were common. The decision to file an appeal must have had policy significance. None of this is

apparent in the correspondence in the case file, but it appears likely that the Department of Justice wanted a judicial ruling against customary-law defences. This would have occurred at a time when both plains Indians and Northwest Coast Indians were mounting such defences.

32 This defence undermines the *mens rea* of intending a criminal act. See Keedy, 'Ignorance and Mistake in the Criminal Law,' *Harvard Law Review*, vol. 22 (1908), 75; Rollin Perkins, 'Ignorance and Mistake in the Criminal Law,' 88 *University of Pennsylvania Law Review*, vol. 88 (1939), 35. This was probably the strongest defence argument, missed by the original defence attorney.

33 *R. v. Machekequonabe*, 311. Correspondence relating to the appeal and a hand-written outline of the appellate argument is held in the National Archives of Canda, RG 13, vol. 2089. Attorney J.K. Kerr of Toronto argued the appeal, billing the Indian Department $120.08 for his services.

34 This case is unreported. The case file is held in the Archives of Ontario, RG 3, file 181 (1906).

35 Letter, deputy minister of justice to deputy attorney general of Ontario, 15 March 1906, Archives of Ontario, RG 3, file 181 (1906).

36 Ten years later Canadian law arrived in the farthest corner of the country when a NWMP patrol reached the Arctic Ocean at the mouth of the Copper River to arrest Sinnisiak and Uluksuk, two Copper Inuit accused of the murder of two Roman Catholic priests. R.G. Moyles, *British Law and Arctic Men: The Celebrated 1917 Murder Trials of Sinnisiak and Uluksuk, the First Inuit Tried Under White Man's Law* (Saskatoon: Western Prairie Books 1979)

37 On the symbolic purposes of early Canadian law in the Arctic, see Sidney L. Harring, 'Rich Men of the Country: Canadian Law in the Land of the Copper Inuit, 1914–1930,' *Ottawa Law Review*, vol. 21 (1989), 63. On the symbolic use of law against potlatching in the Northwest Coast, see Douglas Cole and Ira Chaikin, *An Iron Hand upon the People: The Law Against the Potlatch on the Northwest Coast* (Vancouver: Douglas and MacIntyre 1900), 14–24. More generally, see Katherine Pettipas, *Severing the Ties That Bind*, 17–41.

38 See *Queen vs. Payoo and Npaysoosee*, an unreported Northwest Territories case of 1899, printed in 'The Killing of Moostoos the Wehtigoo,' in Archaelogical Report, appendix to the Report of the minister of education, Ontario, 1903, *Ontario Sessional Papers*, vol. 36, pt. 5, 1904, 128–41.

39 'The Killing of Moostoos the Wehtigoo,' 129. Her remembering 'nothing' other than the bare fact of the killing is probably a fiction, designed to limit her exposure on the witness stand.

40 The report confuses the nature of the leadership of a Cree hunting band, claiming that while Entominahoo was not a 'chief' he was looked up to as a medicine man of considerable authority. A hunting band, often composed of

members of an extended family (as these people were), would not have a chief. Rather, leadership would be informal, based on prestige and experience. The evidence is clear that Entominahoo performed this role.

41 Ibid., 130.
42 Ibid., 131.
43 Chuckachuck and Apishchikisaynis were both Moostoos's brothers-in-law.
44 Ibid., 131–3.
45 Ibid., 133–4. During the day and a half over which these events took place there was a recurrent resort to sorcery to cure Moostoos, but to no avail.
46 Ibid., 135.
47 Ibid., 138–9.
48 Ibid., 140.
49 Ibid., 140.
50 Ibid., 141. Charlebois, Dressy Man, and Bright Eyes were convicted of killing She Wills, an old woman, in the aftermath of Frog Lake in the Northwest Rebellion. She had announced that she would turn into a wendigo unless someone killed her. The band selected three warriors to kill her: Charlebois struck her in the head with a club, Bright Eyes shot her three times, and Dressy Man cut off her head with a saber and threw it into the bush. During the Battleford trials, Judge Charles Rouleau sentenced Bright Eyes to twenty years in jail for manslaughter and Charlebois and Dressy Man to death for murder. The two death sentences were later commuted to life. Bob Beal and Rod Macleod, *Prairie Fire: The 1885 North-West Rebellion* (Edmonton, Hurtig Publishers 1984), 212–13.
51 It might be pointed out that, in terms of modern criminal law, this is still most often true. If any member of a criminal collaboration takes responsibility for the event with an explanation that exculpates the others, that is ordinarily the end of the case. The law is satisfied if some culprit is punished, even if few people really believe a story that limits the culpability of others.
52 A full transcript of this case is printed in the Archaeological Report, *Ontario Sessional Papers*, 1908, 91–120. This transcript is the core of a book, augmented with oral histories and other government documents: Robert R. Stevens and Chief Thomas Fiddler, *Killing the Shaman* (Winnipeg: Penumbra Press 1986). There is also an extensive NWMP file on the case, held in the National Archives of Canada, RG 13, vol. 1452, file 386.
53 Robert Stevens and Thomas Fiddler, *Killing the Shaman*, 111–15. This book essentially parallels the archival record and represents a much more accessible account of the arrest and trial of the Fiddlers.
54 Ibid., 109.
55 Ibid., 116.

56 'Letter, Sergeant Daisy Smith to commanding officer, NWMP, Regina, 1 Oct 1906.' in 'Joseph Fiddler' file, RG 13, vol. 1452, file 386. These various reports are the basis of the account given in *Killing the Shaman*. Sergeant Smith's story seems too naive to be real. For example, the idea that these killings followed from fever or delerium, which must have been common given the state of public health of the day, was probably false, and it exaggerates the frequency of the killings. Similarly, Smith must have been aware of the wendigo killing phenomenon since the NWMP in that region had been involved in earlier cases and the 'wendigo killings' were a part of northern lore.

57 Commissioner Aylesworth Bowen, NWMP, to Sergeant Smith, 28 Dec. 1906, RG 13, vol. 1452, file 386. See also J. Garth Taylor, 'Northern Algonquians on the Frontiers of "New Ontario," 1890–1945,' in Edward S. Rogers and Donald Smith, *Aboriginal Ontario*, 344–73, 352–3.

58 Constable O'Neil, 'Report,' RG 13, vol. 1452, file 386.

59 Ibid.

60 Ibid.

61 The Indians of northern Manitoba signed adhesions to Treaty 5 during 1908, 1909, and 1910. Frank Tough, 'Economic Aspects of Aboriginal Title in Northern Manitoba: Treaty 5 Adhesions and Metis Scrip,' *Manitoba History*, vol. 15 (1988), 3–16. Kenneth Coates and William Morrison, *Treaty Five, 1875–1908* (Treaty Research Report, Treaties and Historical Research Centre, Department of Indian and Northern Affairs, Ottawa 1986), is a complete account of the two treaty 5 processes. The original treaty, negotiated in 1875, covered part of central Manitoba. A second treaty phase, begun in 1908, signed adhesions covering the area in Manitoba north of the original Treaty 5 lands.

62 Letter, NWMP Inspector E.A. Pelletier to Commissioner A. Bowen Perry, June 1906, RG 13, vol. 1452, file 386.

63 Letter, C.E. Saunders to assistant commissioner, NWMP, 20 Aug. 1906, ibid.

64 Constable Daisy Smith, 'Report,' ibid.

65 It is not easy to determine the number of whites living at Norway House in October 1906. It seems that neither Mounties nor missionaries, whites who did live at Norway House, served on the jury. In addition to a number of employees of the fur-trading post, and perhaps commercial fishermen, there would have been schoolteachers, government clerks, and other government functionaries.

66 Robert Stevens and Thomas Fiddler, *Killing the Shaman*, 88.

67 Ibid., 89–90.

68 Ibid., 90.

69 Ibid., 92, 93.

70 Ibid., 95

71 Ibid., 97–8.

72 Ibid., 99.

73 Ibid., 99.

74 Ibid., 100.

75 Ibid., 101

76 Ibid., 103. McKerchar may also be disingenuous here in the way this killing was raised in court. His final question is incongruous as a final question: why would he ask if any other people were sick at the end of his direct examination unless this was intended to prompt Rae to raise this very killing? It seems that Rae had, in fact, told the Mounties everything, so they knew of this killing all along. McKerchar, at the close of the crown case, raised the specter of a wave of wendigo killings.

77 Ibid., 105–6.

78 Ibid., 106–7.

79 Ibid., 106.

80 Ibid., 106. This obviously accounts for Paupanakiss's strange testimony, as well as the fact that the crown attorney called Paupanakiss to the stand only to testify that he had never heard of any of this or ever visited the Sucker band in over sixteen years. Thus, Paupanakiss's complete lack of knowledge about the case became powerful evidence against Fiddler, used to deny his main defence, that he was acting according to tribal custom. Paupanakiss apparently allowed his testimony to be used in this way, perhaps because he, as a Christian, wanted to suppress Cree traditional beliefs. He could, for example, have simply told the court about the place of wendigo killings in Ojibwa society, information that he, as an Ojibwa, must have known and that would have helped Fiddler's case.

81 Ibid., 107–8.

82 Ibid., 108.

83 The practice of setting an example by criminally punishing powerful native people was common in Canada: Brendan O'Brien, *Speedy Justice: The Tragic Last Voyage of His Majesty's Vessel* Speedy (Toronto: Osgoode Society and University of Toronto Press 1992), 49–53; Douglas Cole and Ira Chaikin: *Iron Hand upon the People: The Law Against the Potlatch on the Northwest Coast* (Vancouver: Douglas and McIntyre 1990), 14–39; Sidney L. Harring, 'The Rich Men of the Country'; Katherine Pettipas, *Severing the Ties that Bind*, 9–16; Hamar Foster, 'Letting Go the Bone: Indian Title in British Columbia,' in Hamar Foster and John McLaren, *Essays in the History of Canadian Law, vol. 6, British Columbia and the Yukon* (Toronto: Osgoode Society and University of Toronto Press 1995), 28–85 at 43–5, and '"The Queens' Law Is Better Than Yours": International Homicide in Early British Columbia,' in Jim Phillips, Tina Loo, Susan Lewthwaite, *Essays in the*

History of Canadian Law, vol. 5, *Crime and Criminal Justice* (Toronto: Osgoode Society and University of Toronto Press 1994), 41–111 at 61–80.

84 Commissioner Perry to minister of justice, 30 Oct. 30, 1907. Since this letter was sent two weeks after the trial, it seems impossible to conclude anything other than that Perry had deliberately misinstructed the jury on the issue of the role of Ojibwa law in this case. He could only have done so with the intention of eliminating any possiblity that the jury would use this information as a basis to acquit Fiddler of the murder charge.

85 Robert Stevens and Thomas Fiddler, *Killing the Shaman,* 110–11.

86 Ibid., 111.

87 Ibid., 112.

88 Ibid., 111–12.

89 Ibid., 113–14.

90 Ibid., 115.

91 Ibid., 116.

92 'Queen v. Paul Sabourin,' R.G. 13, vol. 1439, file 315, National Archives of Canada, transcript, 1–2.

93 Transcript, 1–6, ibid.

94 Transcript, 7, ibid.

95 Unpaginated, undated memorandum in case file. 'Queen v. Paul Sabourin.'

96 Telegram, governor general to Joseph Pope, undersecretary of state, 4 Dec. 4 1899, 'Queen v. Paul Sabourin.'

97 Telegram, A.G. Irvine to inspector of penitentiaries, 20 Nov. 1902, 'Queen v. Paul Sabourin.'

98 Smart to minister of justice, 15 Nov. 1899, quoted in René Fumoleau, *As Long As This Land Shall Last* (Toronto: McClelland and Stewart 1976), 99.

99 It seems that none of the common law jurisdictions recognized self- defence claims arising from a native person's honestly held belief. Reasonable belief of an immanent threat to life, however, is at the core of the law of self-defence. The common law casts the reasonableness of such belief in culturally biased terms, reflecting a reasonable English male. See Katherine Pettipas, *Severing the Ties That Bind: Government Repression of Indigenous Religious Ceremonies on the Prairies* (Winnipeg: University of Manitoba Press 1994), chapter 1, 'Imperial Policy and Local Customs,' 17–41.

CHAPTER 11

1 Helen Buckley, *From Wooden Ploughs to Welfare: Why Indian Policy Failed in the Prairie Provinces* (Montreal: McGill-Queen's University Press 1992); Sarah Carter, *Lost Harvests: Prairie Indian Reserve Farmers and Government Policy*

(Montreal: McGill-Queen's University Press 1990); Gerald Friesen, *The Canadian Prairies: A History* (Toronto: University of Toronto Press 1984), 129–61.

2 R.C. Macleod, *The North-West Mounted Police and Law Enforcement, 1873–1905* (Toronto: University of Toronto Press 1976).

3 Alexander Morris wrote a contemporary account of the treaty process, through Treaty 7. *The Treaties of Canada with the Indians of Manitoba and the North-West Territories including the Negotiations on Which They Were Based* (Saskatoon, Fifth House Publishers 1991, facsimile of original ed., 1880). Morris's own detailed account of his negotiations on treaties 4, 5, and 6 (with revisions of treaties 1 and 2) are at 77–244.

4 Olive Patricia Dickason, *Canada's First Nations: A History of Founding Peoples from Earliest Times* (Toronto: McClelland and Stewart 1992), 273–86.

5 This view of the rebellion is the revisionist view presented by Blair Stonechild and Bill Waiser, *Loyal till Death: Indians and the North-West Rebellion* (Saskatoon: Fifth House Publishers 1997). The alternative view, dominant in Canadian historiography prior to the publication of this work, was that there was a Metis and Indian rebellion in the Northwest in 1885. George F. Stanley, *The Birth of Western Canada: A History of the Riel Rebellions* (Toronto: University of Toronto Press 1992; originally published 1936), and Bob Beal and Rod Macleod, *Prairie Fire: The 1885 Northwest Rebellion* (Edmonton: Hurtig Publishers 1984).

6 Cochin to Taché, 14 Aug. 1885, Taché Papers, Saskatchewan Archives Board, quoted in Bob Beal and Rod Macleod, Prairie Fire, 309. A similar mistranslation may have occurred during the trial of Big Bear. Hugh Dempsey, *Big Bear: The End of Freedom* (Lincoln: University of Nebraska Press 1984), 185. See also the account in Blair Stonechild and Bill Waiser, *Loyal till Death*, 199–200.

7 F.W. Spicer and John Hawkes, *Story of Saskatchewan and Its People*, quoted in Hugh Dempsey, *Big Bear: The End of Freedom*, 185. Although the trial is unreported, its details are found in 'The Queen v. Big Bear,' Canada, *Sessional Papers*, 1886, 221.

8 Desmond H. Brown, 'The Meaning of Treason in 1885,' *Saskatchewan History*, vol. 28, no. 2 (spring 1975), 65–73. Brown concludes, perhaps correctly, that Louis Riel was properly tried for treason under Canadian law. Following this logic, it might be concluded that the Indians of the northwest, as a legal and political matter, owed allegiance to the English crown and were punishable under the treason statute, but it still does not follow that the individual Indians convicted had the respective *mens reas* of treason under these circumstances. Blair Stonechild and Bill Waiser claim in *Loyal Till Death* that the Indians did not intend to join the rebellion.

9 Richard Price, ed., *The Spirit of the Alberta Treaties* (Edmonton: Pica Pica Press 1987), 168; Frank J. Tough, 'Aboriginal Rights versus the Deed of Surrender:

The Legal Rights of Native Peoples and Canada's Acquisition of the Hudson's Bay Company Territory,' *Prairie Forum*, vol. 7, no. 2 (1992), 225–50.

10 The Cree undoubtedly knew that the Saulteaux had forced the crown into Treaty 3 by blocking the Dawson Route across northwestern Ontario. George F. Stanley, *The Birth of Western Canada*, 210–13; John L. Taylor, 'Two Views on the Meanings of Treaties Six and Seven,' in Richard Price, ed., *The Spirit of the Alberta Treaties*, 9–45; Jean Friesen, 'Magnificent Gifts: The Treaties of Canada with the Indians of the Northwest, 1869–76,' *Transactions of the Royal Society of Canada*, series 5, vol. 1 (1986), 41–51.

11 Hugh Dempsey, *Treaty Research Report: Treaty Seven* (Ottawa: Treaties and Historical Research Centre, Department of Indian and Northern Affairs 1987). Treaty 7 Elders and Tribal Council, *The True Spirit and Original Intent of Treaty 7* (Montreal- McGill-Queen's University Press 1996), 209.

12 Robert A. Williams, Jr., *Linking Arms Together: American Indian Treaty Visions of Law and Peace, 1800–1860* (New York: Oxford University Press 1997), analyses the complex meaning of treaties to Indians. Although focusing on the United States, his work also is relevant to the experience of Canadian Indians.

13 There is a substantial literature on the origins of the NWMP. R.C. Macleod, *The North-West Mounted Police and Law Enforcement, 1873–1905* (Toronto: University of Toronto Press, 1976); Desmond Morton, 'Cavalry or Police: Keeping the Peace on Two Adjacent Frontiers, 1870–1900,' *Journal of Canadian Studies*, 27–37; Hugh Dempsey, *Men in Scarlet* (Calgary: McClelland and Stewart West 1974).

14 R.C. Mcleod, *The North-West Mounted Police*, 35–6.

15 Ibid., 40.

16 John N. Jennings, 'The Northwest Mounted Police and Indian Policy, 1874–1896' (Ph.D. dissertation, University of Toronto 1979), 7–11.

17 R.C. Macleod, *The North-West Mounted Police*, 19–20.

18 Barbara J. Mayfield, 'The Northwest Mounted Police and Blackfoot Peoples, 1874–1884' (M.A. thesis, University of Victoria 1979).

19 John Jennings, 'The Northwest Mounted Police,' 51.

20 Hamar Foster: 'Sins against the Great Spirit: The Law, The Husdon's Bay Company, and the Mackenzie River Murders, 1835–1839,' *Criminal Justice History: An International Annual*, 1989; John Phillip Reids 'Certainty of Vengeance: The Hudson's Bay Company and Retaliation- in-Kind against Indian Offenders in New Caledonia,' *Montana: The Magazine of Western History*, vol. 43, (winter, 1993), 4–17.

21 John Jennings, 'The Northwest Mounted Police,' 303.

22 Ibid., 182–5.

23 Hugh Dempsey, *Big Bear*, 123. On Big Bear generally see also W.B. Fraser, 'Big Bear, Indian Patriot,' *Alberta Historical Review*, vol. 4, no. 2 (1966), 1–13.

24 John Jennings, 'The Northwest Mounted Police,' 303–5.

25 David Lee, 'Foremost Man, and His Band,' *Saskatchewan History*, vol. 36, no. 3 (1983), 94–101, 98.

26 John Jennings, 'The Northwest Mounted Police,' 329–44.

27 Ibid., 337–8.

28 Hugh Dempsey, *Charcoal's World* (Saskatoon: Western Producer Prairie Books 1978).

29 Jennings, 'The Northwest Mounted Police,' 304–5.

30 J.D. Macdonald to E. Dewdney, 20 Nov. 1885, quoted in Blair Stonechild and Bill Waiser, *Loyal till Death*, 221.

31 George F.G. Stanley, *The Birth of Western Canada*; Bob Beal and Rod Macleod: *Prairie Fire*; Blair Stonechild and Bill Waiser, *Loyal Till Death*. Stonechild and Waiser list by name and offence fifty-five Indians convicted of crimes occurring during the rebellion. See appendix five, 'Indian Convictions,' 261–3.

32 Blair Stonechild and Bill Waiser, *Loyal Till Death*, argue that the Indians had a distinct agenda in the rebellion and were *not* allies of the Metis. Bob Beal and Rod Macleod, *Prairie Fire*, analyse the details of the Metis/Indian alliance in detail. While neither side fully trusted each other (at 116), they did recognize common interests, chiefly in their land rights. Riel calculated that, if there were 1.1 billion acres of land in the northwest, each Indian and each Metis 'owned' 11,000 acres. Unimproved Indian lands were, in his calculation, worth 12.5 cents per acre, while 'improved' Metis lands were worth 25 cents per acre. Exactly how, in Riel's analysis, the Metis came to own as much land as the Indians is unclear and reveals the weakness of this alliance: Riel had created an artificial equality of interests (at 123). Only a few Indians served under Metis direction in the actual rebellion.

33 William Bleasdell Cameron, *Blood Red the Sun* (Calgary: Kenways 1950); Stuart Hughes, *The Frog Lake 'Massacre:' Personal Perspectives on Ethnic Conflict* (Toronto: McClelland and Stewart 1996), collects the major primary sources on the killings.

34 Blair Stonechild and Bill Waiser, *Loyal till Death*, 85–125.

35 Desmond H. Brown, 'The Meaning of Treason in 1885.'

36 The simplest view of this issue, that most favourable to the crown position, and deeply embedded in British law, is that fealty to one's country follows the flag, and thus Indians, like Irish rebels, could not argue that their country was not 'Canadian.' But the remaining issue, that of the *mens rea* of treason, the intent to make war on the sovereign, still remained. In the politically charged atmosphere of the treason trials, there was no willingness to entertain this argument.

37 Bob Beal and Rod Macleod, *Prairie Fire*, 310.

38 Sandra Estlin Bingaman, 'The Trials of Poundmaker and Big Bear, 1885,' *Saskatchewan History* vol. 28, no. 3 (1975), 81–102.

39 Bob Beal and Rod Macleod, Prairie Fire, 310–33. It seems clear, even by the standards of 1880s common law, that Robertson was right on this point and the judge's ruling in error. Presence, itself, at a treasonous event was an evidentiary fact that the jury could have properly considered, but, by itself, it did not prove treason absent additional evidence. Beal and Macleod (at 329) believe that Judge Robertson was ignorant of the elements of the law of treason. Since such charges are extremely rare, this is possible, although it is probably more likely that he deliberately misapplied the law in order to ensure that the accused were convicted.

40 Eighteen Metis, the most prominent members of the council, accepted a plea bargain on treason-felony charges and plead guilty in return for short sentences. Eleven were sentenced to seven years in jail, three to three years, and four to one year. Ibid., 309.

41 Sandra Eslin Bingaman, 'The Trials of Poundmaker and Big Bear, 1885'; Blair Stonechild and Bill Waiser, Loyal till Death, 235. They were sentenced to three years in prison in August 1885. Poundmaker was released on 4 March 1886, sick with tuberculosis, and died four months later at the age of forty-six. One Arrow, also sentenced in August 1885, was released in April 1886, too sick to travel home, and died in Winnipeg before the month was over. Big Bear, convicted at the same time, served the longest but was released on 27 Jan. 1887 because he was sick and the government did not want him to die in prison. He lived another year.

42 Beal and Macleod, Prairie Fire, 311–12, 329–30. The precise legal issue is that treason clearly requires a narrow mens rea: proof beyond a reasonable doubt of an intent to take up arms against the crown. Defence attorney Robertson repeatedly pointed out that the crown had to show that a defendant 'participated in it, or at least knew it was happening' (ibid., 311). The crown took the view that, once a rebellion was shown, the onus was on the defendant to show he was present innocently, which improperly shifts the burden of proof. Although the judge apparently understood the issue, his jury instructions never clarified the point, allowing racially prejudiced juries to draw an inference of treason from mere presence among Indians in the region of the rebellion. This interpretation of the law would have made many Indians and Metis in northern Saskatchewan guilty of treason by their mere armed presence in the region.

43 Bob Beal and Rod Macleod, Prairie Fire, 328, 331. Only one Indian, White Cap, won an acquittal in all of the trials (328).

44 Bob Beal and Rod Macleod, Prairie Fire, 323.

45 Ibid., 323. David Mandelbaum, The Plains Cree: An Ethnographic, Historical, and Comparative Study (1940; repr. Regina: Great Plains Research Centre, University of Regina 1979), 106–10.

46 Beal and Macleod, *Prairie Fire*, 309–12.

47 Ibid., 327–30.

48 Gontran Laviolette, *The Dakota Sioux in Canada* (Winnipeg: DLM Publications 1991), 252–5.

49 Bob Beal and Rod Macleod, *Prairie Fire*, 325–7.

50 Blair Stonechild and Bill Waiser, *Loyal till Death*, lists all of the Indian convictions with their respective sentences at appendix five, 261–3. There were fifty-five convictions in all, omitting several resulting in only six month sentences.

51 Quoted, in Bob Beal and Rod Macleod, *Prairie Fire*, 331. Andre was an Oblate priest from the Batoche area. Stonechild and Waiser, *Loyal till Death*, 110.

52 Assistant Commissioner Hayter Reed to Lieutenant. Governor Dewdney, quoted in Bob Beal and Rod Macleod, *Prairie Fire*, 331.

53 Ibid., 332.

54 William Cameron, *How Red the Sun*, 146–8.

55 Bob Beal and Rod Macleod, *Prairie Fire*, 331–2.

56 John Leonard Taylor, 'Two Views on the Meaning of Treaties Six and Seven.'

57 John Leonard Taylor, 'Canada's Northwest Indian Policy in the 1870s: Traditional Premises and Necessary Innovations,' in Richard Price, ed, *The Spirit of the Alberta Treaties*, 3–7.

58 John L. Tobias, 'The Origins of the Treaty Rights Movement in Saskatchewan,' in F. Laurie Barron and James Waldram, *1885 and After: Native Society in Transition* (Great Plains Research Centre, University of Regina 1986), 241–52. A number of Indian elders give the views of these treaties that have been handed down through oral history. See 'Interviews with Elders,' in Richard Price, ed., *The Spirit of the Alberta Treaties*, 113–60, and Treaty 7 Elders and Tribal Council, *The True Spirit and Original Intent of Treaty 7* (Montreal: McGill-Queen's University Press 1996), 67–82; 111–45.

59 J.E. Foster, 'The Saulteaux and the Numbered Treaties: An Aboriginal Rights Position,' in Richard Price, ed., *The Spirit of the Alberta Treaties*, 161–80 at 168.

60 D.J. Hall, 'A Serene Atmosphere? Treaty 1 Revisited,' *Canadian Journal of Native Studies*, vol. 4, no. 2 (1984), 321–58.

61 Arthur J. Ray, *Indians in the Fur Trade: Their Role As Hunters, Trappers, and Middlemen in the Lands Southwest of Hudson Bay, 1660–1870* (Toronto: University of Toronto Press 1974), 195–230.

62 Sarah Carter, *Lost Harvests*, 15–49.

63 Richard Price, ed., *Spirit of the Alberta Treaties*, 42–3, 113–27.

64 Hugh Dempsey, *Big Bear*, 75. The exchange is reported in Alexander Morris, *The Treaties of Canada*, 240.

65 'Treaty Number Six,' in Alexander Morris, *The Treaties of Canada with the Indians of Manitoba and the North-West Territories*, vol. 1: 354.

66 Treaty 7 Elders and Tribal Council, *The True Spirit and Original Intent of Treaty 7* (Montreal: McGill-Queen's University Press 1996), 23–5.

67 Alexander Morris, *The Treaties of Canada*, vol. 1: 353.

68 'Report,' G. McDougall to Lieutenant Governor Morris, 23 Oct. 1875, ibid., 174–5.

69 The treaty process and treaty rights are repeatedly discussed in the various *St. Catherine's* opinions because of the argument that the treaty process was related to Indian title. The dominant position, taken by a number of judges and, ultimately, the Privy Council, was that the Indian rights were political, rather than legal, in nature, 'dependant on the good will of the sovereign.' (1888), 14 A.C. 46, 54–5. See the discussion in chapter 6.

70 Jean Friesen, 'Alexander Morris,' *DCB*, vol. 11 (1982), 608–14

71 There is a substantial nineteenth-century British literature on treaties, generally discussed in chapter 1. The leading case up to the time of the numbered treaties was *The Mohegan Indians* v. *Connecticut* (1770), in Joseph Henry Smith, *Appeals to the Privy council from the American Plantations* (New York: Octagon Books 1965). The case is also analysed in Paul Williams, 'To Determine According to Justice and Equity' Ottawa: Treaties and Historical Research Centre, Department of Indian and Northern Affairs 1980). Although the case arose in the United States, it went to the Privy Council before the American revolution and therefore represented the first determination of the legal rights of an Indian tribe under British law. In the United States, the Marshall court constructed the legal meaning of British Indian treaties in *Cherokee Nation* (1831) and in *Worcester* v. *Georgia*, (1832) holding them legally binding.

72 Morris, *Treaties of Canada*, 352. John L. Taylor, 'Two Views on the Meaning of Treaties Six and Seven,' 9. See also Treaty 7 Elders and Tribal Council, *The True Spirit and Original Intent of Treaty 7*, 297–304.

73 Hugh Dempsey, *Big Bear*, 63.

74 Ibid., 79.

75 The belief that Treaty 3 Indians tricked crown negotiators into paying a far higher price than the lands were worth was at the core of Ontario's litigation with the dominion in *Province of Ontario* v. *The Dominion of Canada, 1898*. The idea that Indian negotiating tactics were 'tricks' and that their oratorical statements were 'dishonest' was a common nineteenth-century Canadian view of the treaty process.

76 Dempsey, *Big Bear*, 120.

77 The process of the making of these treaties has been described in detail in individual treaty reports. Treaty 7 Elders and Tribal Council, *The True Spirit and Intent of Treaty 7*, 191–229; John L. Taylor, 'Two Views on the Meaning of Treaties Six and Seven.'

78 Quoted in D. Hall, 'A Serene Atmosphere? Treaty 1 Revisited,' 321.
79 'And further, Her Majesty agrees to maintain a school on each reserve hereby made, when ever the Indians of the reserve should desire it' Treaty 1). Alexander Morris, *The Treaties of Canada*, 315. Each of the numbered treaties contains some version of this clause in approximately the same language.
80 Vankoughnet to Provencher, 12 March 1873, quoted in Vic Savino and Erica Schumacher, 'Whenever the Indians of the Reserve Should Desire It': An Analysis of the First Nation Treaty Right to Education,' *Manitoba Law Journal* vol. 19 (1992), 476–97, 490.
81 Ibid., 490.
82 Alexander Morris, *The Treaties of Canada*, 77–245. Morris's account is rich and detailed and contains numerous accounts of miscommunication and confusion, some deliberate, some perhaps accidental. For example, at pages 99–100, there is an account of an exchange between The Gambler and Morris at the negotiations for Treaty 4, the Qu'Appelle Treaty, in which The Gambler pushes the issue of the HBC and its interest in Indian lands. Morris clearly does not want to discuss the issue and deflects the question of why he slept in the 'Company's house' (at 99), surely metaphoric, with the flattering (and disingenuous) answer that he was not as strong as the Indians: 'I never slept in a tent in my life before and was only too glad to find a home to go to' (at 100). Even without the record of these awkward exchanges, it is obvious to any lawyer, linguist, or anthropologist that the complex legal and cultural issues involved in these treaties could not have been understood in the same way by Canadians and Indians. Treaty 7 elders remember translation difficulties and believe that they were deliberate, designed to cover up that the core of the treaty was a land surrender. Treaty 7 Elders and Tribal Council, *The True Spirit and Original Intent of Treaty 7*, 324.
83 Treaty 7 Elders and Tribal Council, *The True Spirit and Original Intent of Treaty 7*, is the most complete account of the misunderstanding and confusion endemic in the treaty process. While it focuses on Treaty 7, many of the issues it explores apply to the other treaties as well. Richard Price, ed., *The Spirit of the Alberta Treaties*, also contains a number of essays that illustrate the complexity of native understanding of the substance of the treaties. See particularly John L. Taylor, 'Two Views on the Meaning of Treaties Six and Seven' and Richard Daniel, 'The Spirit and Terms of Treaty Eight.'
84 'T.A.R.R. Interviews with Elders Program,' in Richard Price, ed., *The Spirit of the Alberta Treaties*, 113–43, is an oral history of the tribe's understandings of the treaties. Treaty 7 Elders and Tribal Council, *The True Spirit and Original Intent of Treaty 7*, includes both oral histories and academic analysis in a similar study. See also John L. Taylor, 'Two Views on the Meaning of Treaties Six

and Seven,' and John Tobias, 'Canada's Subjugation of the Plains Cree, 1879–1885,' *Canadian Historical Review*, vol. 64, no. 4 (1983), 519–48.

85 Irene Spry, 'The Tragedy of the Loss of the Commons in Western Canada,' in A. Getty and A. Lussier, *As Long As the Sun Shines and Water Flows A Reader in Canadian Native Studies* (Vancouver: University of British Columbia Press 1984), 203–28.

86 Plains Indians faced periodic game shortages, particularly in winter. The ordinary ranges of buffalo were always irregular, and so some years hunts were sparse. The Cree, inhabitants of the mixed forest and plain parkland south of the boreal forest, had access to the resources of the forests as well and did not face such seasonal shortages. Irene Spry, 'The Tragedy of the Loss of the Commons in Western Canada,' 205–6. John Milloy, '"Our Country": The Significance of the Buffalo Resource for a Plains Cree Sense of Territory,' in Kerry Abel and Jean Friesen, *Aboriginal Resource Use in Canada: Historical and Legal Aspects* (Winnipeg: University of Manitoba Press 1991), 51–70, discusses the place of the Buffalo in Plains Cree culture.

87 Bob Beal and Rod Macleod, *Prairie Fire*, 38.

88 Henry Youle Hind, *Northwest Territory. Report of the Assiniboine and Saskatchewan Exploring Expeditiion* (Toronto, 1859), quoted in Spry, 'The Tragedy of the Loss of the Commons in Western Canada,' 210.

89 Alexander Morris, *The Treaties of Canada*, vol. 1: 171.

90 Ibid., 168–9; Arthur Ray, *Indians in the Fur Trade*, 227.

91 Alexander Morris, *Treaties of Canada* ... (Toronto: Bedford and Clarke 1880), 170. This warning of an Indian war is probably exaggerated, or it may have been influenced by the wars in the United States. Christie's next paragraph points out that these Indians will come to the HBC for relief from starvation and that there was no force in the northwest sufficient to stop them from simply taking what relief they wanted.

92 Alexander Morris, *Treaties of Canada*, 171.

93 Treaty 7 Elders and Tribal Council, *The True Spirit and Original Intent of Treaty 7*, 324.

94 Deputy minister of the interior E.A. Meredeth to minister, n.d. (probably spring 1874), quoted in Noel E. Dyck, 'The Administration of Federal Indian Aid in the Northwest Territories, 1879–1885' (M.A. thesis, University of Saskatchewan 1970), 21.

95 DHC, quoted in ibid., 22.

96 Noel Dyke, 'The Administration of Federal Indian Aid,' 23–4.

97 George F.G. Stanley, *The Birth of Western Canada*, 222–3.

98 Ibid., 223.

99 Ibid., 223. Sitting Bull's presence in Saskatchewan was viewed as a kind of

'wild card' by all participants in the treaty process. The Dakota, an American tribe, did not take treaty in Canada. At the same time, their presence in Canada stemmed directly from their role in two United States wars, the Minnesota Uprising of 1863 and the Sioux War of 1876, leading to the victory over General George Custer. The spectre of Indian wars was not simply the application of U.S. history on the Canadian prairies: the Canadian government was concerned about the Dakota's continued presence. Peter Douglas Elias, *The Dakota of the Canadian Northwest: Lessons for Survival.* (Winnipeg: University of Manitoba Press 1988).

100 Noel Dyke, 'The Administration of Federal Indian Aid,' 23.

101 Christie and Dickieson to the minister of the interior, 7 Oct. 1875, quoted in George Stanley, *The Birth of Western Canada,* 218.

102 J.R. Miller, *Skyscrapers Hide the Heavens: A History of Indian-White Relations in Canada* (Toronto: University of Toronto Press 1989), attributes the decline of the buffalo to a number of factors, including an American policy of eliminating the buffalo hunt in an effort to starve the tribes, particularly in the context of the Sioux War of 1876, into submission (171–2).

103 George Stanley, *Birth of Western Canada,* 222; Noel Dyke, 'An Opportunity Lost: The Initiation of the Reserve Agricultural Programme in the Prairie West,' in F. Laurie Barron and James B. Waldram, *1885 and After,* 24–5.

104 Treaty 6 was signed on 23 Aug. 1876. The Indian Act (1876) had been passed on 12 April 1876. It consolidated and expanded the 1869 Indian Act, which had consolidated Ontario and Quebec Acts. There was no systematic effort to post the act in the northwest, and no one has argued that Indians at Fort Carlton were aware of its provisions. The existence and meaning of the act was not a part of treaty negotiations, and so the crown must have chosen not to use the opportunity of the meeting of a large assembly of Indians to make its provisions known. It is possible that the crown thought that it might have angered the Indians and this made the signing of the treaty problematic.

105 L. VanKoughnet, memorandum to Indian Branch, Department of the Interior, 22 Aug. 1876, RG 10 (red series). vol. 1995, file 6886, National Archives of Canada.

106 John Leslie and Ron Maguire, *The Historical Development of the Indian Act,* 2nd ed, (Ottawa: treaties and Research Centre, Research Branch, Department of Indian and Northern Affairs 1978).

107 Peter Douglas Elias, *The Dakota of the Canadian Northwest,* 88.

108 Quoted in Don McLean, *1885: Metis Rebellion or Government Conspiracy?* (Winnipeg: Pemmicen 1985), 58.

109 Dempsey, *Big Bear,* 123.

110 John Jennings, 'The Northwest Mounted Police,' 217.

111 J.R. Miller, *Shingwauk's Vision* (Toronto: University of Toronto Press 1997), 129.
112 Ibid., 219–20; R.C. Macleod, *The North-West Mounted Police and Law Enforcement*, 146; J.R. Miller, 'Owen Glendower, Hotspur, and Canadian Indian Policy,' in J.R. Miller, *Sweet Promises:A Reader on Indian-White Relations* (Toronto: University of Toronto Press 1991), 323–52, 327.
113 B. Bennett, 'Study of Passes for Indians to Leave Their Reserves,' (Ottawa: Department of Indian and Northern Affairs, Treaties and Historical Research Centre 1974), 1–2. Blair Stonechild and Bill Waiser, *Loyal till Death* (1997), makes it clear that, aside from isolated instances, the Indians were mostly on their reserves, although they were not legally required to reside there.
114 B. Bennett, 'Study of Passes for Indians,' 2. Dewdney to J.M. Rae, Indian agent, Treaty 6, 23 June 1885, quoted in ibid., 2–3.
115 Reed to Dewdney, 16 Aug. 1885, quoted in ibid., 3.
116 Ibid., 3, 8.
117 Steele to Commissioner, NWMP, nd. [1891], quoted in ibid., 4.
118 Reed to superintendent general of Indian Affairs, 10 Dec. 1891, quoted in ibid., 5.
119 For Treaty 6, for example, see Alexander Morris, *The Treaties of Canada*, 215, 218, 353. The other treaties carry parallel language.
120 John Jennings, 'The Northwest Mounted Police,' 219–20. The Indian Act (1876) had no vagrancy provisions, but such provisions would have been redundant since Indians were subject to all the laws of Canada, both civil and criminal.
121 Begg to Indian commissioner, Regina, 26 July 1894, quoted in B. Bennett, 'Study of Passes,' 5.
122 A.E. Forget, Indian commissioner, Regina, confidential circular to Indian agents, 30 July 1894, 'Forget to Indian agents, 8 April 1889, Forget, circular, 29 March 1889, all quoted in ibid., 5–6.
123 There are two full-length studies of these provisions. Katherine Pettipas, *Severing the Ties That Bind: Government Repression of Indigenous Religious Ceremonies on the Prairies* (Winnipeg: University of Manitoba Press 1994), and Douglas Cole and Ira Chaikin, *An Iron Hand upon the People: The Law against the Potlatch on the Northwest Coast* (Vancouver: University of British Columbia Press 1990).
124 Katherine Pettipas, *Severing the Ties That Bind*, 1–41.
125 47 Vic, c. 27 (1884).
126 Hamasak (or Ha-mer-ceeluc), of Mamalillikulla, had twice called tribes for a potlatch. He was arrested after a scuffle and sentenced to six months in jail by his Indian agent, sitting as a justice of the peace. Begbie, in *R. v. Hamasak*,

held that the statute was so overbroad that it was not clear what specific conduct was prohibited by it. Douglas Cole and Ira Chaikin, *An Iron Hand upon the People*, 35–9; Robin Fisher, *Contact and Conflict: Indian-European Relations in British Columbia, 1774–1890* (Vancouver: University of British Columbia Press 1977), 207. It is a fundamental principle of the English common law that a penal statute has to indicate clearly the kind of conduct prohibited.

127 Department of Indian and Northern Affairs, *The Historical Development of the Indian Act* (Ottawa), 95.

128 Katherine Pettipas, *Severing the Ties That Bind*, 95–96; Hugh Dempsey, *Big Bear*, 123–30.

129 Katherine Pettipas, *Severing the Ties that Bind*, 116. The Department of Indian Affairs believed that Piapot held the only sun dance in Canada in 1895. His reserve was a centre of traditional religion, listed as 85 per cent 'pagan' in 1896. David Lee, 'Piapot: Man and Myth,' *Prairie Forum*, vol. 17, no. 2 (1992), 251–62, 258.

130 Pettipas, *Severing the Ties that Bind*, 118–19. Thus, Piapot, although arrested twice for holding religious ceremonies, was arrested once on charges of drinking and once for resisting arrest, indicating the reluctance of the police to charge him directly with holding religious ceremonies under the Indian Act.

131 J.R. Miller, *Shingwauk's Vision*, 129; 343–74.

132 Whisky traders and cattle thieves were concentrated along the international border while buffalo roamed everywhere, making this kind of law enforcement somewhat simpler than enforcing hunting regulations.

CONCLUSION

1 Anthony Hall, 'Treaties, Trains, and Troubled National Dreams: Reflections on the Indian Summer in Northern Ontario, 1990,' in Louis A. Knafla and Susan W.S. Binnie, *Law, Society, and the State: Essays in Modern Legal History* (Toronto: University of Toronto Press 1995), 290–320. This article represents First Nations legal history in an important anthology. It is not conventional legal history but an analysis of a contemporary legal struggle in its historical context. It is also 'micro' legal history, an analysis of one small community. This is the way that aboriginal legal history needs to be approached. Each community has its own legal history; each treaty its own interpretative problems.

2 Ibid., 294.

3 Ibid.

4 Miles Goldstick, *People Resisting Genocide*, (Montreal: Black Rose Books 1987), 37.

5 On the making of Treaty 8 see Richard Daniel, 'The Spirit and Terms of Treaty Eight,' in Richard Price, ed., *The Spirit of the Alberta Treaties*, (Edmonton: Pica Press 1987), 47–100, 71–82.
6 Darlene Abreu Ferreira, 'Oil and Lubicons Don't Mix: A Land Claim in Northern Alberta in Historical Perspective,' *Canadian Journal of Native Studies*, vol. 12, no. 1 (1992) 1–35.
7 These agreements, between the provinces and the crown, are discussed in Anthony G. Gulig, 'In Whose Interest?: Government-Indian Relations in Northern Saskatchewan and Wisconsin, 1900–1940' (Ph.D. dissertation, University of Saskatchewan 1997). The Saskatchewan Natural Resource Transfer Agreement of 1930 is discussed at 203–8. See also Frank Tough, 'Introduction to Documents: Indian Hunting Rights, Natural Resources Transfer Agreements and Legal Opinions from the Department of Justice,' *Native Studies Review*, vol. 10, no. 2 (1995), 121–67, and Jack Woodward, *Native Law* (Toronto: Carswell 1989), 317–23. A native student gave this excuse to me in the fall of 1994 when I taught at the College of Law of the University of Saskatchewan.
8 Russel Lawrence Barsh and James Youngblood Henderson, 'The Supreme Court's Van der Peet Trilogy: Naive Imperialism and Ropes of Sand,' *McGill Law Journal*, vol. 42 (1997) 993, 1005–1006, argues that the case–by–case approach to 'existing aboriginal rights' set out in *Van der Peet* means that there are '600 individual First Nation boxes ... with the Heiltsuk box ... containing a different mix of traditions and practices from the Sheshaht box.' It then asks the question: 'Does this case by case approach to decision making qualify as "Law"?' This 'illegality' refers here to jurisprudential method but extends to matters of substance as well.
9 *McGregor v. R; Boyer v. R.* (1979), 102 D.L.R. (3rd.) 602 at 613 (Fed. T.D.); *Nowegijick v. R.*, [1983] 1 S.C.R. 29. See, generally, Jack Woodward, *Native Law*, 403–6; and Bradford Morse, ed., *Aboriginal Peoples and the Law: Indian, Metis and Inuit Rights in Canada* (Ottawa: Carleton University Press 1985).
10 Brian Slattery, 'The Legal Basis of Aboriginal Title,' in Frank Cassidy, ed., *Aboriginal Title in British Columbia: Delgamuukw v. The Queen*, (Lantzville, B.C.: Oolichan Books 1992), 113–32, has argued (at 121–8) for a broad interpretation of the Royal Proclamation as a fundamental legal document protecting a broad range of aboriginal rights across Canada. See also Jack Woodward, *Native Law*, 75–6. Some case law also directly suggests that sharp dealing or trickery in treaties cannot be condoned by Canadian courts. See *R. v. Taylor* (1981), 34 O.R. (2d.) 360 (C.A.); *R. v. Batisse* (1977), 19 O.R. (2d.) 145 (Ont. Dist. Ct.).
11 Franklin S. Gertler and Peter Hutchins, 'The Marriage of History and Law in *R. v. Sioui*,' *Native Studies Review*, vol. 6, no. 2 (1990), 115–93.

12 *R.* v. *Sioui* [1990] 1 R.C.S. 1025. This represents one case in which Canadian
   courts have adopted a 'large and liberal' reading of treaty rights. At the same
   time, however, the Siouis were arrested as common criminals for these trivial
   offences and the immediate result of the case was simply that their convictions
   were reversed. It is fundamental to common law reasoning that each case governs only its own facts. While there is some precedential value to each Indian
   rights case, their factual complexity limits their value as precedent.

13 Justice Allan McEachern of the Supreme Court of British Columbia, commenting on his own judgment in *Delgamuukw* v. *the Queen*, wrote that 'the difficulties facing the Indian populations of the territory ... will not be solved in the
   context of legal rights.' McEachern further characterized such legal terms as
   'ownership,' 'sovereignty,' and 'rights,' foundational to Anglo-Canadian jurisprudence, as 'fascinating legal concepts' which would not solve the underlying social and economic problems of the First Nations. He then dismissed
   most of the evidence of the hereditary chiefs and denied the claims of the Gitksan and Wet'suwet'en. This perfunctory dismissal occurred after McEachern
   had presided over the longest and perhaps most historically detailed indigenous rights trial in the world. *Delgamuukw,* brought by traditional Gitksan and
   Wet'suwet'en chiefs, sought the restoration of a vast tract of northern British
   Columbia, alienated from Indian ownership in the late nineteenth century
   without any treaty. *Delgamuukw* v. *the Queen in Right of the Province of British
   Columbia and the Attorney General of Canada*, No. 0843 Smithers Registry (1990)
   at 299. This case is reported as 48 B.C. 211 (1990). The judgment was partially
   reversed by the British Columbia Court of Appeal, [1993] 5 W.W.R. 97; then
   reversed by the Supreme Court of Canada, File no. 23799, Dec. 11, 1997 (unreported).

14 Medig'm Gymak (Neil Sterritt), 'It Doesn't Matter What the Judge Said,' in
   Frank Cassidy, ed., *Aboriginal Title in British Columbia*, 303–7.

15 Satsan (Herb George), 'The Fire within Us,' in Frank Cassidy, ed., *Aboriginal
   Title in British Columbia*, 53–7, 55–6.

16 Wigetimstochol (Dan Michell), 'Deep within Our Spirit,' in Frank Cassidy, ed.,
   Aboriginal Title in British Columbia 62–5.

17 Chief Justice McEachern in *Delgamuukw* v. *British Columbia* [1991] 3 W.W. R. 97
   appears to have completely misunderstood the lengthy testimony about Gitksan and Wet'suwet'en law and characterized these legal systems as a 'most
   uncertain and highly flexible set of customs which are frequently not followed
   by the Indians themselves.' He continued: 'I head many instances of prominent Chiefs conducting themselves other than in accordance with these rules,
   such as logging or trapping on another chief's territory, although there always
   seemed to be an aboriginal exception which made almost any departure from

aboriginal rules permissible. In my judgement these rules are so flexible and uncertain that they cannot be classified as laws' (at 379–80).

18 Quoted by Satsan, in Frank Cassidy, ed., *Aboriginal Title in British Columbia*, 55.

19 Any short characterization of a comparison between two complex legal orders is an oversimplification. Justice McEachern, for example, confused the character and form of Gitksan and Wet'suwet'en law with evidence of its effectiveness in governing the lives of complex and changing Native societies – something he would surely not do for Canadian law, which is also, of course, frequently violated. Canadian judges never hold that because Canadian law is often violated it is not really 'law.' Antonia Mills, *Eagle Down Is Our Law* (Vancouver: University of British Columbia Press 1984), provides a detailed description of Wet'suwet'en law. This description, based on research done by Mills on behalf of the Wet'suwet'en traditional chiefs in preparation for their case, was part of the evidence before Justice McEachern.

20 Brian Slattery has argued that the Royal Proclamation and the subsequent history of recognition of Indian land rights has created a common law of aboriginal rights. Brian Slattery, 'The Legal Basis of Aboriginal Title,' *British Columbia: Delgamuukw v. The Queen*, 113–32, 121–8.

21 Bruce Clark, *Native Liberty, Crown Sovereignty: The Existing Aboriginal Right of Self-Government in Canada* (Montreal: McGill-Queen's University Press 1990), argues, among other things, that Indians retain a broad range of rights to self-government. While he offers a number of legal reasons for this, one is simply that Indians have continuously re-asserted these rights in Canada, over hundreds of years.

22 David Ricardo Williams, ordinarily categorized as a traditional legal historian best known for his judicial biography of Matthew Baillie Begbie, *The Man for a New Country: Matthew Baillie Begbie* (Sydney, B.C.: Gray Publishers 1977), made a remarkably prescient observation that is anything but traditional legal history in a paper, 'Native Land Claims: The Rule of History or the Rule of Law,' given at the Canadian Law in History Conference, Ottawa, in July 1987: 'At least in some types of cases history cannot be distinguished from law, or to put it the other way around, history is so bound up as an issue in a certain type of case that it becomes part of the tissue of that case. Certainly land claim cases afford an example of the intertwining of history and law. In these cases, history and not some abstract principle of law determines the legal outcome ... Judges have an opportunity to be historical researchers themselves ... I believe land claim cases will form a growth industry for both lawyers and historians, let legal history rejoice.'

23 [1990] 1 S.C.R. 1075; [1996] 137 D.L.R. (4th) 289; [1996] 137 D.L.R. (4th) 648; [1996] 137 D.L.R. (4th) 528. For example, Dorothy Van der Peet, a Sto:lo, on 11

Sept. 1987 sold ten salmon that Charles Jimmy, her common-law husband, and Steven Jimmy, his brother, had caught under the authority of an Indian food-fish licence. She was arrested under the British Columbia Fishery (General) Regulations, SOR/84–248 s. 27(5): 'No person shall sell, barter or offer to sell or barter any fish caught under the authority of an Indian food fish license.' Her defence was that she had an aboriginal right to sell fish. The case went through Canadian courts for ten years before she ultimately lost, dividing the Supreme Court of Canada on the proper test for determining the nature of her aboriginal rights.

24 Clinton Rickard, *Fighting Tuscarora* (Syracuse: Syracuse University Press 1984).

25 Geoffrey York, *The Dispossessed: Life and Death in Native Canada* (London: Vintage 1990), is an introduction to these issues. There is a substantial literature in the social sciences on the social problems of native people but these problems are derivative from legal issues and do not determine the structure of First Nations/Canadian relations. For example, it is clear that, historically, the policy of legal dualism, for the most part (but not entirely) *preceeds* the social disorganization. But, even if this is true, this does not mean that Canadian paternalism *causes* the social disorganization endemic of reserve life. There are a number of complex issues related to this social disorganization that can benefit from historical research. R.C. Macleod, *The North-West Mounted Police and Law Enforcement, 1873–1905* (Toronto: University of Toronto Press 1976), for example, shows that there was relatively little crime on the northwest reserves in the late nineteenth century (144–8). The high crime rates of today are a product of twentieth-century historical developments.

26 Brendan O'Brien, *Speedy Justice: The Tragic Last Voyage of His Majesty's Vessel Speedy* (Toronto: Osgoode Society/University of Toronto Press 1992), 49–53.

27 Susan Zimmerman, 'The Revolving Door of Despair: Aboriginal Involvement in the Criminal Justice System,' *University of British Columbia Law Review*, Special Edition, Aboriginal Justice: 1992, 367–426. Appendix B, at 413, contains data that show that Indians are imprisoned at 7 to 8 times their proportion of the population in the prairie provinces; 1.5 to 2.5 their proportion in Northwest Territories and Yukon.

28 Richard White, *The Middle Ground: Indians, Empires, and Republics in the Great Lakes Region, 1650–1815* (Cambridge, U.K.: Cambridge University Press 1991), has characterized this politically as a 'middle ground.' Jeremy Webber, 'Relations of Force and Relations of Justice: The Emergence of Normative Community between Colonists and Aboriginal Peoples,' *Osgoode Hall Law Journal*, vol. 33 (1995), 624. White's thesis, incorporated into Webber's compelling legal argument, is historically limited to a period – before the War of 1812 – when Indians were powerful political players in the Great Lakes region. The indige-

nous legal tradition was not respected in succeeding years and White's 'middle ground' thesis does not describe Indian/white relations after 1815.

29 Antonia Mills, *Eagle Down Is Our Law*, based on research done for the *Delgamuukw* case, illustrates the kind of indigenous legal history that can be written about one First Nation. One might imagine what Canadian legal history would look like if there were ten, twenty, or fifty such studies. In many ways Justice McEachern's failure to take this law seriously meant that Wet'suwet'en law had an even greater impact than if he had recognized it. His blindness to Wet'suwet'en law and legal tradition made his decision look illegitimate and undermined the integrity of all of his legal conclusions. There is a voluminous literature on this case. See, for example, the articles in Frank Cassidy, *Aboriginal Title in British Columbia: Delgamuukw v. The Queen*, and a special issue of *B.C. Studies* (1992), 3–65.

30 'Nisga'a Treaty Negotiations: Agreement-in-Principle,' issued jointly by the government of Canada, the province of British Columbia, and the Nisga'a Tribal Council, 15 Feb. 1996.

31 *Delgamuukw* v. *British Columbia*, file no. 23799, Supreme Court of Canada, decided 11 Dec. 1997 and unreported at the time of this writing.

32 Grand Council of the Crees, *Sovereign Injustice: Forcible Inclusion of the James Bay Crees and Cree Territory into a Sovereign Quebec* (Nemaska, Eeyou Astchee (Quebec), 1995), 1–17; 219–51. An irony here is that the relationship between the crown and the First Nations is one of the forces that binds Canada together, from coast to coast, and is thus potentially a unifying force in Canada.

33 See, for example, 'Amended Statement of Claim, between the Six Nations of the Grand River Band of Indians and the Attorney General of Canada and Her Majesty the Queen in Right of Ontario,' Ontario Court of Justice, General Division, Brantford, Ontario, file no. 406/95, 26 April 1995. This complex and lengthy claim is based on detailed historical research and resolving it will require litigating many complex historical questions.

34 Brian Slattery, 'The Legal Basis of Aboriginal Title'; *Delgamuukw v. The Queen*, (Montreal: Institute for Research on Public Policy 1992),113–32, 117–21; Jeremy Webber, 'Relations of Force and Relations of Justice.'

35 Douglas Sanders, 'The Nishga Case,' *B.C. Studies*, vol. 19 (1973), 3, 15, makes the point that, at the time of *Calder*, Canadian courts hardly took the Nisga'a claims seriously. The fact that they do now is a product of the interaction between the continued process of bringing forward claims of Indian land rights and the evolution of Canadian law: Canadian law would never have reinterpreted this law in the way that it has without the substantial legal arguments that the First Nations brought forward.

Photo Credits

Wet'suwet'en territories, from the *Historical Atlas of Canada: Addressing the Twentieth Century*, vol. 3, Donald Kerr and Deryck W. Hodsworth, eds. (Toronto: University of Toronto Press, 1990), plate 2

Index

to, 57; J.B. Robinson as member of, 66; William Robinson as member of, 84

assimilation, 30, 33, 53–4, 108, 204, 264; and Six Nations, 38, 54–60; 98–9

Assiniboine nation, 240

Attorney General for Ontario v. *Bear Island Foundation et al*, 4, 131, 147

Attorney General of Ontario v. *Francis et al*, 92, 143–4

Attorney General of Ontario v. *St. Catherine's Milling and Lumber Company*, 12, 13, 64, 79, 83, 92, 125–47, 155, 165, 253; joint appendix, 141

Australia, 14, 19, 23, 24, 32, 101, 165, 196

Badger Bay (Nlfd.), 177

Bagot, Sir Charles, 31. *See also* Commission of Inquiry/Indian Affairs

Banfield, William, 201

Baptiste, 149

barbarians, Indians as, 137–172

Barry, James, 208

Barsh, Russel, 6

Bastien v. *Hoffman*, 173–4

Bathurst, Lord, 115

Batoche, Battle of, 246, 248, 249

Battleford (Sask.), 227, 247–9

Bear Island reserve, 156–7

Beardsley, Bartholomew, 113

Beaver, 198,

Begbie, Mathew, 202–10, 212, 268

Begg, Magnus, 267

Bella Coola nation, 190

Beothuk, 19, 25, 176–8, 185

Big Bear, 240, 243–9, 252–5, 264, 271

Blackfoot Confederacy, 243, 252, 253, 257, 271

Blackstone's Commentaries, 63

Blackwood, H.P., 154

Blake, Edward, 134, 143

Blake, William Hume, 72, 81

Blanshard, Richard, 192, 199, 200

Blood nation, 244, 271

Board of Trade, Great Britain, 177

Borrows, John, 6, 108, 150–2, 163

Bown v. *West*, 66, 71–2, 85, 86, 126, 136

Boyd, John Alexander, 11, 12, 132–4, 137–9, 142–5

Brant County (Ont.), 159

Brant, Issac, 110–11

Brant, John, 37; elected to Legislative Assembly, 57, 101

Brant, Joseph (Thayendanegea), 9, 19, 27–39, 43, 45, 47, 73, 102, 110, 111, 158

Brantford (Ont.), 48, 49, 59, 120, 157–63

Bright Eyes, 249

British Columbia, 14, 19, 21, 92, 106, 165, 193, 186–216, 280

'British justice': and indigenous peoples, 24, 109, 159

British North America Act (BNA Act), 104, 126, 133, 135, 137–40, 142, 145, 147

Brock, Isaac, 43, 44

Buctouche reserve, 183

buffalo, 250, 251, 257–62

Bull's Head, 264

burden of proof: in land claim, 274

Burn's Justice, 196

Burns, Robert Easton, 74, 75, 82, 83

Burston, Mangus, 247

Burton, George, 139

Bushby, James 22

Caban, François, 208

Calder v. *Attorney General of British Columbia*, 4, 14, 147, 186, 188, 215

Caldwell v. *Fraser*, 92, 186

PUBLICATIONS OF THE OSGOODE SOCIETY FOR CANADIAN LEGAL HISTORY

1995   David Williams, *Just Lawyers: Seven Portraits*
Hamar Foster and John McLaren, eds., *Essays in the History of Canadian Law: Volume 6 – British Columbia and the Yukon*
W.H. Morrow, ed., *Northern Justice: The Memoirs of Mr. Justice William G. Morrow*
Beverley Boissery, *A Deep Sense of Wrong: The Treason Trials and Transportation to New South Wales of Lower Canadian Rebels after the 1838 Rebellion*

1996   Carol Wilton, ed., *Essays in the History of Canadian Law: Volume 7 – Inside the Law: Canadian Law Firms in Historical Perspective*
William Kaplan, *Bad Judgment: The Case of Mr. Justice Leo A. Landreville*
Murray Greenwood and Barry Wright, eds., *Canadian State Trials: Volume I – Law, Politics, and Security Measures, 1608–1837*

1997   James W. St.G. Walker, *'Race,' Rights, and the Law in the Supreme Court of Canada: Historical Case Studies*
Lori Chambers, *Married Women and Property Law in Victorian Ontario*
Patrick Brode, *Casual Slaughters and Accidental Judgments: Canadian War Crimes and Prosecutions, 1944–1948*
Ian Bushnell, *A History of the Federal Court of Canada, 1875–1992*

1998   Sidney Harring, *White Man's Law: Native People in Nineteenth-Century Canadian Jurisprudence*
Peter Oliver, *'Terror to Evil-Doers': Prisons and Punishments in Nineteenth-Century Ontario*